STROUD'S
JUDICIAL DICTIONARY
OF
WORDS AND PHRASES

AUSTRALIA
LBC Information Services
Sydney

CANADA and USA
Carswell
Toronto

NEW ZEALAND
Brooker's
Auckland

SINGAPORE and MALAYSIA
Thomson Information (S.E. Asia)
Singapore

STROUD'S
JUDICIAL DICTIONARY

OF

WORDS AND PHRASES

*FOURTEENTH CUMULATIVE SUPPLEMENT TO
THE FIFTH EDITION*

up-to-date to July 31, 1999

BY

The Late John S. James
Barrister

Daniel Greenberg
*of Lincolns Inn, Barrister and of the Office of the
Parliamentary Counsel*

and

Alexandra Millbrook
*of Middle Temple, Barrister and the Intervention Board
Executive Agency*

LONDON
SWEET & MAXWELL
1999

Published in 1999 by
Sweet & Maxwell Ltd of
100 Avenue Road, London NW3 3PF.
http://www.smlawpub.co.uk
Typeset by Dataword Services Limited, Chilcompton
Printed and bound in Great Britain by
MPG Books Ltd, Bodmin, Cornwall

No natural forests were destroyed to make this product;
only farmed timber was used and re-planted.

ISBN   Supplement 0–421–673–10–9
ISBN   Main work 0–421–36630–3

TABLE OF ABBREVIATIONS

ECR = European Court Reports.
E.C.S.C. = European Coal and Steel
Community.
Ed.Law. = Education and the Law.
E.E.C. = European Economic Community.
EG = Estates Gazette.
EGCS = Estates Gazette Case Summaries.
EGLR = Estates Gazette Law Reports.
E.I.P.R. = European Intellectual Property
Review.
E.H.R.R. = European Human Rights
Reports.
ELR = Education Law Reports.
E.L.Rev. = European Law Review.
E.O.R. = Equal Opportunities Review.
E.P.L. Leaflet = Excess Profits Levy
Leaflet.
E.P.T. Leaflet = Excess Profits Tax Leaflet.
E.T. = Estates Times.
Ent.L.R. = Entertainment Law Review.
Env.L.R. = Environment Law Reports.

F.C.R. = Family Court Reporter.
Fed.L.R. = Federal Law Reports.
FLR = Family Law Reports.
Fin.LR = Financial Law Reports.
F.S.R. = Fleet Street Reports.
FTLR = Financial Times Law Reports.
Fam. = Family Division (Law Reports).
Fam.Law = Family Law.

Gazette = Law Society Gazette.
G.W.D. = Green's Weekly Digest.

H.L. = House of Lords.
H.L.R. = Housing Law Reports.
Harv.L.R. *or* Harvard L.R. = Harvard Law
Review.

I.B.F.L. = Butterworths Journal of
International Banking and Financial Law
I.B.L. = International Business Lawyer.
I.C.C.L.R. = International Company and
Commercial Law Review.
I.C.L.Q. = International and Comparative
Law Quarterly.
I.C.L.R. = International Construction Law
Review.
I.C.R. = Industrial Cases Reports.
IFL Rev = International Financial Law
Review.
I.L.J. = Industrial Law Journal.
I.L.P. = International Legal Practitioner.
I.L.R.M. = Irish Law Reports Monthly.
I.L.T. *or* Ir.L.T. = Irish Law Times
I.L.T.R. = Irish Law Times Reports.
I.M.L. = International Media Law.
ImmAR = Immigration Appeals Reports.
Imm. and Nat.L. & P. = Immigration and
Nationality Law and Practice.
Ins.L. & P. = Insolvency Law & Practice.

Int.Med.Law = International Medical Law.
I.P.B. = Intellectual Property in Business.
I.R. *or* Ir.R. = Irish Reports (Eire).
IRLR = Industrial Relations Law Reports.
Ir.Jur. = Irish Jurist.
Ir.Jur.(N.S.) = Irish Jurist (New Series).
Ir.Jur.Rep. = Irish Jurist Reports.
I.T.R. = Industrial Tribunal Reports.

J. *and* JJ. = Justice, Justices.
J.A.L. = Journal of African Law.
J.B.L. = Journal of Business Law.
J.C. = Justiciary Cases.
J.C.L. = Journal of Criminal Law.
J.Ch. Law = Journal of Child Law.
J.C.L. & Crim. = Journal of Criminal Law
and Criminology.
J.Crim.L., C. & P.S. = Journal of Criminal
Law, Criminology and Police Science.
J.E.R.L. = Journal of Energy and Natural
Resources Law.
J.I.B. = Journal of the Institute of Bankers.
J.I.B.L. = Journal of International Banking
Law.
J.L.A. = Jewish Law Annual.
J.L.H. = Journal of Legal History.
J.L.S. = Journal of the Law Society of
Scotland.
J.M.L. & P. = Journal of Media Law and
Practice
J.P. = Justice of the Peace Reports.
J.P.L. = Journal of Planning and
Environment Law.
J.P.N. = Justice of the Peace Journal.
J.R. = Juridical Review.
J.S.W.L. = Journal of Social Welfare Law.
Jam. = Jamaica.

K.B. = King's Bench (Law Reports).
K.I.R. = Knight's Industrial Reports.

L.C. = Lord Chancellor.
L.C.J. *or* C.J. = Lord Chief Justice.
L.Exec. = Legal Executive.
L.G.C. = Local Government Chronicle.
L.G.R. = Local Government Review.
L.G.Rev = Local Government Review.
L.J. = Law Journal Newspaper.
L.J. *and* L.JJ. = Lord Justice, Lord Justices.
L.J.A.C.R. = Law Journal Annual Charities
Review.
L.J.N.C.C.R. = Law Journal Newspaper
County Court Reports.
L.J.R. = Law Journal Reports.
L.M.C.L.Q. = Lloyd's Maritime and
Commercial Law Quarterly.
L.P. = Reference to denote Lands Tribunal
decisions (transcripts available from the
Lands Tribunal).
L.Q.R. = Law Quarterly Review.
L.R. = Law Reports.

L.R.R.P. = Reports of Restrictive Practices Cases.
L.S. = Legal Studies.
L.S.Gaz. = Law Society's Gazette.
L.T. = Law Times.
L.Teach. = Law Teacher.
L.T.J. = Law Times Journal.
L.V.App.Ct. = Lands Valuation Appeal Court (Scotland).
L.V.C. = Reference to denote Lands Tribunal decisions (transcripts available from the Lands Tribunal).
L. & J. = Law and Justice.
Ll.Rep. = Lloyd's List Reports (before 1951).
Ll.P.C. = Lloyd's Prize Cases.
Law M. = The Law Magazine.
Lit. = Litigation.
Liverpool L.R. = Liverpool Law Review.
Lloyd's Rep. = Lloyd's List Reports (1951 onwards).

M.L.J. = Malayan Law Journal.
M.L.R. = Modern Law Review.
M.R. = Master of the Rolls.
McGill L.J. = McGill Law Journal.
Mag.Ct. = Magistrates' Court.
Mal. = Malaya.
Mal.L.R. = Malaya Law Review.
Man.Law = Managerial Law.
MedLR = Medical Law Reports.
Med.Sci. & Law = Medicine, Science and the Law.
Melbourne Univ.L.R. = Melbourne University Law Review.
Mel.L.J. = Melanesian Law Journal.

NATO R. = NATO Review.
N.I. = Northern Ireland; Northern Ireland Reports.
N.I.J.B. = Northern Ireland Judgment Bulletin.
N.I.L.Q. = Northern Ireland Legal Quarterly.
N.I.L.R. = Northern Ireland Law Reports.
N.Z.L.R. = New Zealand Law Reports.
N.Z.U.L.R. = New Zealand Universities Law Review.
New L.J. = New Law Journal.
New L.R. = New Law Reports, Ceylon.
NPC = New Property Cases.
Nig.L.J. = Nigerian Law Journal.

O.G.L.T.R. = Oil & Gas Law and Taxation Review.
O.H. = Outer House of Court of Session.
O.J. = Official Journal of the European Communities.
O.J.L.S. = Oxford Journal of Legal Studies.
Oklahoma L.R. = Oklahoma Law Review.
O.P.L.R. = Occupational Pensions Law Reports.

Ord. = Order.
Osgoode Hall L.J. = Osgoode Hall Law Journal.

P. = Probate, Divorce and Admiralty (Law Reports).
P.A.D. = Planning Appeal Decisions.
P. & C.R. = Property and Compensation Reports.
P.C. = Privy Council.
PCC = Palmer's Company Cases.
P.C.L.B. = Practitioners' Child Law Bulletin.
P.C.L.J. = Practitioners' Child Law Journal.
P.I.Q.R. = Personal Injury and Quantum Reports.
P.L. = Public Law.
PLR = Planning Law Reports.
P.N. = Professional Negligence.
P.S. = Petty Sessions.
P.S.L.G. = Public Service and Local Government.
P.T. = Profits Tax Leaflet.
Pr.A.S.I.L. = Proceedings of the American Society of International Law.

Q.B. = Queen's Bench (Law Reports).
Q.J.P.R. = Queensland Justice of the Peace Reports.
Q.L.R. = Queensland Law Reporter.
Q.S. = Quarter Sessions.
Q.S.R. = Queensland State Reports.

r. = Rule.
RA = Rating Appeals.
R. & I.T. = Rating and Income Tax.
R. & V. = Rating and Valuation.
R.C.N. = Rating Case Notes.
Rep. L.R. = Green's Reparation Law Reports.
R.F.L. = Reports of Family Law (Canadian).
R.I.C.S. = Royal Institution of Chartered Surveyors, Scottish Lands Valuation Appeal Reports.
R.P.C. = Reports of Patent, Design and Trade Mark Cases.
R.P.Ct. = Restrictive Practices Court.
R.P.R. = Real Property Reports (Canada).
R.R.C. = Ryde's Rating Cases.
RTR = Road Traffic Reports.
RVR = Rating and Valuation Reporter.
reg. = Regulation.
Reg.Acct. = Registered Accountant.
Rep. of Ir. = Republic of Ireland.

s. = Section (of Act of Parliament).
S. *or* Scot. = Scotland.
S.A. = South Africa.
S.A.L.J. = South African Law Journal.
S.A.L.R. = South African Law Reports.
S.A.S.R. = South Australian State Reports.

S.C. = Session Cases.
S.C.C.R. = Scottish Criminal Case Reports.
S.C.(H.L.) = Session Cases (House of Lords).
S.C.(J.) = Session Cases (High Court of Justiciary).
S.C.L.R. = Scottish Civil Law Reports.
SCOLAG = Journal of the Scottish Legal Action Group
S.I. = Statutory Instrument.
S.J. = Solicitors' Journal.
S.J.(LB) = Solicitors Journal (Lawbrief).
S.J.Suppl. = Supplement to the Solicitors' Journal.
S.L.C.R. = Scottish Land Court Reports.
S.L.C.R.App. = Scottish Land Court Reports (appendix).
S.L.G. = Scottish Law Gazette.
S.L.R. = Scottish Law Reporter (Reports 1865–1925).
S.L.R. = Scottish Law Review (Articles 1912–63).
S.L.R. = Scottish Law Review (Sheriff Court Reports 1885–1963).
S.L.R. (and date) = Statute Law Reform Act (Statute Citator only).
S.L.R. = Statute Law Revision.
S.L.T. = Scots Law Times.
S.L.T.(Land Ct.) = Scots Law Times Land Court Reports.
S.L.T.(Lands Tr.) = Scots Law Times Lands Tribunal Reports.
S.L.T.(Lyon Ct.) = Scots Law Times Lyon Court Reports.
S.L.T.(News) = Scots Law Times, News section.
S.L.T.(Notes) = Scots Law Times Notes of Recent Decisions (1946–1981).
S.L.T.(Sh.Ct.) = Scots Law Times Sheriff Court Reports.
S.N. = Session Notes.
S.P.L.P. = Scottish Planning Law and Practice.
S.R. & O. = Statutory Rules and Orders.
STC = Simon's Tax Cases.
Sc.Jur. = Scottish Jurist.

Sh.Ct.Rep. = Sheriff Court Reports (Scottish Law Review) (1885–1963).
Sol. = Solicitor.
Stat.L.R. = Statute Law Review.
Sydney L.R. = Sydney Law Review.

TC *or* Tax Cas. = Tax Cases.
T.C. Leaflet = Tax Case Leaflet.
T.L.R. = Trading Law Reports.
T.P.G. = Town Planning and Local Government Guide.
T.U.L.B. = Trade Union Law Bulletin.
Tas.S.R. = Tasmanian State Reports.
Tax. = Taxation.
Tax.Int. = Taxation International.
Tr.L. = Trading Law.
Tr.L.R. = Trading Law Reports.
Traff.Cas. = Railway, Canal and Road Traffic Cases.
Trial. = Trial.
Trib. = Tribunal.
Trust L. & P. = Trust Law and Practice.
Tulane L.R. = Tulane Law Review.

U.G.L.J. = University of Ghana Law Journal.
U.S. = United States Reports.
U.T.L.J. = University of Toronto Law Journal.

V. & D.R. = Value Added Tax & Duties Reports.
VATTR = Value Added Tax Tribunal Reports.
V.L.R. = Victorian Law Reports.

W.A.L.R. = West Australian Law Reports.
W.I.A.S. = West Indies Associated States.
W.I.R. = West Indian Reports.
W.L.R. = Weekly Law Reports.
W.N. = Weekly Notes (Law Reports).
W.W.R. = Western Weekly Reports.
Washington L.Q. = Washington Law Quarterly.

Yale L.J. = Yale Law Journal.

TABLE OF CASES

TABLE OF STATUTES

TABLE OF STATUTORY INSTRUMENTS

TABLE OF EUROPEAN TREATIES, CONVENTIONS AND LEGISLATION

A

ABANDON. Whether or not a merger "proposal . . . has been abandoned" within the meaning of s.75(5) of the Fair Trading Act 1973 (c. 41) is a question of fact for the Monopolies and Mergers Commission, though not for the chairman alone (*R.* v. *Monopolies and Mergers Commission, ex p. Argyll Group* [1986] 1 W.L.R. 763).

An animal was "abandoned" within the meaning of section 1(1) of the Protection of Animals Act 1911 (c. 27), as applied by the Abandonment of Animals Act 1960, if the owner, at the time of leaving the animal, had totally disregarded his duty to make arrangements for the welfare of the animal (*R.* v. *Roulden* (1947) 41 Cr.App.R. 105 considered) (*Hunt* v. *Duckering* [1993] Crim.L.R. 678).

ABANDONMENT. Stat. Def., in relation to a mine, Water Resources Act 1991 (c. 57), s.91A(1) inserted by Environment Act 1995 (c. 25), s.58.

ABNORMAL. "Abnormal amount by way of dividend," see WHEREBY.

Massive drug importation, given the many anti-social effects, was an "abnormal crime" which justified the imposition of a heavy sentence (*R.* v. *Richardson* [1994] 15 Cr.App.R.(S.) 876).

ABNORMALITY. "Abnormality of mind" (Homicide Act 1957 (c. 11), s.2(1)). To establish the defence of "abnormality of mind" "induced by" the "disease" of alcoholism within the meaning of this section it is necessary to show that the craving for drink was such as to render the accused's use of it involuntary. A woman who drank nine-tenths of a bottle of vodka before strangling her daughter was held to have drunk it voluntarily, so that her admitted alcoholism did not amount to an "abnormality of mind" (*R.* v. *Tandy* (1988) 87 Cr.App.R. 45). Ignorance of the precise nature or strength of alcoholic content does not make drinking "involuntary" where the accused knew that he was drinking alcohol (*R.* v. *Allen* [1988] Crim.L.R. 698).

ABODE. See PLACE.

ABOUT. "About 15.5 knots." Where a charter provided that a vessel was capable of maintaining "about 15.5. knots" in moderate weather it was held that the margin imported in the word "about" could not be fixed as a matter of law. It was for the arbitrators to decide in each case (*Arab Maritime Petroleum Transport Co.* v. *Luxor Trading Corp. and Geogas Enterprise S.A., The Al Bida* [1987] 1 Lloyd's Rep. 124).

ABSENT. "Absent from work" (Employment Protection (Consolidation) Act 1978 (c. 44), Sched. 13, para. 9(1)(*b*)). See TEMPORARY(5).

(C.C.R., Ord. 37, r.2). A legal representative was "absent" for the purposes of Ord. 37, r.2 if he lacked the authority to act on behalf of a party, although he was physically present at the hearing (*Kirton* v. *Augustus Ltd* [1996] 9 C.L. 75, C.A.).

ABSTRACTION. (Water Resources Act 1963 (c. 38), s.135(1)). Occupiers of land who pumped water from an adjacent outfall channel connected to, but not forming part of a canal, thereby inducing a gravitational flow from the canal to the channel of the same volume of water, were not making an "abstraction" of water from the canal within the meaning of this section (*British Waterways Board* v. *National Rivers Authority* [1992] NPC 100).

"Abstraction of electricity" (Theft Act 1968 (c. 60), s.13). The use of electricity with no intention of paying for it is sufficient to amount to an offence under this section, and there is no requirement that the electricity meter in question should have been tampered with (*R.* v. *McCreadie, The Times*, June 10, 1992).

ABSOLUTELY ENTITLED. "Person absolutely entitled as against the trustees" (Development Land Tax Act 1976 (c. 24), s.28(1)(*a*)). A football club that was an unincorporated association was held to be a "person absolutely entitled as against the trustees" of the club within the meaning of this section (*Worthing Rugby Football Club Trustees* v. *I.R.C.* [1987] 1 W.L.R. 1057).

ABUSE. "Abuse . . . of a dominant position" (Treaty of Rome, Article 86). A copyright action cannot by itself be an abuse of a dominant position (*Ransburg Gema* v. *Electrostatic Plant Systems* [1990] F.S.R. 287). Withholding further supplies of goods to an insolvent company until goods already supplied had been paid for was not an "abuse of a dominant position" for the purposes of Art. 86 (*Leyland Daf* v. *Automotive Products* [1993] BCC 389).

ACCEPTANCE. "Acceptance" (Theft Act 1968 (c. 60), s.20(2)), has, in relation to valuable securities, its ordinary proper commercial meaning and is used in the technical sense of acceptance of a bill of exchange; mere receipt of a stolen security is not "acceptance" (*R.* v. *Nanayakkara* [1987] 1 W.L.R. 265). Payment of a cheque or a credit card voucher by a bank does not constitute its "acceptance" for the purposes of this section (*R.* v. *Kassim* [1991] 3 W.L.R. 254).

ACCIDENT. Death as a result of heatstroke was held not to be death sustained as a result of "accidental bodily injury caused solely and directly by outward violent and visible means" within the meaning of this clause in an insurance policy (*De Souza* v. *Home and Overseas Insurance Co., The Times*, September 19, 1990).

"Accident arising out of and in the course of his employment" (Social Security Act 1975 (c. 14), s.50). Where a woman, by the nature of her employment, was obliged to inhale smoke arising from her fellow employees' cigarettes, such inhalation could be an "accident" within the meaning of this section (Social Security Decision No. R(1) 6/91).

In *R.* v. *Cullen* [1993] Crim.L.R. 936, the term "accident" was held not to apply in the context of an act done by a person in such a state of self-induced intoxication that he failed to appreciate the risks of what he was doing.

ACCIDENTAL MEANS. "Caused by accidental means" in an insurance policy requires an inquiry into the cause of injury and whether it occurred by accidental means (*Dhak* v. *Insurance Co. of North America (U.K.) Ltd* [1996] 1 W.L.R. 936).

ACCOMMODATION. In a series of cases there had been some disagreement as to the effect the quality and adequacy of a habitation had on the decision as to whether it constituted "accommodation" within the meaning of s.1(1) of the Housing (Homeless Persons) Act 1977 (c. 48). In *R.* v. *Wyre Borough Council, ex p. Parr* (1983) 2 H.L.R. 71 it was held that a housing authority providing accommodation under s.4(5) of the 1977 Act was under a duty to ensure that the accommodation was suitable both as to quality and location. But in *R.* v. *South Herefordshire District Council, ex p. Miles* (1983) 17 H.L.R. 82, it was suggested that the test was whether a reasonable housing authority could take the view that the applicant had accommodation which was capable of being so described for himself and his family. In *R.* v. *Preseli District Council, ex p. Fisher* (1984) 17 H.L.R. 147 it was held that "accommodation" in s.1 meant appropriate accommodation. In *R.* v. *Hillingdon London Borough Council, ex p. Puhlhofer* [1985] 3 All E.R. 734, the Court of Appeal held that *Parr's* case being a decision under s.4 was not relevant to and of no help in construing s.1, and they preferred the test adumbrated in *Miles's* case to *Fisher's* in deciding that a local housing authority were justified in concluding that a family's place of habitation, although severely overcrowded, inappropriate and inadequate to their needs, constituted "accommodation" within the meaning of s.1. This decision was upheld in the House of Lords [1986] A.C. 484. Section 1(1) of the 1977 Act was amended by s.14 of the Housing and Planning Act 1986 (c. 63) by the insertion after subs. (2) of the following words "(2A) A person shall not be treated as having accommodation unless it is accommodation which it would be reasonable for him to continue to occupy." So now see REASONABLE.

The reference to "accommodation" in s.2(1)(*c*)(ii) of the Car Tax Act 1983 (c. 43) was to additional accommodation behind the driver's seat and not to the overall accommodation of the particular vehicle, and that accommodation had to be fitted with side windows if tax was to be charged under this Act (*R.* v. *Commissioners of Customs and Excise, ex p. Nissan (U.K.)* [1988] 3 W.L.R. 837).

"Accommodation which she . . . has an express or implied licence to occupy" (Housing Act 1985 (c. 68), s.58(2)(*b*)). Where a homeless woman was offered a job as a housekeeper it was held that the accommodation which went free with the job was not "accommodation which she had a licence to occupy" within the meaning of this subsection once she had turned the job down (*R.* v. *Kensington and Chelsea London Borough Council, ex p. Minton* (1988) 20 H.L.R. 648). (Housing Act 1985 (c. 68), ss.58, 60(1), 65(2)) "Suitable accommodation" meant a place which it would be reasonable to occupy having regard to general local authority housing conditions and did not have to be permanent or settled (*R.* v. *Hillingdon London Borough Council, ex p. Pulhofer* [1986] C.L.Y. 1619 considered) (*R.* v. *Brent London Borough Council, ex p. Awua* [1995] 3 W.L.R. 215; [1995] 3 All E.R. 493).

(Housing Act 1985 (c. 68), s.65). "Accommodation" was intended to have the same meaning throughout the 1985 Act so that a local authority discharged its duty under s.65(2) by offering an assured shorthold tenancy, provided the accommodation was suitable (*R.* v. *Brent London Borough Council, ex p. Awua* [1996] 1 A.C. 55 followed) (*R.* v. *Wandsworth London Borough Council, ex p. Mansoor and Wingrove* [1996] 3 All E.R. 913).

"Roofed accommodation," see ROOF. "Shared accommodation," see SHARED ACCOMMODATION.

ACCOUNT. "On account of a ship," see DISBURSEMENT.

An inadvertent overpayment of a current debt was simply payment under a mistake of fact and not a payment "on account", so that liability for VAT did not arise since the payee was under a legal obligation to make an immediate repayment (*Customs and Excise Commissioners* v. *British Tele-communications plc* [1996] 1 W.L.R. 1309).

ACCOUNTING RECORDS. (Companies Act 1985 (c. 6), s.221). Sale and purchase invoices, cheque books, paying-in books and bank statements remained accounting records within the meaning of s.221, even though the accountant had collated the information contained in the documents for the purposes of preparing accounts (*DTC (CNC) Ltd* v. *Gary Sargeant & Co. (a firm)* [1996] 2 All E.R. 369).

ACCRUE. (4) An action in tort "accrues" within the meaning of the Limitation Act 1980 (c. 58), s.2 at the time the act complained of was committed. So that where acts infringing a patent were committed after publication of the complete specification but before letters patent had been granted a cause of action in respect of those acts accrued when they were committed even though, under the Patents Act 1949 (c. 87), s.13(4), proceedings could not be started until the patent had been sealed (*Sevcon* v. *Lucas CAV* [1986] 1 W.L.R. 462).

An obligation to comply with a noise abatement notice "accrued" within the meaning of the Interpretation Act 1978 (c. 30), s.16(1)(*b*) in respect of breaches which occurred after the repeal of the Control of Pollution Act 1974 (c. 40), s.58(1), under which the noise abatement notice had been served (*R.* v. *Folkestone Justices, ex p. Kibble, The Times*, March 1, 1993 wrongly decided) (*Aitken* v. *South Hams District Council* [1994] 3 W.L.R. 333).

"Arising or accruing," see ARISING.

ACCUSE. "Accused of some offence" (Extradition Act 1870 (c. 52), s.3(3)). A person who had appeared before justices to answer a charge which, with the justices' permission, had been withdrawn by the prosecution, had not been "accused of some offence" within the meaning of this section (*R.* v. *Governor of Pentonville Prison, ex p. Herbage* (*No. 3*) (1987) 84 Cr.App.R. 149).

The words "the accused" in s.20(3) of the Magistrates' Courts Act 1980 (c. 43) include the plural, and therefore jointly charged defendants must be tried together; thus if, on a charge triable either way, one elects trial by jury all must be so tried (*R.* v. *Brentwood Justices, ex p. Nicholls* [1991] 3 W.L.R. 201).

(Prosecution of Offences Act 1985 (c. 23), s.16(5)). The "accused" in s.16(5) included a parent or guardian so that a local authority as guardian of a child in care should be liable to a costs order imposed under the 1985 Act (*R. v. Preston Crown Court, ex p. Lancashire County Council* [1999] 1 W.L.R. 142).

(Extradition Act 1989 (c. 33), s.1(1)(a)). While more than a mere suspicion of the commission of an offence by an individual was required to render him an "accused" for the purposes of s.1(1)(a), it was unwise to impose too rigid a definition given the differences between criminal procedures in the U.K. and those of the civil law jurisdictions. A purposive approach should be adopted so that a person who was wanted for pre-trial investigations in another jurisdiction, where the foreign judge and public prosecutor had been satisfied that there was sufficient evidence to justify criminal proceedings, could be an "accused" within the meaning of s.1 (*Re Ismail* [1998] 3 W.L.R. 495).

ACQUIESCE. "Acquiesced in the removal" (Child Abduction and Custody Act 1985 (c. 60), Sched. 1, art. 13(a)). Acquiescence within the meaning of this article might be active or passive, and could be constituted by a single event provided that the acquiescing parent was aware of his rights against the other parent. (*Re A (Minors) (Abduction; Acquiescence)*, [1992] Fam. 106). Deliberately misleading statements about a party's intentions, coupled with expeditious prosecution of a custody suit, could not amount to acquiescence within the meaning of this article (*Re A (Minor) (Abduction: Arizona)* [1991] 2 F.L.R. 241).

"Subsequently acquiesced" (Hague Convention on Civil Aspects of International Child Abduction, Art. 13(*a*)). The father of a child abducted to England could be said to have "acquiesced" in the abduction for the purposes of this section, notwithstanding that he did not know (at the time of the acts alleged to constitute acquiescence) of his rights under the Convention (*Re A (Minor) (Abduction: Acquiescence)*, *The Times*, August 25, 1992).

"Acquiescence to wrongful retention of a child" (Hague Convention, *supra,* Art. 13(*a*)) was conduct inconsistent with the summary return of a child to its habitual residence and did not have to be a long term acceptance of an existing state of affiars (*Re AZ (A Minor (Abduction: Acquiescence)* [1993] 1 FLR 682, C.A.

ACQUIRE. (15) "Interest in property . . . acquired before the coming into force of this section" (Forfeiture Act 1982 (c. 34), s.2(7)). "Acquired" in this sentence means actually transferred to the person entitled to it as a result of the operation of the forfeiture rule. Property which was still held by a personal representative who had not completed the administration of the estate, had not been acquired within the meaning of this section (*Re K (Dec'd)* [1985] 3 W.L.R. 234).

"Land which has been acquired for development" (Housing Act 1985 (c. 68), Sched. 1, para. 3). Where a local authority replaces an earlier authority under the provisions of the Local Government Act 1972 (c. 70), and land held by the predecessor authority now vests in the authority, such land can become land "acquired for development" within the meaning of this paragraph, and accordingly the tenancy of a dwelling house on the land will not be secure (*Attley* v. *Cherwell District Council* [1989] 21 H.L.R. 613).

ACQUISITION. Stat. Def., Administration of Justice Act 1985 (c. 61), s.11.

ACT. (10) "Act or default of some other person" (Trade Descriptions Act 1968 (c. 29), s.23). The "other" person who may be charged under this section is not limited to persons acting in the course of a trade or business (*Olgeivsson* v. *Kitching* [1986] 1 W.L.R. 304).

(11) "When the act complained of was done" (Race Relations Act 1976 (c. 74), s.68(1)). The "act complained of" for the purposes of starting a complaint of racial discrimination at work under this section is the determination of the employer's internal appeal procedure (*Adekeye* v. *Post Office* [1993] I.C.R. 464).

"Does acts calculated to interfere with the peace or comfort of the residential occupier" (Protection from Eviction Act 1977 (c. 43), s.1(3)). The failure by a landlord to take steps to complete building works which had already been started was not the doing of an "act" so as to render him liable under this section (*R.* v. *Ahmad* (1986) 130 S.J. 554).

"Act as director of . . . a company" (Company Directors Disqualification Act 1986 (c. 46), s.11(1)). The offence of acting as the director of a company while an undischarged bankrupt is an absolute offence requiring no guilty intent (*R.* v. *Brockley, The Times,* November 25, 1993).

"Acting in the execution of this Act" (Immigration Act 1971 (c. 77), s.26(1)(*c*)). A police officer to whom false statements were made by an immigrant, while the officer was investigating another matter, was not "acting in the execution of" the Act (*R.* v. *Clarke* [1985] 2 All E.R. 777).

"Act, or thing done . . . by the rating authority" (General Rate Act 1967 (c. 9), s.7(1)(*c*)). Refusal by the rating authority to grant a remission or reduction of the rates was an "act done" within the meaning of this section, thus giving the ratepayer the right to appeal as a person "aggrieved" (*Investors in Industry Commercial Properties* v. *Norwich City Council* [1986] 2 All E.R. 193).

"Any act which constitutes sex discrimination" (Sex Discrimination Act 1975 (c. 65), s.23). The closure of the only single sex boys' school while two girls' schools remained open was held to be such an act, and therefore unlawful (*R.* v. *Secretary of State for Education and Science, ex p. Keating, The Times,* December 3, 1985). By providing a system of selective education which had fewer places for girls than boys, and which required higher marks from a girl than a boy, the council were doing an "act" which constituted "sex discrimination" within the meaning of this section (*R.* v. *Birmingham City Council, ex p. Equal Opportunities Commission* [1989] 2 W.L.R. 520).

(Finance Act 1985 (c. 54), s.13). The phrase "does any act or omits to take any action" applied to a dishonest failure to register and was not limited to evasion due to dishonest declarations (*Customs and Excise Commissioners* v. *Stevenson, The Times,* August 15, 1996).

"Act extending over a period," see PERIOD.

Stat. Def., includes omission (Employment Rights Act 1996 (c. 18), s.235(1); United Nations Personnel Act (c. 13), s.8).

ACTION. (16) An application for leave to issue execution on a judgment, or to extend the process of execution, was not an "action" within s.38(1) of the Limitation Act 1980 (c. 58) (*National Westminster Bank* v. *Powney* [1990] 2 W.L.R. 1084).

(Limitation Act 1980 (c. 58), s.19). Section 19 applies to actions against the guarantor of the lessor's undertaking to pay the rent reserved by the lease notwithstanding that both the lease and guarantee are under seal as well as to actions against the lessee (*Romain* v. *Scuba TV Ltd* [1996] 2 All E.R. 377).

(Limitation Act 1980 (c. 58), s.24(1)). Bankruptcy proceedings based on a statutory demand for money due under a previous judgment constituted an "action . . . brought upon a judgment" within the meaning of section 24(1) of the 1980 Act and were not a means of enforcing or executing that judgment and would therefore be statute barred if brought more than six years after the date of the previous judgment (*Re a Debtor (No. 50A-SD-1995)* [1997] 2 W.L.R. 57).

(Limitation Act 1980 (c. 58), s.24). "Action" in s.24 did not include execution proceedings so that a fresh action on a judgment could be brought but not enforcement proceedings after six years (*Lowsley* v. *Forbes (t/a L.E. Design Services)* [1998] 3 All E.R. 897).

(19) "Action (short of dismissal)" (Employment Protection (Consolidation) Act 1978 (c. 44), s.23(1)) includes omission, so that the failure of the National Coal Board to pay to two members of the National Union of Mineworkers wages at the increased rates agreed with the Union of Democratic Mineworkers was held to be "action" . . . "taken against" them "as an individual" for the purposes of this section (*Ridgeway* v. *National Coal Board* [1987] I.C.R. 641). The action of a company in terminating an agreement with a union did not amount to "action (short of dismissal) taken against" an employee member of the union "as an individual" for the purposes of this section (*Associated Newspapers* v. *Wilson* [1992] IRLR 440). The withholding of a pay increase from employees who refused to sign individual contracts is not "action short of dismissal" under ss.23(1)(*a*) and 153(1) (*Associated Newspapers* v. *Wilson*; *Associated British Ports* v. *Palmer* [1995] I.C.R. 406). Where, in the interest of greater flexibility, the employers offered enhanced terms embodying higher wage increases for those employees who relinquished union representation than to those who did not, it was held that the employers' treatment of the appellant (who had refused the new terms) was "action . . . taken against him . . . for the purpose of . . . penalising him for" being a member of a trade union (*Associated British Ports* v. *Palmer* [1993] IRLR 366).

An employers' failure to renew a contract of employment when it expired by effluxion of time constituted dismissal and could not amount to "action short of dismissal" (*Johnstone* v. *BBC Enterprises* [1994] I.C.R. 180).

"Action" was not apt to include as an "omission" the withholding by an employer from an employee of a benefit that was conferred on other employees (*Associated Newspapers* v. *Wilson*).

"Action or proceeding" (Companies Act 1948 (c. 38), s.231, now Companies Act 1985 (c. 6), s.525(2)). Distress, levied on the goods of a company by the Customs and Excise in respect of unpaid value added tax, was an "action or proceeding" within the meaning of this section (*Re Memco Engineering* [1985] 3 All E.R. 267).

"Any action, execution, or other legal process" (Insolvency Act 1986 (c. 45), s.285(1)). A committal warrant against a debtor for non-payment of rates is not an "action" within the meaning of this section (*Re Smith (A Bankrupt*), *ex p. Braintree District Council* [1988] 3 W.L.R. 327).

"No action shall be brought" (Solicitors Act 1974 (c. 47), s.69). A statutory demand in bankruptcy proceedings was not an "action" within the meaning of this section (*Re a Debtor (No. 88 of 1991*) [1992] 4 All E.R. 301).

(Civil Jurisdiction and Judgments Act 1982 (c. 27), s.25.) An application under s.25 for a Mareva injunction made by way of originating summons was an "action" within the meaning of the Supreme Court Act 1981, s.151 (*Balkanbank* v. *Taher and ors* [1995] 2 All E.R. 904).

The right to compensation for the compulsory purchase of land could only be enforced through the Lands Tribunal and amounted to an "action to recover" a sum of money within the meaning of s.9(1) of the 1980 Act (*Hillingdon LBC* v. *Arc Ltd* [1998] 3 W.L.R. 754).

Stat. Def., Administration of Justice Act 1985 (c. 61), s.56; Latent Damage Act 1986 (c. 37), s.5.

ACTIVE. Proceedings before a coroner remained "active" within the meaning of s.2(3) and para. 12 of Sched. 1 to the Contempt of Court Act 1981 (c. 49) notwithstanding that the hearing had been adjourned *sine die* before the hearing of any contentious evidence (*Peacock* v. *London Weekend Television* (1986) 150 J.P.N. 47). Criminal proceedings are "active" from arrest without warrant (*Solicitor-General* v. *Henry and News Group Newspapers* [1990] C.O.D. 307).

ACTIVITY. "Activity has been carried out" (Town and Country Planning Act 1971 (c. 78), s.90(2), as substituted by Town and Country Planning (Amendment) Act 1977 (c. 29), s.1). The erection of a revolving multiple display advertisement did not constitute the same "activity" as the erection of hoardings bearing advertisements (*Arora* v. *Hackney London Borough Council* [1991] C.O.D. 342).

(Council Directive 79/7 on equal treatment for men and women in matters of social security, Art. 2). The term "activity" in Art. 2 referred to economic activity, so that a wife who cared for her paraplegic husband but had neither given up work nor abandoned any attempts to find work was not part of the working population for the purposes of the Social Security Equal Treatment Directive (*Zuchner* v. *Handelskrankenkasse (Ersatzkasse) Bremen (C77/95)*, *The Times*, December 9, 1996).

ACTUAL. "The actual cost of attendance" (Supplementary Benefit (Requirements) Regulations 1983 (No. 1399), Sched. 4, Pt. 11, para. 10) means actual expenditure. So that, in a case where the daughter of the recipient of supplementary benefit needed, after an operation, the full-time attention of the claimant's wife, the resultant loss of the wife's earnings could not be taken into account in calculating the additional requirement that the claimant was entitled to under reg. 11 (*Kynaston* v. *Chief Adjudication Officer* [1988] L.S.Gaz, Sept. 28, 48).

"Actual resources" (Supplementary Benefits (Resources) Regulations 1981 (No. 1527), reg. 5) held to include money held by a solicitor on behalf of the claimant (*Thomas* v. *Chief Adjudication Officer*, February 11, 1987 (Court of Appeal Transcript No. 109)).

"Actually paid". The term "actually paid" in an ultimate net loss clause in common usage in the loss reinsurance market means the net amount for which a reinsurer is liable (*Charter Reinsurance Co. Ltd* v. *Fagan* [1996] 2 W.L.R. 726).

"Actual occupation," see OCCUPATION.

ACTUAL BODILY HARM. (Domestic Violence and Matrimonial Proceedings Act 1976 (c. 50), s.2(1)), To establish "actual bodily harm" within the meaning of this section there must be evidence of real psychological damage and real change in the psychological condition. Just being too frightened of the husband to return home is not enough (*Kendrick* v. *Kendrick* [1990] 2 F.L.R. 107).

(Offences against the Person Act 1861 (c. 100), s.47) is capable of including psychiatric injury but does not include mere emotions, such as fear, distress or panic (*R.* v. *Chan-Fook* [1994] 1 W.L.R. 689). See also ASSAULT.

ACTUARY. Stat. Def. Pensions Measure 1997 (No. 1), s.9(1).

ADAPT. "Designed or adapted" (Firearms Act 1968 (c. 27), s.5(1)(*b*)). The word "adapted" in this section has a narrow meaning which imports some alteration to make the object fit for the use in question; so that a washing-up liquid bottle, although containing hydrochloric acid, was held not to have been "adapted for the discharge of any noxious liquid" for the purposes of this section (*R.* v. *Formosa*; *R.* v. *Upton* [1990] 3 W.L.R. 1179).

See also DESIGNED.

ADDITIONAL DAMAGES. See DAMAGES.

ADDITIONALITY PRINCIPLE. The "additionality principle" contained in E.C. regulations for the administration of the European Social Fund was fulfilled where the provision of the grant meant that other initiatives could be undertaken which, in the absence of the grant, might or would not have seen fruition and which would have genuine economic impact on the policy area concerned and a grant from the Fund did not have to be applied to those projects for which it was made (*Birmingham City Council* v. *Birmingham College of Food and Sutton Coldfield College*; *Cheshire County Council* v. *Halton College* [1996] E.L.R. 1).

See also SPECIFICITY PRINCIPLE.

ADDRESS. The ordinary meaning of address, in the context of the County Court Rules, does not include a place at which the defendant is never present and at which the process does not come to his notice, albeit that it is a place which, in the circumstances of this case, may well have had a direct and immediate connection with him (*Willowgreen* v. *Smithers* [1994] 1 W.L.R. 833).

"Home address", Stat. Def., Sex Offenders Act 1997 (c. 51), s.2(7).

(R.S.C., Ord. 10, r.1(2)(b)). The "usual or last known address" of a professional person was his business address or the place where he practised his profession (*Barclays Bank of Swaziland Ltd* v. *Hahn* [1989] 1 W.L.R. 506 and *Forward* v. *West Sussex County Council* [1995] 1 W.L.R. 1469 applied) (*Marsden* v. *Kingswell Watts* [1992] 2 All E.R. 239 not followed) (*Robertson* v. *Banham & Co.* [1997] 1 W.L.R. 446).

ADEQUATE. (Allotments Act 1925 (c. 61), s.8). "Adequate" for the purposes of section 8 should be construed with reference to reasonable needs (*R.* v. *Secretary of State for the Environment, ex p. Gosforth Allotments and Gardens Association* (1996) 72 P. & C.R. D38).

ADMINISTER. (2) (Offences against the Person Act 1861 (c. 100), s.24). It has been held that squirting a solution of household ammonia at a man was not "administering" a noxious thing; on the grounds that "administer" was used in the Act in a quasi-medical sense and was not intended to cover this sort of case (*R.* v. *Dones* [1987] Crim.L.R. 682). It has since been held that direct physical force is not necessary and that it is enough that the noxious thing is brought into contact with the victim's body. So that CS gas sprayed from a canister into a person's face is "administered" for the purpose of this section (*R.* v. *Gillard* (1988) 87 Cr.App.R. 189).

ADMINISTRATIVE RECEIVER. (Insolvency Act 1986 (c. 45) s.29(2)). A receiver appointed to an overseas company was an "administrative receiver" within the meaning of the definition contained in this section (*Re International Bulk Commodities* [1992] BCC 463).

ADMISSIBILITY. (Immigration Rules (H.C. 395), para. 345). "Admissibility" in para. 345 dealt with the practical question of the physical admission of a person to a safe third country (*R.* v. *Secretary of State for the Home Department, ex p. Carvalho* [1996] 8 C.L. 362).

ADMISSION. "Admission for treatment" (Mental Health Act 1983 (c. 20), s.3) is restricted to treatment in hospital as an in-patient and does not extend to out-patients who are to be admitted and detained for a very short period and to whom no treatment is to be given (*R.* v. *Hallstrom, ex p. W.* (*No.* 2); *R.* v. *Gardner, ex p. L* [1986] 2 All E.R. 306).

(County Court Rules 1981, Ord. 9, r.10). "Admission" meant the admission of the whole of the plaintiff's claim so that a pleading which put in issue all the heads of damage in a plaintiff's claim could not be an "admission" within the meaning of Ord. 9, r.10 (*Limb* v. *Union Jack Removals Ltd* [1998] 2 All E.R. 513; *Watkins* v. *Toms* [1998] 2 All E.R. 534).

ADOPT. "Contracts of employment adopted by him" (Insolvency Act 1986 (c. 45), s.19(5)). For the purposes of this section the word "adopted" means that the administration had procured the company to continue to carry out the contracts of employment, and did not impose personal liability on him (*Re Paramount Airways (in Administration), The Times,* September 14, 1993). Where an administrator retained and continued to employ members of staff after 14 days after his appointment as administrator, without negotiating fresh contracts of employment, he had impliedly adopted the existing contracts (*Powdrill* v. *Watson, Re, The Times,* March 23, 1995.

Continuing to employ and pay employees in accordance with their previous contracts so as to give rise to separate liability in the administration or receivership amounted to the "adoption of the contract" under s.19(5)(*b*) of the 1986 Act and could not be avoided by the administrator or receiver telling the employees that their contracts were not being adopted or only on certain terms (*Powdrill* v. *Watson* [1995] 2 W.L.R. 312).

Acts or acquiescence by a receiver after 14 days from his appointment was indicative of an intention to treat a contract as continuing in force and amounted to the "adoption of a contract" under the Insolvency Act 1986 (c. 45), s.44(1)(*b*) (*Re Paramount Airways (No. 3)* [1993] BCC 662 and *Powdrill* v. *Watson* [1995] 2 W.L.R. 312 followed) (*Re Leyland Daf; Ferranti Intl, Re; Talbot* v. *Cadge* [1994] 4 All E.R. 300).

ADOPTIVE. "Adoptive parent" (Statement of Changes in Immigration Rules February 1983 (H.C. 169), rule 50). These words are to be interpreted in their widest sense. They do not necessarily connote some legally recognisable adoptive process and require no more than a *de facto* adoption (*R.* v. *Immigration Appeal Tribunal, ex p. Ali Tohur* (1988) 18 Fam. Law 289). But see also *R.* v. *Secretary of State for the Home Department, ex p. Dhahan, The Times,* January 15, 1988 where the applicant was refused permission to bring his nephew from India for the purpose of adoption in the United Kingdom.

ADVENTURE. "Adventure insured" (Marine Insurance Act 1906 (c. 41), s.41). A contract of non-marine insurance in respect of goods alone was not in respect of an "adventure" within the meaning of this section (*Euro-Diam* v. *Bathurst* [1988] 2 All E.R. 23).

"Adventure activities". Stat. Def., Activity Centres (Young Persons' Safety) Act 1995 (c. 15), s.1(3).

ADVERSE EFFECT. "Adverse effect on the fairness of the proceedings" (Police and Criminal Evidence Act 1984 (c. 60), s.78). The fact that a police officer, making a test purchase of intoxicating liquor from premises with no licence, with a view to adducing evidence for a prosecution, had not announced his office, was held not to be likely to have an "adverse effect" on the fairness of the proceedings (*DPP* v. *Marshall* [1988] 3 All E.R. 683). Evidence of an interview with an accused who had not been informed of the duty solicitor scheme was held to be inadmissible as likely to have an "adverse effect on the fairness of the proceedings" (*R.* v. *Vernon* [1988] Crim.L.R. 449). The fairness under this section is a matter for the discretion of the judge, with which the Court of Appeal has expressed itself to be unwilling to interfere (*R.* v. *O'Leary* (1988) 87 Cr.App.R. 387). Evidence obtained by undercover police, who opened a jewellers shop purporting to be willing to buy stolen property, was held not be such as to be likely to have an "adverse effect on the fairness of the proceedings," and was therefore admissible at the trial of customers who had offered recently stolen jewellery for sale (*R.* v. *Christou; R.* v. *Wright (Christopher),* [1992] 3 W.L.R. 228). "Fairness of the proceedings" involves a consideration not only of fairness to the accussed but also of fairness to the public (*R.* v. *Smurthwaite*; *R.* v. *Gill, The Times,* October 5, 1993).

ADVERSE POSSESSION. (Limitation Act 1939 (c. 21), s.10(1); Limitation Act 1980 (c. 58), s.15, Sched. 1, para. 8(1)). Possession authorised by licence cannot be "adverse" for the purposes of these Acts (*B.P. Properties* v. *Buckler, The Times*, August 13, 1987). To establish "adverse possession" it is not necessary to show an intention to own or acquire ownership of the land. Factual possession coupled with a shown intention to possess is sufficient. (*Buckinghamshire County Council* v. *Moran* [1989] 2 All E.R. 225). The mere sending by the owner of land, and the receipt by the person in possession, of a letter demanding possession, would not by itself have the effect of making the property cease to be in "adverse possession" (*Mount Carmel Investments* v. *Peter Thurlow Ltd.* [1988] 1 W.L.R. 1078). A claim to the ownership of a plot of land based on 12 years' "adverse possession" failed because the claimants had accepted an assertion by the holder of the paper title of a right to restrict the claimants' activities on the land (*Morrice* v. *Evans, The Times*, February 27, 1989). The claim by the lessee of a factory to have acquired a title, by adverse possession, to an adjacent plot used by him as a car park failed because he had previously requested the present owner's predecessors (the original owners of the land) to carry out repair work on it (*Pavledes* v. *Ryesbridge Properties* [1989] 58 P. & C.R. 459). The occupier of a caravan stationed for several months in an abandoned quarry, and who described herself as having adopted "the travelling way of life" was held not to have shown that she had the necessary intention to establish title by adverse possession (*R.* v. *Secretary of State for the Environment, ex p. Davies* (1990) 61 P. & C.R. 487). An occupier who acknowledges that his occupation of land has not been adverse possession cannot subsequently rely on a claim of adverse possession against the same party in a second set of proceedings (*Colchester Borough Council* v. *Smith* [1992] 2 W.L.R. 728). A person having no documentary title to land was held not to have established a right by "adverse possession" where the only act of possession was the temporary erection of a fence (*Marsden* v. *Miller* [1992] NPC 6). An oral acknowledgment by the occupier of land of the registered holder's title was held not to be sufficient to interrupt the 13 years uninterrupted adverse possession, and thus acquisition of ownership, by the occupier. An acknowledgment of title to land must be in writing (*Browne* v. *Perry* [1991] 64 P. & C.R. 228). A landowner who from time to time, and at his neighbour's request, cleaned out the intervening ditch, failed in his claim for adverse possession because his acts had not shown any intention of excluding the public, nor had he been in actual possession of the ditch (*Bladder* v. *Phillips* [1991] EGCS 109). A claim for adverse possession failed in circumstances where third parties were being allowed to use the land for purposes for which the true owner wished it to be used (*Pulleyn* v. *Hall Aggregates (Thames Valley)* (1992) 65 P. & C.R. 276). Where a trespasser claims adverse possession of land, the court requires clear and affirmative evidence that he not only had the requisite intention to possess but had also made such intention clear to the world (*Wilson* v. *Martin's Exors* [1993] 24 EG 119).

ADVERTISEMENT. (Town and Country Planning (Control of Advertisements) Regulations 1984 (No. 421), reg. 2(1)). A dutch blind over a shop front which bore the words "Bally of Switzerland" was an "advertisement" for the purposes of this regulation (*Westminster City Council* v. *Secretary of State for the Environment and Bally Group (U.K.)* [1990] 1 P.L.R. 30).

The words "an advertising circular or other advertisement issued to the public" in s.4(1)(*b*) of the Trade Marks Act (c. 22) included a manual issued to its sales distributors by a pyramid selling company (*Chanel* v. *L'Arome* (*UK*), *The Times*, November 26, 1992).

Stat. Def., Building Societies Act 1986 (c. 53), s.50(10); Financial Services Act 1986 (c. 60), s.207(2); Town and Country Planning Act 1990 (c. 8), s.336; Food Safety Act 1990 (c. 16), s.53; Employment Act 1990 (c. 38), s.3; Town and Country Planning (Scotland) Act 1997 (c. 8), s.277(1).

ADVERTISER. (Town and Country Planning (Control of Advertisements) Regulations 1992, reg. 8 (S.I. 1992 No. 666)). A person whose particular interests were being publicised in an advertisement constituted an "advertiser" within the meaning of reg. 8 of the 1992 Regulations (*O'Brien* v. *Croydon LBC*, *The Times*, July 27, 1998).

ADVICE. See LEGAL ADVICE.

ADVOCATE. Stat.Def., Courts and Legal Services Act 1990 (c. 41), s.27.

AFFAIRS OF THE COMPANY. (Insolvency Act 1986 (c. 45), s.14(1)) ("The administrator of a company (a) may do all . . . as may be necessary for the management of the affairs, business and property of the company . . .")

The general power conferred by s.14(1) covered all matters which realistically touched or concerned the company's business and property, including the administration of the company's pension scheme (*Denny* v. *Yeldon and ors* [1995] 3 All E.R. 624).

AFFECTING. "Any writ or order affecting land," see LAND.

AFFRAY. An ingredient of the common law offence of "affray" is that a bystander has to be in terror for his own safety. Fear for the safety of some other person is not enough (*R.* v. *Plastow* (1989) 88 Cr.App.R. 48).

There are two limbs to the offence of affray: first, the use or threat of unlawful violence towards another, and, secondly, that the conduct was such as would cause a person of reasonable firmness to fear for his own personal safety. It was here held, however, that such a person did not necessarily have actually to be there (*R.* v. *Davison* [1992] Crim.L.R. 31).

In order to prove a charge of affray it is not necessary for the prosecution to prove each separate allegation which constitutes part of the offence, provided that the evidence shows that the accused used or threatened unlawful violence against someone in such manner as would cause them to fear for their safety (*Cobb* v. *DPP* (1992) 156 J.P.N. 330).

Although the test in s.3(1) of the Public Order Act 1986 (c. 64) is objective, justices are entitled to take account of evidence showing where the incident occurred, the fact that the violence was restricted and that those present were not afraid (*DPP* v. *Cotcher*, *The Times*, December 29, 1992).

AGE. (3) "The time at which a person attains a particular age expressed in years shall be the commencement of the relevant anniversary of the date of his birth" (Family Law Reform Act 1969 (c. 46), s.9). This effectively overtakes the interpretation of the word in *R.* v. *Shurey* [1918] 1 Ch. 263 [see Main Work, p. 80].

AGENCY. (Commercial Agents (Council Directive) Regulations 1993 (S.I. 1993 No. 3053), reg. 17). For the purposes of reg. 17 "agency contract" referred to the entire period during which the agency relationship subsisted and the word "contract" added nothing, so that the agent was entitled to an indemnity during that period to be calculated according to the principles set out in reg. 17 (*Moore* v. *Piretta PTA Ltd* [1999] 1 All E.R. 174).

AGENT. "Claim by . . . agent in respect of disbursements" (Supreme Court Act 1981 (c. 54), s.20(2)(*p*)). An insurance broker is not an "agent" for the purposes of this section (*Bain Clarkson* v. *Owners of Sea Friends, The Times,* April 18, 1991).

Local managers of a companies who entered into agreements without the express or ostensible authority of their employers did so as the representatives or "agents" of the companies and it followed that the companies could be in breach of restraining injunctions issued by the Restrictive Practices Court (*Re Supply of Ready Mixed Concrete (No. 2)* [1995] 1 All E.R. 135).

"Agent to insure" within the meaning of the Marine Insurance Act 1906 (c. 41), s.19 only encompassed those who dealt with insurers and made an insurance contract, so that underwriting agents who had acted through brokers when concluding contracts for reinsurance were not "agents to insure" (*P.C.W. Syndicates* v. *P.C.W. Reinsurers* [1996] 1 W.L.R. 1136).

AGENT PROVOCATEUR. Police who left an unattended van as a trap for thieves were not *agents provocateurs* because they had not incited, procured or commissioned the perpetration of any crime (*Williams and O'Hare* v. *DPP* [1993] Crim.L.R. 775).

AGGRAVATED VEHICLE-TAKING. Being in a car, having been party to its taking without consent amounted to aggravated vehicle-taking (*R.* v. *Harding* [1995] Crim.L.R. 733).

AGGRIEVED. (3) "Person aggrieved" (Trade Marks Act 1938 (c. 22), s.26(1)). An applicant for rectification of the Register of Trade Marks might be a "person aggrieved'" by an entry in the register, and hence have *locus standi*, notwithstanding that he had sought relief wider than that to which he was entitled (*Re Warrington Inc's Application, The Times,* February 9, 1987). The efforts of the proprietor of a trade mark to discourage firms from selling the goods of an applicant for rectification of the Trade Marks Register did not make the applicant a "person aggrieved" within the meaning of this section (*Bach Flower Remedies Trade Mark* [1992] R.P.C. 439).

(Trade Marks Act 1938 (c. 22), ss.11, 15(1), 38, 39(1)(*a*); Copyright Act 1911 (c. 46), s.5) A person in the same trade as the registered proprietor of the mark in question who is prevented from lawfully doing something which he would otherwise have been unable to do had the mark not been registered is a "person aggrieved" (*AUVI Trade Mark* [1995] F.S.R. 288).

(12) "Person aggrieved" (Public Health Act 1936 (c. 49), s.301). A local authority against whom justices had awarded the costs of a hearing was a "person aggrieved" within the meaning of this section and therefore entitled to appeal to the Crown Court (*Cook* v. *Southend Borough Council* (1989) 133 S.J. 1133).

"Person aggrieved" (Public Health Act 1936 (c. 49), s.99). A person could not be a "person aggrieved" under this section in relation to a whole building where the statutory nuisance of which he complained related only to the flat which he occupied (*Birmingham District Council* v. *McMahon* (1987) 19 H.L.R. 452).

(17) "Person aggrieved" (London County Council (General Powers) Act 1947 (c. xlvi), s.64) does not include a local council licensing authority (*R.* v. *Southwark Crown Court, ex p. Watts* [1990] 88 L.G.R. 86).

(31) "Person . . . aggrieved" (Town and Country Planning Act 1971 (c. 78), s.245). A successor in title to land subject to a planning appeal could be a person "aggrieved" for the purposes of challenging the planning decision under this section (*Times Investment* v. *Secretary of State for the Environment* (1990) 3 P.L.R. 111). A local authority is a "person aggrieved" and has the right of appeal from the justices where the decision has been adverse to the contentions of the authority, and where the matter is not criminal in nature (*Cook* v. *Southend Borough Council* [1990] 2 Q.B. 1).

"Person aggrieved" (Criminal Justice Act 1988 (c. 33), s.159(1)(*b*). A journalist excluded from two criminal trials while the judge in each case heard an application by counsel in chambers, was not a "person aggrieved" within the meaning of this section. It would not be right, where the public is excluded, to make an exception in favour of the press (*Re Cook (Timothy)* [1992] 2 All E.R. 687).

See ACT.

AGIST. "Agisted livestock." Stat. Def., Agricultural Holdings Act 1986 (c. 5), s.18(5).

AGREE. "Agreed to the making of the adoption order" (Adoption Act 1958 (c. 5), s.34(1), as substituted by s.29 of the Children Act 1975 (c. 72)). It is not necessary that the agreement under this section should be in writing (*Re T (A Minor)* [1986] 1 All E.R. 817).

"Person who agrees to become a member" (Companies Act 1985 (c. 6), s.22(2)). Any person who, even without any antecedent contract for membership, consents to become a member of a company "agrees" within the meaning of this section (*Re Nuneaton Borough Association Football Club* [1989] BCLC 454.

AGRICULTURAL. (9) "Agricultural land"; "Agricultural unit" (Agriculture Act 1947 (c. 48)). A dwelling-house and its curtilage could constitute part of an agricultural unit or of agricultural land for the purposes of this Act. Whether or not it can be said to be used for agriculture is a question of fact and degree in every case (*Hancock* v. *Secretary of State for the Environment; Tyack* v. *Same* [1988] 3 P.L.R. 78).

(13) "Agricultural machine" (Vehicles (Excise) Act 1971 (c. 10), Sched. 3, Pt. 1, para. 2). The question of whether a vehicle is an "agricultural tractor," and therefore an "agricultural machine" within the definition

contained in this paragraph, is a question of fact for the justices (*DPP* v. *Free's Land Drainage Co.* [1990] RTR 37).

A farmhouse and garden set to one side of a farm was not agricultural property for the purposes of relief from income tax. "Agricultural land" within the meaning of the Inheritance Tax (formerly Capital Transfer Tax) Act 1984 (c. 51), s.115(2) meant underdeveloped land, similar to pasture, used for agricultural purposes (*Starke* v. *I.R.C., The Times*, May 29, 1995).

"Agricultural operations" (General Rate Act 1967 (c. 9), s.26(4)(*a*)); "Agricultural building" (Rating Act 1971 (c. 39), s.2(1)(*a*)). To be exempt from rating under these Acts a building had to be one which was used for a purpose contributing to human subsistence; so that buildings used for the breeding, rearing and keeping of thoroughbred horses did not qualify for exemption (*Hemens* v. *Whitsbury Farm and Stud* [1988] 2 W.L.R. 72).

"Agricultural tenancy" (Agricultural Holdings Act 1986 (c. 5), s.1). A contract of tenancy of land for grazing from year to year was not necessarily disqualified by s.2(3)(*a*) of the 1986 Act from being an agricultural tenancy on account of the existence of certain limits imposed on the grazing (*Brown* v. *Tiernan* [1993] 18 EG 134).

"Agricultural activities," Stat. Def., Health and Safety (Enforcing Authority) Regulations 1998 (No. 494), reg. 2(1).

"Agricultural holding," "agricultural land," Stat. Def., Agricultural Holdings Act 1986 (c. 5), s.1.

"Agricultural merchant," Stat. Def., Medicines (Exemption for Merchants in Veterinary Drugs) Order 1998 (No. 1044), art. 2(1).

AGRICULTURE. "Worked whole-time in agriculture" (Rent (Agriculture) Act 1976 (c. 80), Sched. 3, para. 1). A person who worked as a sales assistant in a farm shop which, in addition to what was produced by the farm, sold other produce as well, was held not to have worked in "agriculture" within the meaning of this section (*Baird* v. *Newell*, Chichester County Court, May 15, 1992).

(Town and Country Planning Act 1990 (c. 8), s.336). Food processing and cheese making on a significant scale was held not to come within the definition of "agriculture" in this section (*Salvatore Cumbo* v. *Secretary of State for the Environment and Dacorum Borough Council* [1992] J.P.L. 366). Worm culture, and sale of the compost thus produced from dung produced as a result of intensive rabbit breeding, did not fall within the definition of "agriculture" in this section (*Powell* v. *Secretary of State for the Environment* [1993] J.P.L. 455).

(Agriculture (Safety, Health and Welfare Provision) 1956 (c. 49), s.24). Peat cutting was not agriculture since the formation of peat was a natural incident of processes which were the antithesis of cultivation, and the removal of naturally forming deposit from the soil was not agriculture. The definition of agriculture in s.24 was wide enough to encompass the consumption and use of produce for purposes incidental to farming including personal consumption (*Pottinger* v. *Peterson* 1997 S.L.T. 387).

Stat. Def., Agricultural Holdings Act 1986 (c. 5), s.96; Town and Country Planning Act 1990 (c. 8), s.336; Agricultural Tenancies Act 1995 (c. 8), s.38(1); Dogs (Fouling of Land) Act 1996 (c. 20), s.1(6); Town and Country Planning (Scotland) Act 1997 (c. 8), s.277(1).

AIRCRAFT. Stat. Def., Consumer Protection Act 1987 (c. 43), s.45.

AIR WEAPON. An "air weapon" within the meaning of s.1(3)(*b*) of the Firearms Act 1968 (c. 27) is a weapon actuated by air, so that a weapon depending upon compressed carbon dioxide cannot be regarded as an air weapon (*R.* v. *Thorpe* [1987] 1 W.L.R. 383). See also FIREARM.

AIRPORT. Stat. Def., Airports Act 1986 (c. 31), s.82.

ALARM. See PERSON.

ALCOHOL. See LIQUOR.

ALLEGED PARTNER. (C.C.R., Ord. 29, r.5). The term "alleged partner" applied to cases where there was a dispute as to whether a person was a partner at the relevant time (*Turner* v. *Haworth Associates* [1996] 7 C.L. 71, C.A.).

ALLOW. "Allowed to borrow by way of overdraft" (Theft Act 1968 (c. 60), s.16(2)(*b*)). A bank customer was "allowed to borrow by way of overdraft" within the meaning of this section when his account became overdrawn upon presentation of cheques supported by a cheque guarantee card; notwithstanding that no overdraft limit had been agreed, and the customer had been specifically told not to overdraw (*R.* v. *Bevan* (1987) 84 Cr.App.R. 143).

ALLOWANCE. (Finance Act 1965 (c. 25), s.56(2)). By the ordinary meaning of the word an "allowance" cannot be automatic and has first to be claimed. Therefore for corporation tax purposes capital allowances to which a company is entitled should not be credited to it automatically (*Ellis* v. *BP Oil Northern Ireland Refinery* [1987] S.T.C. 52).

ALLOWING ESCAPE. The offence of "allowing" a dangerous dog to escape under the Dangerous Dogs Act 1991 (c. 65), s.3(3) could include both acts of commission and omission, so that an owner who had taken inadequate precautions to ensure that his dog was securely tied up so that the dog escaped into a private place and attacked a child was guilty of the offence (*Greener* v. *D.P.P., The Times*, February 16, 1996).

ALTER. "Fraudulently alters or uses . . . any licence", see USE.

ALTERATION. "Alteration" (Industrial Training (Construction Board) Order 1980 (No. 1274), Sched. 1, para. 1(*a*)(*c*), as amended by Industrial Training (Construction Board) Order 1964 (Amendment) Order 1982 (No. 922)). Companies engaged in the manufacture and installation of double glazing units were held not to be engaged in the construction industry as such operations did not involve the "alteration" or "repair" of buildings within the meaning of this regulation (*Construction Industry Training Board* v. *Chiltern Insulations* [1986] I.C.R. 394).

"Alteration" (Town and Country Planning Act 1971 (c. 78), s.55(1)). Repainting the exterior of a listed building in such a manner that its character as a building of special architectural and historic interest was affected was capable of being an "alteration" within the meaning of this section (*Windsor and Maidenhead Borough Council* v. *Secretary of State for the Environment* (1988) 86 L.G.R. 402).

"Alteration or enlargement" (Value Added Tax Act 1983 (c. 55), Sched. 5, Group 8, Item 2, Note (9)(*a*); as substituted by Finance Act 1989 (c. 26), Sched. 3). The construction of a garage 12 yards from a building could not be regarded as an "alteration or enlargement" of that building (*Bradfield (J.H.)* v. *Customs and Excise Commissioners* (1991) 1 VATTR 22).

"Alteration of a listed building" (Planning (Listed Buildings and Conservation Areas) Act 1990 (c. 9), s.27(1)(a)). The alteration of a listed building was a question of fact and degree and had to be considered in the context of the building as a whole and not merely in the context of that part of the structure that had been listed. The removal of chimney breasts and chimney stacks of a listed building could amount to works of alteration rather than demolition (*Shimizu (U.K.) Ltd* v. *Westminster City Council* [1997] 1 W.L.R. 1698).

ALTERNATIVE ACCOMMODATION. See SUITABLE.

AMALGAMATION. (3) "Amalgamation" (Finance Act 1927 (c. 10), s.55). For there to be an "amalgamation" within the meaning of this section there must be a welding or blending of two or more concerns into one. Where the companies concerned retained separate entities there was no amalgamation (*Swithlands Investments* v. *I.R.C.* [1990] S.T.C. 448).

AMEND. Stat. Def., "includes repeal and apply (with or without modifications)" (Human Rights Act 1998 (c. 42), s.21(1)).

AMENITIES. "Amenities of the locality" (General Rate Act 1967 (c. 9), s.20(1)(*b*)). "Amenities" embraces factors of an intangible nature as well as physical factors and applies to those aspects of the locality which are capable of affecting all the hereditaments in the locality, and not merely a separate class such as commercial premises (*Addis* v. *Clement* [1988] 1 W.L.R. 301).

AMMUNITION. Primed bullet cases or blank cartridges constituted "ammunition" for the purposes of ss.1, 19 of the Firearms Act 1968 (c. 27) (*R.* v. *Stubbings*, [1990] Crim.L.R. 811).

AMOUNT. "The amount of the share capital" (Companies Act 1985 (c. 6), s.2(5)(*a*)) does not have to mean a single total amount, and although the "fixed amount" (*ibid.*) of each share cannot be stated in more than one currency it can be stated in different currencies for different classes of share. Thus the share capital which has to be stated in the company's memorandum can comprise a number of amounts in different currencies (*Re Scandinavian Bank Group* [1987] 2 W.L.R. 752).

"Amount recovered" (County Court Rules 1981, Ord. 38, r.4). Interest and costs were to be included in the definition of "amount recovered" for the purposes of Ord. 38, r.4 (*Dataschool Ltd* v. *Sandhu* [1998] 2 C.L. 45).

ANCESTOR. The word "ancestor" in British Nationality Act 1948 (c. 56), s.32(7) includes a father (*R.* v. *Secretary of State for Foreign and Common-wealth Affairs, ex p. Ross-Clunis* [1991] C.O.D. 221).

ANCILLARY. "Ancillary to a dwelling-house" (Common Land (Rectifica-tion of Registers) Act 1989 (c. 18), s.1(2)). Where the owner of an orchard was the tenant of a dwelling-house near but not adjoining the orchard from which he picked fruit, the orchard could properly be described as land used "ancillary" to the dwelling-house within the meaning of this section (*Sir Richard Storey* v. *The Commons Commissioner* (1993) 66 P. & C.R. 206).

"Ancillary to purposes of a retail shop" (Capital Allowances Act 1968 (c. 3), s.7). For a building to be used as for a purpose ancillary to the purposes of a retail shop, it had to be subordinate and subservient to retail selling, so that a warehouse development which was used as a storage and distribution depot and also for the purpose of carrying on its own separate and independent trade was not entitled to allowances under the 1968 Act (*Sarsfield (Inspector of Taxes)* v. *Dixons Group plc* [1997] S.T.C. 283).

"Any ancillary matter relating to" (Supreme Court Act 1981 (c. 54), s.9(7)). The trial of the remaining counts on a severed indictment was not an "ancillary matter relating to" the first trial nor did it constitute proceedings arising out of that trial for the purposes of s.9(7) (*R.* v. *Lord Chancellor, ex p. Maxwell* [1996] 4 All E.R. 751).

AND. "Give evidence himself and to call witnesses" (Magistrates' Courts Rules 1981 (No. 552(L1)). "And" in this rule is to be read disjunctively (*R.* v. *Blyth Valley Justices, ex p. Fawcus, The Times*, April 30, 1986).

AND read as OR. "The proposition that 'and' can sometimes mean 'or' is true neither in law nor in English usage" *per* Blackburn J. (*Re The Licensing Ordinance* (1968) 13 F.L.R. 143).

ANIMAL. "Fighting or baiting of any animal" (Protection of Animals Act 1911 (c. 27), s.1(1)(*c*)). By virtue of s.15(*a*) of this Act "animal" in s.1 means "any domestic or captive animal" and would therefore exclude a badger (*DPP* v. *Barry* [1989] Crim.L.R. 645).

ANNUAL PAYMENT. See ANNUITY.

ANNUAL PROFITS. "Annual profits or gains" (Income and Corporation Taxes Act 1970 (c. 10), s.67, Sched. A). A once-and-for-all payment received by a landowner in return for allowing motorway contractors to tip sub-soil on a part of his property was of a capital and not income nature and thus not "annual profits or gains" (*McClure* v. *Petre* [1988] S.T.C. 749).

ANNUITY. "Any annuity or other annual payment" (Income and Corpora-tion Taxes Act 1970 (c. 10), s.52(1)). Covenanted payments made to a county council by the father of a handicapped child as reimbursement for expenditure incurred by the council on special education for his son were not instalments of an annuity or annual payments within the meaning of this section (*Essex County Council* v. *Ellam* [1989] 2 All E.R. 494). A scheme designed to increase a taxpayer's taxable income by exploiting the fiscal treatment of annuities was struck down by the principles set out in *W.T. Ramsay* v. *I.R.C.* [1982] A.C. 300, rendering self-cancelling tax avoidance schemes fiscal nullities, nothwithstanding that the House of Lords had earlier, in *I.R.C.* v. *Plummer* [1980] A.C. 896, declared that particular scheme effective (*Moodie* v. *I.R.C.*; *Sotnick* v. *Same* [1993] 1 W.L.R. 266). The tax avoidance principle laid down by *Ramsay* v. *I.R.C.* applies to settlement of property made for the admitted purpose of avoiding liability to capital transfer tax (*Hatton* v. *I.R.C.* [1992] S.T.C. 140).

ANOTHER. "Supply . . . to another" (Misuse of Drugs Act 1971 (c. 38), s.4(3)). Where a number of people were charged with unlawfully supplying drugs "to another," the "another" could not be one of those charged (*R.* v. *Lubren and Adepoju* [1988] Crim.L.R. 378).

ANOTHER PERSON. "Causes the death of another person" (Road Traffic Act 1972 (c. 20), s.1, as substituted by s.50(1) of the Criminal Law Act 1977 (c. 45)). A foetus *in utero* at the time of the accident, who was subsequently born alive but died the following day could be "another person" within the meaning of this section (*McCluskey* v. *H.M. Advocate, The Times,* January 12, 1989). But see also OTHER PERSON.

"Another person" (Offences Against the Person Act 1861 (c. 100), s.16, as substituted by Criminal Law Act 1977 (c. 45), Sched. 12). A foetus is not "another person" within the meaning of this section (*R.* v. *Tait* [1989] 3 W.L.R. 891).

The words "to another person" in the Criminal Justice and Public Order Act 1994 (c. 33), s.51, did not restrict the offence to acts carried out in the presence of the victim, and therefore an act done by telephone communication could constitute an offence (*DPP* v. *Mills* [1996] 3 W.L.R. 1093).

ANTARCTICA. Stat. Def., Antarctic Act 1994 (c. 15), s.1(1).

ANTE-NUPTIAL SETTLEMENT. See POST NUPTIAL SETTLEMENT.

ANY. (34) A covenant in a lease prohibiting the assignment or underletting of "any part of the premises" also prohibited the assignment or underletting of the whole (*Field* v. *Barkworth* [1986] 1 All E.R. 362).

"The authority . . . may enter any premises" (Water Act 1989 (c. 15), Sched. 19, para. 10(1). For the purposes of this paragraph "any premises" can include land other than that on which work is to be done, and in the ownership of a third party (*Dwr Cymru Cyfynagedig* v. *Williams, The Times,* October 9, 1991).

Any annuity, see ANNUITY.

ANY DAY. (Licensing Act 1964 (c. 26), s.76(2)(*a*)(*b*)). "Any day" for the purposes of this section does not apply to Sundays (*Carey, Smithers* v. *DPP* [1989] Crim.L.R. 368).

ANY INHERENT CAUSE. (Homicide Act 1957 (c. 11), s.2(1)). Functional mental illness including a paranoid psychosis amounted to "any inherent cause" within the meaning of s.2(1) (*R.* v. *Sanderson (Lloyd)* (1994) 98 Cr.App.R. 325).

ANY OTHER. "Any other new claim" (Limitation Act 1980 (c. 58), s.35(1)(*b*)). A claim by one defendant against another defendant for contribution was "any other new claim" for the purposes of this section, and related back to the date of the original action in which the contribution was claimed (*Kennet* v. *Brown* [1988] 1 W.L.R. 582).

ANY PARTY. "Any party to the proceedings" (Arbitration Act 1975 (c. 3), s.1(1)) is restricted to the parties to the arbitration agreement and those claiming through or under them (*Etri Fans* v. *NMB (UK)* [1987] 2 All E.R. 763).

ANY PAYMENT. The words "any payments" in s.2(1)(*a*) of the Drug Trafficking Offences Act 1986 (c. 32) do not mean net profits after deduction of expenses, but any payment in money or in kind (*R.* v. *Smith (Ian)* [1989] 1 W.L.R. 765).

ANY PERSON. "Any person" (Bankruptcy Act 1914 (c. 59), s.25(1)) would not include a person who was not at the relevant time in England (*Re Tucker (A Bankrupt), ex p. Tucker* [1988] 1 All E.R. 603).
    "Any person" (Insolvency Act 1986 (c. 45), s.133). Held to include a person in any of the classes specified by the section even though he might be out of the jurisdiction (*Re Seagull Manufacturing Co. (in liquidation)* [1991] 3 W.L.R. 307).
    (Insolvency Act 1986 (c. 45), s.236(2)). "Any person" was not confined to persons resident in the jurisdiction of the court or who had been personally served with a petition within the jurisdiction, but extended to any person whether within or outside the jurisdiction (*McIsaac and Wilson* (O.H.), January 13, 1995).
    "Any person" (Insolvency Act 1986 (c. 45), s.238) is to be construed literally and is not subject to any implied limitation. Thus the section has unrestricted extra-territorial effect and allows service of process on a foreign bank not carrying on business in the U.K. (*Re Paramount Airways (in Administration)* [1992] 3 All E.R. 1).
    "Where any other person holds an interest in the property" (Drug Trafficking Offences Act 1986 (c. 32), s.5(4)(*a*). Where a house was purchased by a wife, partially with a gift from her husband of money deriving from his drug dealings and partially with a mortgage from a building society, it was held that the building society was a person holding an interest in the property within the meaning of this section (*R.* v. *Chapman, The Times,* November 18, 1991).
    "Any person or body carrying out functions of care and conservation" for the purposes of the Care of Churches and Ecclesiastical Jurisdiction Measure 1991, s.1 did not apply to Chancellors of the Consistory Court (*Re St. Luke the Evangelist, Maidstone* [1995] 1 All E.R. 323).
    (Fair Trading Act 1973 (c. 41), s.93A). The right to enforce undertakings given to the Secretary of State in s.93 of the 1973 Act was given to the Crown alone rather than to any private person (*Mid Kent Holdings plc* v. *General Utilities plc* [1996] 4 All E.R. 132).

ANYONE. The word "anyone" in s.17(1) of the Forestry Act 1967 (c. 10), is to be given its ordinary meaning and is not restricted to those persons entitled to apply for a licence to fell trees under s.10 as "persons having an estate or interest in land" (*Forestry Commission* v. *Frost* (1990) 154 J.P. 14).

ANYTHING. "Anything suffered," see SUFFER.

"Anything . . . for the purpose of making a counterfeit" (Forgery and Counterfeiting Act 1981 (c. 45), s.17(1)). A chromolin or printer's proof, which was used as part of the process of making a counterfeit, was caught by s.17(1) (*R.* v. *Maltman, The Times*, June 28, 1994).

"Anything" under the Misuse of Drugs Act 1971 (c. 38), s.27 did not extend to real property (*R.* v. *Khan* (Sultant Ashraf applied) (*R.* v. *Pearce (John Frederick) The Times*, February 22, 1996). (Transfer of Undertakings (Protection of Employment Regulations 1981 (S.I. 1981 No. 1794), reg. 5).

The right to recover a redundancy payment erroneously made was not "anything done . . . in respect of . . . a person employed in that undertaking" (*Mediguard Services Ltd* v. *McVeigh* 1996 S.C.L.R. 1097).

APPARATUS. "Apparatus coupled by means of any material substance" (Wireless Telegraphy Act 1949 (c. 54), s.19(1) as amended by Telecommunications Act 1984 (c. 12), s.92(3)). A claim that records and audio cassettes were "coupled" to the radio equipment by way of the stylus and tape head failed, so that they were not "apparatus" within the meaning of this section. Loudspeakers used for monitoring were, however, held to be "apparatus" (*Rudd* v. *Secretary of State for Trade and Industry* (1986) 130 S.J. 504); upheld by the House of Lords, [1987] 1 W.L.R. 786. See also USE.

"Apparatus" (Mines and Quarries Act 1954 (c. 70), s.81(1)) held to include a fixed steel access ladder within a vertical shaft underground in a colliery (*Brebner* v. *British Coal Corporation, The Times*, July 23, 1988).

Stat. Def., "includes any vessel, vehicle or hovercraft, any structure, any diving plant or equipment and any other form of equipment" (Merchant Shipping Act 1995 (c. 21), s.88(4)).

APPARENT. (2) (Wills Act 1837 (c. 26), s.21). Where the signatures on a will were so effectively obliterated by overscoring with a pen that they were illegible they ceased to be "apparent" within the meaning of this section, and the will was therefore revoked (*Re Adams (Dec'd.)* [1990] 2 W.L.R. 924).

See also DESTROY.

APPEAL. Stat. Def., Drug Trafficking Act 1994 (c. 37), s.40(2).

APPEAR. "Appearing to the Court" (Drug Trafficking Offences Act 1986 (c. 32), s.2(3)(*a*)) means that there has to be prima facie evidence which entitles the judge to make any of the assumptions specified in this section (*R.* v. *Dickens* [1990] 2 Q.B. 102).

APPELLANT. "The appellant . . . if dissatisfied" (Taxes Management Act 1970 (c. 9), s.56(1)). In circumstances where a single partner, acting against the wishes of his co-partners, sought to bring an appeal by way of case stated against a determination by general commissioners of the partnership's income tax liability, the single partner could not properly be described as an "appellant" who was "dissatisfied" with the commissioners' determination for the purposes of this section (*Sutherland* v. *Gustar* (*Inspector of Taxes*) [1994] Ch. 304.

APPLICATION. "Application for judicial review" (R.S.C., Ord. 53, r.4(1)) is not restricted to the substantive application itself. The application for leave to apply for judicial review is an "application" within the meaning of the rule (*R.* v. *Stratford-on-Avon District Council, ex p. Jackson* [1985] 3 All E.R. 769).

"Application . . . in any civil proceedings" (Supreme Court Act 1981 (c. 54), s.42(1A)(*c*), as amended by section 24 of the Prosecution of Offences Act 1985 (c. 23), s.24(3). Substantive appeals to the Court of Appeal are applications in any civil proceedings within the meaning of this section (*Att.-Gen.* v. *Jones* [1990] 1 W.L.R. 859; *Henry J. Garrett & Co.* v. *Ewing* [1991] 1 W.L.R. 1356.

Any request to the court for relief whether interlocutory or final amounted to an "application" in civil proceedings for the purposes of the Supreme Court Act 1981 (c. 54), s.42(1A) (*Mephistopheles Debt Collection Service* (*a firm*) v. *Lotay* [1994] 1 W.L.R. 1064).

"Application for an emergency prohibition order" (Food Safety Act 1990 (c. 16), s.12(1)(*a*)) means the process whereby an application is made to the court by the council's environmental health officer and not the hearing of the application itself (*Farrand* v. *Tse, The Times*, December 10, 1992).

"Application" (Highways Act 1980 (c. 66), s.116). An application under this section is to be treated as being by way of complaint and, accordingly, a highway authority can be ordered to pay the costs of objectors entitled to be heard at the hearing (*Lincolnshire County Council* v. *Brewis, The Times*, August 18, 1992).

(R.S.C., Ord. 31, r.1). An application, the real purpose of which was to obtain an early release of capital before the final resolution of claims for ancillary relief under the Matrimonial Causes Act 1973 was not "an application relating to land" within the meaning of Ord. 31, r.1 (*Wicks* v. *Wicks* [1998] 1 All E.R. 977).

APPLICATION FOR A SUPERVISION ORDER. An application to extend a supervision order under the Children Act 1989 (c. 41), s.35 and Sched. 3, para. 6 was not an "application for a supervision order" and there was no requirement for the threshold criteria under s.31(5)(*b*) to be satisfied (*Re A.* (*A Minor*) (*Supervision Order: Extension*) [1995] 1 W.L.R. 483).

APPLY. "Goods to which a false trade description is applied" (Trade Descriptions Act 1968 (c. 29), s.1(1)(*b*)). The words "is applied" describe a state of affairs and not an act, and so it was enough that a defendant supplied a car with a false trade description (odometer false reading) even though it was not he who had first applied it to the car (*Swithland Motors* v. *Peck* [1991] RTR 322).

"Applies to a local housing authority" (Housing Act 1985 (c. 68), s.62). For the purposes of this section an application can be made on behalf of a person under a disability by someone else acting on their behalf even though the disability was such as to render the sufferer unable to consent to the application (*R.* v. *Tower Hamlets London Borough Council, ex p. Begum* (*Ferdous*) (1991) 24 H.L.R. 188).

APPOINTMENT. What amounted to an "appointment" for the purposes of art. 10(*a*) of the Agricultural Holdings (Arbitration on Notices) Order 1987 (No. 710) defended on the facts of each case. Clear evidence of receipt and acceptance by the arbitrator of a letter of appointment from both parties was sufficient (*Malik* v. *Bank of Credit and Commerce International SA, The Times,* February 23, 1994).

APPROPRIATE. "Appropriate adult" (Police and Criminal Evidence Act 1984 (c. 60), s.66, Codes of Practice, Code C). An estranged parent whose presence had been expressly and specifically objected to by a juvenile was not an "appropriate adult" to accompany the juvenile to an interview or for the taking of a confession (*DPP* v. *Blake* [1989] 1 W.L.R. 432). A father (neither estranged nor unwanted) who attends the interview of a juvenile may be an "appropriate adult" even if he intervenes robustly during the interview (*R.* v. *Jefferson* [1994] 1 All E.R. 270, C.A.). An adult incapable of giving advice was not an "appropriate adult" (*R.* v. *Morse* [1991] Crim.L.R. 195).

Even mental incapacity does not prevent an adult from being an "appropriate adult" provided he is capable of fulfilling the functions of an appropriate adult and can deal rationally with the situation (*R.* v. *W.* [1994] Crim.L.R. 130).

APPROPRIATION. (Military Lands Act 1892, s.14(1)). "Appropriated" meant set aside or allocated for a specific purpose and was not concerned with the use of the land in question (*DPP* v. *John, The Times,* January 28, 1999).

(Theft Act 1968 (c. 60), s.3(1)). The use of a cheque card to guarantee payment of a cheque drawn on an account with inadequate funds was not an "assumption" of the rights of the bank and was not, therefore, an "appropriation" within the meaning of this section (*R.* v. *Navvabi* [1986] 3 All E.R. 102). But the presentation and negotiation through a bank of a forged cheque constituted an "assumption" of the rights of the bank's customer to the debt owed by the bank to the customer, and was therefore an "appropriation" within the meaning of s.4(1) of the Hong Kong Theft Ordinance (which is couched in the same terms as s.3(1) of the 1968 Theft Act) (*Chan Man-sin* v. *The Queen* [1988] 1 W.L.R. 196). By drawing cheques on his employer's account at the bank, and using the proceeds for his own use, an offender assumes the rights of an owner and therefore "appropriates" the debt owed by the bank to the employing company. Whether or not the bank had authority to honour the cheque is irrelevant (*R.* v. *Wille* (1988) 86 Cr.App.R. 296). Where a defendant, without a customer's authority, dishonestly issued a cheque drawn on the customer's account, the "appropriation" was made when the cheque was drawn, notwithstanding that the funds might not yet have been debited. Thus, where dishonest instructions are sent by telex to withdraw money from a bank account, the sending of the telex is an "appropriation" within the meaning of this section (*R.* v. *Governor of Pentonville Prison, ex p. Osman* [1989] 3 All E.R. 701). "Appropriation," under the Theft Act, which is done by an officer, agent or employee of a company means "misappropriation," and cannot normally involve an act done with the express or implied authority of the company (*R.* v. *McHugh*; *R.* v. *Tringham* (1989) 88

Cr.App.R. 385). But it is not necessary for the prosecution to establish that the appropriation was without the owner's consent or authority (*R.* v. *Philippou* (1989) 89 Cr.App.R. 290). Where property was obtained with express authority of the owner but that authority was obtained by a false representation, the obtaining of that property did not amount to an "appropriation" (*R.* v. *Gomez* [1991] 3 All E.R. 394). Where a person in authority signed a false invoice intending that innocent people should take further steps which resulted in money being debited from a bank account there was an "appropriation" within the meaning of this section (*R.* v. *Stringer and Banks* (1992) 94 Cr.App.R. 13). A person cannot be charged with theft in respect of an authorised act, even when that act was committed in order to do an unauthorised act, since the authorised act could not amount to "appropriation" under s.3(1) (*R.* v. *Nadir, The Independent*, June 24, 1992). Trading-in a hired motorcar outside the jurisdiction was held not to be an act of appropriation that could justify a charge of theft of the motorcar (*R.* v. *Morgan* (*Oliver*) [1991] RTR 365). An act done with the authority or consent of the owner of goods could amount to an "appropriation" of those goods for the purposes of the section where such authority or consent had been obtained by deception (*R.* v. *Gomez* [1992] 3 W.L.R. 1067). A sum of money represented by a figure in an account fell within the phrase "other intangible property" in s.4(1) and accordingly a transaction, although effected by electronic means, was an appropriation of intangible property (*R.* v. *Crick, The Times,* August 18, 1993).

"Appropriation" is an objective description of an act irrespective of the mental state either of the owner of the property or the accused (*R.* v. *Gallasso* (*Lesley Caroline*) (1994) 98 Cr.App.R. 284).

(Town and Country Planning Act 1990 (c. 8), s.226). "Appropriation", in the context of land which a council already owns, is the equivalent of compulsory purchase of a council's own land. *R.* v. *Leeds City Council, ex p. Leeds Industrial Co-operative Society Ltd* (1997) 73 P. & C.R. 70).

APPROVE. "And the court . . . . . . approves the sale" (Companies Act 1985 (c. 6), s.456(3)(*b*)). This means approved of the fact of the sale. It should not be construed as meaning only approval of the terms of the sale (*Re Greers Gross, The Times*, August 18, 1987).

"A practitioner approved for the purposes of this section" (Mental Health Act 1983 (c. 20), s.12(2)). In deciding whether a registered medical practitioner is "approved," under this section, to make medical recommendations to admit a patient to a mental hospital the Secretary of State for Health, or his delegate, is entitled to have regard to the fitness of the particular practitioner for the task in hand (*R.* v. *Trent Regional Health Authority, ex p. Somaratue, The Times,* December 10, 1993).

APPURTENANCE. (Leasehold Reform, Housing and Urban Development Act 1993 (c. 28), s.62). A storeroom on the sixth floor which was an "appurtenance" to a flat which was on the second floor did not need to have to be passed under an assignment without express mention but had to belong to or be enjoyed by the flat (*Cadogan* v. *McGirk* [1996] 8 C.L. 414, C.A.).

Where a loan was secured by a first mortgage on a vessel covering, amongst other things, "appurtenances". It was held that the appurtenances did not include the ship's bunker oil (*The Pan Oak* [1992] 2 Lloyd's Rep. 36).

ARABLE. "Arable land." Stat. Def., Agricultural Holdings Act 1986 (c. 5), s.15.

ARBITRATION. A rent review clause in a lease which gave a unilateral right to the lessee to refer disputes to arbitration was first held not to be an "arbitration agreement" on the grounds that it is an essential ingredient of an arbitration agreement that each party should be entitled to refer a dispute to arbitration (*Tote Bookmakers* v. *Development and Property Holding Co.* [1985] 2 All E.R. 555). But it has since been held that that is not an essential ingredient of an "arbitration agreement" for the purposes of the Arbitration Acts 1950 (c. 27) and 1975 (c. 3). The terms of a lease conferring a unilateral right to refer on the lessee could still be an arbitration agreement (*Pittallis* v. *Sherefettin* [1986] 2 All E.R. 227). The decision of an adjudicator appointed pursuant to the terms of the DOM/1 sub-contract is not an award on an "arbitration agreement" within the meaning of section 26 of the 1950 Act (*Cameron (A)* v. *John Mowlem & Co.* (1990) 52 BLR 24).

AREA. "Area used for milk production" (Dairy Produce Quota Regulations 1984 (No. 1047), Sched. 2, para. 6(3)) includes not merely the area used to support cows which are actually lactating, but also those areas, including buildings and yards, used to support cows between lactations and those destined for subsequent inclusion in the herd (*Puncknowle Farms* v. *Kane* [1985] 3 All E.R. 790).

ARISE. "If any dispute or difference shall arise . . . as to the construction of this contract" (JCT Form (July 1977 revision)). A dispute between building owners and contractors, based upon alleged mistake, misrepresentation or misstatement, was one which arose as to the construction of the contract within the meaning of this clause (*Ashville Investments* v. *Elmer Contractors* [1988] 2 All E.R. 577).

The phrase "disputes arising under a contract" in an arbitration agreement was held not to be wide enough to include disputes which did not concern obligations created by or incorporated in that contract (*Fillite (Runcorn)* v. *Aqua-Lift* (1989) 45 Build.L.R. 27).

ARISING. (6) "Arising or accruing" (Income and Corporation Taxes Act 1970 (c. 10), s.108, Sched. D). Income of a trust that was administered abroad, and whose income arose from foreign assets held for the benefit of non-resident beneficiaries, and which was not remitted to the United Kingdom, did not "accrue" to the one trustee, out of three, who resided in the United Kingdom (*Dawson* v. *I.R.C.* [1989] 2 W.L.R. 858.

"Arising out of or under this contract" (GAFTA 30/86, clause 31). These words when incorporated into an arbitration agreement could be given a wide interpretation so as to cover all disputes other than one as to the very existence of the contract itself (*Ethiopian Oilseeds and Pulses Export Corporation* v. *Rio Del Mar Foods* [1990] 1 Lloyd's Rep. 86).

(Road Traffic Act 1988 (c. 52), s.145). The phrase "arising out of" contemplated a more remote consequence than was embraced by "caused by" in s.145 so that in circumstances where D ran across the road in order to obtain assistance with restarting her car, her involvement in an accident with a passing vehicle was closely and causally connected with her use of her car so that the accident "arose out of" such use rendering her insurers liable (*Dunthorne* v. *Bentley* [1996] RTR 428).

"Arising out of and in the course of employment." See IN THE COURSE OF.

ARMED. "Armed with . . . or other offensive weapon" (Vagrancy Act 1824 (c. 83), s.4). The offence is not the actual use of the weapon but the premeditated carrying of it, so that where a man, trying to deny entry, slammed the front door in the face of two police officers, thereby breaking the glass, and then lunged at them with a piece of the glass, he was not guilty of an offence under this section (*Wood* v. *Commissioner of Police for the Metropolis* [1986] 1 W.L.R. 796).

"Is armed" (Customs and Excise Management Act 1979 (c. 2), s.86). For a person to be "armed" within the meaning of this section it is not necessary to prove an intent to use the arms should the situation require it. Thus the captain of a ship engaged in the importation of cannabis resin was held to be "armed" when two unloaded guns were found in a locker in the wheelhouse (*R.* v. *Jones* (*K.D.*) [1987] 1 W.L.R. 692).

ARMS. (Firearms Act 1968 (c. 27), s.57). Air rifles in normal working order were "arms" within the meaning of s.57, since they could maim or kill if aimed at vulnerable parts of the body (*Castle* v. *DPP*, *The Times*, April 3, 1998).

ARRAIGNMENT. (Prosecution of Offences (Custody Time Limits) Regulations 1987 (No. 299), r.5). A pre-trial review, at which the prosecution counsel told the judge the intended pleas of the defendants, was not an "arraignment" within the meaning of this regulation (*R.* v. *Bristol Crown Court, ex p. Commissioners of Customs and Excise* [1990] C.O.D. 11).

ARRANGE. "Handles stolen goods . . . or . . . arranges to do so" (Theft Act 1968 (c. 60), s.22(1)). To constitute the offence it is necessary that any arrangement to do so must take place after the goods have been stolen. A prior arrangement is not sufficient (*R.* v. *Park* (1988) 87 Cr.App.R. 164).

ARRANGEMENT. "Transaction" or "arrangement" (Dairy Produce Quotas Regulations 1984 (No. 1047), para. 17(3)). A verbal arrangement which is not legally enforceable is capable of amounting to a "transaction" or "arrangement" within the meaning of this paragraph (*R.* v. *Dairy Produce Quota Tribunal for England and Wales, ex p. Lifely* [1988] 27 E.G. 79).

"Shares or securities in respect of which arrangements exist" (Finance Act 1973 (c. 51), Sched. 12, para. 5(3)). The existence of an option to buy shares does not deprive the current owner of beneficial ownership, nor does it constitute an "arrangement" with the meaning of this paragraph (*Sainsbury (J.)* v. *O'Connor* [1991] S.T.C. 318).

(9) "Disposition . . . arrangement or transfer of assets" (Income and Corporation Taxes Act 1970 (c. 10), s.444(2)). See SETTLEMENT.

Stat. Def., Companies Act 1985 (c. 6), ss.44, 103, 131, 425.

ARREST. An offender was arrested when he was detained by automatic activation of the door locks inside a motor vehicle specially adapted by the police as a trap. The arrest was made lawful when the police informed the offender as soon as practicable of his arrest and the grounds (*Dawes* v. *DPP, The Times,* March 2, 1994).

(Arrest Convention 1952, Art. 7). "Arrest" related to the character of the legal process rather than to the motivation of the party initiating the arresting process (*Anna H., The* [1995] 1 Lloyd's Rep. 11).

ARRESTABLE OFFENCE. (Police and Criminal Evidence Act 1984 (c. 60), s.25). Where an intervener sought to prevent the arrest of a person who was himself being unlawfully arrested the arrest of the intervener was also unlawful and, therefore not an "arrestable offence" within the meaning of this section (*Edwards* v. *DPP, The Times,* March 29, 1993).

ARTICLE. "Breaking up or demolition of any article" (Factories Act 1961 (c. 34), s.175(1)(*b*)). It was held that a kiln could not properly be described as an "article" within the meaning of this section (*R.* v. *A.I. Industrial Products* [1987] I.C.R. 418).

A motor vehicle part, which had no independent life as an article of commerce and was merely an adjunct to a larger item, was not an "article" within s.1(1) of the Registered Designs Act 1949 (c. 88), as substituted by s.265(1) of the Copyright, Designs and Patents Act 1988 (c. 48) (*R.* v. *Registered Designs Appeal Tribunal, ex p. Ford Motor Co.* [1995] 1 W.L.R. 18).

(Obscene Publications Act 1959 (c. 66), ss.1(2), (3), 2(1)). A print of a photograph was a record of a picture and constituted an "article" for the purposes of the 1959 Act (*R.* v. *Taylor (Alan)* [1995] 1 Cr.App.R. 131).

"Article" in the definition of "industrial process" in the Town and Country Planning Development Order 1988, Sched. 2, Part 8, Class D should be construed to include walls, buildings, roads, driveways and paths (*Kent County Council* v. *Secretary of State for the Environment and R. Marchant and Sons Ltd* CO/604/95, July 13, 1995).

ARTIFICIAL LIGHTING. Light which came from low pressure lamps which could be seen from a house, but where the amount of light which fell on the ground around the houses was infinitesimally small, amounted to "artificial lighting" and came within the Land Compensation Act 1973 (c. 26), Pt. I (*Blower* v. *Suffolk County Council* (1994) 67 P. & C.R. 228).

ARTISTIC. "Artistic work" (Copyright Act 1956 (c. 74), s.3). The manufacturer's drawing of a car's exhaust pipe is capable of being an "artistic work" within the meaning of this section (*British Leyland Motor Corporation* v. *Armstrong Patents Co.* [1986] 2 W.L.R. 400).

Circuit diagrams relating to an electronic dust meter were "artistic works" (*Anacon Corp.* v. *Environmental Research Technology* [1994] F.S.R. 659).

"Artistic work." Stat. Def., Copyright, Designs and Patents Act 1988 (c. 48), s.4.

ASCERTAINED. A number of cases or bottles of identical wine which had been kept separately or segregated from a company's trading stock in store for customers were "ascertained" for the purposes of the Sale of Goods Act 1979 (c. 54), s.16, even though they were not immediately appropriated to the individual customer (*Re Stapylton Fletcher* [1994] 1 W.L.R. 1181).

AS SOON AS POSSIBLE. (Prison Rules 1964 (No. 338), as amended). This is a mandatory requirement which was not satisfied by the Board of Visitors when laying a charge on May 2 in respect of an incident which took place on February 16 (*R. v. Board of Visitors of Dartmouth Prison, ex p. Smith* [1986] 3 W.L.R. 61).

AS SOON AS PRACTICABLE. Where formal notice of complaints made against them was not given to five police officers until two and a half years after the complaints were made it was held that notice had not been served "as soon as practicable," as is required by the Police (Discipline) Regulations 1977 (No. 580), reg. 7 (*R. v. Chief Constable of the Merseyside Police, ex p. Calveley* [1986] Q.B. 424). Eleven weeks was held to be far beyond being "as soon as practicable" (*R. v. Chief Constable of the Merseyside Police, ex p. Merrill* [1989] 1 W.L.R. 1077).

(Bail Act 1976 (c. 63), s.7). The requirement for a detainee to be brought before a justice of the peace "as soon as reasonably practicable and in any event within 24 hours of his arrest" was an absolute requirement, so that merely bringing the detainee into the precincts of the court was insufficient to satisfy the section (*R. v. Governor of Glen Parva Young Offenders Institution, ex p. G (a minor)* [1998] 2 All E.R. 295).

See also PRACTICABLE; REASONABLY PRACTICABLE.

AS SUCH. (Genocide Act 1969 (c. 12), s.1). The use of the words "as such" in the definition of genocide in s.1 meant that the crime referred to acts aimed at the destruction of all or part of a national, racial, ethnic or religious group and could not be taken to mean all or part of the human race (*Hipperson* v. *DPP* [1996] 10 C.L. 116, C.A.).

ASSAULT. (Offences against the Person Act 1861 (c. 100), s.47). A person who, in a moment of panic, poured concentrated sulphuric acid into a hot air hand drier was guilty of "assault" occasioning actual bodily harm when the acid injured the next person to use the machine; notwithstanding that it had been his intention to deal with the acid before the next use of the machine. Taking the risk that the machine would be used by another before he could render it safe amounted to recklessness (*DPP* v. *K* [1990] 1 All E.R. 331). A sado-masochistic act of violence is an "assault" for the purposes of this Act, notwithstanding that it is made with the consent of, and for the sexual pleasure of the victim (*R.* v. *Brown* [1993] 2 W.L.R. 556).

Recognisable psychiatric illnesses, which affected the central nervous sytem, can amount to "bodily harm" under ss.20 and 47 of the 1867 Act; the making of silent phone calls which caused psychiatric injury was capable of amounting to an assault under s.47 (*R.* v. *Ireland*) [1997] 3 W.L.R. 534).

Post-traumatic stress disorder as a psychological and physiological reaction as a consequence of violent external stimuli could constitute an accidental bodily injury (*Connelly* v. *New Hampshire Insurance Co.* (1997) S.C.L.R. 459).

"Assaults an officer of the court while in the execution of his duty" (County Courts Act 1984 (c. 28), s.14(1)). A person was not punishable under this section if, at the time, he honestly but mistakenly believed that the victim was not an officer of the court or was not acting in the execution of his duty (*Blackburn* v. *Bowering* [1994] 3 All E.R. 380).

(Criminal Justice Act 1988 (c. 33), ss.39, 40). "Assault" in s.40 of the 1988 Act was to be defined in the same manner as in s.39 and included assault and battery (*R.* v. *Lynsey (Jonathan Simon)* [1995] 3 All E.R. 654).

"Wilfully assaults, ill-treats, neglects. . . . " See ASSAULT; ILL-TREAT.

ASSESSMENT. (Children Act 1989 (c. 41), s.38(6)). "Assessment" should be given a broad construction to include the relationship between a child and his parents, and the court could order any assessment of a child which would provide the evidence to assist the court in deciding whether a full care order should be made (*Re C (A Minor) (Interim Care Order: Residential Assessment)* [1996] 3 W.L.R. 1098).

ASSET. Stat. Def., "means any form of property or rights" (Finance Act 1997 (c. 16), Sched. 12, para. 30(1)).

ASSETS. (7)(8) Notwithstanding *Re Barleycorn Enterprises* [1970] Ch. 465 [see Main Work, p. 196] "assets" for the purposes of s.115 of the Insolvency Act 1986 (c. 45) means "assets available for distribution to the general body of creditors" and would not include assets subject to a valid floating charge (*Re M. C. Bacon (No. 2)*, *The Times*, April 12, 1990).

(15) "Assets" (Finance Act 1965 (c. 25), s.22; Capital Gains Tax Act 1979 (c. 14), s.20). Money received by a company in return for a five-year covenant not to compete was held not to accrue from the disposal of any "asset" and thus could not give rise to a chargeable gain (*Kirby* v. *Thorn EMI* [1986] 1 W.L.R. 851). This decision was reversed by the Court of Appeal which ruled that a sum received in return for giving a covenant not to compete was a sum received for a disposal of goodwill, and goodwill constituted an "asset" ([1987] S.T.C. 621).

(4) The milk quota formerly registered in the name of a farming partnership could not properly be regarded as property or a right or interest in property, separate and distinct from the holding in respect of which it was registered, and would not therefore be available as partnership "assets" in a dissolution under the Partnership Act (c. 39), s.39 to meet the debts and liabilities of the partnership (*Faulks* v. *Faulks* [1992] 15 E.G. 15).

Stat. Def., Local Government (Contracts) Act 1997 (c. 65), s.1(4); Bank of England (Information Powers) Order 1998 (No. 1270), art. 1(2).

See also FIXED ASSETS.

ASSIGNMENT. Stat. Def., Landlord and Tenant (Covenants) Act 1995 (c. 30), s.28(1).

ASSIST. (6) "Assists in or induces" (Misuse of Drugs Act 1971 (c. 38), s.20). A person cannot be guilty of assisting in the commission of an offence, within the meaning of this section, if that offence was never in fact committed (*R.* v. *Panayi*; *R.* v. *Karte* [1987] Crim.L.R. 764). Where drugs, which had been concealed in a consignment of raisins intended for importation into Holland, were not claimed on arrival and were subsequently sent to Belgium by an innocent third party, the person responsible for shipping the drugs to Holland was guilty of "assisting in the commission of an offence" in Belgium contrary to section 20 (*R.* v. *Ahmed* [1990] Crim.L.R. 648, C.A.).

"Assist in the management of a brothel" (Sexual Offences Act 1956 (c. 69), s.33). Where women in a massage parlour not only performed lewd acts but, among other things, discussed the nature of the acts to be performed and negotiated the terms of payment for their services, they were assisting in the management of a brothel within the meaning of this section (*Elliott* v. *DPP*; *Dublides* v. *DPP*, *The Times*, January 19, 1989). Taking advertisements to the post office and paying for them to be displayed could amount to assisting in the management of the brothel within the meaning of this section (*Jones* v. *DPP*, *The Times*, June 4, 1992). It is not necessary, in order to establish that an offence has been committed under this section, to show that the accused has been exercising some sort of control over its management (*Jones and Wood* v. *DPP* (1993) 96 Cr.App.R. 130).

ASSOCIATE. (3) "Associated employer" (Employment Protection (Consolidation) Act 1978 (c. 44), s.153(4)). For two companies to be "associated" one of them must "control" the other or they must both be under the control of a third person or company. Where a single person dominated and to all intents and purposes controlled the operations of a number of companies, but did not hold a majority of the shares of any of them, it was held that he did not "control" them within the meaning of this section and that therefore they were not "associated" (*South West Launderettes* v. *Laidler* [1986] I.C.R. 455). Where four brothers owned 80 per cent. of the shares in company A and their father the remaining 20 per cent., and the four brothers owned 20 per cent. of company B and their father and mother the remaining 80 per cent., the companies were not "associated" within the meaning of s.153(4) (*Strudwick* v. *IBL* [1988] 1 IRLR 457). A group of people controlling a company can be an "associated employer" for the purposes of this section (*Harford* v. *Swiftrim* [1987] I.C.R. 439). An employer who controls a company and who then becomes a sole trader is an "associated employer" in relation to any employees whom he continues to employ after the change, and such employees have continuity of employment (*Secretary of State for Employment* v. *Chapman* [1989] I.C.R. 771). Two companies, run by the same man, but in one of which his wife was a fellow director (each holding one share), were, notwithstanding the wife's equal shareholding, held to be under the same "control" and therefore "associated" within the meaning of this section (*Payne* v. *Secretary of State for Employment* [1989] IRLR 352). Two companies can be "associated employers" within the meaning of s.153(4) notwithstanding that one of them is British and the other American (*Hancil* v. *Marcon Engineering*, [1990] IRLR 51).

(Equal Pay Act (c. 41), s.1(6), as amended; E.E.C. Treaty, Art. 119). The critical question for the purpose of Art. 119 was whether the applicant and the comparators were employed in the same establishment or service, whether those establishments were directly or indirectly controlled by a third party, the extent and nature of that control and whether common terms and conditions were observed (*Scullard* v. *Knowles* [1996] I.C.R. 399). See also CONTINUOUSLY (3).

"Associated operations" (Finance Act 1975 (c. 7), s.20(4)). Where trustees of a discretionary settlement permitted certain valuable paintings, part of the trust fund, to go into the custody of a connected person, but one excluded from the beneficial interest, and then appointed a life interest in them to a beneficiary, these were "associated operations" within the meaning of this section, and the disposition was "made in a transaction intended to confer . . . gratuitous benefit" on the life interest beneficiary, so that capital transfer tax was payable (*I.R.C.* v. *Macpherson* [1988] 2 W.L.R. 1261). See also VALUE.

"One other offence associated with it" (Criminal Justice Act 1991 (c. 53), s.1(2)(*a*)). An offence for which the accused was given a suspended sentence was not, when the suspended sentence was activated, an offence "associated" with another (*R.* v. *Crawford* (1994) 98 Cr.App.R. 297).

Stat. Def., Administration of Justice Act 1985 (c. 61), s.39; Insolvency Act 1985 (c. 65), s.233; Banking Act 1987 (c. 22), s.105; Finance Act 1987 (c. 16), s.37); Companies Act 1989 (c. 40), s.52.

ASSOCIATION. "Any partnership, association or company" (Companies Act 1985 (c. 6), s.665). The International Tin Corporation, being an international body created by treaty, was plainly not a "partnership" or "company," and was here also held not to be an "association," and therefore not an "unregistered company" for the purposes of this section (*Re International Tin Council* (1988) 4 BCC 653).

ASSUME. "Any obligation assumed," see OBLIGATION.

ASSUMPTION. See APPROPRIATION.

ASYLUM. (Asylum and Immigration Appeals Act 1993 (c. 23), s.1). A person could, during a single uninterrupted stay in the United Kingdom, make more than one "claim for asylum" for the purposes of s.1 and the test was whether comparing the fresh claim with that earlier rejected and excluding material on which the claimant could reasonably be expected to rely in the earlier claim, the new claim was sufficiently different from the earlier claim to admit of a realistic prospect that a favourable view would be taken of the new claim (*R.* v. *Secretary of State for the Home Department, ex p. Onibiyo* [1996] 2 All E.R. 901).

AT. "At a police station" (Police and Criminal Evidence Act 1984 (c. 60), Code of Practice D). A suspect walking out of a police station could still be "at" the police station for the purposes of the Code (*R.* v. *Nagah* [1991] Crim.L.R. 55).

"At an establishment in Great Britain," see ESTABLISHMENT.

AT BUYER'S CALL. In considering the meaning and effect of these words in clause 7 of GAFTA form 119 it was held that they meant something very similar to "on buyer's call," although weaker than "on buyer's demand"; so that failure by the seller to make prompt delivery at the buyer's call was a breach of condition (*Tradax Export S.A.* v. *Italgrani di Francesco Ambrosio* [1983] 2 Lloyd's Rep. 109).

AT ONCE. "Proceeding at once to another country" (Statement of Changes of Immigration Rules (H.C. 169), para. 9). "At once" should be allowed some flexibility given the delays normal in air travel and could perhaps mean "within a reasonable time" (*R.* v. *Secretary of State for the Home Department, ex p. Caunhye, The Times,* April 21, 1988).

AT OR NEAR. "At or near his own place of work" (Trade Union and Labour Relations Act 1974 (c. 52), s.15(1)(*a*), as substituted by Employment Act 1980 (c. 42), s.16(1)). Where, pursuant to a trade dispute, various employees of a company, whose place of work was situated in a trading park, set up a picket at the park entrance, it was held that for the purposes of this section the picket was "at or near" the place of work, notwithstanding that the premises were more than half a mile from the entrance, as it was the nearest they could get without trespassing on the park (*Rayware* v. *Transport and General Workers Union* [1989] 1 W.L.R. 675).

AT THE TIME. "At the time of . . . the arrest" (Police and Criminal Evidence Act 1984 (c. 60), s.28(3)). The requirements of this section were fulfilled when a short but reasonable time before the arrest the accused had been informed of the ground for the arrest (*Nicholas* v. *Parsonage* [1987] RTR 199).

"At the time of the transfer" (Employment Protection (Consolidation) Act 1978 (c. 44), Sched. 13, para. 17(2)). In construing this phrase the courts should favour an interpretation that gives effect to continuity of service. The words should not be given the restrictive meaning of a moment in time (*Macer* v. *Abafast* [1990] I.C.R. 234).

"Specimen provided by the accused was divided at the time it was provided" (Road Traffic Offenders Act 1988 (c. 53), s.15(5)(*a*)). "At the time" should not be construed as "there and then" and it is not necessary that the division should be made in the presence of the accused (*DPP* v. *Elstob* [1992] RTR 45).

"And at the time has with him any . . . weapon of offence" (Theft Act 1968 (c. 60), s.10(1)). When determining whether a change of aggravated burglary under this section was committed by use of a weapon of offence the relevant "time" for consideration was the time the theft actually occurred (*R.* v. *Kelly (R.P.)* (1993) 97 Cr.App.R. 245, C.A.).

Where the terms of a licence to assign imposed upon the assignee an obligation to pay the rents reserved by the lease "at the time and in the manner therein provided for", the assignee was bound to pay the rents payable during the whole of the term (*Estates Gazette* v. *Benjamin Restaurants* [1995] 1 All E.R. 129).

(Landlord and Tenant Act 1987 (c. 31), s.12(6)). The words "at any time since the original disposal" meant that changes in circumstances up to the contract or conveyance could be taken into account, including any increase in the value of property resulting from a regulated tenant's death (*Twinsectra Ltd* v. *Jones* [1998] 23 EG 134).

AT WORK. "For use at work" (Health and Safety at Work Act 1974 (c. 37), s.6(1)). A dummy mine undergoing its first trials and demonstration could not be said to have been designed or manufactured "for use at work" but rather to determine whether it could be used at work (*McKay* v. *Union Pyrotechnics* [1991] Crim.L.R. 547.

ATTACHED. "The site . . . to which the balloon is attached" (Town and Country Planning (Control of Advertisements) Regulations 1984 (No. 421). A balloon can be "attached" to a "site" for the purposes of these regulations if it is flown from any object on the premises heavy enough to prevent it blowing away, such as, in this case, a motor vehicle (*Wadham Stringer (Fareham)* v. *Fareham Borough Council* (1987) 53 P. & C.R. 336).

ATTEMPT. (9) "Attempting to commit the offence" (Criminal Attempts Act 1981 (c. 47), s.1(1)). An attempt to commit an offence under this section is still an attempt even though on the facts of the case the offence the accused set out to commit was in law impossible. In deciding that a man who brought a packet from India, believing it contained heroin, was guilty of attempting to deal with a controlled drug, notwithstanding that the packet only contained snuff, the House of Lords ruled that *Anderton* v. *Ryan* [see Main Work (9)] was wrongly decided (*R.* v. *Shivpuri* [1987] A.C. 1). For an act to constitute an attempt to commit a crime it must form part of a series of acts which would constitute its actual commission if it were not interrupted. The defendant must have gone beyond mere preparation and actually embarked on the commission of the offence proper. So that a man who jumped on to the track during a greyhound race, in the hope that the steward would declare "no race," thus entitling him to recover his stake from the bookmaker, was held to be performing an act which was "merely preparatory" within the meaning of the section. He was not guilty of "attempting to commit" a theft (*R.* v. *Gullefer* [1990] 1 W.L.R. 1063). When considering the question whether a particular act is "more than merely preparatory" within the meaning of this section the court is entitled to look at the tests that were applied prior to the passing of the 1981 Act. Damaging the door of a flat with the intention of entry and theft is "more than merely preparatory" (*R.* v. *Boyle and Boyle* (1987) 84 Cr.App.R. 270). But it has since been held that as the 1981 Act was a codifying statute the correct approach was to look first at the natural meaning of the statutory words, not to turn back to the earlier case law and seek to fit some previous test to the words of the section (*R.* v. *Jones (Kenneth Henry)* [1990] 1 W.L.R. 1057). On this basis it was held that a man arrested outside a sub-post office wearing a crash helmet and gloves, and carrying something heavy in his pocket, along with an imitation gun and a threatening note, could not be convicted of attempted robbery as up to that point all his actions had been "merely preparatory" (*R.* v. *Campbell* [1991] Crim.L.R. 269). On a charge of attempted rape it is not incumbent on the prosecution, as a matter of law, to prove that the defendant physically attempted to penetrate the woman's vagina with his penis. It is sufficient if there is evidence from which the intent could be inferred; as, in this case, the complainant's distress, the state of her clothing and the position in which she was seen (*Att.-Gen.'s Reference (No. 1 of 1992)* [1993] 1 W.L.R. 274).

ATTEND. Where, in an insurance risk delimiting clause, the owners of cash and carry business premises warranted that a cash kiosk would be "attended" at all times during business hours the term "attended" meant a permanent presence and did not extend to a person being within the vicinity of the kiosk (*C.T.N. Cash and Carry* v. *General Accident Fire and Life Assurance Corp.* [1989] 1 Lloyd's Rep. 299).

ATTENDANCE. "Board or attendance," see BOARD.

ATTENTION. "Attention throughout the day in connection with his bodily functions". Social Security Contributions and Benefits Act 1992 (c. 4), s.72(1)(*b*)(i).
  "Attention" denoted personal service of an active nature rather than "supervision" which was essentially passive. Guidance of a blind person walking in unfamiliar surroundings constituted "attention in connection with bodily functions" (*R.* v. *National Insurance Commissioner, ex p. Secretary of State for Social Services* [1981] 1 W.L.R. 1017 and *Woodling* v. *Secretary of State for Social Security* [1984] 1 W.L.R. 348 applied) (*Mallinson* v. *Secretary of State for Social Security* [1994] 1 W.L.R. 630).
  [(Social Security Contributions and Benefits Act 1992 (c. 4), s.72(1)(*b*)(i))] "Frequent attention . . . in connection with . . . bodily functions" included attention which was reasonably required to enable a deaf person to carry on, as far as possible, a normal social life and was not confined to attention which was merely essential to maintain life (*Secretary of State for Social Security* v. *Fairey, The Times*, June 22, 1995 H.L.).
  In order for an activity to constitute "attention" within the meaning of s.64(2)(a) of the 1992 Act, it was necessary for it to be performed in the presence of the applicant and for such attention to be "in connection with" the bodily functions of the applicant which was directed primarily to those activities which the fit person normally performed for himself and which involved a high degree of physical intimacy. The taking away of laundry was neither "attention" nor a sufficiently personal service as to be in connection with a bodily function (*Cockburn* v. *Chief Adjudication Officer* [1997] 1 W.L.R. 799).

ATTRIBUTABLE. Where a gardener employed by the GLC continued to do the same job when the property was transferred to Wandsworth Borough Council, but was later dismissed when Wandsworth decided to privatise its gardening services, it was held that his loss of employment was entirely due to the need to economise and was not "attributable to" the transfer of property order under s.23(2) of the London Government Act 1963 (c. 33) within the meaning of regs. 4, 11(1) of the Greater London Council Housing (Compensation) Regulations 1980 (No. 646) (*Fleming* v. *Wandsworth London Borough Council* (1985) 84 L.G.R. 442).
  In deciding whether any action or omission is "attributable" to the existence of a monopoly situation within the meaning of s.48(*d*) of the Fair Trading Act 1973 (c. 41) it was sufficient for the Monopolies and Mergers Commission to find a causal link between the action in question and the

existence of the monopoly situation, although that did not exclude the possibility of other concurrent causes for the action (*R.* v. *Monopolies and Mergers Commission, ex p. National House Building Council, The Times,* January 25, 1994).

AUTHOR. Stat. Def., Copyright, Designs and Patents Act 1988 (c. 48), s.9.

AUTHORISE. "Authorised to do so by the court" (Magistrates' Courts Act 1980 (c. 43), s.87(3)). Where the clerk of the court was "authorised" to obtain a garnishee order nisi in the High Court and this was dismissed on a procedural technicality, it was held that the authority extended to the application for a second garnishee order (*Gooch* v. *Ewing (Allied Irish Bank, garnishee)* [1985] 3 All E.R. 654).

"Payment or reward authorised by the court" (Adoption Act 1958 (c. 5), s.50(3)). There is nothing in the word "authorise" to suggest that authorisation under this section could only be given in advance of payment. Thus the court could authorise a payment or reward that had already been made (*Adoption Application: Surrogacy AA* 212/86, [1987] 3 W.L.R. 31).

"Authorise" (Copyright Act 1956 (c. 74), s.1(1)). The respondents made and sold twin-deck tape-recording machines which could be used to reproduce one tape directly on to another, and which were capable therefore of being used by an infringer of copyright. The advertising, although likely to encourage home-taping, made it clear that some copying required permission. It was held that neither the sale nor the advertising "authorised" a breach of copyright within the meaning of this section (*C.B.S. Songs* v. *Amstrad Consumer Electronics* [1988] 2 W.L.R. 1191).

AUTOMATISM. A person who drives without awareness, although able to steer and react to stimuli, is not in a state of "automatism" (*Att.-Gen.'s Reference (No. 2 of 1992)* [1993] 3 W.L.R. 982).

A driver, suffering a hypoglycaemic episode, had been able to undertake various manoeuvres and where although his manner of driving was erratic, there was no complete loss of voluntary control but rather a gradual loss of control, was not able to raise the defence of automatism (*Chelsea Girl* v. *Alpha Omega Electrical Services*, May 9, 1994, Mayor's and City of London County Court).

AUTREFOIS ACQUIT. Where a totally defective information was replaced by a properly drafted alternative, and no evidence was offered upon the original information, the defence of *autrefois acquit* was not a defence to the second information in circumstances where the original information had been so defective that the defendant could never have been in "jeopardy" upon it (*DPP* v. *Porthouse* [1989] RTR 177). Similarly defendants in proceedings for civil contempt and sequestration had not been in "jeopardy" where the plaintiffs' motion was dismissed on the ground that the supporting affidavit evidence was inadmissible. Accordingly on a fresh application founded on the same facts, but supported by evidence in proper form, the defendants could not rely on a plea of *autrefois acquit* (*El Capistrano SA* v. *ATO Marketing Group* [1989] 1 W.L.R. 471). Where an information had been dismissed for want of prosecution, and duplicate proceedings started, the plea of *autrefois acquit* was not open to the defendant as there had been no trial on the merits (*R.* v. *Willesden Justices, ex p. Clemmings* (1988) 87 Cr.App.R. 280). A plea of *autrefois acquit* failed where the acquittal had been of a conspiracy to supply cocaine and the second charge was of a conspiracy to import cocaine (*R.* v. *Norman Griffiths* [1990] Crim.L.R. 181). A plea in bar before justices failed where a charge had been dismissed before the defendant pleaded (*Williams* v. *DPP* [1991] 3 All E.R. 651).

Where a charge was dismissed because it was defective, either as a matter of law, or because the evidence was insufficient to sustain a conviction, or as a rationalisation or reorganisation of the prosecution case, it could not properly be said that the defendant had ever been in jeopardy of a conviction; so that the *autrefois acquit* principle would not apply (*R.* v. *Dabhade* [1992] 4 All E.R. 796).

There was no risk of double jeopardy where a defendant had been acquitted of one charge before proceedings commenced on new charges (*DPP* v. *Riches* [1993] C.O.D. 457).

AUTREFOIS CONVICT. A plea of *autrefois convict* could only be sustained by evidence that the offence with which the defendant stood charged had already been the subject of a complete adjudication against him by a court of competent jurisdiction comprising both the decision establishing his guilt, whether it was the decision of the court or of the jury or the entry of his own plea, and the final disposal of the case by the court by passing sentence or making some other order such as an order of absolute discharge (*Richards* v. *R.* [1992] 3 W.L.R. 928).

AVAILABLE. (14) "Available market" (Sale of Goods Act 1979 (c. 54), s.50(3)). If a seller actually offers goods for sale there is no "available market" within the meaning of this section unless there is one actual buyer, on that day, at a fair price; but, if there is only a hypothetical sale for the purposes of this section, there is no "available market" unless, on that day, there are sufficient traders in touch with each other to evidence a market in which the seller can, if he wishes, sell the goods (*Shearson Lehman Hutton* v. *Maclaine Watson & Co.* [1989] 2 Lloyd's Rep. 570).

(17) "Nearest available route" (Education Act 1944 (c. 31), s.39(5)). A route to be "available" within the meaning of this section had to be a route along which a child, accompanied as necessary, could walk with reasonable safety to school. It did not fail to qualify as "available" because of dangers which would arise if the child was unaccompanied (*Rogers* v. *Essex County Council* [1986] 3 W.L.R 689). In considering availability the local authority should take into account not only the age of the child and the nature of any route he could reasonably be expected to take if accompanied, but also whether, under the circumstances, it was reasonable for him to be so accompanied by a parent or some other person (*Devon County Council* v. *George, sub nom. R.* v. *Devon County Council, ex p. G.* [1988] 3 W.L.R. 1386).

A suitable vacancy is "available" within the meaning of the Employment Protection (Consolidation) Act 1978 (c. 44), s.45(3), notwithstanding that by offering it the employers would cease to qualify for funding from the Manpower Services Commission. The word "available" should not be qualified by considerations of what was economic or reasonable (*Community Task Force* v. *Rimmer* [1986] I.C.R. 491).

"Available for his occupation and which it would have been reasonable for him to continue to occupy" (Housing Act 1985 (c. 68), s.60(1)). Accommodation would be "available for his occupation" by a person within the meaning of this section notwithstanding that it was owned by his mother. The important fact was that it was available and not who owned it. As to whether it was "reasonable for him" to occupy the accommodation regard may be had to what could be considered reasonable under the customs and living style of the applicant's own community in Bangladesh (*R.* v. *Tower Hamlets London Borough Council, ex p. Monaf, Ali and Miah* (1988) 20 H.L.R. 529).

A defendant, who was not in detention or immediately available for arrest, but was an escapee who had tried to evade detection and arrest, was "available" to stand on an identity parade (*R.* v. *Kitchen* [1994] Crim.L.R. 684).

AVOIDABLY IMPAIRED OR NEGLECTED. (Children and Young Persons Act 1969 (c. 54), s.1(2)(*a*)). It is possible to form the opinion that the health of a child has been "impaired or neglected" within the meaning of this section while it is still unborn; as, for instance in this case, where the mother was taking drugs (*Re D* [1986] 3 W.L.R. 85).

B

BADGER. Stat. Def., Protection of Badgers Act 1992 (c. 51), s.14.

BAIL. "Court decided not to grant . . . bail" (Bail Act 1976 (c. 63), Sched. 1, Part IIA, para. 2 as substituted by the Criminal Justice Act 1988 (c. 33), s.154). Where justices, in accordance with Schedule 1, Part I, para. 5 of the 1976 Act, came to the conclusion that the defendant "need not be granted bail" because it had not been practicable to obtain sufficient information to enable them to decide whether or not to grant it, that was not a decision "not to grant bail" within the meaning of paragraph 2 (*R.* v. *Calder Justices, ex p. Kennedy, The Times,* February 18, 1992).

BALLAST. Stat. Def., Weights and Measures Act 1985 (c. 72), Sched. 4.

BALLOT. (Trade Union Act 1984 (c. 49), s.10(3) as amended by the Employment Act 1990 (c. 38), Sched. 2, para. 2). A single question asking whether a member of an union supported strike action could be a ballot within the meaning of s.10(3) (*West Midlands Travel* v. *Transport and General Workers' Union* [1994] I.C.R. 978).

BAND. In musical context, Stat. Def., Public Processions (Northern Ireland) Act 1998 (c. 2), s.17(1).

BANK. Stat. Def., Housing Act 1985 (c. 68), s.622; Housing Association Act 1985 (c. 69), s.106; Finance Act 1994 (c. 9), s.177(1).

BANK DEPOSIT. Dictum in *Re Heilbronner* (see main entry) approved in *Re Norman* (*dec'd*) [1994] 1 All E.R. 804.

BANK HOLIDAYS. (Bank Holiday Act (c. 17)). The term "bank holidays" was a term of art, the meaning of which was to be drawn from statutory provisions. Banks were not obliged to close on such holidays and so an employee was not entitled to a paid holiday on each bank holiday (*Turnbull* v. *TSB Scotland plc*, 1999 S.C. 121).
   Stat. Def., Banking and Financial Dealings Act 1971 (c. 80), s.1; Representation of the People Act 1985 (c. 50), s.19(4).

BANKER. (5) "Bankers' book" (Bankers' Books Evidence Act 1879 (c. 11), s.9). Paid cheques and paying-in slips, retained in bundles by a bank after the conclusion of the transactions to which they related, were held not to be "bankers' books" or "other records" within the meaning of this section. "Other records" is to be read *ejusdem generis* with the rest of the definition in this section (*Williams* v. *Williams*; *Tucker* v. *Williams* [1987] 3 W.L.R. 790).

BANKING. An Isle of Man bank which made a loan to a United Kingdom property company was not "carrying on a bona fide banking business in the United Kingdom" within the meaning of s.54(2) of the Income and Corporation Taxes Act 1970 (c. 10) (*Hafton Properties* v. *McHugh* (1986) TC Leaflet No. 3069).

BANKRUPTCY. (Civil Jurisdiction and Judgments Act 1982 (c. 27), Sched. 1, art. 1). A claim brought by a trustee in bankruptcy for a declaration that a bankrupt's halfshare in a property registered in Spain vested in the trustee in bankruptcy and that its transfer to a third party was void, while it depended on the bankruptcy, was essentially a claim to recover assets from a third party and was relief which could be obtained outside the bankruptcy jurisdiction so that art. 1 of the 1982 Act applied (*Re Hayward (dec'd)* [1997] 1 All E.R. 32).

BANKRUPTCY DEBT. A bankruptcy debt under the Insolvency Act 1986 (c. 45), s.382 can include indebtedness under a periodical payments order (*Bradley-Hole (A Bankrupt)*, *Re*; [1995] 1 W.L.R. 1097).

BAR. "Barred from all relief" (County Courts Act 1959 (c. 22), s.19(1)(*c*)) means barred from obtaining all relief whatsoever, including relief that might be obtained otherwise than under this section (*Di Palma* v. *Victoria Square Property Co.* [1985] 2 All E.R. 676).

BARE TRUSTEE. Stat. Def., Banking Act 1987 (c. 22), s.106.

BATTERY. It is not necessary to prove an intention to injure to support an action in battery. Intentional hostile touching is sufficient (*Wilson* v. *Pringle* [1986] 3 W.L.R. 1). A doctor who administered blood transfusions to a Jehovah's Witness, knowing that he carried a card stating that no blood was to be administered under any circumstances, was held to be liable in battery (*Macette* v. *Shulman* [1991] 2 Med. L.R. 162).

BEAT. (Criminal Justice Act 1988 (c. 33), s.39) "Beat" involved physical contact, and referred to a battery (*D.P.P.* v. *Cross* [1995] C.O.D. 382).

BECAME. "Day on which the company . . . became insolvent" (Company Directors Disqualification Act 1986 (c. 46), s.7(2)). A company "became insolvent" for the purposes of this section when a winding-up order was made rather than when the winding-up petition was presented (*Re Walter L. Jacob*; *Official Receiver* v. *Jacob* [1993] BCC 512).

BEFORE. (7) "Person who . . . is before the court" (Justices of the Peace Act 1968 (c. 69), s.1(7)). A person who was the subject of an unconditional witness order to be a witness for the prosecution, and who presented himself at the courthouse but was not required to give evidence, was not "before the court" for the purposes of this section (*R.* v. *Kingston upon Thames Crown Court, ex p. Guarino* [1986] Crim.L.R. 325). Again, a person who attended court to give evidence, but was not in the event called on to give evidence, was not "before the court" (*R.* v. *Lincoln Crown Court, ex p. Jones* [1990] C.O.D. 15).

"Before the date specified" (Town and Country Planning (Enforcement Notices and Appeals) Regulations 1981 (No. 1742), reg. 4). An appeal under these regulations delivered *on* the date specified was too late (*R.* v. *Secretary of State for the Environment, ex p. JBI Financial Consultants* [1989] 1 P.L.R. 61).

"Before taxation" (RSC Ord. 62, App. 2, Pt I, para. 2(1)(a)). "Before taxation" meant before the taxing officer or master had taxed counsel's fees (*Spath Holme Ltd* v. *Chairman of the Greater Manchester and Lancashire Trent Assessment Committee* [1998] 3 All E.R. 909).

BEGIN. "Begins to carry on the activities of the trade" (Income and Corporation Taxes Act 1988 (c. 1), s.343(8)). Where a successor company, which previously sold goods, takes over their manufacture from a predecessor company it "begins to carry on the activities of the trade" for the purposes of loss relief under this section (*Falmer Jeans* v. *Rodin* [1990] S.T.C. 270).

"Period of three months beginning with the effective date of termination" (Employment Protection (Consolidation) Act 1978 (c. 44), s.67(2)). This means that the effective date of termination had to be counted as part of the three-month period (*University of Cambridge* v. *Murray* [1993] I.C.R. 460).

"Where the court has . . . begun to try the information summarily" (Magistrates Courts Act 1980 (c. 43), s.25(2)). Something more than a plea of guilty must occur before the trial which initiated the plea can be said to have begun for the purposes of s.25(2). The consideration of a preliminary point of law which had a direct and immediate bearing on the conduct and content of the trial was one such circumstance so that the trial process did not have to begin only with the taking of evidence (*R.* v. *Horseferry Road Magistrates' Court, ex p. K.* [1996] 3 All E.R. 719).

BELIEVED AND AVERRED. The formula "believed and averred" should be used where the pleader was averring a fact sought to be inferred from other averments of primary facts (*Strathmore Group* v. *Credit Lyonnais* (O.H.), 1994 S.L.T. 1023).

BELONG. (27) "Any foreign ship to which he does not belong" (Merchant Shipping Act 1894 (c. 60), s.686(1)). Passengers do not "belong" to a ship for the purposes of this section (*R.* v. *Cumberworth* [1989] Crim.L.R. 591).

"The machinery belongs . . . to him" (Finance Act 1971 (c. 68), s.44(1); see now Capital Allowances Act 1990 (c. 1), s.24). Central heating equipment purchased by a finance company, and leased to a local authority for installation in council houses, was held not to "belong" to the finance company for the purposes of this section (*Melluish* v. *BMI (No. 3) and related appeals, The Times,* February 15, 1994).

Central heating equipment which was leased from the taxpayer company no longer "belonged" to the taxpayer company once it had been installed into local authority property for the purposes of the Finance Act 1971 (c. 68), s.44(1). (*Melluish* v. *B.M.I. (No. 3)* [1995] 3 W.L.R. 631).

"Belonging to another" (Theft Act 1968 (c. 60), s.15(1)). A person who obtained a mortgage advance by deception did not commit the offence of dishonestly obtaining property belonging to another, since in the circumstances no property belonging to another was obtained by the person practising the deception by the debiting of one person's bank account and the corresponding crediting of another's bank account (*R.* v. *Preddy* [1996] 3 All E.R. 481).

BENEFICIAL. Where a service charge agreement allowed the landlord to recover the costs of providing "any other beneficial services" it was held that "beneficial services" did not include the decoration or repairs of the common parts of the property, but did cover the provision of management services (*Lloyds Bank* v. *Bowker Orford* [1992] 31 EG 68).

BENEFICIARY. "By a beneficiary" (Limitation Act 1980 (c. 58), s.21(3)). A claim made by the Attorney-General to enforce a public trust for the benefit of the public at large was not made "by a beneficiary" within the meaning of this section (*Attorney-General* v. *Cocke* [1988] 2 W.L.R. 542).

A board of management set up by trustees to run a school was not a "beneficiary" under the trust within the meaning of s.41(1) of the Landlord and Tenant Act 1954 (c. 56).

Stat. Def., Administration of Justice Act 1985 (c. 61), s.50.

BENEFIT. "Benefits" (Fatal Accidents Act 1976 (c. 30), s.4, as amended by the Administration of Justice Act 1982 (c. 53), s.3). An allowance based on the husband's pension and paid by his former employers to his widow following his death in a road accident was a "benefit" to be disregarded within the meaning of this section (*Pidduck* v. *Eastern Scottish Omnibuses* [1990] 1 W.L.R. 993). "Benefits" to be disregarded under this section are not limited to pecuniary benefits and could include the benefit accruing to a minor by virtue of the fact that the fatal accident to his unreliable mother resulted in his father marrying a more reliable woman (*Stanley* v. *Saddique* [1991] 2 W.L.R. 459).

The benefit to a child of being absorbed into another family following the death of its mother was to be disregarded for the purposes of assessing damages for loss of dependency (*R.* v. *Criminal Injuries Compensation Board, ex p. K (minors)* [1999] 2 W.L.R. 948).

"The cost of a benefit" (Finance Act 1976 (c. 40), s.63(2), now Income and Corporation Taxes Act 1988 (c. 1), s.156(1)). Where, under a concessionary fees scheme, members of the staff of a school, whose sons were educated at the school, received a taxable benefit, the "cost" of that "benefit" for the purposes of this section was limited to the additional cost to the school of providing those boys with such items as food, laundry and stationery; disregarding the costs to the college of its overhead expenses (*Pepper* v. *Hart* [1992] 3 W.L.R. 1032).

"For the benefit of the child" (Guardianship of Minors Act 1971 (c. 3), s.11B as inserted by s.12 of the Family Law Reform Act 1987 (c. 42). The "benefit" need not be restricted to mean financial benefit, and the transfer by the father to the mother of his interest in the family property could be for the benefit of the child" for the purposes of this section (*K.* v. *K.* [1992] 1 W.L.R. 530).

"Benefit, improvement or development of their area" (Local Government Act 1972 (c. 70), s.120(1)(*b*)). The banning of stag hunting over land acquired by a local authority was in excess of the statutory powers granted by this section as, being based on councillors' moral objections, it was not conducive to the "benefit, improvement or development" of the area (*R.* v. *Somerset County Council, ex p. Fewings* [1995] 1 All E.R. 513).

(Council Regulation (E.E.C.) No. 1408/71, arts. 12(2), 46a(1), as amended.)

A retirement pension granted by one member state on the basis of periods of insurance completed in that state and a retirement pension obtained by the same person in another member state as a divorcee based on the periods of insurance completed by the former spouse were not "benefits of the same kind" within the meaning of arts. 12(2) and 46a of Regulation No. 1408/71, as the benefits did not have the same purpose and object and were calculated or provided on the basis of the periods of employment of two different persons (*Schmidt (Christel)* v. *Rijksdienst voor Pensionen* [1996] I.C.R. 91).

"Benefits secured under the scheme" meant future benefits not just benefits already accrued (*Lloyd's Bank Pension Trust Corp.* v. *Lloyd's Bank plc* [1996] O.P.L.R. 181).

(Income and Corporation Taxes Act 1988 (c. 1), s.739). A settlement which provided for the possibility of resettling trusts so that a person presently excluded might benefit in the future provided a potential benefit whereby income could be enjoyed and so was liable to tax (*I.R.C.* v. *Botner* [1998] STC 38).

Stat. Def., Social Security Contributions and Benefit Act 1992 (c. 4) s.122; Social Security Administration Act 1992 (c. 5), s.81.

BERTH. "Whether in berth or not," see WHETHER.

BESET. "Watch or beset" (Conspiracy and Protection of Property Act 1875 (c. 86), s.7). To mount a charge successfully under this section the prosecution had to prove that a defendants "watching and besetting" of premises where an activity took place "compelled" another to obtain from doing something which he had a legal right to do. Persuasion was not enough (*DPP* v. *Fidler* [1992] 1 W.L.R. 91).

BEST. "The best information available to him" (Local Government Planning and Land Act 1980 (c. 65), s.66). The use by the Secretary of State of figures supplied to him by the Registrar General of the Office of Population Censuses and Surveys satisfied the requirement under this section that, when assessing the number of people in a council area for the purpose of determining the level of rate support grant, he should use the "best" information available (*R.* v. *Secretary of State for the Environment, ex p. North Tyneside Borough Council* [1990] C.O.D. 195).

BEST ENDEAVOURS. A covenant to use "best endeavours" to procure the fulfilment of a condition on a sale of shares was not breached where to fulfil would mean giving bad advice (*Rackham* v. *Peek Foods* [1990] BCLC 895).

BETTER PERFORMANCE. "Better performance of his duties" (Housing Act 1985 (c. 79), Sched. 1, para. 2(1)). Where a school caretaker, after living in a house unconnected with the school for two years, moved, at the insistence of the local authority, into a house owned by them, there was held to be an implied term of the contract of employment that he was required to reside at the house for the "better performance of his duties" as a caretaker within the meaning of this paragraph (*South Glamorgan County Council* v. *Griffiths* (1992) 24 H.L.R. 334).

BEYOND. The Channel Islands are "beyond the seas" for the purposes of the Civil Evidence Act 1968 (c. 64), s.8(2)(*b*) and R.S.C., Ord. 38, r.25 (*Rover International* v. *Cannon Films Sales* [1987] 1 W.L.R. 1597).

BLASPHEMY. The common law offence of blasphemy is restricted to vilification of the Christian religion (*R.* v. *Bow Street Magistrates' Court, ex p. Choudhury* [1990] 3 W.L.R. 986).

BOARD. "By boarding him out" (Child Care Act 1980 (c. 5), s.21(1)(*a*)). A child in the care of the local authority who at their request was then placed in the care of a foster parent selected by an organisation such as Dr. Barnardo's had still been boarded out by the local authority within the meaning of this section (*Kininmonth* v. *Chief Adjudication Officer* [1987] 1 F.L.R. 498).
  "Board or attendance" (Rent Act 1977 (c. 42), s.7(1)). A dwelling-house let at a rent which included payments for the provision of a continental breakfast was held to have been "let at a rent which includes payments in respect of board or attendance" within the meaning of this section (*Otter* v. *Norman* [1988] 3 W.L.R. 321). "Attendance" in this section would include the taking away of dirty linen and the supply of clean linen (*Nelson Developments* v. *Taboada* (1992) 24 H.L.R. 462).

BOARDING HOUSE. (Fire Precautions (Hotels and Boarding Houses) Order 1972 (No. 238), reg. 3). Premises at which the owner let out rooms for low-cost accommodation were held to be boarding houses within the meaning of this regulation, and not houses in multiple occupation under the Housing Acts, notwithstanding that the length of stay was sometimes six months or more. An establishment at which the owner is in business to receive those that present themselves, if acceptable to him, and for money to provide them with accommodation and refreshment, is a boarding house (*R.* v. *Mabbott* [1987] Crim.L.R. 826).

BODILY FUNCTIONS. (Social Security Act 1975 (c. 14), s.35(1)). Walking in unfamiliar surroundings, in connection with which a blind man needed assistance, was not a bodily function for the purposes of this section (*Mallinson* v. *Secretary of State for Social Security, The Times*, April 2, 1993) See also ATTENTION.

BODILY HARM. See ASSAULT.

BODILY INJURY RESULTING IN DEATH. The term "bodily injury" in an insurance policy was not restricted to injury to the exterior of the body and could include the introduction of some foreign agent into the body or some particular of it which caused physiological changes to the structure of the body, such as asphyxia caused by the inhalation of vomit (*Dhak* v. *Insurance Co. of North America (U.K.) Ltd* [1996] 1 W.L.R. 936).

BODY. Stat. Def., "includes unincorporated association" (Scotland Act 1998 (c. 46), s.126(1)).

BONA FIDE USE OF COURT'S PROCESS. (R.S.C., Ord. 18, r.19). The phrase "bona fide" suggested some activity by solicitors in the prosecution of their client's case (*Parr* v. *Bolton* [1996] 8 C.L. 81).

BOOKMAKER. Blank diaries and address books which were designed primarily to be written in rather than read or looked at were not "books" or "booklets" in the ordinary sense of the words and did not fall to be zero-rated under the Value Added Tax Act 1983 (c. 55), Sched. 5, Group 3, item 1 (*Customs and Excise Commissioners* v. *Colour Offset* [1995] STC 85).
    Stat. Def., Deregulation and Contracting Out Act 1994 (c. 40), Sched. 8, para. 1(1).

BORDER RIVERS. Stat Def., "the Rivers Tweed and Esk" (Scotland Act 1998 (c. 46), s.111(4)).

BORROW. "A local authority . . . may borrow money" (Local Government Act 1972 (c. 70), Sched. 13). Advances from a loan fund account to spending committees formed a part of the total "borrowings" by the authority for the purposes of this Schedule (*Stockdale* v. *Haringey London Borough Council* (1988) 28 RVR 177).

BREACH. (Town and Country Planning Act 1990 (c. 8), ss.187A and 171B). A "breach of the condition notice" in s.187A required a notice to be served in accordance within the time limits under s.171B and thus a valid notice (*Dilieto* v. *Ealing Borough Council* [1998] 2 All E.R. 885).

BREACH OF THE PEACE. A police constable could arrest a person for conduct which in his opinion was "likely to cause a breach of the peace" even if it occurred on private premises with no other member of the public present (*McConnell* v. *Chief Constable of Greater Manchester Police* [1990] 1 W.L.R. 364).

BREAD. Stat. Def., Bread and Flour Regulations 1998 (No. 141), reg. 2(1).

BREAKDOWN VEHICLE. (Goods Vehicles (Plating and Testing) Regulations 1982 (No. 1478), reg. 3(1)). Appropriately constructed vehicles were not prevented from being "breakdown vehicles" within the meaning of this regulation by virtue of the fact that they were being used to transport two disabled vehicles (*Kennet* v. *Holding and Barnes* [1986] RTR 334). See also RECOVERY VEHICLE; SPECIALISED.

BREAKS OF . . . 15 MINUTES EACH. (Council Regulation 3820/85, Arts. 7(1) and (2)). Where a driver had taken 45 minutes' break either as a single break or as several breaks of at least 15 minutes' duration during or at the end of a four-and-a-half hour period, the calculation provided for by Art. 7(1) began afresh without taking into account the driving time and breaks previously completed by the driver (*Charlton* v. *DPP* [1994] R.T.R. 133).

BREATH TEST. Stat. Def., Road Traffic Act 1988 (c. 52), s.11.

BRIDLEWAY. Stat. Def., Road Traffic Act 1988 (c. 52), s.192; Horses (Protective Headgear) Act 1990 (c. 25), s.3.

BRINGING OF PROCEEDINGS. See PROCEEDINGS.

BROADCAST. "Broadcast to be made" (Marine Broadcasting (Offences) Act 1967 (c. 41), s.3). "Broadcast" in this section refers to the manner of the broadcast, not to the persons making the broadcast (*R.* v. *Murray* [1990] 1 W.L.R. 1360).
Stat. Def., Copyright, Designs and Patents Act 1988 (c. 48), s.6.

BROKER. Stat. Def., Finance Act 1986 (c. 41), Sched. 18, para. 6(3).

BROTHEL. (5) Where premises were used by a team of prostitutes, but on any one day only one prostitute was present, the premises still constituted a "brothel" within the meaning of s.33 of the Sexual Offences Act 1956 (c. 69) (*Stevens* v. *Christy* [1987] Crim.L.R. 503).
See ASSIST.

BROUGHT. "An action must be brought . . ." (Carriage by Air Acts (Applications of Provisions) Order 1967 (S.I. 1967 No. 480), art. 28(1)). "Brought" in art. 28 embraces both the initiation and pursuit of an action (*Milor S.r.L.* v. *British Airways plc* [1996] 3 W.L.R. 642).
(Civil Jurisdiction and Judgments Act 1982 (c. 27), s.34). Proceedings commenced in one jurisdiction before judgment in respect of the same issues had been concluded in another were "brought" within the meaning of s.34 of the 1982 Act (*Republic of India* v. *India Steamship Co. Ltd* [1997] 3 W.L.R. 818).

BROUGHT UNDER ANY ENACTMENT. (Race Relations Act 1976 (c. 74), s.54(2)). An appeal brought under the FIMBRA rules was not an appeal "brought under any enactment" within the meaning of s.54(2) of the 1976 Act since the power to enforce the rules and to hold an appeal came not from any statutory enactment or any subordinate legislation but from the FIMBRA articles of association (*Zaidi* v. *Financial Intermediaries Managers and Brokers Regulatory Association* [1995] I.C.R. 876).

BUILDING. A steel and concrete frame clad with corrugated sheeting but without a roof was a "building" (*R.* v. *Ealing London Borough Council, ex p. Zainuddain* [1994] 3 P.L.R. 1).

(Theft Act 1968 (c. 60), s.9). Unhitched trailers, left on their wheels and struts in a place where buildings had been, and used as temporary storage space during building redevelopment, were held not to be "buildings" within the meaning of this section (*Norfolk Constabulary* v. *Seekings and Gould* [1986] Crim.L.R. 167).

"Building or engineering work involved in the construction, improvement, maintenance or repair of buildings" (Local Government Planning and Land Act 1980 (c. 65), s.20(1)) held to include painting (*Wilkinson* v. *Doncaster Metropolitan Borough Council* (1986) 84 L.G.R. 257).

"Building" (Landlord and Tenant Act 1987 (c. 31), s.1(2)). The gardens and other appurtenances included in the demise of a flat to a tenant were part of the "building" for the purposes of this section, and were thus part of the premises which the tenant could require the landlord to transfer by virtue of a purchase notice served under s.12(1) of the Act (*Denetower* v. *Toop* [1991] 3 All E.R. 661).

"Building" (Landlord and Tenant Act 1985 (c. 70), s.29(1)) here means a building or buildings under the same service charge regime (*R.* v. *London Rent Assessment Panel, ex p. Trustees of Henry Smith's Charity Estate* (1988) 20 H.L.R. 103).

"Building" (Town and Country Planning Act 1971 (c. 78), s.22). Where a structure was erected as a single building, but had two identifiable component parts, each part could, for planning purposes, be treated as a separate building and be permitted development (*Hendricks (J.M.)* v. *Secretary of State for the Environment and Eastbourne Borough Council* (1990) 59 P. & C.R. 443).

"Demolition or alteration of those buildings" (Town and Country Planning Act 1971 (c. 78), s.92(1)). Where, after the service of an enforcement notice, planning permission is granted for the retention of buildings to which the enforcement notice relates, the words "those buildings" in s.92(1) refer to the buildings for the retention of which planning permission has been granted subsequent to the service of the enforcement notice (*R.* v. *Chichester Justices, ex p. Chichester District Council* [1990] C.O.D. 297. See also DEVELOPMENT.

"Demolition of a listed building" (Planning (Listed Buildings and Conservation Areas) Act 1990 (c. 9), s.7)). Twenty-seven self-built wooden chalets were, for the purposes of this section, held to be "buildings," even though not incorporated in the realty, as they had been erected with the prospect of permanence and that fulfilment had affected the quality of the land (*Ellestone's Application for Judicial Review* [1993] NPC 74).

A restrictive covenant requiring preliminary approval of any "building work" was held to cover also extension work done later (*Cryer* v. *Scott Brothers (Sunbury)* (1988) 55 P. & C.R. 183).

(Local Government Act 1972 (c. 70), s.100B). Wooden, self-built chalet-type dwellings were structures or erections and were "buildings" for the purposes of the planning legislation (*R.* v. *Swansea City Council, ex p. Elitestone* [1993] 46 E.G. 181).

(Value Added Tax Act 1983 (c. 55), s.40, Sched. 5). A roofless barn which had two-thirds of its walls missing was not a building within the meaning of the 1983 Act (*Customs and Excise Commissioners* v. *Lewis, The Times*, June 22, 1994).

(4) The cleaning of windows did not amount to a "building operation" when the window glass did not form part of the structure of the building (*Edie* v. *Edie* (O.H.) *The Scotsman*, September 20, 1995).

The provision of access to plant which was not part of the construction of a building did not qualify as "building operations" within the meaning of the Construction (Working Places) Regulations 1966 (S.I. 1966 No. 94), regs. 2 and 6(2)) (*Ballantyne* v. *John Young & Co. (Kelvinhaugh)* (O.H.) 1996 S.L.T. 358).

Stat. Def., Town and Country Planning Act 1990 (c. 8), s.336; includes structure (Environment Act 1995 (c. 25), s.7(7)); Town and Country Planning (Scotland) Act 1997 (c. 8), s.277(1).

BUILDING LAND. (Sixth Council Directive 77/388 on a common system for VAT Arts. 4 and 13). "Building land" in Arts. 4 and 13 referred to land which had been defined by member states as land intended for building, irrespective of whether or not it had been improved (*Gemeente Emmen* v. *Belastingdienst Grote Ondernemingen* [1996] 1 All E.R. (E.C.) 372).

BUILDING REGULATIONS. Stat. Def., Housing Act 1985 (c. 68), s.622.

BUILDING SOCIETY. Housing Act 1985 (c. 68), s.622; Building Societies Act 1986 (c. 53), ss.5, 119.

BULK. Stat. Def., in relation to sale of goods, Sale of Goods Act 1979 (c. 54), s.61(1) as amended by Sale of Goods (Amendment) Act 1995 (c. 28), s.2(*a*).

BURDEN. Stat. Def., Deregulation and Contracting Out Act 1994 (c. 40), s.1(5)(*b*).

BURIAL GROUND. Stat. Def., Channel Tunnel Rail Link Act 1996 (c. 61), s.56(1); Town and Country Planning (Scotland) Act 1997 (c. 8), s.197(5).

BURST. Property damage caused by a fractured sprinkler system pipe was not cause by "flood" or "bursting . . . of . . . pipes" within the meaning of clause 22C:1.3 of the JCT Standard Building Contract (1980) (*Computer and Systems Engineering* v. *John Lelliott (Ilford)* 54 BLR 1).

BUS. Stat. Def., Transport Act 1985 (c. 67), s.19.

BUSINESS. "Disposes . . . of the whole or part of a business" (Finance Act 1965 (c. 25), s.34(1); Capital Gains Tax Act 1979 (c. 14), s.124(1); Finance Act 1985 (c. 54), s.69(2)(*a*)). Land, for a farmer, is a business asset, and the disposal of part of his land is the disposal of an asset and not a disposal "of the whole or part of a business" within the meaning of this section (*Atkinson* v. *Dancer*; *Mannion* v. *Johnston* [1988] S.T.C. 758). The sale by a farmer of a cattle yard for which he had acquired planning permission was not "a disposal of the whole or part of a business" for the purposes of s.69(2)(*a*) of the 1985 Act (*Pepper* v. *Daffurn* [1993] 41 E.G. 184).

(15) Occupied "for the purposes of a business" (Landlord and Tenant Act 1954 (c. 56), s.23). A small open space improved and maintained by a local authority for local inhabitants' leisure was held to be occupied "for the purposes of a business carried on" by the local authority within the meaning of this section (*Wandsworth London Borough Council* v. *Singh* [1991] 33 E.G. 90). Premises occupied as a residence, but where the occupier also carried on the incidental business of dog breeding and kennelling were not occupied for "business purposes" within the meaning of this section (*Gurton* v. *Parrott* [1991] 18 E.G. 161). The tenant of a market hall who had fitted out the market and managed it by sub-letting to stallholders, who had exclusive possession of their stalls, did not occupy the hall "for the purposes of a business" within the meaning of this section (*Graysim Holdings* v. *P. & O. Holdings* [1992] NPC 120). Where a school management board appointed a caretaker who was required to live in a cottage of which trustees, holding property in trust for the school, were the tenants, then it was the board of management, which had appointed the caretaker, that was in occupation "for the purposes of a business" within the meaning of this section (*Trustees of the Methodist Secondary Schools Trust Deed* v. *O'Leary* [1992] NPC 149).

"Business" (Value Added Tax Act 1983 (c. 55), s.15(1)(*a*)). An activity which neither makes nor is intended to make taxable supplies is not a business for the purposes of this section (*Neuvale* v. *Customs and Excise Commissioners* [1989] S.T.C. 395).

"Any contract entered into . . . by way of business" (Financial Services Act 1986 (c. 60), s.63(2)). Contracts for "differences" based on the prospective progress of a selection of stock market indices, under which clients of the plaintiff acquired certain rights, were held to have been entered into "by way of business" and were thus exempted from the terms of s.18 of the Gaming Act 1845 (c. 109) (*City Index* v. *Leslie* [1991] 3 W.L.R. 207). See GAMING.

"Business . . . is transferred" (Employment Protection (Consolidation) Act 1978 (c. 44), Sched. 13, para. 17(2)). This paragraph was held to apply where part only of a business was transferred (*Gibson* v. *Motortune* [1990] I.C.R. 740).

"Consumer credit business" (Consumer Credit Act 1974 (c. 39), ss.21, 189). A private one-off offer of a loan made by a person in business did not amount to a business activity, so that the person making the offer was not in the "consumer credit business" for the purposes of this section (*Hare* v. *Schurek, The Times*, May 28, 1993).

The transfer of an undertaking's business to another undertaking which thereby assumed the obligations of an employer towards employees was "part of a business" within the meaning of the Council Directive (77/187/ EEC), Art. 1 (*Schmidt* v. *Spar-und Leihkasse der früheren Amter Bordesholm, Kiel und Cronshagen* (Case C–392/92) [1995] I.C.R. 237).

(Finance Act 1985 (c. 54), s.69). On a true construction of s.69(2), the words "a business" denoted any business of the person making the disposal and where the person carrying on the business disposed of an asset in the business, that disposal did not qualify of for retirement relief (*Plumbly (Personal Representatives of the Estate of Harbour)* v. *Spencer (Inspector of Taxes)* [1997] STC 301.

"In the course of any business of his", see HIS.

An interest rate swap contract was held to have been "entered into by way of business" (*Morgan Grenfell & Co.* v. *Welwyn Hatfield District Council (Islington London Borough Council, third party*) [1995] 1 All E.R. 1).

Stat. Def., Business Names Act 1985 (c. 7), s.8; Insolvency Act 1985 (c. 65), s.232; Consumer Protection Act 1987 (c. 43), s.45; Food Safety Act 1990 (c. 16), s.1; "includes any trade, profession or vocation" (Value Added Tax Act 1994 (c. 23), s.94(1)); "includes a trade or profession" (Trade Marks Act 1994 (c. 26), s.103(1)); Civil Evidence Act 1995 (c. 38), s.9(4); Employment Rights Act 1996 (c. 18), s.235(1).

BY MEANS OF. (Interception of Telecommunications Act 1985 (c. 5), ss.1(1) and 9(1)). A telephone conversation involving a defendant who was using a cordless telephone, which was not passing through the public system was not intercepted by police officers "by means of" a public telecommunication system (*R.* v. *Effik* [1994] 3 W.L.R. 583).

BY VIRTUE OF. Stat. Def., "includes 'by' and 'under' " (Scotland Act 1998 (c. 46), s.126(11)).

C

CALCULATED TO DECEIVE. (Road Traffic Act 1988 (c. 52), s.173(1)(c)). Uncompleted bogus forms of insurance certificates could constitute documents so closely resembling genuine insurance certificates so as to be calculated to deceive within s.173(1)(c) of the 1988 Act (*R.* v. *Aworinde* [1996] RTR 66).

CALCULATED TO SUBJECT. (Administration of Justice Act 1970 (c. 31), s.40(1)). "Calculated to subject" within the meaning of s.40(1) meant "likely to subject" and not "intended to subject" so that a written demand for payment for an alleged debt, the liability for which was denied and the recalibration of an electricity meter to collect the debt could amount to conduct contrary to s.40(1) (*Norweb plc* v. *Dixon* [1995] 3 All E.R. 952).

CAN. (7) "Can comply with it" (Sex Discrimination Act 1975 (c. 65), s.1(1)(*b*)(i)). The proportion of qualified women librarians with dependent children who could comply with a requirement of full-time work was not smaller than the proportion of men in a similar situation (*Clymo* v. *Wandsworth London Borough Council* [1989] I.C.R. 250). See also DETRIMENT; JUSTIFIABLE.

(8) "Can comply with it" (Race Relations Act 1976 (c. 74), s.1(1)(*b*)(i)). Imposing a requirement that applicants for a clerical job should have "O" Level English could be discrimination against applicants of Asian birth as, with the examination set in what is to them a second language, fewer of them "can comply" with the required qualification (*Raval* v. *Department of Health and Social Security* [1985] I.C.R. 685).

"Can most effectively be provided" (Race Relations Act 1976 (c. 74), s.5(2)(*b*)). When considering whether services "can most effectively be provided" by a particular class of person a tribunal must consider whether services would be less effective if provided by others, and is not limited to the question whether they can only be provided by one class of person (*Tottenham Green Under Fives' Centre* v. *Marshall* [1989] I.C.R. 214).

CAN READILY ASCERTAIN. (Trade Union and Labour Relations (Consolidation) Act 1992 (c. 52), ss.226A(2)(c), 234A(3)(a) (as inserted by the Trade Union and Employment Rights Act 1993 (c. 19), ss.18(2), 21). A notice served on employers by a union had to specify a category of employee or name the employees to comply with s.226A(2)(c) to enable the employer "readily to ascertain" which of his employees were to be balloted or to be called to take industrial action (*Blackpool and Fylde College* v. *National Association of Teachers in Further and High Education* [1994] I.C.R. 648).

CANNOT. "Cannot be obtained" (National Conditions of Sale (20th edition) condition 11(5)). These words mean "cannot ever be obtained," and would not cover a case where the landlord's consent to the assignment of a lease is not yet forthcoming but might be obtained in the future (*29 Equities* v. *Bank Leumi (U.K.)* [1987] 1 All E.R. 108).

CAPABLE. (12) "Capable of remedy" (Law of Property Act 1925 (c. 20), s.146(1)(b)). Whether a breach of covenant is "capable of remedy" depends on whether the harm suffered by the landlord is capable of being remedied in practical terms. It was held in this case that the failure of a tenant to honour a covenant to reconstruct the interior of the relevant premises by a certain date was "capable of remedy" (*Expert Clothing Service and Sales* v. *Hillgate House* [1985] 2 All E.R. 998).

"Child capable of being born alive" (Infant Life (Preservation) Act 1929 (c. 34), s.1.) A foetus of between 18 and 21 weeks, whose cardiac muscle was contracting and which showed signs of primitive movement, but which was incapable of breathing, was not "capable of being born alive" (*C.* v. *S.* [1987] 2 W.L.R. 1108). If a child could live and breathe through its own lungs it was "capable of being born alive" for the purposes of this Act and may therefore not be aborted (*Rance* v. *Mid-Downs Health Authority* (1990) 140 New L.J. 325).

"Design capable of registration" (Copyright Act 1956 (c. 74), Sched. 7, para. 8(2)). This refers to designs possessing, when they were made, those essential characteristics which qualified them as designs under the definition contained in s.1(3) of the Registered Designs Act 1949 (c. 88) (*Interlego A.G.* v. *Tyco Industries* [1988] 1 W.L.R. 678).

CAPITAL. (7) "Capital withdrawn from, or any sum employed or intended to be employed as capital in, the trade" (Income and Corporation Taxes Act 1970 (c. 10), s.130(f)). An exchange loss sustained by a retail trading company when it repaid a five-year foreign currency loan was not deductible in computing the company's profits for corporation tax purposes, since the borrowing of a definite sum for a fixed term of five years did not form part of the company's day-to-day activities in earning profits and was a capital transaction (*Beauchamp* v. *F.W. Woolworth* [1989] 3 W.L.R. 1). Anticipated expenditure to be incurred by an oil company at some future time on the termination of its operations in the North Sea was expenditure of capital within the meaning of this section, and not deductible in computing corporation tax liability (*RTZ Oil and Gas* v. *Elliss* [1987] 1 W.L.R. 1442). A cash injection of £50 million into an insolvent bank by its taxpaying parent company in return for the Bank of England agreeing to purchase the bank for a nominal sum was not "employed as capital" within the meaning of this subsection, and was "expended for the purposes of the trade" of the taxpayer within the meaning of s.130(*a*) (*Lawson* v. *Johnson Matthey* [1991] S.T.C. 259).

Land sites acquired by a company for waste disposal purposes were capital and not current assets; so that neither the expenditure incurred on setting them up, nor on restoring them when infilling was completed, was allowable against profits when computing corporation tax liability (*Rolfe* v. *Wimpey Waste Management* [1989] S.T.C. 454).

Payments made by a company to a trust fund set up to provide pension and retirement benefits for its employees were held not to be capital expenditure for the purposes of the Income Tax Acts. As revenue expenditure they were deductible in computing the company's profits (*Jeffs* v. *Ringtons* [1986] 1 All E.R. 144). A payment made by the taxpayer company to the Bank of England to persuade it to mount a rescue operation to enable the taxpayer's wholly owned subsidiary company to continue trading, and so preserve confidence in the taxpayer's own business, was held to be a revenue payment deductible from its profits for Corporation tax (*Lawson* v. *Johnson Matthey* [1992] 2 W.L.R. 826).

(Law of Property Act 1925 (c. 20), s.2(1)(ii). "Capital money" in the Law of Property Act 1925 was not to be confined to money arising under the powers and provisions of the Settled Land Act 1925 (*State Bank of India* v. *Sood* [1997] 2 W.L.R. 421).

"Capital receipts" (Local Government Planning and Land Act 1980 (c. 65), s.75). Statutory transfers of housing are not disposals for which the local authority is entitled to payment either as agreed or assessed by the Secretary of State and they are therefore not "an authority's capital receipts" within the meaning of this section (*R.* v. *Secretary of State for the Environment, ex p. Newham London Borough Council* (1987) 85 L.G.R. 737). Sums paid to a local authority by a purchaser under an agreement by which the local authority agreed to sell expected receipts from future sales of land did not qualify as "capital receipts" within s.72(3)(*d*) as they were not sums received in respect of "disposals" of land within the meaning of s.75(1)(*a*) (*R.* v. *Wirral Metropolitan Borough Council, ex p. Milstead* (1989) 21 RVR 66).

"Capital sum . . . derived from assets" (Capital Gains Tax Act 1979 (c. 14), s.20(1)). Sums awarded as compensation under s.164 of the Town and Country Planning Act 1971 (c. 78) for loss of income and other costs incurred as the result of the revocation of an original planning permission were capital sums derived from assets within the meaning of this section (*Pennine Raceway* v. *Kirklees Metropolitan Council (No. 2)* [1989] S.T.C. 122).

"Capital payments". Stat. Def., Taxation of Chargeable Gains Act 1992 (c. 12), s.97).

See also ANNUAL PROFITS; DISPOSAL; VOTING SHARE CAPITAL.

CAPITAL ALLOWANCE. See QUALIFY.

CAPTIVITY. The cruel maiming of a hedgehog by repeated beating with a stick did not make it a "captive animal" within the meaning of s.15(c) of the Protection of Animals Act 1911 (c. 27) (*Hudnott* v. *Campbell, The Times*, June 27, 1986).

(Protection of Animals Act 1911, s.15(c)). A temporary inability to get away or a restraint incidental to capture would not suffice for "captivity or confinement" within the meaning of the Act. Some period of time during which acts of dominion were exercised over the animal was required before it could be said to be in captivity or confinement (*Barrington* v. *Colbert* (1998) 162 J.P. 642).

CAR. Stat. Def., Income and Corporation Taxes Act 1988 (c. 1), s.168.
See PRIVATE VEHICLE.

CARAVAN. (Caravan sites and Control of Development Act 1960 (c. 62), s.29(1)). A chalet which lacked wheels but could be moved was a "caravan" within the definition contained in s.29(1) and therefore escaped the planning ban on any fresh "structures" on the site (*Wyre Forest District Council* v. *Secretary of State for the Environment* [1990] 2 W.L.R. 517). A structure which consisted of four prefabricated panels brought to the site by lorry then bolted together and dragged on to a concrete base by a mechanical digger was not a "caravan" within the meaning of this section. A caravan had to be fit for human habitation and had to be capable of being towed by a single motor vehicle or trailer (*Carter* v. *Secretary of State for the Environment* [1994] 1 W.L.R. 1212).

CARD. "Stored value card," Stat. Def., Cash Ratio Deposits (Eligible Liabilities) Order 1998 (No. 1130), art. 2(1).

CARE. (8) (Children Act (c. 41), ss.20, 105; Child Benefit Act 1975 (c. 61); Child Benefit (General) Regulations 1976; Social Security Contributions and Benefits Act 1992 (c. 4), Sched. 9).

There was no distinction to be drawn between the reception of a child into "care" pursuant to a court order under s.31 of the Children Act 1989 and the provision of accommodation where a child was placed voluntarily in the care of the local authority under s.20 when assessing a person's entitlement to receive child benefit under Sched. 9 of the 1992 Act (*McLavey* v. *Secretary of State for Social Security, The Times*, May 10, 1996).

"Institution providing care" (Value Added Tax Act 1983 (c. 55), Sched. 5, Group 16, Item 5). For the purposes of this item "care" is provided in a contest where the provider himself provides, or assumes the responsibility for providing, something in the nature of a continuing state of care for a handicapped person (*Medical Care Foundation* v. *Customs and Excise Commissioners* (1991) 1 VATTR 28).

CAREER. Stat. Def., Education Act 1997 (c. 44), s.43(6).

CARRIAGE. Where an express term in a charterparty provided that deck cargo was to be "carried" at the charterers' risk it was held that "carriage" included loading and stowage, both of which were the responsibility of the charterers (*Exercise Shipping Co.* v. *Bay Marine Lines; The Fantasy* [1992] 1 Lloyd's Rep. 235).

(Carriage by Air Acts (Application of Provisions) Order 1967 (S.I. 1967 No. 480), Sched. 1). The articles of Sched. 1 were sufficiently widely expressed that they encompassed carriage under a time charter of the helicopter for the purposes of surveillance and detection work by the police so that the owners of the helicopter were liable for the death of a police officer during a flight (*Herd* v. *Clyde Helicopters* [1997] 1 All E.R. 775).

CARRY ON. (14(*b*)). "Has carried on business" (Insolvency Act 1986 (c. 45), s.265(1)(*c*)(ii)). These words have the same meaning as in the Bankruptcy Act 1914 (c. 59). A debtor does not cease carrying on a business until all trading debts have been discharged (*Re A Debtor* (*No. 784 of 1991*) [1992] 3 W.L.R. 119).

(Insurance Companies Act 1982 (c. 50), s.2). For the purposes of s.2(1) of the 1982 Act "to carry on insurance business" included not only the conclusion of a contract but also the pre-contract negotiation which began later than the issue of an invitation to treat and the solicitation of such business so that a person who sought insurance business having issued a brochure and held himself out as having authority both to make insurance contracts and to receive premiums on behalf of an insurer did carry on insurance business (*R.* v. *Wilson* [1997] 1 All E.R. 119).

(Companies Act 1985 (c 6)). The mere holding of a right in heritable property was not "carrying on business" (*McShane* v. *Comet Group*, 1994 S.C.L.R. 1077).

CASH. Stat. Def., "includes coins and notes in any currency" (Drug Trafficking Act 1994 (c. 37), s.48(1)).

CASH PRICE. The "cash price" (Consumer Credit (Advertisement) Regulations 1980 (No. 54), reg. 1(2)) is the price at which a person indicated that he was willing to sell goods to cash purchasers. So that where a car dealer offered a discount off the manufacturer's list price for cash customers, the "cash price" for the purposes of this regulation was the discounted price and not the manufacturer's list price (*R.* v. *Boldwins Garage* (*Warrington*) [1988] Crim.L.R. 438).

CASTING VOTE. Does not carry any special meaning or requirement of impartiality (except for Speaker in Parliament)—(*R.* v. *Bradford, ex p. Wilson* [1990] 2 Q.B. 375, *same, ex p. Corris* [1990] 2 Q.B. 363).

CATEGORY C WATERS. The Merchant Shipping Act 1988 (c. 12) lacked a clear definition of the waters within which a ship might be competently detained (*Ullapool Harbour Trustees* v. *Secretary of State for Transport* (O.H.), *The Scotsman*, April 13, 1995).

CATERING. "A supply in the course of catering" (Value Added Tax Act 1983 (c. 55), Sched. 5, Group 1(*a*)). Supplying from a snack bar in a small room in a large building to people working in the building, for consumption elsewhere in the building, was held not to be "a supply in the course of catering," notwithstanding that the snack bar was also used to a small extent by visitors and members of the public (*R.* v. *Customs and Excise Commissioners, ex p. Sims* (*T/A Supersonic Snacks*) [1988] S.T.C. 210). See also PREMISES.

CATHEDRAL COMMUNITY. Stat. Def., Cathedrals Measure 1999 (No. 1), s.35(1).

CATTLE. Stat. Def., Cattle Identification Regulations 1998 (No. 871), reg. 2.

CAUSE. "Cause or matter" (R.S.C., Ord. 36, r.1(2)). An application for leave to appeal against the decision of an arbitrator is a "cause or matter" within the meaning of this rule (*Tate and Lyle Industries* v. *Davy McKee (London)* [1989] 2 All E.R. 641).

(R.S.C., Ord. 62, r.8). The words "cause or matter" should be given a more restricted meaning in the context of wardship proceedings where the hearing of the originating summons was the final hearing and so the time limit for lodging a bill of costs for taxation was within three months of the final hearing (*Enfield London Borough Council* v. *P* [1996] 1 FLR 629).

"Good and sufficient cause," see GOOD CAUSE.

CAUSE, To. "Causes or permits" (Transport Act 1968 (c. 73), s.97(4)(*b*)). A company's wilful ignorance of the fact that an employee driver was not filling in his tachograph could not of itself be said to have "caused" the driver to omit to do so (*Redhead Freight* v. *Shulman* [1989] RTR 1).

(13) "Causes . . . any trade effluent . . . to be discharged into any relevant waters" (Control of Pollution Act 1974 (c. 40), s.32(1)(*a*); now Water Act 1989 (c. 15) s.107(1)(*c*)). Some positive act by the owners or occupiers of land in the chain of operations that give rise to pollution is necessary for them to be found guilty under this section (*Welsh Water Authority* v. *Williams Motors (Cymru)*, *The Times*, December 5, 1988). Where, due to a blocked drain following heavy rain, polluting liquid escaped into a stream, the respondent landowners were held to have "caused" the discharge within the meaning of s.32(1)(*a*). The question of causation is to be approached in a common sense way. A defendant may cause an escape without being negligent. Whilst an act of God may be a defence, that was not the case here as the rainfall was not an operation of natural forces so unpredictable as to excuse the respondents from liability (*Southern Water Authority* v. *Pegrum* [1989] Crim.L.R. 442). A conviction under this section could only be sustained if the defendant took some positive or deliberate action to cause the pollution; failure to prevent it was not enough (*Wychavon District Council* v. *National Rivers Authority* [1993] 1 W.L.R. 125).

"Causes . . . any . . . noxious or polluting matter . . . to enter any controlled waters" (Water Act 1989 (c. 15), s.107(1)(*a*)). A water authority was held to have "caused" a pollutant to enter controlled waters notwithstanding that the sewage treatment plant was gravity fed and that the pollutant had been released into the plant by an unknown third party (*National Rivers Authority* v. *Yorkshire Water Services* [1995] 1 All E.R. 225).

A company which participated in an active operation or chain of operations resulting in the pollution of controlled waters was guilty of an offence under s.107(1)(*a*)) (*Att.-Gen.'s Reference (No. 1 of 1994)* [1995] 2 All E.R. 1007).

(Water Resources Act 1991 (c. 57), s.85(1)). A person "caused" a pollutant to enter controlled waters if he actively did something, with or without the occurrence of other factors, which produced a situation in which the polluting matter could escape, even if he was not the immediate cause of the pollution (*Empress Car Co. (Abertillery) Ltd* v. *National Rivers Authority* [1998] 1 All E.R. 481).

In an action where P argued that D's breach of contract had delayed his performance of his obligations under the contract, it was held that loss of productivity because of a succession of events could be demonstrated in a number of ways without pointing to a particular event which affected productivity (*Ralph M. Lee Pty Ltd* v. *Gardner & Naylor Industries Pty Ltd* (1996) 12 Const.L.J. 125).

"Causing" grievous bodily harm was wide enough to include "inflicting" grievous bodily harm (*R.* v. *Mandair* [1994] 2 W.L.R. 700).

(Offences against the Person Act 1861 (c. 100), ss.18 and 20).

CAUSE OF ACTION. (8) The breach of an implied term to honour an arbitration award was a "cause of action" within the meaning of s.7 of the Limitation Act 1980 (c. 58), distinct from the original cause of action for breach of contract which was the subject-matter of the submission to arbitration (*Agromet Motoimport* v. *Maulden Engineering (Beds)* [1985] 2 All E.R. 436).

A claim for financial provision under the Inheritance (Provision for Family and Dependants) Act 1975 (c. 63), s.1 did not give rise to a "cause of action" and was not, therefore, capable of surviving for the benefit of the claimant's estate where the claimant died before proceedings were commenced (*Re Bramwell (Dec'd)*; *Campbell* v. *Tobin* [1988] 2 F.L.R. 263).

"Cause of action" was a broad concept denoting the factual or legal basis out of which a claim arose (*William Grant & Sons* v. *Marie-Brizard & Roger International S.A.*), *The Times*, July 1, 1996 O.H.).

CAUTION. Stat. Def., Police Act 1997 (c. 50), s.126(1).

CHAMPAGNE. A non-alcoholic, carbonated drink made from elderflowers, sugar, citric acid and lemons was not "champagne" (*Taitinger* v. *Allbev Ltd* [1994] 4 All E.R. 75).

CHANCE. "Chance that . . . in the future the injured person will . . . suffer some serious deterioration" (Supreme Court Act 1981 (c. 54), s.32A; (added by the Administration of Justice Act 1982 (c. 53), s.6)). "Chance" covers a wide range, but the possibility has to be measurable rather than fanciful. "Serious deterioration" means a clear risk of deterioration beyond what could normally be expected (*Wilson* v. *Ministry of Defence* [1971] 1 All E.R. 638).

CHANGE. "Any change in the use of any land" (Finance Act 1974 (c. 30), Sched. 3, para. 9(2)(*e*)). A mere cessation of use does not amount to a "change in the use of any land" (*Smith* v. *Squires* [1989] S.T.C. 60).

"Change of use of any building to use as a single dwellinghouse" (Town and Country Planning Act 1990 (c. 8), s.172(4)(*c*)). Where a house, grounds and outbuildings formed one planning unit there was no "change of use" when the family moved from one building to another within the unit, but a change of use did occur upon the changing of one building within the unit into a separate unit (*Pope* v. *Secretary of State for the Environment* [1991] EGCS 112). The conversion of a single unit of residential accommodation into two flats was a "change of use" within the meaning of this section (*Worthing Borough Council* v. *Secretary of State for the Environment* [1991] EGCS 113).

"Change in the workforce" (Transfer of Undertaking (Protection of Employment) Regulations 1981 (No. 1794), reg. 8(2)). A change in the functions of employees can amount to a change in the workforce, so that where the same workforce is engaged in a different occupation there is a "change in the workforce" within the meaning of this regulation (*Crawford* v. *Swinton Insurance Brokers* [1990] 1 R.L.R. 42).

CHARACTER. "His character and antecedents" (Magistrates' Courts Act 1980 (c. 43), s.38). This phrase covers anything which reflects on the defendant's character, and could include a circumstance of the offence, provided that it was not known to the magistrates before they took the decision to try the case summarily, and that it amounted to more than simply the filling in of detail in some matter which is already known (*R.* v. *Doncaster Justices, ex p. Goulding* [1993] 1 All E.R. 435).

IN HIS CHARACTER AS A MEMBER. See MEMBER.

CHARGE. (16) "A charge on book debts" (Companies Act 1985 (c. 6), s.396(1)(*e*)). A reservation of title in a contract for the sale of goods from one company to another constitutes a "charge" over the buyer's book debts within the meaning of this section and should therefore be registered under s.395 (*Re Weldtech Equipment, The Times*, December 7, 1990).

A charge-back, such as that created when a depositor purports to charge deposits made to a bank by way of security, does not create and vest in the charges a proprietary interest in the debt which he owes to the chargor, and is not therefore a charge within the meanings of s.395 (*Re Bank of Credit and Commerce International S.A.) (No. 8)* [1996] 2 All E.R. 121).

"Charged with the duty of investigating offences" (Police and Criminal Evidence Act 1984 (c. 60), s.67(9)). A store detective could be a person "charged with the duty of investigating offences" within the meaning of this section (*R.* v. *Bayliss (Roy)* (1994) 98 Cr.App.R. 235).

"Is in charge of a vehicle" (Road Traffic Act 1988 (c. 52), s.5(1)(*b*)). The presence of a wheel clamp on a motor vehicle could not be disregarded by the court when considering under this section the likelihood of the person in charge of the vehicle being able to drive it while over the limit (*Drake* v. *DPP* [1994] R.T.R. 411).

(European Convention on Human Rights 1950, s.6(1)). A "charge" could be defined as the official notification to an individual by the competent authority of an allegation that he was accused of committing a criminal offence (*Serves* v. *France* (1998) B.H.R.C. 446).

"Fixed charge", Stat. Def., in relation to Tenancy, Landlord and Tenant (Covenants) Act 1995 (c. 30), s.17(6).

CHARGEABLE. "Chargeable transaction" (Finance Act 1973 (c. 51), s.47), see INCREASE.

"Chargeable gain". Stat. Def., Taxation of Chargeable Gains Act 1992 (c. 12), s.15.

CHARITABLE PURPOSES. (17)(*a*) A gift for the saying of Masses is prima facie charitable (*Re Hetherington (Dec'd)*; *Gibbs* v. *McDonnell* [1989] 2 All E.R. 129).

Campaigning, in the sense of seeking to influence public opinion on political matters, is not a charitable purpose (*Webb* v. *O'Doherty*, *The Times*, February 11, 1991).

"Charitable purposes" (Finance Act 1955 (c. 7), Sched. 6, para. 10(3)). A testator's bequest of residue "for the use in connection with the sports centre in North Berwick or some similar purpose in connection with sport" was held to be charitable within the meaning of this paragraph (*Guild* v. *I.R.C.* [1992] 2 W.L.R. 397).

But a gift of land to a local authority for use as "recreation ground and for no other purposes" did not create a charitable trust requiring the authority to maintain the land for recreational purposes in perpetuity in the absence of any of the formalities applicable to a transfer of land to be held on charitable trust (*Liverpool City Council* v. *A.G., The Times,* May 1, 1992).

Stat. Def., Charities Act 1992 (c. 41), s.58.

CHARITY. (Charities Act 1993 (c. 10)). A foreign charity operating in the UK was not a "charity" within the meaning of the Charities Act 1993 (*Gaudiya Mission* v. *Brahmachary* [1997] 4 All E.R. 957).

Stat. Def., National Lottery etc. Act 1993 (c. 39), s.25A(9) inserted by National Lottery Act 1998 (c. 22), s.11(1); National Minimum Wage Act 1998 (c. 39), s.42(5).

CHARITY PROCEEDINGS. Proceedings instituted between governors of a charity, on a motion in an action concerning the affairs of the charity, were "charity proceedings" requiring an order of the Charity Commissioners authorising them under s.28 of the Charities Act 1960 (c. 58) (*Brooks* v. *Richardson* [1986] 1 W.L.R. 385).

For the purposes of s.33 "charity proceedings" could include an application for judicial review of a discretionary decision in the management of trust property by a charitable public body (*Ex p. Scott* [1998] 1 W.L.R. 226).

CHARITY TRUSTEES. Stat. Def., Care of Places of Worship Measure 1999 (No. 2), Sched. 1, para. 6.

CHEMICAL WEAPONS. Stat. Def., Chemical Weapons Act 1996 (c. 6), s.1.

CHILD. (40) "Child of the family" (Inheritance (Provision for Family and Dependants) Act 1975 (c. 63), s.1(1)(*d*)). A woman, who was 32 years old when her father remarried, and who had never lived in her deceased widowed stepmother's house, and had never been maintained either wholly or in part by her, was nevertheless held to be eligible to apply under this section for financial provision out of the stepmother's estate, as being "a person treated by the deceased as a child of the family" (*Re Leach (Dec'd)*, *Leach* v. *Lindeman* [1985] 2 All E.R. 754).

(Matrimonial Causes Act 1973 (c. 18), s.52). A grandchild, who lived with grandparents because its mother was incapable of looking after it, was a "child of the family" within the meaning of s.52 (*A Child of the Family, Re*; [1998] 1 F.L.R. 347).

"The child of a void marriage" (Legitimacy Act 1976 (c. 31), s.1(1)). A child born before the celebration of a void marriage cannot be a "child of a void marriage" within the meaning of this section (*Re Spence (Dec'd)*, *Spence* v. *Dennis* [1990] 2 W.L.R. 1430).

The protection against deportation extended to a "child of a common-wealth citizen" by s.1(5) of the Immigration Act 1971 (c. 77) is restricted to those who were minors at the material date (*R.* v. *Secretary of State for the Home Department, ex p. Menn, The Times,* December 30, 1991).

"Child in care" (Children Act 1989 (c. 41), s.34(4)) would not include the applicant's mother even though she was in fact herself a child in care (*Birmingham City Council* v. *H (A Minor)* [1994] 2 W.L.R. 31). On an application for a care order the court's paramount consideration was the welfare of the child which was the subject of the application and not the welfare of the child's mother notwithstanding that she also was a child (*F.* v. *Leeds City Council, The Times,* March 10, 1994).

The definition of "child" in Art. 12 of Council Regulation 1612/68 was not subject to an age restriction (*Nordrhein-Westfalen Gaal Landesamt für Auabildungsforderung* (C–7/94), May 7, 1995, ECJ, Sixth Chamber (1995) 8 C.L. 226; [1990] I E.C.R. 1031).

(Housing Act 1985 (c. 68), s.113). A foster child was not a "child" within the meaning of s.113 and so could not succeed to a tenancy as a member of a deceased tenant's family (*Hereford C.C.* v. *O'Callaghan* [1996] 12 C.L. 352).

(Child Abduction Act 1984 (c. 37), s.2, as amended). The phrase "the child in question" in subsections (2) and (3) of s.2 of the 1984 Act referred to a child which had been taken or detained (*R.* v. *Berry (Thomas Clive)* [1996] 2 Cr.App.R. 226).

Stat. Def., Family Law Act 1986 (c. 55), s.42; Children Act 1989 (c. 41), s.105; Child Support Act 1991 (c. 48), s.55; Social Security Contributions and Benefits Act 1992 (c. 4), ss.122, 137, 142.

Stat. Def., "a person under the age of eighteen years" (Family Law Act 1996 (c. 27), s.63(1); Housing Act 1996 (c. 52), s.158(1)); "person aged under 18" (Protection of Children Act 1999 (c. 14), s.12(1)).

"Child of the family." Stat. Def., Children Act 1989 (c. 41), s.105.

"Childbirth." Stat. Def., Employment Rights Act 1996 (c. 18), s.235(1).

CHILD CARE ORGANISATION. Stat. Def., Protection of Children Act 1999 (c. 14), s.12(1).

CHILD CARE POSITION. Stat. Def., Protection of Children Act 1999 (c. 14), s.12(1).

CHILD'S CIRCUMSTANCES. "Child's circumstances" when making a direction under the Children Act 1989 (c. 41), s.37(1) should be widely construed to include any situation which might result in a child suffering significant harm in the future (*Re H. (A Minor) (Section 37 Direction)* [1993] 2 F.L.R. 541).

CHURCHYARD. A consecrated part of a municipal cemetery was a "churchyard" within the meaning of the Churches and Ecclesiastical Jurisdiction Measure 1991 (No. 1), s.13 (*Re West Norwood Cemetery* [1994] 3 W.L.R. 820).

CINEMATOGRAPH EXHIBITION. The operation of a video amusement game was held not to be a "cinematograph exhibition" within the meaning of s.1 of the Cinematograph Act 1909 (c. 30), as amended (*British Amusement Catering Trades Association* v. *Westminster City Council* [1988] 2 W.L.R. 485).

CIRCUMSTANCES. (7) "All the circumstances of the case" (Matrimonial Homes Act 1983 (c. 19), s.1). The circumstances which by virtue of subsection (3) the court had to take into account when hearing an application by a wife under this section for a declaration that she had a right to occupy the former matrimonial home, should include the circumstances of a third party to whom the husband had sold the house (*Kashmir Kaur* v. *Gill* [1988] 3 W.L.R. 39).

"All the circumstances of each case" (Occupiers Liability Act 1957 (c. 31), s.2(2)). The antiquity of a building (in this case Pendennis Castle) was such a "circumstance" (*Hogg* v. *Historic Buildings and Monuments Commission for England* [1989] 3 C.L. 285).

"Circumstances" (Consumer Credit (Agreements) Regulations 1983 (No. 1553), reg. 2, Sched. 1, para. 19). The mere desire of a lender to vary the interest payable on a consumer credit agreement, which allowed him to do so at will, was a "circumstance" sufficient to satisfy the requirements of this regulation, which required the agreement to state the circumstances in which the interest rate might be varied (*Lombard Tricity Finance* v. *Paton* [1989] 1 All E.R. 918).

"Circumstances which, in the ordinary course of business, ought to be known" (Marine Insurance Act 1906 (c. 41), s.18). The dishonesty of an assured's agent was not a "circumstance which, in the ordinary course of a business, ought to be known by the assured (*P.C.W. Syndicates* v. *P.C.W. Reinsurers* [1996] 1 W.L.R. 1136 & *Group Josi Re (formerly Groupe Josi Reassurance S.A.* v. *Walbrook Insurance Co. Ltd* [1996] 1 W.L.R. 1152).

CIVIL EMERGENCY. Stat. Def., Local Government etc. (Scotland) Act 1994 (c. 39), s.117(7).

CIVIL MATTER. "Civil or commercial matter" (Evidence (Proceedings in Other Jurisdictions) Act 1975 (c. 34), s.9(1)). The expression "civil . . . matter" in this section (in respect of which evidence could be obtained for a foreign court) is not restricted to the interpretation that would be given to it in civil law systems, that is private rather than public law (*Re State of Norway's Application* (*Nos. 1 & 2*) [1989] 2 W.L.R. 458).

CIVIL PROCEEDINGS. The words "civil proceedings" in s.139 of the Mental Health Act 1983 (c. 20) do not include proceedings for judicial review (*Re Waldron* [1985] 3 W.L.R. 1090).

Applications to commit for contempt of court in the course of civil litigation were "civil proceedings" for the purposes of s.18 of the Civil Evidence Act 1968 (c. 64) notwithstanding possible penal consequences (*Savings and Investment Bank* v. *Gasco Investments (Netherlands) BV* (*No. 2*) [1988] 1 All E.R. 975). See also INTERLOCUTORY.

"Civil proceedings before a juvenile court" (Children (Admissibility of Hearsay Evidence) Order 1990 (No. 143), art. 2(2)). An appeal to the

Crown Court against an order in a juvenile court is a stage in "civil proceedings before a juvenile court" for the purposes of this article (*Re B. (Appeal to Crown Court; Evidence*) [1992] F.C.R. 153).

"Civil procedings" (Antigua and Barbuda Constitution Order 1981 (No. 1106), s.122(1)(*a*)). Final decisions given by the Court of Appeal on appeals from the Industrial Court are "civil proceedings" giving a right of appeal to the Privy Council (*Sundry Workers (Represented by the Antiguan Workers' Union)* v. *Antigua Hotel and Tourist Association* [1993] 1 W.L.R. 1250).

In Crown Proceedings Act 1947 (c. 44), s.19(2) and in R.S.C., Ord. 77, rr. 1(2), 9(1) and 13(1), "civil proceedings" includes third party proceedings (*St. Martins Property Investments* v. *Phillips Electronics (U.K.) (Secretary of State for the Environment, Third Party)* [1995] 1 All E.R. 378).

Stat. Def., National Minimum Wage Act 1998 (c. 39), s.55(1).

See also CRIMINAL PROCEEDINGS.

CIVIL RIGHT. See RIGHT.

CIVIL SERVANT. The term "civil servants" in Council Reg. 1408/71 Art. 4(4) as amended extended to all civil servants employed by a public authority and persons treated as such (*Vougioukas* v. *Idrima Koinonikon Asphalisseon* [1996] I.C.R. 913).

CIVIL SERVICE. Stat. Def., Scotland Act 1998 (c. 46), s.51(9).

CLAIM. "Claim for damages" (Supreme Court Act 1981 (c. 54), s.31(4)). A claim for outstanding arrears of statutory remuneration, *e.g.* under the Remuneration of Teachers Act 1965 (c. 3), can constitute a "claim for damages" for the purposes of this section (*R.* v. *Liverpool City Council, ex p. Coade, The Times*, October 10, 1986).

A "claim for damages for personal injuries which exceeds £1000" in CCR, Ord. 19, r.3(1A)(*b*) included both the general and special elements of a damages claim (*Couldry* v. *Hull Daily Mail Publications Ltd* [1998] 4 C.L. 67).

"On the making of a claim" (Income and Corporation Taxes Act 1970 (c. 10), s.258). A note on a company's annual accounts submitted to the tax inspector stating that its profits were "subject to group relief" was enough to constitute a "claim" for the purposes of this section (*Gallic Leasing* v. *Coburn* [1991] 1 W.L.R. 1399).

(Leasehold Properties (Repairs) Act 1938 (c. 34, s.1) Where a tenant was in breach of a repairing convenant which expressly conferred upon the landlord the right to carry out the repairs himself and recover the cost from the tenant, an action by the landlord to recover the cost of repairs was a claim in debt for reimbursement of sums spent on the repairs rather than a claim for damages for breach of the covenant to repair and so did not require leave under s.1(3) (*Swallow Securities Ltd* v. *Brand* (1981) 45 P. & C.R. 329 overruled) (*Jervis* v. *Harris* [1996] 1 All E.R. 303).

(Limitation Act 1980 (c. 58), s.35(3)). The making of positive averments by a defendant, without a claim for any form of relief, did not amount to a "claim" within the meaning of s.35(3), so that a new claim founded on a cause of action which was statute-barred could be permitted (*JFS (UK) Ltd* v. *Dwr Cymru CYF* [1999] 1 W.L.R. 231).

"Claims arising out of one event". In ordinary speech, an "event" was something that happened at a particular place, at a particular place and in a particular way, whereas a "cause" could be a continuing state of affairs or the absence of something that was happening (*Axa Reinsurance (U.K.) plc* v. *Field* [1996] 1 W.L.R. 1026).

"Any one claim" in an insurance policy meant a claim by a third party against an insured giving rise to a recoverable loss so that the insured was entitled to make more than one claim against its indemnity policy in respect of its liabilities as a result of separate acts of misappropriation by an employee (*Haydon* v. *Lo & Lo (A Firm)* [1997] 1 W.L.R. 198).

CLAIM, QUESTION OR DIFFERENCE. (Agriculture (Maintenance, Repair and Insurance of Fixed Equipment) Regulations 1973, Sched., para. 15). Once liability had been established, there could be no "claim, question or difference" between a landlord and tenant, so that the tenant was entitled to pursue his remedies through the courts (*Hammond* v. *Allen* [1994] 1 All E.R. 307).

CLASS. A "class of development" for the purposes of s.17(4) of the Land Compensation Act 1961 (c. 33) means a development that can be classified. That development need not concern only land owned by the applicant for compensation, and the likelihood of the development proceeding is not relevant to the issue of a certificate under s.17 of the Act (*Sutton* v. *Secretary of State for the Environment* (1985) 50 P. & C.R. 147).

"Civil proceedings" included proceedings for judicial review within the meaning of the Supreme Court Act 1981 (c. 54), s.42(1A) as amended by the Prosecution of Offences Act 1985 (c. 23), s.24 (*Ewing (No. 2), Re* [1994] 1 W.L.R. 1553).

"Civil proceedings . . . against the Crown" (Crown Proceedings Act 1947 (c. 44), s.19(2) and R.S.C., Ord. 77, r.13(1)) included third party proceedings against the Crown (*St. Martin's Property Investment* v. *Phillips Electronics* (U.K.) (*Secretary of State for the Environment, Third Party*) [1994] 3 W.L.R. 1074).

CLASSROOM ASSISTANT. Stat. Def., Education (Grants for Education Support and Training) (England) Regulations 1998 (No. 656), reg. 2(1).

CLERICAL ERROR. (Administration of Justice Act 1982 (c. 53), 20(1)(*a*). The failure by the draftsman of a will to incorporate a clause exercising a power of appointment as a result of inadvertence rather than a misunderstanding of his instructions was a "clerical error" within the meaning of this section and was a ground for the rectification of the will (*Wordingham* v. *Royal Exchange Trust Co.* [1992] 2 W.L.R. 496).

(Administration Act 1982, s.20(1)). A solicitor's failure to carry out a testator's intentions when drafting his will was a clerical error which could be cured by rectification (*Segelman (Deceased) Re;* [1995] 3 All E.R. 676).

CLERK. "Clerk to a solicitor" (Solicitors Act 1974 (c. 47), s.43(1)) held to include an inquiry agent who, on behalf of a solicitor, had performed the functions of a solicitor's clerk. The words of the section do not necessarily imply a master/servant relationship (*Re B (A Solicitor's Clerk)*, *The Times*, April 19, 1988).

CLIENT. Stat. Def., Solicitors Act 1974 (c. 47), ss.44A, 47A as inserted by Administration of Justice Act 1985 (c. 61), ss.1, 3; Administration of Justice Act 1985 (c. 61), s.39.

CLIPPER. A "clipper" who offered sexual favours for reward, taking money without intending to provide those favours was a prostitute (*R.* v. *De Munck* [1918–1919] All E.R. 499, *R.* v. *Webb* [1963] 3 All E.R. 177 and R. v. *Morris-Lowe* [1985] 1 All E.R. 400 considered) (*R.* v. *McFarlane* [1994] 2 All E.R. 283).

CLOSE COMPANY. Stat. Def., Income and Corporation Taxes Act 1988 (c. 1), s.414); Finance Act 1989 (c. 26), s.104.

CLOSE RELATIVE. "Without other close relatives to turn to" (Immigration Rules 1983 (H.C. 169), r. 52). This phrase is to be interpreted as someone to turn to when in need—any sort of need that may afflict elderly parents, not merely loneliness or financial support. In certain circumstances therefore it was possible that even a brother might not be a sufficiently "close relative" for the purposes of this rule (*Immigration Appeal Tribunal* v. *Singh* (1988) 18 Fam. Law 256).

"Close relative' (Supplementary Benefit (Requirements) Regulations 1983 (No. 1399), reg. 2(1)) held not to include a limited company of which a close relative was a director (Social Security Decision No. R(SB) 9/89).

"Close relation" (Income Support (General) Regulations 1987 (No. 1967), Sched. 4, Pt. 2). Services supplied to a patient by the staff of a nursing home were not provided by a "close relation," notwithstanding that the patient's son and daughter-in-law were the secretary and director respectively. The nursing home was a private limited company with a separate legal entity (*Dawson* v. *Adjudicating Officer*, SSAT Ref. 4; 14 04631, March 6, 1989).

Stat. Def. "husband, wife, father, father-in-law, mother, mother-in-law, son, son-in-law, daughter, daughter-in-law, brother, brother-in-law, sister or sister-in-law" (Mental Health Act 1983 (c. 20), s.25C(10), inserted by Mental Health (Patients in the Community) Act 1995 (c. 52), s.1(1)).

CLOSELY LINKED. The provision of catering at the annual conference of a religious charitable organisation was held to be a supply of services "closely linked" to spiritual welfare within Art. 13A(1)(g) of the Sixth Council Directive (77/388/EEC). (*International Bible Students Association* v. *Commissioners of Customs and Excise, The Times*, December 23, 1987.)

CLOTHING. Stat. Def., "includes footwear" (Education Act 1996 (c. 56), s.579(1)).
See DESIGNED.

COAL, COAL MINE, COAL MINING OPERATIONS. Stat. Def., Coal Industry Act 1994 (c. 21), s.65(1).

COASTAL WATERS. Stat. Def., Water Resources Act 1991 (c. 57), s.104(1)(*b*).

COHABITANTS. Stat. Def., Housing Act 1996 (c. 52), s.178(3).

COIN. Stat. Def., "includes any metal token which was, or can reasonably be assumed to have been, used or intended for use as or instead of money" (Treasure Act 1996 (c. 24), s.3(1)).

COLLATERAL AGREEMENT. Stat. Def., Landlord and Tenant (Covenants) Act 1995 (c. 30), s.28(1).

COLLECTION. "Collection" (House to House Collections Act 1939 (c. 44), ss.1(1), 11). A person who sells from house to house goods made by blind or other disabled people, and who is either properly registered for that purpose or exempted under the Trading Representations (Disabled Persons) Act 1958 (c. 49), is not making a "collection" within the meaning of these sections (*Murphy* v. *Duke* [1985] 2 All E.R. 274). House-to-house visits in order to persuade the purchase of goods, where part of the purchase price was to be applied for charitable purposes, were "collections" within the meaning of s.11(1). (*Cooper* v. *Coles* [1986] 3 W.L.R. 888 following *Carasu* v. *Smith* [1968] 2 Q.B. 383). See Main Work, p. 457.

COLLECTOR'S PIECE. The Court of Justice of the European Communities (Third Chamber) held that, in order to qualify for duty-free admission into the EEC, "collector's pieces" within the meaning of Common Customs Tariff heading 99.05 were those which had the necessary qualities for their inclusion in a collection, namely objects which were relatively rare, which were not normally used for the purpose for which they were originally intended, which were subject to special transactions outside the usual trade in similar usable objects, and which had increased value. Collector's pieces which marked a significant step forward in the development of human achievements or which illustrated a period of that development were to be regarded as of "historical interest" under C.C.T. heading 99.05 (*Daiber* v. *Hauptzollamt, Rentlingen*, Case 200/84; *Collector Guns GmbH* v. *Hauptzollamt Koblenz*, Case 252/84, *The Times*, October 21, 1985).

COLLEGE. Stat. Def., "includes any institution in the nature of a college" (Education Act 1994 (c. 30), s.21(4)).

COMBUSTIBLE. See NON-COMBUSTIBLE MATERIAL.

COME TO ... KNOWLEDGE. The phrase "coming to their knowledge" in an agreement could cover knowledge acquired before the contract as well as after and meant matters known to the sellers whenever such knowledge was acquired (*Niobe Maritime Corp.* v. *Tradax Ocean Transportation S.A.* [1995] 1 Lloyd's Rep. 579).

COMMANDER. In relation to aircraft, Stat. Def., Antarctic Act 1994 (c. 15), s.31(1).

COMMENCE. An arbitration is "commenced" for the purposes of cl. 30(7) of the JCT Standard Form of Building Contract at the same time as it is commenced for the purposes of s.34(3) of the Limitation Act 1980 (c. 58) (*Blackpool Borough Council* v. *Parkinson* 58 BLR 85).

COMMENSURATE. "Commensurate with the seriousness of the offence" (Criminal Justice Act 1991 (c. 53), s.2(2)(*a*)), means commensurate with the punishment and deterrence which the seriousness of the offence requires (*R.* v. *Cunningham, The Times*, December 3, 1992).

COMMENT. "Any comment by the prosecution" (Criminal Evidence Act 1898 (c. 36), s.1(*b*)) means any comment whatsoever, whether favourable or unfavourable (*R.* v. *Everitt; R.* v. *Riley*, (1990) 154 J.P. 637).

COMMERCIAL. A Quaker school with charitable status was held to be an undertaking which was not in the nature of a "commercial venture" for the purposes of reg. 2(2) of the Transfer of Undertakings (Protection of Employment) Regulations 1981 (No. 1794) (*Woodcock* v. *Committee of Friends School* (1986) 83 L.S. Gaz. 1474). The catering and cleaning business contracted out by the Ministry of Defence was not a business "in the nature of a commercial venture" within the meaning of reg. 2 (*Expro Services* v. *Smith* [1991] IRLR 156). A contract to provide a crew for an off-shore ship was not "in the nature of a commercial venture" within the meaning of this regulation (*Stirling* v. *Dietsmann Management Systems* [1991] IRLR 368).

"Proceedings relating to: (a) a commercial transaction" (State Immunity Act 1978 (c. 33), s.3(1)). Commercial transactions did not cease to be "commercial" within the meaning of this section by virtue of the fact that they were performed by diplomats (*Amalgamated Metal Trading* v. *Department of Trade and Industry, The Times*, March 21, 1989).

(State Immunity Act 1978 (c. 33(, s.4(3)). The medical office of a foreign embassy was not engaged in activities of a commercial character for the purposes of s.4 of the 1978 Act (*Arab Republic of Egypt* v. *Gamal-Eldin and ors* [1996] I.C.R. 13).

(Income and Corporation Taxes Act 1970 (c. 10), s.170). To carry on a trade on a "commercial basis" the distinction between commercial and uncommercial traders was between serious traders with an interest in making a profit and amateurs, even where profits and interest were earned from their interests and activities (*Wannell* v. *Rothwell (Inspector of Taxes), The Times*, April 11, 1996).

(Transfer of Undertakings (Protection of Employment) Regulations 1981 (S.I. 1981 No. 1794), reg. 2(1)). A local authority's cleansing services, while they did not make a profit for distribution, were "in the nature of a commercial venture" to which the 1981 regulations applied (*U.K. Waste Control Ltd* v. *Wren and ors* [1995] I.C.R. 974).

"Commercial rent," Stat. Def., "such rent as may reasonably be expected to have been required in respect of the subordinate interest (having regard to any premium given in consideration of the grant of the interest) if the transaction had been at arm's length" (Finance Act 1994 (c. 9), s.120(3)) (new inserted s.4A(10) of Capital Allowances Act 1990 (c. 1)).

COMMERCIAL PROPERTY. "Industrial or commercial property," see INDUSTRIAL PROPERTY.

COMMITTEE. A single person cannot be a "committee" within the meaning of s.10(1) of the Local Government Act 1972 (c. 70) (*R.* v. *Secretary of State for the Environment, ex p. Hillingdon Borough Council* [1986] 1 W.L.R. 807).

COMMODITY. Stat. Def., Building Societies Act 1986 (c. 53), s.9A(9) inserted by Building Societies Act 1997 (c. 32), s.10.

COMMON. "Common" under the Equal Pay Act 1970 (c. 41), s.1(6) means identical, equal or precisely the same (*British Coal Corporation* v. *Smith* [1994] I.C.R. 810).

Stat. Def. (in relation to land), Channel Tunnel Rail Link Act 1996 (c. 61), s.5(6) and Town and Country Planning (Scotland) Act 1997 (c. 8), s.277(1).

COMMON DUTY OF CARE. A licence to use a footpath was merged into a public right of way, subsequently established so that a landowner was not liable for negligent non-feasance to the user of the public right of way under the Occupiers' Liability (Northern Ireland) Act 1957 (c. 25), s.2 and the Occupiers' Liability Act 1957 (c. 31), s.2 (*McGeown* v. *Northern Ireland Housing Executive* [1994] 3 W.L.R. 187).

COMMON LAND. See WASTE LAND.

COMMON LODGING HOUSE. Stat. Def., Housing Act 1985 (c. 68), s.401.

COMMON PARTS. The definition of "common parts" in a lease included anything which was shared or which in any way concerned or benefited the occupiers so that the roof and external walls although not specifically mentioned in the lease fell naturally within the scope of the expression to be included by implication (*Marfield Properties* v. *Secretary of State for the Environment* 1996 S.C.L.R. 749 I.H.).

Stat. Def., Housing Grants, Construction and Regeneration Act 1996 (c. 53), s.58; "those parts of premises used in common by, or for providing common services to or common facilities for, the occupiers of the premises" (Health and Safety (Enforcing Authority) Regulations 1998 (No. 494), reg. 2(1)).

COMMON PROSTITUTE. The term "common prostitute" in the Street Offences Act 1959 (c. 57), ss.1(1), 2(1) applied exclusively to females (*DPP* v. *Bull* [1994] 3 W.L.R. 1196).

COMMON PROSTITUTE. See PROSTITUTE.

COMMON TERMS. "Common terms and conditions" (Equal Pay Act 1970 (c. 41), s.1(6), as amended by Sex Discrimination Act 1975 (c. 65), Sched. 1). "Common" as used in this section should not be construed as meaning "the same" or "identical," and variations in pay or job description did not prevent there being "common terms and conditions" (*Leverton* v. *Clwyd County Council* [1989] 2 W.L.R. 47). See EQUAL VALUE; MATERIAL FACTOR.

The words "common terms and conditions of employment" in s.1(6) meant terms and conditions which were, on a broad basis, substantially comparable rather than identical since the object of the legislation was to establish that for a relevant class the terms and conditions were sufficiently similar for a fair comparison to be made (*British Coal Corporation* v. *Smith* [1996] 3 All E.R. 97).

COMMUNITY. "Community bus service." Stat. Def., Transport Act 1985 (c. 67), s.22.

COMMUNITY LAW. Stat. Def., "any enforceable Community right or any enactment giving effect to a Community obligation" (Chiropractors Act 1994 (c. 17), s.14(11)); Government of Wales Act 1998 (c. 38), s.155(1).

COMMUNITY OBLIGATIONS. The administrative costs resulting from the Agreement on Social Policy comprised expenditure payable out of the Community budget and thus amounted to "Community obligations" within the meaning of the European Communities Act 1972 (c. 68) (*Monckton* v. *Lord Advocate* (O.H.) 1995 S.L.T. 1201).

COMMUTING. Stat. Def., Income and Corporation Taxes Act 1988 (c. 1), Sched. 12A, para. 2(1) inserted by Finance Act 1998 (c. 36), Sched. 10.

COMPANY. "In the case of a company" (Insolvency Act 1986 (c. 45), s.40(1)). A society registered under the Industrial and Provident Societies Act 1965 (c. 12) was not a "company" for the purposes of this section (*Re Devon and Somerset Farmers Ltd.* [1993] BCC 410).
A society registered under the Industrial and Provident Societies Act 1965 was not a "company" within the meaning of the Companies Act 1985 (c. 6), s.735(1), (4) and the Insolvency Act 1986 (c. 45), ss.40 and 251 (*Re International Bulk Commodities* [1993] Ch. 77 distinguished) (*Re Devon and Somerset Farmers* [1994] 1 All E.R. 717).
(Company Directors Disqualification Act 1986 (c. 46), s.16(1)). "A company" referred to the lead company or companies and there was no requirement in the 1986 Act to identify all companies in the notice of intention to apply for a disqualification order against a director (*Official Receiver* v. *Kean, The Times*, January 25, 1999).
Stat. Def., Companies Act 1985 (c. 6), s.735, Sched. 1; Company Directors (Disqualification) Act 1986 (c. 46), s.22(2); Income and Corporation Taxes Act 1988 (c. 1), s.832. See also ASSOCIATE (3).
"UK public company", Stat. Def., Defamation Act 1996 (c. 31), Sched. 1, para. 13(4).

COMPEL. "With a view to compel" (Conspiracy and Protection of Property Act 1875 (c. 86), s.7). The ingredient of the offence under this section is compulsion, not mere persuasion; so that merely standing outside a clinic in order to dissuade women attending the clinic from having an abortion, was not an offence under this section (*DPP* v. *Fidler* [1992] 1 W.L.R. 91).

COMPENSATION. "Compensation" for damages in an insurance policy, included exemplary damages, where the torts included for compensation were of a type which could attract exemplary damages (*Lancashire County Council* v. *Municipal Mutual Insurance Ltd*, *The Times*, April 8, 1996).

"Proper compensation for the damage" (Coal Industry Act 1975 (c. 56), s.2(4)). "Compensation," for the purposes of this section, for damage to land caused by mining subsidence means only compensation for that damage and does not extend to consequential loss, such as disturbance (*Hepworth Building Products* v. *British Coal Corporation, The Times,* March 18, 1994).

Where an insurance policy specifically indemnified the insured for liability for accidental bodily injury, which included the torts of assault, wrongful arrest, malicious prosecution and false imprisonment, an award of exemplary damages was to be regarded as falling within the definition of "compensation" (*Lancashire C.C.* v. *Municipal Mutual Insurance Ltd* [1996] 3 W.L.R. 493).

COMPETITION. (4) (Lotteries and Amusements Act 1976 (c. 32), s.14(1)). Where the publishers of a newspaper, after distributing at random large numbers of cards carrying five-letter codes, published computer prepared grids of rows of letters and other sequences (against which the cardholders could check to see if they had won prizes), it was held that there was no "competition" within the meaning of this section, as no competitive action was required from the reader (*Express Newspapers* v. *Liverpool Daily Post* [1985] 3 All E.R. 680).

See RESTRICTIONS.

COMPLAINT. (Pensions Schemes Act 1993 (c. 48), s.146). A complaint of maladministration which raised issues of law and fact was a "complaint" within the meaning of s.146(1) of the 1993 Act rather than a "dispute" under s.146(2) (*Westminster City Council* v. *Hayward* [1996] 3 W.L.R. 563).

COMPONENT. "Component part" (Firearms Act 1968 (c. 27), s.57(1)). A sub-machine gun from which parts are missing can itself be a "component part" of a prohibited weapon within the meaning of this section (*R.* v. *Clarke (Frederick)* [1986] 1 W.L.R. 209). See also DESIGNED.

COMPOSITION. (7) "Indication . . . of . . . composition" (Trade Descriptions Act 1968 (c. 29), s.2(1)(c)). "Composition" is wider in meaning than that laid down in *British Gas Corporation* v. *Lubbock* [1974] 1 W.L.R. 737). It includes not only the enumeration of various components but also the way in which those components are arranged (*Queensway Discount Warehouses* v. *Burke* (1986) 150 J.P. 17).

COMPRISED IN. (Interception of Communications Act 1985 (c. 56)). A cordless telephone on a privately run system was not "comprised in" the British Telecommunications public telecommunication system for the purposes of the 1985 Act (*R.* v. *Effik* [1994] 3 W.L.R. 583).

COMPUTER. A GR Speedman was a computer and its reading admissible in evidence without a certificate under s.69 of the Police and Criminal Evidence Act 1984 (*Darby* v. *DPP* [1995] R.T.R. 294).

CONCERN. "Concerned in the organisation or management of that entertainment" (Local Government (Miscellaneous Provisions) Act 1982 (c. 30), Sched. 1, para. 12(1)(*a*)). An offence under this paragraph is one of strict liability. All people who take part in the provision of unlicensed musical entertainment, except those who simply attend for the purpose of being entertained, are "concerned" within the meaning of this paragraph (*Chichester District Council* v. *Silvester, The Times,* May 6, 1992).

CONCLUSION. "Twelve hours after the conclusion of his examination" (Immigration Act 1971 (c. 77), Sched. 2, para. 6(1)). The examination by an immigration officer of an applicant for leave to enter the United Kingdom was only "concluded" for the purposes of this paragraph when all relevant information was to hand. So that, notwithstanding that the immigration officer had received a decision by the Home Office that the applicant did not have refugee status, his examination had not been concluded within para. 6(1) until a subsequent interview, conducted by the immigration officer for the purpose of ensuring that all relevant and up-to-date information was to hand, had been concluded (*R.* v. *Secretary of State for the Home Department, ex p. Thirukumar* [1989] Imm.A.R. 270).

"Conclusion of proceedings." See PROCEEDINGS.

CONCLUSIVE. "Conclusive evidence" (Wildlife and Countryside Act 1981 (c. 69), s.56(1)). "Conclusive" here means conclusive unless and until reviewed under s.53 (*R.* v. *Secretary of State for the Environment, ex p. Simms* [1991] 2 Q.B. 354).

CONDITION. "Suffers from a condition . . . for which he has to follow a diet" (Supplementary Benefit (Requirements) Regulations 1983 (No. 1399), Sched. 4, para. 14(*e*)). A man who was 6 ft. 10 in. tall and weighed 23 stone did not suffer from a "condition," and the extra food required was not a "special diet" within the meaning of these regulations (*Adamson* v. *Chief Adjudication Officer* (1988) 18 Fam. Law 210).

"Condition of the grant . . . of a protected tenancy" (Rent Act 1977 (c. 42), s.119(1)). A premium paid to a protected tenant in consideration for the tenant surrendering his tenancy, so that a protected tenancy would be granted to the person paying the premium, was paid "as a condition of the grant" within the meaning of this section and was therefore illegal (*Saleh* v. *Robinson* [1988] 36 EG 180).

An obligation to keep a building in "good and tenantable condition" could amount to a requirement to put the building into a state which would make it reasonably fit for the occupation of a reasonably minded tenant of the class likely to lease it even if the building had never been in that state (*Credit Suisse* v. *Beegas Nominees* [1994] 4 All E.R. 803).

An obligation to leave premises and fixtures and fittings in "good condition and repair" at the end of the term of a lease did not require the tenant to leave the subjects in the same condition as at the commencement of the lease but to leave them in the condition which they ought to have achieved as a consequence of the tenant fulfilling his duties of repair and maintenance under the terms of the lease (*Pacitti* v. *Manganiello (Sh.Ct.)* 1995 S.C.L.R. 557).

CONDUCIVE. "Conducive to the public good." See PUBLIC GOOD.

CONDUCT. Cheating the public revenue was a "conduct" offence for which loss did not have to be proved and not a "result offence" (*R.* v. *Hunt* [1995] STC 819).

"Conduct his undertaking" (Health and Safety at Work Act 1974 (c. 37), s.3(1)). The director of a cleaning and maintenance company which left its cleaning machinery over a week-end at a store it was under a contract to clean (with permission granted to the employees of the store to use it), was held to be "conducting his undertaking" for the purposes of this section when an accident occurred on the Saturday, although neither he nor any of his staff were present and the work then being done had been expressly removed from the ambit of the contract (*R.* v. *Mara* [1987] 1 W.L.R. 87). An employer's mere capacity or opportunity to exercise some control over the activity of an independent contractor was not enough to bring that activity within the ambit of the employer's "conduct" of his undertaking for the purposes of this section (*R.M.C. Roadstone Products* v. *Jester* [1994] 4 All E.R. 1037).

Repair work carried out by an independent contractor could form part of an employer's undertaking to ensure as far as was reasonably practicable that persons not in his employment who might be affected were not exposed to risks to their health and safety under s.3 but this was a question of fact in each case (*RMC Roadstone Products Ltd* v. *Jester* [1994] I.C.R. 456 disapproved) (*R.* v. *Associated Octel Co. Ltd* [1996] 1 W.L.R. 1543).

(Employment Protection (Consolidation) Act 1978 (c. 44), s.73(7B)). Participation in a strike or other industrial action did not by itself amount to "conduct" for the purposes of reducing the compensation payable to a complainant on the grounds of contributory fault, although individual, blameworthy conduct during the period of industrial action could amount to such contributory conduct (*Tracey* v. *Crosville Wales Ltd* [1997] 4 All E.R. 449).

"Conduct of a community home" (Child Care Act 1980 (c. 5), s.40(1)). The word "conduct" is to be given its ordinary meaning. Where no home was being conducted on the premises, which had been closed for over two years, the section did not apply (*R.* v. *Secretary of State for Social Services, ex p. The Official Custodian of Charities, The Times*, February 28, 1984).

A clause in a lease which required premises, which included public lavatories, to be "conducted in a decent, respectable and orderly manner", did not require the tenant to keep the lavatories open and governed the tenant's conduct in relation to the premises rather than the way he ran his business (*Chorley Borough Council* v. *Ribble Motor Services* [1996] 9 C.L. 409).

(Housing Act 1988 (c. 50), s.27(7)). "Conduct" for the purposes of the 1988 Act was to be given its ordinary and natural meaning and was not limited to acts of misfeasance, so that non-payment of rent could amount to conduct (*Regalgrand Ltd* v. *Dickerson* (1997) 29 H.L.R. 620).

Stat. Def., "includes any act, omission or statement" (Finance Act 1996 (c. 8), s.70(1)); 'includes speech" (Protection from Harassment Act 1997 (c. 40), s.7(4) and Criminal Law (Consolidation) (Scotland) Act 1995 (c. 39), s.50A(6) inserted by Crime and Disorder Act 1998 (c. 37), s.33); Late Payment of Commercial Debts (Interest) Act 1998 (c. 20), s.5(5).

CONFER. "Confer an authorisation or qualification . . . needed for . . . a particular profession or trade" (Race Relations Act 1976 (c. 74), s.12). An appointment to the position of sub-postmaster did not amount to the conferring of an authorisation needed for engagement in a particular trade (*Malik* v. *Post Office Counters* [1993] I.C.R. 93).

CONFESSION. A damaging but exculpatory statement is not a "confession" with s.82(1) of the Police and Criminal Evidence Act 1984 (c. 60) (*R.* v. *Sat-Bhambra* [1988] Crim.L.R. 453).

CONFIDENTIAL INFORMATION. Stat. Def., Health Act 1999 (c. 8), s.23(6).

CONFINEMENT. Stat. Def., Social Security Act 1986 (c. 50), s.50; Social Security Contribution and Benefits Act 1992 (c. 4), ss.35, 171.

CONFLICT OF INTEREST. (Solicitors' Practice Rules 1988, r.6.2). "Provided no conflict of interest appears" in r.6.2 had to mean that which was apparent to a reasonable solicitor in the same position as the solicitor under scrutiny (*R.* v. *Solicitors Complaints Bureau, ex p. Hermer* [1996] 6 C.L. 411).

CONNECTED PERSONS. Stat. Def., Companies Act 1985 (c. 6), s.346; Insolvency Act 1985 (c. 65), s.108; Taxation of Chargeable Gains Act 1992 (c. 12), s.286.

CONNECTED WITH. "Reason connected with her pregnancy" (Employment Protection (Consolidation) Act 1978 (c. 44), s.60(1)). Where, out of four staff, one had to be made redundant, and a woman had been selected because she would require maternity leave, it was held that she had been dismissed for a "reason connected with her pregnancy" (*Brown* v. *Stockton-on-Tees Borough Council* [1988] 2 W.L.R. 935). A dentist's receptionist who, a month before she was due to return to work after maternity leave, was dismissed on the grounds that her employer had been unable to find a temporary replacement and had been obliged to take on a permanent assistant, was held to have been dismissed for a "reason connected with her pregnancy" (*Clayton* v. *Vigers* [1989] I.C.R. 713).

"Dispute . . . which is connected with the employment" (Social Security Act 1975 (c. 14), s.19(2)(*b*)). These words were held to be wide enough to cover also any dispute which is connected with the manner in which the employment is carried out (Decision No. R(U) 5/87).

"In connection with the dispensing of hearing aids" (Hearing Aid Council Act 1968 (c. 50), s.7(1)(*b*)). These words were not wide enough to cover alleged cheating in connection with the setting or preparation of the examinations for students of the Hearing Aid Council (*R.* v. *Hearing Aid Disciplinary Committee, ex p. Douglas, The Times,* January 30, 1989).

"Payment . . . in connection with drug trafficking" (Drug Trafficking Offences Act 1986 (c. 32), s.1(3)). The payment of a sum of money to a confessed drug courier to enable her to get through immigration was held to have been made "in connection with drug trafficking" within the meaning of this section (*R.* v. *Osei* [1988] Crim.L.R. 775). The fact that his co-accused knew that the money he had lent the defendant was going to be used for drug trafficking did not mean that the defendant so received it. If he thought it was a loan unconnected with drug trafficking he did not "receive" it within the terms of this section (*R.* v. *Richards,* [1992] Crim.L.R. 134).

"Or in connection with its commission" (Criminal Justice Act 1988 (c. 33), s.71(4)). Payment received by an author in respect of a book he wrote describing an offence he had committed was held to have been received "in connection with" the commission of the offence for the purposes of this section (*Re Randle and Pottle, The Independent,* March 28, 1991).

"In connection with . . . water . . . services" (Council Regulation (EEC) 3820/85, Art. 4(6)). A lorry adapted for winch and lifting work, and used exclusively in the business of drilling water wells, was held to be a vehicle used "in connection with" water services for the purposes of this article (*DPP* v. *Ryan* (1991) 155 J.P.N. 314).

"Connected with any of those referred to" (Brussels Convention on Jurisdiction and Enforcement of Judgments in Civil and Commercial Matters, Art. 12A(4); incorporated into English law by the Civil Jurisdiction and Judgments Act 1982 (c. 27)). The words "connected with" are to be interpreted in the normal sense as synonymous with "ancillary to" (*Charman* v. *WOC Offshore BV, The Times,* October 27, 1992).

"In connection with the management of a company" (Company Directors Disqualification Act 1986 (c. 46), s.2). An offence under the Company Securities (Inside Dealing) Act 1985 (c. 8) is an indictable offence "in connection with the management of a company" within the meaning of s.2 (*R.* v. *Goodman* [1992] BCC 625).

"In connection with any proceedings," see PROCEEDINGS.

"In connection with an offence," see OFFENCE.

[Social Security Act 1975 (c. 14), s.35(1)(*a*)(i)). Attention provided to a person "in connection with" a sight handicap was to enable that person to do what he would be able to do if he had sight (*Mallinson* v. *Secretary of State for Social Security* [1994] 2 All E.R. 295].

(Police Pensions Regulations 1987, reg.K5). The words "offence committed in connection with his service as a member of the police force" should not be limited to cases where the officer was a serving officer and the offence was committed during his service as a police officer, so that an officer convicted of offences including blackmail, contamination of goods with intent to cause economic loss, a threat to kill and attempting to obtain property by deception, committed whilst the officer was on sick leave but in circumstances where the officer would not have had access to the information to commit the offences had he not been a police officer, forfeited his police pension (*Whitchelo* v. *Secretary of State for the Home Department* [1996] 7 C.L. 517).

(Rehabilitation of Offenders Act 1974 (Exceptions) Order 1975, Sched. 1, Part II). The words "in connection with the provision of social services" were not confined to social workers but could include a bursar and an outreach manager and other administrative posts, so that an employer was entitled to take into account an applicant's spent convictions when considering suitability for a post (*Wood* v. *Coverage Care Ltd* [1996] IRLR 264).

CONSENT. A person who borrowed a vehicle and used it at a time and for purposes outside the limitations as to use set by the owner, did not have "the consent of the owner" for the purposes of an insurance policy (*Singh* v. *Rathour* [1988] 1 W.L.R. 422).

"With his consent" (Road Traffic Offenders Act 1988 (c. 53), s.15(4)). For the purposes of this section it is essential that the person required to provide a specimen of blood should "consent" to such a request when conscious of what he was doing and of the request that was being made of him (*Friel* v. *Dickson* [1992] RTR 366).

(Banking Act 1987 (c. 22), ss.3 and 96). A company director, who knows that acts which can only be performed by the company if licensed by the Bank of England are being performed when in fact no licence exists, is guilty of an offence of consenting to the acceptance of a deposit contrary to ss.3 and 96b of the 1987 Act (*Attorney-General's Reference (No. 1 of 1995)* [1996] 4 All E.R. 21).

"Displayed without his knowledge or consent," see KNOWLEDGE.

Stat. Def., includes licence, Landlord and Tenant (Covenants) Act 1995 (c. 30), s.28(1).

CONSEQUENCE. See IN CONSEQUENCE OF.

CONSERVATION. Stat. Def., including protection of animals' environment, Scotland Act 1998 (c. 46), s.111(4).

CONSIDERATION. (13) (Finance Act 1972 (c. 41), s.6(2), as amended by Finance Act 1977 (c. 36), Sched. 6; Value Added Tax Act 1983 (c. 55), s.3(2); and EEC Council Directive (67/228), Art. 2). The House of Lords referred to the European Court the question whether an annual charge imposed on growers by the Apple and Pear Development Council was "consideration" within the meaning of s.6(2) of the Act and Art. 2 of the Directive, and thus whether the exercise of its functions by the Council was a "supply of services" for VAT purposes (*Commissioners of Customs and Excise* v. *Apple and Pear Development Council*, [1986] S.T.C. 192). A payment by a vendor of land to the purchaser as an allowance for sums expended by the purchaser to make the site safe for further development constituted "consideration" for the purposes of the Value Added Tax Act 1983 (c. 55), s.3 (*Commissioners of Customs and Excise* v. *Battersea Leisure* [1992] S.T.C. 213). See also BUSINESS, Main Work, para. (35); SUPPLY, Main Work, paras. (12), (13); TAXABLE SUPPLY.

(Council Directive 77/388, Art. 2). Contributions to a property maintenance fund and drawn out by taxpayers to pay the salaries of staff undertaking maintenance services amounted to consideration obtained by the taxpayers to discharge their duties as trustees of the property and were therefore liable to VAT under Art. 2 (*Trustees of the Nell Gwynn House Maintenance Fund* v. *Customs and Excise Commissioners* [1999] 1 W.L.R. 174).

(Council Directive 77/388, Art. 11A(1)(*a*)). Consideration for the supply of goods could consist of a supply of services if there was a direct link between the supply of goods and the provision of services and the value of the services could be expressed in monetary terms (*Empire Stores* v. *Customs and Excise Commissioners* [1994] 2 All E.R. 90).

CONSOLIDATION. (Town and Country Planning Act 1990 (c. 8), s.288). "Consolidation" of an undesirable use did not imply an increase or intensification but a strengthening of the features supporting a use, rendering it less likely that the use would diminish in intensity or be replaced (*W. H. Tolley & Son Ltd* v. *Secretary of State for the Environment* (1998) 75 P. & C.R. 533).

CONSPIRACY. "Conspiracy to commit the offence" (Criminal Law Act 1977 (c. 45), s.1(1)). In the case of conspiracy, as opposed to the substantive offence, it is necessary to consider what was agreed to be done rather than what was in fact done (*R.* v. *Bolton* (1991) 155 J.P.N. 620).

CONSTABLE. (Race Relations Act 1976 (c. 74), s.16). See EMPLOY.

CONSTRUCTED. "Constructed to carry a load," see LOAD.

CONSTRUCTING. "Person constructing a building" (Value Added Tax Act 1983 (c. 55), Sched. 5, Group 8, Item 1; as substituted by Finance Act 1989 (c. 26), Sched. 3). "Constructing" is limited to buildings actually under construction or recently constructed and hitherto unoccupied (*Link Housing Association* v. *Customs and Excise Commissioners* (1991) 2 VATTR 112).

(Value Added Tax Act 1983 (c. 55), s. 21). "Constructing a building" meant erecting a building as a whole and "constructing a dwelling" could include the conversion of an existing building into a dwelling (*Customs and Excise Commissioners* v. *Arnold* [1996] 12 C.L. 555).

CONSTRUCTION. For the purposes of s.2(4)(*b*) of the Occupiers' Liability Act 1957 (c. 31) "construction" can embrace demolition (*Ferguson* v. *Welsh* [1987] 1 W.L.R. 1533).

"Construction industry" (Industrial Training (Construction Board) Order 1980 (No. 1274), Sched. 1). A firm whose principal business was in replacement windows and patios, including the framework for the windows and doors, was in the "construction industry" for the purposes of this schedule (*Construction Industry Training Board* v. *New View Aluminium Products, The Times*, July 27, 1988).

"Construction, improvement, maintenance" (Local Government Planning and Land Act 1980 (c. 65), s.10(1)). See BUILDING.

"Construction contract", Stat Def., Housing Grants, Construction and Regeneration Act 1996 (c. 53), s.104.

"Construction operations", Stat. Def., Housing Grants, Construction and Regeneration Act 1996 (c. 53), s.105.

CONSULT. "Secretary of State shall consult with organisations . . . concerned" (Social Security and Housing Benefit Act 1982 (c. 24), s.36(1)). To achieve consultation under the requirements of this section sufficient information and sufficient time must be given to the consulted party (*R.* v. *Secretary of State for Social Services, ex p. Association of Metropolitan Authorities* [1986] 1 All E.R. 164).

CONSULT A SOLICITOR AS SOON AS PRACTICABLE. (Police and Criminal Evidence Act 1984 (c. 60), s.58). A policy which refused access by a solicitor to a prisoner held on remand in the cells at the court-house on the sole ground that the request to see the prisoner had been made after 10 a.m. without reference to whether it was practicable to allow access at once or within a reasonable period was unlawful (*R.* v. *Chief Constable of South Wales, ex p. Merrick* [1994] 2 All E.R. 560).

CONSULTATION. (4) The nature of consultation requires a proper consideration of opinions expressed—(*Agricultural Industry Training Board* v. *Aylesbury Mushrooms* [1972] 1 All E.R. 280).

CONSUME. "Consumption on the premises," see PREMISES.
"Consuming" within the meaning of the Road Traffic Act 1988 (c. 52), s.5(1) could embrace ingestion of alcohol into the blood, breath or urine in any form, including by injection (*DPP* v. *Johnson* [1995] 4 All E.R. 53).

CONSUMER. "Deals as consumer" (Unfair Contract Terms Act 1977 (c. 50), s.12). A company operating as shipping brokers and freight forwarding agents which bought a car for the use of a director was dealing as a "consumer" within the meaning of this Act (*R. & B. Customs Brokers Co.* v. *United Dominions Trust* [1988] 1 W.L.R. 321).
The definition of "consumer" in Art. 13 of the Convention on Jurisdiction and Enforcement of Judgments in Civil and Commercial Matters 1968 only applied to a private and final consumer, who was not engaged in trade or professional matters (*Benincasa* v. *Dentalkit Srl* [1998] All E.R. (E.C.) 135).
"Consumer credit business", see BUSINESS.

CONTAINER. Stat. Def., Weights and Measures Act 1985 (c. 72), s.94; Food Safety Act 1990 (c. 16), s.53.

CONTEMPT OF COURT. (Contempt of Court Act 1981 (c. 49), ss.1, 6). Where an interlocutory injunction against publication of certain material has been granted against one person, publication of the same material by another person not specifically bound by the order is capable of constituting contempt of court as tending "to impede or prejudice the administration of justice" (*Att.-Gen.* v. *Observer and Guardian Newspapers, The Times*, May 9, 1989). Intentional interference in the administration of justice by publishing matter which another was restrained by injunction from publishing constituted contempt of court, whether or not publication was in the public interest, and notwithstanding prior publication and the lack of intention of the editors to commit contempt (*Times Newspapers* v. *Att.-Gen.* [1991] 2 W.L.R. 994). The publication by a journal of two articles about a litigant in a libel action against the journal was held to have been for the purpose of deterring the litigant from pursuing the action and was a contempt of court (*Att.-Gen* v. *Hislop* [1991] 1 Q.B. 514). Although mental health review tribunal proceedings are those of a court to which the law relating to contempt of court applies, it was held not to be a contempt to publish the fact of a hearing, or its date, time and place, or its result (*Pickering* v. *Liverpool Daily Post and Echo Newspapers* [1991] 2 A.C. 370). The Queen's Bench Divisional Court, while agreeing that a newspaper was not in contempt of court by having published details of a suspect murderer's previous convictions prior to the initiation of criminal proceedings against him, disagreed on whether contempt could be committed at common law by intentional publication of material (creating a real risk of prejudice to the administration of justice) before a warrant for the arrest of the defendant had been issued (*Att.-Gen.* v. *Sport Newspapers* [1989] Q.B. 110). A person who inspected documents on a court file without leave, knowing that he required leave for that purpose, was held to be in contempt of court (*Dobson* v. *Hastings*, [(1992] 2 W.L.R. 414). An individual could be in contempt of court by publishing inaccurate information about a trial in progress if it created a substantial risk that the course of justice would be seriously impeded or prejudiced, even though it never in fact became necessary to discharge a juror or start a fresh trial (*Att.-Gen.* v. *BBC* [1992] C.O.D. 264). A person in the public gallery of a Crown Court who perpetrated a wolf whistle when the jurors, among whom there was an attractive smartly dressed young lady, was returning to court to deliver their verdict, was guilty of contempt (*R.* v. *Powell*, *The Times*, June 3, 1993).

When applying the strict liability rule under s.2(2) of the 1981 Act in respect of a publication, the court has to consider whether the publication has created a practical, as opposed to theoretical, risk that the course of justice will be seriously impeded or prejudiced (*Att.-Gen.* v. *Guardian Newspapers* [1992] 3 All E.R. 38). The publication by a newspaper of the deliberations of a jury was in contempt of court within the meaning of s.8(1) of the 1981 Act (*Att.-Gen.* v. *Associated Newspapers* [1993] 3 W.L.R. 74).

CONTINUAL. "Continual supervision," see SUPERVISION.

CONTINUALLY. (Town and Country Planning (Control of Advertisements) Regulations 1992 (S.I. 1992 No. 666), Sched. 3, class 13). "Continually" meant regularly recurring rather than continuous (*Westminster City Council* v. *Moran*, *The Independent*, June 22, 1998).

CONTINUING OFFENCE. An offence under s.35 of the Building Act 1984 (c. 55), namely a person acting in breach of the Building Regulations 1985 (No. 1065), was not a continuing offence and therefore the six-month time limit in section 127 of the Magistrates' Courts Act 1980 (c. 43) applied to laying the information (*Torridge District Council* v. *Turner* (1991) 90 L.G.R. 173).

CONTINUOUS EMPLOYMENT. (Employment Protection (Consolidation) Act 1978 (c. 44), s.151, as substituted by Employment Act 1982 (c. 46), Sched. 13). For the purposes of this section continuity was held to have been broken where an employee broke his employment for 12 days to work for another firm (*Roach* v. *C.S.B. (Moulds)* [1991] I.C.R. 349).

CONTINUOUS RESIDENCE. For the purposes of the Secretary of State's extra-statutory concession (by virtue of which an immigrant may be granted indefinite leave to remain after a period of 10 years "continuous residence") these words should be strictly construed. They do not mean "ordinarily resident" (*R.* v. *Secretary of State for the Home Department, ex p. Ali (F)* [1992] Imm.A.R. 316).

"Continuous residence" was a matter of fact and degree and could be broken by period of temporary absence from the U.K. (*R.* v. *Secretary of State for the Home Department, ex p. Ali (Akin)* [1993] Imm.A.R. 610).

CONTINUOUSLY. (3) "Continuously employed" (Employment Protection (Consolidation) Act 1978 (c. 44), s.64(1)(*a*)). Where an employee accepted, for a period of four weeks, an illegal tax-free lodging allowance in addition to his wages, he was held to have been working under an illegal contract and was not therefore "continuously employed" for that period (*Hyland* v. *J. H. Barker (North West)* [1985] I.C.R. 861). A teacher who had been employed under several contracts of employment by the same employer was not entitled to aggregate those periods of employment for the purpose of a claim for wrongful dismissal, and had not therefore been "continuously employed" for the requisite period under this section (*Lewis* v. *Surrey County Council* [1987] 3 W.L.R. 927). A fuel delivery driver regularly employed for seven months a year over 15 years was held not to have been "continuously employed," since the breaks in his employment were more than a temporary cessation of work (*Sillars* v. *Charringtons Fuels* [1989] IRLR 152). An employee was "continuously employed" where he was originally employed by one company within a group and subsequently by a partnership containing three companies also within the group. His original employer and the three companies were "associated employers" within the meaning of s.153(4) of the 1978 Act (*Pinkney* v. *KCA Offshore Drilling Services; sub nom. Pinkney* v. *Sandpiper Drilling* [1989] I.C.R. 389). The continuity of employment was held not to have been broken in the case of a man who worked in Germany until March 31, 1986, and then (under a new contract with the same employer) in the U.K. from April 7, 1986 (*Weston* v. *Vega Space Systems Engineering* [1989] IRLR 429). See also TRANSFER; ORDINARILY WORKS.

(3) "Continuously employed" (Employment Protection (Consolidation) Act 1978 (c. 44), s.81(1)). An employee who was intermittently absent from work, in an irregular pattern over a period of years prior to dismissal, could be considered only temporarily absent for the purposes of Sched. 13, para. 9(1)(*b*) and therefore "continuously employed" within the meaning of this section (*Flack* v. *Kodak* [1987] 1 W.L.R. 31). Trawlermen who had worked for the same company for many years under a system whereby their employment had been regulated by a series of contracts, starting at the beginning of a voyage and ending by mutual consent when the trawler returned to port, were not "continuously employed" within the meaning of this section, and not, therefore, entitled to redundancy payments (*Hellyer Brothers* v. *McLeod* [1986] I.C.R. 122; confirmed by the Court of Appeal [1987] 1 W.L.R. 728). An applicant on a civil service pension scheme who was transferred to a private company (joining their pension scheme), who then received his original civil service pension prior to being made redundant, was held to have been "continuously employed" by the company throughout the entire period of his employment, so that his pension benefits could not be offset against his redundancy claims (*Royal Ordnance* v. *Pilkington* [1989] I.C.R. 737). Continuity of employment was held not to have been broken in a case where a lorry driver, on being dismissed from that job following a driving ban, was, on the following Monday, found work by the same employer, clearing a site (*Tipper* v. *Roofdec* [1989] IRLR 419).

An employee working at a school which was previously funded by the local education authority and which had then become a direct grant-maintained school was, for the purposes of the calculation of redundancy payments, "continuously employed" since the commencement of her employment with the authority (*Pickwell* v. *Lincolnshire County Council* [1993] I.C.R. 87). Where an employee normally worked for 16 hours or more per week she was "continuously employed" within the meaning of this section notwithstanding that her contract stated that she would work such hours as was reasonably required (*Green* v. *Robert* [1992] IRLR 499).

See also TEMPORARY (5); ASSOCIATE.

CONTRACT. (18(*c*)). "Contract to be governed by English law" (R.S.C., Ord. 11, r. 1(*f*)). The relationship between a director and the company is not a "contract" for the purposes of this rule (*Newtherapeutics* v. *Katz* [1990] BCC 362).

(R.S.C., Ord. 11, r.1). "Contract" within the meaning of Ord. 11, r.11(1)(d) included agreements entered into with intent to create legal relations (*DR Insurance Co.* v. *Central National Insurance Co.* [1996] 1 Lloyd's Rep. 74).

"Any other contracts" (Financial Services Act 1986 (c. 60), Sched. 1, para. 9). Wagering contracts entered into by each or either party by way of business, in which clients lost or won variable sums dependent on changes or expected changes in indices were enforceable as "any other contracts" within the meaning of this paragraph (*City Index* v. *Leslie* [1991] 3 W.L.R. 207).

Where an agreement granting an option to purchase land had been executed the words "A contract for the sale or other disposition of an interest in land" in s.2 of the Law of Property (Miscellaneous Provisions) Act 1989 (c. 34) refer to the agreement creating the option, not to the notice by which the option is exercised (*Spiro* v. *Glencrown Properties* [1991] Ch. 537). An option to purchase land could be a "contract for the sale" of land within s.2 of the 1989 Act (*Armstrong and Holmes* v. *Holmes* [1993] 1 W.L.R. 1482.

"In matters relating to a contract" (Civil Jurisdiction and Judgments Act 1982 (c.27), Sched. 4, art. 5(1)). A claim to recover money paid under a contract which was a nullity because of the recipient's lack of capacity to enter into the transaction was a matter relating to a contract for the purposes of art. 5(1) (*Kleinwort Benson* v. *Glasgow City Council* [1996] 2 All E.R. 257).

(Lugano Convention on Jurisdiction and the Enforcement of Judgments in Civil and Commercial Matters 1988, Art. 5(1)). For the purpose of Art. 5(1) of the Convention an action claiming avoidance of a contract on the grounds of misrepresentation or non-disclosure was a "matter relating to a contract" since it was meaningless to talk of the duty of goods faith save by reference to a specific contract (*Agnew* v. *Lansforsakringsbolagens AB* [1997] 4 All E.R. 937).

"Exchange of contracts" (Law of Property (Miscellaneous Provisions) Act 1989 (c. 34), s.2). An option agreement in an agreement for an underlease of commercial premises was an interest in land falling within the 1989 Act and the exchange by the parties of signed facsimiles concerning it did not amount to an exchange of contracts within the meaning of the Act (*Commission for New Towns* v. *Cooper (Great Britain* [1993] NPC 115).

(Employment Protection (Consolidation) Act 1978 (c. 44), s.153(1)). There could be no "contract of employment" in the absence of any mutual obligations for a nurse working for the "nurse bank" where there was no entitlement to regular or continuous work nor to holiday pay or sick leave (*Clark* v. *Oxfordshire Health Authority* [1998] IRLR 125).

"Contract of Employment". Stat. Def., Trade Union and Labour Relations (Consolidation) Act 1992 (c. 52), s.65; Industrial Tribunals Act 1996 (c. 17), s.42(1); Employment Rights Act 1996 (c. 18), s.230(1).

"Contract for the sale . . . of . . . land," see SALE.

"If" contract, see IF.

CONTRARY. "Unless the contrary is shown," see UNLESS.

CONTRAVENTION. Stat. Defs., "includes a failure to comply" (Finance Act 1994 (c. 9), s.17(2)); same (Coal Industry Act 1994 (c. 21), s.65(1)); same (Pensions Act 1995 (c. 26), s.124(1)).

CONTRIBUTORY. Stat. Def., Insolvency Act 1986 (c. 45), s.79.

CONTRIBUTORY NEGLIGENCE. (Law Reform (Contributory Negligence) Act 1945 (c. 28), s.1). Failure to wear a crash helmet (*O'Connell* v. *Jackson* [1972] 1 Q.B. 270), or a seat belt (*Froom* v. *Butcher* [1976] Q.B. 286; *Patience* v. *Andrews* [1983] RTR 447), or to fasten the chin-strap of a crash helmet (*Capps* v. *Miller* [1989] 1 W.L.R. 839) have all been held to amount to contributory negligence for the purposes of this Act.

CONTROL. "Control" in s.153(4) of the Employment Protection (Consolidation) Act 1978 (c. 44) meant control by a majority of votes in general meeting (*Secretary of State for Employment* v. *Newbold* [1981] IRLR 305). This was followed by the Court of Appeal in *South West Launderettes* v. *Laidler* ([1986] I.C.R. 455) where it was held that a single person, notwithstanding that he dominated and to all intents and purposes controlled the operations of a number of companies, did not "control" any of them within the meaning of the section because he did not have a majority holding in any of them. A builder who, with his wife as equal shareholder but playing no part in the management, set up a limited company for the purpose of avoiding the charging of value added tax on a building contract, had "control" of the company within the meaning of this section; the wife was to be regarded as a nominee (*Payne* v. *Secretary of State for Employment* [1989] IRLR 352).

"Supervision, direction or control" (Finance (No. 2) Act 1975 (c. 45), s.38(1)(*a*)). A self-employed doctor filling locum posts in hospitals was held to be under the "control" of the relevant health authorities while doing so (*Bhadra* v. *Ellam* (1988) 85 L.S.Gaz. 37).

"Person having control," see PERSON.

"Controlled waste," see WASTE.

CONTROLLER. Stat. Def., Banking Act 1987 (c. 22), s.105.

CONVENE. "Convene an extraordinary general meeting" (Companies Acts 1948 (c. 38), s.132 and 1985 (c. 6), s.368). Convene here means "fix a date for" or "summon." It does not mean "hold" (*McGuinness v. Petitioners, The Times*, January 15, 1988, following *Re Windward Islands (Enterprises) UK* [1988] BCLC 293).

CONVICT; CONVICTION. "Convicted or sentenced" (Legal Aid Act 1974 (c. 4), s.28(5)). A local authority against which a nuisance order had been made by a magistrates' court had been "convicted or sentenced" within the meaning of this section (*R. v. Inner London Crown Court, ex p. Bentham* [1989] 1 W.L.R. 408).

"Conviction" has been commonly used with two different meanings; often "final disposal of a case"; and not uncommonly "a finding of guilt" (*S (an Infant)* v. *Recorder of Manchester* [1971] A.C. 481).

"Conviction" (Powers of Criminal Courts Act 1973 (c. 62), s.13) is here used in its formal sense and is not synonymous with "finding of guilt" for the purposes of para. 15 of Sched. 2 to the Police (Discipline) Regulations 1977 (No. 580) (*R. v. Secretary of State for the Home Department, ex p. Thornton* [1986] 3 W.L.R. 158).

"Conviction" in s.2(1) of the Criminal Appeal Act 1968 (c. 19) should be given the extended meaning of a finding of guilt; so that the Court of Appeal has jurisdiction under this section to entertain the appeal of an accused found guilty but not yet sentenced (*R. v. Drew* [1985] 1 W.L.R. 914).

"Convicted of an offence" (Police and Criminal Evidence Act 1984 (c. 60), s.74). The meaning of "convicted" in this section is the latter of the two referred to in *S (an Infant)*, *supra*, namely found guilty or pleaded guilty (*R. v. Robertson*; *R. v. Golder* [1987] 3 W.L.R. 327).

"Convicted," "conviction" (Extradition Act 1870 (c. 52), ss.10, 26). A person found guilty of an offence in the United States, but not yet sentenced, was a person "convicted" of an extradition crime within the meaning of these sections (*Morgan v. Attorney-General, The Times*, July 5, 1990).

"Convicted of . . . any offence" (Criminal Evidence Act 1898 (c. 36), s.1(1)(*f*)). The acceptance by a U.S. court of a plea of *nolo contendere* did not amount to a conviction for the purposes of this section (*R. v. McGregor, The Times*, January 29, 1992).

"Before the conviction" (Road Traffic Offenders Act 1988 (c. 53), s.29(1)(*b*)). The date of "conviction" under this section is to be construed as being the date sentence is imposed, not the date of the verdict (*R. v. Brentwood Justices, ex p. Richardson, The Times*, January 1, 1991).

See also AUTREFOIS CONVICT.

(Extradition Act 1989 (c. 33), Sched. 1). A person who pleaded guilty and absconded while awaiting sentence was a "convicted person" for extradition purposes as there was no longer any question as to guilt or innocence by virtue of the guilty plea (*Re Sarig* (Arishalom) [1993] C.O.D. 472).

(Estate Agents Act 1979, s.3(1)(*a*)(i)) "Convicted of an offence" under s.3(1)(*a*)(i) applied to offences committed before the commencement of the 1979 Act and offences committed outside the U.K. (*Antonelli v. Secretary of State for Trade and Industry* [1995] N.P.C. 68).

"Conviction."—Stat. Def., Criminal Justice and Public Order Act 1994 (c. 33), s.25(5).

COPPICE. Stat. Def.,—" 'short rotation coppice' means a perennial crop of tree species planted at high density, the stems of which are harvested above ground level at intervals of less than ten years"—(Finance Act 1995 (c. 4), s.154(3)).

COPY. The unsigned copy of an intoximeter print out was still a "copy" within the meaning of s.10(5) of the Road Traffic Act 1972 (c. 20), as substituted by Sched. 8 of the Transport Act 1981 (c. 56) (*Chief Constable of Surrey* v. *Wickens* [1985] RTR 277). A copy into which the officer conducting the test had inserted the incorrect forename of the accused was still a valid "copy" for the purposes of this section (*Toovey* v. *Chief Constable of Northampton* [1986] Crim.L.R. 475). A handwritten amendment to the top copy of the print out, to read British Summer Time, did not invalidate the "copy" on which it did not appear (*Beck* v. *Scammell* [1986] RTR 162).

Stat. Def., Interception of Communications Act 1985 (c. 56), s.10; Civil Evidence Act 1995 (c. 38), s.13; Magistrates Courts Act 1980 (c. 43), s.5F(4) inserted by Criminal Procedure and Investigations Act 1996 (c. 25), Sched. 1, para. 3.

CORPORATION. See PUBLIC CORPORATION.

COPYRIGHT. Stat. Def., Copyright, Designs and Patents Act 1988 (c. 48), s.1.

COST. "The actual cost of attendance," see ACTUAL COST.

"The cost of a benefit," see BENEFIT.

"The whole cost" (Social Security (Attendance Allowance) Regulations 1991 (S.I. 1991 No. 2740), reg. 7(3)). The reference to paying "the whole cost" in reg. 7(3) of the 1991 Regulations is to be read as meaning the payment of the charge fixed for residents in respect of their individual accommodation (*Steane* v. *Chief Adjudication Officer* [1996] 4 All E.R. 83).

COSTS. "Costs of and incidental to all proceedings" (Supreme Court Act 1981 (c. 54), s.51(1)). The remuneration and expenses of a receiver appointed by the court were not "costs of and incidental" to the proceedings, and could not be recovered from the defendant (*Evans* v. *Clayhope Properties* [1988] 1 All E.R. 444).

The use of "all" in s.51 denoted proceedings before the court and did not allow costs to be awarded for proceedings not incidental to the case before the court (*Zanussi* v. *Anglo Venezuelan Real Estate and Agricultural Development Ltd, The Times*, April 18, 1996).

"Relating only to costs," see RELATING.

The phrase "costs to be paid in full" contemplated something more than standard costs (*Gannon* v. *Chubb Fire Ltd* [1996] P.I.Q.R. P108).

A Tomlin order, that one party pay the "costs of the action" included the costs incurred in the implementation of the order following the date upon which it was made, although disbursements, such as the limiting of structural experts, were not (*Wallace* v. *Brian Gale and Associates, The Times*, March 5, 1998).

COUNSEL. "Aid, abet, counsel or procure" (Accessories and Abettors Act 1861 (c. 94), s.8, as amended by Criminal Law Act 1977 (c. 45), Sched. 12). "Counsel" in this sentence has no implication of any causal connection between the counselling and the principal offence; the offence is established if there was counselling and the principal offence was committed by the person counselled acting within the scope of his authority and not by accident (*R.* v. *Calhaem* [1985] Q.B. 808).

"Counsel" includes a solicitor with a Higher Courts Advocacy Certificate in the Practice Directions applicable to civil appeals (*Practice Direction (House of Lords: Amendments to Procedure (No. 2)* [1995] 1 W.L.R. 1145).

COUNTERCLAIM. (Civil Jurisdiction and Judgments Act 1982 (c. 27), Sched. 1, Art. 11). "Counterclaim" in Art. 11 referred only to a counterclaim against the original plaintiff and not against new parties (*Jordan Grand Prix Ltd* v. *Baltic Insurance Group* [1999] 1 All E.R. 289).

COUPLE. "Apparatus coupled by means of any material substance." See APPARATUS.

See also UNMARRIED COUPLE.

COURSE. See IN THE COURSE.

COURT. (Contempt of Court Act 1981 (c. 49), s.10). Inspectors appointed by the Secretary of State under s.177 of the Financial Services Act 1986 (c. 60) to investigate possible contraventions of ss.1, 2, 4 or 5 of that Act were not a "court" within the meaning of s.10 of the 1981 Act (*Re an Inquiry under the Company Securities (Insider Dealing) Act 1985* (c. 8), *The Times*, May 7, 1987).

"Court" (Contempt of Court Act 1981 (c. 49), s.19). A mental health review tribunal discharging its duties under the Mental Health Act 1983 (c. 20) exercises thereby "the judicial power of the state" and is therefore a "court" within the meaning of this section (*Pickering* v. *Liverpool Daily Post and Echo Newspapers* [1991] 2 A.C. 370).

"Without the leave of the court or tribunal in question" (Supreme Court Act 1981 (c. 54), s.18(1)(*h*)). This does not mean that the leave must be granted by the actual judge whose order was to be appealed against (*Warren* v. *Kilroe (T.) & Sons* [1988] 1 W.L.R. 516). A mental health review tribunal was held not to be a "court" for the purposes of s.1 of the 1981 Act (*Att.-Gen.* v. *Associated Newspaper Group* [1989] 1 All E.R. 604).

"Court of first instance" (Legal Aid Act 1974 (c. 4), s.13(3)). The Divisional Court is not a court of first instance when hearing judicial review proceedings (*R.* v. *Leeds County Court, ex p. Morris* [1990] 1 W.L.R. 175).

"Where a court makes an order for . . . possession" (Housing Act 1980 (c. 51), s.89(1)). The "court" here is the county court (*Bain & Co.* v. *Church Commissioners for England* [1989] 1 W.L.R. 24).

(Criminal Justice Act 1991, Sched. 2) The "court" in the Criminal Justice Act 1991, Sched. 2, para. 8(2)(*b*) referred to the court which originally sentenced the offender and therefore a Crown Court when revoking a community service order could not impose a penalty in excess of the limits of the sentencing powers of the magistrates' court (*R. v. Kosser* [1995] Crim.L.R. followed) (*R. v. Ogden (Dylan Lee), The Times*, March 13, 1996).

(Company Directors Disqualification Act 1986 (c. 46) s.6). A court which has the jurisdiction to wind up a company has jurisdiction to order the disqualification of its directors provided that the proceedings were commenced during the period when the company was being wound up by the court and before its formal dissolution by the Registrar of Companies. In every other case "the court" meant the High Court (*Working Project, Re;* [1995] 1 BCLC 226).

(EC Treaty, Art. 177). Whether a body constituted a "court or tribunal" required consideration of whether the body had been established by law, its permanence and independence, whether its jurisdiction was compulsory and whether it applied rules of law and permitted inter partes procedures (*Dorsch Consult Ingenieurgesellschaft mbH* v. *Bundesbaugesellschaft Berlin mbH (Case C–54/96)* [1998] All E.R. (EC) 262).

Stat. Def., Courts and Legal Services Act 1990 (c. 41), s.119.

COVENANT. Stat. Def., Landlord and Tenant (Covenants) Act 1995 (c. 30), s.28(1).

CRAFT. "Pleasure Craft"—Stat. Def., "any ship of a kind primarily used for sport or recreation"—(Finance Act 1995 (c. 4), Sched. 14, para. 5(1)).

CREAM. Stat. Def., Food Safety Act 1990 (c. 16), s.53.

CREATURE. Stat. Def., Food and Environment Protection Act 1985 (c. 48), s.24.

CREDITOR. (25) "Creditor . . . aggrieved by the company having been struck off the register" (Companies Act 1948 (c. 38), s.353(6); now Companies Act 1985 (c. 6), s.653). "Creditor" is here restricted to those who were creditors on the date when the company was dissolved; so that a creditor of a company whose debt was incurred after the dissolution of the company was not a "creditor" for the purposes of this section (*Re Aga Estate Agencies, The Times*, June 4, 1986, confirming *Re New Timbiqui Gold Mines* [1961] Ch. 319).

"Creditor" within the meaning of s.458 of the 1985 Act meant any person to whom money was owed irrespective of whether the debt could be sued for immediately (*R. v. Smith (Wallace Duncan), The Times*, November 13, 1995).

(Insolvency Act 1986 (c. 45), s.262). A person whose debt may be unascertained, unliquidated or disputed was entitled to vote at a creditors' meeting and qualified as a "creditor" without having to establish his debt to the required civil standard (*Sea Voyager Maritime Inc.* v. *Bielecki (t/a Hughes Hooker & Co.)* [1999] 1 All E.R. 628).

(Insolvency Rules 1986, r.1.17(1) and (3)) A person who was entitled to a future or contingently payable debt, such as future payments of rent under an existing lease, was a "creditor" for the purposes of the Insolvency Rules 1986, r.1.7(1) and (3) and was bound by a company voluntary arrangement

approved at a creditors' meeting of which he had had notice and at which
he was entitled to vote (*Cancol Ltd, Re;* [1996] 1 All E.R. 37).
   (Companies Act 1985 (c. 6), s.653(2)).
   Stat. Def., Insolvency Act 1986 (c. 45), s.383.

CRIME. (7) "Crime of violence" (Compensation for Victims of Crimes of
Violence Scheme 1964 (1969 Revision), para. 5; (1979 Revision),
para. 4(*a*)). It is the nature of the crime, not its likely consequences, that
determines whether it is a "crime of violence" for the purposes of this
scheme. The words "of violence" are adjectival. Thus a psychiatric injury
attributable to an offence under s.34 of the Offences Against the Person
Act 1861 (c. 100) was not attributable to a crime of violence. So that drivers
of trains who suffer shock when someone commits suicide by throwing
himself under their trains are not entitled to compensation (*R.* v. *Criminal
Injuries Compensation Board, ex p. Webb, Warner* [1987] Q.B. 74).

CRIMINAL CAUSE. (11) "Criminal cause or matter" (Supreme Court Act
1981 (c. 54), s.18(1)(*a*)). Orders under appeal in cases where the Central
Criminal Court had issued a witness summons against a person who had
conducted an inquiry into the affairs of a company for the Department of
Trade, and where the Crown Court had granted a summons requiring
production of documents relating to the Lion Intoximeter, were each held
to have arisen in a "criminal cause or matter." *Day* v. *Grant; R.* v.
Manchester Crown Court, ex p. Williams [1987] 3 W.L.R. 537. Garnishee
proceedings taken by a magistrates' court's clerk to enforce payment of
compensation or costs orders made on the conviction of the judgment
debtor for an offence were not a "criminal cause or matter" within the
meaning of this section (*Gooch* v. *Ewing (Allied Irish Bank, garnishee)*
[1985] 3 All E.R. 654. A summons for breach of the peace issued by justices
under s.115 of the Magistrates' Courts Act 1980 (c. 43) is a criminal cause
or matter within the meaning of s.18(1)(*a*) (*R.* v. *Bolton Justices, ex p.
Graeme* (1986) 150 J.P. 129). So also was an application to a Queen's
Bench Divisional Court to quash an order for production of special
procedure material made by a circuit judge under s.9 and Sched. 1 of the
Police and Criminal Evidence Act 1984 (c. 60) (*Carr* v. *Atkins* [1987] 3
W.L.R. 529). The Home Secretary's power under s.17 of the Criminal
Appeal Act 1968 (c. 19) to refer a case to the Criminal Division of the
Court of Appeal for further consideration amounted to an extension of a
convicted person's right to appeal against his conviction or sentence and
was accordingly a "criminal cause or matter" within the meaning of
s.18(1)(*a*) (*R.* v. *Secretary of State for the Home Department, ex p. Garner*
[1990] C.O.D. 457). Where, on an application for judicial review, the
Divisional Court determined a question raised in respect of criminal
proceedings after such proceedings had been concluded, the court's decision was nevertheless made in a "criminal cause or matter," and accordingly the Court of Appeal, pursuant to this section, could entertain no
appeal against it (*R.* v. *Blandford Justices, ex p. Pamment* [1990] 1 W.L.R.
1490). An order requiring the disclosure of assets made in connection with
a restraint order under the Criminal Justice Act 1988 (c. 33) was collateral
to criminal proceedings and accordingly did not arise in a "criminal cause
or matter" (*Re O* [1991] C.O.D. 251).

(Supreme Court Act 1981 (c. 54), s.18(1)(*a*); Extradition Act 1989 (c. 33), s.11(3)(*c*)). Extradition proceedings and a related application for habeas corpus fell within the expression "criminal cause or matter" in s.18(1)(*a*) (*Cuoghi* v. *Governor of Brixton Prison* [1997] 1 W.L.R. 1346).

Restraint orders made for the purpose of aiding the enforcement of an external confiscation order were civil in character and not, therefore, a "criminal cause or matter" so that the Civil Division of the Court of Appeal could entertain an appeal against such an order (*United States Government* v. *Montgomery* [1999] 1 All E.R. 84).

CRIMINAL INJURY. Stat. Def., Criminal Justice Act 1988 (c. 33), s.109.

CRIMINAL OFFENCE. A disciplinary offence charged against a prisoner was not necessarily to be regarded as a "criminal offence" for the purposes of Article 6(3)(*c*) of the Convention for the Protection of Human Rights and Fundamental Freedoms (1953) (Cmd. 8969) (*R.* v. *Board of Visitors of H.M. Prison, The Maze, ex p. Hone* [1988] 2 W.L.R. 177).

CRIMINAL PROCEEDINGS. (R.S.C., Ord. 52, r.1(2)(a)(ii)). Where a person's property was subject to a restraint order under s.8 of the Drug Trafficking Offences Act 1986 (c. 32) or under s.9 of the Act, an application to commit the person for contempt of court was a proceeding for breach of an order made in civil proceedings and not, therefore, within this Order (*Re H, The Times*, April 1, 1988).

In *R.* v. *Crawley Justices, ex p. Ohakwe, The Times*, May 26, 1994, a claim against the detention of moneys alleged to be connected with drug trafficking was not a "criminal proceedings" under the Criminal Justice (International Co-operation) Act 1990 (c. 5), s.25; Legal Aid Act 1988 (c. 34), ss.19, 21 and 26.

(Police and Criminal Evidence Act 1984 (c. 60)). Extradition proceedings, having their origin in acts or conduct punishable under the criminal law, were not criminal proceedings sui generis but were criminal proceedings for the purposes of the 1984 Act (*R.* v. *Governor of Brixton Prison, ex. p. Levin* [1996] 3 W.L.R. 657).

Stat. Def., Legal Aid Act 1988 (c. 34), s.19; Police Act 1997 (c. 50), s.108(1).

Stat. Def., including courts-martial appeals, Human Rights Act 1998 (c. 42) s.5(4).

CRIMINAL PURPOSE. "Items held with the intention of furthering a criminal purpose," see INTENTION.

CROPS. Stat. Def., Food and Environment Protection Act 1985 (c. 48), s.24.

CROWN. "In any proceedings against the Crown" (Crown Proceedings Act 1947 (c. 44), s.21(1)(*a*)). Proceedings against a Health Board constituted under the National Health Service (Scotland) Act 1978 (c. 29) were not "proceedings against the Crown" within the meaning of this section (*British Medical Association* v. *Greater Glasgow Health Board* [1989] 2 W.L.R. 660).

"For the services of the crown" (Patents Act 1977 (c. 37), s.55). The use by a health authority of machines treating kidney stones was use "for the services of the Crown" for the purposes of this section, and did not therefore constitute an infringement of a patent (*Dory* v. *Sheffield Health Authority* [1991] F.S.R. 221).

"Crown or Duchy interest", Stat. Def., Water Industry Act 1991 (c. 56), s.221(7) substituted by Environment Act 1995 (c. 25), Sched. 21, para. 1(1).

A judge, sitting alone, could constitute a "Crown Court" for the purposes of the Crown Court Rules 1982, r.26(14), even though he had not originally determined the case in the Crown Court and the justices who had originally sat with the judge were not part of the later process (*DPP* v. *Coleman* [1998] 1 All E.R. 912).

"Crown land" and "Crown interest," Stat. Def., Town and Country Planning (Scotland) Act 1997 (c. 8), s.242(1).

"Crown land," Stat. Def., Petroleum Act 1998 (c. 58), s.1.

CULTIVATED. See WASTE LAND.

CURRENCY. Stat. Def., Building Societies Act 1986 (c. 53), s.119(1) as amended by Building Societies Act 1997 (c. 32), Sched. 7, para. 53(1).

CURRENT. The term "current price list" in a lease between the landlord of a public house and the tenant under a tied house agreement could refer to the time the lease was made or currency from time to time but where the lease was a standard one which could last for some time, "current price list" for beers sold had the latter meaning (*Greenalls Management Ltd* v. *Canavan (No. 2)*, *The Times*, August 20, 1997).

(Road Traffic Act 1988 (c. 52), s.2A). The word "current" referred only to the state of the vehicle at the time of an alleged offence and the way in which the dangerous condition arose was irrelevant (*Carstairs* v. *Hamilton*, 1997 S.C.C.R. 311).

CURRENT EVENTS. See FAIR DEALING.

CURTILAGE. "Within the curtilage of the building" (Housing Act 1980 (c. 51), Sched. 1, para. 1(1) as amended by Housing and Building Control Act 1984 (c. 29), s.2(1); now Housing Act 1985 (c. 68), Sched. 5, para. 5)). "Curtilage" denotes a small area which is part and parcel of the building it contains or is attached to. So that a house on campus, but at a distance from the college buildings, cannot be said to be "within the curtilage" of the buildings for the purposes of this paragraph (*Dyer* v. *Dorset County Council* [1988] 3 W.L.R. 213). A tennis court constructed on a field some 100 metres from a house, and separated from it by an area of undergrowth, rough grassland, shrubs and trees was not within the "curtilage" of the house (*James* v. *Secretary of State for the Environment and Chichester District Council* (1990) 61 P. & C.R. 234). In determining whether a property was within the curtilage of another the test was whether in a conveyance the one building would pass with the other (*Banwick* v. *Kent County Council* [1992] 24 H.L.R. 341).

See also STRUCTURE.

CUSTODIAL SENTENCE. Stat. Def., Criminal Justice Act 1991 (c.53), s.31.

CUSTODY. "Rights of custody" (Hague Convention on the Civil Aspects of International Child Abduction, 1980, Art. 3, as set out in Schedule 1 to the Child Abduction and Custody Act 1985 (c. 60)). The removal of a child from Australia by his mother without the consent of his father, in breach of an order of the Australian court, was a breach of "rights of custody" within the meaning of this article (*Re C* (*a Minor*), *The Times*, December 19, 1988). "Rights of custody" could include the inchoate rights of those carrying out duties and enjoying the privileges of custodial or parental character, although not recognised or enshrined in law (*Re B. (A Minor) (Abduction)* [1994] 2 F.L.R. 249).

A father who, under the domestic law of his country, had joint custody and was joint guardian of his child with the mother, was capable of exercising rights of custody and asserting that the removal of the child was unlawful under the Child Abduction and Custody Act 1985 (c. 60), Sched. 1 even though he merely exercised his rights of access to the child (*McKiver* v. *McKiver* (O.H.), 1995 S.L.T. 790).

Where a mother had been awarded custody of children on divorce, the father did not have "rights of custody" within the meaning of the 1980 Convention (*Pirrie* v. *Sawacki*, 1997 S.C.L.R. 59).

A right to watch over a child's education and living conditions and a right of access did not amount to "rights of custody" within the meaning of the Civil Aspects of International Child Abduction 1980, Art. 5 (*S.* v. *H.* [1997] 3 W.L.R. 1086).

"Non-custodial sentence" (Criminal Justice Act 1982 (c. 48), s.1(4A)). A conditional discharge does not qualify as a "non-custodial sentence" (*R.* v. *Hunter* [1991] Crim.L.R. 146; *R* v. *Betts* (*Mark*) (1992) 13 Cr.App.R.(S.) 281).

"Custody" (Protection of Animals (Amendment) Act 1954 (c. 40), s.2). A person who held a dog's lead in a public procession for more than an hour, but under the supervision of its owner, was held not to have had "custody" of the dog within the meaning of this section (*Royal Society for the Prevention of Cruelty to Animals* v. *Miller, The Times,* March 8, 1994).

"Surrender to custody," see SURRENDER.

"Police custody," see POLICE.

CUSTOMARY. "Customary for employers to provide living accommodation" (Finance Act 1977 (c. 36), s.33(4)(*b*)), see *Vertigan* v. *Brady* cited EMOLUMENTS.

"In contravention of a customary arrangement" (Employment Protection (Consolidation) Act 1978 (c. 44), s.59). A company which made 304 employees redundant, without first calling for volunteers, was held not to have dismissed them "in contravention of a customary arrangement" since, in order to qualify as such within the meaning of this section the arrangement had to relate directly to actual selection and not merely to the creation of a pool from which selection could be made (*Rogers* v. *Vosper Thornycroft* (*U.K.*) [1989] IRLR 82).

CUSTOMER. (Consumer Protection Act 1987 (c. 43), s.20). The definition of "customer" in s.20 was limited to private individuals who wished to purchase goods for personal use, rather than for other retailers and wholesalers (*MFI Furniture Centres* v. *Hibbert, The Times,* July 21, 1995).

CYCLE. Stat. Def., Road Traffic Act 1988 (c. 52), s.192.

D

DAILY WORKING PERIOD. See WORKING.

DAMAGE. "Damages any property" (Criminal Damage Act 1971 (c. 48), s.1(1)). The erasure of a computer program from the plastic circuit card of a computerised saw was "damage" within the meaning of this section (*Cox* v. *Riley* [1986] Crim.L.R. 460). Anything which impairs the value of a computer disc to its legitimate user was capable of being "damage" for the purposes of this section (*R.* v. *Whiteley* (1991) 93 Cr.App.R. 25). Where a local authority washed away by high pressure jets silhouettes painted on a pavement as part of a protest, it was held that there had been damage within the meaning of this section (*Hardman* v. *The Chief Constable of Avon and Somerset Constabulary* [1986] Crim.L.R. 330).

"Damage to any property" (Nuclear Installations Act 1965 (c. 57), s.7) held not to extend to a risk or increased risk of damage to property, nor to pure economic loss, but only to proved personal injury and actual damage to property (*Merlin* v. *British Nuclear Fuels* [1990] 3 W.L.R. 383).

"Damage" for the purposes of s.7 was caused where there had been some alteration in the physical characteristics of property caused by radiation which rendered the property less useful or valuable (*Blue Circle Industries plc* v. *Ministry of Defence* [1998] 3 All E.R. 385).

"Damage was caused to the vehicle" (Theft Act 1968 (c. 60), s.12A(2)(*d*), as inserted by the Aggravated Vehicle Taking Act 1992 (c. 11), s.1(1)). Damage done to a vehicle in an escape attempt from a lawful arrest constituted "damage" for the purposes of this section (*Dawes* v. *DPP* [1994] R.T.R. 209).

"Any damage to the vehicle" (Road Traffic Act 1988 (c. 52), s.5(3)). The application of a wheel clamp did not constitute "damage" to the vehicle under this section (*Drake* v. *DPP* [1994] R.T.R. 411).

"Damage and destruction" referred to the destruction or damage which a defendant intended to cause or to the risk of which he was reckless and not to the destruction or damage which in fact occurred (*R.* v. *Webster; R.* v. *Warwick* [1995] 2 All E.R. 168).

(Law Reform (Contributory Negligence) Act 1945 (c. 28), s.1(1)). In a claim for damage as a result of a negligent valuation, "damage" for the purpose of s.1(1) of the 1945 Act was the overall loss sustained by the lender as a result of the loan, rather than that part of the loss attributable to the negligent valuation, so that damages against a negligent valuer would be reduced to take into account that an imprudent lending decision had been made by the lender (*Platform Home Loans Ltd* v. *Oyston Shipways Ltd* [1998] 4 All E.R. 252).

Stat. Def., Water Industry Act 1991 (c.56), s.219; Water Resources Act 1991 (c.57), s.221.

DAMAGES. "By way of damages for breach of . . . contract" (Employment Protection Act 1975 (c. 71), s.102(3)). This phrase is to be construed broadly to enable the gross rather than the net amount of any payment to be set off against the protective award made under this Act (*Vosper Thornycroft U.K.* v. *Transport and General Workers Union* [1988] L.S.Gaz., March 2, 469).

(Civil Liability (Contribution) Act 1978, s.1(1)). The relevant damage was the alleged wrong which caused injury and death rather than the damages which the deceased could have recovered for his injury for the purposes of s.1(1) with the result that a concurrent tortfeasor could be liable to a plaintiff notwithstanding a settlement with the other tortfeasor (*Jameson* v. *CEGB* [1997] 4 All E.R. 38).

A claim for an award of damages was a prerequisite to a claim for "additional damages" under the Copyright, Designs and Patents Act 1988 (c. 48), s.97(2) (*Redrow Homes Ltd* v. *Bett Brothers plc and ors* [1998] 2 W.L.R. 198).

DAMAGES FOR PERSONAL INJURIES. (Limitation Act 1980, s.11(1)). An unwanted conception whether as a result of negligent advice or negligent surgery was a "personal injury" in the sense of an "impairment" in the illustrative definition in s.38(1) of the 1980 Act (*Walkin* v. *South Manchester Health Authority* [1995] 1 W.L.R. 1517).

DANCING. Stat Def., "includes any movement apparently to the accompaniment of music" (Licensing (Scotland) Act 1976 (c. 66), s.18A(9) inserted by Licensing (Amendment) (Scotland) Act 1996 (c. 36), s.1(1)).
See MUSIC.

DANGEROUS. "Trees which . . . have become dangerous" (Town and Country Planning Act 1971 (c. 78), s.60(6)). A tree becomes "dangerous" within the meaning of this section at the moment it constitutes a present danger to persons or property (*Smith* v. *Oliver* [1989] 2 P.L.R. 1).

(Factories Act 1961 (c. 34), s.29(1)). "Dangerous" in s.29(1) did not merely mean "not safe" because the two words were antonyms, but that the state of the workplace was a reasonably foreseeable source of injury and that the danger manifested itself in a reasonably foreseeable way (*Mains* v. *Uniroyal Englebert Tyres* (I.H.), *The Times*, September 29, 1995).

Goods were of a "dangerous" nature for the purposes of Art. IV, r.6 of the Hague Rules if they were dangerous to other goods or liable to cause loss by making it necessary to dump the cargo at sea, even though the goods were not dangerous to the vessel itself or liable to cause direct physical damage to other cargo loaded on it (*Effort Shipping Co. Ltd* v. *Linden Management SA* [1998] 1 All E.R. 495).

"Dangerous instruments." Stat. Def., "instruments which have a blade or are sharply pointed" (Criminal Justice and Public Order Act 1994 (c. 33), s.60(11)).

(Dogs Act 1871, s.2). "Dangerous" under the 1871 Act was to be given its ordinary meaning and construed by reference to the nature and disposition of the dog in question, and not to be restricted to meaning dangerous to human beings or specific animals referred to in subsequent statutes and could be applied to a dog involved in a fight with another dog (*Briscoe* v. *Shattock* [1999] 1 W.L.R. 432).

DANGEROUSLY OUT OF CONTROL. (Dangerous Dogs Act 1991 (c. 65), ss.3(1) and 10(3)). A dog is "dangerously out of control" in a public place if it acts in a way which gives grounds for reasonable apprehension that injury might ensue (*R.* v. *Bezzina* [1994] 3 All E.R. 964).

DATA. "Data user" (Data Protection Act 1984 (c. 35), s.1(5)). An accountant who put information provided by clients on computer for the purposes of producing accounts for presentation to the Inland Revenue and other bodies was a "data user" within the meaning of this section (*Data Protection Registrar* v. *Griffin*, *The Times*, March 5, 1993).

Stat. Def., Data Protection Act 1998 (c. 29), s.1(1).

DATE. "Date on which the proceedings were commenced" (Landlord and Tenant Act 1954 (c. 56), s.24A(2)). Where a tenant applied to the county court for the grant of a new tenancy, the "date on which the proceedings were commenced" was the date of the landlord's answer (*Thomas* v. *Hammond & Lawrence* [1986] 2 All E.R. 214).

"Date fixed for the trial" (Legal Aid in Criminal Proceedings (General) Regulations (1968 No. 1231) reg. 6E(2)(*c*), as substituted by Legal Aid in Criminal Proceedings (General) (Amendment) Regulations (1983 No. 1863), reg. 8). These words cannot refer to the date of a defendant's first appearance before justices in a magistrates' court (*R.* v. *Bury Justices*, *ex p. N* (*a Minor*) [1986] 3 W.L.R. 965).

"At the date of application" (British Nationality Act 1964 (c. 22), s.1(5)). This refers to the date on which the application for resumption of citizenship is made rather than the date on which naturalisation was granted or registration effected (*R.* v. *Secretary of State for the Home Department, ex p. Patel (Pratimakumari)* [1991] Imm. A.R. 25).

"Date of death of deceased debtor" (Administration of Insolvent Estates of Deceased Persons Order 1986 (No. 1999), Sched. 1). The date of death of a deceased debtor was the moment of the death and not the first moment of the day on which he died (*Re Palmer* [1994] 3 All E.R. 835).

DATE OF KNOWLEDGE. See KNOWLEDGE.

It was not necessary for the plaintiff to know whether the act or omission was actionable or tortious (*Dobbie* v. *Medway Health Authority* [1994] 4 All E.R. 449).

DAY. The term "day" in article 6(1) of EEC Regulation 3820/85 meant successive periods of 24 hours beginning with the driver's resumption of driving after his last weekly rest period (*Kelly* v. *Shulman* [1988] 1 W.L.R. 1134).

"Days of interruption of employment" had the same meaning for the reduced earning provisions as for the unemployment benefit, sickness benefit and invalidity benefit legislation and means a day of unemployment or a day of incapacity to do work which it would be reasonably expected of a person to do (*Social Security Decision No. R(1) 3/93*).

The reference to "three clear days" in the Local Government Act 1972 (c. 70), s.100B connotes three working days (*R.* v. *Swansea City Council, ex p. Elitestone* [1993] 46 E.G. 181).

(Apportionment Act 1870, s.2; Wages Act 1986 (c. 48)). The phrase "from day to day" in the Apportionment Act 1870, s.2 referred to calendar days and not working days (*Sim* v. *Rotheram MBC* [1986] IRLR 391 and *Miles* v. *Wakefield DC* [1987] IRLR 193 distinguished) (*Thames Water Utilities* v. *Reynolds* [1996] IRLR 186).

"Business Day," Stat. Def., National Debt (Stockholders Relief) Act 1892 (c. 39), s.2(5) inserted by Finance Act 1997 (c. 16), s.108(1).

"Working day," Stat. Def., Interception of Communications Act 1985 (c. 56), s.10; "means any day other than a Saturday, a Sunday, Christmas Day, Good Friday or a day which is a bank holiday under the Banking and Financial Dealings Act 1971 in any part of the United Kingdom" (Intelligence Services Act 1994 (c. 13), s.11(1)(f)).

See also WORKING DAY.

DEAD WILD BIRD. (Wildlife and Countryside Act 1981 (c. 69), s.1(2)(*a*)). A stuffed and mounted golden eagle is still a "dead wild bird" for the purposes of this section (*Robinson* v. *Everett* [1988] Crim.L.R. 699).

DEAL WITH. "Deal with any property" (Matrimonial Causes Act 1973 (c. 18), s.37(2)(*a*)). "Property" in this section cannot apply to the assets of a company, and "deal with" refers only to some positive dealing with property, and not lack of dealing (*Crittenden* v. *Crittenden* [1990] 2 F.L.R. 361).

DEBENTURE. Stat. Def., Companies Act 1985 (c. 6), s.744; "includes debenture stock" (Atomic Energy Authority Act 1995 (c. 37), s.13(1)).

DEBT. "The debt . . . is for a liquidated sum payable . . . either immediately or at some certain future time" (Insolvency Act 1986 (c. 45), s.267(2)(*b*)). An order made under R.S.C., Ord. 29, r.10, requiring a defendant to make an interim payment, created a "debt" within the meaning of this section (*Maxwell* v. *Bishopsgate Investment Management* (*in Liquidation*), *The Times*, February 11, 1993).

Unpaid community charge amounted to a "debt" within the meaning of the County Courts Act 1984 (c. 28) (*Preston Borough Council* v. *Riley* [1995] RA 227).

(Capital Gains Tax Act 1979 (c. 14)). The fact that a debt is secure is not, without more, a "debt on a security" within the meaning of ss.82 and 134(1) of the 1979 Act and the security for the debt did not turn it into an asset, capable of being disposed of at a profit (*Taylor Clark International Ltd* v. *Lewis* (1998) T.C. Leaflet No. 3567).

Stat. Def., Insolvency Act 1986 (c. 45), ss.382, 385.

DECEPTION. "By any deception . . . with intent to make permanent default" (Theft Act 1978 (c. 31), s.2(1)(*b*)). The offence under this subsection might be committed in one of two ways, either by the defendant intending to make permanent default in respect of a personal liability, or by a defendant intending to let another make permanent default in respect of that other's liability (*R.* v. *Attewell-Hughes* (1991) 93 Cr.App.R. 132).

"By any deception . . . obtains any exemption from . . . liability to make a payment" (Theft Act 1978 (c. 31), s.2(1)(*c*)). The "deception" may be by an act of omission as well as commission (*R.* v. *Firth* (1990) 91 Cr.App.R. 217).

"Person who by any deception dishonestly obtains property belonging to another" (Theft Act 1968 (c. 60), s.15(1). A wholesale milkman who for years had overcharged a retailer was guilty of obtaining by "deception" under this section notwithstanding that the retailer had been gullible enough to pay the bills for years unchecked and without question (*R.* v. *Jones* (*Ivor*), *The Times*, February 15, 1993).

Property was not obtained by deception from a company if any employee whose state of mind stood as that of the company knew the true position or falsity of the representation (*R.* v. *Rozeik* [1996] 3 All E.R. 281).

S.15(1) was inapt to cover deception which involved the debiting of one person's bank account and the corresponding crediting of another's bank account so that a person who obtained a mortgage advance by deception was not guilty of an offence (*R.* v. *Preddy* [1996] 3 All E.R. 481).

DECISION. "Decision which is the subject of the appeal" (Supreme Court Act 1981 (c. 54), s.48(1) as amended). "Decision" is here used in a wide sense; so that, on an appeal from justices to a crown court against one of several convictions entered against the defendant on the same occasion, the powers of the crown court under this section, to correct any "order or judgment incorporating the decision which is the subject of the appeal" extend also to those convictions which were not appealed against (*Dutta* v. *Westcott* [1986] 3 W.L.R. 746).

"Any order, judgment or other decision of the crown court" (Supreme Court Act 1981 (c. 54), s.28(1)). "Decision" means "final decision" and would exclude a preliminary ruling (*Loade* v. *DPP* [1989] 3 W.L.R. 1281).

A decision by justices to refuse to adjourn *sine die* a mother's application for access to children in care was a "decision" appealable to the High Court under s.12C(5) of the Child Care Act 1980 (c. 5), as inserted by Health and Social Services and Social Security Adjudications Act 1983 (c. 41), Sched. 1, Pt. 1 (*Southwark London Borough Council* v. *H.* [1985] 1 W.L.R. 861).

"Decision" (Social Security Act 1980 (c. 30), s.14(2)). A social security commissioner's refusal to grant an extension of time to appeal was not a "decision" within the meaning of this section and could not, therefore, be appealed (*White* v. *Chief Adjudication Officer* [1986] 2 All E.R. 905).

"Decision" (Industrial Tribunals (Rules of Procedure) Regulations 1985 (No. 16), reg. 2) would include an oral decision (*Spring Grove Services Group* v. *Hickinbottom* [1990] I.C.R. 111; *Arthur Guinness & Co.* (*Great Britain*) v. *Green* [1989] I.C.R. 241). An interlocutory order was not a "decision" within the meaning of this regulation (*Casella London* v. *Banai* [1990] I.C.R. 215).

"Decision in proceedings on an appeal . . . against an enforcement notice" (Town and Country Planning Act 1971 (c. 78), s.246(1)). An order for costs made by the Secretary of State acting through his inspector is such a "decision" and can therefore be the subject of an appeal to the High Court under this section (*R.* v. *Secretary of State for the Environment, ex p. Bolton, The Times,* March 26, 1991).

"A decision of that judge on such an appeal" (Insolvency Act 1986 (c. 45), s.375(2)). The refusal of a High Court judge to extend time for appealing to him against a bankruptcy order was "a decision of that judge on such an appeal" within the meaning of that section (*Lawrence* v. *European Credit Co.* [1992] BCC 792).

(Bahamas Independence Order 1973 (S.I. 1973 No. 1080), Part III, art. 104). Art. 104(2) contemplates a decision determining a constitutional motion. Where the Court of Appeal of the Bahamas upheld the refusal of a stay of execution pending an appeal against the death penalty on the grounds that it had no prospect of success, the finding was a "decision" for the purposes of art. 104 (*Farrington* v. *Queen* [1996] 3 W.L.R. 177).

DECIDED. (Sex Discrimination Act 1976 (c. 65), s.76(6)(*c*)). "Decided" for the purposes of s.76(6)(*c*) means decided at a time and in circumstances when an alleged discriminator was in a position to implement a decision (*Swithland Motors* v. *Clarke* [1994] I.C.R. 231).

DEDICATION. "Deemed to have been dedicated" (Highways Act 1980 (c. 66), s.31(1)). Use of a footpath by the public purely for the purpose of recreational walking was capable of founding a deemed dedication of the path as a highway under this section (*Dyfed County Council* v. *Secretary of State for Wales* (1989) 59 P. & C.R. 275).

DEDUCTION. "A deduction from his wages," see WAGES.

"Deduction" meant both the process of subtraction and the result where one claim was set off against another and a balance struck (*Connaught Restaurants* v. *Indoor Leisure* [1994] 4 All E.R. 834).

DEER. Stat. Def., Deer Act 1991 (c.54), s.16; Deer (Scotland) Act 1996 (c. 58), s.45(1).

DEFAULT. See WILFUL DEFAULT.

"Default rules." Stat. Def., Companies Act 1989 (c. 40), s.188.

DEFAULTER. (Transport Act 1982 (c. 49), s.36). "Defaulter" in this section can include an unincorporated body (*R.* v. *Clerk to Croydon Justices, ex p. Chief Constable of Kent* [1989] Crim.L.R. 910).

DEFECT. Stat. Def., Consumer Protection Act 1987 (c. 43), s.3.

The phrase "defective in workmanship" in an insurance policy should be construed objectively and did not involve only an inquiry into whether there had been negligence (*Queensland Government Railways and Electric Power Transmission Pty* v. *Manufacturers Mutual Insurance* [1969] 1 Lloyd's Rep. 214 considered) (*Kier Construction* v. *Royal Insurance (U.K.)* (Q.B.D. 1992) 30 Con.L.R. 45).

DEFECTIVE. (Child Support Act 1991 (c. 48), s.2; Child Support (Collection and Enforcement Regulations 1992, reg. 22). An assertion that s.2 of the 1991 Act had not been observed correctly and that the deduction from an earnings order was "defective" was a matter for judicial review and therefore confined to the High Court (*Biggin* v. *Secretary of State for Social Security* [1995] C.O.D. 405).

DEFENCE. Stat. Def., Official Secrets Act 1989 (c. 6), s.2.

DEFEND. "Establishing, preserving or defending his title," see ESTABLISH.

DEFENDANT. "Defendant to an action" (R.S.C., Ord. 23, r.1). A third party against whom a plaintiff has brought interlocutory proceedings is not a "defendant" within the meaning of this rule, and the court, therefore, has no power to order the plaintiff to provide security for costs of such third party (*Taly N.D.C. International N.V.* v. *Terra Nova Insurance Co.* [1985] 1 W.L.R. 1359). "One of a number of defendants" within the meaning of the Civil Jurisdiction and Judgments Act 1982 (c. 27), Sched. 4, art. 6 envisaged a claim by the same plaintiff against multiple defendants (*Barclays Bank* v. *Glasgow City Council* [1994] 4 All E.R. 865).

For the purposes of the C.C.R. (S.I. 1981 No. 1687), Ord. 13, r.8 a party might within the same action be both plaintiff and defendant and even though a wife had been the petitioner in the divorce suit, she could be the defendant to the ancillary relief proceedings which were separate from the main suit (*Penny* v. *Penny* [1996] 1 W.L.R. 1204).

DEFERRED SENTENCE. See SENTENCE.

DEGREE. Stat. Def. (in academic context), Education (Mandatory Awards) Regulations 1998 (No. 1166), reg. 2.

DELAY. The "delay" which s.33(3)(*a*)(*b*) of the Limitation Act 1980 (c. 58) requires the court to consider is that which has occurred between the expiry of the limitation period and the issue of the writ and not the period between the beginning of the limitation period and the issue of the writ (*Eastman* v. *London Country Bus Services*, *The Times*, November 23, 1985; *Donovan* v. *Gwentoys* [1990] 1 W.L.R. 472).

See also INORDINATE DELAY.

DELIBERATE. (Housing Act 1985 (c. 68), Pt. III, s.60(1)). A failure to pay rent as a result of real financial difficulties and a genuine inability to make ends meet was not "deliberate" for the purposes of the Housing Act 1985, s.60(1) (*R.* v. *Wandsworth London Borough Council, ex p. Hawthorne* [1995] 2 All E.R. 331).

DELICT. Stat. Def., "includes quasi-delict" (Private International Law (Miscellaneous Provisions) Act 1995 (c. 42), s.9(8)).

DELIVER. "Deliver" in the County Court Rules 1981, Order 9, rule 2(6) and Order 17, rule 11(11) was to be construed the same way and meant the lodging of a defence with the court by the defendant but not the sending of the defence by an officer of the court to the plaintiff, which was a separate procedure (*Lightfoot* v. *National Westminster Bank plc; Roberts* v. *British Telecommunications plc* [1996] 1 W.L.R. 583).

DEMAND. "Demand (known as the 'Statutory demand')" (Insolvency Act 1986 (c. 45), s.268). A demand purporting to be a "statutory demand" under this section remains a "statutory demand" within the meaning of the section even if it is defective and liable to be set aside (*Re A Debtor (No. 1 of 1987, Lancaster*) [1988] 1 All E.R. 959).

DENOMINATIONAL CHARACTER. In relation to institution, Stat. Def., Education Act 1994 (c. 30), s.19(2).

DEPENDENT. "With whom dependent children reside" (Housing Act 1985 (c. 68), s.59(1)(*b*)). In determining whether a homeless person has a priority need for accommodation under this section it is not a requirement that the children be wholly and exclusively dependent upon that person, or that they reside only with him (*R.* v. *Lambeth London Borough Council, ex p. Vagliviello* [1990] C.O.D. 428). Classification of those in priority need as contained in s.59(1) did not include a dependent child living with its parents (*R.* v. *Oldham Metropolitan Borough Council, ex p. Garlick* [1993] 2 W.L.R. 609).

A young person was in full-time enployment when on a youth training scheme and therefore could not be "dependant" within the meaning of s.59(1)(*b*) (*R.* v. *Kensington and Chelsea RLBC, ex p. Amarfio* (1995) 27 H.L.R. 543).

DEPORTED. The phrase "is or had been ordered to be deported" in s.3(5)(*c*) of the Immigration Act 1971 (c. 77) is to be read as "is to be deported or had been ordered to be deported" and not "is ordered to be deported or had been ordered to be deported" (*R.* v. *Immigration Appeal Tribunal, ex p. Ibrahim* [1989] C.O.D. 272).

DEPOSIT. Deposits taken by a commodity broker from his client for the purpose of securing trading on the client's behalf were not "deposits" within the meaning of s.1 of the Banking Act 1979 (c. 37) (*SCF Finance Co.* v. *Masri (No. 2)* [1987] 2 W.L.R. 58).

"Shall not . . . deposit controlled waste on any land" (Control of Pollution Act 1974 (c. 40), s.3(1)(*a*)). This has been held to refer to the actual deposit of the waste on the dumping site with no realistic prospect of further inspection (*Leigh Land Reclamation* v. *Walsall Metropolitan Borough Council* [1991] Crim.L.R. 298). But this prohibition against depositing and disposing of controlled waste applied not only to waste which was in its final resting place but also to waste which was on the site temporarily (*R.* v. *Metropolitan Stipendary Magistrate, ex p. London Waste Regulation Authority* [1993] All E.R. 113).

(Environmental Protection Act 1990 (c. 43), s.33). A broad interpretation must be given to the meaning of "deposit" in the 1990 Act and did not have to mean only the final resting place of the deposit (*Thames Waste Management Ltd* v. *Surrey C.C.* [1997] 2 C.L. 275).

(Banking Act 1987 (c. 22), s.58(1); Banking Act 1987 (Meaning of Deposit Order 1991 (No. 1776), art. 2(1)).

A "depositor" was prima facie the person who made the original deposit and an assignee of a debt was not a "depositor" holding a protected deposit (*Deposit Protection Board* v. *Barclays Bank* [1994] 2 A.C. 367).

Stat. Def., Banking Act 1987 (c. 22), s.5.

DEPOSITED. Braziers for roasting chestnuts mounted on barrows were "deposited" on the highway within the meaning of the Highways Act (c. 66), s.149(2) (*Scott* v. *Westminster City Council* [1995] RTR 327; 93 L.G.R. 370).

DEPOSITION. "Depositions or statements on oath taken in a foreign state," see FOREIGN.

DEPOSITOR. In the Banking Act 1987, s.58(1), "depositor" means the person who made the original deposit to an institution and does not include a person entitled to a debt by reason of a part-assignment (*Deposit Protection Board* v. *Dalia* [1994] 2 W.L.R. 732).

DERELICT. A ship is "derelict" and therefore a "wreck" if the master and crew abandoned her at sea without any intention of returning to her, and without any hope on their part of recovering her. Furthermore, a vessel which was derelict did not cease to be derelict merely because it sank and was lying on the sea bed (*Pierce* v. *Bemis, The Lusitania* [1986] 1 All E.R. 1011).

DERIVE. "Derived from any business" (Taxes Management Act 1970 (c. 9), s.20(4) as substituted by Sched. 6 to the Finance Act 1976 (c. 40)). Financial gains arising from dealings in assets received from a company were "derived" from the business of that company as much as were gains made as a result of the receipt of the assets themselves (*Monarch Assurance Co.* v. *Income Tax Special Commissioners* [1986] S.T.C. 311).

DESCRIBE. Notice . . . describing . . . the employees . . . entitled to vote" (Trade Union and Labour Relations (Consolidation) Act 1992 (c. 52), s.266A, as inserted by s.18(2) of the Trade Union Reform and Employment Rights Act 1993 (c. 19)). Where a college employing a large number of lecturers did not know which of its academic staff were union members, notices given by the union describing those to be balloted as "all our members employed by the college" did not satisfy the requirement of this section (*Blackpool and Fylde College* v. *National Association of Teachers in Further and Higher Education, The Times,* March 23, 1994).

DESCRIPTION. (6) "Sale of goods by description" (Sale of Goods Act 1979 (c. 54), s.13(1)). A sale by one dealer to another of a painting later discovered to be a forgery, where there had been no reliance by the buyer on the seller's attribution, was not a sale "by description" under the meaning of this section (*Harlingdon and Leinster Enterprises* v. *Christopher Hull Fine Art* [1990] 1 All E.R. 737).

DESIGN. Stat. Def., Copyright, Designs and Patents Act 1988 (c. 48), s.213.

"Design capable of registration," see CAPABLE.

DESIGNED. A sub-machine-gun from which the trigger, pivot pin and magazine were missing remained "designed and adapted" for continuous firing within the meaning of s.5(1)(*a*) of the Firearms Act 1968 (c. 27), and was therefore a "prohibited weapon" within the meaning of s.5(2) (*R.* v. *Clarke (Frederick)* [1986] 1 W.L.R. 209). An unknown fault in a gun, which stopped it working, did not prevent it from being a "prohibited weapon" within the meaning of this section (*Brown* v. *DPP, The Times,* March 27, 1992).

"Articles designed as clothing . . . for young children" (Value Added Tax Act 1983 (c. 55), Sched. 5, Group 17, Item 1). Where an article had been produced to such a state that, even though incomplete as a garment, its design was such that it was suitable only for that purpose, it was an "article designed as clothing" within the meaning of Item 1 (*Customs and Excise Commissioners* v. *Ali Baba Tex* [1992] S.T.C. 590).

DESTROY. "Or otherwise destroying" (Wills Act 1837 (c. 26), s.20). Where, with the intention of revoking a will, the testator's and witnesses' signatures had been so badly scored by a ballpoint pen that it was impossible to discern them by the senses by which a signature is normally discerned, it was held that the will was effectively destroyed within the meaning of this section (*Re the Estate of Adams (Dec'd)* [1990] 2 W.L.R. 924).

DESTRUCTION. "By the destruction or damage" (Criminal Damage Act 1971 (c. 48), s.1(2)(*b*)), see THEREBY.

Stat. Def., "includes making permanently inaccessible or permanently unusable" (Northern Ireland Arms Decommissioning Act 1997 (c. 7), s.10(1)).

DETAIN. "Detained" (Mental Health Act 1983 (c. 20), s.20(3)(*b*), (4)(*c*)). A patient on leave of absence from a hospital could not be regarded as "detained" in a hospital for the purposes of this section (*R.* v. *Garner* [1986] 1 W.L.R. 73).

A patient who had made no attempt to leave and been accommodated on an unlocked ward had not been "detained" within the meaning of s.131 of the 1983 Act (*R.* v. *Bournewood Community and Mental Health NHS Trust, ex p. L* [1998] 3 All E.R. 289).

(Mental Health (Scotland) Act 1984, s.64(1)). The words "liable to be detained" was to be construed with reference to the reasons for the original detention: a regime of supervised care, which had the effect of preventing a deterioration of the symptons of the disorder, but not the disorder itself, could be sufficient to justify continued detention (*Reid* v. *Secretary of State for Scotland* [1999] 2 W.L.R. 28).

DETER. "Deterring him from . . . seeking to become a member of an independent trade union" (Employment Protection (Consolidation) Act 1978 (c. 44), s.23(1)(*a*)(*b*)). The effect of giving employees a pay increase if they gave up rights of collective bargaining was to "deter" the employees within the meaning of this section (*Associated Newspapers* v. *Wilson, The Times*, May 5, 1993). Where a high executive officer, who was also group assistant secretary of his trade union, was denied promotion to a higher grade because of his lack of managerial experience caused by his spending so much time on trade union duties, the failure to promote him was held not to have been an "action . . . for the purpose of . . . deterring him from taking part in the activities of an independent trade union" for the purposes of this section (*Department of Transport* v. *Gallacher, The Times*, March 25, 1994). See also ACTION; PENALISE.

DETERMINATION. (6) "Determination" of an appeal (Taxes Management Act 1970 (c. 9), s.56(2)). A decision on a preliminary issue by commissioners that enabled a taxpayer's capital gains tax liability on the disposal of assets to be quantified did not constitute the "determination" of his appeal for the purposes of this section (*Gibson* v. *General Commissioners for Stroud* [1989] STC 421).

Upon the true construction of a lease the words "at the time of . . . determination," in connection with a rent review clause, meant the review date specified in the lease, even where the actual determination was many years later due to a dispute between the parties (*Glofield Properties* v. *Morley* (*No. 2*) [1989] 32 EG 49).

"Determination" (Employment Act 1988 (c. 19), s.3(5)(*a*)) means a final decision. A recommendation that expulsion from a trade union should be effected in the future could not of itself amount to a "determination" to expel an individual for the purposes of this section (*Transport and General Workers' Union* v. *Webber* [1990] I.C.R. 711).

DETERMINED. (Income Support (General) Regulations 1987 (S.I. 1987 No. 1967), reg. 70(3)(b), as inserted by Social Security (Persons from Abroad) Miscellaneous Regulations 1996 (S.I. 1996 No. 30), reg. 8(3)(c)). An asylum seeker's application for asylum was "determined" when the refusal was recorded on the applicant's file, even though the decision may not be communicated to him at the time and even though there may be subsequent reconsideration of his status by the Secretary of State (*R.* v. *Secretary of State for the Home Department, ex p. Salem* [1999] 2 W.L.R. 1).

DETRIMENT. (3) "Detriment" (Race Relations Act 1976 (c. 74), s.4(2)(*c*)) has to be a detriment or disadvantage in connection with the complainant's employment. A coloured woman had not been subjected to a "detriment" within the meaning of this section by being called a "wog" in her absence (*De Souza* v. *Automobile Association* [1986] IRLR 103).

(2) "Subjecting her to any other detriment" (Sex Discrimination Act 1975 (c. 65), s.6(2)(*b*)). Refusal by a local authority to permit a woman branch librarian to share her job with her husband after the birth of her child was held not to have subjected her to a "detriment" within the meaning of this section. "Detriment" had to be some less favourable treatment arising in the course of her employment and could not amount to a failure to provide an advantage (*Clymo* v. *Wandsworth London Borough Council* [1989] I.C.R. 250). A single act of sexual harassment can amount to

a "detriment" within the meaning of this section (*Bracebridge Engineering* v. *Darby* [1990] IRLR 3). See also CAN; JUSTIFIABLE.

DETRIMENTAL. "Detrimental to good administration" (Supreme Court Act 1981 (c. 54), s.31). Where there had been undue delay in bringing an application for judicial review of a tribunal decision it would have been "detrimental to good administration" for the court to grant relief, notwithstanding that on the merits of the case alone the application would have succeeded (*R.* v. *Dairy Produce Quota Tribunal for England and Wales, ex p. Caswell* [1990] 2 W.L.R. 1320).

DEVELOPMENT. (4) "Constitute or involve development" (Town and Country Planning Act 1971 (c. 78), ss.22, now Town and Country Planning Act 1990 (c. 8), s.55(1)). A change of use of property from self-catering short-term lettings to permanent residential use did not "constitute or involve development" for the purposes of s.53 (*R.* v. *Tunbridge Wells Borough Council, ex p. Blue Boys Development, The Times,* August 18, 1989). Neither did the proposed use of some of the buildings in the old London County Hall complex for office purposes unrelated to local government (*London Residuary Body* v. *Secretary of State for the Environment* (1989) 58 P. & C.R. 370). Demolition is not of itself an "other operation in, on, over or under land", so that the demolition of houses in order to use the site for providing car parking and enhancing the visual aspect of nearby development by high quality landscaping did not constitute "development" within the meaning of these Acts (*Cambridge City Council* v. *Secretary of State for the Environment and Milton Park Investments, sub nom. Secretary of State for the Environment* v. *Cambridge City Council* 90 L.G.R. 275). The use of a caravan for the storage and mixing of cattle food did not constitute a "development" for the purposes of this section (*Wealden District Council* v. *Secretary of State for the Environment* [1988] 08 E.G. 112). A use of land which existed before the coming into force of the town and country planning legislation was capable of being abandoned, so that resumption of the use constituted "development" (*White* v. *Secretary of State for the Environment* [1989] 15 E.G. 193). The reversion to industrial use of land which had been in agricultural use since 1972 constituted "development" even though the land had been used for light industrial purposes from before 1948 to 1972 (*J.L. Engineering* v. *Secretary of State for the Environment, The Times,* March 2, 1993).

"Benefit, improvement or development," see BENEFIT.

Stat. Def., Town and Country Planning Act 1990 (c. 8), s.55.

See INCIDENTAL.

DEVICE. "Any disc, tape, sound track or other device" (Forgery and Counterfeiting Act 1981 (c. 45), s.8(1)(*d*)). "Device" must here be treated *ejusdem generis* with disc, tape and sound track. Thus the electronic impulses used to gain unauthorised access to a computer data bank were not a "device" and therefore could not be an "instrument" within the meaning of this section (*R.* v. *Gold*; *R.* v. *Schifreen* [1988] 2 W.L.R. 984).

DIFFERENCE. "After differences have arisen" (Arbitration Act 1950 (c. 27), s.10). An arbitral "difference" permitting the appointment of an arbitrator by the court under the provisions of this section requires the existence between the parties of a genuinely disputable issue. It is not sufficient for the party seeking such an appointment merely to assert the existence of a claim against the other (*Mayer Newman & Co.* v. *Al Ferro Commodities* [1990] 2 Lloyd's Rep. 290). See also DISPUTE.

DIFFERENT. "Situated in two different countries" (Convention on the Contract for the International Carriage of Goods by Road as set out in the Schedule to the Carriage of Goods by Road Act 1965 (c. 37)). The United Kingdom and Jersey are not "different countries" for the purposes of this Convention (*Chloride Industrial Batteries* v. *F.W. Freight* [1989] 1 W.L.R. 823).

DILIGENCE. See REASONABLE PRECAUTIONS.

DILIGENT. "After making diligent inquiry" (Compulsory Purchase Act 1965 (c. 56), s.5). These words require some reasonable diligence to have been used but they do not involve the making of a very great inquiry (*R.* v. *Secretary of State for Transport, ex p. Blackett* [1992] J.P.L. 1041).

"Direct loss &/or expense" meant loss that flowed naturally or without any intervening cause (*F.G. Minter* v. *Welsh Health Technical Services* (1980) 13 Build.L.R. 1 and *Rees and Kirby* v. *Swansea City Council* (1985) Build.L.R. 1; *Koufos* v. *C. Czarnikow* [1969] A.C. 350). (*Ogilvie Builders* v. *City of Glasgow District Council* (O.H.), 1994 S.C.L.R. 546).

DIRECTING MIND. (Health and Safety at Work Act 1974 (c. 37), ss.2 and 3). A company was responsible at store management level to ensure the safety of its employees (*R.* v. *Gateway Foodmarkets Ltd* (1997) 94(3) L.S.Gaz. 28).

DIRECTIONS. "Such directions . . . as may be appropriate" (R.S.C., Ord. 12, r.8(5)) could include orders for discovery (*Rome* v. *Punjab National Bank*, *The Times*, July 14, 1988).

DIRECTLY. "Research . . . directly undertaken . . . on his behalf" (Capital Allowances Act 1968 (c. 3), s.9(1)(*a*)). "Directly" in this section denotes a close relationship akin to agency between the person claiming a capital allowance and the person doing the research (*Gaspet* v. *Ellis* [1987] 1 W.L.R. 769).

Prospective defendants to proceedings for judicial review were not "directly affected" under R.S.C. Ord. 53, r.5(3) until a full legal aid certificate has been granted and were not entitled to make representations at an appeal against the refusal to grant legal aid (*R.* v. *Legal Aid Board, ex p. Megarry* [1994] C.O.D. 468).

(Patents Act 1977 (c. 37), s.60). A product which had been obtained directly from a patented process was the product with which the patented process ended and could still be considered the direct result of the patented process even after it had undergone further processing provided it retained its identity and did not lose its fundamental characteristics (*Pioneer Electronics Capital Inc.* v. *Warner Music Manufacturing Europe GmbH*, *The Times*, December 10, 1996).

DIRECTLY AFFECTED. (R.S.C. Ord. 53, r.5(3)). A person is "directly affected" if he is affected without the intervention of any intermediate agency so that the Secretary of State was not "directly affected" within the meaning of Ord. 53, r.5(3) and could not be joined as a party even though a local authority were required by virtue of a decision in judicial review proceedings to pay housing benefit to an applicant, and the Secretary of State had a collateral obligation therefore to increase the authority's annual housing benefit subsidy (*R. v. Rent Officer Service ex p. Muldoon and Kelly* [1996] 1 W.L.R. 1103).

DIRECTOR. "Director" (Companies Act 1985 (c. 6), ss.295, 300). For the purposes of applications under these sections seeking to disqualify a person from acting as a director, the word "director" could refer to a person *de facto* acting as a director even though not appointed as such (*Re Lo-Line Electric Motors* [1988] 3 W.L.R. 26).

"Presented . . . by . . . the directors" (Insolvency Act 1986 (c. 45), s.9(1)). An application to the court for an administration order was held to have been properly presented by "the directors," notwithstanding that only five of the seven directors were present at the board meeting which resolved to apply, since once a proper resolution had been passed it became the duty of all the directors, including the absentees, to support it (*Re Equiticorp International* (1989) 5 BCC 599).

Stat. Def., Companies Act 1985 (c. 6), s.741; Insolvency Act 1986 (c. 45), s.251; Financial Services Act 1986 (c. 60), s.207; Banking Act 1987 (c. 22), s.105; Income and Corporation Taxes Act 1988 (c. 1), s.417; Companies Act 1989 (c. 40), s.53; "includes any person occupying the position of director, by whatever name he is called" (Requirements of Writing (Scotland) Act 1995 (c. 7), s.12(1)); "in relation to a body corporate whose affairs are managed by its members, means a member of the body corporate" (Chemical Weapons Act 1996 (c. 6), s.31(4)); "in relation to a body corporate whose affairs are managed by its members, means a member of the body corporate" (Nuclear Explosions (Prohibition and Inspections) Act 1998 (c. 7), s.11(2)).

DISABLED PERSON. Stat. Def., Local Government Housing Act 1989 (c. 42), s.114.

"Totally disabled" (Police (Injury Benefit) Regulations 1987 (S.I. 1987 No. 156), reg. 3). For the purposes of the 1987 regulations, the tribunal had to consider whether the disability had totally destroyed the former officer's capacity to earn any money regardless of whether as an employee or in self-employment (*R. v. Milling, ex p. West Yorkshire Police Authority, The Times*, December 24, 1996).

(Disability Discrimination Act 1995 (c. 50), s.1). A person who suffered from paranoid schizophrenia was a "disabled person" within the meaning of the Act. Even though he was capable of carrying out the ordinary functions of his job, if evidence established that his capacity to carry out those functions had been impaired, he was a "disabled person" within the meaning of Sched. 1, para. 4(1) to the Act (*Goodwin v. Patent Office* [1999] I.C.R. 302).

DISASTER. Unlawful eviction whereby the landlord changed the locks and removed the tenant's belongings could amount to a "disaster" within the meaning of the Housing Act 1985 (c. 68), s.59(1)(*d*) (*R.* v. *Bristol City Council* (1995) 27 H.L.R. 584).

DISABILITY. Stat. Def., "a person has a disability for the purposes of this Act if he has a physical or mental impairment which has a substantial and long-term adverse effect on his ability to carry out normal day-to-day activities" (Disability Discrimination Act 1995 (c. 50), s.1(1)).

DISBURSEMENTS. "Disbursements made on account of a ship" (Supreme Court Act 1981 (c. 54), s.20(2)(*p*)). An insurance premium is not a disbursement on account of a ship, although it might be a disbursement in respect of a ship (*Bain Clarkson* v. *Owners of Sea Friends, The Times*, April 18, 1991).

(Legal Aid Act 1988 (c.34)). Costs incurred by solicitors in obtaining advice on questions of law relating to welfare entitlement from an expert who was neither a solicitor nor a barrister nor employed in the office of a solicitor could not be charged as "disbursements" under Part 3 of this Act (*R.* v. *Legal Aid Board, ex p. Bruce, The Times*, July 8, 1992).

"Claim . . . in respect of disbursements made on account of a ship" (Supreme Court Act 1981 (c. 54), s.20(2)(*p*)). Insurance premiums are not disbursements as they are not made to keep the ship going (*Bain Clarkson* v. *Owners of Ship Sea Friends* [1991] 2 Lloyd's Rep. 322).

DISCARD. (E.C. Council Directive 75/442). "Discard" means "to get rid of" (*Mayer Parry Recycling Ltd* v. *Environment Agency, The Times*, December 3, 1998).

DISCHARGE. "Discharge" (Mental Health Act 1983 (c. 20), ss.72–75) means discharge from hospital. Once a tribunal was satisfied that all conditions of s.73(2) applied they had to discharge a patient. Discharge meant release from hospital and not further treatment at another hospital (*Secretary of State for the Home Department* v. *Mental Health Review Tribunal for Mersey Regional Health Authority* [1986] 1 W.L.R. 1170).

"Discharge of any noxious . . . thing" (Firearms Act 1968 (c. 27), s.5(1)(*b*)). A discharge or emission of electricity from a stunning device was held to be a "discharge" of a "noxious" thing within the meaning of this section (*Flack* v. *Baldry* [1988] 1 W.L.R. 393).

DISCIPLINARY PROCEEDINGS. (Wages Act 1986 (c. 48), s.1(5)(*b*)). Where employers left without giving proper notice, and the employer made deductions from their final salaries on the basis of it being satisfaction for damages for breach of contract, it was held that the deductions had not been made "in consequence of any disciplinary proceedings" within the meaning of this section (*Chiltern House* v. *Chambers* [1990] IRLR 88).

DISCLOSE. (Contempt of Court Act 1981 (c. 49), s.8(1)).

The revelation of jury deliberations by an individual juror and the further disclosure of those deliberations by publication in a newspaper, provided that the publication amounted to disclosure and not the republication of already known facts came within the meaning of "disclose" (*Att.-Gen.* v. *Associated Newspapers* [1994] 2 A.C. 238).

A non-disclosure was innocent if it was not made in bad faith or with the intention of misleading a court (*Kuwait Oil Tanker Co. SAK* v. *Al Bader QBCMI* 95/1178/B, November 27, 1995).

DISCOUNT. "Price discount and rebates" (E.C. Council Directive 77/388, Art. 11A3(*b*)) covers the sale of goods at a reduced price on presentation of a coupon (*Boots* v. *Customs and Excise Commissioners* (No. C–126/88) [1990] S.T.C. 387).

DISCRIMINATE. (Sex Discrimination Act 1975 (c. 65)). The word "discriminate" bears two meanings in this Act. In section 1 it means less favourable treatment on the ground of sex. Section 4 deals with discrimination by way of victimisation. In Parts 2 and 3 of the Act "discriminate" is to be understood as bearing both meanings (*Cornelius* v. *University College of Swansea* [1987] IRLR 141).

"Discriminates against a woman . . . on the ground of her sex" (Sex Discrimination Act 1975 (c. 65), s.1(1)). A woman who was dismissed because she was pregnant was not automatically discriminated against on the ground of her sex. Whether her dismissal for reasons of pregnancy was direct sex discrimination depended on whether the employer treated or would have treated more favourably a man whose relevant circumstances were not materially different, for example, who needed an absence from work because of a medical condition (*Webb* v. *Emo Cargo (U.K.)* [1992] 4 All E.R. 929; *Shomer* v. *B & R Residential Lettings* [1992] IRLR 317; *Brown* v. *Rentokil* [1992] IRLR 302. But see also *Leeds Private Hospital* v. *Parkin* [1992] I.C.R. 571). Since "pensionable age," as defined in the Social Security Act 1975 (c. 14) is itself discriminatory in that it treats women more favourably than men on the ground of their sex, any other differential treatment which adopted the same criterion must be equally discriminatory on the ground of sex within the meaning of this section. Thus, by refusing to provide men with swimming facilities on the same terms as those provided for women, *i.e.* free for women over 60, the local council had discriminated against men (*James* v. *Eastleigh Borough Council* [1990] 3 W.L.R. 55). Where a girls' school had a different retiring age for teachers and for gardeners and that difference was accounted for by ordinary commercial reasons, the difference was not discriminatory by reason of the sex of the employees, although the teachers were female and the gardeners were male (*Bullock* v. *Alice Ottley School* [1992] IRLR 564). A local authority which provided more grammar school places for boys than for girls was guilty of discrimination contrary to s.1 (*R.* v. *Birmingham City Council, ex p. Equal Opportunities Commission* [1989] 2 W.L.R. 520). So also was an authority which, although granting grammar school places to the same percentage of girls as of boys, refused places to some girls who had obtained higher marks than some of the boys who had been accepted (*Equal Opportunities Commission for Northern Ireland's Application* [1989] IRLR 64). The dismissal of a woman from her employment on the ground of her repeated absences from work through sickness did not constitute direct discrimination based upon sex, provided that such absences would lead to the dismissal of a man under the same conditions (*Handels-og-Kontorfunktionaererernes Forbund i Danmark (for Hertz) and Dansk Arbeijdsgiverforening (for Aldi Marked K/S)*, *The Times*, December 20, 1990). An unmarried school matron who was dismissed when she became pregnant and did not intend to get married was held not to have been unlawfully discriminated against on the ground of sex because there was evidence that in the past male teachers who had formed liaisons without benefit of marriage had been similarly treated (*Berrisford* v. *Woodard Schools* (*Midland Division*) [1991] I.C.R. 564). In refusing, pursuant to a long established policy, to publish an advertisement by a man resident in Italy for a cook and housekeeper to work at his residence, whereas an advertisement by a woman would have been accepted, the publishers of a magazine were guilty of unlawful sexual discrimination (*Bain* v. *Bowles* [1991] IRLR 356). An applicant who, being in receipt of an occupational pension from a previous employer, was rejected because he could not comply with the policy of the Authority not to employ those who had retired early from previous employment, was held to have been discriminated against as the proportion of men to women who could comply with the policy was considerably smaller (*Greater Manchester Police Authority* v. *Lea* [1990] IRLR 372). Where a woman teacher, who was promoted on her written agreement to carry out certain additional duties, adopted a daughter and, on returning to school, refused to carry out those extra-curricular activities, it was held that she had been discriminated against on the grounds of sex when, as a result, her pay was reduced to the previous level. It was held that a "requirement" had been applied to her "which was such that the proportion of women who can comply with it is considerably smaller than the proportion of men" (*Briggs* v. *North Eastern Education and Library Board* [1990] IRLR 181). An agreement which provide for a severance payment for employees who had worked a minimum of 38 hours per week was held to be indirectly discriminatory against women within the meaning of EEC Treaty, Art. 119, since the proportion of women who worked part-time was higher than that of men (*Kowalska* v. *Freie und Hansestads Hamburg* [1990] IRLR 447). The restriction, by the Social Security Act 1975 (c. 14), ss.36, 37 as amended, of an entitlement to a severe disablement allowance to those people who had reached pensionable age, defined as 65 years for men and 60 for women, as discriminatory against women and contrary to EEC Directive 79/7 (*Thomas* v. *Chief Adjudication Officer and Secretary of State for Social Security* [1990] IRLR 436). Regulation 10 of the Social Security (Overlapping Benefits) Regulations 1979 (No. 597), which provided that a dependency benefit, such as augmentation of a husband's pension, extinguished a personal benefit, such as an invalid care allowance, was held not to discriminate indirectly on the grounds of sex contrary to Directive 79/7 (*Jones* v. *Chief Adjudication Officer* [1990] IRLR 533). A difference of treatment accorded to a man and a woman on the ground of differing marital or family status did not amount to an indirect form of discrimination on the grounds of sex, and was not therefore contrary to Art. 4 of Directive 79/7 (*Social Security Decision No. R(SB) 6/91*). The requirement that the candidate for a particular job be within a particular age range could be a requirement or condition within the meaning of s.1(1)(*b*) of the 1975 Act without being indirectly discriminatory on the ground of sex (*University of Manchester* v. *Jones* [1993] I.C.R. 474). The enforcement of Sunday trading laws, which would deprive more women than men of job opportunities, did not constitute sexual discrimination contrary to the Sex Discrimination Act 1975 or Directive 76/207 (*Chisholm* v. *Kirklees Metropolitan Borough*

Council; *Kirkless Metropolitan Borough Council* v. *B. & Q., The Times,* May 31, 1993). A Church of England school governing body acted lawfully in stipulating that any applicant for the post of headteacher should be a committed communicant christian (*Board of Governors of St. Mathias Church of England School* v. *Crizzle* [1993] I.C.R. 401).

"Discriminates against a married person" (Sex Discrimination Act 1975 (c. 65), s.3(1)). A married woman living with her husband and their two young children, who had been away from work for over two years because of family commitments, was unlawfully discriminated against on the ground of her marital status when she was refused the child-care payment given under the Employment Training Scheme, because of the requirement imposed by the Training Commission that only a lone parent was entitled to the payment (*Training Commission* v. *Jackson* [1990] I.C.R. 222).

"Discriminates against another . . . on racial grounds" (Race Relations Act 1976 (c. 74), s.1(1)). To provide an interpreter who could assist some of the persons present at a parents' consultative meeting, while others speaking different languages were without an interpreter, was held not to amount to discrimination on racial grounds (*R.* v. *Birmingham City Council, ex p. Darsham Kaur* [1991] C.O.D. 21). An employer who requested an Indian job applicant to produce evidence of his right to work in the U.K. was not thereby discriminating against him on the ground of race (*Dhatt* v. *McDonalds Hamburgers,* [1991] I.C.R. 238). A Thai croupier who was refused English lessons to enable him to qualify for the post of full casino manager was not discriminated against on the ground of race (*Mecca Leisure Group* v. *Chatprachong* [1993] ICR 688).

DISCRIMINATION. The dismissal of a woman from her employment solely because she had attained the qualifying age for state pension, where that age was different for men and for women, constituted discrimination on the ground of sex contrary to EEC Directive No. 76/207, Art. 5(1) (*Marshall* v. *Southampton and South-West Hampshire Area Health Authority (Teaching)* [1986] Q.B. 401). But see also *Duke* v. *G.E.C. Reliance (formerly Reliance Systems)* [1988] 2 W.L.R. 359 where the House of Lords held that a woman forced to retire on reaching the age of 60 (the pensionable age for women under the policy operated by the employers) had not been discriminated against. The construction of a British statute was a matter of judgment to be determined by the British courts, and therefore the provisions of the Equal Treatment Directive (76/207/EEC) (OJ 1975 No. L 45, p. 19) did not affect the construction of s.6(4) of the Sex Discrimination Act 1975 (c. 65) which provided that the discrimination provisions of the earlier subsections did not apply "in relation to . . . retirement." Since only a woman could be refused employment on the ground of pregnancy, such a refusal constituted direct discrimination based upon sex contrary to Directive No. 76/207 (*Dekker* v. *Stichting Vermingscentrum voor Jong Volwassenen Plus* [1991] IRLR 27). The enforcement of section 47 of the Shops Act 1950 (c. 28) prohibiting retail stores from opening on Sundays thereby depriving a large number of women than men of job opportunities did not constitute sexual "discrimination" contrary to the Sex Discrimination Act 1975 (c. 65) or Directive 76/207 (*Chisholm* v. *Kirklees Metropolitan Borough Council*; *Kirklees Metropolitan Borough Council* v. *B & Q, The Times,* May 27, 1993). See also IN RELATION TO.

Article 7 of the EEC Treaty prohibits discrimination on the ground of nationality. R.S.C., Ord. 23, r.1(1)(*a*), which empowers the court to order security for a defendant's costs against a plaintiff resident outside the jurisdiction, was held not to discriminate either overtly or covertly on the ground of nationality contrary to Art. 7, since Ord. 23 applied equally to those residing outside the EEC, irrespective of nationality (*Berkeley Administration* v. *McClelland* [1990] 2 W.L.R. 1021).

Where a company's scheme provided pensions for men at the age of 65 and women at the age of 60 there was discrimination contrary to Art. 119 EEC in a case where a man, on becoming redundant, took an early pension at the age of 60 and received a pension smaller than that which would have been received by a woman of that age (*Clarke D.W.* v. *Cray Precision Engineering* [1989] 1 C.M.L.R. 465; *Roscoe* v. *Hick Hargreaves & Co.* [1991] I.C.R. 501). Compliance by a local education authority with s.6 of the Education Act 1980, which required the authority to comply with a parent's request for a child to be sent to a preferred school, was not an act of discrimination (*R.* v. *Cleveland County Council, ex p. Commission for Racial Equality* 91 L.G.R. 139).

Provisions in the Merchant Shipping Act 1988 (c.12) which require that conditions of British citizenship, residence and domicile must be satisfied before a fishing vessel can be registered as British and allowed to fly the British flag are discriminatory and contrary to Art. 52 of the EEC Treaty, and are therefore ineffective in relation to other E.C. states (*R.* v. *Secretary of State for Transport, ex p. Factortame* [1991] 3 All E.R. 769).

"Act which constitutes sex discrimination," see ACT.

See JUSTIFIABLE.

DISEASE. "Induced by disease" (Homicide Act 1957 (c. 11), s.2(1)). To establish the defence of "abnormality of mind" "induced by" the "disease" of alcoholism within the meaning of this section it is necessary to show that the craving for drink was such as to render the accused's use of it involuntary. A woman who drank nine-tenths of a bottle of vodka before strangling her daughter was held to have drunk it voluntarily, so that her admitted alcoholism did not amount to a "disease" (*R.* v. *Tandy* (1988) 87 Cr.App.R. 45).

For the purposes of as statutory scheme dealing with compensation or pension entitlements, "injury" or "disease" meant an impairment of a person's physical or mental condition, so that illness caused by stress of work amounted to an "injury" or "disease" (*Bradley* v. *London Fire and Civil Defence Authority* [1995] IRLR 46).

DISEMBARKING. An arriving passenger using a "travelator" at Heathrow Airport, prior to immigration and customs formalities, was not in the course of disembarking" from an aircraft within the meaning of the Warsaw Convention, art. 17, given effect by the Carriage by Air Act 1961 (c. 27), s.1 (*Adatia* v. *Air Canada* [1992] P.I.Q.R. P238).

DISGRACEFUL CONDUCT IN ANY PROFESSIONAL RESPECT. The employment of two veterinary surgeons who were not registered under the Veterinary Surgeons Act 1966 (c. 36), s.5A, although they were entitled to be registered because they had the prescribed European qualifications and had applied for registration did not amount to "disgraceful conduct in any professional respect" (*Plenderleith* v. *Royal College of Veterinary Surgeons* [1996] 1 W.L.R. 224).

DISHONESTY. "Dishonesty uses . . . any electricity" (Theft Act 1968 (c. 60), s.13). To establish dishonest use of electricity, within the meaning of this section, it is not necessary to prove that an electricity meter has been tampered with (*R.* v. *McCreadie (Malcolm)*; *R.* v. *Tume (William John)* (1993) 96 Cr.App.R. 143).

DISMISS; DISMISSAL. "Dismissal" (EEC Directive No. 76/207, Art. 5(1)) should be given a wide interpretation (*Burton* v. *British Railways Board*, Case 19/81 [1982] Q.B. 1080). Consequently, an age limit for the compulsory dismissal of workers pursuant to an employer's general policy concerning retirement fell within the term "dismissal" in this article (*Marshall* v. *Southampton and South-West Hampshire Area Health Authority (Teaching)* [1986] Q.B. 411).

"Dismissal" (Employment Protection (Consolidation) Act 1978 (c. 44), s.55). Where an apprentice plumber had been sentenced to Borstal training after conviction of conspiracy to assault it was held that his training service contract had been frustrated, and that the refusal of his employers to take him back on release could not amount to "dismissal" within the meaning of this section (*Sherrpherd, F.C. and Co.* v. *Jenom* [1986] 3 W.L.R. 801). Where, for an employee to be granted an extended holiday, there was a condition that her contract of employment would be automatically terminated if she failed to return by a certain date, and, because of illness, she failed to do so and was thus informed that her employment was automatically terminated, it was held that she had been "dismissed" within the meaning of s.55(2) (*Igbo* v. *Johnson, Matthey Chemicals* [1986] I.C.R. 505). A full time teacher and head of department who, on returning to work after an absence due to illness, was told he could not continue as a department head, but could continue to teach part time on a reduced salary, was held to have been constructively dismissed (*Hogg* v. *Dover College* [1990] I.C.R. 39). An auxiliary nurse who smoked 30 cigarettes a day and who resigned after the Board introduced a policy of no smoking in its hospitals had not been constructively dismissed (*Dryden* v. *Greater Glasgow Health Board* [1992] IRLR 469).

An employer's failure to renew a contract of employment when it expired by effluxion of time amounted to "dismissal" (*Johnstone* v. *BBC Enterprises* [1994] I.C.R. 180).

"Dismissal" for the purposes of the 1978 Act meant the determination of the employee's actual employment, not the date on which the employee was given notice that the employment was to be brought to an end (*Alboni* v. *Ind Coope Retail Ltd* [1998] IRLR 131).

"Selected for dismissal in contravention of a customary arrangement . . . relating to redundancy" (Employment Protection (Consolidation) Act 1978 (c. 44), s.59(*b*)). Where there had been a customary arrangement whereby the employer would first select for redundancy from a pool of volunteers, and the employer then selected employees for redundancy without calling for volunteers, those employees had not been "selected" in contravention of this section since it applied only where the actual selection of the relevant employee had itself been in contravention of such an arrangement (*Rogers* v. *Vosper Thornycroft* (*U.K.*) [1989] IRLR 82).

"Dismissed . . . by reason of redundancy" (Social Security Act 1975 (c. 14), s.20(3A), as amended by the Social Security Act 1985 (c. 53), s.10). Where, in anticipation of future redundancies an employer and employee mutually agree when and on what terms the employee will leave the employment, the employee has been "dismissed" by reason of redundancy for the purposes of this section. The use of the word "dismissed" in this section is not confined to the technical meaning of dismissal in ss.83 and 85 of the Employment Protection (Consolidation) Act 1978 (c. 44) (*Social Security Decision No. R(U)3/91* [1993] 5 CL 391).

(Employment Rights Act (c. 18), s.214). Where employment had continued after a takeover of the employer's business and the employees' contract of employment had not come to an end or been brought to an end, there had been no "dismissal" for the purposes of s.214(2) (*Lassman* v. *Secretary of State for Trade and Industry* [1999] I.C.R. 416).

Stat. Def., Employment Rights Act 1996 (c. 18), ss.136 to 138 and 181(1).

DISORDERLY. (1) Where a defendant was charged at common law with keeping a disorderly house the prosecution had to show disorderly use of the premises on more than one occasion. A single indecent performance was not enough (*Moores* v. *DPP* [1991] 3 W.L.R. 549).

DISORDERLY BEHAVIOUR. (Public Order Act 1986) (c. 64), s.5). There was no requirement for violence to be present or threatened for there to be disorderly behaviour so that protestors who interfered with the work of a surveyor by putting their hands in front of a measuring instrument was disorderly and caused harrassment (*Chambers* v. *DPP* [1995] C.O.D. 321).

DISPLAY. "Displays any writing" (Public Order Act 1986 (c. 64), s.5(1)(*b*)). The writer of threatening or abusive words, which were then concealed in an envelope and sent to a woman through the post was held not to be displaying the writing contrary to this section (*Chappell* v. *DPP* [1989] C.O.D. 259).

DISPOSAL. "Disposals . . . of land" (Local Government, Planning and Land Act 1980 (c. 65), s.75(2)). A transfer of housing accommodation made under s.23(3) of the London Government Act 1963 (c. 33) was not a "disposal" for the purposes of Pt. VIII of the 1980 Act and any payment received did not constitute a capital receipt within the meaning of s.75 of the 1980 Act (*R.* v. *Secretary of State for the Environment, ex p. Newham* (1987) 85 L.G.R. 737). Sums paid to a local authority by a purchaser under an agreement by which the local authority agreed to sell expected receipts from future sales of land were not sums received in respect of "disposals" of land within the meaning of s.75 (*R.* v. *Wirral Metropolitan Borough Council, ex p. Milstead* (1989) 21 RVR 66). See also CAPITAL.

(8) "Disposal" (Finance Act 1965 (c. 25), Sched. 7, para. 4(2)). For the circumstances in which a share exchange, forming part of a complicated series of transactions, was held to be for a proper commercial purpose, and therefore ensuring that ultimately there was no "disposal" for the purposes of this paragraph, see *Craven* v. *White* [1988] 3 W.L.R. 423. The transfer of

an asset by one company to its subsidiary in exchange for an allotment of shares was a "disposal" (*Westcott* v. *Woolcombers* [1987] S.T.C. 600). The receipt by a company of a capital sum in consideration for it agreeing to surrender an option was a "disposal" within the meaning of s.22 of the Finance Act 1965 (c. 25). Such a transaction was not excluded from a charge to corporation tax by virtue of the provisions of Sched. 7, para. 14(3) (*Powlson* v. *Welbeck Securities* [1987] S.T.C. 468).

"Disposal" in a public liability policy should be given its ordinary dictionary definition. The disposal of waste which had been placed in a landfill site ended with the covering of the waste with earth and did not include the process of degradation so that the site owners were not liable under the terms of their insurance policy which excluded liability for loss or damage arising from the disposal of waste unless arising from an accident in the method of disposal for damage to persons and property arising out of the build-up of gasses from the breakdown of the waste (*Middleton* v. *Wiggin* [1996] Env.L.R. 17).

A subsequent escape of gas which occurred because the site chosen for the disposal of waste was unsafe because of its geological structure could not be part of the "method of disposal" within the meaning of a clause in an insurance policy which excluded liability for damage "arising from the disposal of waste materials in the way the insured . . . intended to dispose of them unless such claim arises from an accident in the method of disposal" (*Middleton* v. *Wiggins*, *The Independent*, August 31, 1995).

(Landlord and Tenant Act 1987 (c. 31), s.4). A "relevant disposal" within the meaning of s.4 referred to a completed conveyance and not an exchange of contracts for the sale of premises to which Part I of the 1987 Act applied (*Mainwaring* v. *Trustees of Henry Smith's Charity* [1996] 2 All E.R. 220).

"Exempt disposal," see EXEMPT.

Stat. Def., Housing Act 1985 (c. 68), s.262; Town and Country Planning Act 1990 (c. 8), s.336; Water Industry Act 1991 (c. 56), s.219; Water Resources Act 1991 (c. 57), s.221; Housing Act 1996 (c. 52), s.39(2).

DISPOSE OF. "Until the charge is disposed of or withdrawn" (Fugitive Offenders Act 1967 (c. 68), s.99(2)). An order for a count to lie on the file did not dispose of it for the purposes of this section (*R.* v. *Central Criminal Court, ex p. Raymond* [1986] 1 W.L.R. 710; *Oskar* v. *Government of Australia* [1988] 2 W.L.R. 82.

"Disposed of by the trustee" (Capital Gains Tax Act 1979 (c. 14), s.54(1)). The appointment, by trustees exercising discretionary powers, of trust assets to be held on new exhaustive trusts, did not create a new and separate settlement giving rise to a deemed disposal of the appointed assets within the meaning of this section (*Swires* v. *Renton* [1991] S.T.C. 490).

"May dispose of . . . that property or right" (Companies Act 1985 (c. 6), s.655(1)). A Crown disclaimer of property which became *bona vacantia* on the removal of a company from the register was not a disposition for the purposes of this section (*Allied Dunbar Assurance* v. *Fowle, The Times,* February 22, 1994).

Although the future duration of P's business looked uncertain after he had surrendered a tenancy in favour of a licence, the fact that he was carrying on the same business activities as before did not mean that he had "disposed of the whole or part of his business" within the meaning of s.69(2)(*a*) of the Finance Act 1985 (c. 54) (*Barrett (Inspector of Taxes)* v. *Powell* [1998] STC 283).

DISPOSITION. An order made by the court under s.24 of the Matrimonial Causes Act 1973 (c. 18), ordering the transfer of property by a person against whom a bankruptcy petition had been presented, was a "disposition" by the bankrupt and void under s.284 of the Insolvency Act 1986 (c. 45) (*Re Flint (a Bankrupt)* [1993] 2 W.L.R. 53).

(Matrimonial Causes Act 1973 (c. 18), s.37(2)(b)). A tenant, who brought a periodic tenancy to an end by the service of a notice to quit, did not make a "disposition" of property after the tenancy had expired by reason of effluxion of time, since there was no longer any property to dispose of. A notice to quit was not a dispositive act, merely the indication of an intention that the tenant no longer wanted the tenacy to continue (*Newlon Housing Trust* v. *Alsulsaimen* [1998] 4 All E.R. 1).

(Hire Purchase Act 1964 (c. 53), ss.27 and 29). Where a vehicle had been sold to a third party by one of two or more parties to a finance agreement covered by the 1964 Act, the requirements of s.27(1) were satisfied so that a disposition had been made by one of the bailees (*Keeble* v. *Combined Lease Finance plc* [1996] 7 C.L. 610).

"Where . . . dispositions . . . are varied," see VARY.

Stat. Def., Administration of Justice Act 1985 (c. 61), s.11; "includes the creation of a term of years" (Law of Property (Miscellaneous Provisions) Act 1994 (c. 36), s.1(4)).

DISPOSITION OF THE COMPANY'S PROPERTY. The payment of moneys into a company's bank account which was in credit after the commencement of winding up proceedings was not a "disposition of the company's property" and so void under the Insolvency Act 1986 (c. 45), s.127 (*Re Barn Crown* [1995] 1 W.L.R. 147).

DISPOSITION OF AN EQUITABLE INTEREST. A deposit of title deeds to property by one joint tenant without the consent of the other could not operate as a disposition of an equitable interest under the Law of Property Act 1925 (c. 20), s.53(1)(*c*) (*United Bank of Kuwait* v. *Sahib* [1995] 2 All E.R. 973).

"Some other disposition" (Transfer of Undertakings (Protection of Employment) Regulations 1981 (No. 1794), reg. 3). A business which retained its identity in the hands of its directors and shareholders, with the same assets and employees, although the undertaking was not transferred on its dissolution, could amount to a transfer of an undertaking by "some other disposition" within the meaning of reg. 3 (*Charlton* v. *Charlton Thermosystems* [1995] I.C.R. 57).

DISPUTE. (1)–(4) In the context of an arbitration the words "disputes" and "differences" should be given their ordinary meanings. Because one man could be said to be indisputably right and the other indisputably wrong, that did not necessarily mean that there had never been any dispute between them (*Hayter* v. *Nelson* (1990) 2 Lloyd's Rep. 265). An arbitration clause in a bill of lading expressed to apply to "any dispute arising in any way whatsoever out of this bill of lading" is wide enough to cover a claim in conversion in a short delivery dispute as well as a claim for breach of contract or duty (*Ulysses Compania Naviera S.A.* v. *Huntingdon Petroleum Services; The Ermoupolis* [1990] 1 Lloyd's Rep. 160). See also DIFFERENCE.

(Arbitration Act 1996 (c. 23)). A "dispute" to be referred for arbitration included any claim which the other party refused to admit or did not pay, whether or not there was any answer to the claim in fact or in law (*Tradax Internacional S.A.* v. *Cerrahogullari T.A.S.* [1981] 3 All E.R. 344; *Ellerine Bros (Pty.) Ltd* v. *Klinger* [1982] 1 W.L.R. 1375 and *Hayter* v. *Nelson* [1990] 2 Lloyd's Rep. 265 applied) (*Halki Shipping Corporation* v. *Sopex Oils Ltd* [1997] 1 W.L.R. 1268).

Stat. Def., "includes any difference" (Arbitration Act 1996 (c. 23), s.82(1)).

DISPUTE ARISING OUT OF THE OPERATIONS OF A BREACH. (Convention on Jurisdiction and Enforcement of Judgments in Civil and Commercial Matters 1968, Art. 5(1)(5)). The courts of a country where a contract was concluded had jurisdiction to determine any dispute arising under the contract, although the contract had been performed in another country (*Lloyd's Register of Shipping* v. *Societe Campenon Bernard* [1995] All E.R. 531 (E.C.)).

DISQUALIFICATION. "Disqualification, disability, prohibition or other penalty" (Rehabilitation of Offenders Act 1974 (c. 53), s.5(8)). An endorsement of a driving licence was no more than a record of the particulars of a conviction and not a disqualification or prohibition and would be spent after five years (*Powers* v. *Provincial Insurance plc* [1998] RTR 60).

(Road Traffic Offenders Act 1988 (c. 53), s.44(1)). "If the court orders him to be disqualified" referred to a disqualification on any charge, not just to the offence in question (*Ahmed (Baria)* v. *McLeod*, 1998 S.C.C.R. 486).

DISREPAIR. (Landlord and Tenant Act 1985 (c. 70), s.11). "Disrepair" meant deterioration to such an extent that it no longer performed the function it was designed to perform and the presence or absence of hazard was not relevant (*Windever (Christine)* v. *Liverpool City Council* (June 13, 1994; Mr Recorder Stockdale Liverpool County Ct.)).

DISTRAINING. "Distraining or having distrained" (Companies Act 1948 (c. 38), s.319(7), now Companies Act 1985 (c. 6), s.614(4)). These words denote a continuous process rather than a single act (*Re Memco Engineering* [1985] 3 All E.R. 267).

DISTRESS. "No distress may be levied" (Insolvency Act 1986 (c. 45), s.11(3)(*d*)). The detention by a creditor of the debtor's aircraft was not a "distress" for the purposes of this section (*Re Paramount Airways* [1990] BCC 130). See PERSON.

DISTURB. See WILFULLY.

DO. "Does acts," see ACT.

DOCK. (10) The discharge of wet fish from a cargo vessel in the port of Hull did not constitute "dock work" for the purposes of the Dock Labour Scheme for Hull and Goole 1967 (*National Dock Labour Board* v. *Hull Fish Landing Company, The Times*, May 17, 1988).

(11) "Dock work" (Dock Workers Employment Scheme 1967). Where a product was carried by river from a waterside factory at one point on the Thames to another point, at which it was discharged for distribution, that was no longer the work of a "waterside manufacturer" but remained in the province of "dock work" (*National Dock Labour Board* v. *Blue Circle Industries* [1989] C.O.D. 444). See also WATERSIDE MANUFACTURER.

Stat. Def., in shipping context, Merchant Shipping Act 1995 (c. 21), s.191(9).

DOCUMENT. (Supreme Court Act 1981 (c. 54), s.33(2)). A written instrument or any other object carrying information such as a photograph, tape recording or computer disc could be both "document" for the purposes of this section and "property" for the purposes of s.33(1) (*Huddleston* v. *Control Risks Information Services* [1987] 2 All E.R. 1035).

"Document" (R.S.C., Ord. 24). A computer database which formed part of the business records of a company was, so far as it contained information capable of being retrieved and converted into a readable form, a "document" for the purposes of Ord. 24 (*Derby & Co.* v. *Weldon (No. 9)* [1991] 1 W.L.R. 652.

Computer files and information they contained were "documents" which were discoverable under R.S.C. Ord. 24, r.7(2) (*C.* v. *P.B.P.* (1995) 12 C.L. 448).

"Document produced by a computer" (Police and Criminal Evidence Act 1984 (c. 60), s.69). It is unlikely that a document produced by a word processor, rather than by typewriter or pen, could be one to which s.69 applies in respect of its admissibility (*R.* v. *Blackburn*; *R.* v. *Wade, The Times*, December 1, 1992).

Information stored by a computer is a "document" within the meaning of a court order relating to discovery (*Alliance and Leicester Building Society* v. *Gharemani* [1992] 32 RVR 198).

(Misuse of Drugs Act 1971 (c. 38), s.23). The means of recording did not deprive information from its character as a "document" and it was immaterial that the information required to be processed by means of a translation, decoding, or electronic retrieval so that information stored on a "Memomaster" or electronic notepad amounted to a "document" for the purposes of s.23(3) (*Rollo* v. *HM Advocate* (1996) S.C.C.R. 874).

"Statements made by a person in a document" (Criminal Justice Act 1988 (c. 33), s.23(1)). A deathbed statement made to the police which was recorded by them contemporaneously and which was confirmed by the deceased as being accurate was a "document" for the purposes of this section; notwithstanding that because of his condition the deceased had been unable to sign it (*R.* v. *McGillvray* (1993) 96 Cr.App.R. 232).

"Document of identity." A "document of identity" need not be a travel document for the purposes of the Immigration Act 1971 (c. 77), Sched. 2, para. 8(c)(ii), (iv) (*R.* v. *Secretary of State for the Home Department, ex p. Akram (Mohammed)* [1994] Imm.A.R. 8).

"Documents of title" in a mortgage indemnity insurance policy included the mortgage document (*Metropolitan Mortgage Corp.* v. *Eagle Star Insurance Co.* [1994] N.P.C. 33).

A judgment in chambers was a public document (*Forbes* v. *Smith* [1998] 1 All E.R. 973).

(Criminal Justice Act 1988, (c. 33), ss.23(1), 26). A video recording was a "document" and admissible, subject to the exercise of the judge's discretion, even if the recording itself was incomprehensible without its transcript (*R.* v. *Duffy* [1998] 3 W.L.R. 1060).

"Statement in a document," see STATEMENT.

"Orally or in a document", see ORALLY.

Stat. Def., Companies Act 1985 (c. 6), s.744; Banking Act 1987 (c. 22), s.106; "includes information recorded in any form" (Finance Act 1994 (c. 9), s.43); "includes records, of whatever form and in whatever medium, which convey or are capable of conveying information" (Local Government (Wales) Act 1994 (c. 19), s.60(7)); includes in addition to a document in writing maps, plans, graphs, drawings, photographs, and certain discs, tapes, sound tracks, films, negatives and the like (Criminal Justice (Scotland) Act 1995, (c. 20), s.20(3)); "anything in which information of any description is recorded" (Civil Evidence Act 1995 (c. 38), s.13, and Police Act 1996 (c. 16), s.81(3) and Magistrates Courts Act 1980 (c. 43), ss.5A(4) and 5B(6), &c. inserted by Criminal Procedure and Investigations Act 1996 (c. 25), Sched. 1, para. 3); Sea Fishing (Enforcement of Community Quota Measures) Order 1998 (No. 268), art. 2(2); "includes information recorded otherwise than in legible form" (School Standards and Framework Act 1998 (c. 31), s.2(8)); "means anything in which information is recorded in any form" (Scotland Act 1998 (c. 46), s.126(1)).

DOG. "Guide dog", "Hearing dog", Stat. Def., Disability Discrimination Act 1995 (c. 50), s.37(11).

DOMESTIC. "Domestic property." Stat. Def., Local Government Finance Act 1988 (c. 41), s.66.

"Domestic premises." Stat. Def., Children Act 1989 (c. 41), s.71(12).

"Domestic purposes." Stat. Def., Water Industry Act 1991 (c. 56), s.218.

DOMICILE. The word "domicile" in article 34(3) of the Commonwealth Games Constitution was rightly given its ordinary popular meaning by the Commonwealth Games Federation, as opposed to the legal meaning that would be given it under the English law of domicile (*Cowley* v. *Heatly and Others, The Times,* July 24, 1986).

DONATIO MORTIS CAUSA. (9) The Court of Appeal held that land was capable of passing by way of a *donatio mortis causa,* so that a deathbed oral gift of a house, with constructive delivery of the title deeds, was a valid gift (*Sen* v. *Headley* [1991] 2 All E.R. 636). The fact that a car given to his son by a man who died shortly thereafter was not accompanied by the log book or a second set of keys did not prevent the gift qualifying as a *donatio mortis causa,* as in the circumstances there was sufficient parting of domination by the donor (*Woodard* v. *Woodard* [1991] Fam. Law 470).

DONE. "Said or done," see SAID.

DOOR-TO-DOOR. Delivery of concessionary coal to miners was not "door-to-door" selling within the meaning of reg. 4(3) of the Community

Road Transport Rules (Exemptions) Regulations 1978 (No. 1158), because there was no sale (*DPP* v. *Digby* [1992] RTR 204).

DOWNLOADING. The "downloading" of information from a computer meant the transfer of information from one storage device to another and did not require the writing of that information onto disk (*R.* v. *City of London Magistrates Court, ex p. Green* [1997] 3 All E.R. 551).

DRAIN. Stat. Def., Water Industry Act 1991 (c. 56), s.219.

DRAINAGE. Stat. Def., Water Resources Act 1991 (c. 57), s.113; Land Drainage Act 1991 (c. 59), s.72 substituted by Environment Act 1995 (c. 25), s.100(2).

DRAMATIC. "Dramatic work." Stat. Def., Copyright, Designs and Patents Act 1988 (c. 48), s.3.

DRIVE; DRIVER; DRIVING. (9) "Driving" (Road Traffic Act 1972, (c. 20), s.6 as substituted by the Transport Act 1981 (c. 56), Sched. 8, now Road Traffic Act 1988 (c. 52), s.5). A person who knelt on the driving seat of a vehicle to release the handbrake, and then had to attempt to reapply the handbrake to stop the vehicle, could be held to have been "driving" the vehicle within the meaning of this section (*Rowan* v. *Chief Constable of Merseyside, The Times,* December 10, 1985). A defendant wearing motor-cyclist's clothing and a crash helmet, standing with legs astride a motor cycle, and who had been controlling the movement and direction of the motor cycle by pushing and steering it while its ignition and lights were on, without riding it, could properly be held to have been "driving" it within the meaning of this section (*McKoen* v. *Ellis* [1987] 3 RTR 26). Where two occupants of a motor vehicle were each charged with an offence under s.6 it was held to be unnecessary for the prosecution to establish which of them drove and which abetted so long as each of them knew that the other was unfit to drive through drink (*Smith* v. *Mellors and Soar* [1987] Crim.L.R. 421).

(9) "Driving" (Road Traffic Act 1972 (c. 20), s.7(1) as substituted by the Transport Act 1981 (c. 56), Sched. 8, now Road Traffic Act 1988 (c. 52), s.6). If the accused admits having driven on a particular day, and on the same day has given a specimen over the limit, the burden is on him to show that he had not driven whilst over the limit (*Patterson* v. *Charlton* [1986] RTR 18).

"Driving" (Greater London Council (Restriction of Goods Vehicles) Order 1985, art. 3). A limited company cannot be convicted of "driving" a vehicle without a permit (*Richmond-upon-Thames London Borough Council* v. *Pinn & Wheeler* [1989] RTR 354).

"A person driving a motor vehicle" (Road Traffic Act 1988 (c. 52), s.163). A person in the driver's seat of a stationary vehicle who turned on the engine and put his hand on the steering wheel was held not to be a "person driving" within the meaning of this section (*Leach* v. *DPP* [1993] RTR 161).

"A person who drives a motor vehicle" (Road Traffic Act 1988 (c. 52), s.2). The question of whether a person is driving a car is one of fact and degree and the act of a passenger who seized the steering wheel was held to be an act of interfering with the driver rather than of driving (*DPP* v. *Hastings* [1993] RTR 205).

A defendant who sat astride a moped which would not start because of a fault and propelled it down a road using his feet had control over the moped so as to "drive" it within the meaning of the section (*McKoen* v. *Ellis* [1987] 3 R.T.R. 26 followed; *R.* v. *MacDonagh* [1974] R.T.R. 372 distinguished) (*Gunnell* v. *DPP* [1994] R.T.R. 151).

(Road Traffic Act 1988 (c. 52), s.103). A police officer who arrested A on suspicion of driving whilst disqualified when A was out of the car and talking to B in his garden was not acting in the execution of his duty since A was not driving at the time of his arrest (*James* v. *DPP* [1997] 5 C.L. 569).

"Driver." Stat. Def., Road Traffic Act 1988 (c. 52), s.192; Road Traffic Offenders Act 1988 (c.53), s.89.

DRUG. Stat. Def., Road Traffic Act 1988 (c. 52), s.11.

DRUG MONEY LAUNDERING. Stat. Def., Drug Trafficking Act 1994 (c. 37), s.52(7).

DRUG TRAFFICKING. Stat. Def., Drug Trafficking Act 1994 (c. 37), s.1.

DRUGS. In medical context, Stat. Def., National Health Service Act 1977 (c. 49), Sched. 12A, para. 7(1) inserted by Health Act 1999 (c. 8), s.4(1).

DUE CARE. "Due care and diligence" (Social Security Act 1975 (c. 14), s.119(2)). A claimant was held not to have used "due care and diligence" to avoid overpayment of benefit, as required by this section, when he obtained one-parent child benefit without disclosing that he was not permanently separated from his wife living in Pakistan (*Sadiq* v. *Chief Adjudication Officer*, *The Times*, March 28, 1988). See also REASONABLE PRECAUTIONS.

DUE DILIGENCE. A solicitor who made inquiry of another professional person, who did not remember that he had access to material which might be helpful, could not be said to have failed to use due diligence to obtain the material which might have been adduced as further evidence on appeal (*Gibbs* v. *Bartlett*, *The Times*, April 20, 1989). See also DUE CARE.

DUE EXPEDITION. "With all due expedition" (Prosecution of Offences Act 1985 (c. 23), s.22(3)(*b*)). Where an application is made by the prosecution to extend the time limits for keeping the defendant in custody, the court, when looking at the question whether the prosecution acted "with all due expedition," must look at delays by the prosecution as a whole, including the police (*R.* v. *Birmingham Crown Court ex p. Ricketts* [1991] RTR 105). When considering whether the prosecution had acted with "all due expedition" the court was not required to approach the case as though that was the only question it was concerned with. Whether the prosecution acted with due expedition meant due expedition in the circumstances (*R.* v. *Norwich Crown Court, ex p. Parker* (1993) 96 Cr.App.R. 68).

"All due expedition" (Criminal Appeal Act 1968 (c. 19), s.8, as amended by s.43 of the Criminal Justice Act 1988 (c. 33). "Due" means "reasonable" or "proper" So that where an order for re-trial was made by the Court of Appeal in respect of an accused and the prosecution could give no reason for failing to re-arraign him within the time limit set by this section the prosecution could not claim to have acted with "due expedition" (*R.* v. *Horne* [1992] Crim.L.R. 304). "Expedition" means promptness or speed. "Due" means reasonable or proper (*R.* v. *Coleman* (1992) Cr.App.R. 345).

"Due expedition" in the 1985 Act, s.22(3) had to be aimed at achieving a contested rather than an unopposed committal within the prescribed 70 day period (*R.* v. *Leeds Crown Court, ex p. Briggs (No. 2)*, *The Times*, March 10, 1998).

DURESS. To establish the defence of duress it is necessary to show that the fear engendered by threats caused the accused to lose complete control of his will (*DPP* v. *Bell* [1992] Crim.L.R. 176).

Imminent peril was a necessary precondition to the establishment of the defence of duress (*R.* v. *Cole* [1994] Crim.L.R. 582).

DUTY. "Duty" in s.2(1) of the Official Secrets Act 1911 (c. 28), s.2(1) means an official duty rather than a moral, contractual or civic duty (*R.* v. *Ponting* [1985] Crim.L.R. 318). See also INTEREST.

"Duty of a local education authority . . . to comply with any preference expressed" (Education Act 1980) (c. 20), s.6(2)). This section imposes a single mandatory duty upon the authority, and s.18 of the Race Relations Act 1976 (c. 74) does not qualify the duty to comply with a parental request made under s.6 of the 1980 Act. The parents' reasons for making the request are irrelevant (*R.* v. *Cleveland County Council ex p. Commission for Racial Equality* (1991) 135 S.J.(LB) 205).

DWELLING. "Inside a dwelling" (Public Order Act 1986 (c. 64), s.4(2)). "Dwelling" connotes those areas which lay behind closed doors, and did not include common landings which were merely means of access to the dwelling (*Rukwira* v. *DPP* [1993] Crim.L.R. 882).

A floating home was a "dwelling" under the Local Government Finance Act 1992, s.3(2) and so liable to council tax (*Nicholls* v. *Wimbledon Valuation Office Agency* [1995] RVR 171).

Stat. Def., Landlord and Tenant Act 1987 (c. 31), s.60; Local Government and Housing Act 1989 (c. 42), ss.100, 138, 172; Local Government Finance Act 1992 (c. 14), s.3; Social Security Contributions and Benefits Act 1992 (c. 4), s.137; Social Security Administration Act 1992 (c. 5), s.191; Noise Act 1996 (c. 37), s.11(1); Housing Act 1996 (c. 52), ss.63(1) and 220(7); Housing Grants, Construction and Regeneration Act 1996 (c. 53), s.101; Water Industry Act 1991 (c. 56), Sched. 4A, para. 1(2), inserted by Water Industry Act 1999 (c. 9), s.1(2).

DWELLING-HOUSE. (28) (Capital Gains Tax Act 1979 (c. 14), s.101). A caravan parked in the courtyard of an uninhabitable farmhouse being renovated by the owner was not a "dwelling-house" for the purposes of this section (*Moore* v. *Thompson* [1986] S.T.C. 170, distinguishing *Makins* v. *Elson*, see Main Work, para. (28)).

"Dwellinghouse" (Common Land (Rectification of Registers) Act 1989 (c. 18), s.1) could include an unoccupied house or even one which had become derelict and unfit for human habitation (*Re* 1–4 *White Row Cottages, Bewerley* [1991] 3 W.L.R. 229).

Stat. Def., Insolvency Act 1986 (45), s.385; Housing Act 1985 (c. 68), ss.112, 183; Coal Mining Subsidence Act 1991 (c. 45), s.52; Northern Ireland (Emergency Provisions) Act 1996 (c. 22), s.58; Family Law Act 1996 (c. 27), s.63(1).

See also MAIN RESIDENCE; OCCUPY; PRIVATE DWELLING-HOUSE.

E

EARN. "Earned income." Stat. Def., Income and Corporation Taxes Act 1988 (c. 1), s.833.

EARNING CAPACITY. (Matrimonial Causes Act 1973 (c. 18), s.25(1)(*a*), as substituted by Matrimonial and Family Proceedings Act 1984 (c. 42), s.3). The fact that an applicant under this Act has had a child by a man not the respondent following their separation was to be taken into consideration when assessing the applicant's "earning capacity" under this section (*Fisher* v. *Fisher* (1989) 153 J.P.N. 217).

EARNINGS. (Social Security Act 1975 (c. 14), s.4). The value of petrol obtained by an employee for private use by means of his employer's charge card was to be taken into account in calculating the employee's "earnings" for the purposes of this section (*Re Charge Card Services* [1988] 3 W.L.R. 764; *R.* v. *Department of Social Security, ex p. Overdrive Credit Card* [1991] 1 W.L.R. 635).

(11) "Earnings of prostitution" (Sexual Offences Act 1956 (c. 69), s.30(1)). A person might fairly be said to be living on the earnings of prostitution if he supplied goods as services to prostitutes for payment which he would not have supplied but for the fact that they were prostitutes (*R.* v. *Howard* [1991] Crim.L.R. 847). A man who lived off the earnings of a woman who offered sexual services, took money and then reneged on the offer, lived on the earnings of prostitution (*R.* v. *MacFarlane* [1994] Q.B. 419). See also PROSTITUTION.

Stat. Def., Social Security Contributions and Benefits Act 1992 (c. 4), ss.3, 4, 112.

ECONOMIC. "Economic . . . reason" (Transfer of Undertakings (Protection of Employment) Regulations 1981 (No. 1794), reg. 8(2)). The fact that, as the prerequisite of the purchase of an hotel, three employees had to be dismissed did not amount to an "economic reason" sufficient to justify their dismissal. A mere desire to ensure a sale or to obtain an enhanced price was held not to amount to an "economic reason" within the meaning of this regulation (*Gateway Hotels* v. *Stewart* [1988] IRLR 287).

The dismissal of employees designed to make an uneconomic business saleable was not an "economic reason" within the meaning of reg. 8(2) (*Anderson* v. *Dalkeith Engineering* [1985] I.C.R. 66 not followed) (*Ibex Trading Co.* v. *Walton* [1994] I.C.R. 907).

ECONOMIC ACTIVITY. (Sixth Council Directive 77/388 on a common system for VAT Arts. 4, 13B and 17). The sale of shares by a charitable trustee in the course of the management of the charity's assets was not an economic activity within the meaning of Art. 4 and so fell outside the scope of VAT because a charity was prohibited from engaging in such activities for commercial purposes (*Wellcome Trust Ltd* v. *Customs and Excise Commissioners* (C155/94), *The Times*, July 10, 1996).

The concept of "economic activity" was one usually performed for consideration and connected with economic life. It was not an essential characteristic that it should be carried on for profit or commercial reasons and the provision of licensing functions was not the carrying out of a business even though services were supplied and a fee payable. (*Institute of Chartered Accountants in England and Wales* v. *Customs and Excise Commissioners* [1998] 4 All E.R. 115).

ECU. Stat. Def., Cash Ratio Deposits (Eligible Liabilities) Order 1998 (No. 1130), Art. 2(1).

EDUCATION. Where a residuary bequest in a will set up a trust for the "education and welfare" of Bahamian children it was held that as "education" and "welfare" had to be construed disjunctively, and as "welfare" was non-charitable, the bequest failed as a charitable trust (*Attorney-General of the Bahamas* v. *Royal Trust Co.* [1986] 3 All E.R. 423).

"Special educational provision" (Education Act 1981 (c. 60), s.1) could include speech therapy (*R.* v. *Lancashire County Council, ex p. Moore* (*a Minor*) (1990) 154 L.G.Rev. 112).

(Education Act 1993 (c. 35), Part III). Nursing care for a child suffering from epilepsy and cerebral palsy did not amount to "educational provision" so that a statement of special educational needs could not include a claim for nursing care while at school (*Bradford M.B.C.* v. *A* [1996] 9 C.L. 231).

(Education Act 1993 (c. 35), s.298). A "suitable education" was to be determined solely by reference to educational considerations, namely its efficiency and suitability to a child's age, aptitude and ability and any special education needs rather than by reference to the resources of the education authority to provide that education (*R.* v. *Essex County Council, ex p. Tandy* [1998] 2 All E.R. 769).

Stat. Def., "includes training and the provision of activities for children" (National Lottery Act 1998 (c. 22), s.6(8)).

EDUCATIONAL ESTABLISHMENT. Stat. Def., "includes any university, college, school or other educational establishment" (Employment Rights Act 1996 (c. 18), s.43K(3) inserted by Public Interest Disclosure Act 1998 (c. 23), s.1).

EFFECT. "By his signature to give effect to the will" (Wills Act 1837 (c. 26), s.9(*b*), as substituted by s.17 of the Administration of Justice Act 1982 (c. 53), see VALID.

EFFECTED BY A SERIES OF TWO OR MORE TRANSACTIONS. A draft contract for sale, a payment on account and subsequent negotiations prior to the agreement for sale were not a series of two or more transactions by which a transfer of an employers' undertaking was "effected" within the meaning of the Transfer of Undertakings (Protection of Employment) Regulations 1981 (No. 1794), reg. 5(3) (*Wheeler* v. *Patel* [1987] I.C.R. 631 applied) (*Longden* v. *Ferrari* [1994] I.C.R. 443).

EFFECTING. (Insurance Companies Act 1982 (c. 50), s.2). The word "effecting" in s.2 included the negotiation of a contract which could begin when the invitation to treat was made so that the offence of carrying on an insurance business without authoritisation could be committed before a contract had been formed (*R.* v. *Wilson (Rupert), The Times*, August 14, 1996).

EFFECTIVE. (4) "Effective provision" of "sufficient and suitable lighting" (Factories Act 1961 (c. 34), s.5(1)). These words impose an absolute duty on employers, which will be breached even by the mere failure of a light bulb immediately before the occurrence of an accident (*Davies* v. *Massey Ferguson Perkins* [1986] I.C.R. 580).

(5) "Effective date of termination" (Employment Protection (Consolidation) Act 1978 (c. 44), s.67(2)). The day on which an employee was told in writing that she was "dismissed with immediate effect" constituted the "effective date of termination" of her contract of employment under this section notwithstanding that such an immediate dismissal was in breach of a code incorporated in the contract of employment (*Batchelor* v. *British Railways Board* [1987] IRLR 136). For the purposes of this section the effective date of termination of a contract is the date it takes effect, and this applies also to cases of constructive dismissal (*B.M.K.* v. *Logue* [1993] I.C.R. 601).

"Effective notice in writing," see NOTICE.

EFFLUENT. Stat. Def., Water Industry Act 1991 (c. 56), s.219; Water Resources Act 1991 (c. 57), s.221).

ELECTRONIC. Stat. Def., Copyright, Designs and Patents Act 1988 (c. 48), s.178.

ELIGIBLE INVESTOR. An "eligible investor" under the Financial Services (Compensation of Investors) Rules 1990, r.2.02.2(a) was the person who made the investment and did not include a personal representative, who could only pursue a claim of a deceased eligible investor (*R.* v. *Investors Compensation Scheme, ex p. Bowden* [1994] 1 All E.R. 525).

EMANATION. (Transfer of Undertakings (Protection of Employment) Regulations 1981 (S.I. 1981 No. 1794), regs. 2(1), 8; E.C. Directive 77/187, Arts. 1, 3).

Education in a voluntary-aided school, while a public service, is provided by the governing body of the school, which was not under the control of the state and not therefore an "emanation" or agency of the state (*N.U.T.* v. *Governing Body of St. Mary's C. of E. (Aided) Junior School* [1995] I.C.R. 317).

EMBARRASS. "The plaintiff is embarrased by the payment" (R.S.C., Ord. 22, r.1(5)). The extent to which the difficulty experienced by the plaintiff, where the defendant has paid into court a single sum in respect of more than one cause of action, can amount to "embarrassment" within the meaning of this rule was considered in *Driscoll* v. *Nye Saunders and Partners (a Firm)*, *The Times*, June 27, 1988. A plaintiff is "embarrassed" if he is placed in a difficulty which he ought not fairly to have to face (*Walker* v. *Turpin* [1994] 1 W.L.R. 196).

Two plaintiffs may be "embarrassed" by a single payment into court without apportionment between them, where one plaintiff was unable to accept the payment in or continue the action, without the concurrence of the other (*Walker* v. *Turpin* [1994] 1 W.L.R. 196).

EMERGENCY. See CIVIL EMERGENCY.

EMERGENCY VEHICLE. See VEHICLE.

EMOLUMENTS. (13) Payments made by the Government to Civil Service employees as compensation for removing their rights to belong to a union and certain other rights under the employment protection legislation, were held to be "emoluments" for the purposes of s.181 of the Income and Corporation Taxes Act 1970 (c. 10); now s.19 of the Income and Corporation Taxes Act 1988 (c. 1), and therefore chargeable to tax under Schedule E (*Hamblett* v. *Godfrey* [1987] 1 W.L.R. 357). Capital payments made, on the winding-up of two company funds, to an employee after the termination of his employment were held to be "emoluments" within the meaning of this section. But as for tax purposes, payments can only be attributable to the year in which they are made, and as, in this case, they were made after the "termination" of employment their source had ceased to exist and they could not be charged to income tax (*Bray* v. *Best* [1989] 1 W.L.R. 167). The benefit of free living accommodation provided for a horticultural nurseryman by his employer was held to be an emolument for Schedule E tax purposes, since it could not be shown that, in these circumstances, it was "customary for employers to provide living accommodation" (Finance Act 1977 (c. 36), s.33(4)(*b*)) (*Vertigan* v. *Brady* [1988] S.T.C. 91). A living allowance, paid by an employer to an employee required to work away from his home for long periods, was held to be part of the employee's "emoluments" chargeable under Schedule E (*Elderkin* v. *Hindmarsh* [1988] S.T.C. 267). A fee paid to a professional footballer by his club as an inducement to him to consent to his transfer to another club, was an emolument, chargeable to Schedule E income tax as it was "from his employment" with the new club (*Shilton* v. *Wilmshurst* [1991] 2 W.L.R. 530). And a footballer's income derived from a loan made by his club to Jersey trustees, and held for the footballer's benefit, was held to be an emolument of his employment chargeable to tax, notwithstanding that the income was never remitted to the U.K. (*O'Leary* v. *McKinlay* [1991] S.T.C. 42). A redundancy payment is not an emolument from employment so therefore a payment in consideration of the release of a contingent right to receive a redundancy payment was also not an emolument (*Mairs* v. *Haughey* [1993] 3 W.L.R. 393). Monetary benefits which, by virtue of an agreement, became due on the occurrence of certain events were, when laid, emoluments for the purposes of s.19 from which PAYE should be deducted in accordance with s.203 of the 1988 Act (*Booth* v. *Mirror Group Newspapers* [1992] STC 615). See also THEREFROM.

"Emoluments for duties performed outside the United Kingdom" (Income and Corporation Taxes Act 1970 (c. 10), s.184(1)). For the purposes of calculating an international airline pilot's overseas earning relief for short absences from the U.K. his emoluments for periods in the U.K. when he was not working were not "emoluments for duties performed outside the United Kingdom" within the meaning of this section (*Leonard* v. *Blanchard*, *The Times*, February 16, 1993).

Stat. Def., Income and Corporation Taxes Act, 1988 (c. 1), s.131.

EMPLOY. "Employed under a person who holds office under her Majesty" (Official Secrets Acts 1911 (c. 28), s.2(1) and 1920 (c. 75), s.7). A person who worked exclusively at a police station taking instructions from a police officer was "employed under a person who holds office under her Majesty," *i.e.* the police officer, notwithstanding that his contract of employment was with the County Council (*Loat* v. *Andrews*, *sub nom. Lout* v. *James* [1986] Crim.L.R. 744.

"A person employed by him" (Race Relations Act 1976 (c. 74), s.4(2)). A special constable is a "constable" within the meaning of s.16 and therefore a "person employed" for the purposes of s.4 (*Sheik* v. *Anderton* [1989] 2 W.L.R. 1102).

(Transfer of Undertakings (Protection of Employment) Regulations 1981 (S.I. 1981 No. 1794), reg. 5(1)). An employee did not have to be exclusively employed in the undertaking or part of the undertaking transferred to come within the scope of reg. 5(1) (*Buchanan-Smith* v. *Schleicher & Co. International Ltd* [1996] I.C.R. 613).

EMPLOYEE. "Every employee shall have the right not to be unfairly dismissed" (Employment Protection (Consolidation) Act 1978 (c. 44), s.54(1)). A minister of the Presbyterian Church of Wales was not an "employee" for the purposes of this section (*Davies* v. *Presbyterian Church of Wales* [1986] 1 W.L.R. 323). Similarly a Sikh appointed as a priest at a Sikh temple in the United Kingdom was not an *employee* of the temple (*Santokh Singh* v. *Guru Nanak Gurdwara*, [1990] I.C.R. 309). An equity partner is not an "employee" as he does not have any employment relationship with his other partners; such relationship being governed by the contract of partnership and the partnership legislation (*Cowell* v. *Quilter Goodison Co. and Q.G. Management Services* [1989] IRLR 392).

A person who worked for an employment agency on a series of temporary contracts, which stated that he was self-employed and where he was not obliged to accept an offer of work, but if he did, he was subject to duties of fidelity, confidentiality and obedience to instructions, and was not entitled to holiday pay, sick pay or pension rights was an "employee" of the agency who could instruct him to end an assignment and could dismiss him for improper conduct (*McMeeschan* v. *Secretary of State for Employment* [1995] I.C.R. 444).

"Health . . . at work of all his employees" Health and Safety at Work Act 1974 (c. 37), s.2(1)). The employer's duty under this section was owed to all empoloyees, not just to those engaged in work in which particular plant was used or available (*Bolton Metropolitan Borough Council* v. *Malrod Insulations* [1993] I.C.R. 358).

A gamekeeper who had round the clock responsibilities was not at work during a search of a premises since once he had been cautioned he was acting on his own behalf (*Thomson* v. *Barbour*, 1994 S.C.C.R. 485).

The terms "employee" in the Race Relations Act 1976 excluded a person whose employment had ceased at the time of the act of discrimination so that where an employee had been unconditionally dismissed with immediate effect, an internal appeal was not part of the dismissal process and an aggrieved party could not rely on s.4 of the 1976 Act (*Post Office* v. *Adekeye* [1997] I.C.R. 110).

(Transfer of Undertakings (Protection of Employment) Regulations 1981 (No. 1794), reg. 2(1)). A person employed under a contract of service could not also work for another body which was not his employer so as to fall within the definition of "employee" within the meaning of reg. 2(1) (*Governing Body of Clifton Middle School* v. *Askew* [1997] I.C.R. 808).

An ordained priest of the Church of England was called to an office recognised by law and charged with functions set out in the Book of Common Prayer. A curate was not employed by his diocese, which was not a legal person nor by the Church Commissioners or the Diocesan Board of Finance, notwithstanding their power to remove him from office nor by his bishop with whom he had a relationship which was governed by the church rather than a contract and so that he could not be an "employee" (*Diocese of Southwark* v. *Coker* [1998] I.C.R. 140).

(Employment Rights Act 1996 (c. 18), s.230). A sole shareholder could, depending on the facts, be an employee of a company and eligible for redundancy payments (*Bottrill* v. *Secretary of State for Trade and Industry* [1998] IRLR 120).

Stat. Def., Social Security Act 1986 (c. 50), s.84; Social Security Contributions and Benefits Act 1992 (c. 4), ss.163, 171; "in relation to a body corporate, includes any director or other officer of that body" (Deregulation and Contracting Out Act 1994 (c. 40), s.79(1)); Industrial Tribunals Act 1996 (c. 17), s.42(1); Employment Rights Act 1996 (c. 18), s.230(1).

EMPLOYER. "His employer" (Employment Protection (Consolidation) Act 1978 (c. 44), s.84(1)). This phrase included, for any employee, an associated company of the company last employing him before it dismissed him, and thus an offer of employment by such associated company precluded redundancy (*Lucas* v. *Henry Johnson* (*Packers and Shippers*) [1986] I.C.R. 384).

The Secretary of State was excluded form being an "employer" in the set off provision of s.190(3) of the Trade Union and Labour Relations (Consolidation) Act 1992 (c. 52) (*Secretary of State for Employment* v. *Mann* [1996] IRLR 4).

(Sex Discrimination Act Act 1975, (c. 65), s.12). An organisation of the self-employed and small businesses was an organisation of employers within the 1975 Act, and was therefore required to entertain a member's complaint that renewal of membership had been refused contrary to s.12 (*National Federation of Self-employed and Small Businesses Ltd* v. *Philpott*, *The Times*, February 13, 1997).

(Employment Protection (Consolidation) Act 1978 (c. 44), s.127). The test of insolvency in s.127(1) was to be applied to an employee, so that in the case of a partnership each partner had to have been adjudicated bankrupt for an application to qualify under the section (*Secretary of State for Trade and Industry* v. *Forde* [1997] I.C.R. 231).

Employer (Income Tax (Employment) Regulations 1973 (No. 334), reg. 29), see TRADE.

Stat. Def., Social Security Act 1986 (c. 50), s.84; Social Security Contributions and Benefits Act 1992 (c. 4), ss.163, 171.

EMPLOYMENT. A man was held to have "lost employment . . . due to a trade dispute" within the meaning of s.19(1) of the Social Security Act 1975 (c. 14), notwithstanding that two weeks before the commencement of the dispute he had been given 12 weeks' notice of the termination of his employment on the ground of redundancy (*Cartlidge* v. *Chief Adjudication Officer* [1986] 2 W.L.R. 558).

The word "employment" (Employment Act 1980 (c. 42), s.4) is to be construed widely as meaning employment in a particular field of industry, rather than narrowly as referring to a specific job (*Clark* v. *Society of Graphical and Allied Trades 1982* [1986] I.C.R. 12).

"The employment is wholly outside Great Britain" (Employment Protection (Consolidation) Act 1978 (c. 44), s.141(5)(*a*)). In the case where a merchant seaman had been engaged to work on board a British registered vessel used solely for cruising in the Caribbean and South America the "employment" for the purposes of this section was held to refer to that part of the employment which related to working on board ship, and was therefore "wholly outside Great Britain," notwithstanding that he had been engaged in Southampton and had been given air tickets to enable him to join the ship (*Wood* v. *Cunard Line* [1990] IRLR 281).

"Employment" (Sex Discrimination Act 1975 (c. 65), s.82(1)). The appointment of a general practitioner is not "a contract personally to execute any work or labour" and so does not constitute "employment" (*Ealing, Hammersmith and Hounslow Family Health Services Authority* v. *Shukla* [1993] I.C.R. 710); (*Wadi* v. *Cornwall and Isles of Scilly Family Practitioner Committee* [1985] I.C.R. 492 followed; *Roy* v. *Kensington and Chelsea and Westminster Family Practitioner Committee* [1990] 1 Med.L.R. 328 not followed).

(Equal Pay Act 1970 (c. 41), s.1(6)). A male comparator from a separate establishment was to be treated as in the same employment as a woman if the terms and conditions of employment for men of the relevant class at his establishment were the same as those of men of the relevant class employed at the woman's establishment or which would be available for male employees for that work at her establishment, although the terms and conditions of employment need not be the same at both establishments (*British Coal Corporation* v. *Smith* [1994] I.C.R. 810).

For the purpose of determining whether men or women were to be treated as being in the "same employment" within s.1(2)(c) of the 1970 Act, the words "common terms and conditions of employment" meant terms and conditions that were broadly substantially comparable rather than identical (*British Coal Corporation* v. *Smith* [1996] 3 All E.R. 97).

(Equal Pay Act 1970 (c. 41), s.2(4) (as amended)). The "employment" in s.2(4) of the 1970 Act referred to a particular contract of service rather than a series of different contracts with the same employer (*Preston* v. *Wolverhampton NHS Trust* [1998] I.C.R. 227).

(Housing Act 1985 (c. 68), s.61(1)(*b*)). A local authority erred in discounting a homeless applicant's voluntary work as a qualifying circumstance when considering his local connection with the district (*R.* v. *Ealing London Borough Council, ex p. Fox, The Times*, March 9, 1998).

(Fair Employment (Northern Ireland) Act 1976, s.57). Since the definition of "employment" in s.57 includes "a contract personally to execute any work or labour", a sole practitioner could claim he was seeking to be employed when applying for membership of a panel of solicitors engaged to carry out legal services and could be the victim of discrimination. Similarly, the definition of "employment" was sufficiently wide to enable a partner in a firm to be regarded as employed where one partner undertook to do and be responsible for the work (*Kelly* v. *Northern Ireland Housing Executive* [1998] 3 W.L.R. 735).

(Employment Rights Act 1996 (c. 18), s.211). Where an employee had been employed by different departments of the same employer, the presumption in favour of continuous employment, required the entire employment relationship to be considered, including whether an employee had two or more employments with the same employer for the purposes of establishing continuity of employment under the 1996 Act (*Bradford Metropolitan District Council* v. *Dawson* [1999] I.C.R. 312).

Stat. Def., Social Security Contributions and Benefits Act 1992 (c. 4), s.122; "includes an office" (Income and Corporation Taxes Act 1988 (c. 1), Sched. 12A, para. 1(2) inserted by Finance Act 1998 (c. 36), Sched. 10); and see "Office-holder" under Office; wide definition including unpaid work, etc., Protection of Children Act 1999 (c. 14), s.12(1).

"Contract of employment," Stat. Def., Asylum and Immigration Act 1996 (c. 49), s.8(8).

See also EMOLUMENTS; IN THE COURSE; OFFICE.

EMPTY. "Empty" within the meaning of the Control of Pollution Act 1974 (c. 40), s.3(2)(*d*) depended on the context and could include a vessel less than 1 per cent. full (*Durham County Council* v. *Thomas Swan & Co., The Times*, July 24, 1994).

ENACTMENT. "And any other enactment" (Local Government Act 1972 (c. 70), s.111(1)). The word "enactment" is apt to include delegated legislation (*Allsop* v. *North Tyneside Metropolitan Borough Council* [1992] RVR 104).

Stat. Def., "includes a local enactment and an enactment contained in subordinate legislation within the meaning of the Interpretation Act 1978" (Conservation (Natural Habitats, etc.) Regulations 1994 (No. 2716), reg. 2(1)); "includes an enactment contained in a statutory instrument" (Requirements of Writing (Scotland) Act 1995 (c. 7), s.12(1)); "includes subordinate legislation and any Order in Council" (Disability Discrimination Act 1995 (c. 50), s.68(1)); "includes an enactment comprised in subordinate legislation (within the meaning of the Interpretation Act 1978)" (Chemical Weapons Act 1996 (c. 6), s.27(7)); "includes an enactment contained in Northern Ireland legislation" (Arbitration Act 1996 (c. 23), s.82(1)); "includes an enactment comprised in subordinate legislation (which here has the same meaning as in the Interpretation Act 1978)" (Criminal Procedure and Investigations Act 1996 (c. 25), s.20(5)(b)); same, Housing Act 1996 (c.52), s.230; "includes an enactment in any local or private Act of Parliament, and an order, rule, regulation, byelaw or scheme made under an Act of Parliament, including an order or scheme confirmed by Parliament" (Town and Country Planning (Scotland) Act 1997 (c. 8), s.277(1)); "includes any instrument made under any enactment" (Regional Development Agencies Act 1998 (c. 45), s.37(10)); including Scotland and Nothern Ireland legislation, Scotland Act 1998 (c. 46), s.126(1); see also Northern Ireland Act 1998 (c. 47), s.98(1); "includes an enactment whenever passed or made" (Health Act 1999 (c. 8), s.64); see also Legislation.

"Local enactment", Stat. Def., "means a local or private Act, or an order confirmed by Parliament or brought into operation in accordance with special Parliamentary procedure" (Merchant Shipping Act 1995 (c. 21), s.151(1)); note also "local statutory provision," Stat. Def., Environment Act 1995 (c. 25), s.121(7).

ENFORCE. (Hire Purchase Act 1965 (c. 66), s.34(1)). The use of the word "enforce" requires there to be some coercive action (*Chartered Trust* v. *Pitcher* [1988] RTR 72).

ENFORCEMENT. "Recognition and enforcement" under the Hague Convention on the Civil Aspects of International Child Abduction 1980, as enacted by the Child Abduction and Custody Act 1985 (c. 60), Sched. 2, art. 10(1)(*b*) should be construed disjunctively since "enforcement" did not follow automatically from "recognition" (*Re H. (A Child) (Foreign Custody Order: Enforcement*) [1994] 1 All E.R. 812).

ENGINEERING PLANT. A rigid-bodies goods vehicle specially constructed with a boiler for transporting molten asphalt fell within the definition of "engineering plant" and was exempt under the Goods Vehicles (Planting and Testing) Regulations 1988 (No. 1478), Sched. 2 (*DPP* v. *Derbyshire* [1994] R.T.R. 351).

ENLARGEMENT. "Enlargement of any existing building" (Value Added Tax Act 1983 (c. 55), s.21(3)(*b*)). A new building, wholly different in style and size from an existing building, was held not to be an "enlargement" of the existing building, notwithstanding a communicating door between the two (*Waterways Services* v. *Customs and Excise Commissioners* [1990] VATTR 37).

ENQUIRE. "Enquiring into an offence" (Magistrates' Courts Act 1980 (c. 43), s.6(1)). Examining justices were not "enquiring into an offence" within the meaning of this section, despite having heard argument as to abuse of process, in circumstances where the prosecution had not opened the case, no witnesses had been called and no other step pertinent to the committal of the case for trial had taken place (*R.* v. *Worcester Magistrates' Court, ex p. Leavesley, The Times,* January 14, 1993).

ENROL. The Immigration Appeal Tribunal has held that the word "enrolled" in H.C. 169 para. 107 means that the student in question shall have an unconditional confirmed place on a course (*Chinwo* v. *Secretary of State for the Home Department* [1985] Imm.A.R. 74).

ENTER. "Entered at Customs House" for the purpose of a laytime provision in a voyage charterparty means "entered a final entry" and the filing of a prior entry was not sufficient (*President of India* v. *Diamantis*

Pateras (Hellas) Marine Enterprises; The Nestor [1987] 2 Lloyd's Rep. 649). A chartered vessel is "entered", and can give valid notice of readiness to discharge, even if the inwards entry registers is not yet complete, if it has completed the prior entry procedure at an Indian port and been granted free pratique (*The Antclizo (No. 2), The Financial Times,* February 26, 1992).

ENTERING AN APPEARANCE. The admission of liability and submission of an application for a time-to-pay direction amounted to "entering an appearance" within the meaning of the Civil Jurisdiction and Judgments Act 1982 (c. 27), Sched. 4, art. 18 (*Clydesdale Bank* v. *Ions*, 1993 S.C.L.R. 964).

ENTITLED. (15) "Receiving or entitled to the income" (Income and Corporation Taxes Act 1970 (c. 10), s.114(1)). A taxpayer who deposited a sum of money in a special bank account, which was to secure debts owed to the bank by a company, and over which the bank had complete control, was not "entitled" to the interest credited to the account (*Macpherson* v. *Bond* [1985] 1 W.L.R. 1157, distinguishing *Dunmore* v. *McGowan*, Main Work, para. (15)). Where a taxpayer maintained a frozen bank deposit account in his name, as security for an unpaid foreign debt, his personal liability to repay the debt, if required to do so, made him assessable under the provisions of s.114(1) as the person "entitled to the income" accruing to the account, notwithstanding that he himself would never receive any of it (*Peracha* v. *Miley* [1990] S.T.C. 512; distinguishing *Macpherson* v. *Bond*, *supra*, and following *Dunmore* v. *McGowan*). A trustee of a discretionary trust administered abroad who was, of the three trustees, the only one resident in the United Kingdom was not "entitled" to the unremitted trust income for the purposes of this section (*Dawson* v. *Inland Revenue Commissioners* [1989] 2 W.L.R. 858).

"Are not entitled to do so" (Copyright Designs and Patents Act 1988 (c. 48), s.298(2)). Persons who were not authorised by or on behalf of the provider of encoded satellite television programmes to receive the programmes or other transmissions were "not entitled to do so" within this section (*BBC Enterprises* v. *Hi-Tech Xtravision* [1991] 2 A.C. 327).

"To which the company appears to be entitled" (Insolvency Act 1986 (c. 45), s.234(2)). Where there was an exclusive jurisdiction clause in an agreement between motor manufacturers and their hauliers that required any diputes to be dealt with by the Dutch courts, the English court was precluded from determining whether, for the purposes of this section, the manufacturers were "entitled" to the new unsold vehicles stored by the hauliers (*Re Leyland Daf (No. 2), The Times,* January 19, 1994).

(Employment Protection (Consolidation) Act 1978 (c. 44), s.122). The phrase "entitled" in s.122(1)(b) meant legally entitled (*Secretary of State for Employment* v. *Wilson and B.C.C.I.* [1996] IRLR 330).

"Entitled to vote," see RESIDENT.

ENTRANT. "New entrant" in a contractual clause meant every new entrant and could not exclude new entrants who joined a company as a result of a merger or a transfer of business (*Adams* v. *British Airways plc* [1995] IRLR 577).

ENTRIES ON THE REGISTER. Cautions are "entries" on the land register within the meaning of the Charging Orders Act 1979 (c. 53), s.2(1)(*b*)(iii) (*Clark* v. *Chief Land Registrar* [1994] 4 All E.R. 96).

ENTRUST. "Entrusted to either of the parties" (Matrimonial Causes Act 1973 (c. 18), s.43(1)). "Entrusted" in this section has a wider meaning than just care and control (*Re L* (*Minors*) (1989) 153 J.P.N. 820).

ENVIRONMENT. Stat. Def., Environmental Protection Act 1990 (c. 43), s.1; "includes the living and social environment" (National Lottery Act 1998 (c. 22), s.6(8)).

ENVIRONMENTAL CONSERVATION. Stat Def., Environment Act 1995 (c. 25), s.97(8).

EQUAL VALUE. (Equal Pay Act 1970 (c. 41), s.1(2)(*c*)). A woman could not succeed on a claim that her work was of "equal value" to that of men employed by the same employer at a different establishment unless the terms and conditions of the men's employment were broadly similar to those of her employment (*Leverton* v. *Clwyd County Council* [1989] 2 W.L.R. 47; See MATERIAL FACTOR.

EQUAL WORK. See LIKE WORK.

EQUALITY OF OPPORTUNITY. Stat. Def., Northern Ireland Act 1998 (c. 47), s.75(1).

EQUALLY ADVANTAGEOUS. (Acquisition of Land Act 1981 (c. 67), s.19(1)(*a*)). In considering whether land to be exchanged for open-space land is, for the purposes of this section, "equally advantageous" it is permissible to have regard to predicted development, or future occurrences which would affect either piece of land. It is not necessary that there should be precise correspondence between the advantages of each piece of land (*Greenwich London Borough Council* v. *Secretary of State for the Environment*: *Yates* v. *Secretary of State for the Environment*, *The Times*, March 2, 1993).

EQUIPMENT. "Equipment" for the purposes of s.1(1)(*a*) of the Employer's Liability (Defective Equipment) Act 1969 (c. 37) was held to be wide enough to include a ship of whatever size, notwithstanding that ships are not specifically mentioned in the definition of "equipment" in subsection (3), whereas vehicles and aircraft are (*Coltman* v. *Bibby Tankers* [1987] 3 W.L.R. 1181). A flagstone was held to be "equipment" within the meaning of this section (*Knowles* v. *Liverpool City Council* [1994] I.C.R. 243).

(Transport Act 1968 (c. 73), s.97; Council Regulation 3821/85 on recording equipment in road transport). The phrase "recording equipment in use according to articles 13 and 15" extended to record sheets which had been removed from the inside of a tachograph machine as well as those currently inside the machine (*Birkett* v. *Wing*, *The Times*, June 10, 1997).

(Employer's Liability (Defective Equipment) Act 1969 (c. 37), s.1(3)). Wooden packaging was "equipment" within the meaning of s.193) of the

1969 Act where it had been supplied for the purpose of transporting a load from one place to another (*Davison* v. *A. R. Allen* (*t/a Allen's Transport*) [1998] 2 C.L. 333).

Stat Def., "does not include clothing" (Education Act 1996 (c. 56), s.462(1)); "includes vehicles, apparatus, furniture, fittings, accoutrements and clothing" (Police (Northern Ireland) Act 1998 (c. 32), s.73(1)).

"Fixed equipment." Stat. Def., Agricultural Tenancies Act 1995 (c. 8), s.19(10).

EQUITY. "Equity security." Stat. Def., Companies Act 1985 (c. 6), s.94.

ERROR OF COMPUTATION. An employer's failure to make a payment because he believed he was contractually entitled to do so was not an "error of computation" under the Wages Act 1986 (c. 48), s.8(3), (4) (*Yemm* v. *British Steel* [1994] I.R.L.R. 117).

ESSENTIAL TO PROVIDE FAIR COMPENSATION. Compensation under the Financial Services (Compensation of Investors) Rules 1990, r.2.04.1 had to be determined in accordance with common law principles and considerations of fairness to other investors and the difficulty of making judgments of valuation were irrelevant to the issue of what was "essential to provide fair compensation under the scheme" (*R.* v. *Investors Compensation Scheme, ex p. Bowden* [1995] 1 All E.R. 214).

ESTABLISH. "Established place of business in England" (Companies Act 1948 (c. 38), s.106). Where an overseas company acquired four garage sites and, before trading, charged them to the petrol company, the overseas company had not at that time "established a place of business in England" (*Re Oriel* [1986] 1 W.L.R. 180).

"Establishing, preserving or defending his title" (Finance Act 1965 (c. 25), Sched. 6, para. 4(1)(*b*); now Capital Gains Tax Act 1979 (c. 14), s.32(1)(*b*)). Where a residuary legatee who, at the time of the death of the testatrix, had no interest in any particular asset of the estate, paid to the executors the difference in value between the residue and the house of the testatrix, so that they could transfer it to him, such expenditure was incurred neither in "establishing" nor in "preserving or defending" his title to the house (*Passant* v. *Jackson* [1986] S.T.C. 164).

"Company or association established in the United Kingdom" (British Nationality Act 1981 (c. 61), Sched. 1, para. 1(1)(*d*)(ii). A company incorporated abroad but registered as an overseas company with a place of business in the U.K. was a company "established in the United Kingdom" for the purposes of this paragraph (*R.* v. *Secretary of State for the Home Department, ex p. Mehta* [1992] Imm.A.R. 512).

(Education Act (c. 20), s.12). "Establish" meant putting into action a train of procedures necessary for the establishment of a school in a specified area (*R.* v. *Buckinghamshire C.C. ex p. Milton Keynes Borough Council* [1996] 12 C.L. 187).

ESTABLISHMENT. "Establishment in Great Britain" (Sex Discrimination Act 1975 (c. 65), ss.6(2), 10(1)). A person employed by an English company to work on a German registered cross-Channel ferry based at Sheerness but spending most of its time outside territorial waters was not "employed . . . at an establishment in Great Britain" within the meaning of these sections (*Haughton* v. *Olau Line (U.K.)* [1986] 1 W.L.R. 504).

"Establishment in Great Britain" (Race Relations Act 1976 (c. 74), ss.4(1), 8(1)). A ship which, at the time the crew was recruited, was not expected to sail to Britain, was held not to be an "establishment in Great Britain" within the meaning of these sections, notwithstanding that at the end of the voyage, by reason of unforeseen circumstances, three hours had been spent in territorial waters (*Deria* v. *General Council of British Shipping* [1986] 1 W.L.R. 1207).

ESTATE. "The bankrupt's estate" (Insolvency Act 1986 (c. 45), s.306). A non-assignable secure periodic tenancy being a mere personal right did not form part of the bankrupt's "estate" vested in the trustee in bankruptcy under this section (*London City Corp.* v. *Brown* (1990) 60 P. & C.R. 42).

"Estate of a deceased person." The unsevered interest of a deceased person under a joint tenancy did not form part of his estate for the purposes of the Insolvency Act 1986 (c. 45), s.421 (*Re Palmer (Deceased)* (*A Debtor*) [1994] 3 All E.R. 835).

ESTATE AGENT. Stat. Def., Disability Discrimination Act 1995 (c. 50), s.22(6).

ESTATE CONTRACT. (Land Charges Act 1972 (c. 61), s.2(4)). A renewal covenant in a lease under which the lessee was granted an option to renew the lease for a further term was an "estate contract" within the meaning of this section (*Phillips* v. *Mobil Oil Co.* [1989] 1 W.L.R. 888).

ETHNIC. "Ethnic . . . origins" (Race Relations Act 1976 (c. 74), s.3(1)). English-speaking Welsh and Welsh-speaking Welsh do not have separate ethnic origins and are not therefore of different racial groups within the meaning of this section. So that refusing to employ a person because she could not speak Welsh was not racial discrimination (*Gwynedd County Council* v. *Jones* [1986] I.C.R. 833). Gypsies, by reason of their shared history, common geographical origin, customs, language and culture are of common ethnic origin and therefore identifiable as a separate racial group (*Commission for Racial Equality* v. *Dutton* [1989] 2 W.L.R. 17). Rastafarians are not a separate ethnic group for the purposes of this section. Accordingly a Rastafarian who had been considered unsuitable for employment as a government van driver because of his long hair (a style adopted by Rastafarians) had not been racially discriminated against (*Dawkins* v. *Crown Supplies (PSA) (now Department of Environment)*, *The Times*, February 4, 1993). See also RACIAL.

EVASION. (Value Added Tax Act 1983 (c. 55), s.39(1)) "Evasion" within s.39(1) meant a deliberate non-payment when payment was due and the Crown did not have to prove intent to make permanent default of the existing liability (*R.* v. *Dealy (John Clark)* [1995] 1 W.L.R. 658).

(Customs and Excise Management act 1979 (c. 2), s.170(2)). S, who delivered a quantity of heroin in Pakistan to an informer of a drugs enforcement agency who arranged for the transportation of the heroin to

London where it was to be collected by S, but where a customs officer delivered packages to S, which had been contrived to look like heroin, was guilty of an offence under s.170(2) (*R* v. *Latif and Shahzad* [1996] 1 All E.R. 353).

EVENT. Where a policy of insurance gave an indemnity against "events occurring during the period of the policy" the "events" referred to the happening of any of the specified insured perils not the damage caused as a result (*Kelly* v. *Norwich Union Fire and Life Insurance* [1989] 2 All E.R. 888).

"Event or events" within the Life Assurance Act 1774, s.2 did not include claims by employees against an employer (*Siu Yin Kwan* v. *Eastern Insurance Co.* [1994] 1 All E.R. 213).

EVIDENCE. "Evidence sufficient to justify proceedings" (Immigration Act 1971 (c. 77), s.28(1)(*a*)). Information given to a police officer over the telephone is not sufficient evidence to satisfy the requirements of this section (*Enaas* v. *Dovey*, *The Times*, November 25, 1986).

"Evidence on which the prosecution proposes to rely" (Police and Criminal Evidence Act 1984 (c. 60), s.78) includes all the evidence which might be introduced into a trial, including evidence of confessions and admissions (*R.* v. *Mason (Carl)* [1988] 1 W.L.R. 139).

"Does not give oral evidence" (Criminal Justice Act 1988 (c. 33), s.23(3)(*b*)). Refusing to continue giving evidence through fear could come within the meaning of this phrase (*R.* v. *Ashford Justices, ex p. Hilden* [1993] 2 W.L.R. 529).

"The discovery by the authority of evidence" (Wildlife and Countryside Act 1981 (c. 69), s.53(3)(*c*)). In this section "evidence" is to be given its ordinary meaning, and is not to be restricted to new evidence or evidence not previously considered (*Mayhew (Margaret)* v. *Secretary of State for the Environment* (1992) 65 P. & C.R. 344).

(9) "Evidence in support of an alibi" (Criminal Justice Act 1967 (c. 80), s.11)). Evidence, whether from a defendant or from any other person, which merely indicated that the defendant was not present at the place where an offence was committed was not "evidence in support of an alibi" within this section. Evidence in support of an alibi has to be evidence that this defendant was at some other place (*R.* v. *Johnson (Aldin)* [1995] 2 Cr.App.R.1).

"Other evidence," see OTHER.

Under the Criminal Justice (International Co-operation) Act 1990 (c. 5), s.4 "evidence" included the evidence to be used at trial and also any documents which may lead to the discovery of further evidence (*R.* v. *Secretary of State for the Home Department, ex p. Finninvest SpA* [1996] 12 C.L. 146).

(Criminal Procedure (Attendance of Witnesses) Act 1965 (c. 69), s.2 and Magistrates Courts Act 1980 (c. 43), s.97). To be "material evidence" documents must not only be relevant and admissible to the issues arising in the criminal proceedings. Documents which were desired merely for the purposes of cross-examination were not admissible and so not material either for the purposes of either s.2 of the 1965 Act or s.97 of the 1980 Act (*R.* v. *Azmy* [1996] 7 Med. L.R. 415).

EXAMINE. "Examined . . . by an immigration officer" (Immigration Act 1971 (c. 77), Sched. 2, para. 2(3)). The mere fact that a person had passed through immigration controls in the normal way did not mean that he had been "examined" in accordance with this paragraph (*R.* v. *Secretary of State for the Home Department, ex p. Kumar* [1990] Imm. A.R. 265).

"Examination (including any further examination)" (Immigration Act 1971 (c. 77), Sched. 2, para. 6(1)). "Examination" of a person for the purposes of this paragraph includes the period taken to make exquiries about that person as well as any initial and subsequent interview (*Labiche (Francis)* v. *Secretary of State for the Home Department* [1991] Imm. A.R. 263).

EXCEPTIONAL. "Exceptional hardship" (Transport Act 1981 (c. 56), s.19(6)(*b*)). The approach to cases involving "exceptional hardship" within the meaning of this section is not the same as for "special reasons" cases under s.93(1) of the Road Traffic Act 1972 (c. 20). It was not necessary, therefore, for justices to hear evidence in mitigation before deciding whether or not to disqualify a driver because he might otherwise suffer exceptional hardship (*Owen* v. *Jones* [1988] RTR 102).

(11) "Exceptional need" (Supplementary Benefits Act 1976 (c. 71), s.3(1) as amended by Sched. 2 to the Social Security Act 1980 (c. 30)). The cost of conveying the unemployed claimant's two children from the home of his ex-wife, who had custody, to his own for the purpose of weekend access, was not an "exceptional need" within the meaning of this section (*Vaughan* v. *Social Security Adjudication Officer* (1987) 151 J.P.N. 15. See also SINGLE PAYMENT.

"Exceptional circumstances of that case" (Powers of Criminal Courts Act 1973 (c. 62), s.22(2)(*b*), as substituted by s.5(1) of the Criminal Justice Act 1991 (c. 53)). What are exceptional circumstances depends on the facts of each individual case. However, taken on their own or in combination, good character, youth and an early plea was not "exceptional circumstances" justifying a suspended sentence (*R.* v. *Okinikan* [1993] 1 W.L.R. 173). The expression "exceptional circumstances" in this section is sufficiently wide to allow the court to take into account all the relevant circumstances surrounding the offence, the offender and the background circumstances (*R.* v. *Sanderson* [1993] Crim.L.R. 224; *R.* v. *Lowery* [1993] Crim.L.R. 225).

A person's good character, his remorse and the dependence upon him of his wife and mother-in-law were not "exceptional circumstances" to justify the suspension of a sentence for unlawful wounding (*R.* v. *Sanderson* [1993] Crim.L.R. 224). The circumstances of a sub-postmistress who falsified accounts over two years, to repay loans taken out to purchase the post office business, who was now bankrupt, with an ill husband, were not "exceptional" to justify the suspension of a sentence imposed for theft and false accounting (*R.* v. *Robinson (Yvonne)* (1993) 14 Cr.App.R. 559). The health problems of a defendant who suffered from a paranoid psychosis which had affected his concentration and judgment at the time of the commission of the offence constituted an "exceptional circumstance" which justified the suspension of a sentence (*R.* v. *Ullah Khan* [1993] Crim.L.R. 982). A decision by a local authority that it was in the interests of the children to be rehabilitated to their natural family was an "exceptional circumstance" which justified the suspension of a sentence imposed for assault on a child occasioning actual bodily harm, even though assault on a defenceless child always a serious matter (*R.* v. *Cameron* (*John McDougall*) (1993) 14 Cr.App.R. 5801). The theft of £37,000 by a daughter from her mother over eight years while she was looking after her mother who was ill and cantankerous, and where some of the money was spent on the mother amounted to "exceptional circumstances" to justify the suspension of any sentence (*R.* v. *Edney* [1994] 15 Cr.App.R.(S.) 889).

No legal definition could or should be given for the words "exceptional circumstances of the case" in reg. 3(4)(*c*)(iii) of the Legal Aid in Family Proceedings (Remuneration) Regulations (S.I. 1991 No. 2038) and must include the circumstances of a particular case at whatever level of court it was heard. "Exceptional circumstances" could include innate difficulties in communicating with the client, conflict of detailed expert evidence, a hearing in excess of two days without counsel and where the child had instructed his own solicitor and conflict between the guardian of *ad litem* and the child. A solicitor-advocate's membership of the Law Society's Children Panel was an "exceptional circumstance" in care proceedings which gave the taxing officer discretion to allow a larger amount of costs than that specified in the relevant costs' regulations (*Children Act 1989* (*Taxation of Costs*), *Re;* [1994] 2 F.L.R. 934).

Exceptional circumstances of the case" (Legal Aid in Criminal and Care Proceedings (Costs) Regulations 1989 (No. 343), Sched. 1, para. 3(*b*)). In determining whether, within the meaning of this paragraph, circumstances are "exceptional" comparison should be made with the generality of criminal cases, and should not be restricted to comparisons with other similar cases (*R.* v. *Legal Aid Board, ex p. R.M. Broudie (a Firm), The Times,* April 11, 1994).

(Housing Act 1985, (c. 68), s.65). A complaint of racial abuse did not amount to an exceptional circumstance which justified the pursuit of an appeal against the offer of accommodation before the offeree moved into the premises (*R.* v. *Mayor and Burgesses of Newham London Borough Council, ex p. Begum* [1996] 7. C.L. 294).

(Crime (Sentences) Act 1997 (c. 43), s.21). "Exceptional" meant out of the ordinary, unusual, special or uncommon. There were no exceptional circumstances to avoid the imposition of a mandatory life sentence where a defendant had committed an offence when a juvenile some 18 years before, where the evidence demonstrated that he was a threat to the public, despite differences between the two offences and a good record maintained in between (*R.* v. *Kelly (Edward), The Times,* December 29, 1998).

EXCESSIVE. "Damages . . . are excessive" (Courts and Legal Services Act 1990 (c. 41), s.8(1)). A jury award of libel damages which was disproportionately large in comparison to the harm suffered by the plaintiff was held to be "excessive", within the meaning of this section (*Rantzen* v. *Mirror Group Newspapers, The Times,* April 6, 1993).

A jury award would have to be twice the amount a reasonable jury might be expected to award on similar facts to be "excessive" (*Currie* v. *Kilmarnock and Loudoun District Council* (I.H.), *The Scotsman,* December 1, 1995).

EXCHANGE. (7) "Exchange contract" (Bretton Woods Fund Agreement Order 1946 (No. 36), Art. VIII, s.2(*b*)) is to be interpreted narrowly, and is confined to contracts to exchange the currency of one country for that of another. It does not include contracts entered into in connection with sale of goods which require currency conversion in order to effect payment (*United City Merchants (Investments)* v. *Royal Bank of Canada* [1983] 1 A.C. 168). In *Mansouri* v. *Singh* [1986] 1 W.L.R. 1393 the Court of Appeal remitted to the judge for retrial the question whether an agreement whereby the plaintiff bought airline tickets in Iran with Iranian currency, had them sent to England, and obtained a sterling refund, was an "exchange contract" contrary to the Bretton Woods Agreement.

"Exchange of contracts." See CONTRACT.

EXCLUDE. "Excluded material" (Police and Criminal Evidence Act 1984 (c. 60), s.11(1)). Hospital records of patients' admission and discharge from hospital were "excluded material" within the meaning of this section as they related to the physical or mental health of persons who "could be identified from them" (s.12) (*R.* v. *Cardiff Crown Court, ex p. Kellam, The Times*, May 3, 1993).

EXCLUSION. (Trade Union and Labour Relations (Consolidation) Act 1992 (c. 52), s.174). The word "exclusion" in s.174(1) of the 1992 Act was limited to a refusal to admit a person to membership of a trade union and did not cover a mere suspension of the privileges of trade union membership (*National Association of Colliery Overmen, Deputies and Shotfirers (NACODS)* v. *Gluchowski* [1996] IRLR 252).

EXCLUSIVE JURISDICTION. (Civil Jurisdiction and Judgments Act 1982 (c. 27), Sched. 1, art. 17). The parties to an "exclusive jurisdiction" agreement were presumed to have intended that all matters in dispute would be tried in one jurisidiction (*Continental Bank NA* v. *Aeakos Cia Naviera SA* [1994] 2 All E.R. 540).

EXCLUSIVE OCCUPATION. See OCCUPIER.

EXCURSION OR TOUR. Stat. Def., Transport Act 1985 (c. 67), s.137.

EXCUSE. See LAWFUL EXCUSE.

EXECUTION. (25) "In the execution of his duty" (Police Act 1964 (c. 48), s.51). An arrest made at a time when it was not yet practicable to inform the accused of the grounds for the arrest did not become unlawful under s.28(3) of the Police and Criminal Evidence Act 1984 (c. 60), and was therefore made by police officers acting in the "execution" of their duties (*DPP* v. *Hawkins* [1988] 1 W.L.R. 1166). It is an essential element in the offence of an assault on a police officer in the execution of his duty that the officer's actions be lawful (*Riley* v. *DPP* (1990) 90 Cr.App.R. 14). A police officer who, on intervening in a fight between two persons, was assaulted by one of them, was still acting in the execution of his duty when he arrested that person notwithstanding that at the time the police officer was unknowingly a trespasser (*R.* v. *Lamb* [1990] Crim.L.R. 58). Where, during a demonstration, the accused was seen obstructing a uniformed (but unidentified) police officer, the justices were entitled to draw the inference that the unidentified officer was acting "in the execution of his duty" (*Plowden* v. *DPP* [1991] Crim.L.R. 850).

The restraint of a person by a police officer acting under the mistaken belief that the person was under arrest did not amount to the police officer acting under a duty so that any resulting struggle or striking of the officer was not an assault on a police officer in the "execution of his duty" (Police Act 1964 (c. 48), s.51(1)) (*DPP* v. *Kerr, The Times*, August 5, 1994).

(14) For the purposes of the Legal Aid Act 1988 (c. 34), s.17(3)(*b*) a charging order was a form of execution and therefore prohibited under the section (*Parr* v. *Smith* [1995] 2 All E.R. 1031).

(23) "Procures the execution of a valuable security" (Theft Act 1968 (c. 60), s.20(2)). The cashing of a cheque by a bank did not constitute the execution of a valuable security within the meaning of this section. "Execution" means doing something to the face of a document, such as signing it, or the due performance of all formalities necessary to give it validity. It does not mean "give effect to" (*R.* v. *Kassim* [1991] 3 W.L.R. 254). A Clearing House Automated Payment System order, by which a bank makes an electronic transfer of money, is a valuable security, and is "executed" when the bank official keys the transfer into the computer and completes the appropriate form (*R.* v. *King* [1991] 3 W.L.R. 246).

(27) "In the execution of his office" (Justices of the Peace Act 1979 (c. 55), s.52). A justice of the peace was held to be acting in the execution of his office within the meaning of this section notwithstanding that he was acting in excess of jurisdiction (*R.* v. *Waltham Forest Justices, ex p. Solanke* [1986] 3 W.L.R. 315).

"Execution . . . in respect of the debt . . . has been returned unsatisfied" (Insolvency Act 1986 (c. 45), s.268). A writ of fieri facias returned by a bailiff endorsed to the effect that he had failed to gain access to the debtor's property on a number of occasions with a view to seizing goods and chattels did not amount to an execution of the judgment debt which was unsatisfied so as to justify the institution of bankruptcy proceedings against the debtor. An execution would have to take place before s.268(1)(b) could apply (*Re a Debtor (No. 340 of 1992), ex p. The Debtor v. First National Commercial Bank plc* [1996] 2 All E.R. 211).

EXECUTIVE. Stat. Def., Trade Union and Labour Relations (Consolidation) Act 1992 (c. 52), s.119.

EXEMPT. "Exempted disposal" (Housing Act 1985 (c. 68), s.160(1)). The sale of the former matrimonial home, a council house jointly purchased by the parties, following a consent order made in ancillary matrimonial proceedings was not an "exempted disposal" for the purposes of this section, and the parties were therefore required to account to the local authority in respect of the discount they had received on acquiring the property (*R.* v. *Rushmoor Borough Council, ex p. Barrett* [1988] 2 W.L.R. 1271).

EXERCISE. A council tenant's right to buy under the Housing Act 1980 (c. 51) was not only "exercised" (within the meaning of s.2(4)(*b*) and Sched. 1, Pt. 11) when he gave the first notice of his intention, but was "exercised" each time he took a step towards the implementation of that right (*Enfield London Borough Council* v. *McKeon* (1986) 130 S.J. 504).

For the purposes of s.44 of the Compulsory Purchase Act 1965 (c. 56) powers of compulsory purchase were duly "exercised," within the requisite period of three years from the date upon which the compulsory purchase orders became operative, by service of notices under s.3 of the Compulsory Purchase (Vesting Declarations) Act 1981 (c. 66) (*Westminster City Council* v. *Quereschi* (1990) 60 P. & C.R. 380).

EX FACTORY. The term "ex factory People's Republic of China" in a contract of insurance took effect in the place where the goods were produced rather than when they left the processing plant (*Wunsche Handelsgesellschaft International MBH* v. *Tai Ping Insurance Co. Ltd* [1998] 2 Lloyd's Rep. 8).

EXHIBITION. "Exhibition of moving pictures," see MOVING PICTURES.

EXIST. "Existing liability to make a payment" (Theft Act 1978 (c. 31), s.2(1)). A Consumer Credit Act 1974 regulated agreement that was improperly executed and only enforceable with the leave of the court was an "existing liability" within the meaning of s.2(1) notwithstanding the absence of such leave (*R.* v. *Modupe* (1992) 11 Tr.L.R. 59).

EXPECTED. "Expected to realise" (Land Compensation Act 1961 (c. 33), s.5(2)). Where the value of land is being assessed by reference to this section the words "expected to realise" refer to the expectations of properly qualified persons who have informed themselves of all the particulars ascertainable about the property, its capabilities and the likely demand for it (*Church Cottage Investments* v. *Hillingdon London Borough* [1990] 15 E.G. 51).

EXPEDITION. See DUE EXPEDITION.

EXPEDITIOUS MEANS. Oral rejection of documents amounted to notification by "expeditious means" for the purposes of the Uniform Customs and Practice for Documentary Credits ICC No. 400 Art. 16 (*Seaconsfar Far East Ltd* v. *Bank Markazi Jomhouri Islami Iran* [1997] 2 Lloyd's Rep. 89).

EXPENDITURE. "Expenditure reasonably incurred by the assignor" (Rent Act 1977 (c. 42), s.120(3)(*b*)). The exception contained in this subsection is not restricted to expenditure incurred after the grant of the lease (*Steele* v. *McMahon* [1990] 44 E.G. 65).

"The expenditure the authority estimates it will incur" (Competition and Service (Utilities) Act 1992 (c. 43), s.43(2)(*a*)). An amount deducted by the Secretary of State from the revenue support grant to a council to recoup sums in respect of the maintenance grant made by central government to grant-maintained schools in the council's area constituted "expenditure" by the council within the meaning of s.43(2)(*a*) (*R.* v. *Secretary of State for Wales, ex p. Gwent County Council, The Times,* March 16, 1994).

(Drug Trafficking Offences Act 1986 (c. 32), s.2(2)(3)). "Expenditure" meant any form of disbursement including a gift (*R.* v. *Clark (Paul)* [1997] 1 W.L.R. 557).

EXPENSES. "Expenses . . . incurred by him in . . . defence" (Costs in Criminal Cases Act 1973 (c. 14), s.1(3)). A solicitor's fees and disbursements incurred in acting for himself in defending a criminal charge before a magistrates' court were "expenses" within the meaning of this section (*R.* v. *Stafford, Stone and Eccleshall Magistrates' Court, ex p. Robinson* [1988] 1 All E.R. 430).

(International Convention on Salvage 1989, art. 14). "Expenses . . . incurred" by a salvor denoted amounts either disbursed or borne rather than earned as profits, so that an award of special compensation which was intended to recompense or reimburse a salvor for his expenses was not intended to yield or be a source of profit (*Semco Salvage and Marine Pte Ltd* v. *Lancer Navigation Co. Ltd* [1997] 1 All E.R. 502).

EXPERIENCE. "Persons of experience in education" (Education Act 1944 (c. 31), Sched. 1, Part II, para. 5). These words are to be given their ordinary and natural meaning and do not require that every member of the education committee of a local education authority should have undergone training or experience as a teacher (*R.* v. *Croydon London Borough Council, ex p. Leney* (1987) 85 L.G.R. 466).

"Experience" is not a finite definition but a continuing test and meant a real and sufficient fund of experience and not merely having encountered a particular subject or topic (*R.* v. *Wandsworth London Borough Council, ex p. M* [1997] 11 C.L. 240).

EXPERT. "Expert advice" (Limitation Act 1980 (c. 58), s.14(3)(*b*)). A party's solicitor is not an "expert" for the purposes of this section which is directed to experts in the sense of expert witnesses (*Fowell* v. *National Coal Board, The Times,* May 28, 1986).

"Expert" within the Legal Aid Act 1988 (c. 34), s.22(2)(*d*) qualified cross-examination and not the nature of the witness being cross-examined (*R.* v. *Liverpool City Magistrates, ex p. McGhee* [1993] Crim.L.R. 609).

Special knowledge of a police officer, not held by a jury, amounted to "expert evidence" (*R.* v. *Leaney, R.* v. *Steele* and *R.* v. *Howe* considered) (*R.* v. *Clare and Peach, The Times,* April 7, 1995).

(R.S.C., Ord. 40). There was nothing in Ord. 40 to restrict its use to cases in which the assistance of a court expert was required in order to resolve questions of a scientific, technical or subsidiary nature if the appointment was otherwise appropriate, nor did the expert have to have direct firsthand knowledge but was to be regarded as an ordinary valuation expert who having made careful and appropriate inquiries was entitled to rely on what reasonably appeared to him to be reliable information (*Abbey National Mortgages plc* v. *Key Surveyors Nationwide Ltd* [1996] 3 All E.R. 1814).

Stat. Def., Companies Act 1985 (c. 6), s.62; "a person appearing to the Secretary of State to have knowledge or experience which would be relevant in determining the question of fact requiring special expertise" (Social Security Act 1998 (c. 14), s.11(3)); Social Security Contributions (Transfer of Functions, etc.) Act 1999 (c. 2), s.9(3).

EXPLOITATION. "Exploitation of a tangible or intangible asset" (Sixth Directive No. 77/388/EEC of the Council of May 17, 1977, articles 2, 4, 17). A holding company which did not carry out any other activities than those which were concerned with the holding of shares in various subsidiaries were not exploiting an asset within the meaning of articles 2 and 4, and were not, therefore, a "taxable person" within the meaning of article 17 (*Polysar Investments Netherlands BV* v. *Inspecteur der Invoerrechten en Accijnzen te Arnhem, The Times,* October 3, 1991).

EXPLOSION. (2) The fracturing and shattering of the casing and impeller of a compressed air blower, caused by a piece of the impeller breaking off and flying outwards by centrifugal force, was not an "explosion" within the terms of an insurance policy (*Commonwealth Smelting* v. *Guardian Royal Exchange Assurance* [1986] 1 Lloyd's Rep. 121).

EXPLOSIVE. "Explosive substance" (Offences against the Person Act 1861 (c. 100), s.29). A petrol bomb, made from a milk bottle containing petrol and air and a wick was held to be an "explosive substance" within the meaning of this section (*R.* v. *Howard* [1993] Crim.L.R. 213).

Stat. Def., Aviation and Maritime Security Act 1990 (c. 31), s.46; Northern Ireland (Emergency Provisions) Act 1996 (c. 22), s.58.

EXPOSE. "Exposing his person" (Vagrancy Act 1824 (c. 83), s.4). For a defendant to be convicted of an offence under this section it was not necessary for there to be direct evidence that his penis was seen by a witness. There merely had to be evidence from which it could be inferred that at the material time his penis was exposed (*Hunt* v. *DPP* [1990] Crim.L.R. 812).

"Exposed to risks to their health or safety" (Health and Safety at Work etc. Act 1974 (c. 37), s.3(1)). For the purposes of this section it is sufficient for the prosecution to prove that members of the public were exposed to a possibility of danger. It is not necessary to show that there had actually been a danger (*R.* v. *Board of Trustees of the Science Museum* [1993] 1 W.L.R. 1171).

EXTENSION. A wall can be an "extension" to a building under the Town and Country Planning General Development Order 1988 (No. 1813), even though it does not enlarge the owner's living space (*Richmond upon Thames London Borough Council* v. *Secretary of State for the Environment* [1991] 2 P.L.R. 107).

EXTORTIONATE. (Consumer Credit Act 1974 (c. 39), s.138). The unconscionable conduct of a third party cannot of itself render the terms of a commercial loan "extortionate" within the meaning of this section (*Coldunell* v. *Gallon* [1986] 1 All E.R. 429). A credit bargain, charging interest at 25.785 per cent. per annum over 10 years, was not "extortionate" within the meaning of this section where the borrower had been warned of the cost of the credit and where the risk taken by the lender justified the rate of interest charged and the rate was not out of line with that charged by other lending bodies (*Davies* v. *Directloans* [1986] 1 W.L.R. 823).

EXTRADITION. "Extradition arrangements"; "extradition crime"; "extradition procedures." Stat Def., Criminal Justice Act 1988 (c. 33), s.1; Extradition Act 1989 (c. 33), ss.2, 3.

F

FACILITATE. "Calculated to facilitate . . . the discharge of . . . their functions" (Local Government Act 1972 (c. 70), s.111(1)). See FUNCTIONS.

FACILITATING. "Facilitating the commission of any offence" (Powers of Criminal Courts Act 1973 (c. 62), s.43(1)(*a*)). A car used by a burglar can be said to be "facilitating" the commission of his offence and could therefore properly be the subject of a forfeiture order under this section (*R. v. Stratton, The Times*, January 15, 1988).

A car which was driven by the defendant in such a way to block the passage of the victim's car, forcing it to stop immediately prior to the assault committed by the defendant was "facilitating the commission of an offence" (*R. v. Patel (Rajesh)* [1995] RTR 421).

"Facilitating the entry into the United Kingdom of . . . illegal entrant" (Immigration Act 1971 (c. 77), s.25(1)). The provision of false documents to those wishing to travel to the U.K., where the documents were not used as the recipients sought political asylum instead, did not constitute the offence of facilitating the entry of illegal immigrants (*R. v. Naillie; R. v. Kanesarajah* [1993] 2 W.L.R. 927).

FACILITIES. Stat. Def., National Health Service (Private Finance) Act 1997 (c. 56), s.1(5).

FACILITY. "Facilities for the common use of all the occupants" (Wireless Telegraphy (Broadcast Licence Charges and Exemptions) Regulations 1984 (No. 1053), Sched. 2, para. 1(*b*)). The provision of a housing steward responsible for the welfare of the occupants of "accommodation for residential care" provided by the local authority was a "facility" shared by all the occupants for the purposes of this regulation (*R. v. Secretary of State for the Home Department, ex p. Kirklees Borough Council, The Times*, June 24, 1987).

"Facilities and advantages" (Value Added Taxes Act 1983 (c. 55), s.47). "Facilities" were means, resources or conveniences, which made its easier to achieve a purpose, while "advantages" were benefits or gains (*Customs and Excise Commissioners v. British Field Sports Society* [1998] STC 315).

FACTS. "Facts relevant to [the] cause of action" (Limitation Act 1980 (c. 58), s.32A). "Facts relevant to the cause of action" in s.32A of the 1980 Act referred to the relevant facts which a plaintiff had to prove to establish a prima facie cause of action and did not extend to facts which might rebut any possible defence (*C. v. Mirror Group Newspapers* [1997] 1 W.L.R. 131).

FAIL. (16) "Fails to provide a specimen when required" (Road Traffic Act 1972 (c. 20), s.8(7), as substituted by Transport Act 1981 (c. 56), Sched. 8; now Road Traffic Act 1988 (c. 52), s.7(6)). A person who refuses to provide a second specimen of breath when lawfully required to do so commits an offence under this section notwithstanding that the first specimen he supplied may have been within the prescribed limits and that he could not, therefore, be convicted of the offence of driving with excess alcohol in his blood (*Stepniewski v. Commissioner of Police of the Metropolis* [1985] RTR

330). An accused who the justices were satisfied had tried as hard as he could, albeit unsuccessfully, to provide a specimen of breath for analysis was not guilty of failure under this section (*Cotgrove* v. *Cooney* [1987] RTR 124). A motorist who refused to provide a specimen of blood was guilty of failing to provide a specimen under this section, notwithstanding that he had offered to supply a urine sample instead (*Grix* v. *Chief Constable of Kent* [1987] RTR 193). To be guilty of failing to supply specimens under this section a motorist must have been warned of the penal consequences of refusal and to have understood the warning (*Chief Constable of Avon and Somerset Constabulary* v. *Singh* [1988] RTR 107). A motorist who, following a positive roadside breath test, had been taken to a police station, where the breath testing device was inoperative, and had there refused to provide a blood specimen, was not guilty under this section because the officer concerned had omitted to inform him of the urine sample alternative (*DPP* v. *Gordon* [1990] RTR 29). A defendant who neither refused nor agreed to provide a specimen of breath, but remained silent, was held to have failed to provide a specimen within the meaning of this section (*Campbell* v. *DPP* [1989] RTR 256). The offence of failure to provide a breath specimen without reasonable excuse under s.7(6) of the 1988 Act is a single offence (*Shaw* v. *DPP*; *R.* v. *Bournemouth Crown Court, ex p. Yates* (1992) 142 New L.J. 1683). Motorists were not guilty of failing to provide specimens for analysis in circumstances where they were not given opportunities to express their own preferences as to which samples, blood or urine, should be taken (*Holding* v. *DPP* [1992] RTR 192; *Renshaw* v. *DPP* [1992] RTR 186). The offence of failing to provide a speciment of breath does not depend upon whether the motorist was driving or attempting to drive with excess alcohol, or being in charge while unfit (*Crampsie* v. *DPP* [1993] RTR 383).

FAIR AND REASONABLE. (4) (Unfair Contract Terms Act 1977 (c. 50), s.11(3)). Where a surveyor engaged by a building society to carry out a visual inspection of a property negligently failed to discover a structural defect which he would have discovered had he exercised proper care, it was not "fair and reasonable" to allow him to rely on general disclaimers of liability for negligence contained in his report and in the mortgage application (*Smith* v. *Bush, Eric S. (a firm)*; *Harris* v. *Wyre Forest District Council* [1989] 2 W.L.R. 790).

A provision in an option for renewal of a lease that the rent was to be "a fair and reasonable market rent at the time" envisaged the rent at which the demised premises might reasonably be expected to be let in the open market (*ARC* v. *Schofield* [1990] E.G. 113).

"Fair and reasonable" (Truck Act 1896 (c.14), s.1(1)(*d*)), see FINE.

FAIR DEALING. "Fair dealing . . . reporting current events" (Copyright Act 1988 (c. 48), s.30(2)). The defence of fair dealing under this section is not limited to current events in general news programmes. The 1990 World Cup football finals were "current events" and the showing by one television broadcasting company of film of another broadcasting company's live broadcasts was "fair dealing" (*British Broadcasting Corporation* v. *British Satellite Broadcasting* [1991] 3 W.L.R. 174).

The defence of "fair dealing", while an objective one, depended on the user's subjective intentions for the material concerned (*Pro Sieben A.G.* v. *Carlton Television Ltd* [1999] 1 W.L.R. 605).

FAIR RATE. Costs recovered by salvors under the International Convention on Salvage 1989, Art. 14(3) did not include an element for profit but did cover all expenses incurred during the salvage operation including the costs of having the resources required for the operation readily available (*Semco Salvage and Marine Pte. Ltd* v. *Lancer Navigation Co. Ltd (The Nagasaki Spirit)* [1997] 1 All E.R. 502).

FAIR RENT. (Rent Act 1977 (c. 42), s.70). The test of what is a "fair rent" in a climate where there was no scarcity of comparable rented accommodation is the fair market rent (*B.T.E.* v. *Merseyside and Cheshire Rent Assessment Committee and Jones* (1991) 24 H.L.R. 514).

Fair rents should be assessed by reference to market rent comparables where they were available, rather than already registered fair rents unless the market rents approach was established to be wrong (*Curtis* v. *London Rent Assessment Committee* [1998] 3 W.L.R. 1427).

FAIRNESS. "Fairness of the proceedings," see ADVERSE EFFECT.

FALSE. "Representation which he knows to be false," see REPRESENTATION.

FALSE IMPRISONMENT. A lawfully detained prisoner retained such residual liberty as was left to him under the provisions of the Prison Rules 1964 (No. 388) and to confine a prisoner, without lawful authority, in a segregation cell, or in a strip cell, deprived him of that residual liberty and was false imprisonment (*Weldon* v. *Home Office* [1990] 3 W.L.R. 465). A defendant was not liable on a claim in damages for false imprisonment where he merely gave information to the prosecuting authority, which effected the plaintiff's arrest and detention and had not himself instigated or procured it (*Davidson* v. *Chief Constable of the North Wales Police, The Times*, April 26, 1993).

An intention to frighten a victim so that she could not move or escape was sufficient to found a charge of false imprisonment (*R.* v. *James (Anthony David)*, *The Times*, October 2, 1997).

FALSE INSTRUMENT. "An instrument is false" (Forgery and Counterfeiting Act 1981 (c. 45), s.9(1)). The accused stole a cheque made out in favour of an individual, and with it opened a building society account in the name of the individual. The withdrawal form which the accused made and signed in the name of the individual, and then presented to the building society, was held not to be a "false instrument" within the meaning of this section (*R.* v. *More* [1987] 3 All E.R. 825).

The gaining of unauthorised access to a computer system by means of the improper use of passwords or control numbers does not amount to the making of an "instrument" within the meaning of s.8(1) of the Forgery and Counterfeiting Act 1981 (c. 45) (*R.* v. *Gold*; *R.* v. *Shifreen* [1988] 2 W.L.R. 984).

FALSE REPRESENTATION. (H.C. 169, para. 13(a)). It is enough to constitute a "false representation" for the purposes of this paragraph if it had been made inaccurately rather than fraudulently (*Akhtar (Tahzeem)* v. *Immigration Appeal Tribunal* [1991] Imm. A.R. 326).

FALSE STATEMENT. "Makes a false statement" (Agriculture Act 1970 (c. 40), s.29(5)). For the purposes of this section the statement is) "made" at the time and place at which the addressee of the statement receives it (*Lawrence* v. *M.A.F.F.* [1992] Crim.L.R. 874).

FALSE TRADE DESCRIPTION. (2) (Trade Descriptions Act 1968 (c. 29), s.1). Where a motor dealer had applied the description "new" to motor cars registered previously in his name, it was open to the jury to find that a false trade description had been applied, although the cars concerned had been sold in mint condition and with low delivery mileage only (*R.* v. *Anderson* [1988] 2 W.L.R. 1017). A trade description applied to goods for sale can be "false" for the purposes of this section, even when it is scientifically correct, if it is likely to mislead a customer without specialised knowledge (*Dixons* v. *Barnett* (1989) 8 Tr. L. 37). An advertisement in a shop for a package of items was held to be a "false trade description" if some of the items were temporarily unavailable, unless the customer had been so informed at the time of purchase (*Denard* v. *Smith* [1991] 1 Crim.L.R. 63). An odometer reading can be a "trade description" within the meaning of this section (*Swithland Motors* v. *Peck* [1991] Crim.L.R. 386). A general disclaimer in an auction catalogue is ineffective to a charge of applying a false trade description to a particular item (*May* v. *Vincent* (1991) 10 Tr.L.R. 1). An odometer reading can be a false trade description notwithstanding the car was sold with a disclaimer on the invoice saying that that the reading was not warranted, and the purchaser was under no illusion as to the accuracy of the reading (*Southend Borough Council* v. *White* [1991] C.O.D. 345).

FALSIFY. "Falsifies . . . any document . . . required for any accounting purpose," see REQUIRE.

FAMILY. (14) "Member of the original tenant's family" (Rent Act 1977 (c. 42), Sched. 1, para. 3). A woman who had been residing with the tenant in what appeared to be a state of permanence and stability was held to be a protected member of his "family," notwithstanding that the relationship had existed for only two years (*Chios Investment Property Co.* v. *Lopez* [1988] 05 E.G. 57).

(14) "Member of the first successor's family" (Rent Act 1977 (c. 42), Sched. 1, para. 7). "Family" in this context has to be given its ordinary everyday meaning; so that a woman who had been living with the daughter of the original tenant was not a member of the daughter's "family," and was not, therefore, a protected tenant when the daughter died, notwithstanding that she had always been accepted by the family as a member and had lived in the house for 46 years (*Sefton Holdings* v. *Cairns* [1988] 20 H.L.R. 124).

A surviving partner in a stable and permanent homosexual relationship could not claim succession rights since the concept of family meant an entity bound together by ties of kinship, including adoptive status or marriage (*Fitzpatrick* v. *Sterling Housing Association* [1997] 4 All E.R. 991).

The objectives of the International Covenant on Civil and Political Rights 1966 required that "family" should be given a broad interpretation, so as to include all those comprising the family as understood in the society in question together with its cultural traditions (*Hopu* v. *France* 3 B.H.R.C. 597).

"Treated . . . as a child of the family," see CHILD.

Stat. Def., Finance Act 1985 (c. 54), Sched. 20, para. 1; Insolvency Act 1985 (c. 65), s.211; Social Security Act 1986 (c. 50), s.20(11); Social Security Contributions and Benefits Act 1992 (c. 4), s.137; Taxation of Chargeable Gains Act 1992 (c. 12), Sched. 6, para. 1(2); Jobseekers Act 1995 (c. 18), s.35(1)); Child Support Act 1995 (c. 34), s.10(7).

"Member of family," Stat. Def., Housing Act 1996 (c. 52), s.140(1).

"Immediate family," Stat. Def., Merchant Shipping (Fire Protection: Small Ships) Regulations 1998 (No. 1011), reg. 1(2).

FAMILY ASSOCIATION. (Housing Act 1996 (c. 52), s.199). The words "family association" were not restricted in s.199 and so could include an association where there was no blood tie or legal relationship (*Munting* v. *Hammersmith and Fulham LBC* [1998] 2 C.L. 361).

FAMILY COMPANY. Stat. Def., Finance Act 1985 (c. 54), Sched. 20, para. 1; Taxation of Chargeable Gains Act 1992 (c. 12), Sched. 6, para. 1(2)).

FAMILY LIFE. (European Convention on Human Rights, Art. 8). "Family life" under Art. 8 did not relate solely to families created by marriage (*X, Y and Z* v. *United Kingdom* (1997) 94 (17) L.S.Gaz. 25).

FAMILY PROCEEDINGS. (Children Act 1989 (c. 41), s.8). An application to the justices by a local authority under s.25 of the 1989 Act for an order that a child in their care be placed in secure accommodation was held to be a family proceeding within the meaning of s.8 (*R.* v. *Oxfordshire County Council* [1992] 3 W.L.R. 88).

FARM. "Farmland," "farming." Stat. Def., Income and Corporation Taxes Act 1988 (c. 1), s. 832.

FAVOURABLE. "Less favourable to the woman" (Equal Pay Act 1970 (c. 41), s.1(2)(*c*)). In considering whether any term of a woman's contract was "less favourable" to her than a term of a similar kind in men's contracts it is necessary to compare the terms and conditions of their respective contracts of employment as a whole and not just their basic wage and overtime rates (*Hayward* v. *Cammell Laird Shipbuilders* (*No.* 2) [1987] 3 W.L.R. 20).

"Less favourably than he treats . . . other persons" (Race Relations Act 1976 (c. 74), s.1(1)(*a*)). Acts designed to discourage an applicant from continuing with an application for employment, based on grounds of race or religion, were capable of amounting to treatment less favourable than that given to other persons (*Simon* v. *Brimham Associates* [1987] I.C.R. 596).

FERTILITY SERVICES. Stat. Def., Human Fertilisation and Embryology Act 1990 (c. 37), s.3A added by Criminal Justice and Public Order Act 1994 (c. 33), s.156.

FILM. Stat. Def., Films Act 1985 (c. 21), Sched. 1; Copyright, Designs and Patents Act 1988 (c. 48), s.5.

FINAL. "Pending the final determination" (Town and Country Planning Act 1971 (c. 78), s.88(10) as added by the Schedule to the Local Government and Planning (Amendment) Act 1981 (c. 41)). An appeal under s.246 of the 1971 Act is a part of the s.88 appeals procedure and not necessarily "final" for the purposes of subsection (10) (*R.* v. *Kuxhaus* [1988] 2 W.L.R. 1005).

(Asylum and Immigration Appeals Act 1993 (c. 23), s.9). The remittance of a case for a fresh hearing did not amount to a "final determination" within the meaning of s.9(1) and consequently there was a right of appeal from that decision (*R.* v. *Secretary of State for the Home Department, ex p. Kara (Hussein)* [1995] Imm.A.R. 584).

FINANCIAL ASSISTANCE. Stat. Def., Companies Act 1985 (c. 6), s.152.

FINANCIAL RESOURCES. "Other financial resources" (Matrimonial Causes Act 1973 (c. 18), s.25(1)(*a*), as amended by s.3 of the Matrimonial and Family Proceedings Act 1984 (c. 42)). Assets held outside the jurisdiction on discretionary trusts in favour of one spouse were "other financial resources" which could properly be taken into account in considering the other spouse's application in matrimonial proceedings for financial relief under ss.23 and 24 of the Act (*Browne* v. *Browne* [1989] 1 F.L.R. 291). Funds held on discretionary trusts were "other financial resources" within the meaning of this section (*J.* v. *J.*, (*C intervening*) [1989] 1 All E.R. 1121). The word "resources" in s.25 is unqualified and the court, when considering appropriate financial provision, should take into account all the available resources, includng after-acquired assets where relevant (*Schuller* v. *Schuller* [1990] 2 F.L.R. 193). An award of damages for serious personal injuries to a husband was a "financial resource" for the purposes of this section (*Wagstaff* v. *Wagstaff* [1992] 1 All E.R. 275).

FINANCIAL TRADER. Stat. Def., Finance Act 1994 (c. 9), s.177(1).

FINANCIAL YEAR. Stat. Def., Companies Act 1985 (c. 6), s.742; Companies Act 1989 (c. 40), s.3.

FINE. "For or in respect of any fine" (Truck Act 1896 (c. 44), s.1). A contract of employment which provided under its disciplinary rules for the deduction of losses from the wages of an employee, but which failed to provide for any means of ascertaining the amount of the loss in circumstances where the employee was in a position to check the calculation, was a contract "for or in respect of any fine" within the meaning of this section. As the deductions were entirely at the arbitrary discretion of the company the amounts of the fines, £20 per week on one occasion, could not be regarded as "fair and reasonable" within the meaning of s.1(1)(*d*) (*Sealand*

Petroleum v. *Barratt* [1986] 1 W.L.R. 700). "Fine" in s.1 bore its natural meaning of financial loss agreed upon in the case of non-fulfilment of some contractual obligation, and punishment did not have to be its predominant characteristic or purpose. Thus deductions from an employee's wages pursuant to an agreement to make good losses, whether or not caused by his acts or omissions, are "fines" within the meaning of this section (*Bristow* v. *City Petroleum Co.* [1987] 1 W.L.R. 529).

(Magistrates' Courts Act 1980 (c. 43), s.35). Back-duty, due to be paid by an accused guilty of keeping a vehicle on the road without an excise licence, was not a "fine" within the meaning of this section (*Patterson* v. *Charlton* [1986] RTR 18).

Stat. Def., Criminal Justice Act 1991 (c. 53), s.24(4).

FINGERPRINTS. Stat. Def., "includes palm prints" (Armed Forces Act 1996 (c. 46), s.11(4)).

FIRE. "Fire" in a marine insurance policy was not confined to accidental fire but included, at least, a fire started deliberately by a stranger to the insurance contract (*Schiffshypothekenbank zu Livebeck* v. *Compton* (*The Alexion Hope*) [1988] 1 F.T.L.R. 270).

FIREARM. (2) (3) A revolver with six chambers from which pellets could be shot by the release of carbon dioxide gas from a cylinder, and which was capable of causing injury from which death might result, was held to be a "lethal weapon" and therefore a "firearm" within the meaning of ss.1(1)(*a*) and 57(1) of the Firearms Act 1968 (c. 27), but not an "air weapon" (*q.v.*) within s.1(3)(*b*) (*R.* v. *Thorpe* [1987] 1 W.L.R. 383).

Neither the lack of any explosion or detonation in firing nor that of a continuous barrel precluded a spear gun from being a lethal barrelled weapon and so a "firearm" within the Firearms Act 1968 (c. 27), s.57(1) (*Boyd* v. *McGlennan*, 1964 S.L.T. 1148).

The decision of the Divisional Court in *Moore* v. *Goodeham* [1960] 1 W.L.R. 1308 [see Main Work p. 981] is not to be treated as authority for the proposition that every air rifle or airgun is a "firearm" within the meaning of these sections (*Grace* v. *DPP* [1989] Crim.L.R. 365). The discharger of signalling flares was capable of being a "firearm" within the meaning of s.57(1) (*R.* v. *Singh* [1989] Crim.L.R. 724).

Stat. Def., includes an air gun or air pistol (Northern Ireland (Emergency Provisions) Act 1996 (c. 22), s.58).

FIRST CONSIDERATION. (Matrimonial Causes Act 1973 (c. 18), s.25(1) as substituted by Matrimonial and Family Proceedings Act 1984 (c. 42), s.3). Whereas the welfare of any child is, by this section, to be the "first consideration" that does not mean that it should in all cases be paramount or overriding (*Suter* v. *Suter and Jones* [1987] 3 W.L.R. 9).

FIRST INSTANCE. "Court of first instance," see COURT.

FISH. Stat. Def., Food and Environment Protection Act 1985 (c. 48), s.24; Food Safety Act 1990 (c. 16), s.53.

FISHING. "Fishing boat." Stat. Def., Food and Environment Protection Act 1985 (c. 48), s.24.

"Fishing vessel." Stat. Def., Safety at Sea Act 1986 (c. 23), s.13; Merchant Shipping Act 1988 (c. 12), s.12.

FIT. Where a rent review clause provided for the determination of the open market rent on the assumption that the premises were vacant "but fit for immediate occupation and use" it was held that these words meant "free from defects" and not "fitted out" and did not necessarily require that the premises should be ready for full beneficial occupation (*Pontsarn Investments* v. *Kansallis* [1992] NPC 56).

"Fit to live in" was to be construed in accordance with the Housing Act 1985 (c. 68), s.604, which set the standard of fitness for human habitation (*Johnson* v. *Sheffield City Council* [1994] 6 C.L. 124).

"Fit for human habitation." Stat. Def., Housing Act 1985 (c. 68), s.604; Landlord and Tenant Act 1985 (c. 70), s.10.

FITTED. (Road Vehicles Lighting Regulations 1989 (S.I. 1989 No. 1794) reg. 16). "Fitted" within the meaning of reg. 16 meant "equipped" so that an operational blue magnetic mounted roof lamp similar to that carried by police and fire brigade personnel which was found on the rear parcel shelf of a vehicle not authorised to carry such a lamp was in breach of reg. 16 and it was irrelevant that the lamp was moveable where the impression was given that the vehicle was fitted with a warning lamp (*Brown* v. *McGlennan, The Scotsman*, November 22, 1995).

FIX. "Fixed or determinable future time" (Bills of Exchange Act 1882 (c. 61), s.83). Documents which undertook to repay a loan "on or before" a certain date or "by" a certain date were held not to have satisfied the definition of promissory note in this section, since they gave the payer an option to repay on any day he chose up to the specified time. There was thus no unconditional promise to pay at a "fixed or determinable future time" (*Williamson* v. *Rider* [1963] 1 Q.B. 89, followed by *Claydon* v. *Bradley* [1987] 1 All E.R. 522.

"Object or structure fixed to a building" (Town and Country Planning Act 1971 (c. 78), s.54(9)). A wall connected to a manor but separately owned was held not to be listed when the manor became listed as it was not "fixed" to the manor (*Watts* v. *Secretary of State for the Environment* [1991] P.L.R. 61).

Fixed amount, see AMOUNT.

FIXED ASSETS. Stat. Def., Cash Ratio Deposits (Eligible Liabilities) Order 1998 (No. 1130), Art. 2(1).

FIXED ENGINE. A net placed or suspended in tidal waters, unattended by the owner, was a "fixed engine" within the meaning of s.41 of the Salmon and Freshwater Fisheries Act 1975 (c. 51) and s.33(1) of the Salmon Act 1986 (c. 62), notwithstanding that it was not placed with the intention of taking salmon or trout (*Gray* v. *Blamey* [1991] 1 All E.R. 1).

FIXED EQUIPMENT. (Agricultural Holdings Act 1986 (c. 5), Sched. 2, para. 4(1)(*b*)). Although the surrender of a farm house can be a change in "fixed equipment" within the meaning of this paragraph, a surrender of a holding, or part of a holding, even if it is comprised partly or entirely of the building, is not a change in "fixed equipment" (*Mann* v. *Gardner* (1991) 61 P. & C.R. 1).

FIXED ESTABLISHMENT. (Sixth Council Directive 77/388 on a common system of VAT, Art. 9(1)). The leasing of vehicles did not create a "fixed establishment" for the purposes of the Directive so that interest on refunds of VAT to a company based in another Member State could only be on the same basis as refunds to residents (*Lease Plan Luxembourg SA* v. *Belgium* [1998] STC 628).

FIXTURE. Stat. Def., Capital Allowances Act 1990 (c. 1), s.51.
  "Fixtures" as opposed to chattels required an object and purpose of permanent and substantial improvement of a building so that carpets, light fittings, curtains, blinds, fitted gas fires, bathroom and kitchen fittings and electrical white goods, *inter alia*, were all fixtures (*TSB Bank plc* v. *Botham* [1995] EGCS 3).

FLAT. Stat. Def., Housing Act 1985 (c. 68), s.183; Landlord and Tenant Act 1985 (c. 70), s.30; Landlord and Tenant Act 1987 (c. 31), s.60; Local Government and Housing Act 1989 (c. 42), s.138; Housing Grants, Construction and Regeneration Act 1996 (c. 53), s.58.
  "Block of flats," Stat. Def., Housing Act 1996 (c. 52), s.2(6).

FLEETING GLANCE. The evidence of a witness who had observed the incident over minutes rather than seconds in a position where both he and the site of the incident were illuminated by street lighting and where he had seen the accused on two occasions shortly before the incident did not render his identification of the accused a "fleeting glance" case (*Rose* v. *R.* [1995] Crim.L.R. 939).

FLOATING CHARGE. (Insolvency Act 1986 (c. 45), s.40). A fixed charge of a company's existing and future book debts contained in a debenture issued to its bankers did not become a "floating charge" upon the assignment of the debenture to another (*William Gaskell Group* v. *Highley* [1993] BCC 200). Where a debenture is expressed as a fixed charge over the book debts and the debenture holder has a right to give directions as to how the debts and proceeds are to be dealt with, but no such directives are actually given, then where the company is left free to deal with the debts the charge is deemed to be a floating one (*Re New Bullas Trading* [1993] BCC 251).

FLOOD. See Burst.

FLOOR. (2) A duckboard was held to be a "floor" within the meaning of s.28(1) of the Factories Act 1961 (c. 34) (*Harper* v. *Mander and Germain*, *The Times*, December 28, 1992).

FLOUR. Stat. Def., Bread and Flour Regulations 1998 (No. 141), reg. 2(1).

FOLD. "Folding pocketknife" (Criminal Justice Act 1988 (c. 33), s.139(2)). A folding knife which was secured in an open position by a locking device was not a "folding pocketknife" within the meaning of this section as it could not be immediately folded by means of a folding action alone but required the pressing of a button to release the locking mechanism (*Harris* v. *DPP*; *Fehmi* v. *Same* [1993] 1 W.L.R. 94).

FOOD. Stat. Def., Consumer Protection Act 1987 (c. 43), s.19; Food Safety Act 1990 (c. 16), s.1.

FOOTPATH. Stat. Def., Road Traffic Act 1988 (c. 52), s.192; Horses (Protective Headgear) Act 1990 (c. 25), s.3.
    An alley-way at right angles to a road was not a "footpath by the side of a road" under the Highways Act 1835 (c. 50), s.72 (*Selby* (*Justin*) v. *DPP* [1994] R.T.R. 157).

FOR. "Admitted for settlement" (Statement of Immigration Rules for Control of Entry (HC 81) 1973, r. 38(c)). The word "for" means "for the purpose of" or "with the object of" (*R.* v. *Immigration Appeal Tribunal, ex p. Rashida Bibi* [1988] Imm.A.R. 298). See SETTLEMENT.

FORCE MAJEURE. (E.C. Commission Reg. 1687/76, Art. 11). The theft of beef, which had been held in intervention storage, and which was stolen whilst on its way to being exported from the EEC, did not amount to "force majeure" within the meaning of this article, and did not therefore justify the failure of the purchaser to meet his obligation to export it (*Anthony McNicholl* v. *Minister for Agriculture* (No. 296/86) [1988] 2 C.M.L.R. 275).
    Means different things in different Member States, but falls short of absolute impossibility (*Organisationen Danske Slagterier pro Jydske Andelsslagteriers Konservesfabrik AmbA (JAKA)* v. *Landebrugsministeriet* [1994] 1 C.M.L.R. 729 (338/89)).

FORCIBLE. Where the phrase "entry to . . . premises by forcible and violent means" was used in an insurance policy, "forcible" was held to denote the application of energy, so that entry to the insured's premises by using stolen keys was sufficient to satisfy the "forcible" condition (*Nash t/a Dino Services* v. *Prudential Assurance Co.* [1989] 1 All E.R. 422). See also VIOLENT.

FOREIGN. "Foreign state" (Extradition Act 1870 (c. 52), s.14) is not restricted to the foreign state applying for extradition. So that statements taken on oath in Bolivia were admissible evidence in extradition proceedings at the suit of the West German Government (*R.* v. *Secretary of State for the Home Department, ex p. Rees* [1986] A.C. 937).
    "Any foreign ship" (Merchant Shipping Act 1894 (c. 60), s.686(1)). For the purposes of determining the extent of the jurisdiction of English courts under this section a French ship does not cease to be a "foreign ship" even though it was alongside in a French port with the passenger gangway still in position. The submission that at the material time the ship was annexed to

the land and notionally part of France failed (*R.* v. *Cumberworth* [1989] Crim.L.R. 591).

"Foreign currency," Stat. Def., Finance Act 1987 (c. 16), s.69.

"Foreign state." Stat. Def., Criminal Justice Act 1988 (c. 33), s.1; Extradition Act 1989 (c. 33), s.3.

FORMED. "Has not been formed" (Companies Act 1985 (c. 6), s.36(4)). A company awaiting from the registrar of companies a certificate of incorporation on alteration of its name was not a company that "has not been formed" within the meaning of this section (*Oshkosh B'Gosh* v. *Dan Marbel* (1988) 4 BCC 795).

FORTHWITH. The requirement in an Anton Piller order that the defendant "forthwith" permit the plaintiff to enter the search means after a reasonable period to obtain legal advice (*Bhimji* v. *Chatwani* [1991] 1 All E.R. 705).

FOSSIL FUEL. Stat. Def., Electricity Act 1989 (c. 29), s.32.

FOSTER CHILD. (Foster Children Act 1980 (c.6), s.1). Where parents informally placed their child with a carer while temporarily abroad it was not open to the local authority to conclude that the family was not in priority need of accommodation on the ground that the child was being fostered (*R.* v. *Lewisham London Borough Council, ex p. Creppy* (1991) 24 H.L.R. 121).

FOUNDATION. Stat. Def., Party Wall etc. Act 1996 (c. 40), s.20.

FOUNDED. (Criminal Appeal Act 1968 (c. 19), s.2(1), as amended by Criminal Appeal Act 1995). Only where a plea of guilty had been influenced by an erroneous ruling on the law which rendered an acquittal legally impossible that an acquittal could be said to be "founded upon" that ruling (*R.* v. *Chalkley* [1998] 2 All E.R. 155).

(County Courts Act 1984 (c. 28), s.15). A claim in relation to a statutory superannuation scheme, which was not precluded by statutory provision, arose from a plaintiff's contract of employment and so was an action "founded in contract or tort" (*Hutchings* v. *Islington LBC* [1998] 3 All E.R. 445).

FRAUD. (14) "A claim based . . . on an allegation of fraud" under R.S.C., Ord. 14, r.1(2) is to be confined to an allegation of fraud where the cause of action is deceit (*Newton Chemicals* v. *Arsenis* [1989] 1 W.L.R. 1297).

(Limitation Act 1980 (c. 58), s.21). "Actual fraud" within the meaning of s.21 meant "actual dishonesty" (*Armitage* v. *Nurse* [1995] N.P.C. 110).

FRAUDULENT DEVICE. "Fraudulent device or contrivance" (Representation of the People Act 1983 (c. 2), s.115(2)(*b*)). A leaflet issued by Liberal election candidates purporting to be from their Labour opponents was a "fraudulent device or contrivance" contrary to this section notwithstanding that its contents were true (*R.* v. *Local Government Election Commissioner, ex p. Mainwaring* [1992] C.O.D. 367).

FRAUDULENT EVASION. "Fraudulent evasion . . . of any prohibition" (Customs and Excise Management Act 1979 (c. 2), s.170(2)). The words "fraudulent evasion" include more than merely entering the United Kingdom with goods concealed and no intention of declaring them; they extend to any conduct which is directed and intended to lead to the importation of goods covertly in breach of a prohibition on import (*R. v. Latif; R. v. Shahzad* [1995] 1 Cr.App.R. 270).

FRAUDULENT PREFERENCE. (6) "Fraudulent preference" (Companies Act 1985 (c. 6), s.615); "preference" (Insolvency Act 1986 (c. 45), s.239). Where an employee is entitled on the liquidation of a company, to some level of compensation for redundancy or breach of contract, a payment far in excess of that sum could amount to a "fraudulent preference" within the meaning of s.615 (now repealed) or a "preference" within the meaning of s.239 (*Re Clasper Group Services* (1988) 4 BCC 673). See PREFERENCE.

FRAUDULENT PURPOSE. (2) "Or for any fraudulent purpose" (Companies Act 1948 (c. 38), s.332(1), as amended by Companies Act 1981 (c. 62), s.96). Indictments under this section are not limited to offences against creditors (*R. v. Kemp* [1988] 2 W.L.R. 975).

FRAUDULENTLY. "Fraudulently alters or uses . . . any licence," see USE.

FREE. "Free to come into . . . the United Kingdom" (Immigration Act 1971 (c. 77), s.1(5)). A person whose hopes and expectations of being given leave to enter depended on the exercise of their discretion by immigration officers could not be said to be "free to come into" the United Kingdom (*R. v. Immigration Appeal Tribunal, ex p. Ruhul* [1987] 1 W.L.R. 1538). See also SHALL.

FREEHOLD. "Freehold" (Leasehold Reform Act 1967 (c. 88), ss.1(1), 8(1)) should not be construed as embracing all superior or intermediate interests (*Gratton-Storey v. Lewis* (1987) 283 E.G. 1562).

FREESTANDING CLAIM. Claims based on the E.C. Treaty, Art. 119 were free-standing in the sense that they derived from a legal order superior in force to U.K. domestic law (*Biggs v. Somerset County Council* [1995] IRLR 452).

FREQUENT ATTENTION THROUGHOUT THE DAY. Assistance provided to a blind person in connection with his bodily functions of bathing, eating and walking in unfamiliar surrondings could be "frequent attention throughout the day" within the meaning of the Social Security Act 1975 (c. 14), s.35(1)(*a*)(i) (*Mallinson v. Secretary of State for Social Security* [1994] 2 All E.R. 295).

FRESHWATER FISH. The definition of "freshwater fish" included those fish which migrated between fresh water and the sea (*McLeod v. Keith (Derek Alexander)*, 1997 S.C.C.R. 475).

FRIVOLOUS. (Magistrates' Courts Act 1980 (c. 43), s.111). The refusal to state a case by magistrates under s.111 on the grounds that it was "frivolous" meant that the application was futile, misconceived, hopeless or academic (*R.* v. *Mildenhall Magistrates' Court, ex p. Forest Heath District Council, The Times*, May 16, 1997).

FULL AND FINAL SATISFACTION OF ... CLAIM. A payment into court "in full and final satisfaction" of a claim, where no counterclaim had been entered, did not preclude a subsequent action being commenced where the particulars were substantially the same as in the first action (*Hoppe* v. *Titman* [1996] 1 W.L.R. 841).

Satisfaction of a claim by one tortfeasor which was expressed to be in "full and final settlement" had the effect of extinguishing all claims against other concurrent tortfeasors since a plaintiff could not recover more by way of damages than the amount of his loss but for his accident (*Jameson* v. *C.E.G.B.* [1999] 1 All E.R. 193). Similarly, where a creditor accepted a lesser sum in full and final settlement of a joint debt from a debtor, the debt was extinguished in the absence of any express or implied agreement that the creditor's rights against the remaining debtor had been preserved (*Morris* v. *Wentworth-Stanley* [1999] 2 W.L.R. 470).

FULL EXTENT. See NORMAL.

FUNCTIONS. The activities carried out by local authorities pursuant to their duties under the Education Act 1944 (c. 31), s.8, such as the provision of selective education, were "functions" within the meaning of the Sex Discrimination Act 1975 (c. 65), s.23 (*R.* v. *Birmingham City Council, ex p. Equal Opportunities Commission* [1989] 2 W.L.R. 520). But the court was not satisfied that the exercising by a local education authority of its duty to comply with parental expressions of preference made under s.6 of the Education Act 1980 (c. 20) was truly a "function" of the authority to which s.18 of the Race Relations Act 1976 (c. 74) was directed (*R.* v. *Cleveland County Council, ex p. Commission for Racial Equality* (1991) 135 S.J.(LB) 205).

"Calculated to facilitate . . . the discharge of any of their functions" (Local Government Act 1972 (c. 70), s.111(1)). Although charging a fee for advice given to persons contemplating making a planning application was held to be conducive to facilitating the giving of such advice by a local authority it was held on appeal that as the giving of such advice was not a local authority "function" within the meaning of this section they were not authorised to charge for it. (*McCarthy & Stone (Developments)* v. *Richmond upon Thames London Borough Council, sub nom. R.* v. *Richmond upon Thames London Borough Council, ex p. McCarthy & Stone (Developments)* [1991] 3 W.L.R. 941). A local authority has no power under this section to made redundancy payments which are for amounts in excess of those which it is obliged to make (*North Tyneside Metropolitan Council* v. *Allsop* [1992] RVR 104).

Stat. Def., "includes powers, duties and obligations" (Goods Vehicles (Licensing of Operators) Act 1995 (c. 23), s.58(1)); "includes powers and duties" (Education Act 1996 (c. 56), s.579(1) and Teaching and Higher Education Act 1998 (c. 30), s.43(1)).

FUNDS AVAILABLE. (Bills of Exchange Act 1882 (c. 61), s.53). An overdraft facility could not create "funds available" to be assigned under s.53(2) as the contractual right which a customer had in respect of an overdraft was a right to have cheques paid notwithstanding that he did not have available funds, which right could not be assigned to a payee of a cheque drawn upon that facility, the customer was not provided with a credit balance on which an assignment could operate (*Sutherland* v. *Royal Bank of Scotland plc*, 1997 S.L.T. 329).

FUNERAL. "Funeral" in reg. 8(1)(*c*) of the Supplementary Benefit (Single Payment) Regulations 1981 (No. 1528) is used in the sense of burial rather than of the ceremonial or religious services which accompany burial or cremation. The funeral or cremation must take place wholly within the United Kingdom to qualify for payment (Decision No. R(SB) 23/86).

FURNISH. "Furnish . . . a return" (Value Added Tax (General) Regulations 1985 (No. 886), reg. 58(1)). A return posted in a pre-paid and pre-printed envelope supplied for that purpose was "furnished" when posted (*Hayman* v. *Griffiths* [1987] 3 W.L.R. 1125).

FURNITURE. (Value Added Tax (Special Provisions) Order 1981 (No. 1741), reg. 8 as amended; see now Value Added Tax (Input Tax) Order 1992 (No. 3222), reg. 6(2)(*b*)). Built-in wardrobes are not fitted furniture within the meaning of these regulations (*Customs and Excise Commissioners* v. *McLean Homes Midland* [1993] S.T.C. 335).

FURTHER OR DIFFERENT DIRECTIONS. Directions setting out steps to be taken to prosecute an action, which were sent after the action had been transferred from another county court, which had also earlier issued directions regarding the prosecution of the action, amounted to "further or different directions" within the meaning of C.C.R., Ord. 17, r.11(4)(*a*) (*McIntosh and Partners* v. *Dudley* [1995] 6 C.L. 319).

FURTHERANCE. (4) "In . . . furtherance of a trade dispute" (Trade Union and Labour Relations Act 1974 (c. 52), s.13(1); now Trade Union and Labour Relations (Consolidation) Act 1992 (c. 52), s.219). Employees made redundant as a result of their employer losing a contract to clean offices were not acting in "furtherance" of a trade dispute within the meaning of this section when they picketed the offices concerned in an effort to induce the employees of the new contractor to break their contracts of employment (*J. & R. Kenny Cleaning Services* (*a Firm*) v. *Transport and General Workers Union*, *The Times*, June 15, 1989). Registered dock workers were held to be under a contractual and not a statutory duty to work, notwithstanding that the supply of dock labour was regulated by the Dock Workers (Regulation of Employment) Order 1947 (No. 1252); so that the union's action in calling for industrial action was in "furtherance" of a trade dispute and was therefore within the statutory immunity conferred by s.13 (*Associated British Ports* v. *Transport and General Workers Union* [1989] 1 W.L.R. 939). Teachers who boycotted certain duties in relation to national curriculum assessment which they considered unreasonable were acting "in furtherance" of a trade dispute (*Wandsworth London Borough Council* v. *National Association of School Masters and Union of Women Teachers*, *The Times*, April 7, 1993). See TRADE DISPUTE.

"In the . . . furtherance of a . . . profession or vocation, accepts any office" (Value Added Tax Act 1983 (c. 55), s.47(4)). There can be no "furtherance" within the meaning of this section where the acceptance of the office precedes the establishment of the profession (*Gardner (James Jesse)* v. *Customs and Excise Commissioners* [1989] V.A.T.T.R. 132).

FUTURE INDEBTEDNESS. "Future indebtedness" could include cases where there was an obligation to pay an unliquidated sum in the future, or in the arising of a contingency and cases where an obligation only arose in the future (*Banner Lane Realisations Ltd (In Liquidation)* v. *Berisford plc* [1997] 1 C.L. 325).

G

GAIN. (10) "With a view to a gain" (Theft Act 1968 (c. 60), s.21). By forcing a doctor at gun-point to give an injection the defendant "gained" the property contained in the syringe and thereby made a "gain" of property for himself (*R.* v. *Bevans* (1988) 87 Cr.App.R. 64).

(10) "With a view to gain" (Theft Act 1968 (c. 60), s.17(1)) means gain by keeping money or other property. So that the falsification of bills of exchange with a view to securing a bank's forbearance from enforcing its rights on earlier bills did not constitute falsification "with a view to gain" within the meaning of this section (*R.* v. *Golechha* [1989] 1 W.L.R. 1050).

"Where a person realises a gain" (Income and Corporation Taxes Act 1970 (c. 10), s.186). A gain realised by the exercise of a right to acquire shares in a company is, by virtue of this section, chargeable to tax under Sched. E, and remains a gain so chargeable notwithstanding that the original grant of the option had been taxed as an emolument (*Ball* v. *Phillips* [1990] S.T.C. 675).

"The amount of the gain" (Finance Act 1982 (c. 39), s.86(2)). Gain here means "chargeable gain" and not the whole gain (*Smith* v. *Scholfield* [1992] 1 W.L.R. 639).

"Similar gainful employment" in an insurance contract meant an occupation which could generate a living wage (*Johnson* v. *IGI Insurance Co. Ltd* [1997] 6 C.L. 358).

GAME. A shooting right reserved in respect of "all game, woodcocks, snipe and other wild fowl, hares, rabbits and fish" was held not to include deer (*Inglewood Investment Co.* v. *Forestry Commission* [1988] 1 W.L.R. 1278).

GAME OF CHANCE. Stat. Def., Value Added Tax Act 1994 (c. 23), s. 23(4).

GAMING CONTRACT. "All contracts or agreements by way of gaming or wagering" (Gaming Act 1845 (c. 109), s.18; Gaming Act 1892 (c. 9), s.1). A contract to purchase chips at a casino is not by way of "gaming or wagering" within the meaning of this section (*Lipkin Gorman* v. *Karpnale* [1989] 1 W.L.R. 1340). Swap contracts entered into by parties or institutions involved in the capital market and in the making or receiving of loans are not wagering contracts for the purposes of this section (*Morgan Grenfell & Co.* v. *Welwyn Hatfield District Council* (*Islington London Borough Council, third party*) [1995] 1 All E.R. 1). See also BUSINESS.

GAMING MACHINE. Stat. Def., Value Added Tax Act 1994 (c. 23), s.23(4).

GANGWAY. See MAIN GANGWAY.

GARDEN. "Garden" (Common Land (Rectification of Registers) Act 1989 (c. 18), s.1(3)). Pasture land was held not to be a "garden" within the meaning of this section (*Re Land at Freshfields*, *The Times*, February 1, 1993). But an acre of unfenced and impenetrable woodland over which, before the 1987 hurricane, the public had exercised a right of entry was held to be a "garden" for the purposes of this section.

A public right of way over land did not prevent it from being a "garden" (*Land at Mooredge Farm* [1994] N.P.C. 65).

GAS. Stat. Def., Gas Act 1986 (c. 44), s.48; Environmental Protection Act 1990 (c. 43), s.79.

"Oil or gas."—Stat. Def., "means—(a) any mineral oil or any relative hydrocarbon which, in its natural state, is not a solid; or (b) methane or any other natural gas"—(Coal Industry Act 1994 (c. 21), s.9(6)).

GENERAL PARAMOUNT CLAUSE. A general paramount clause required the incorporation of the Hague Rules where they had been enacted, or the legislation in the country where the Rules had not been enacted or the Convention which incorporated the Rules or, where the Hague Visby Rules were compulsorily applicable to the trader in question, the legislation enacting those rules (*The "Bukhta Russkaya"* [1997] 2 Lloyd's Rep. 744).

GENERALLY. "Generally, children aged 18 or over must qualify . . . in their own right; but subject to . . . " (Statement of Immigration Rules for Control on Entry (1973) H.C. 79). The use of the word "generally" does not here confer any discretion. It has to be read together with "but" so that the latter formed or contained the exceptions, and the only exceptions, to the former (*R.* v. *Immigration Appeal Tribunal, ex p. Mukith*, *The Times*, November 14, 1987).

GENUINELY DUE TO A MATERIAL FACTOR WHICH IS NOT THE DIFFERENCE OF SEX. (Equal Pay Act 1970 (c. 41), s.1(3), as amended). The re-employment of women on a lower hourly rate and with no sick pay and less holiday pay from men similarly employed as a result of compulsory competitive tendering was not "genuinely due to a material factor which is not the difference of sex" within the meaning of s.1(3), as amended (*Ratcliffe and ors* v. *North Yorkshire County Council* [1995] 3 All E.R. 597).

GIPSIES. "Gipsies" (Caravan Sites Act 1968 (c. 52), ss.6, 16). Travelling showmen who travelled as members of an organised group "travelling together as such" in the summer months, and were thus excluded from the definition of "gipsies" in this section, did not come within the definition during the winter months when they ceased travelling and stayed in winter quarters (*Hammond* v. *Secretary of State for the Environment*; *Smith* v. *Same* [1988] 3 P.L.R. 90). A gypsy who has lost the nomadic way of life ceases to be a gypsy for the purposes of this Act (*Horsham District Council* v. *Secretary of State for the Environment, The Independent*, October 31, 1989). But it has been held that a local authority did not act irrationally or perversely in finding that a family were "gypsies" within the meaning of s.6 despite the fact that travelling had not been in evidence for some time (*R.* v. *Shropshire County Council, ex p. Bungay* (1990) 23 H.L.R. 195). A person may be a gypsy within the definition in section 16 if he leads a nomadic life only seasonally and returns regularly for part of the year to the same place (*A. J. and G. Cuss* v. *Secretary of State for the Environment and Wychavon District Council* [1991] J.P.L. 1033). The definition contemplates that class of persons whose means of getting an independent living necessarily involves their wandering from place to place (*R.* v. *Dorset County Council, ex p. Rolls, The Times,* February 1, 1994). See also NOMADIC.

Stat. Def., "means persons of nomadic habit of life, whatever their race or origin, but does not include members of an organised group of travelling showmen, or person engaged in travelling circuses, travelling together as such"—(Criminal Justice and Public Order Act 1994 (c. 33), s.80(2) (amending Caravan Sites and Control of Development Act 1960 (c. 62), s.24)); note *R.* v. *South Hams District Council, ex p. Gibb* [1994] 4 All E.R. 1012 for interpretation of similar wording in Caravan Sites Act 1968, s.16 as requiring connection between travelling and means of seeking livelihood.

GIVE. "Given to the tenant" (Landlord and Tenant Act 1954 (c. 56), s.4(1)). A notice under this section served on the tenant's solicitors had been "given" to him within the meaning of this section (*Galinski* v. *McHugh* [1989] 05 E.G. 89).

GIVE UP. "Gives up regular employment" (Social Security Act 1975 (c. 14), s.59B(1)). A claimant for a reduced earnings allowance cannot be considered to have given up regular employment if he has been dismissed from that employment through no fault of his own (*Social Security Decision No. R(1) 2/93*).

GOOD AND TENANTABLE CONDITION. See CONDITION.

GOOD CAUSE. "Good and sufficient cause" (Prosecution of Offences Act 1985 (c. 23), s.22(3)). A defence request for more time could, in certain circumstances, constitute "good and sufficient cause" for allowing an extension of the time a defendant could be held in custody under the Prosecution of Offences (Custody Time Limits) Regulations (1987 No. 299) (*White* v. *Director of Public Prosecutions* [1989] Crim.L.R. 375). The seriousness of the offence charged and the fact that the delay would be only a few days were not "good and sufficient causes" for extending the custody time limits (*R.* v. *Governor of Winchester Prison, ex p. Roddie; R.* v. *Southampton Crown Court, ex p. Rose* [1991] 1 W.L.R. 303). The protection of a member of the public is capable, as a matter of law, of being a "good and sufficient cause" for an extension of the custody time limit (*R.* v. *Luton Crown Court, ex p. Neaves* [1992] Crim.L.R. 721). The lack of a court or the non-availability of a judge to hear the trial could be a "good and sufficient cause" for an extension (*R.* v. *Norwich Crown Court, ex p. Cox, The Times*, November 3, 1992). But an extension of the custody time limit for 14 days was not made for "good and sufficient cause" when the earliest trial date was in not less than 93 days (*R.* v. *Maidstone Crown Court, ex p. Schultz, The Times*, December 2, 1992). There can be no "good and sufficient cause" for extending the custody time limit in circumstances where arraignment would not have taken place until 144 days after committal and where there was no satisfactory explanation as to why arraignment could not have been within the 112-day limit (*R.* v. *Norwich Crown Court, ex p. Stiller* [1992] Crim.L.R. 501).

The protection of the public was not in itself a "good and sufficient cause" for extending the custody time limit, but the unavailability of a judge or court to try a defendant in custody could amount to a "good and sufficient cause" as could the interests of justice that jointly charged defendants should be tried together (*R.* v. *Central Criminal Court, ex p. Abu-Wardeh* [1997] 1 All E.R. 159).

"Good and sufficient reason." The lack of a court room and judge to hear a criminal trial did not amount to a good and sufficient reason for extending the custody time limits under regulation 5(3) of the Prosecution of Offenders (Custody Time Limits) Regulations 1987 (No. 299). (*R.* v. *Norwich Crown Court, ex p. Stiller, The Times*, February 4, 1992). But the protection of a member of the public from violence was capable of being a "good and sufficient cause" for extending the custody time limit of a defendant awaiting trial for the purposes of s.22(3)(*a*) of the Prosecution of Offences Act 1985 (c. 23) (*R.* v. *Luton Crown Court, ex p. Neaves, The Times*, June 9, 1992).

Where an extension of time was academic because the defendant was already in custody was a "good and sufficient cause" for exercising the discretion under s.22(3)(*b*) (*R.* v. *Woolwich Crown Court, ex p. Gilligan* [1998] 2 All E.R. 1).

GOOD FAITH. See IN GOOD FAITH.

GOOD REASON. Delay in applying for leave to make an application for judicial review caused by the time taken to obtain legal aid may be a "good reason" for extending the time under R.S.C. Ord. 53, rule 4(1) (*R.* v. *Stratford-on-Avon District Council, ex p. Jackson* [1985] 1 W.L.R. 1319). The fact that a defendant already knew of possible claims against him could be a relevant consideration in deciding whether, within the meaning of R.S.C., Ords. 6, 8(2) and 53, r.4, a "good reason" for the extension of the validity of a writ had been shown; and, where leave had previously been granted to serve the writ out of the jurisdiction, an important consideration would be whether leave would have been granted to serve a fresh writ out of the jurisdiction (*Goldenglow Nut Food Co.* v. *Commodin (Produce)* [1987] 2 Lloyd's Rep. 569). Where there were matters which could, potentially at least, constitute "good reason" for extension, balance of hardship should be a relevant consideration in deciding whether an extension might be granted or refused (*Kleinwort Benson* v. *Barbrak* [1987] A.C. 597; *Waddon* v. *Whitecroft Scovill* [1988] 1 W.L.R. 309). It was doubtful whether confusion in the mind of a solicitor, causing him to transpose the date of expiry of the validity of a writ, could amount to a "good reason" for extending the writ's validity under Order 6, rule 8 (*Doble* v. *Haymills* (*Contractors*) (1988) 132 S.J. 1063). An application by trustees for an order authorising proceedings does not constitute a good reason for failing to serve a write in time (*Dagnell* v. *Freedman & Co.* (*A Firm*) [1993] 1 W.L.R. 388). Where a litigant applied for an extension of the validity of a writ under this rule the application had to be made during the validity of the writ. Only one extension not exceeding four months could be granted on a particular application (*Singh* (*Joginder*) v. *Duport Harper Foundries, The Times,* November 15, 1993).

"Good reason" was a different expression from "reasonable excuse," and failure to throw away a spike after using it did not amount to a "good reason" (*DPP* v. *Gregson* [1993] 96 Cr.App.R. 240 followed) (*Lister* v. *Lees,* 1994 S.C.C.R. 548).

(Juries Act 1974 (c. 23), s.9(2)). Religious or conscientious belief was not of itself a "good reason" why a person "should be excused from attending" for jury service within the meaning of this section (*R.* v. *Guildford Crown Court, ex p. Siderfin* [1989] 3 All E.R. 73).

"Good reason . . . for having the article with him" (Criminal Justice Act 1988 (c. 33), s.139(4)). Forgetfulness is not a "good reason" within the meaning of this section (*DPP* v. *Gregson* (1993) 96 Crim.App.R. 240). A defendant did not discharge the burden of showing "good reason" merely by providing an explanation which was un-contradicted by any prosecution evidence (*Godwin* v. *DPP* (1992) 156 J.P.N. 716).

GOODS. "Goods . . . are of merchantable quality" (Sale of Goods Act 1979 (c. 54), s.14(2)). In this section "goods" includes the packaging and the instructions as to their use (*Wormell* v. *R.H.M. Agricultural* (*East*) [1986] 1 W.L.R. 336).

Computer software could be "goods" within the meaning of the Sale of Goods Act 1979 (c. 54) (*St. Alban's City and District Council* v. *International Computers* [1995] F.S.R. 686).

"Goods . . . supplied to a ship for her operation" (Supreme Court Act 1981 (c. 54), s.20(2)(*m*)). Containers, hired by the defendant from the plaintiff, delivered to shippers for their use at specified depots and used interchangeably on a number of vessels owned or chartered by the defendant, were not sufficiently closely connected with the defendant's ships to qualify as "goods supplied to a ship for her operation" within the meaning of this section (*The River Rima* [1988] 1 W.L.R. 758).

Lottery activities were not "goods" for the purposes of the EEC Treaty, Art. 30 (*Customs and Excise Commissioners* v. *Schindler* [1994] 2 All E.R. 193).

The crystallisation of a floating charge on the appointment of administrative receivers which had the effect of completing the assignment of goods to a third party so that they were no longer "goods of" a company over which distress for rates may be levied under the Non-Domestic Rating (Collection and Enforcement) (Local Lists) Regulations 1989 (No. 2260), reg. 14 (*Re ELS* [1994] 2 All E.R. 833).

"Goods to be sold . . . by retail" (Value Added Tax Act 1983 (c. 55), Sched. 4, para. 3). A business, which in part consisted in selling goods to its agents for resale was taxable under Sched. 4, para. 3 (*Fine Art Developments plc* v. *Customs and Excise Commissioners* [1996] 1 All E.R. 888).

"Goods and chattels." A bequest of "my farm together with dwelling house and out-office, cattle and stock, goods and chattels therein and thereon" included all the goods in and on the farm but not the deceased's personal estate (*Mackessy* v. *Fitzgerald* [1993] 1 I.R. 520).

"Goods of a dangerous nature." Groundnuts infested with khapra beetle were "goods of a dangerous nature" within the meaning of the Hague-Visby Rules, Art. IV, r.6 as the loss of the other cargo was natural and not unlikely (*Effort Shipping Co.* v. *Linden Management SA; The Giannis NK, The Times*, May 5, 1994).

A computer disk is within the definition of "goods" contained in s.61 of the Sale of Goods Act 1979 (c. 54) and s.18 of the Supply of Goods and Services Act 1982 (c. 29) but a computer program was not (*St. Alban's City and District Council* v. *International Computers Ltd* [1996] 4 All E.R. 481).

(Capital Allowances Act 1990 (c. 1), s.18(1)(e)). "Goods" referred to merchandise or wares and should be given its ordinary meaning in a commercial context. Thus cheques and other pieces of paper carrying out requests or instructions did not amount to "goods" with the result that the building in which they were processed could not qualify for industrial building allowance (*Girobank plc* v. *Clarke (Inspector of Taxes)* [1998] 4 All E.R. 312).

Stat. Def., Consumer Protection Act 1987 (c. 43), s.45; Prevention of Terrorism (Temporary Provisions) Act 1989 (c. 4), Sched. 5, para. 4 inserted by Prevention of Terrorism (Additional Powers) Act 1996 (c. 7), s.3(1).

Stat. Def., "includes property of any description and a right to, or interest in, property" (Fair Trading Act 1973 (c. 41), s.118(8) as substituted by Trading Schemes Act 1996 (c. 32), s.1).

GOODS VEHICLE. Stat. Def., "a vehicle constructed or adapted for use and used for the conveyance of goods or burden of any description, whether in the course of trade or not"—(Vehicle Excise and Registration Act 1994 (c. 22), s.62(1)).

GOVERNING BODY. Stat. Def., "the executive governing body which has responsibility for the conduct of affairs of the establishment and the management and administration of its revenue and property"—(Education Act 1994 (c. 30), s.21(5)).

GOVERNMENT. Recognition of the government of a state required consideration of whether it was the constitutional government of that state, the degree, nature and stability of the administrative control exercised over its territory, whether the United Kingdom had dealings with it and the extent of its international recognition as the government of a state (*Sierra Leone Telecommunications Ltd* v. *Barclays Bank plc* [1998] 2 All E.R. 821).

GOVERNMENT DEPARTMENT. Stat. Def., Scotland Act 1998 (c. 46), s.126(1).

GOVERNOR. "Foundation governor," Stat. Def., School Standards and Framework Act 1998 (c. 31), Sched. 9, para. 2.

GRANDCHILD. Stat. Def., "means a child of a child" (Finance Act 1998 (c. 36), s.131).

GRANT OF FACILITIES FOR PARKING A VEHICLE. Where an unqualified lease was granted of a lock-up garage or converted stables by necessary implication arising from the nature of the premises, there had been a grant of facilities for parking a vehicle (Value Added Tax Act 1983 (c. 55), Sched. 1, Group 1, Item 1(*g*)) (*Customs and Excise Commissioners* v. *Trinity Factoring Services, The Times,* June 30, 1994).

GRAPHIC. "Graphic work." Stat. Def., Copyright, Designs and Patents Act 1988 (c. 48), s.4.

GRATUITOUS BENEFIT. See ASSOCIATE.

GREAT BRITAIN. "At an establishment in Great Britain," see ESTABLISHMENT.

GROSS. "Gross amount thereof" (Family Income Supplements (General) Regulations 1980 (No. 1437), reg. 2(3) means gross before tax but after deduction of expenses (*Chief Adjudication Officer* v. *Hogg* [1985] 1 W.L.R. 1100; Decision No. R (FIS) 2/88).

GROUP. The provisions of the Fair Trading Act 1973 (c. 41) do not require that the member of a "group," found to have conducted their respective affairs in the manner described by s.7(2), must have acted pursuant to any agreement or arrangement (*R.* v. *Monopolies and Mergers Commission and the Secretary of State for Trade and Industry, ex p. Ecaudo Systems, Philbeach Events and Earls Court and Olympia* [1993] C.O.D. 89).

A body of people linked only by their employment does not constitute a "particular social group" for the purposes of the Convention Relating to the Status of Refugees 1951, Art. 1A(2) (*Ouanes* v. *Secretary of State for the Home Department, The Times,* November 26, 1997).

GROUPS OF COMPANIES. Stat. Def., Finance Act 1985 (c. 54), Sched. 20; Financial Services Act 1986 (c. 60), s.207; Banking Act 1987 (c. 22), s.106; Finance Act 1989 (c. 26), s.138.

GUARANTEE. Stat. Def., Companies Act 1985 (c. 6), s.331. A guarantee which had no legal validity remained an enforceable guarantee (*Gulf Bank KSC* v. *Mitsubishi Heavy Industries (No. 2)* [1994] 3 Bank L.R. 74).

GUARANTEED. The use of the word "guaranteed" in a pension scheme contract was inconsistent with anything other than a binding commitment for the period during for which it was given (*Miller* v. *Stapleton* [1997] 2 All E.R. 449).

GUARDIAN. (Children and Young Persons Act 1933 (c. 12), s.107). A father of an illegitimate child who had *de facto* care and control was the "guardian" of that child for the purposes of this Act (*R.* v. *Telford Juvenile Court, ex p. E* [1989] 2 F.L.R. 101).

"Guardian of a child." Stat. Def., Children Act 1989 (c. 41), s.105.

GUN. "Machine gun," Stat. Def., "any firearm which is so designed or adapted that, if pressure is applied to the trigger, missiles continue to be discharged until pressure is removed from the trigger or the magazine containing the missiles is empty" (Firearms (Northern Ireland) Order 1981 (S.I. 1981/155 N.I. 2), Art. 6(1).

GYPSIES. See NOMADIC.
(Caravan Sites Act 1968 (c. 52), s.16). "Gypsies" were persons whose habit of life was nomadic, where habit of life meant a manner of living so settled as to become customary (*Re Gibbs* [1994] N.P.C. 78) and whose means of obtaining an independent living necessarily involved a nomadic existence (*R.* v. *Dorset County Council, ex p. Rolls, The Times*, February 1, 1994).

There had to be some recognisable connection between the travelling and the means whereby the persons concerned sought their livelihood (*R.* v. *South Hams District Council, ex p. Gibb* [1994] 4 All E.R. 1012).

H

HABITUAL RESIDENCE. (Child Abduction and Custody Act 1985 (c. 60), Sched. 1; Hague Convention on the Civil Aspects of International Child Abduction 1980, Art. 3). A person might cease to be "habitually resident" in a country in a single day if he left it with a settled intention not to return but he could not become habitually resident in a new country in a single day (*F.* v. *F.* (*Abduction: Habitual Residence*) [1993] Fam.Law 199).

In *Re B.* (*Minors*) (*Abduction*) (*No. 2*) [1993] 1 F.L.R. 993, a family was found to be "habitually resident" in a country in which it had settled to provide a base for reconciliation and to plan its future and where they had remained for an appreciable period.

Where parents have equal rights of custody, the habitual residence of their children can only be altered by agreement or acquiescence (*Re S.* (*Minors*) [1994] 1 All E.R. 237).

"Habitual residence" required a physical presence in the place or country in question immediately prior to the wrongful removal which was both voluntary and for settled purposes so that the children of a serviceman, who had been posted overseas in the course of his service career with his family, were habitually resident in that country where they lived voluntarily and with the requisite degree of continuity and not in the country which he served, however much life on the military base resembled ordinary life in the native country (*A (Minors) (Abduction: Habitual Residence) Re;* [1996] 1 All E.R. 24).

(Income Support (General) Regulation 1987, reg. 21(3)). In order to be habitually resident for the purposes of the 1987 regulations, a claimant had to be living in the country voluntarily, with a settled purpose and for an appreciable length of time, which was a question of fact in each case (*Nessa* v. *Chief Adjudication Officer* [1998] 2 All E.R. 728).

HACKNEY CARRIAGE. Stat. Def., Vehicle Excise and Registration Act 1994 (c. 22), Sched. 1, para. 3(3); Private Hire Vehicles (London) Act 1998 (c. 34), s.36.

HAIR. "Hair" in the Police and Criminal Evidence Act 1984 (c. 60), s.65 was to be construed as including the inner sheath that was inevitably withdrawn when hair was pulled and was therefore a non-intimate sample and its taking was authorised subject to the statutory procedural requirements (*R.* v. *Cooke (Stephen)* [1995] 1 Cr.App.R. 318).

HANDED TO. "Handed to" (Road Traffic Act 1972 (c. 20), s.10(5) as substituted by the Transport Act 1981 (c. 56), Sched. 8). Putting an intoximeter printout on the desk in front of the accused and leaving it there, does not amount to handing it to him (*Walton* v. *Rimmer* [1986] RTR 31).

HANDICAPPED. Stat. Def., "means chronically sick or disabled"— (Finance Act 1994 (c. 9), s.70(10)(*a*)).

HANDLE. "While he is handling open food" (Food Hygiene (Market Stalls and Delivery Vehicles) Regulations 1966 (No. 791). "Handling" in this regulation is not confined to the actual touching of open food, so that a market trader who, between serving customers with vegetables, smoked a cigarette, could be held to have been smoking while handling the vegetables within the meaning of this regulation (*Cuckson* v. *Bugg* (1986) 85 Cr.App.R. 643).
"Handles stolen goods . . . or . . . arranges to do so," see ARRANGE.

HARASSMENT. (Public Order Act 1986 (c. 64), s.5(1)). There was no requirement that a person had to be apprehensive about his safety to found an offence under s.5(1), so that protestors who placed their hands in front of measuring equipment used by a surveyor caused him harrassment (*Chambers* v. *DPP* [1995] C.O.D. 321).
(Protection for Harassment Act (c.40), ss.1 and 7). In an action brought against the landlord of the property the existence of noisy tenants and the failure to maintain the garden of the leased property did not amount to harassment of a person within the meaning of the 1997 Act (*B.* v. *MHA Ltd* [1999] 2 C.L. 372).
Failure to engage in normal social contact and courtesies following a dispute was not a course of conduct amounting to harassment (*Morris* v. *Knight* [1999] 2 C.L. 373).
Stat. Def., "includes causing the person alarm or distress" (Criminal Law (Consolidation) (Scotland) Act 1995 (c. 39), s.50A(6) inserted by Crime and Disorder Act 1998 (c. 37), s.33).
See PERSON.

HARBOUR. Stat. Def., Pilotage Act 1987 (c. 21), s.1; Merchant Shipping Act 1995 (c. 21), s.313(1).
See TIDAL WATER.

HARD COPY. Stat. Def., "in relation to information held electronically, means a printed out version of that information"—(Finance Act 1995 (c. 4), Sched. 28, para. 9).
(Criminal Justice and Public Order Act 1994 (c. 33), s.51(2)). "Harm" in s.51(2) meant physical harm, either threatened or sustained by a victim, so that spitting in a victim's face did not constitute harm within the meaning of the Act (*R.* v. *Normanton* (*Lee*) [1997] 11 C.L. 136).

HARM. (Criminal Justice and Public Order Act 1994 (c. 33), s.51(2)). "Harm" in s.51(2) meant physical harm, either threatened or sustained by the victim, so that spitting in a victim's face was not harm (*R.* v. *Normanton* (*Lee*) [1997] 11 C.L. 136). Stat. Def., Environment Protection Act 1990 (c. 43), s.78A(4) inserted by Environment Act 1995 (c. 25), s.57.

Stat. Def., in relation to children and young persons, Family Law Act 1996 (c. 27), s.63(1) and Housing Act 1996 (c. 52), s.158(1).

HAS. "A third party has a better right than the plaintiff" (R.S.C., Ord. 15, r.10A(2)). This means "has at the time of the alleged tort." It is not restricted to the date of the application or its hearing (*De Franco* v. *Commissioner of Police of the Metropolis, The Times,* May 8, 1987).

"Has with him" (Prevention of Crime Act 1953 (c. 14), s.1(1)). Forgetfulness is not enough to prevent the state of possession continuing. So that a man who had a cosh in his car still had it "with him" notwithstanding that he had forgotten that it was there (*R.* v. *McCalla* (1988) 152 J.P. 481). See also POSSESSION; REASONABLE EXCUSE (8).

"Has with him any article for use in the course of . . . theft" (Theft Act 1968 (c. 60), s.25(1)). A person who comes into possession of articles after he has started preparing for theft can still be convicted of having them with him for the purposes of this section. It is immaterial whether or not the theft is achieved (*Minor* v. *DPP* (1988) 86 Cr.App.R. 378).

"Having upon him . . . any instrument" (Vagrancy Act 1824 (c. 83), s.4). The offence is not the actual use of the weapon but the premeditated carrying of it; so that where a man, trying to deny entry, slammed the front door in the face of two police officers, thereby breaking the glass, and then lunged at them with a piece of the glass, he was not guilty of an offence under this section (*Wood* v. *Commissioner of Police of the Metropolis* [1986] 1 W.L.R. 796).

"Would have to go" (H.C. 169, para. 134) means "would have no practical alternative but to go" (*R.* v. *Immigration Appeal Tribunal, ex p. Miller* [1988] Imm.A.R. 358).

"To have with him a firearm" (Firearms Act 1968 (c. 27), s.18(1)). A robber has "with him" a firearm within the meaning of this section if it is readily accessible to him as he is about to commit a robbery, even if it is in fact some distance away (*R.* v. *Pawlicki; R.* v. *Swindell* [1992] 1 W.L.R. 827).

"Has to work" (Factories Act 1961 (c. 34), s.29). A worker ordered to work on the roof of a factory "has to work" there within the meaning of this section (*Dexter* v. *Tenby Electric Accessories* [1991] C.O.D. 288).

HEALTH CARE. Stat. Def., "services for or in connection with the prevention, diagnosis or treatment of illness" (Health Act 1999 (c. 8), s.18(4)).

HEALTH PROFESSIONAL. Stat. Def., Data Protection Act 1998 (c. 29), s.69.

HEARSAY. Stat. Def., Civil Evidence Act 1995 (c. 38), s.1(2)(a).

HEDGEROW. Stat. Def., "includes any stretch of hedgerow" (Environment Act 1995 (c. 25), s.97(8)).

HELD. "Held by him since his conviction" (Drug Trafficking Offences Act 1986 (c. 32), s.2(3)). The words "held by him since his conviction" applied to any property or funds held by the defendant on the date of his conviction (*R.* v. *Clark* [1997] 4 All E.R. 803).

HEREDITAMENT. "The hereditament" referred to in paras. 2(*a*) and 2(*b*) of Sched. 1 of the General Rate Act 1967 (c. 9) applied to a unit of property that was sufficiently identified by an entry in the valuation list whether or not the description of the hereditament in that entry appropriately described the purpose for which it might lawfully be occupied (*Hailbury Investments* v. *Westminster City Council* [1986] 1 W.L.R. 1232).
    Stat. Def., Local Government Finance Act, 1988 (c. 41), s.64.
    A floating home was a "hereditament" within the meaning of the General Rate Act (c. 9), s.115 and so liable to council tax (*Nicholls* v. *Wimbledon Valuation Office Agency* [1995] RVR 171).

HERITABLE SECURITY. Stat. Def., Building Societies Act 1986 (c. 53), s.119.

HIGH-CLASS. "High-class accommodation." The reference under this paragraph in the Main Work, p. 1165, should be to *Patoner* v. *Lowe* (1985) 275 E.G. 540.

HIGHWAY. See WAY.

HIRE. "Carrying passengers for hire or reward", see PUBLIC SERVICE VEHICLE.

HIRE OR REWARD. See PUBLIC SERVICE VEHICLE.

HIS. "In the course of any business of his" (Consumer Protection Act 1987 (c. 43), s.20(1)). These words mean any business of which the defendant was either the owner or in which he had a controlling interest. So that where the defendant employee placed a special offer notice outside one of a group's shops he was not acting in the course of any business of "his" (*R.* v. *Warwickshire County Council, ex p. Johnson* [1993] 2 W.L.R. 1).

HISTORICAL INTEREST. See COLLECTOR'S PIECE.

HISTORY. "History of failure to respond to non-custodial penalties" (Criminal Justice Act 1982 (c. 48), s.1(4A)(*a*) as amended by s.123(3) of the Criminal Justice Act 1988 (c. 33)). The word "history" involves plurality. Consequently a young offender who had only one previous appearance could not qualify for a custodial sentence under this subsection (*R.* v. *Southwark Crown Court, ex p. Ager* [1990] Crim.L.R. 531). Followed in *R.* v. *Robertson* [1990] Crim.L.R. 822. An offender does not have a "history" within the meaning of this section unless he has had at least two previous appearances and two failures to respond (*R.* v. *Smith* (*Catherine Elizabeth*) (1992) 13 Cr.App.R.(S.) 17). A conditional discharge did not qualify as a non-custodial penalty for the purposes of deciding whether a defendant had "a history of failure to respond to non-custodial penalties" (*R.* v. *Betts* [1992] Crim.L.R. 218).

See also SERIOUS.

HOLDER IN DUE COURSE. (3) (Bills of Exchange Act 1882 (c. 61), s.29(1)). The holder of a cheque who had received it as indorsee from the payee in payment of an antecedent debt smaller than the amount of the cheque was the "holder in due course" within the meaning of this section, as he had taken it "for value" within the meaning of s.29(1)(*b*) (*Mac-Kenzie Mills* v. *Buono, The Times*, July 31, 1986). An endorsee of a cheque who acquires it in good faith for value by conditional delivery becomes a "holder in due course" on satisfaction of the condition (*Clifford Chance* v. *Silver* [1992] NPC 103).

HOLDING COMPANY. (Income and Corporation Taxes Act 1970 (c. 10), s.258(5)(*b*), now Income and Corporation Taxes Act 1988 (c. 1), s.413(3)(*b*)). "Holding company" within the meaning of ss.5(*b*) and 7 meant companies resident in the United Kingdom, so that a business which did not consist wholly or mainly in the holding of shares and securities of subsidiary companies within s.285(5)(*b*) was not entitled to consortium relief (*ICI* v. *Colmer* [1996] 1 W.L.R. 469).

Stat. Def., Companies Act 1985 (c.6), s.736; Finance Act 1985 (c. 54), Sched. 1; Income and Corporation Taxes Act 1988 (c. 1), s.229; Companies Act 1989 (c. 40), s.144; Taxation of Chargeable Gains Act 1992 (c. 12), Sched. 6, para. 1(2)).

HOLY TABLE. See TABLE.

HOME. A "home" within the meaning of s.9(3) of the Children Act 1975 (c. 72) must provide some element of regular occupation with the likelihood of permanency; *e.g.* the fixed residence of a family or a household providing the comforts of home (*Re Y.* (*Minors*) (*Adoption: Jurisdiction*) [1985] 3 W.L.R. 601).

"Principal home" (Housing Act 1985 (c. 68), s.81). For a dwelling-house to be a person's "home" for the purposes of this section it was not necessary that he should be in actual physical occupation of it. It was sufficient if there was some sign of occupation, *e.g.* the presence of furniture, and that the person intended to return to live there. A person could have more than one "home" at any one time, and which one constituted the "principal home" was a question of fact for the judge. (*Crawley Borough Council* v. *Sawyer* (1988) 20 H.L.R. 98).

"The home" (Supplementary Benefits (Resources) Regulations 1981 (No. 1527), regs. 5, 7). Where part of a family occupied one house, and the other part occupied a second house three eighths of a mile away, in circumstances where all meals were taken together in one of the houses and neither of them could accommodate the whole family, the two houses together were held to satisfy the definition of "the home" in these regulations (Social Security Decision No. R(SB) 10/89).

"Home address", see ADDRESS.

"Mobile home", see MOBILE HOME.

HOMELESS. (Housing Act 1985 (c. 68), s.58(2A), as inserted by s.14 of the Housing and Planning Act 1986 (c. 63)). A housekeeper who, following an argument with her employer, was asked to leave, and did so, became "homeless" within the meaning of this section, notwithstanding that the employer expressed a willingness to take her back. The contract of employment had been terminated and in its absence there was no "licence to occupy" within the meaning of s.58(2)(*b*) (*R.* v. *Kensington and Chelsea Royal Borough, ex p. Minton* (1988) 20 H.L.R. 648). In considering whether an applicant is homeless within the meaning of this section an authority must have regard to overcrowding even where the accommodation is not statutorily overcrowded (*R.* v. *Westminster City Council, ex p. Alouat* (1989) 21 H.L.R. 447), and must have regard to all relevant factors including, but not limited to, the quality of the accommodation available, and which might include, as in this case, violence or threats of violence (*R.* v. *Broxbourne Borough Council, ex p. Willmoth* (1989) 22 H.L.R. 118). In considering whether persons had settled accommodation and were therefore not homeless a relevant factor was their intention in relation to the accommodation and the intention of the person who allowed them to occupy it (*R.* v. *Hammersmith and Fulham London Borough Council, ex p. Lusi* [1991] C.O.D. 290). A child whose parents' application under s.62 has been rejected is not "homeless" for the purposes of s.58 (*R.* v. *Bexley London Borough Council, ex p. B*; *R.* v. *Oldham Metropolitan Borough Council, ex p. G* (1992) 24 H.L.R. 726).

Stat. Def., Housing Act 1985 (c. 68), s.58.

See also ACCOMMODATION; REASONABLE.

HOMEWORKER. Stat. Def., Wages Act 1986 (c. 48), s.26.

HORSE. Stat. Def., Horses (Protective Headgear) Act 1990 (c. 25), s.3.

HOSPITAL. Stat. Def., Road Traffic Act 1988 (c. 52), s.11.

HOSTEL. Stat. Def., Housing Act 1985 (c. 68), s.622; Housing Associations Act 1985 (c. 69), s.106; Housing Act 1996 (c. 52), s.63(1).

HOUR. "Employment for sixteen hours or more weekly" (Employment Protection (Consolidation) Act 1978 (c. 44), Sched. 13, para. 4). A teacher's free periods, which are normally used for preparing and marking work, can be taken into account in computing his hours of employment (*Society of Licensed Victuallers* v. *Chamberlain* [1989] IRLR 421).

HOUSE. (40)–(42) A building comprising two maisonettes, one above the other, is a "house" for the purposes of ss.2(1), 2(1)(*b*) of the Leasehold Reform Act 1967 (c. 88) notwithstanding that the entrance to the top unit was via a ground floor hall separated vertically from the hall of the lower unit by a wall (*Sharpe* v. *Duke Street Securities NV* (1987) 283 E.G. 1558). Similarly, a building divided horizontally into two maisonettes could be called a "house" within the meaning of these sections, notwithstanding that the building had two front doors (*Malpas* v. *St. Ermin's Property Co.* [1992] RVR 68.

(Leasehold Reform Act 1967 (c. 88), s.2(1)). Where a dwelling which would otherwise be a "house" under the 1967 Act had a material part of its accommodation under the structure of another property it fell within the exclusionary provisions of the Act and was not enfranchiseable (*Duke of Westminster* v. *Birrane* [1995] 2 W.L.R. 270).

(Leasehold Reform Act 1967 (c. 88), s.2). The ground floor of a mews house which was used as a garage together with a separate house was a "house and premises" for the purposes of s.2 (*Dugan-Chapman* v. *Grosvenor Estates* [1997] 10 E.G. 152).

"House" (Housing Act 1957 (c. 56), s.9(1A) (now s.190 of the Housing Act 1985 (c. 68)). A building originally constructed as a single dwelling-house did not cease to be a "house" within the meaning of this Act when it was internally converted into flats which were then sold on long leases. It could therefore be argued, as here, that a modern purpose-built block of flats was a "house" for the purposes of the Act (*Pollway Nominees* v. *Croydon London Borough Council* [1987] A.C. 79). But a flat in a block is not a "house" within the meaning of this section (*R.* v. *Lambeth London Borough Council, ex p. Clayhope Properties* [1987] 3 W.L.R. 854).

"House" (Public Health Act 1936 (c. 49), s.72). A university hall of residence is not a "house" for the purposes of this section, so that refuse generated by the occupants is not "house refuse" (*Mattison* v. *Beverley Borough Council* (1987) 151 J.P. 499).

Stat. Def., Housing Act 1985 (c. 68), ss.56, 183, 207, 322, 399, 457, 575, 602, 623; Housing Associations Act 1985 (c. 69), s.106; Water Industry Act 1991 (c. 56), s.219; Housing Act 1996 (c. 52), s.63(1).

HOUSEBOAT. Stat. Def., Finance Act 1989 (c. 26), s.21; Value Added Tax Act 1994 (c. 23), Sched. A1, para. 3(4) (Sched. inserted by Finance Act 1995 (c. 4), s.21(3)); Housing Grants, Construction and Regeneration Act 1996 (c. 53), s.78(5).

HOUSE REFUSE. See REFUSE.

HOW. "How . . . the deceased came by his death" (Coroners Act 1988 (c. 13), s.11(5)(*b*)(ii)). The word "how" is specific and means "by what means" rather than such concept as "in what broad circumstances" (*R.* v. *H. M. Coroner for Birmingham, ex p. Secretary of State for the Home Department* (1991) 155 J.P. 107). (*R.* v. *H.M. Coroner for Birmingham* followed in *R.* v. *H.M. Coroner for North Humberside and Scunthorpe, ex p. Jamieson* [1994] 3 W.L.R. 82).

HUMAN CONSUMPTION. Stat. Def., Food and Environment Protection Act 1985 (c. 48), s.24.

HUMAN RIGHTS. Stat. Def., including, but not limited to, rights under Convention on Human Rights, Norther Ireland Act 1998 (c. 47), s.69(11)(b).

I

"IF" CONTRACT. An "if contract" must contain the necessary terms and include an unequivocal term that it was to apply if no formal agreement reached (*Monk Construction* v. *Norwich Union Life Assurance Society* (C.A. 1992) 62 B.L.R. 107).

IF SUED. (Law Reform (Married Women and Tortfeasors) Act 1935 (c. 30), s.6(1)(*c*)). These words neither impose nor relate to a time limit in the action (*Forte's Service Areas* v. *Department of Transport* (1985) 31 Build.L.R. 1).

ILL-TREAT. "Wilfully assaults, ill-treats, neglects, abandons or exposes" (Children and Young Persons Act 1933 (c. 12), s.1(1), as amended by the Children and Young Persons Act 1963 (c. 37)). A prosecutor had the burden of choosing the precise word in the subsection to describe the conduct complained of. In stating this in an appeal against conviction of cruelty by ill-treatment, in a case where there was no evidence of ill-treatment but there was of neglect, their Lordships concluded that the conviction would have had to have been quashed, because ill-treatment and neglect could not sensibly be equated, were it not that they were bound by the decision in *R.* v. *Hayles* [1969] 1 Q.B. 364 [see Main Work, p. 1205] (*R.* v. *Beard* (1987) Cr.App.R. 395).
    "Ill-treat or wilfully to neglect" (Mental Health Act 1983 (c. 20), s.127). Persons drafting indictments should bear in mind that "ill-treat" is not the same as "wilfully to neglect" (*R.* v. *Newington* (1990) 91 Cr.App.R. 247).
    "Ill-treatment," Stat. Def., Housing Act 1996 (c. 52), s.158(1).

ILLEGAL ENTRANT. (Immigration Act 1971 (c. 77), s.33(1)). A person who had entered the U.K. by deception was an "illegal entrant" within the meaning of this section (*R.* v. *Secretary of State for the Home Department, ex p. Kumar* [1990] Imm. A.R. 265). A person whose entry into the United Kingdom was obtained through a deception by a third party was also an "illegal entrant," notwithstanding that he played no part in the deception and was unaware of it at the time (*R.* v. *Secretary of State for the Home Department, ex p. Khaled* [1987] Imm.A.R. 67). Permission to enter the United Kingdom granted to a number of persons by an immigration officer, who erroneously believed that they were British citizens, did not prevent those persons from being "illegal entrants" for the purposes of this section (*R.* v. *Secretary of State for the Home Department, ex p. Mokuolo* [1989] C.O.D. 210, C.A.). Failing to tell the immigration officer of an intention to study in the U.K. was obtaining leave to enter by fraud and rendered the person concerned an "illegal entrant" for the purposes of s.33 and Sched. 2 (*R.* v. *Secretary of State for the Home Department, ex p. Nwanarve* [1992] Imm. A.R. 39). A Filipino who had entered the U.K. as the servant of a Kuwaiti family with the intention of escaping from them as soon as a chance arose was not an "illegal entrant" by deception as she had not made or been asked to make any representations about her intentions (*R.* v. *Secretary of State for the Home Department, ex p. Dordas* [1992] Imm. A.R. 99). A person who obtained leave to enter the U.K. by means of a work permit illegally obtained for him was an "illegal entrant" notwithstanding the fact that he had no personal knowledge of the invalidity of the work permit (*R.* v. *Immigration Officer, ex p. Chan* [1992] 1 W.L.R. 541). Disembarkation from a plane or a ship is not of itself entry into the country, so that person who disembarked without a right of entry were not automatically illegal entrants (*R.* v. *Naillie; R.* v. *Kanesarajah, The Times,* May 27, 1993). A person in breach of a restriction placed on his temporary admission to the U.K. is an "illegal entrant" within the meaning of the section (*Akhtar (Raya Waheed)* v. *Governor of Pentonville Prison* [1993] ImmAR 424, C.A.).

A person was not an "illegal entrant" for the purposes of s.33(1) of the 1971 Act when he had entered the United Kingdom in breach of the immigration laws where his work permit was merely inappropriate having been issued by mistake, rather than invalid since it contained no false information and was not a forgery (*R.* v. *Secretary of State for the Home Department, ex p. Ku* [1995] 2 All E.R. 981).

IMMEDIATE. "Immediate unlawful violence" (Public Order Act 1986 (c. 64), s.4(1)(*b*)). For the purposes of this section the word "immediate" does not mean instantaneous; a relatively short time interval might elapse between the act which was threatening, abusive or insulting and the unlawful violence (*R.* v. *Horseferry Road Justices, ex p. Siadatan* [1990] Crim.L.R. 598) and *Valentine* v. *DPP* 1997] 6 C.L. 159).

IMMEDIATELY. (14) "Immediately before the transfer" (Transfer of Undertakings (Protection of Employment) Regulations 1981 (No. 1794) r.5). An employee who was dismissed by the transferors of a business after contracts of sale had been exchanged but before completion was still employed "immediately before the transfer" for the purposes of this regulation (*Kestongate* v. *Miller* [1986] I.C.R. 672; *Wheeler* v. *Patel* [1987] I.C.R. 631). Employees dismissed at 11 a.m. were held not to have been employed "immediately before the transfer" of the business which took place at 2 p.m. on the same day (*Secretary of State for Employment* v. *Spence* [1986] I.C.R. 651). And, where an employee ceased working for the old owners on March 1, and completion of the sale of the business was not until March 31, he had not been employed "immediately before the transfer" within the meaning of this regulation (*Brook Lane Finance Co.* v. *Bradley* [1988] I.C.R. 423). An employee dismissed shortly before the transfer of a business, for a reason connected with the transfer, was deemed to have been a person employed "immediately" before the transfer and to have been unfairly dismissed by the transferor. In effect that involved reading reg. 5(3) as if there were inserted after the words "immediately before the transfer" the words "or would have been so employed if he had not been unfairly dismissed in the circumstances described in reg. 8(1)" (*Litster* v. *Forth Dry Dock & Engineering Co.* [1989] 2 W.L.R. 634). See also TRANSFER.

IMMORAL. "Immoral purposes" (Sexual Offences Act 1956 (c. 69), s.32). An immoral purpose for the purposes of this section had to be some kind of sexual activity (*R.* v. *Kirkup (David)* [1993] 2 All E.R. 802).

IMPAIRMENT. (Sexual Offences Act 1956 (c. 69), s.45, as amended), see SEVERE.

IMPAIRED OR NEGLECTED. See AVOIDABLY IMPAIRED OR NEGLECTED.

IMPARTIAL. "Impartial discharge of his duties" (Police Regulations 1979 (No. 1470), Sched. 2). Impartiality, for the purposes of these regulations, bears a wide meaning, not restricted as between alternatives, and involves the proper performance of the police officer's duties free from conflict of interest (*Champion* v. *Chief Constable of Gwent Constabulary* [1990] 1 W.L.R. 1).

IMPOSE. "Impose imprisonment", See IMPRISONMENT.

IMPRISONMENT. "Impose imprisonment" (Magistrates' Courts Act 1980 (c. 43), s.133) means "pass a sentence of imprisonment" (as defined in s.150(1)) so that s.133 does not apply to the activation of a suspended sentence (*R.* v. *Chamberlain* (1992) 156 J.P.N. 172).

"Imprisonment or detention," Stat. Def., Criminal Justice Act 1961 (c. 39), s.38(3) as amended by Criminal Justice and Public Order Act 1994 (c. 33), Sched. 10, para. 12(5).

IMPROPER. "Unnecessary or improper act" (Prosecution of Offences Act 1985 (c. 23), s.19(1)). The word "improper" does not necessarily connote some grave impropriety, used as it is in conjunction with the word "unnecessary." It would cover an act or omission which would not have occurred if the party concerned had conducted his case properly (*DPP* v. *Denning* [1991] 3 W.L.R. 235).

"Improper, unreasonable or negligent" (Supreme Court Act 1981 (c. 54), s.51(6)). "Improper" covered any significant breach of a substantial duty imposed by a professional body and conduct regarded as "improper" according to a consensus of professional opinion. "Unreasonable" conduct was conduct which was vexatious, which harassed the other side rather than advanced the resolution of the case and incapable of a reasonable explanation. "Negligent" denoted a failure to act with the competence reasonably expected of the profession (*Ridehalgh* v. *Horsfield* [1994] 3 All E.R. 848).

IMPROVEMENT. The meaning of "improvement" in article 9(4) of the Local Government Reorganisation (Property, etc.) Order 1986 (No. 148) was not restricted to work on existing structures or in any other way. The word is here used in a sufficiently broad sense to cover development (*Coin Street Community Builders* v. *Barking and Dagenham London Borough Council, The Times*, July 20, 1988).

"Tenant's improvement," Stat. Def., Agricultural Tenancies Act 1995 (c. 8), s.15.

"Benefit, improvement, or development," see BENEFIT.

Stat. Def., Housing Act 1985 (c. 68), ss.187, 237, 518, 525; "includes alteration and enlargement" (Housing Grants, Construction and Regeneration Act 1996 (c. 53), s.101).

IN ANY CAUSE. (Exchequer Court (Scotland) Act 1856 (c. 56), s.24). "In any cause" in s.24 related to a cause in which one of the parties was the Crown (*Meekison* v. *Uniroyal Englebert Tyres* (Sh.Ct.) 1995 S.C.L.R. 273).

IN CHARGE. (5) "In charge of a vehicle" (Road Traffic Act 1972 (c. 20), s.5(2) as amended by Transport Act 1981 (c. 56), Sched. 8). A person who at the time he was arrested had been round the corner and in a different street from where his own vehicle was parked was held not to have been "in charge" of it for the purposes of this section (*Director of Public Prosecutions* v. *Webb* [1988] RTR 374). For a defendant to be "in charge of a vehicle" there must be a close connection between him and the control of the vehicle, but it is not necessary to prove that there was a likelihood of him actually driving the vehicle (*R.* v. *Watkins* [1989] 1 All E.R. 1126).

A person could be "in charge" of a motor vehicle even when it had been immobilised by means of a wheel clamp (*DPP* v. *Watkins* [1989] R.T.R. 324 applied) (*Drake* v. *DPP* [1994] R.T.R. 411).

IN CONNECTION WITH. See CONNECTED WITH.

IN CONSEQUENCE OF. (16) "During and in consequence of a trade dispute" (Local Government Superannuation (Amendment) (No. 2) Regulations 1981 (No. 1509) reg. (1A)). A person who, on the advice but not the instruction of his union, was absent from duty in support of a strike was held to have been absent "in consequence of a trade dispute" within the meaning of this regulation, notwithstanding that his absence was voluntary (*Povey* v. *Secretary of State for the Environment*, *The Times*, July 17, 1986).

(17) The words "in consequence of" in the Housing Act 1985 (c. 68), s.60(1) required a local authority to decide the question of the cause of an applicant's homelessness by applying the ordinary principles of remoteness (*R.* v. *Havant Borough Council, ex p. Marten* (CO/3110/94), January 19, 1995 9 C.L. 255).

IN GOOD FAITH. "Act or omission in good faith" (Housing Act 1985 (c. 68), s.60(3)). An act or omission can be "in good faith" within the meaning of this section notwithstanding that it was unreasonable that the appellant should be unaware of a relevant fact (*R.* v. *Tower Hamlets London Borough Council, ex p. Rouf* (1991) 23 H.L.R. 38).

IN PURSUANCE OF. See PURSUANCE.

IN RECEIPT OF ALLOWANCE. A child must satisfy the conditions of entitlement to be "in receipt of the attendance allowance" for the purposes of the Income Support (General) Regulations 1987 (No. 1967) Sched. 2, para. 13 and had the same meaning in para. 14 (*Social Security Decision No. R(IS) 10/94*).

IN RELATION TO. "In relation to . . . retirement" (Sex Discrimination Act 1975 (c. 65), s.6(4)) means "about" and not "consequent upon" (*Roberts* v. *Cleveland Area Health Authority* [1979] I.C.R. 558; *Duke* v. *Reliance Systems* [1988] 2 W.L.R. 359).

IN RESPECT OF. "A payment in respect of . . . the supply" (Value Added Tax Act 1983 (c. 55), s.5(1)). A deposit paid on placing an order for made-to-order goods became a payment "in respect of" the supply of those goods as soon as accepted, even though the order might be cancelled (*Bruce Banks Sails* v. *Customs and Excise Commissioners* (1990) 3 VATTR 175).

(Value Added Tax (General) Regulations 1985 (S.I. 1985 No. 886). reg. 23(1)(a) (as substituted by Value Added Tax (General) (Amendment) Regulations 1989 (S.I. 1989 No. 1132), reg. 5). An inadvertent overpayment of a current debt amounted to a payment made under a mistake of fact and as such could not be characterised as a payment "on account" before the services were performed or as being received "in respect of" future supplies within reg. 23(1) (*Customs and Excise Commissioners* v. *British Telecommunications plc* [1996] 1 W.L.R. 1309).

"In respect of, or relating to any land," see RELATING.

IN SO FAR AS. "In so far as it covers one or more of the risks set out in Article 12A" (Brussels Convention on Jurisdiction and Enforcement of Judgments in Civil and Commercial Matters, Art. 12(5); incorporated into English Law by the Civil Jurisdiction and Judgments Act 1982 (c. 27)). The words "in so far as" are to be interpreted literally as synonymous with "to the extent that", and not as equivalent to "if" or "provided" (*Charman* v. *WOC Offshore BV, The Times*, October 27, 1992).

IN THE COURSE. (1) "Arising out of and in the course of employment" (Social Security Act 1975 (c. 14), s.50(1)) "Arises out of and in the course of his employment" (s.107(5)(*a*)). Whether an accident happens in the course of employment is an issue of fact, and those adjudicating should adopt a broad approach in weighing all the factors material to a particular claim, and should then consider the aggregate of such factors in the final evaluation (*Nancollas* v. *Insurance Officer; Ball* v. *Insurance Officer* [1985] 1 All E.R. 833). Members of a fire brigade who, while operating a "go slow" policy, took so long to reach a fire that the building and its contents were almost completely destroyed, were held not to have been acting "in the course of" their employment, so that their employer was not liable for the damage resulting from their action (*General Engineering Services* v. *Kingston and St. Andrew Corporation* [1988] 3 All E.R. 867). An employee required by his employer to travel from his ordinary residence to a place which was some distance from his usual workplace to carry out a job of work, and who was paid wages for travelling time, was acting in the course of his employment, notwithstanding that the employee was allowed to choose the manner and time of travel (*Smith* v. *Stages* [1989] 2 W.L.R. 529). But a man on deployment at a depot away from his regular workplace, for which inconvenience he had been granted a travelling allowance, was held not to have been acting "in the course of" his employment when he was involved in an accident on the way home from work, on the basis that a flat-rate travelling allowance was not "wages" within the meaning of s.107 (*Social Security Decision No. R(1)(1/91)*). A police officer who was injured while playing for a police football team had not been injured "in the course" of his employment (*Faulkner* v. *Chief Adjudication Officer, The Times,* April 8, 1994).

(Race Relations Act 1976 (c. 74), s.32). In order to give effect to the legislative purpose of the Act it was necessary to give the phrase "in the course of his employment" in s.32(1) a wide interpretation. Vicarious liability under the common law and liability under the Act were not sufficiently similar to justify the application of common law principles to the interpretation of s.32(1). The purpose of the Act was to deter racial harassment in the workplace by making employers liable for the acts of their employees, unless they could show themselves to have taken reasonable steps to prevent the discrimination and it would be wrong and contrary to the purpose of the Act to permit an employer to escape liability for serious harassment by seeking to apply principles drawn from a completely separate area of law (*Jones* v. *Tower Boot Co. Ltd* [1997] I.C.R. 254).

(Social Security Contributions and Benefits Act 1992 (c. 4), s.94(1)). An assault on an employee, committed when she was on sick leave, which took place for a reason connected with her employment, was not committed "in the course of employment", since at the time of the assault the victim was not engaged on her work duties nor doing something reasonably incidental to the performance of those duties (*Chief Adjudication Officer* v. *Rhodes* [1999] I.C.R. 178).

"In the course of an investigation" (Road Traffic Act 1972 (c. 20), s.8(1) as substituted by the Transport Act 1981 (c. 56), Sched. 8). Where there was reason to suspect that any one of three suspects was the driver of a vehicle, it was held to be lawful to request samples from all three as the requests were made "in the course of an investigation" within the meaning of this section (*Pearson* v. *Commissioner of Police of the Metropolis* [1988] RTR 276).

"In the course of the winding up of a company" (Insolvency Act 1986 (c. 45), s.214). The words "if in the course of the winding up of a company" in s.214 of the 1986 Act meant "if it appeared to the court" and thereby governed the period within which the court had jurisdiction to make an order rather than imposing a limitation period on the commencement of proceedings (*Moore* v. Gadd, *The Times*, February 17, 1997).

A body charged with statutory functions to regulate and control the investment industry, auditors and insolvency practitioners did not act in the course of or furtherance of a business for the purposes of s.4 of the Value Added Tax 1994 (c. 23), even though charges were made for the services offered by the body (*Institute of Chartered Accountants in England and Wales* v. *Customs and Excise Commissioners* [1998] 4 All E.R. 115).

"In the course of catering" (Value Added Tax Act 1994 (c. 23), Sched. 8). Party trays of cold food made to order by a delicatessen was not a supply "in the course of catering" within the 1994 Act, Sched. 8 (*Customs and Excise Commissioners* v. *Safeway Stores plc* [1997] STC 163).

Freshly cooked food delivered to customers to eat while still hot amounted to supplies "in the course of catering" and liable to VAT (*Malik* (*t/a Hotline Foods*) v. *Customs and Excise Commissioners* [1998] STC 537).

IN THE METHOD OF DISPOSAL. See DISPOSAL.

IN THE NAME OF AND ON BEHALF OF. See NAME.

An application by a liquidator under the Insolvency Act 1986 (c. 45), s.242 for a declaration that a payment made by the company was unlawful was not made "in the name of and on behalf of" the company (*Dyer* v. *Hyslop*, 1994 S.C.C.R. (Sh.Ct.) 171).

IN THE NATURE OF A COMMERCIAL VENTURE. (Transfer of Undertakings (Protection of Employment Regulations) 1981 (No. 1794), reg. 2(1)). The words "in the nature of" showed that a venture did not have to be a commercial venture to qualify under the regulations, so that a local authority's cleansing services where no profit for distribution was made was "in the nature of a commercial venture" (*U.K. Waste Control Ltd* v. *Wren and ors* [1995] I.C.R. 974).

INABILITY. Inability to walk, see UNABLE.

INADEQUATE. (C.C. Rules (S.I. 1981 No. 1687), Ord. 38, r.9). The word "inadequate" in Ord. 38, r.9 should be considered in relation to the work done which, in all the circumstances, it would be reasonable to charge a losing party (*Daniels* v. *London Borough of Lambeth* [1997] 10 C.L. 51).

INCAPABLE. "Incapable of work", see WORK.

INCIDENTAL. "Of and incidental to" (Supreme Court Act 1981 (c. 54), s.51(1)). Where two actions were heard together, the respondent in the first being the applicant in the second, the costs in the second were not "of and incidental to" the first, so that there was no power to order the applicant in the first action to pay the costs of the second action (*Aiden Shipping Co.* v. *Interbulk* [1985] 1 W.L.R. 1222).

(22) "Merely incidental to the discussion" (Contempt of Court Act 1981 (c. 49), s.5). A television broadcast and a newspaper article which created serious prejudicial risks to criminal proceedings by appearing during the trial, were more than "merely incidental to the discussion"; so that the newspaper and the television company concerned were guilty of contempt of court (*Att.-Gen.* v. *TVS Television, The Times*, July 7, 1989).

"Incidental to the enjoyment of the dwellinghouse" (Town and Country Planning Act 1971 (c. 78), s.22(2)(*d*); now Town and Country Planning Act 1990 (c. 8), s.55(2)(*d*)). Siting a canal narrow boat in the front garden while it was being refurbished and refitted by the owner's family was a use "incidental to the enjoyment of the dwellinghouse" and did not therefore involve development (*Chiltern District Council and Peters* (1988) 3 P.A.D. 201). For the use of proposed buildings to be considered as "incidental" to the use of a dwelling-house both the nature and scale of the proposed activities to be conducted in the buildings had to be considered; the size of the building being relevant to that consideration, but in no way decisive (*Emin* v. *Secretary of State for the Environment* (1989) 58 P. & C.R. 416). The keeping of a large number of dogs, 44 at one point, in a cottage in Wales involved a "material change of use" and was not exempted as a "purpose incidental to the enjoyment of the dwelling-house as such" within the meaning of s.22(2)(*d*) (*Wallington* v. *Secretary of State for Wales* [1991] 1 P.L.R. 87). The retail sale of plants grown upon the property was held to be "incidental and ancillary" to the growing of the plants on the land (*Allen* v. *Secretary of State for the Environment and Reigate and Banstead Borough Council* (1990) 1 P.L.R. 25).

The placing of a replica Spitfire and a fibreglass fish on a roof were not "incidental to the enjoyment of the dwelling-house" which involved a concept of objective reasonableness and was not solely a matter for the whim of the individual owner or occupier (*Croydon London Borough Council* v. *Gladden* [1994] 1 P.L.R. 30).

"Incidental to the discharge of any of their functions" (Local Government Act 1972 (c. 70), s.111(1)). "Functions" embraces all the duties and powers of a local authority and therefore includes its borrowing powers. Interest rate swap transactions are not "incidental" to the borrowing powers conferred by this Act on local authorities and are not therefore incidental to their functions (*Hazell* v. *Hammersmith and Fulham London Borough Council* [1991] 2 W.L.R. 372).

"Costs of and incidental to all proceedings," See COSTS.

INCLUDES. (Town and Country Planning Act 1971 (c. 78), s.52). "Includes'" is capable of two interpretations: either "means" or "comprises" (*Wiggins* v. *Arun District Council* [1997] 74 P. &. C.R. 64).

INCOME. (31) "Income of the person to whom it is paid" (Finance Act 1973 (c. 51), s.17). Payments made from the capital of a discretionary trust fund to pay for the cost of nursing care for an elderly beneficiary were not "income" within the meaning of this section (*Stevenson* v. *Wishart* [1987] 2 All E.R. 428).

Borrowings by way of a bank overdraft secured by capital and used for day-to-day living expenses constituted "income" for the purposes of regulation 16(4) of the Housing Benefit Regulations 1985 (No. 677) (*R.* v. *West Dorset District Council, ex p. Poupard* (1988) 28 RVR 40).

(Income and Corporation Taxes Act 1988 (c. 1), s.393(8)). Investment income which accrued when the making of investments was not part of the taxpayer's business and which was not employed in any way in the taxpayer's business was not "trading income" within the meaning of s.393(1) and (8) (*Nuclear Electric plc* v. *Bradley (Inspector of Taxes)* [1996] 1 W.L.R. 529).

(Insolvency Act 1986 (c. 45), s.310(7). The collection of contractual rights under a pension policy was a chose in action and therefore constituted "property" within the meaning of s.436 of the 1986 Act so that the benefits of the policy, which vested in a trustee in bankruptcy by virtue of s.306, and an annuity payable under the policy were not the "income of the bankrupt" (*Landau (a bankrupt), Re* [1997] 3 W.L.R. 225).

Stat. Def., "means receipts of any description, including capital receipts"—(Education Act 1994 (c. 30), s.21(3)).

"Chargeable to income," see EXPENSES.

See also ANNUAL PROFITS.

INCREASE. "Increase in the capital" (Finance Act 1973 (c. 51), s.47). A resolution by directors in the course of a company merger allotting shares in the company in exchange for part of the share capital of another company effected an "increase in the capital" of the company giving rise to a liability to stamp duty on a "chargeable transaction" within the meaning of this section (*Rothschild (J) Holdings* v. *I.R.C.* [1989] S.T.C. 645).

INDECENT. "Indecent photograph of a child" (Protection of Children Act 1978 (c. 37), s.1(1)(*a*)). In determining whether a photograph of a child is "indecent" within the meaning of this section the age of the child is a material consideration; so that it is possible that a photograph which, if judged intrinsically, is not indecent on the face of it, can be indecent within the meaning of this section by virtue of the fact that it was of a girl of 14 (*R.* v. *Owen* (*Charles*) [1988] 1 W.L.R. 134). The circumstances in which a photograph of a child was taken and the motives of the photographer were not relevant to the question whether the photograph was, in fact, "indecent" within the meaning of this section (*R.* v. *Graham-Kerr* [1988] 1 W.L.R. 1098).

For the common law crime of indecent exposure the test of indecency is whether the act outraged public decency. A mere wilful public exposure of the person is not necessarily indecent (*R.* v. *Clifford* [1988] 8 C.L. 86).

INDEMNITY COVER. In medical context, Stat. Def., National Health Service Act 1977 (c. 49), s.43C(3) inserted by Health Act 1999 (c. 8), s.9(1).

INDEPENDENT PERSON. (Social Security Pensions Act 1975 (c. 60), s.57C(2)(*a*) as inserted by para. 1 of Sched. 4 of the Social Security Act 1990 (c. 27)). A solicitor who, on being appointed trustee of a pension plan pursuant to this section, procured the services of partners in his own firm to assist him was not an "independent person" within the meaning of s.57C (*Re Scientific Investment Pension Plan, Clark* v. *Hicks, The Times*, December 10, 1992).

Stat. Def., "a knowledgeable and willing party dealing at arm's length" (Finance Act 1996 (c. 8), s.103(1)).

INDEPENDENT TRADE UNION. Stat. Def., Employment Rights Act 1996 (c. 18), s.235(1).

INDICATION. "Indication of quantity." Stat. Def., Weights and Measures Act 1985 (c. 72), s.94.

INDICTABLE OFFENCE. Where completed offence was triable either way, an attempt to commit that offence was an "indictable offence" even though the offence would have been tried summarily by virtue of the value of the damage that would have been done had the commission of the offence taken place (*R.* v. *Bristol Justices, ex p. E* [1999] 1 W.L.R. 390).

INDICTMENT. "Relating to trial on indictment," see RELATING.

INDIVIDUAL. "Action . . . taken against him as an individual" (Employment Protection (Consolidation) Act 1978 (c. 44), s.23(1), as amended). Action taken against a union, however much it may affect the individual members and officers, was not action against "an individual" within the meaning of this section (*National Coal Board* v. *Ridgway* [1987] 3 All E.R. 582).

"The council may arrange for any of its functions . . . to be discharged by . . . (*c*) an individual whether or not a member of the Society's staff" (Solicitors Act 1974 (c. 47), s.79 as substituted by s.97 of the Courts and

Legal Services Act 1990 (c. 41)). The Council of the Law Society, when delegating some of its functions to an "individual" pursuant to this section, is entitled to delegate to the holder of an office as such, and there is no obligation on the council to familiarise itself with the individual's name (*R.* v. *Law Society, ex p. Curtin, The Times,* December 3, 1993).

INDUSTRIAL ACTION. (Trade Union and Labour Relations (Consolidation) Act 1992 (c. 52), s.65). In order to constitute "industrial action" there must be some action directed against the employer with the object of securing some advantage for the employees, so that a union's opposition to full time fire fighters being additionally employed on retained fire fighting contracts was not "other industrial action" (*Fire Brigades Union* v. *Knowles* [1996] 4 All E.R. 653).

Stat. Def., Employment Act 1988 (c. 19), s.1; Trade Union and Labour Relations (Consolidation) Act 1992 (c. 52), s.62).

INDUSTRIAL BUILDING. A processing centre where cheques were sorted, encoded and their data electronically stored was an "industrial building" within the meaning of the Capital Allowances Act 1990 (c. 1), s.18(1)(e) since the process carried on in the centre did not need to be industrial nor alter the character of the goods and materials subjected to them (*Girobank plc* v. *Clarke (Inspector of Taxes), The Times*, March 21, 1996).

INDUSTRIAL PROPERTY. "Industrial or commercial property" (EEC Treaty, Art. 36) would cover a patent granted under s.50 of the Patents Act 1949 (c. 87) (*Thetford Corp.* v. *Fiamma Spa (Case No. 35/87)* [1990] 2 W.L.R. 1394).

INDUSTRIAL RELATIONS. "Duties concerned with industrial relations" (Employment Protection (Consolidation) Act 1978 (c. 44), s.27(1)(a)). Union officials who attended a meeting of trade union officials to discuss the implications of the repeal of a particular statute, were held to be carrying out "duties concerned with industrial relations" between an employer and his employees within the meaning of this section (*Adlington* v. *British Bakeries (Northern)* [1989] IRLR 218).

INEXCUSABLE DELAY. See INORDINATE DELAY.

INFERIOR COURT. An industrial tribunal is an "inferior court" within the meaning of R.S.C., Ord. 52, r.1(2)(a)(iii), since it has many of the characteristics of a court of law, is a body which discharges judicial rather than administrative functions as part of the judicial system and fulfils the definition of a court within the meaning of the Contempt of Court Act 1981 (c. 49), s.19 (*Peach Grey & Co. (a firm)* v. *Sommers* [1995] 2 All E.R. 513).

INFIRMITY. "Incapacitated by old age or infirmity" (Income and Corporation Taxes Act 1970 (c. 10), s.16(1)(a)). Youth as such is not an "infirmity." Accordingly, relief from income tax under this section could not be given to a taxpayer in respect of his infant children (*Eglen* v. *Butcher* [1988] S.T.C. 782).

INFLICT. Offences against the Person Act 1861 (c. 100), s.20). A stalker was capable of "inflicting" grievous bodily harm even though no direct or indirect violence had been applied to the victim (*R.* v. *Burstow, The Times,* July 30, 1996).

(Offences against the Person Act 1867 (c. 100), ss.20 and 47). "Inflict" included the infliction of psychiatric injury on another and did not mean the direct application of violence to the victim (*R.* v. *Ireland* [1997] 3 W.L.R. 534).

INFLUENCE. (Sexual Offences Act 1956 (c. 69), s.31). The meaning of "influence" in s.31 should be given its ordinary meaning and did not imply any form of sanction and necessity; compulsion and persuasion were not necessary ingredients of influence (*Re Attorney-General's Reference (No. 2 of 1995)* [1996] 3 All E.R. 860).

INFORMATION. A request to justices to issue a warrant under s.7(1) of the Bail Act 1976 (c. 63) did not constitute an "information" within the meaning of s.127 of the Magistrates' Courts Act 1980 (c. 43) (*Schiavo* v. *Anderton* (1986) 150 J.P. 264).

(Consumer Credit Act 1974 (c. 39), s.186; Consumer Credit Advertisement Regulations 1989). The phrase "information supplied" covered the giving of advice as well as the giving of factual information (*Coventry City Council* v. *Lazarus* (1996) 160 J.P. 188).

INFORMATION TECHNOLOGY. Stat. Def., "includes any computer or other technology by means of which information or other matter may be recorded or communicated without being reduced to documentary form" (Police Act 1997 (c. 50), s.109(6)).

INHERENT VICE. Where leather gloves, packed into containers in Calcutta during the monsoon season, were damaged in transit by moisture falling on to them from the roof of the containers in which they were packed, it was held that the damage was due to the "inherent vice or nature of the subject matter insured" within the terms of an exclusion clause in an insurance policy (*T.M. Noten B.V.* v. *Paul Charles Harding* [1990] 2 Lloyd's Rep. 283).

INHUMAN AND DEGRADING PUNISHMENT. (Bahamas Independence Order 1973 (S.I. 1973 No. 1080), art. 17(1)). The fact that the appellant had been tried for other offences whilst he was awaiting trial for capital muder did not amount to "inhuman or degrading punishment", nor could the period on remand before trial be taken as founding a complaint under art. 17, since complaints about pre-trial delay amounted to an attack on the trial process itself rather than concentrating on the punishment post conviction (*Fisher* v. *Minister of Public Safety and Immigration* [1998] 3 W.L.R. 201).

INITIAL. Stat. Def., Business Names Act 1985 (c. 7), s.8.

INJUNCTION. A stay under R.S.C., Ord. 53, r.3(10)(*a*) pending the resolution of an application for judicial review is not an "injunction," and decisions of ministers of the Crown can therefore be stayed (*R*. v. *Secretary of State for Education and Science, ex p. Avon County Council* [1990] C.O.D. 237).

"In the nature of an injunction" (County Court Rules 1981 (No. 1687), Ord. 29, r. 1(3)). A consent order in standard form made in the county court giving joint custody was not "in the nature of an injunction" within the meaning of this rule (*Re P.* (*Minors*) (*Custody Order-Penal Notice*) [1990] 1 W.L.R. 613).

INJURY. "Personal injury" (Supplementary Benefits (Resources) Regulations 1981 (No. 1527), regs. 4(7), 6(1)). "Injury" includes a disease and any injury suffered as a result of a disease (Social Security Decision No. R(SB) 2/89).

For the purposes of the Fireman's Pension Scheme Order 1992 (No. 129) "injury" meant impairment of physical or mental condition (*Bradley* v. *London Fire and Civil Defence Authority*, [1995] I.R.L.R 46).

"Personal injury", Stat. Def., "includes any disease and any impairment of a person's physical or mental condition" (Civil Evidence Act 1995 (c. 38), s.10(3), also Industrial Tribunals Act 1996 (c. 17), s.3(5)).

"Serious injury", Stat. Def., "A fracture, damage to an internal organ, impairment of bodily function, a deep cut or a deep laceration" (Police Act 1996 (c. 16), s.65); National Crime Squad (Complaints) Regulations 1998 (No. 638), reg. 2; Police (Northern Ireland) Act 1998 (c. 32), s.50(1).

INLAND WATERS. Stat. Def., Town and Country Planning (Scotland) Act 1997 (c. 8), s.26(6).

INLAND WATERWAY. Stat. Def., Transport and Works Act 1992 (c. 42), s.67.

INORDINATE DELAY. This means the lapse of a period of time materially longer than that usually regarded by the courts and the profession as acceptable (*Tabata* v. *Hetherington, The Times*, December 15, 1983). On an application to strike out an action for want of prosecution the court, when considering whether there had been "inordinate and inexcusable delay," could take into account not only those periods when nothing had been done by either side, but also periods when steps were being taken in a desultory fashion (*Lev* (*t/a Michael Lev & Co.*) v. *Fagan, The Times*, March 15, 1988).

"Inordinate and inexcusable delay" (Arbitration Act 1950 (c. 27), s.13A, as inserted by s.102 of the Courts and Legal Services Act 1990 (c. 41)). An arbitrator has power under this section to dismiss a claim on the ground of "inordinate and inexcusable delay" occurring before this section came into force on January 1, 1992 (*Yamashita-Shinnihon Steamship Co.* v. *L'Office Cherifien des Phosphates and Unitramp SA, The Times,* December 17, 1993).

INSOLVENCY. Stat. Def., Insolvency Act 1986 (c. 45), s.247; Banking Act 1987 (c. 22), s.59.

INSANITY. A state of mind bordering on "insanity" had to be a state of mind in the form of mental illness or mental disorder and a personality disorder was not sufficient to establish the defence of "diminished responsibility" (*Williamson* v. *H.M. Advocate*, 1994 S.C.C.R. 358).

INSOLVENT. A company for which a receiver was appointed in relation to "the book debts" and other debts comprised in and charged by a debenture which created, *inter alia*, a fixed charge over those debts and a floating charge over the other assets of the company was not "insolvent" within the meaning of the Employment Protection (Consolidation) Act 1978 (c. 44) as amended by the Insolvency Act 1985 (c. 65), s.218(2) and the Employment Act 1990 (c. 38), Sched. 2, para. 127(1)(*c*) (*Secretary of State* v. *Stone* [1994] I.C.R. 761).

INSPECTION. "Inspection . . . of property" (Supreme Court Act 1981 (c. 54), s.33(1)(*a*)). It was held that the powers of the court to make an order under this section, providing for the "inspection" of "property," did not extend to making a document available to an applicant who simply wished to read it in order to discover whether it was defamatory (*Huddleston* v. *Control Risks Information Services* [1987] 1 W.L.R. 701).

INSTITUTED. (10) For the purposes of s.7(1) of the Explosive Substances Act 1883 (c. 3) proceedings were not "instituted" against the defendants until, following a number of occasions when the case was remanded, they were arraigned for the purpose of committal proceedings (*R.* v. *Whale*; *R.* v. *Lockton* [1991] Crim.L.R. 692).

INSTITUTION. Stat. Def., Banking Act, 1987 (c. 22), s.106.
See PRISON.

INSTITUTIONAL AND RESIDENTIAL CARE. The provision of accommodation in a hostel run by a charity for single persons and where counselling was offered by an allocated social worker did not amount to "care" within the meaning of the Social Security Act 1986 (c. 50) and the Social Fund Directions (*R.* v. *Social Fund Inspector, ex p. Ali* (1994) 6 Admin. L.R. 205).

INSTITUTION STANDING IN EXTENSIVE GROUNDS. There was no legal definition of "institution standing in extensive grounds" and whether a proposed development met the description was a matter of fact and degree and planning judgment (*Northavon District Council* v. *Secretary of State for the Environment and the Trustees of the Congregation of Jehovah's Witnesses* [1993] J.P.L. 761).

INSTRUMENT. (Vagrancy Act 1824 (c. 83), s.4). See HAVE. See also DEVICE; FALSE INSTRUMENT.
"In pursuance of any instrument," see PURSUANCE.
"Proper instrument of transfer" (Companies Act 1985 (c. 6), s.183). The omission of the amount of consideration from an instrument transferring legal title to company shares was a mere irregularity which did not prevent the instrument from being a "proper instrument" within the meaning of this section (*Nisbet* v. *Shepherd, The Times,* July 1, 1993).

Stat. Def., "includes orders, rules, regulations, schemes, licences, agreements and other documents" (National Lottery Act 1998 (c. 22), Sched. 1, para. 1).

INSUFFICIENT. "Insufficiency of enquiry" (Coroners Act 1988 (c. 13), s.13(1)(*b*)). On an application for a fresh inquest under this section it cannot be argued that there was "insufficiency of enquiry" merely because other experts disagree with the expert evidence given at the inquest (*R. v. H.M. Coroner for Wiltshire, ex p. Taylor (Geoffrey)* (1990) 154 J.P. 933).

INSULT. "Insulting behaviour" (Metropolitan Police Act 1839 (c. 47), s.54(13)). An overt display of homosexual conduct in a public place could be "insulting behaviour" within the meaning of this section, even though not aimed at any particular person or persons (*Masterson v. Holden* [1986] 1 W.L.R. 1017).

(County Courts Act 1984 (c. 28), s.118). Threats to a witness returning from court could amount to a contempt of court (*Manchester City Council v. McCann* [1999] 2 W.L.R. 590).

INSURANCE. "Jurisdiction in matters relating to insurance" in the Brussels Convention 1968 is not restricted to insurance for domestic or private purposes (*New Hampshire Insurance Company v. Strabag Bau Aktiengesellschaft, The Times,* November 26, 1991).

Reinsurance business and retrocession arrangements for the reinsurance of such reinsurance business are "insurance business" within the meaning of the Insurance Companies Act 1982 (c. 50), s.49(1) (*Re N.R.G. Victory Reinsurance* [1995] 1 W.L.R. 239).

"Insurance services," Stat. Def., Disability Discrimination Act 1995 (c. 50), s.1(1).

INSURANCE ON THE LIFE OF. A policy which paid the same benefits on the death of the life assured as on the surrender of the policy was not a contract of insurance within the meaning of the Life Assurance Act 1774 (c. 48), s.1 (*Fuji Finance Inc. v. Aetna Life Insurance Co.* [1994] 3 W.L.R. 1280).

INSURED. (Road Traffic Act 1988, (c. 52), s.151). A person who had stolen and driven a car was not "insured" within the meaning of s.151(8) (*Gibson v. Paynter* [1996] 8 C.L. 100).

INSURER. (Lugano Convention on Jurisdiction and the Enforcement of Judgments in Civil and Commercial Matters 1988, Art. 11). "Insurer" in Art. 11 did not include a reinsurer because of the conceptual differences in the subject matter and definitions of risk between the two (*Agnew v. Lansforsakringsbolagens AB* [1997] 4 All E.R. 937). "Insurer" in Art. 11 referred to any insurer and not just one domiciled in a contracting state (*Jordan Grand Prix v. Baltic Insurance Group and others* [1999] 1 All E.R. 289).

(R.S.C. Ord. 29, r.11(2)(a)). "Insurer concerned" under Ord. 29, r.11(2)(a) did not only refer to cases where there was an insurance policy in place, which was subsequently voided, but could refer to the MIB, which would meet the liability of an uninsured tortfeasor *Sharp* v. *Pereria* [1998] 4 All E.R. 145).

INSURRECTION. An "insurrection" for insurance purposes is an organised and violent uprising within a country, the main purpose of which is to overthrow or supplant that country's government (*National Oil Company of Zimbabwe (Private)* v. *Sturge* [1991] 2 Lloyd's Rep. 281).

INTEND. (1) "The landlord intends" (Landlord and Tenant Act 1954 (c. 56), s.30(1)(*f*)). In order to establish the intention, required by this section, to carry out a reconstruction of premises forming part of a larger area of land, it is necessary to prove not only an intention to develop the whole site but also the means and ability to carry it into effect (*Edwards* v. *Thompson* [1990] 29 E.G. 41). An undertaking given by the landlord's counsel that the landlord would proceed with plans to occupy the holding even if he failed to secure possession of adjoining premises was held to be sufficient to establish the intention to occupy required by s.30(1)(*g*) (*London Hilton Jewellers* v. *Hilton International Hotels* [1990] 20 E.G. 69). In a case where a local council had opposed the tenant's application for a new business tenancy of a bowling club on the grounds that it intended to occupy the holding for the purposes of a business to be carried on by it, namely a bowling club to be managed on the council's behalf by outside agents, it was held that the necessary intention to occupy had been established (*Teesside Indoor Bowls* v. *Stockton on Tees Borough Council* [1990] 46 E.G. 116). The entering by a landlord into an agreement for the development of the land in question was enough to show intention for the purposes of this section (*Peter Goddard & Sons* v. *Hounslow London Borough Council* [1992] 1 EGLR 281).

"The landlord intends" (Housing Act 1985 (c. 68), Sched. 2, ground 10). Although in the case of a local authority or other corporation a resolution passed by the body was not essential to prove intent, nevertheless the intention had to be clearly defined and settled (*Wansbeck District Council* v. *Marley, The Times*, November 30, 1987).

INTENDED. (7) By s.190 of the Road Traffic Act 1972 (c. 20) a motor vehicle is defined as "a mechanically propelled vehicle intended or adapted for use on roads." "Intended" in this context does not mean intended by the user of the vehicle, either at the time or for the future, nor the intention of the manufacturer, wholesaler or retailer. The test is whether a reasonable person looking at the vehicle would say that one of its uses would be a road use. Once it was established that a vehicle as manufactured was intended for road use it would require a very substantial alteration before it could be said to be no longer a motor vehicle. The mere absence of items required by the regulations to make the use of the vehicle legal would not be enough. (*Chief Constable of Avon and Somerset* v. *Fleming* [1987] 1 All E.R. 318). A fork lift truck with an enclosed cab, lights, a horn and various other accessories suitable for road use, but with no speedometer or wing mirrors, poor visibility and a tendency to over-heat, was held to be "intended" for road use within the meaning of this section (*Percy* v. *Smith* [1986] RTR 252).

"Intended to confer," See ASSOCIATE.

INTENT. (12) "Intent . . . to endanger life" (Firearms Act 1968 (c. 27), s.16). For the purposes of this section the intent had to be an unlawful intent (*R.* v. *Georgiades* [1989] 1 W.L.R. 759). The intent which must be proved to establish an offence under this section is an intent to act with a gun so as to endanger life. It is not necessary to prove specific or ulterior intent (*R.* v. *East* [1990] Crim.L.R. 413).

(14) "Intent to avoid payment" (Theft Act 1968 (c. 60), s.3(1)). On a charge of making off without payment contrary to this section there must be an intent permanently to avoid payment. An intent to delay payment is insufficient (*R.* v. *Allen* (*Christopher*) [1985] 3 W.L.R. 107).

"With intent to commit an offence" (Criminal Attempts Act 1981 (c. 47), s.1(1)). These words mean, when applied to rape or attempted rape, "with intent to have sexual intercourse with a woman in circumstances where she does not consent and the defendant knows or could not care less about her absence of consent" (*R.* v. *Khan* [1990] 1 W.L.R. 813).

(Race Relations Act 1976 (c. 74), s.57(3)). s.57(3) of the 1976 Act was not concerned with motivation but with the state of mind of a respondent in relation to the consequences of his actions (*J.H. Walker Ltd* v. *Hussain* [1996] I.C.R. 291).

"Intent to supply," see SUPPLY.

INTENTION. "Items held with the intention of furthering a criminal purpose" (Police and Criminal Evidence Act 1984 (c. 60), s.10(2)). The intention is not limited to that of the solicitor holding the items but extends to cover a client who, whether knowingly or unknowingly, was furthering a criminal purpose by laundering the proceeds of drug trafficking. The "criminal purpose" could be that of a third party (*R.* v. *Central Criminal Court, ex p. Francis and Francis* [1988] 3 W.L.R. 989).

(8) "Intention of permanently depriving" (Theft Act 1968 (c. 60), s.15(1)). Where a person was charged under this section with obtaining credit and charge cards by deception it was held that not only was it necessary to prove that the cards were dishonestly obtained by deception but also that at the time he applied for and obtained them he had the "intention" of using them to cheat the issuing companies (*R.* v. *Atwal* [1989] Crim.L.R. 293). Where a manager took money without permission from a company safe it was held that the "intention of permanently depriving" the owner of the money was established, notwithstanding that he intended to return it later, albeit of necessity with different notes and coins (*R.* v. *Velumyl* [1989] Crim.L.R. 299).

Where a person set up a company to which third parties paid moneys owed to another, each time a payment was made by a third party there was an "intention permanently to deprive" (*R.* v. *Mitchell* [1993] Crim.L.R. 788).

(Theft Act 1968 (c. 60), s.6(1)). Where a defendant removed a door from one council property to replace a damaged door at another council property, he had treated the property as his own, regardless of the council's rights, and had manifested an intention permanently to deprive (*DPP* v. *Lavender* [1994] Crim.L.R. 297).

INTENTIONALLY. "Homeless intentionally" (Housing (Homeless Persons) Act 1977 (c. 48), s.17(1); Housing Act 1985 (c. 68), s.60). A woman who voluntarily abandoned a flat in Bristol, which she had occupied with her husband until he left her, was held to be "intentionally" homeless when she applied for accommodation in Gloucester, notwithstanding that by the time of her application the Bristol flat had been vandalised by her husband, and was uninhabitable (*R.* v. *Gloucester City Council, ex p. Miles* (1985) 83 L.G.R. 607). A person does not become homeless "intentionally" just because he does not contest his landlord's action for possession, in circumstances where he could not reasonably have done so (*R.* v. *Exeter City Council, ex p. Gliddon* [1985] 1 All E.R. 493). A wife who believed assurances that the family would be rehoused when her husband resigned from a tied accommodation occupation could not be said to have acquiesced in her husband's resignation, and was, therefore, herself not "homeless intentionally" when they had to move out (*R.* v. *Mole Valley District Council, ex p. Burton* (1988) 20 H.L.R. 479). A person can be "intentionally homeless" if she voluntarily leaves her present home to seek work elsewhere (*R.* v. *Kensington and Chelsea London Borough Council, ex p. Cunha* (1989) 21 H.L.R. 16). The intentionality of the homelessness was not vitiated by an intervening period of temporary accommodation (*R.* v. *Merton London Borough Council, ex p. Ruffle* (1989)) 21 H.L.R. 361). Immigrants who left settled accommodation in Bangladesh made themselves homeless "intentionally" (*R.* v. *Tower Hamlets London Borough Council, ex p. Monaf* (1988) 20 H.L.R. 529). A tenant who left a secure tenancy following threats to herself and her child was nevertheless "intentionally" homeless (*R.* v. *London Borough of Croydon, ex p. Toth* (1988) 20 H.L.R. 576). A person who left private accommodation to go abroad for a period of some months without making arrangements to keep his accommodation available for his return was held to be "intentionally" homeless (*R.* v. *Wycombe District Council, ex p. Mahsood* (1988) 20 H.L.R. 683). Persons who left their homes in Northern Ireland as a result of death threats brought about by evidence of their criminal and anti-social behaviour were nevertheless "intentionally" homeless for the purposes of this Act (*R.* v. *London Borough of Hammersmith and Fulham, ex p. P* [1989] 22 H.L.R. 21). A person who has been found to be intentionally homeless does not cease to be homeless merely by occupying temporary accommodation (*R.* v. *Merton London Borough Council, ex p. Ruffle* (1989) 21 H.L.R. 361). In assessing whether or not applicants' behaviour was such as to make them intentionally homeless when asked to leave by their family it was incumbent on the authority, having regard to the known domestic emotional difficulties, to make full enquiries and to allow the applicants an opportunity to explain (*R.* v. *Dacorum Borough Council, ex p. Brown* (1989) 21 H.L.R. 405). A local housing authority was entitled to decide that a Filipina, working and living for part of every year in the United Kingdom, was "intentionally" homeless by reason of her giving up other accommodation available to her in Manila (*R.* v. *Kensington and Chelsea (Royal) London Borough Council, ex p. Bayani,* (1990) 22 H.L.R. 407. A woman who, on becoming pregnant (and on being told to do so by the landlord), left premises which, as a mere licensee, she had no right to occupy, did not thereby become "intentionally" homeless (*R.* v. *Hammersmith and Fulham London Borough Council, ex p. O'Sullivan* [1991] EGCS 110). Where a person obtained a mortgage by deliberately giving false information to the building society, and was dispossessed of her home as a result of the fraud being discovered, that person was intentionally homeless within the meaning of s.60 of the 1985 Act (*R. v. Barnet London Borough Council, ex p. Rughooputh, The Times*, May 11, 1993). Where a person ceased to occupy property of which she was a joint owner, surrender of her legal interest over two years later did not render her intentionally homeless within the meaning of section 60 of the 1985 Act (*R. v. Wandsworth London Borough, ex p. Oteng, The Times*, June 23, 1993). In deciding whether or not an applicant for housing had acted reasonably in leaving his accommodation for the purposes of determining his intentional or unintentional homelessness under this section, a local authority should have regard to his former accommodation in the context of accepted standards within that local community and should not compare that accommodation with the housing standard of the area to which he had applied (*R. v. Newham London Borough Council, ex p. Tower Hamlets London Borough Council* (1991) 23 H.L.R. 62). See also *R. v. Swansea City Council, ex p. Evans* (1990) 22 H.L.R. 467; *R. v. Barnet London Borough, ex p. O'Connor* (1990) 22 H.L.R. 486. See also AVAILABLE.

A Roman Catholic family living in Belfast, where it had been subjected to regular attacks from the Protestant community, was held to have become intentionally homeless when it left its house. It was considered reasonable for the family to remain where it was, or in available temporary accommodation, while pursuing a priority transfer to alternative accommodation in Northern Ireland (*McIlroy v. Newham London Borough Council* [1991] N.P.C. 76). Where a woman vacated her flat claiming harassment by two men from the floor above, no gas, faulty toilet and a loose dog, it was held that it was reasonable in all the circumstances for her to return, and that she was therefore homeless "intentionally" (*R. v. Cardiff City Council, ex p. Barry* [1991] C.O.D. 112). A person who had sold his house because of his inability to keep up the mortgage payments despite there being no threat of repossession of the house was held to be intentionally homeless (*Adamiec v. Leeds City Council* [1992] C.O.D. 206). When an unintentionally homeless person in intermediate short-term accommodation refused an offer of permanent accommodation, the subsequent eviction from the intermediate accommodation rendered him "intentionally" homeless within the meaning of this section (*R. v. Brent London Borough Council, ex p. Awua* (1993) 25 H.L.R. 628). Housing applicants who had left a secure tenancy to go to live in Australia but who, for lack of the necessary visas, has been deported back to England, were held to be "intentionally" homeless (*R. v. Croydon London Borough Council, ex p. Easom* (1992) 25 H.L.R. 262). A woman who, by false representations, obtained a mortgage on a flat was held to be intentionally homeless when the building society repossessed (*R. v. Barnet London Borough Council, ex p. Rughooputh* (1993) 25 H.L.R. 607). The test as to whether an applicant is intentionally homeless within the meaning of the Act is a subjective one (*R. v. Brent London Borough Council, ex p. McManus* (1993) 25 H.L.R. 643). An authority should not asume that applicants for accommodation are intentionally homeless simply because payments to them of income support (calculated to provide sufficient means for a family to live on) included sums in respect of mortgage interest (*R. v. Shrewsbury and Atcham Borough Council, ex p. Griffiths* (1993) 25 H.L.R. 613).

In deciding whether for the purposes of the Housing Act 1985 (c. 68), s.60(1), an applicant's failure to pay rent was deliberate, the local authority had to consider whether the failure was caused by the inadequacy of resources to meet reasonable living expenses before asserting that there was wilful and persistent refusal to pay rent (*R.* v. *Wandsworth London Borough Council, ex p. Hawthorne* [1994] 1 W.L.R. 1442).

"Intentionally homeless." Stat. Def., Housing Act 1985 (c. 68), s.60.

INTER PARTES. *"Inter partes"* (Police and Criminal Evidence Act 1984 (c. 60), Sched. 1, para. 7). The requirement of this paragraph that an application for an order to produce special procedure material (such as the state of an accused's bank and building society accounts) should be made *inter partes* did not mean that the accused had to be informed of the application (*R.* v. *Leicester Crown Court, ex p. DPP* [1987] 3 All E.R. 654). Reference to the application being *inter partes* meant the applicant and the person against whom the order was sought (*R.* v. *Manchester Crown Court, ex p. Taylor* [1988] 1 W.L.R. 705).

INTEREST. "In the interest of the State" (Official Secrets Act 1911 (c. 28), s.2(1)) means in the interests of the State according to its recognised organs of government and the policies of the particular Government of the day (*R.* v. *Ponting* [1985] Crim.L.R. 318). See also DUTY.

"In the interests of the company" (Companies Act 1985 (c. 6), s.153(2)(*b*)). The transfer by a company of half its assets to another company, for no consideration, to finance the acquisition of shares in the first company was held not to be "in the interests of" that company within the meaning of this section (*Brady* v. *Brady* (1987) 3 BCC 535).

"If by reason of interest in the vessel" (Institute Time Clauses Hulls Port Risks policy, clause 3). "Interest" for the purposes of this clause is not restricted to proprietary interest; it could also embrace an operational interest (*Turner* v. *Manx Line* [1990] 1 Lloyd's Rep. 137).

"The interests of justice so require" (Social Security Commissioners Procedure Regulations 1987 (No. 214), reg. 25(1)(*c*)). This phrase is confined to cases where there have been obvious mistakes or procedural mishaps, where there was no real debate as to fact or law (Social Security Decision No. R(S) 3/89).

"Any person who claims an interest in the disclaimed property" (Insolvency Act 1986 (c. 45), s.181). The term "interest" is not confined to a proprietary interest: it extends to any financial interest in the subsistence or otherwise of a lease. So that a statutory tenant had *locus standi* to apply to have a lease vested in him under this section where a liquidator had disclaimed the head lease as onerous property pursuant to s.178 (*Re Vedmay, The Times,* October 21, 1993).

The phrase "interest in the insured property" in a material damage proviso did not cover an insurable interest which was not a personal property interest of the insured, and the word "interest" could mean any insurable interest in a broad sense, such as a contractual right in respect of insured goods or an insurable interest of a more limited kind, depending on the context (*Glengate-KG Properties Ltd* v. *Norwich Union Fire Insurance Society Ltd* [1996] 2 All E.R. 487).

"Person interested in a charity," see PERSON INTERESTED.

"In the interests of justice," see NECESSARY.

Stat. Def., "in relation to a loan, includes any introductory or other fee or charge which is payable in accordance with the terms on which the loan is made or is otherwise payable in connection with the making of the loan" (Income and Corporation Taxes Act 1988 (c. 1), s.798(3) inserted by Finance Act 1998 (c. 36), s.103(1).

INTEREST IN LAND. "A person having an interest in the land" (Town and Country Planning Act 1971 (c. 78), s.88 as substituted by the Schedule to the Local Government and Planning (Amendment) Act 1981 (c. 41)). A person living in a caravan in a caravan site in a quarry was held not to have a sufficient "interest" in the land to establish the right to appeal against an enforcement notice under this section (*R.* v. *Secretary of State for the Environment, ex p. Davies* [1991] 1 P.L.R. 78).

"So far as it relates to the creation of an interest in land" (Unfair Contract Terms Act 1977 (c. 50), Sched. 1, para. 1(*b*)). A lease was still a "contract" relating to the creation of "an interest in land" within the meaning of this paragraph notwithstanding that it contained a term for the payment of rent "without any deduction or set-off whatsoever" (*Electricity Supply Nominees* v. *IAF Group* [1992] EGCS 145).

(Adoption Act 1976 (c. 36), s.42(4)). "An interest so vested" meant an interest vested in possession so that a child's interest in a will survived the making of an adoption order (*Staffordshire County Council* v. *B* [1998] 1 FLR 261).

Stat. Def., Finance Act 1985 (c. 54), s.44, Sched. 17, para. 1(2).

"Interest in or charge on land," see PENDING LAND ACTION.

INTERESTED. "A properly interested person" (Coroners Rules 1984 (No. 552), r.20(2)(*h*)). A senior member of the deceased's family is not necessarily by virtue of that fact a "properly interested person" for the purposes of this rule (*R.* v. *Portsmouth City Coroner, ex p. Keane* [1990] C.O.D. 7).

(Merchant Shipping Act 1894 (c. 60), s.30). An order pursuant to s.30 of the 1894 Act could not be made on the application of creditors since they were not an "interested person" within the meaning of that section (*NCNB Texas National Bamk* v. *Evensong Co.*; *The Mikado* [1992] 1 Lloyd's Rep. 163).

A transferor who had exchanged property which was the subject of the dispute was an "interested person" within the meaning of s.30. A mere creditor was not an "interested person" (*Richard Hughes* v. *Vail Blyth Clewly (The Siben)* [1994] 2 Lloyd's Rep. 421).

(Charities Act 1993 (c. 10), s.33(1)). An interested party had to have an interest materially greater than or different from that possessed by ordinary members of the public, so that one of the statutory purposes of the National Trust in preserving the red deer population amounted to sufficient interest within the meaning of s.33(1) of the 1993 Act (*Scott* v. *National Trust for Places of Historic Interest or Natural Beauty* [1998] 2 All E.R. 705).

INTERESTED IN. (11) "Person interested . . . in any land" (Land Registration Act 1925 (c. 21), s.54(1)). A tenant who, acting on behalf of himself and other tenants, commenced an action against the landlord for breach of repairing covenants was "interested" in the property for the purposes of this section (*Clayhope Properties* v. *Evans* [1986] 1 W.L.R. 1223.

"Person interested in land" (Town and County Planning Act 1971 (c. 78), s.52). The beneficiary of a restrictive covenant is a "person interested in land" for the purposes of this section (*Re Martin's Application* [1989] 05 E.G. 85).

"Any person interested in the ship" (Merchant Shipping (Liability of Shipowners and Others) Act 1958 (c. 62), s.3(1)). This means a person having a legal or equitable interest in the ship, and the wholly owned subsidiary of the company owning a tug was not such a person (*McDermid* v. *Nash Dredging and Reclamation Co.* [1987] 3 W.L.R. 212).

See also PERSON INTERESTED.

INTERLOCUTORY. (9) Applications to commit for contempt of court were "interlocutory proceedings" within R.S.C., Ord. 41, r.5(2) if they were ancillary to the issues raised in the action (*Savings and Investment Bank* v. *Gasco Investments* (*Netherlands*) *BV* (*No. 2*) [1988] 1 All E.R. 975). See also CIVIL PROCEEDINGS.

INTERNATIONAL CARRIAGE. The carriage of goods from Manchester to Jersey was not "international carriage" for the purposes of the Convention on the Contract for the International Carriage of Goods by Road (*Chloride Industrial Batteries* v. *F. & W. Freight* [1989] 1 W.L.R. 45).

INTERNATIONAL ORGANISATION. Stat. Def., Finance Act 1996 (c. 8), s.103(1).

INTERRUPT. "Wilfully interrupts" (Contempt of Court Act 1981 (c. 49), s.12(1)(*b*)). For the purposes of this section the interruption can be inside or outside the court (*Bodden* v. *Commissioner of Police of the Metropolis* [1990] 2 W.L.R. 76).

INTERVENING DAYS. Days which occur after the taxpayer has finally returned from abroad cannot be brought into account as "intervening days" for the purposes of the Finance Act 1977 (c. 36), Sched. 7, para. 1(3). To qualify as "intervening days" the days must fall between a period of absence from the United Kingdom and a previous period of qualifying absence. (*Robins* v. *Durkin* [1988] S.T.C. 588).

INTERVIEW. (Code C, para. 12.12 of the Codes of Practice made under the Police and Criminal Evidence Act 1984 (c. 60), s.66). The questioning of a suspect at or near the scene of a suspected crime, to elicit an explanation which if true or accepted would exculpate him, was not an "interview" for the purposes of the Codes of Practice (*R.* v. *Maguire* (1990) 90 Cr.App.R. 115). But normally any discussion or talk between a suspect or prisoner and a police officer about an alleged crime would amount to an "interview," whether instigated by the suspect or prisoner, or the police officer (*R.* v. *Matthews* (1990) 91 Cr.App.R. 43). Questioning the accused in his flat about cocaine and scales found there, and further questioning in a police car en route to the police station, were "interviews" within the meaning of the code (*R.* v. *Kingsley Brown* [1989] Crim.L.R. 500). Questions concerning the selling of drugs, put by a police officer to an accused on bail for possessing cannabis, for the purpose of securing evidence for a fresh charge of threatening behaviour, amounted to an "interview" (*R.* v. *Absolam* (1988) 89 Cr.App.R. 332). A conversation between police officers and the accused at the conclusion of a search of the accused's home was held to be an "interview" within the meaning of the code (*R.* v. *Manji* [1990] Crim.L.R. 512). The statutory procedure under ss.7 and 8 of the Road Traffic Act 1988 (c. 52) for obtaining specimens from drivers suspected of driving over the alcohol limit does not constitute an "interview" for the purposes of this Code (*DPP* v. *D (a Juvenile); DPP* v. *Rous* (1992) 94 Cr.App.R. 185). A casual conversation between the accused and the police escort during which admissions had been made was not an "interview" for the purposes of the Code of Conduct (*R.* v. *Younis and Ahmed* [1990] Crim.L.R. 425). But a friendly informed conversation between the accused and a police officer, who was not the investigating officer, during which further admissions were made by the accused, was held to have been an "interview" (*R.* v. *Sparks* [1991] Crim.L.R. 128). An informal unrecorded conversation with the accused was not an "interview" as it did not relate to the alleged offences (*R.* v. *Pullen* [1991] Crim.L.R. 457). Where a police officer questioned a suspect in order to establish whether there were grounds for making an arrest, it was a question of fact, bearing in mind the nature of the questioning, its length, sequence and the place where such enquiries were conducted whether it then became an "interview" (*R.* v. *Weekes, The Times,* May 15, 1992). Whether questioning of a suspect amounted to an "interview" within Code C had to be considered within the framework of the police officer's decision to arrest, the suspect's arrest, his arrival at the police station and notification of his right to free legal advice (*R.* v. *Cox (Rodney William)* (1993) 96 Cr.App.R. 464). Where questions were asked of a suspect at his home on arrest after caution with the aim of obtaining admission on which proceedings might be brought, the questioning was an "interview" (*ibid.*). Where the accused, following his arrest, was questioned, in the police car, as to why he had a knife in his possession, the conversation, not recorded at the time, amounted to an "interview" for the purposes of Code C (*R.* v. *Hunt* [1992] Crim.L.R. 582). A roadside inquiry by means of exploratory questions might at a certain point, become an "interview" within the meaning of this section (*R.* v. *Park, The Times,* July 30, 1993). A single question and answer could amount to an "interview" (*R.* v. *Ward* (1994) 98 Cr.App.R. 337). A customs officer's series of questions designed to elicit an incriminating response came within the spirit and letter of an interview (*R.* v. *Weerdesteyn* [1995] 1 Cr.App.R. 405). Where a suspect detained at a police station volunteered information of which officers mades notes for their own records, that did not amount to an "interview" (*R.* v. *Menard, The Times,* March 23, 1994).

A conversation between the appellant and a customs officer in uniform, acting in accordance with his duty and who was manifestly in authority and exercising control over immigration and customs which was not recorded contemporaneously and where the appellant had not been cautioned nor reminded of his legal rights amounted to an "interview" (*R.* v. *Okafor* [1994] 3 All E.R. 741).

INTIMATE. "Intimate body search" (Police and Criminal Evidence Act 1984 (c. 60), s.18(1)). An intimate body search, as defined by this section, requires some physical intrusion into a body orifice; some physical examination rather than mere visual examination or any attempt as in this case, to cause the person to extrude what was contained in a body orifice (*R.* v. *Hughes* [1994] 1 W.L.R. 876).

INTOXICATING LIQUOR. Stat. Def., Weights and Measures Act 1985 (c. 72), s.94.

INTOXICATION. Stat. Def., Public Order Act 1986 (c. 64), s.6.

INTRODUCED. An estate agent who sent particulars of a property to a potential purchaser did not "introduce" the purchaser to the vendor, but merely gave an indication that the property was for sale (*Christie Owen & Davis plc* v. *King*, 1998 S.C.L.R. 149).

INVALID CARRIAGE. Stat. Def., Road Traffic Act 1988 (c. 52), s.185.

INVALIDITY BENEFIT. A mobility allowance granted under s.37A(1) of the Social Security Act 1975 (c. 14) qualified as an "invalidity benefit" within the meaning of Art. 4(1)(*b*) of Council Regulation (EEC) No. 1408/71 and could not therefore be withdrawn on the sole ground that the recipient was resident in the territory of a different Member State (*Newton* v. *Chief Adjudication Officer, The Times,* September 23, 1991).
  Stat. Def., Social Security Contributions and Benefits Act 1992 (c. 4), s.20.

INVESTIGATE. "Investigate any suspected offence," see SUSPECT.

INVESTIGATING. "The duty of investigating offences" (Police and Criminal Evidence Act 1984 (c. 60), s.67(9)). Department of Trade and Industry inspectors making enquiries pursuant to s.434 of the Companies Act 1985 (c. 6) were not "investigating offences" within the meaning of s.67(9) and therefore were not subject to the Police and Criminal Evidence Act 1984 (s.66) Codes of Practice, and did not have to caution the defendants before questioning them (*R.* v. *Seelig*; *R.* v. *Lord Spens* (1991) 141 New L.J. 638).

INVESTIGATION. "In the course of an investigation," see COURSE.

INVESTMENT. Stat. Def., Financial Services Act 1986 (c. 60), s.1, Sched. 1.

INVESTMENT BUSINESS. (Financial Services Act 1986 (c. 60), s.105). Activities carried out before this section came into effect could not be "investment business" within the meaning of the Act (*R.* v. *Secretary of State for Trade and Industry, ex p. R.* [1989] 1 W.L.R. 372).
  Advice to enter into a home income plan, the purchase of investments to be held in a discretionary fund and the management of a portfolio in accordance with the FIMBRA rules amounted to "investment business" within the meaning of Financial Services Act 1986 (c. 60) (*R.* v. *Investors Compensation Scheme, ex p. Weyell* [1994] Q.B. 749).
  Stat. Def., Financial Services Act 1986 (c. 60), s.1, Sched. 1.

INVESTMENT COMPANY. Stat. Def., Companies Act 1985 (c. 6), s.266; Income and Corporation Taxes Act 1988 (c. 1), s.130.

INVITE. "Document inviting him to borrow money" (Consumer Credit Act 1974 (c. 39), s.50(1)(*a*)). A building society which sent a child a leaflet advertising loans was not guilty of sending a minor a document "inviting him to borrow money" because the leaflet specified that loans were not available to applicants under the age of 18 (*Alliance and Leicester Building Society* v. *Babbs* [1993] CCLR 77).

INVOLUNTARY CAUSE OF ANOTHER'S INJURY. The witness of the death of an old and close working colleague was not the "involuntary cause of another's injury" (*Robertson* v. *Forth Road Bridge Joint Board, The Scotswoman*, March 8, 1995).

IRREGULARITY. "Formal defect or irregularity" (Insolvency Rules 1986 (S.I. 1986 No. 1925), reg. 7.55). The failure by a sheriff to carry out the command in a writ of fieri facias was not a "formal defect or irregularity" under r.7.55, which referred only to irregularities in the proceedings and not to the carrying out of the conditions precedent to the presentation of a bankruptcy petition (*Re A Debtor (No. 340 of 1992), ex p. The Debtor* v. *First National Commercial Bank plc* [1996] 2 All E.R. 211). See also MATERIAL IRREGULARITY.

IRREVOCABLY SUBMITS TO THE JURISDICTION OF THE ENGLISH COURTS. See EXCLUSIVE JURISDICTION.

IS BEING. These words in s.1(2)(*a*) of the Children and Young Persons Act 1969 (c. 54) refer to a continuing rather than an instant situation; so that in considering whether the "proper development" of a child "is being avoidably prevented," or her health "is being avoidably impaired," the justices are entitled to have regard to the fact that the mother, a drug addict, had persisted in taking excessive narcotic drugs throughout her pregnancy (*Re D (a Minor)* [1986] 3 W.L.R. 1080).

IS SUFFERING. "The child concerned is suffering" (Children Act 1989 (c. 41), s.31(2)(*a*)). In *Northamptonshire County Council* v. *S.* it was held that the words "is suffering" relate to the period immediately before the process of protecting the child concerned is first put into motion. The words "is suffering" relate to the time when the local authority initiated the procedure to protect the child (*Re M. (A Minor) (Care Order: Threshold Conditions)* [1994] 3 All E.R. 298).

ISSUE. (17) "Equally among such of the daughters who shall then be living and the issue of any of them who may be dead." Where directions to trustees contained these words it was held that "issue" meant issue through all degrees and not just children (*Drummond* v. *Foster* (1986) 130 S.J. 635).

ISSUE OF LAW. "Any issue in those proceedings" (Police and Criminal Evidence Act 1984 (c. 60), s.74). The word "issue" covers not only an issue which was an essential ingredient of the offence charged, but also less fundamental issues, including those of an evidential nature arising during the course of the proceedings (*R.* v. *Robertson*; *R.* v. *Golder* [1987] 3 W.L.R. 327), such as the reliability of an identification (*R.* v. *Castle* [1989] Crim.L.R. 567).

"Facts as are already in issue on any claim" (Limitation Act 1980 (c. 58), s.35(5)(*a*)) means facts material to the claim. It is not restricted to meaning facts which were already in dispute (*Fannon* v. *Backhouse, The Times,* August 22, 1987).

ISSUED. A convening order was "issued" for the purposes of s.134(3) of the Army Act 1955 (c. 18) if it was signed by the convening officer and directed a court to convene at a particular time and place (*R.* v. *Amos, The Times,* March 18, 1986).

"Issued by the Commissioners" (Finance Act 1985 (c. 54), s.20(2)(*b*); as substituted by the Finance Act 1988 (c. 39), s.20). The word "issued" implies actual delivery of the direction to pay to the person claiming the repayment (*Aston* (*Antony Albert*) v. *Customs and Excise Commissioners* (1991) VATTR 170).

"Shares in a company issued on or after March 16, 1993" (Income and Corporation Taxes Act 1988 (c. 1), s.299A as inserted by s.111 of the Finance Act 1933 (c. 34)). Shares were "issued" when an application had been followed by allotment and allocation and completed by entry on the register (*National Westminster Bank* v. *I.R.C.* [1994] 3 W.L.R. 159).

ITEM. "Items subject to legal privilege" (Police and Criminal Evidence Act 1984 (c. 60), s.9). A blood sample taken by a scientist carrying out a DNA test was held to be an "item" within the meaning of this section (*R.* v. *R.* [1994] 1 W.L.R. 758).

J

JEOPARDY. See AUTREFOIS ACQUIT.

JOBBER. Stat. Def., Company Securities (Insider Dealing) Act 1985 (c. 8), s.3. See now MARKET MAKER.

JOINT TENANCY. See TENANCY.

JOINTLY. "Jointly charged" (Police and Criminal Evidence Act 1984 (c. 60), s.80(3)). A husband and wife charged on separate counts in the same indictment had not been "jointly charged" within the meaning of this section (*R.* v. *Woolgar* [1991] Crim.L.R. 545).

(Magistrates Courts Act 1980, s.24(1)(*b*), as amended). Where in respect of one incident two persons were charged respectively, one with driving and the other with allowing himself to be carried, albeit in different counts of the indictment, they were properly to be considered jointly charged (*R.* v. *Peterborough Justices, ex p. Allgood* [1996] RTR 26).

"Jointly occupies" (Housing Benefit (General) Regulations 1987 (No. 1971), reg. 3(2)). These words envisage a situation when there is a joint tenancy under which both the claimant and the joint occupier are liable to pay rent to the landlord. So that an adult son living with the claimant, but with no liability for the rent, did not "jointly" occupy the premises with the claimant (*R.* v. *Chesterfield Borough Council, ex p. Fulwood* (1992) 24 H.L.R. 706).

(Income Support (General) Regulations 1987 (S.I. 1987 No. 1967, reg. 3(2)(c)). "Jointly occupies" within the meaning of reg. 3(2)(c) connoted a legal relationship, and not merely co-residence in fact (*Bate* v. *Chief Adjudication Officer* [1996] 1 W.L.R. 814).

"Jointly occupies" (Housing Benefit (General) Regulations 1987 (No. 1971), reg. 3(2)(*d*)), see OCCUPY.

JOURNEY. Under Council Directive 91/628, Art. 2, place at which it was loaded a journey included the whole of the transport of an animal from the point of departure until it reached its final destination, unless there had been an interruption of at least 10 hours, during which the animals were cared for (*Ken Lane Transport* v. *North Yorkshire County Council* [1995] 1 W.L.R. 1416).

JUDGMENT. Where a form required the person filling it in to state whether he had ever had "judgment" entered against him it was held that "judgment" would here include a bankruptcy (*R.* v. *Stokes* [1988] Crim.L.R. 110).

The word "judgment" in s.17 of the Judgments Act 1838 (c. 110) means final judgment for a quantified sum, not interlocutory judgment (*Thomas* v. *Bunn* [1991] 2 W.L.R. 27). But an interlocutory judgment with costs has also been held to constitute a "judgment" for the purposes of attracting interest under this section (*Hayes* v. *Fibreglass*, Manchester Crown Court, May 17, 1991).

"Judgment" (EEC Judgments Convention 1968, Art. 25). An order for the taking of evidence abroad was not a "judgment" for the purposes of this Article (*S.A. Trailgaz* v. *Firma Krupp Industrie technik* [1989] E.C.C. 442).

JUDGMENT DEBT. (Judgments Act 1838 (c. 110), s.17) An order for the payment of costs to be taxed was a "judgment debt" within the meaning of this section, and interest ran on the costs from the date when the judgment was pronounced (*Hunt* v. *R. M. Douglas* (*Roofing*) [1988] 3 W.L.R. 975). Sections 17 and 18 of this Act do not apply to criminal proceedings; so that an award from central funds in a criminal cause or matter did not create a "judgment debt" for the purposes of these sections and no interest was payable (*Westminster City Council* v. *Wingrove, Lord Chancellor intervening* [1991] 1 Q.B. 652). In any case in which liability and damages are separately determined the relevant judgment for the purposes of this section is that which created the judgment debt and not that which established or decreed that there was a liability (*Lindop* v. *Goodwin Steel Castings, The Times,* June 19, 1990); *Thomas* v. *Bunn, Wilson* v. *Graham, Lea* v. *British Aerospace* [1991] 1 A.C. 362).

JUDICIAL ACT. A "judicial act" required independent judgment by a judicial officer or authority (*Pounds* v. *Pounds* [1994] 4 All E.R. 777).

Stat. Def., Human Rights Act 1998 (c. 42), s.9(5).

JUNCTION. For the purposes of the Road Vehicles Lighting (Standing Vehicles) (Exemption) (General) Regulations 1975 (No. 1494), reg. 4(2)(*b*) where curving kerbs exist at a road junction, the "junction" is to be regarded as beginning where the kerbing begins to curve (*R.* v. *Derby Crown Court, ex p. Sewell* [1985] RTR 251).

JUST. "Just and equitable" (Employment Protection (Consolidation) Act 1978 (c. 44), s.74(1)). This phrase has to be considered in the light of good industrial practice, and it was held not to be just and equitable to deduct salary paid in lieu of notice from a compensatory award for unfair dismissal (*Addison* v. *Babcock F.A.T.A.* [1987] I.C.R. 805).

"Just and reasonable" (Matrimonial Homes Act 1983 (c. 19), s.1(3)). In proceedings under this section it was held not to be "just and reasonable" to issue an injunction restraining the husband from returning to the flat merely because of the wife's greater need for accommodation (*Wiseman* v. *Simpson* [1988] 1 W.L.R. 35). Where a wife found it impossible to live with her husband because of dissention caused by his jealous, argumentative and unyielding nature, it was held that such conduct by the husband, although short of violence or the threat of violence, was of sufficient severity to make it "just and reasonable" for an order under this section to be issued (*B.* v. *B., The Times,* October 6, 1993).

(8) "Just and equitable" (Insolvency Act 1986 (c. 45), s.122(1)(*g*)). It was held to be "just and equitable" to wind up a company formerly dealing in securities if, had it still been dealing in securities, it would have been just and equitable to wind it up. The fact that the company ceased to carry on that business immediately before the winding-up petition was presented made no difference (*Jacob* (*Walter L.*) *and Co., Re* [1989] B.C.L.C. 345). Notwithstanding that a failure to pay dividends applied to all the members, and was not therefore discriminatory, a failure to meet the reasonable expectations of members to receive a dividend could provide a "just and equitable" ground for a winding-up (*Re A Company* (*No. 00370 of 1987*), *ex p. Glossop* [1988] 1 W.L.R. 1068).

"Just and equitable" (Companies Act 1985 (c. 6), s.404). In a case where a building society failed to register, within the time required, particulars of a mortgage to a property development company it was held that as the failure was accidental it was "just and equitable" to allow late registration (*Re Chantry House Developments* [1990] BCC 646).

"Just excuse" (Criminal Procedure (Attendance of Witnesses) Act 1965 (c. 69), s.3(1)). For the purposes of this section culpable forgetfulness could never amount to a "just excuse" for disobeying a witness order (*R.* v. *Lennock* (1993) 97 Cr.App.R. 228, C.A.).

JUSTICE. "In the interests of justice," see NECESSARY.

JUSTICIABLE. The decision-making process of a legal aid committee in awarding a contract to solicitors for the conduct of a multi-party action was justiciable in public law, since the nature and purpose of the selection process and its consequences, the function exercised by the committee, the purposes for which they were required to act and the consequences of their decision-making process and the public dimension of the matter were of a quality which made it justiciable in public law (*R.* v. *Legal Aid Board, ex p. Donn and Co. (a firm)* [1996] 3 All E.R. 1).

JUSTIFIABLE. (1) "Justifiable" (Race Relations Act 1976 (c. 74), s.1(1)(*b*)(ii)). The requirement that all personnel working in a carriage repair shop, including Sikhs, should wear protective headgear, was discriminatory but "justifiable" within the meaning of this section (*Singh* v. *British Rail Engineering* [1986] I.C.R. 22). The Labour Party rule that only those people who had been resident in Great Britain for one year were eligible for party membership was held to be "justifiable" under this section (*McAlister* v. *Labour Party, The Times*, June 5, 1986). Making it a condition that applicants for the post of head teacher of a Church of England voluntary aided school had to be committed communicant Christians was "justifiable" and there was therefore no breach of the Race Relations Act 1976 (c. 74) (*Board of Governors of St. Matthias Church of England School* v. *Crizzle, The Times*, February 26, 1993).

(2) "Justifiable" (Sex Discrimination Act 1975 (c. 65), s.1(1)(*b*)(ii)). A local authority requirement that the post of branch librarian should be a full-time occupation was held to be "justifiable" (*Clymo* v. *Wandsworth London Borough Council* [1989] I.C.R. 250). See also CAN; DETRIMENT. The requirement that selection for the community programme, a scheme operated by the Manpower Services Commission to provide projects for the young long-term unemployed, should be restricted to those claiming unemployment benefit or supplementary benefit, although discriminatory against married women, was held to be "justifiable" within the meaning of this section (*Cobb* v. *Secretary of State for Employment* [1989] I.C.R. 506).

K

KEEP. "The opening or keeping open of the refreshment house" (Late Night Refreshment Houses Act 1969 (c. 53), s.7(1)). A restaurant was not being kept open after its licensed hours when the only customers present after hours were those who had been admitted within the permitted hours and who were finishing off their meals (*Amin* v. *DPP, The Times*, April 9, 1993).

KEEPER. (Highways Act 1980 (c. 66), s.155). A person can still be a "keeper" of cattle within the meaning of this section notwithstanding that he derives no personal benefit from them and that they may also be in the possession of another person (*DPP* v. *Turton, The Guardian*, June 8, 1988).

KEEPER. Stat. Def. (in relation to animals), Cattle Identification Regulations 1998 (No. 871), reg. 2(1).

KNACKER'S YARD. Stat. Def., Food Safety Act 1990 (c. 16), s.53).

KNEW. "That the accused neither knew nor had reasonable grounds to believe" (Video Recordings Act 1984 (c. 39), s.11(2)(*b*)). Where a company was charged under this Act with supplying a video to a person under the age specified in the classification it is the knowledge of the employee who made the sale which is relevant and can be imputed to the company (*Tesco Stores* v. *Brent London Borough Council, The Times*, February 16, 1993).

KNIFE. Stat. Def., "an instrument which has a blade or is sharply pointed" (Knives Act 1997 (c. 21), s.10).

KNOW-HOW. Stat. Def., Income and Corporation Taxes Act 1988 (c. 1), s.533.

KNOWINGLY. (34) "Knowingly concerned in" (Customs and Excise Management Act 1979 (c. 2), s.170(2)). A person can be "knowingly concerned in any fraudulent evasion . . . of any prohibition" on the importation of goods contrary to this section where he believed that he was carrying pornographic material but was actually carrying cannabis; notwithstanding that the prohibitions are contained in different statutes (*R.* v. *Ellis and Street* (1987) 84 Cr.App.R. 235; following *R.* v. *Hennessey* (1979) 68 Cr.App.R. 419). The *mens rea* for an offence contrary to this section required a specific intent to be knowingly concerned in any fraudulent evasion of a prohibition. It was not enough just to be reckless as to whether or not one was concerned in such an evasion (*R.* v. *Panayi, R.* v. *Karte* [1989] 1 W.L.R. 187). A person who keeps an unsolicited consignment of drugs posted to him from Bolivia could be "knowingly" concerned in the evasion of the prohibition on their importation (*R.* v. *Caippara* (1988) 87 Cr.App.R. 316). Merely being present in a car modified to enable the smugglers of cannabis past Customs officers was not enough to establish that the accused was "knowingly concerned in" the importation of the drugs (*R.* v. *Suurmeijer* [1991] Crim.L.R. 773). It is not necessary for a person to be fraudulently as well as knowingly concerned in a fraudulent evasion for the commission of an offence under s.170(2) (*R.* v. *Latif (Mohammed)* [1996] 1 W.L.R. 104).

To establish the offence of "knowingly" using or permitting the use of premises as a sex establishment, except under licence, contrary to Sched. 3, paras. 6(1), 20(1) of the Local Government (Miscellaneous Provisions) Act 1982 (c. 30) it must be proved that the accused knew not only that the premises were used as a sex establishment but also that the use was otherwise than under and in accordance with the terms of the licence (*Westminster City Council* v. *Croyalgrange* [1986] 1 W.L.R. 674).

"Knowingly concerned in the contravention" (Financial Services Act 1986 (c. 60), ss.6(2), 61(1)). Solicitors acting for the contravening party could be "knowingly concerned" within the meaning of this section (*Securities and Investments Board* v. *Pantell (No. 2)* [1991] 3 W.L.R. 857).

A defendant who had knowledge of all the relevant facts giving rise to a contravention of s.3 of the 1986 Act by another was "knowingly concerned" for the purposes of s.6(2) (*Securities and Investments Board* v. *Scandex Capital Management A/S* [1998] 1 All E.R. 514).

(Environmental Protection Act 1990 (c. 43), s.33). Knowledge of the breach of waste management licence conditions was not necessary to establish an offence under s.33(1); the word "knowingly" in that section related only to causing or permitting the controlled waste to be deposited (*Shanks and McEwan (Teeside) Ltd* v. *Environment Agency, The Times*, January 28, 1997).

KNOWLEDGE. "Knowledge and belief" (Finance Act 1975 (c. 7), Sched. 4, para. 2(1)(*b*)) is confined to the personal knowledge of the person required to prepare the accounts in question, and includes any information contained in documents in his possession. The words do not impose an obligation to go out and seek information from others (*Re Clore (Dec'd) (No. 3), I.R.C.* v. *Stype Trustees* [1985] 2 All E.R. 819).

"Date of knowledge" (Limitation Act 1980 (c. 58), ss.11(4)(*b*), 14(1)). Anxiety caused by a suspicion or belief that a significant injury has been suffered is not enough to constitute "knowledge" for the purposes of these sections (*Stephen*) v. *Riverside Health Authority, The Times*, November 29, 1989). In cases involving surgical operations a plaintiff's date of "knowledge" that an injury she had suffered was attributable to an operation did not arise until she became aware of some act or omission which could have affected the safety of the operation (*Bentley* v. *Bristol and Western Health Authority* [1991] 2 Med.L.R. 359). While, in personal injury cases involving surgical operations, a plaintiff's date of knowledge that an injury was attributable in whole or in part to an operation could well have depended on the date when she had received an expert's report, in a less complicated case the date of knowledge arose when she appreciated that her problems were attributable to the operation, even if the precise terms of what had gone wrong were not known (*Hendy* v. *Milton Keynes Health Authority* [1992] Med.L.R. 114). A plaintiff who, as a child, had been sexually abused by her adoptive father and brother, and had suffered resultant mental disturbance, was held to be entitled to proceed with her action, notwithstanding that the writ had not been issued until 12 years after she had reached the age of majority, as she had not had the requisite knowledge as to the significance and cause of her injuries until within three years of the issue of the writ (*Stubbings* v. *Webb* [1991] 3 W.L.R. 383). "Knowledge" within the meaning of s.14 is constituted where a plaintiff has sufficient confidence of the relevant facts to justify preparing the litigation; ignorance of the availability of a remedy is an irrelevant consideration (*Halford* v. *Brookes* [1991] 1 W.L.R. 428). An injured plaintiff could rely, for the purposes of establishing his "date of knowledge" within the meaning of s.14, on the fact that he had limited resources and that his solicitors had to work within the limitations of the legal aid granted (*Khan* v. *Ainslie* [1994] 4 Med LR 319). An injured plaintiff had constructive knowledge for the purposes of s.14 of the 1980 Act, where she appreciated in general terms that her problem was capable of being attributed to an operation even if the particular facts of what went wrong were not known (*Bentley* v. *Bristol and Weston Health Authority* [1991] 2 Med. L.R. 369 overruled) (*Broadley* v. *Guy Chapman & Co.* [1993] 4 Med LR 328). Where the plaintiff had claimed that a survey report was negligent, and had been aware at the time of exchange of contracts of some of the defects to which the report failed to refer, she was not debarred from relying upon the extended limitation period in respect of other defects of which he only became aware several years after exchange (*Felton* v. *Gaskill Osborne & Co.* [1993] 43 EG 118). Awareness that treatment had not worked did not imbue a plaintiff with relevant knowledge that an operation had failed until the date of an expert medical opinion on his condition (*Smith (Michael John)* v. *West Lancashire Health Authority* [1995] 10 C.L. 575).

"Displayed without his knowledge or consent" (Town and Country Planning Act 1990 (c. 8), s.224(5)). The words "knowedge or consent" are to be construed disjunctively so that even though a person had or had acquired knowledge of the display of an advertisement, it was still open to him to establish a defence by reason of the fact that he had not consented to it (*Edmonds* v. *Merton London Borough Council; Tyndall* v. *Same, The Times,* July 6, 1993).

KNOWN. (4) (Animals Act 1971 (c. 22), s.2(2)). Actual knowledge of an animal's alleged abnormal characteristics was required to found liability under s.2(2)(*c*) (*Hunt* v. *Wallis* [1994] P.I.Q.R. P128).

L

LABELLING. (Council Reg. (EEC) 2392/89). "Labelling" is defined as all descriptions and other references, signs, designs or brand names which distinguish the product and which appear on the same container, including its sealing device or the tag attached to its container (Criminal Proceedings Against Voisine (C–46/94), July 5, 1995, ECJ, Fourth Chamber).

LACK OF CARE. "Lack of care" in the context of an inquest was more appropriately described as "neglect" and meant a gross failure to provide adequate food, shelter or medical attention for a person in a state of dependency (*R.* v. *North Humberside and Scunthorpe Coroner, ex p. Jamieson* [1994] 3 W.L.R. 82).

LAND. "Any writ or order affecting land" (Land Charges Act 1972 (c. 61), s.6(1)(*a*)). An undivided share in the proceeds of sale of land held on trust for sale was not "land" within the meaning of this section (*Perry* v. *Phoenix Assurance* [1988] 3 All E.R. 60).

The reversion of a lease was "land" for the purposes of the common law rule that the benefit of a convenant which touched and concerned land ran with the land (*P. & A. Swift Investments* v. *Combined English Stores Group* [1988] 2 All E.R. 885).

A building to which waste was removed was "land" within the meaning of the Control of Pollution Act 1974 (c. 40), s.91(1) (*Gotech Industrial and Environmental Services* v. *Friel*, 1995 S.C.C.R. 22). See AGRICULTURAL.

(Local Government Finance Act 1988 (c. 41), s.64). A wall to which an advertising hoarding attached to battens was bolted was "land" for the purposes of s.64 and not the advertising hoarding itself (*O'Brien* v. *Secker, The Times*, June 3, 1996).

Stat. Def., Public Order Act 1986 (c. 64), s.39; Town and Country Planning Act 1990 (c. 8), s.336; Environmental Protection Act 1990 (c. 43), s.29; "includes any ice-shelf" (Antarctic Act 1994 (c. 15), s.31(1)); includes buildings and other structures, land covered with water, and any interest in land" (Education Act 1996 (c. 56), s.579(1)); similar definition, Town and Country Planning (Scotland) Act 1997 (c. 8), s.277(1)).

"Disposing of land", Stat. Def., School Standards and Framework Act 1998 (c. 31), s.142(6).

LANDLORD. "The landlord condition" for the purposes of the Housing Act 1980 (c. 51), s.28(2) is not satisfied where the premises belong jointly to two bodies one of which is not a body mentioned in s.28(4) (*R.* v. *Plymouth City Council, ex p. Freeman* (1987) 19 H.L.R. 328).

"Used by the landlord pending development" (Housing Act 1985 (c. 68), Sched. 1, para. 3(1)). For the purposes of this paragraph it is not necessary for the "landlord" to be the person who had acquired the land for development (*Hyde Housing Association* v. *Harrison* (1991) 23 H.L.R. 57).

Stat. Def., Landlord and Tenant Act 1987 (c. 31), ss.2, 59, 60; Landlord and Tenant Act 1988 (c. 26), s.5; Landlord and Tenant (Covenants) Act 1995 (c. 30), s.28(1); Family Law Act 1996 (c. 27), Sched. 7, para. 1.

LARD. For the purposes of the Trade Descriptions Act 1968 (c. 29) and regulation 8 of the Food Labelling Regulations 1980 (No. 1849) the meaning of "lard" is not confined to pig fat (*Wolkind and Northcott* v. *Pura Foods* (1987) 85 L.G.R. 782).

LARGE. "Larger purpose," see PURPOSE.

(Sunday Trading Act 1994, Sched. 1, para. 4). The fact that part of a shop remained closed during Sunday opening did not mean that the premises ceased to be a "a large shop" for the purposes of the 1994 Act (*Haskins Garden Centres Ltd* v. *East Dorset District Council, The Times*, May 7, 1998).

LAST KNOWN ADDRESS. (R.S.C., Ord. 10). The "last known address" under Ord. 10(1) could be construed as a business address and in particular in the case of a solicitor and his client, it was acceptable for that address to be the business address of the solicitor (*Robertson* v. *Banham & Co., The Times,* November 26, 1996).

LAUNDERING. See DRUG MONEY LAUNDERING.

LAWFUL ACT OF DURESS. The exertion of commercial pressure by threatening to withdraw credit facilities was not an act of duress (*CTN Cash and Carry* v. *Gallaher* [1994] 4 All E.R. 714).

LAWFUL AUTHORITY. See LAWFUL EXCUSE.

LAWFUL EXCUSE. (3) "Lawful authority or excuse" (Highways Act 1980 (c. 66), s.137). The question whether an activity is obstructing the highway without lawful excuse has to be decided according to whether it is reasonable or unreasonable; "excuse and reasonableness are really the same ground" (*per* Lord Parker in *Nagy* v. *Weston* [1965] 1 W.L.R. 280). This case was followed by the Divisional Court when allowing the appeal of two animal rights supporters who had been convicted of obstructing the highway by demonstrating outside a furrier's shop (*Hirst* v. *Chief Constable of West Yorkshire* [1987] Crim.L.R. 330). The operation of a stall in the same position for several years and the payment of rates did not of itself constitute "lawful authority" to cause an obstruction within the meaning of this section (*Pugh* v. *Pidgen* (1987) 151 J.P. 644).

"Lawful authority or excuse" (Highways Act 1980 (c. 66), s.131(1)). Absence of *mens rea* is no lawful excuse for making an excavation in a highway. It is an absolute offence under this section (*Greenwich London Borough Council* v. *Millcroft Construction* (1986) 85 L.G.R. 66).

(6) A company director who, for fraudulent purposes, set fire to his company building was not entitled to claim "lawful excuse" under s.1(1) of the Criminal Damage Act 1971 (c. 48), notwithstanding that it was his own building and he must be taken as having consented to the damage. In distinguishing *R.* v. *Denton* [1982] 1 All E.R. 65 [see Main Work, para. 6] it was held that a man could not be held to be entitled to consent to a fraudulent purpose (*R.* v. *Appleyard* (1985) 81 Cr.App.R. 319). A defendant's genuine belief that he was carrying out God's instructions did not provide a defence of "lawful excuse" to a charge of criminal damage under s.1(1) of the 1971 Act (*Blake* v. *DPP*, *The Times*, January 19, 1993). A political motive, in this case a demonstration against nuclear weapons, is not a "lawful excuse" for the possession of an article intended to be used for the damage of property contrary to s.5 of this Act (*R.* v. *Ashford and Smith* [1988] Crim.L.R. 682). Where a person is charged with the possession of an article with intent to damage property, contrary to s.3 of the 1971 Act, the question whether the act concerned could amount to "protection of property," and thus provide a "lawful excuse" under s.5, is an objective one (*R.* v. *Hill*; *R.* v. *Hall* (1989) Cr.App.R. 74).

The demolition of a wall which was obstructing a right of way in order to avoid litigation and to avoid any suggestion of acquiescence could amount to a lawful excuse under s.5 (*Chamberlain* v. *Lindon* [1998] 2 All E.R. 538).

(8) (Firearms Act 1968 (c. 27), s.19). The existence of a valid firearms certificate issued under s.26 of the 1968 Act was not of itself "lawful authority" for the possession of a firearm and ammunition in a public place (*R.* v. *Jones* [1995] 3 All E.R. 139).

LAWFUL MANNER. "In any lawful manner" (Oaths Act 1978 (c. 19), s.1(3)). Whether administration of an oath to a witness was "lawful" within this section did not depend on the intricacies of the witness's religion but on whether it was an oath which appeared to the court to be binding on the witness's conscience and, if so, whether it was an oath which the witness himself considered to be binding on his conscience (*R.* v. *Kemble* [1990] 1 W.L.R. 1111).

LAWFUL USE. "Lawful use of the highway" (Animals Act 1971 (c. 22), s.5(5)). Letting livestock wander at will on the highway was not a "lawful use of the highway" within the meaning of this section, notwithstanding that the highway in question was within the geographical area of the common land over which the owner of the livestock had grazing rights (*Mathews* v. *Wicks*, *The Times*, May 25, 1987).

LAWFULLY. "Other person lawfully acting in the execution of this Act" (Immigration Act 1971 (c. 77), s.26(1)(c)): A police officer who, in the course of an investigation into another matter, became suspicious that the accused was illegally in the United Kingdom, was not a person who could "lawfully" act in the execution of the Act, and was not therefore entitled to interrogate him (*R.* v. *Clarke* (*Ediakpo*) [1985] 3 W.L.R. 113). See also PERSON.

A refugee presenting himself to the immigration authorities and being refused entry by them was not a refugee "lawfully" in the United Kingdom within the meaning of article 32(1) of the Geneva Convention Relating to the Status of Refugees 1951 (Cmnd. 9171) (*R.* v. *Secretary of State for the Home Department, ex p. Bugdaycay* [1987] A.C. 514), and it makes no difference if he holds a valid re-entry visa (*R.* v. *Secretary of State for the Home Department, ex p. H, The Times,* March 24, 1988).

LAWYER. "Qualified lawyer," Stat. Def., Disability Discrimination Act 1995 (c. 50), s.9(4A) inserted by Employment Rights (Dispute Resolution) Act 1998 (c. 8), Sched. 1, para. 11.

"Lawyer," Stat. Def., "a person who holds a legal qualification in the United Kingdom" (Northern Ireland (Sentences) Act 1998 (c. 35), s.1(5)).

LAYING. Stat. Def. (in relation to shellfish), Food Safety (Fishery Products and Live Shellfish) (Hygiene) Regulations 1998 (No. 994), reg. 2(1).

LAYING AN INFORMATION. "Unless the information was laid . . . within six months" (Magistrates' Courts Act 1980 (c. 43), s.127(1)). Where informations were laid by computer link between the police station and the magistrates' court they were "laid" for the purposes of this section at the time of the computer input, not at the time of the print-out (*R.* v. *Pontypridd Juvenile Magistrates' Court, ex p. B.* (1989) 153 J.P. 213).

"Where an information is laid before a justice of the peace" (Costs in Criminal Cases Act 1973 (c. 14), s.12(3)). An information was "laid" within the meaning of this section when its contents were brought to the notice of the justices' clerk (*Patel* v. *Blakey* [1988] RTR 65).

LEASE. "Leased to the landlord" (Housing Act 1985 (c. 68), Sched. 1, para. 6). The word "leased" in this paragraph meant that the landlord local authority's interest in the property was something less than freehold (*Tower Hamlets London Borough Council* v. *Miah* [1992] 1 Q.B. 622). A letter confirming that a quarterly tenancy at a specific rent from a certain date was merely evidence of a lease and had no dispositive effect and therefore did not amount to a "lease in writing" within the meaning of the Law of Property Act 1925 (c. 20), s.54 (*Long* v. *Tower Hamlets LBC, The Times,* March 29, 1996).

(Limitation Act 1980 (c. 58), Sched. 1, para. 5(1)). A written document was not a "lease in writing" for the purposes of Sched. 1, para. 5(1) of the 1980 Act if the writing, whatever its terms and however comprehensively it set out the terms of the lease, was merely evidence of the existence of a lease, the document had to be dispositive in that it created in law and by itself a leasehold estate in land (*Long* v. *Tower Hamlets London Borough Council* [1996] 3 W.L.R. 317).

Stat. Def., "includes a tenancy, sub-lease or sub-tenancy and an agreement for a lease, tenancy, sub-lease or sub-tenancy" (Disability Discrimination Act 1995 (c. 50), s.16(3)); Finance Act 1997 (c.16), Sched. 12, para. 30(1)).

LEASING OR LETTING OF IMMOVABLE PROPERTY. Where a given transaction such as the "letting of immovable property" fell within the scope of an exemption provided for by the Sixth Directive, a change in the contractual relationship such as a surrender of the lease for consideration was to be regarded as falling within the scope of the exemption (*Lubbock Fine and Co.* v. *Customs and Excise Commissioners* [1994] 3 W.L.R. 261).

Stat. Def., Housing Act 1985 (c. 68), s.621; Landlord and Tenant Act 1985 (c. 70), s.36; Landlord and Tenant Act 1987 (c. 31), s.59; Town and Country Planning Act 1990 (c. 8), s.336.

LEGAL ADOPTION. To show a "legal adoption" within the meaning of s.33(1) of the Immigration Act 1971 (c. 77), a Bangladeshi applicant had to show that he had been an "overseas adoption" under s.72(2) of the Adoption Act 1976 (c. 36) (*R.* v. *Secretary of State for the Home Office, ex p. Tahid, The Times*, October 10, 1990).

LEGAL ADVICE. "Giving of legal advice" (Police and Criminal Evidence Act 1984 (c. 60), s.10(1)(*a*)). The document known as "the conveyance," consisting as it does of records of the financing of the purchase of a house, cannot be called "advice," and is not therefore protected under this section (*R.* v. *Inner London Crown Court, ex p. Baines and Baines* [1988] 2 W.L.R. 549).

LEGAL PRIVILEGE. See Privileged Communication. See also Item; Made.

LEGAL PROCEEDINGS. An arrest did not fall within the meaning of "legal proceedings" in s.4(1) of the Contempt of Court Act 1981 (c. 49) so that the justices had no power under s.4(2) to prohibit the broadcasting of a film of the defendant's arrest (*R.* v. *Rhuddlan Justices, ex p. H.T.V.* [1986] Crim.L.R. 329). See also Other.

Stat. Def., "any proceedings before a court or tribunal" (Finance Act 1997 (c. 16), s.47(11)).

LEGAL PROCESS. "Or other legal process" (Insolvency Act 1986 (c. 45), ss.11(3)(*d*), 285(1)). These words were held to include the process in Part VI of the General Rate Act 1967 (c. 9) for the recovery of unpaid rates, including proceedings for committal (*Re Smith (a Bankrupt), ex p. Braintree District Council* [1989] 3 W.L.R. 1317). The use of the word "legal" before the word "process" means a process which requires the assistance of the court and does not extend to the service of a contractual notice, whether or not the notice was a necessary precondition to bringing legal proceedings (*Olympia and York Canary Wharf; American Express Europe* v. *Adamson* [1993] BCC 154).

LEGAL REPRESENTATIVE. Stat. Def., Children and Young Persons Act 1933 (c. 12), s.49(11) as substituted by Criminal Justice and Public Order Act 1994 (c. 33), s.49.

LEGALLY ASSISTED PARTY. (Legal Aid Act 1988 (c. 34), s.17). Where the steps for which a legal aid certificate had been granted had been accomplished, the certificate should be regarded as spent without the need for any formal discharge, and the assisted person was not a "legally assisted person" in respect of any procedural steps taken thereafter (*Turner* v. *Plasplugs Ltd* [1997] 2 All E.R. 939).

LEGISLATION. A national regulation on social security matters whose effects extended to persons carrying out or who had carried out activities partially or wholly outside the Community was to be regarded as "legislation" within the meaning of Art. 2 of EEC Regulation No. 1408/71 (*Van Roosmalen* v. *Bestuur van de Bedrijfsvereniging voor de Gezondheid, The Times*, October 29, 1986).

"Private legislation in Parliament", Stat. Def., Environment Act 1995 (c. 25), s.28(3); see also ENACTMENT.

LEGITIMATE. "Legitimate child of his parents" (Legitimacy Act 1976 (c. 31), s.1(1)). A person born before his parents entered into a void marriage cannot become "legitimate" by virtue of this section (*Spence* (*Dec'd.*), *Re Spence* v. *Dennis* [1990] 2 W.L.R. 1430).

LESS. "Less favourable to the woman," see FAVOURABLE.

"Less free to come into . . . the United Kingdom," see FREE.

"Less favourably than he treats . . . other persons," see FAVOURABLE.

LESS THAN. See NOT LESS THAN.

LESSEE. The expression "the lessee" in s.138(7) of the County Courts Act 1984 (c. 28) applies only to the tenant in whom the lease is or was vested and who is the defendant in the relevant forfeiture proceedings (*United Dominions Trust* v. *Shellpoint Trustees* [1992] 39 EG 144).

(County Courts Act 1984 (c. 28), s.138(2)(7)). The term "lessee" in this section includes an underlessee and a mortgagee (*United Dominions Trust* v. *Shellpoint Trustees* [1993] 4 All E.R. 310).

For the purposes of s.138, a "lessee" meant a person deriving legal title to the lease under the original lessee so that a beneficial co-owner was not entitled to relief from forfeiture (*Bassett Road Housing Association* v. *Gough* [1998] 6 C.L. 362).

LETHAL WEAPON. (2) A revolver from which pellets could be shot by the release of carbon dioxide gas, and which was capable of causing injury from which death might result, was a "lethal weapon" and therefore a "firearm" (*q.v.*) within the meaning of s.57(1) of the Firearms Act 1968 (c. 27) (*R.* v. *Thorpe* [1987] 1 W.L.R. 383).

LETTING VALUE. The words "letting value" in the proviso to s.4(1) of the Leasehold Reform Act 1967 (c. 88) mean the annual rent obtainable in the open market having regard to any limit imposed by the Rent Acts, but with an addition for the decapitalised value of any premium lawfully obtainable (*Johnston* v. *Duke of Westminster* [1986] A.C. 839; *Duke of Westminster* v. *Johnston* (1987) 53 P. & C.R. 36).

LEYS. Stat. Def., Agricultural Holdings Act 1986 (c. 5), Sched. 8, para. 11(3).

LIABILITY. "Liability" (Civil Liability (Contribution) Act 1978 (c. 47), s.1). For the purposes of this section the liability did not need to be procedurally enforceable so long as it had the character of a liability at the time the damage was suffered (*Lister* (*R.A.*) *& Co.* v. *Thomson* (*E.G.*) (*Shipping*), (*No. 2*); *The Benarty* (*No. 2*) [1987] 3 All E.R. 1032).

Where there was cover in an insurance policy against "liability at law" it was held that "liability at law" was not restricted to liability arising at common law but included also contractual liability (*M/S Aswan Engineering Establishment Co.* v. *Iron Trades Mutual Insurance Co.* [1989] 1 Lloyd's Rep. 289).

"Liability to make a payment" (Theft Act 1978 (c. 31), s.2(1)(*b*). The liability referred to in this subsection is necessarily a liability of the person seeking to evade it, and not a liability of someone else (*R.* v. *Attewell-Hughes* (1991) 93 Cr.App.R. 132).

"Liability to make a payment" (Theft Act 1978 (c. 31), s.2(1)(*c*)). These words are not restricted to an existing liability and could cover an expected or future liability (*R.* v. *Firth* (1990) 91 Cr.App.R. 217).

(Carriage by Air Act 1961 (c. 27), Sched. 1, arts. 22(2)(*a*), 25). A special declaration of value of diamonds which were lost while in the custody of an airline was a "limit of liability" for the purposes of art. 25 so that the carrier was deprived of all limitations of liability conferred by art. 22 when the damage was caused by wilful misconduct (*Antwerp International B.V.B.A. and anr* v. *Air Europe* [1995] 3 W.L.R. 396).

Stat. Def., Companies Act 1985 (c. 6), ss.152, 154, 265, Sched. 9, para. 32; Insolvency Act 1985 (c. 65), s.211; "includes obligation" (Education Act 1996 (c. 56), s.579(1)); "includes any liability whether conditional or unconditional, whether present or future, and whether vested or contingent" (Bank of England (Information Powers) Order 1998 (No. 1270), Art. 1(2)).

LIABLE. (23) "Sums which the insured shall become liable at law to pay as damages." Where these words were used in the indemnity clause of an insurance policy the liability "at law" was not restricted to liability in tort, but extended also to liability incurred under contract (*M/S Aswan Engineering Establishment Co.* v. *Iron Trades Mutual Insurance Co.* [1989] 1 Lloyd's Rep. 289).

(24) "Liable" means legally liable under the Social Security Contributions and Benefits Act 1992 (c. 4), s.130(1)(*a*) (*R.* v. *Sheffield City Council Housing Benefit Review Board, ex p. Smith* [1995] 93 L.G.R. 139).

(Drug Trafficking Offences Act 1986 (c. 32), s.6). "Liable to serve a term of custody" meant currently liable rather than contingently liable so that a liability to pay under a confiscation order lasted for the duration of a sentence even though the defendant had been released from prison on licence (*R.* v. *Hastings and Rother Magistrates' Court, ex p. Anscombe* [1998] 4 C.L. 150).

LICENCE. "Licence to occupy," see HOMELESS.
See TENANCY.

LICENSEE. See TENANT.

LIEN. (Marine Insurance Act 1906 (c. 41), s.53(2)). A "lien on the policy" in s.53(2) was confined to a physical possessory lien on the policy and not a right to annex or set off the proceeds collected under the policy in discharge of a debt owed to the holder of the policy, although it could be used to discharge the debt protected by the lien (*Eide UK Ltd* v. *Lowndes Lambert Group Ltd* [1998] 1 All E.R. 946).

LIFE INSURANCE POLICY. The essence of life insurance is that the rights to the benefits are related to life or death, so that a policy where all the rights remained contingent on the death or survival of the assured was a policy of life insurance within the Life Assurance Act 1774 (c. 48), s.1 (*Fuji Finance Inc.* v. *Aetna Life Insurance Co. Ltd* [1996] 3 W.L.R. 871).

LIFE PRISONER. "A discretionary life prisoner" (Criminal Justice Act 1991 (c. 53), s.45(5)). A life prisoner who became a mental patient under detention nevertheless remained a "life prisoner" for the parole provisions of this Act (*R.* v. *Secretary of State for the Home Department, ex p. Hickey* [1994] Q.B. 378).

LIKE SUM. See PREMIUM.

LIKE WORK. (Equal Pay Act 1970 (c. 41), s.1(4)). Women canteen assistants were held not to be doing "like work" with a male canteen worker who worked permanently at night and alone (*Thomas* v. *National Coal Board*; *Baker* v. *National Coal Board* [1987] I.C.R. 757). The principle that men and women should receive equal pay for "equal work." (EEC Treaty, Art. 119) or "like work" (Irish Anti-Discrimination (Pay) Act 1974) was held to extend to a case where the lower paid worker was engaged in work of higher value than that of the person with whom the comparison was made (*Murphy* v. *Bord Telecom Eireann* (European Court Case 157/86 [1988] 1 W.L.R. 692).

LIKELY. (8) Carry . . . any load so heavy as to be likely to cause injury to him" (Factories Act 1961 (c. 34), s.72, as amended). The likelihood of injury is to be assessed with regard to whether the weight of the load is appropriate to the sex, build, physique or other obvious characteristic of the employee in question, and not to any individual weakness or predisposition; in this case the congenital condition of the plaintiff's back of which the defendants were unaware (*Whitfield* v. *H. & R. Johnson* (*Tiles*), *The Times*, March 6, 1990).

(11) "Breach of the peace . . . likely to be occasioned" (Public Order Act 1936 (c. 6), s.5). In circumstances where a constable has to make a spur of the moment decision in an emergency it is reasonable for him to conclude that a mere disturbance could be "likely" to occasion a breach of the peace (*G.* v. *Chief Superintendent of Police, Stroud* [1987] Crim.L.R. 269).

(12) "Is likely to be able to give material evidence" (Magistrates' Courts Act 1980 (c. 43), s.97(1)). In considering whether, on an application for a witness summons under this section, the witness "is likely to be able to give material evidence," the justices have to inquire into the nature of the evidence to be given and whether it is material. It is not sufficient that the applicant merely wants to discover whether the potential witness could give any material evidence (*R.* v. *Peterborough Magistrates' Court, ex p. Willis* [1987] Crim.L.R. 692). Since a witness summons could not be issued to enable an accused to gain access to privileged information between a client and his solicitor, since the privileged information could not be subject to the provisions of the Criminal Procedure Act 1865, the evidence of the proposed witness was not therefore "likely to be material evidence" (*R.* v. *Derby Magistrates' Court, ex p. B.* [1995] 3 W.L.R. 681).

"Likely to interfere with the impartial exercise of his duties" (Police Regulations 1979 (No. 1470), Sched. 2, para. 1). It was held that a police constable's membership, as a parent governor, of the appointments sub-committee of a local comprehensive school was not "likely" to give the impression to members of the public that it might interfere with the impartial discharge of his police duties (*Champion* v. *Chief Constable of Gwent Constabulary* [1990] 1 W.L.R. 1).

"Is likely to have in the foreseeable future" (Matrimonial Causes Act 1973 (c. 18), s.25(2)(*a*)). In certain circumstances an interest which a person might inherit under the will of an existing person could constitute property which she is "likely to have in the foreseeable future" within the meaning of this section, but uncertainties both as to the fact of the inheritance and as to the time at which it would occur would make it rare for a court so to hold (*Michael* v. *Michael* [1986] 2 F.L.R. 398).

"Likely to achieve . . . the purposes mentioned below" (Insolvency Act 1986 (c. 45), s.8(1)(*b*)). The word "likely" as used in this section means there is a "real prospect" of achieving the relevant statutory purpose (*Re S.C.L. Building Services* (1989) 5 BCC 746). It is not necessary for the court to be satisfied on the balance of probability that the purposes of an administration order will be achieved before making the order, but only that it is likely. The word "likely" in this section is not restricted to meaning "more likely than not" (*Re Primlaks* (*U.K.*) [1989] BCLC 734).

"Likely to cause . . . nuisance to other persons" (Sexual Offences Act 1985 (c. 44), s.1(1)(*b*)). In convicting a man under this section, justices were entitled to apply their knowledge of the area concerned and conclude that his activities had been "likely" to cause a nuisance even though there was no direct evidence that a nuisance had actually been caused (*Paul* v. *DPP* (1990) 90 Cr.App.R. 173).

"Likely to cause . . . suffering or injury" (Children and Young Persons Act 1933 (c. 12), s.1). In this section the word "likely" extends beyond probability to something which could well happen. It is to be construed as excluding only what would fairly be described as highly unlikely (*R.* v. *Wills* [1990] Crim.L.R. 714).

"Was likely to cause" (Animals Act 1971 (c. 22), s.2(2)(*a*)). In many contexts "likely" meant "probable" or "more probable than not." But in other contexts it might have a wider meaning so that, as in this case, a likely event included an event "such as might happen" or "such as might well happen." Thus the keeper of a dog known to have a propensity to attack other dogs was liable in damages to a plaintiff who had sustained a fracture of his leg after being knocked over by the aggressive dog when it lunged to attack the plaintiff's dog (*Smith* v. *Ainger, The Times*, June 5, 1990).

"Likely to suffer significant harm" (Children Act 1989 (c. 41), s.31(2)). For the purposes of this section "likely to suffer" should be interpreted with reference to evaluating the future likelihood of significant harm and not by reference back to past events (*Newham London Borough Council* v. *A.G.* [1993] 1 FLR 281).

The threshold criteria for making a care order was satisfied if it was shown that there was a real possibility that a child would suffer significant harm, which conclusion had to be based on facts and not just suspicion (*H. and ors (Minors) (Sexual Abuse: Standard of Proof)* [1996] 1 All E.R. 1).

LIMIT OF LIABILITY. See LIABILITY.

LINE. A stretch of railway track which formed part of a direct route between two stations was a "line" within the meaning of s.56(7) of the Transport Act 1962 (c. 46), thus obliging the Railways Board to comply with the statutory procedures for closure set out in that section, notwithstanding that it proposed to re-route the existing passenger service via another station (*R.* v. *British Railways Board, ex p. Bradford City Metropolitan Council, The Times,* December 8, 1987).

LIQUIDATED SUM. A statutory demand for payment of the total debt less the estimated value of any security, which could be ascertained by an arithmetical calculation, was a "liquidated sum" within the meaning of the Insolvency Act 1986 (c. 45), s.267(2)(*b*) (*Re A Debtor (No. 64 of 1992)* [1994] 1 W.L.R. 264).

LIQUOR. Stat. Def., "means spirits, wine, beer, cider, perry and any other fermented, distilled or spirituous liquor" (Merchant Shipping Act 1995 (c. 21), s.118(6)).

LISTED BUILDING. (Planning (Listed Buildings and Conservation Areas) Act 1990 (c. 9), s.1). "Listed building" could include a part of a listed building (*Shimizu (U.K.) Ltd* v. *Westminster City Council* [1997] 1 W.L.R. 168).

LITIGANT IN PERSON. (Litigants in Person (Costs and Expenses) Act 1975 (c. 47), s.1). A company is not a litigant in person for the purposes of s.1 of the Litigants in Person (Costs and Expenses) Act 1975 and cannot therefore recover costs under C.C.R., Ord. 38, r.17 (*Jonathan Alexander Ltd* v. *Proctor* [1997] 2 All E.R. 334).

The Official Receiver was not a "litigant in person" for the purposes of recovering costs even though he was acting as a servant of the Crown in proceedings for the disqualification of a company director, since a servant or agent could not be regarded as acting in person (*Re Minotaur Data Systems Ltd* [1998] 4 All E.R. 500).

LITTER. (3) (Environmental Protection Act 1990 (c. 43), s.87). "Litter" in s.87(1) of the 1990 Act was miscellaneous rubbish left lying about and included street waste, domestic household waste and commercial waste awaiting collection by removal contractors (*Westminster City Council* v. *Riding* (1995) 94 L.G.R. 489).

LITERARY. (4) "Original literary . . . work" (Copyright Act 1956 (c. 74), s.2(1)). Where the publishers of a newspaper, after distributing at random large numbers of cards carrying five letter codes, published computer prepared grids of rows of letters and other sequences (against which the cardholders could check to see if they had won prizes), it was held that these grids and sequences were "literary works" under this Act on the grounds that they afforded information (*Express Newspapers* v. *Liverpool Daily Post* [1985] 3 All E.R. 680).

A "literary work" had to be written down and contain information which could be read by another, as opposed to being merely appreciated with the eye and could include circuit diagrams relating to an electronic dust meter (*Anacon Corp.* v. *Environmental Research Technology* [1994] F.S.R. 659).

"Literary work." Stat. Def., Copyright, Designs and Patents Act 1988 (c. 48), s.3.

LIVE MUSIC. Where a condition in a planning permission granting a change of use to a public house banned "live music" it was held that the appearance of well-known artists miming to their recordings, although live entertainment, was not live music and therefore there was no breach of the condition (*Shepway District Council and South Coast Leisure* (1988) 3 P.A.D. 178).

LIVE TOGETHER. "Live together as husband and wife" (Housing Act 1985 (c. 68), s.113(1)). To establish that a couple had been living together "as husband and wife" within the meaning of this section it is necessary to show that the parties had a settled intention to be so regarded (*City of Westminster* v. *Peart* (1992) 24 H.L.R. 389).

LIVESTOCK. "The rearing of stock as an agricultural operation must be the rearing of stock which produces or contributes to the production of the means of human subsistence" (*Forth Stud* v. *East Lothian Assessor* (1969) R.A. 35, *per* Lord Avonside). This was confirmed by the House of Lords which held that "livestock" in s.2(1)(*a*) of the Rating Act 1971 (c. 39) did not include racehorses (*Hemens* (*Valuation Officer*) v. *Whitsbury Farm and Stud* [1988] 2 W.L.R 72).

Stat. Def., Agricultural Holdings Act 1986 (c. 5), ss.18(5), 96; Agricultural Tenancies Act 1995 (c. 8), s.38(1).

"Any creature kept for the production of food, wool, skins or fur or for the purpose of any agricultural activity" (Health and Safety (Enforcing Authority) Regulations 1998 (No. 494), reg. 2(1)).

LIVING WITH. "Has his wife living with him" (Income and Corporation Taxes Act 1970 (c. 10), s.8(1)(*a*)(i)). A husband who shared a home with his wife but effectively lived in it as a separate household did not have his wife "living with him" for the purposes of this section (*Holmes* v. *Mitchell* [1991] S.T.C. 25).

LOAD. A dog was a "load" within the meaning of the Road Traffic Act 1972 (c. 20), Sched. 4, column 4(*a*) (*Simpson* v. *Vant* [1986] RTR 247).

"Constructed to carry a load" (Road Traffic Regulation Act 1984 (c. 27), ss.136(6)(7), 137(2)). A heavy breakdown recovery vehicle equipped with a special boom to assist in the lifting and moving of vehicles was held to have been "constructed to carry a load" within the meaning of these sections (*DPP* v. *Holtham* [1991] RTR 5).

LOAN. (Finance Act 1976 (c. 40), s.66). Where an employer made an interest-free advance of salary to assist an employee with the purchase of a house, in circumstances where the employee had been required to move from one place to another, this constituted a "loan" for the purposes of this section (*Williams* v. *Todd* [1988] S.T.C. 676).

Stat. Def., "includes any advance of money" (Finance Act 1996 (c. 8), s.103(1)).

LOCAL AUTHORITY. (Local Government Act 1972 (c. 70), ss.222(1), 270(1)). An urban development corporation is not a "local authority" within the meaning of these sections (*London Docklands Corporation* v. *Rank Hovis* (1985) 84 L.G.R. 101).

Stat. Def., Sunday Trading Act 1994 (c. 20), s.8; Value Added Tax Act 1994 (c. 23), s.96(4); Police and Magistrates' Courts Act 1994 (c. 29), s.69(10); Deregulation and Contracting Out Act 1994 (c. 40), s.79(1); Jobseekers Act 1995 (c. 18), s.33(10); Water Resources Act 1991 (c. 57), s.91B(8) inserted by Environment Act 1995 (c. 25), s.58; Environment Act 1995 (c. 25), s.91(1); Dogs (Fouling of Land) Act 1996 (c. 20), s.7(1); Defamation Act 1996 (c. 31), Sched. 1, para. 11(2); Noise Act 1996 (c. 37), s.11(1); Education Act 1996 (c. 56), s.579(1).

LOCAL CONNECTION. Stat. Def., Housing Act 1985 (c. 68), s.61.

A Muslim wishing to visit the Central London Mosque every day and send his children to a particular Muslim school in the area was held to have no "local connection" with the area within the terms of s.61 (*R.* v. *Westminster City Council, ex p. Benniche, The Times*, April 15, 1996).

LOCAL GOVERNMENT. "Relevant local government service" (Redundancy Payment (Local Government) (Modification) Order 1983 (No. 1160) did not include employment with a water authority (*Liversidge* v. *London Residual Body* [1989] I.C.R. 228; *Deebank* v. *West Midlands Residuary Body* [1990] I.C.R. 349).

LOCAL GOVERNMENT ELECTION. Stat. Def., including City of London municipal elections, etc., European Parliamentary Elections Act 1978 (c. 10), s.3C(7), inserted by European Parliamentary Elections Act 1999 (c. 1), s.1.

LOCAL PEOPLE. Stat. Def., "in relation to an area, means people who live or work in the area" (Housing Grants, Construction and Regeneration Act 1996 (c. 53), s.126(3)).

LOCAL RADIO STATION. Stat. Def., Education (Publication of Local Education Authority Inspection Reports) Regulations 1998 (No. 880), reg. 2.

LOCALITY. (Housing Act 1996 (c. 52), ss.152 and 153). The use of the word "locality" in the Housing Act 1996, ss.152 and 153 was intended to extend the powers and rights of local authorities and housing associations so that a neighbourhood office which was three-quarters of a mile away from the tenant's flat could still be regarded as within the "locality" of the flat for the purposes of granting injunctive relief (*Circle 33* v. *Watt* [1999] 4 C.L. 355).

When considering what was the "relevant locality" for the purposes of paragraph 12(3)(*d*)(i) of Sched. 3 to the Local Government (Miscellaneous Provisions) Act 1982 in connection with an application for a licence to use premises as a sex shop, the local authority had to look at the premises and the general area surrounding them. The locality did not need to be defined in terms of drawing boundaries on a map (*R.* v. *Peterborough City Council, ex p. Quietlynn* (1987) 85 L.G.R. 249).

LOCK-OUT. "Lock-out" (Employment Protection (Consolidation) Act 1978 (c. 44), s.62) is to be given its ordinary meaning. The definition in para. 24 of Sched. 13 is restricted to the operation of that schedule and is not to be incorporated into the main body of the Act. The question whether the employer had been in breach of contract was a relevant consideration in determining whether there had been a lock-out, although it could be possible to institute one without breach of contract (*Express and Star* v. *Bunday* [1987] IRLR 422).

Stat. Def., Employment Rights Act 1996 (c. 18), s.235(4).

LOCK-OUT AGREEMENT. An agreement that D. would not consider any other offer for the purchase of his property, provided P. exchanged contracts within a specified period of receiving the draft contract, was an enforceable "lock-out agreement" (*Pitt* v. *PHH Asset Management* [1993] 40 E.G. 149).

LODGING-HOUSE. Stat. Def., Housing Act 1985 (c. 68), s.56.

LONDON. Stat. Def., Private Hire Vehicles (London) Act 1998 (c. 34), s.36.

LONG LEASE. Stat. Def., Companies Act 1985 (c. 6), Sched. 4, para. 83, Sched. 9, para. 32; Landlord and Tenant Act 1987 (c. 31), s.59.

LONG TENANCY. (Leasehold Reform Act 1967 (c. 88), s.3). A lease which is held to be for the term or terms of 500 years can be construed as a lease for a term certain and therefore, a "long tenancy" within the meaning of this section (*Re 51 Bennington Road, Aston, The Times,* July 21, 1993).

Stat. Def., Housing Act 1985 (c. 68), ss.115, 187.

LONG TERM BUSINESS. Long term reinsurance business and retrocession arrangements for the reinsurance of reinsurance business was "long term business" within the meaning of the Insurance Companies Act 1982 (c. 50), s.49(1) (*Re N.R.G. Victory Reinsurance* [1995] 1 W.L.R. 239).

LOSS. (33)–(35) "Sustains a loss in any trade" (Income and Corporation Taxes Act 1970 (c. 10), s.168(1)), now 1988 (c. 1), s.380(1). A limited partner was held to have sustained losses entitling her to relief against income tax under this section, notwithstanding that her share of the trading losses sustained by the partnership greatly exceeded the amount of her capital contribution to the partnership (*Reed* v. *Young* [1986] 1 W.L.R. 649).

(35) "Incurs a loss in the trade" (Income and Corporation Taxes Act 1970 (c. 10), s.177, and see now 1988 (c. 1), s.393). A company which, as a result of currency fluctuation, incurred substantial losses on borrowings had not incurred a loss in its "trade" for the purposes of this section, since a transaction cannot be a trading transaction unless it is undertaken for a commercial purpose and not merely to obtain a tax advantage (*Overseas Containers (Finance)* v. *Stoker* [1989] 1 W.L.R. 606).

"Sustains a loss in the trade" (Income and Corporation Taxes Act 1988 (c. 1), s.381(1)). Payments made by a taxpayer in acquiring trading assets under the terms of a financing agreement were allowable expenditure in computing for tax purposes the taxpayer's loss for the year in which the payments were made (*Threlfall* v. *Jones*; *Gallagher* v. *Same*, *The Times*, February 10, 1993).

"Loss of earnings" (Law Reform (Personal Injuries) Act 1948 (c. 41), s.2(1)). An award for loss of earning capacity is to be treated as an award for "loss of earnings" within the meaning of this section (*Foster* v. *Tyne and Wear County Council* [1986] 1 All E.R. 567).

"Loss in consequence of dishonesty on the part of a solicitor" (Solicitors Act 1974 (c. 47), s.36(2)(*a*)). The loss referred to resulting from a solicitor's dishonesty is limited to the loss to the client of moneys entrusted to him for the client's purposes (*R.* v. *The Law Society, ex p. Reigate Projects* (1991) 141 New. L.J. 273).

(12) (13) "Loss or damage" (United States Carriage of Goods by Sea Act 1936, s.3(6); Carriage of Goods by Sea Act 1924 (c. 22), Sched., Art. III, r.6(3)). Following *Gouladris* v. *Goldman* [1958] 1 Q.B. 74 [See Main Work p. 1502] it was held that in these contexts "loss or damage" was to be given a wide construction and extended to loss or damage relating to the goods and not just physical loss of or damage to them (*Cargill International SA* v. *C.P.N. Tankers* (*Bermuda*) [1993] 2 Lloyd's Rep. 435, C.A.).

(Companies Act 1985 (c. 6), s.320(1)(b) and s.322(3)(b)). The object of ss.320(1)(b) and 322(3)(b) was to ensure that shareholders were protected from transactions, which were beneficial to the directors but not to the shareholders, so that losses occasioned by the fall in value of the property after the transaction had taken effect were to be taken into account in assessing damages as a result of the transaction (*Duckwari plc* v. *Offerventure Ltd (No. 2)*, *The Times*, May 18, 1998).

LOTTERY. (6) (Lotteries and Amusements Act 1976 (c. 32), s.2(1)). Where the publishers of a newspaper, after distributing at random large numbers of cards carrying five letter codes, published computer prepared grids of rows of letters and other sequences (against which the cardholders could check to see if they had won prizes), it was held that there was no "lottery" within the meaning of this section, as no payment was required from the reader (*Express Newspapers* v. *Liverpool Daily Post* [1985] 3 All E.R. 680).

LUGGAGE. Stat. Def., Convention relating to the Carriage of Passengers and their Luggage by Sea, art. 1(5)—reproduced in Sched. 6 to Merchant Shipping Act 1995 (c. 21).

M

MACHINE. "Machine or implement moved by mechanical power" (Factories Act 1961 (c. 34), s.163). A heavy goods vehicle is a "machine" within the meaning of this section (*Robinson* v. *R. Durham and Sons*, *The Times*, June 10, 1992).

MACHINERY. (3) A machine which had been installed in a factory for the purposes of its development and modification and which, if the development and modification were successful, was to be used as part of the manufacturing process at the factory, was "machinery" within the fencing provisions of s.14 of the Factories Act 1961 (c. 34) (*TBA Industrial Products* v. *Laine* [1987] I.C.R. 75).

MADE. (27) For the purposes of ss.34–40 of the Taxes Management Act 1970 (c. 9) an assessment to tax was "made" on the date that it was entered by a tax inspector into the assessment books of his district, not on the date of service of notice of the assessment (*Honig* v. *Sarsfield* [1986] S.T.C. 246).

"Make an assessment" (Income Tax (Sub-Contractors in the Construction Industry) Regulations 1975 (No. 1960), reg. 12(1)). An assessment was "made" by a tax inspector once he had decided so to do and had calculated the amount that should be claimed by it, and was not invalidated by reason of it being signed by one tax inspector acting on the instructions of another (*Burford* v. *Durkin* [1991] S.T.C. 7.

"Application . . . is made" (Town and Country Planning (Compensation) Act 1985 (c. 19), ss.1, 2). An application for planning permission is not "made," for the purposes of this Act, until it is communicated to or received by the planning authority (*Camden London Borough Council* v. *ADC Estates* (1990) 3 P.L.R. 121).

"Made in pursuance of an arbitration agreement" (Arbitration Act 1975 (c. 3), s.7(1)). In deciding where an arbitral award was "made" for the purposes of this section it is necessary to look at the arbitration as a whole, not merely the place of signature. An arbitration award was "made" when the arbitrator, being no longer able to revoke or vary the award, had expressed his final determination (*Hiscox* v. *Outhwaite* [1991] 3 W.L.R. 297).

"Made" within the context of the Police and Criminal Evidence Act 1984 (c. 60), s.10(1)(c) meant brought into existence and was wide enough to include a blood sample taken by a scientist carrying out a DNA test (*R.* v. *R.* [1994] 4 All E.R. 260).

"Made in connection with legal proceedings" meant lawfully made and did not extend to forged documents (*R.* v. *Leeds Magistrates' Court, ex p. Dumbleton* [1993] Crim.L.R. 866).

(Aviation Security Act 1982 (c. 36), s.4). A butterfly knife was *per se* "made . . . for causing injury (*DPP* v. *Hynde* [1998] 1 All E.R. 649).

MAIN GANGWAY. The short, hinged extension linking the end of a ship's gangway to the quayside did not form part of the "main gangway" for the purposes of regulation 7 of the Shipbuilding and Ship-repairing Regulations 1960 (No. 1932) and did not therefore need to be fitted with handrails (*Williams* v. *Swan Hunter Shipbuilders, The Times*, March 24, 1988).

MAIN RESIDENCE. (Capital Gains Tax Act 1979 (c. 14), s.101). A self-contained detached staff bungalow, which had as many bedrooms as the main house, from which it was separated by a large paddock, was held not to be a part of the "main residence" for capital gains tax purposes (*Markey* v. *Saunders* [1987] 1 W.L.R. 864). *Batey* v. *Wakefield* [1982] 1 All E.R. 61 [Main Work, p. 799] was distinguished on the grounds that in *Batey* the two buildings were much closer together. However a single-storey lodge occupied by the taxpayer's domestic help formed part of the taxpayer's "main residence" although situated some 200 metres distant from the main house (*Williams* v. *Merrylees* [1987] 1 W.L.R. 1511). For the purposes of this section a separate building was not to be treated as part of the main house unless it was within the curtilage of, and appurtenant to it. So that a converted oast house cottage, 569 feet from the main house and lived in by the gardener, and which was a part of the "set-up" of the taxpayer's way of life, did not form part of the taxpayer's own dwelling-house, which was her main residence. (*Lewis* v. *Rook* [1992] S.T.C. 171). A self-contained flat which had provided accommodation for family members and which was situated in a square with three other flats belonging to the taxpayer did not form part of his "main residence" (*Honour* v. *Norris* [1992] E.G.C.S. 35). A taxpayer owning two houses can elect, within two years of owning the second, which is his "main residence" for the purposes of this section (*Griffin* v. *Craig-Harvey, The Times*, November 29, 1993).

"Sole or main residence" (Local Government Finance Act 1988 (c. 41), s.2(1)(*b*)). A merchant ship could not constitute a person's "residence"; so that for community charge purposes a merchant seaman's house on shore was his "sole or main residence" (*Bradford City Metropolitan Council* v. *Anderton* [1991] RA 45). A small barn within the curtilage of a cottage, and connected to all the main services of the cottage was held to be part of the "main residence" within the meaning of this section (*Cherwell District Council* v. *Hodges* (1991) 31 RVR 163).

(Local Government Finance Act 1992 (c. 14), s.6). A wife, whose husband who was only able, by virtue of his employment, to live in the matrimonial home during his leave, was not entitled to the single person's discount for community charge, because the property was also her husband's sole or main residence. The meaning of "sole or main residence" was the same for the purposes of the Local Government Finance Act 1988, s.2(1)(b) (*Doncaster BC* v. *Stark* [1998] RVR 80).

See also CURTILAGE; DWELLING-HOUSE.

MAINTAIN. (22) "Maintained . . . by the deceased" (Inheritance (Provision for Family and Dependants) Act 1975 (c. 63), s.1(1)(*e*)). A woman, who had supported and cared for the elderly man with whom she lived while he was in bad health, was not to be regarded as thereby having given full valuable consideration for the provision, by the man, of a secure home, and she was therefore entitled to be treated as having been "maintained" by the man for the purposes of this section (*Bishop* v. *Plumley* [1991] 1 All E.R. 236).

MAINTENANCE. "Works of maintenance" (Local Authorities (Goods and Services) Act 1970 (c. 39), s.1(4)). The conversion of a flat roof to a pitched roof, renewal of a roof, replacement of windows, doors and walkway handrails and renewal of external cladding were all held to be capable of constituting "works of maintenance" within this section (*R.* v. *Hackney London Borough Council, ex p. Secretary of State for the Environment* (1990) 88 L.G.R. 96).

"Construction, improvement, maintenance" (Local Government Planning and Land Act 1980 (c. 65), s.20(1)). See BUILDING.

"Maintain repair amend renew." The total recladding of premises could fall within an obligation in a lease to "amend" and renew" (*Graysim Holdings* v. *P. & O. Holdings* [1994] 1 W.L.R. 992).

Orders for lump sum payment and property transfer property were to be regarded as "maintenance" and fell within the scope of the Brussels Convention (*Van den Boogaard* v. *Laumen* [1997] 3 W.L.R. 284).

A person bringing an action for maintenance for the first time was a "maintenance creditor" and in the same position as a person who had obtained an order for maintenance in their favour for the purposes of the Convention on Jurisdiction and the Enforcement of the Judgments in Civil and Commercial Matters 1968, Art. 5(2) (*Farrell* v. *Long* [1997] 3 W.L.R. 613).

"Maintenance agreement." Stat. Def., Family Law Reform Act 1987 (c. 42), s.15; Child Support Act 1991 (c. 48), s.9.

"Maintenance order". Stat. Def., Social Security Administration Act 1992 (c. 5), s.107.

MAKE. See MADE.

MAKER OF STATEMENT. For the purposes of the Criminal Justice Act 1984, s.24 the "maker" of a statement was the person who made the statement it was intended to adduce and not anyone who supplied information contained in that statement (*Brown* v. *Secretary of State for Social Security, The Times*, December 7, 1994).

MAKING OFF WITHOUT PAYMENT. The Theft Act 1978 (c. 60), s.3 did not require payment on any particular "spot" and there was no requirement that the act of "making off" had to take place in the paying place (*R.* v. *Aziz* [1993] Crim.L.R. 708).

MALADMINISTRATION. "The action constitutes . . . maladministration" (Building Societies Act 1986 (c.53), Sched. 12, Part III, para. 2(*a*)(*d*). A basic valuation made negligently by the employee of a building society amounted to "maladministration" within the meaning of this paragraph (*Halifax Building Society* v. *Edell*) [1992] 3 W.L.R. 136.

MALICE; MALICIOUS. (8)(9) "Malicious wounding" (Offences against the Person Act 1861 (c. 100), ss.20, 23). Where the defendant had released his dog saying "kill that man," and the dog had bitten the complainant, the Court of Appeal (Criminal Division) was able to avoid deciding whether it was indeed the law that the offence of malicious wounding could be committed by using a dog as a weapon. The appeal was allowed on the grounds that the trial jury had been given insufficient instruction on the questions of *actus reus*, *mens rea* and whether the act was the proximate cause of the injury (*R.* v. *Dume* (*Constantine*), *The Times*, October 16, 1986). Where an accused is charged with "malicious wounding" under these sections the jury should be directed to apply the subjective test laid down in *R.* v. *Cunningham* [1957] 2 Q.B. 396 [see Main Work, p. 1534] (*R.* v. *Farrell* [1989] Crim.L.R. 376; *R.* v. *Rainbird* [1989] Crim.L.R. 505). The defendant must be shown to have foreseen some physical harm resulting from his actions (*R.* v. *Savage* (1990) 91 Cr.App.R. 317). In a case of unlawful wounding contrary to s.20 it was correct to direct the jury that a defendant was acting maliciously if he was acting deliberately and was aware that some physical harm might, not would, result (*R.* v. *Rushworth* (1992) 95 Cr.App.R. 252.

MAMMAL. "Wild mammal," Stat. Def., Wild Mammals (Protection) Act 1996 (c. 3), s.3.

MAN. "Manned by two drivers" (Council Regulation (EEC) No. 543/69, Art. 11(3)) means that two drivers must be aboard so long as the vehicle is in motion (*Williams* v. *Boyd* [1986] RTR 185).

MANAGEMENT. "Management of houses and other property" (Local Government and Housing Act 1989 (c. 42), Sched. IV, Part II, Item 1). This phrase when used to denote items of expenditure which a local housing authority could properly charge to its housing revenue account should be given a wide construction (*R.* v. *Ealing London Borough Council, ex p. Lewis, The Times,* April 15, 1992). See also Assist; Connected with.

MANAGER. (Fire Precautions Act 1971 (c. 40), s.23). An employee in charge of a shop while the general manager was away on holiday was held not to be a "manager" for the purposes of this section so as to be guilty of criminal offences for breach of the premises' fire certificate (*R.* v. *Boal (Francis)* [1992] 2 W.L.R. 890).
  Stat. Def., Banking Act 1987 (c. 22), s.105.

MANUFACTURED DIRECTLY. (Council Regulation 1600/95). "Manufactured directly" did not impose a condition that milk or cream should be transformed directly and immediately into butter, thus precluding the creation of an identifiable product in-between the process (*Customs and Excise Commissioners* v. *Anchor Foods Ltd, The Independent,* July 13, 1998).

MARINE POLLUTION. Stat. Def., Merchant Shipping (Salvage and Pollution) Act 1994 (c. 28), s.8(5).

MARK. See Trade mark.

MARKET GARDEN. Stat. Def., Income and Corporation Taxes Act 1988 (c. 1), s.832).
  A "market garden" supplied a market for buying produce for consumption, not for buying and selling the means for eventually developing that produce (*Twygen* v. *Assessor for Tayside Region* (*L.V.A.C.*), 1991 S.C. 98).

MARKET MAKER. Stat. Def., Finance Act 1986 (c. 41), Sched. 18, para. 6(3).

MARKET OVERT. "Goods . . . sold in market overt" (Sale of Goods Act 1893 (c. 71), s.22(1)). A sale in a private market held on property adjacent to a properly constituted market was not made in "market overt" and did not therefore pass the title to the purchaser (*Long* v. *Jones and Skinner* [1991] 10 Tr.L.R. 113).

MARKET PRICE. "Market price" as specified in the default clause of a FOSFA contract meant that price obtainable in an available market on the day of default and not the price at which it had been agreed to re-sell the goods (*Czarnikow (C.)* v. *Bunge & Co.* [1987] 1 Lloyd's Rep. 202).

MARKET VALUE. Stat. Def., Taxation of Chargeable Gains Act 1992 (c. 12), ss.272–274.

MARKETING. Stat. Def., Copyright, Designs and Patents Act 1988 (c. 48), s.263.

MARRIED COUPLE. Stat. Def., Social Security Act 1986 (c. 50), s.20; Social Security Contributions and Benefits Act 1992 (c. 4), s.137.

MASTER. (1) (Rules of the Supreme Court 1981, Ords. 1, 58). The expression "master" in Ord. 58, r.1 could not be enlarged to include a taxing master (*Macro (Ipswich Ltd, Re;* [1996] 1 W.L.R. 145).
   Stat. Def., Food and Environment Protection Act 1985 (c. 48), s.24.
   In relation to vessel, Stat. Def., Antarctic Act 1994 (c. 15), s.31(1).

MATERIAL. "Materials" for the driver's own use (Community Drivers' Hours and Recording Equipment (Exemptions and Supplementary Provisions) Regulations 1986 (No. 1456), Sched., Part I, para. 7(1)). Fruit and vegetables in course of transit between the wholesalers and the driver's stall were not "materials" for the driver's own use in the course of his work within the meaning of this paragraph. "Material" should be given its ordinary meaning and did not extend to stock in trade for sale to the general public (*DPP* v. *Aston* [1989] RTR 198).
   "Material" was to be defined as "serious" or "important" in a partnership deed where the parties agreed that a material breach by one would entitle the other to purchase the interest of the one in breach (*DB Rare Books Ltd* v. *Antiqbooks* [1995] 2 BCLC 306).
   (Construction (General Provisions) Regulations 1961 (No. 1580), reg. 46(1)). A coping stone amounted to an "article or material" within the meaning of reg. 46(1) since the words in the regulation were not qualified in any way and were not confined to items such as tools or scaffolding materials (*Penman* v. *A & S Scaffolding* (1997) Rep. L.R. 125).

MATERIAL CHANGE. "Material change in the use of any buildings" (Town and Country Planning Act 1990 (c. 8), s.55(2)(*d*)). Notwithstanding that the conversion of a detached garage to a garage with living accommodation over it would provide a certain degree of independence it would not create a separate planning unit from the main house, so that as long as the planning unit remained in single family occupation no material change of use was involved (*Uttlesford District Council* v. *Secretary of State for the Environment and White* [1992] J.P.L. 171). Where a planning application for continued use as a farm shop, selling local and home grown produce, asked for permission to sell imported produce as well, it was rejected on the grounds that this would constitute a material change of use to a retail unit within class A1 (*Brill* v. *Secretary of State for the Environment* [1992] EGCS 60). See INCIDENTAL.

MATERIAL CIRCUMSTANCE. Within the meaning of the Marine Insurance Act 1906 (c. 41), s.18, a "material circumstance" was one that would influence, though not necessarily decisively, the mind of a prudent underwriter either as to whether to accept the risk or as to the premium to be charged (*Pan Atlantic Insurance Co.* v. *Pine Top Insurance Co.* [1994] 3 W.L.R. 677).

MATERIAL CONSIDERATIONS. (2) "Any other material considerations" (Town and Country Planning Act 1971 (c. 78), s.29(1); now Town and Country Planning Act 1990 (c. 8), s.70(2)). The House of Lords has held that the test of what is a "material consideration" in the preparation of local plans or in the control of development is whether it serves a planning purpose relating to the character of the use of the land (*Westminster City Council* v. *Great Portland Estates* [1985] 1 A.C. 661). The Court of Appeal has since held that this would not exclude financial considerations from being treated as "material" in appropriate cases. The fact that finances made available from a commercial development would enable desirable works to be carried out on a listed building was capable of being a "material consideration" for the purposes of this section (*R.* v. *Westminster City Council, ex p. Monahan* [1989] 3 W.L.R. 408). Fear of creating a precedent to be followed by other planning applicants can be a material consideration (*Poundstretcher* v. *Secretary of State for the Environment* [1988] 3 P.L.R. 69). Modifications to a structure plan made after an inspector's hearing might be a material consideration (*Wokingham District Council* v. *Secretary of State for the Environment* [1989] 3 P.L.R. 93). The retention of an existing use is capable of being a material consideration and could thus constitute a valid planning objection, provided it is shown that the land in dispute will effectively be put to the existing use (*London Residuary Body* v. *Secretary of State for the Environment; Secretary of State for the Environment* v. *Lambeth London Borough Council* [1989] 58 P. & C.R. 370). The requirement in this section that the planning authority "shall" have regard to any other "material considerations" does not impose a legal obligation to apply a so-called competing needs test under which the need for and desirability of preserving the existing use would be weighed on its planning merits against the need for and the desirability of the proposed new use or uses (*London Residuary Body* v. *Lambeth London Borough Council* [1990] 1 W.L.R. 744). National policy, as set out in Circular 16/87 and Planning Policy Guidance Notes 2 and 7, can be a material consideration for the purposes of this section (*Charnwood Borough Council* v. *Secretary of State for the Environment* (1990) 60 P. & C.R. 498). Misstatements made to the committee which had heard a planning application were "material considerations" for the purposes of s.29 (*R.* v. *Lewes District Council, ex p. Saunders* [1991] C.O.D. 75). A previous appeal decision indistinguishable from the extant case must ordinarily be a "material consideration" for the purposes of this section (*North Wiltshire District Council* v. *Secretary of State for the Environment and Clover* [1992] J.P.L. 955). In the context of s.70(2) of the 1990 Act "material" is synonymous with "relevant" (*Fairclough Homes & Rayford Properties* v. *Secretary of State for the Environment and Canterbury City Council* [1992] J.P.L. 247). An emerging consultative draft local plan was a material consideration for the purposes of this section and was therefore one which the inspector had to take into consideration (*Kissel* v. *Secretary of State for the Environment, The Times,* July 22, 1993). Personal circumstances could constitute material consdierations (*Fowler* v. *Secretary of State for the Environment* [1992] 3 PLR 140). Undertakings given by applicants for planning permission to enter into agreements under s.106 of the 1990 Act to provide community benefits, including a contribution of £1m towards the cost of providing highway and drainage infrastructure for an industrial site, were "material considerations" within the meaning of s.70(2) (*R.* v. *Plymouth City Council, J. Sainsbury, Tesco Stores, ex p. Plymouth and South Devon Co-operative Society* [1993] 36 EG 135). Where the harmful effects of one development are offset by benefits at another, these are "material considerations" (*Wansdyke District Council* v. *Secretary of State for the Environment and Bath Football (Rugby) Club* (1993) 1 P.L.R. 15). Personal circumstances might be "material considerations" within the meaning of this section but they could only carry considerable weight, and thus outweigh planning considerations, if the latter were finely balanced (*Fowler* v. *Secretary of State for the Environment and Berwick Trust* [1993] J.P.L. 365).

MATERIAL DIFFERENCE. "Material difference (other than the difference of sex)" (Equal Pay Act 1970 (c. 41), s.1(3), as substituted by s.8(1) of the Sex Discrimination Act 1975 (c. 65)). Where, in order to attract into the National Health Service specialists employed by private contractors, it was found necessary to pay them more than those who had entered direct, this difference in pay was held to be a "material difference (other than the difference of sex)" within the meaning of this section (*Rainey* v. *Greater Glasgow Health Board* [1986] 3 W.L.R. 1017).

See also MATERIAL FACTOR.

MATERIAL FACT. "Non-disclosure or misrepresentation . . . of a material fact" (Social Security Act 1975 (c. 14), s.110). A fact was a "material fact" for the purposes of this section if it was a fact which would have influenced the judgment of the body making the decision, in the sense that it was one to which it would have wished to direct its mind (*Saker* v. *Secretary of State for Social Services, The Times,* January 16, 1988).

Concealment of "material facts" (Immigration Rules 1983 (H.C. 169) sub-paras. (a) and (b)). Where, through fear of the possible consequences, a Bangladeshi girl, who was granted entry clearance to join her father, concealed the fact that she intended to marry, it was held that this did not constitute concealment of a "material fact" within the meaning of these rules (*R.* v. *Immigration Appeal Tribunal, ex p. Begum (Suily)* [1990] Imm. A.R. 226).

(Marine Insurance Act 1906, s.18(2)(3)). An insurer was entitled to avoid a contract of insurance for material non-disclosure or misrepresentation only if it were proved that the prudent underwriter would have taken that fact when assessing the risk and where the underwriter had actually been induced by the misrepresentation to enter into the contract and it was not necessary for a fact to be material that it should lead to an increased risk rather than a diminished risk, which was only relevant when considering the question of inducement (*St. Paul Fire and Marine Insurance Co. (U.K.) Ltd* v. *McConnell Dowell Constructors Ltd and ors* [1996] 1 All E.R. 96).

(Criminal Injuries Compensation Scheme 1964 (rev. 1990), para. 24(c)). "Material facts" and "conclusions" in para. 24(c) referred to the primary facts and to the conclusions of a factual nature which fell to be drawn from the primary facts and were to be distinguished from the board's ultimate decision (*R. v. Criminal Injuries Compensation Board, ex p. Dickson* [1997] 1 W.L.R. 58).

MATERIAL FACTOR. "Material factor which is not the difference of sex" (Equal Pay Act 1970 (c. 41), s.1(2)(*c*), as amended by reg. 2 of the Equal Pay (Amendment) Regulations 1983 (No. 1794)). Where a man and a woman were doing work of equal value, and the man was paid more because he had retained the salary pertinent to a job from which he had been demoted, the difference in pay was "due to a material factor which is not the difference of sex" within the meaning of this section (*Forex Neptune (Overseas) v. Miller* [1987] I.C.R. 170). In a case where a man and a woman were employed on work which an industrial tribunal had adjudged to be of equal value, the fact that the employer laid greater stress on a particular factor and was prepared to pay more for it, was a "material factor" within the meaning of this section (*McGregor v. General Municipal Boilermakers and Allied Trades Union* [1987] I.C.R. 505). Where severe financial constraints forced an employer to appoint a woman lecturer at a salary less than that of a man already employed by them, this amounted to a "material difference" between her case and his and was thus a "material factor" which was not the difference of sex so long as the financial crisis lasted (*Benveniste v. University of Southampton* [1989] IRLR 122). Differences in working hours and holiday entitlements can amount to a "material factor" other than sex within the meaning of this section (*Leverton v. Clwyd* [1989] 2 W.L.R. 47). Where a female secretary sought a declaration that she was employed on work of equal value with a male comparator in the accounts department of her firm, it was held that as the male spent much of his time in livestock markets, where conditions were unpleasant, and that he carried out a more demanding role, it was held that the variation in pay was due to a "material factor which is not the difference of sex" (*Davies v. McCartneys* [1989] I.C.R. 705). In defence of a claim for equal pay an employer was held to be able to rely on his own mistake in paying the employee a salary above that fixed on the relevant scale as a "material factor" which was not the difference of sex (*Yorkshire Blood Transfusion Service v. Plaskitt, The Times,* August 17, 1993).
　　See also MATERIAL DIFFERENCE.

MATERIAL FORM. Materialisation of race cards and forecast information on a television monitor was a "material form" within the meaning of the Copyright Act 1956 (c. 74) (*Bookmakers' Afternoon Greyhound Services v. Wilf. Gilbert (Staffordshire)* [1994] F.S.R. 723).

MATERIAL IRREGULARITY. (2) The supply of a dictionary to a jury who needed to look up a word comprising part of the offence charged, when made by an usher without consulting the judge or counsel, was not a "material irregularity" within the meaning of s.2(1)(*c*) of the Criminal Appeal Act 1968 (c. 19) (*R. v. Wallace (Sonia); R. v. Sayles; R. v. Wallace (Sandra)* [1990] Crim.L.R. 433). But the provision of weighing scales to a jury in retirement to enable it to conduct experiments in the jury room was a material irregularity (*R. v. Stewart* (1989) 89 Cr.App.R. 273). But giving a surveyor's tape to a jury in retirement, without objection or inquiry as to why they should want it, was held not to be a "material irregularity" within the meaning of this section (*R. v. Maggs* [1990] RTR 129). There would be no material irregularity in allowing the jury to take with them on retirement tape recordings of interviews which had been given in evidence, so long as the tapes had been edited to remove any parts of the interviews which had not been given in evidence (*R. v. Emmerson* (1991) 92 Cr.App.R. 284). The admission of evidence of private conversations between judge and counsel was a "material irregularity" within the meaning of this section (*R. v. Harper-Taylor; R. v. Bakker (Note)* [1991] RTR 76). Failure by a prosecution expert witness to disclose the results of certain tests could be a "material irregularity" (*R. v. Maguire* [1992] 2 W.L.R. 767). In a case where a jury, after being given a majority direction, still failed to reach a verdict it was a "material irregularity" that the judge did not re-assemble the jury in court to inquire as to the prospects of a verdict being reached (*R. v. Wharton* [1990] Crim.L.R. 877). The threat by a judge to compel forcibly a reluctant defendant to re-enter the witness box was a "material irregularity" (*R. v. O'Boyle* (1991) 92 Cr.App.R. 202). Where, after the jury had retired at the end of a trial, the sending by one of them, via the jury bailiff, of a note to her brother asking him to wait for her to finish and give her a lift home as she was not feeling very well, was not a "material irregularity" (*R. v. Anderson and Mason* [1990] Crim.L.R. 873). Where a judge invites counsel to his private room and there, by his remarks, puts pressure on the defendant through his counsel to change his plea, that amounts to a "material irregularity" (*R. v. Pitman* [1991] 1 All E.R. 468). There was a material irregularity when prosecution witnesses were allowed, in effect, to rehearse their evidence in chief by being interviewed and filmed by a television company before a trial, even though the film was not shown until after the trial (*R. v. Dye; R. v. Williamson* [1992] Crim.L.R. 449). There was a "material irregularity" within the meaning of this section where, after retirement, the jury had received new unexplained evidence (*R. v. Devichand* [1991] Crim.L.R. 446). The holding of part of the proceedings *in camera* with the defendants and solicitors excluded, amounted to a "material irregularity" (*R. v. Preston, The Times,* May 13, 1992). While it was plainly an "irregularity" where, after the summing-up in a criminal trial, a juror separated himself from the other jurors and was not for that period under the control of the jury bailiff, it was not of such a character that it constituted a departure from the established rules of criminal procedure and was not, therefore a "material" irregularity (*R. v. Chandler, The Times,* April 16, 1992). Failure on the part of the prosecution to disclose to the defence material documents or information which ought to have been disclosed may be a "material irregularity" in the course of a trial (*R. v. Maguire* [1992] 2 All E.R. 433). Where public interest immunity was claimed for a video tape it was held that the failure of the judge himself to examine the tape and the evidence in dispute before ruling on the competing claims of immunity and fairness amounted to a "material irregularity" (*R. v. K. (D.T.)* (1992) 136 S.J.(LB) 328). The use by Customs officers, for the purposes of refreshing their memory, of schedules drawn from the written records of one of them, unconfirmed by the other, was a material irregularity (*R. v. Eleftheriou (Costas and Leftevakis), The Times,* March 2, 1993). The trial judge's failure to direct the jury about the effect of the accused not giving evidence was a "material irregularity" (*R.* v. *Forbes* [1992] Crim.L.R. 593). The presence on the jury of a juror who lived next door to the brother of the convicted accused, but did not discover the fact until after the trial, did not amount to a "material irregularity" (*R.* v. *Gough* (*Robert*) [1992] 4 All E.R. 481). It was not a "material irregularity" for a judge to allow a jury to listen again, in the jury room, to a tape recording which had already been played in open court and of which there was an agreed transcript (*R.* v. *Tonge, The Times*, April 16, 1992). It was held that there was no "material irregularity" where a jury was permitted to hear, after they retired, a tape-recorded police interview, a full transcript of which had been read at the trial (*R.* v. *Riaz; Same* v. *Burke* (1992) 94 Cr.App.R. 339). Where, part way through a trial, two members of the jury indicated that internal dissension was disrupting their concentration, it was held that there had been a "material irregularity" when the recorder questioned the two jurors in the absence of the rest of the jury (*R.* v. *Orgles* (*Kevin*); *R.* v. *Orgles* (*Julie*), *The Times*, June 9, 1993). Failure by the police to disclose a witness's earlier statement, inconsistent with the one produced in court, was a "material irregularity" (*R.* v. *Taylor* (*Michelle Ann*); *R.* v. *Taylor* (*Lisa Jane*), *The Times*, June 15, 1993). Failure of counsel to inform the trial judge of his intention to cross-examine the witness as to her character was a breach of his duty. Furthermore, to cross-examine the witness regarding a conviction upon which she had never been adjudicated guilty was a "material irregularity" (*R.* v. *McGregor* (*Beverley Elaine*) (1992) 95 Cr.App.R. 240). The destruction before trial of documents relating to intercepted telephone calls did not amount to a material irregularity since, by virtue of s.2(2) of the Interception of Communications Act 1985 (c. 56), the investigating authority was under a duty to destroy the documents as soon as they were no longer required "for the purpose of preventing or detecting serious crime," a phrase which was held not to extent to the prosecution of such crime (*R.* v. *Preston* (*Stephen*) (1992) 95 Cr.App.R. 355). The failure by the prosecution to disclose an admission of guilt by a man other than the accused was a material irregularity (*R.* v. *Wood* (*Lee*) [1993] 11 C.L. 130). The introduction by a judge in his summing up, of an alternative verdict of careless driving in a trial where all attention had been devoted to the charge of causing death by reckless driving was a material irregularity (*R.* v. *Hammett* (*Peter David John*) [1993] RTR 275). Where, while travelling to a view, the prosecutor went in a car with the magistrates and their clerk and returned in the car with the magistrates alone, this was held to have been a material irregularity (*R.* v. *Ely Justices, ex p. Burgess* [1992] Crim.L.R. 888). Where justices indicated that they would not take "any real notice of" evidence improperly admitted at a committal hearing, the irregularity was held not to have been "material" (*R.* v. *Manchester City Magistrates' Court, ex p. Birtles*). While it is conventional not to mention to the jury the time at which a majority direction might be given it was not necessarily a "material irregularity" to do so if the effect was to alleviate any anxiety the jury might feel (*R.* v. *Guthrie, The Times*, February 23, 1994). A session with an Ouija board by jurors in a murder trial, while they were being accommodated overnight during their deliberations, purporting to ask questions and receive answers from the deceased, which went to the heart of the case and to the matters which they were supposed to decide and which were highly prejudicial to the defendant amounted to a "material irregularity in . . . course of . . . trial (*R.* v. *Young* (*Stephen*) [1995] 2 W.L.R. 430).

MATERIAL PART. For a part of a house to be a "material part" within the meaning of the Leasehold Reform Act 1967 (c. 88), s.2(2), it had to be of substantial substance or significance to make it likely that enfranchisement would prejudice the enjoyment of the house (*Duke of Westminster* v. *Birrane* [1995] 2 W.L.R. 270).

MATRIMONIAL PROCEEDINGS. Stat. Def., Domicile and Matrimonial Proceedings Act 1973 (c. 45), Sched. 1, para. 2 substituted by Family Law Act 1996 (c. 27), Sched. 3, para. 3.

MATTERS IN QUESTION IN THE ACTION. (R.S.C. 1981 Ord. 24, r.2(5) ". . . the parties . . . shall make discovery . . . of the matters in question in the action . . ." The ambit of discovery was not limited to matters in question at the first or any other stage of the action, although the court retained a discretion to limit the discovery in the interests of the parties and justice and in the saving of costs (*Baldock* v. *Addison* [1995] 3 All E.R. 437).

MATTERS RELATING TO A CONTRACT. A contract void *ab initio* came within the provisions of the Civil Jurisdiction and Judgments Act 1982 (c. 27), art. 5(1) (*Barclays Bank plc* v. *Glasgow City Council* [1994] 4 All E.R. 865).

(Brussels Convention of Jurisdiction and Enforcement of Judgments in Civil and Commercial Matters 1968, Art. 5).

The application of Art. 5(1) was not confined to actions to enforce an unchallenged or unchallengeable contract or to obtain recompense for its breach but could apply to cases where one party was asserting that a contract did not exist, since the appropriate test for determining whether a writ should be set aside under Art. 5(1) was whether the Plaintiffs had established a good arguable case (*Boss Group Ltd* v. *Boss France S.A.* [1997] 1 W.L.R. 352).

MATTERS RELATING TO TORT. A claim for unjust enrichment was not a matter of tort within the provisions of the Civil Jurisdiction and Judgments Act 1982 (c. 27), art. 5(3) (*Barclays Bank plc* v. *Glasgow City Council* [1994] 4 All E.R. 865).

(Brussels Convention on Jurisdiction and Enforcement of Judgments in Civil and Commercial Matters 1968, Art. 5). "Matters relating to tort" meant all actions relating to the liability of a defendant and which are not related to a contract (*Source Ltd* v. *TUV Rheinland Holding AG, The Times,* March 28, 1997).

MAY. Under section 9(1)(*e*) of the General Rate Act 1967 (c. 9) the rating authority "may refund" any amount which has been paid by a person who was not liable to make that payment. The use of the word "may" gives the authority some discretion in determining whether to make a repayment, but it was held that it does not relieve them of the duty to take into consideration the object of section 9, which was to remedy any injustice (*R.* v. *Tower Hamlets London Borough Council, ex p. Chetnik Developments* [1988] 2 W.L.R. 654).

"May become entitled" (Variation of Trusts Act 1958 (c. 53), s.1(1)(*b*)). Where the interest held by persons under a trust is contingent and very remote those persons cannot be held to be persons who "may become entitled" within the meaning of this section (*Knocker* v. *Youle* [1986] 1 W.L.R. 934).

"He may make an order" (Drug Trafficking Offences Act 1986 (c. 32), s.27(2)). "May" is discretionary and is not to be construed as meaning "must" or "shall" (*R.* v. *Southwark Crown Court, ex p. Commissioners of Customs and Excise* [1989] 3 W.L.R. 1054).

"He may be charged instead" (Income and Corporation Taxes Act 1970 (c. 10), s.118(1)(*b*)). In the circumstances provided for by this section these words were held to impose a mandatory duty on the tax inspector to raise additional Schedule D assessments, and not just the granting of a general discretion (*Baylis* v. *Roberts* [1989] S.T.C. 693).

(National Assistance Act 1948 (c. 29), ss.21, 26(1), as amended). "May include" within the meaning of s.26(1) could consist wholly of arrangements made with voluntary organisations or other persons and there was no obligation on local authorities to make any direct provision for residential care under their own control (*R.* v. *Wandsworth LBC, ex p. Beckwith* [1996] 1 W.L.R. 60; [1996] 1 All E.R. 129).

MEANS. "Means . . . of proceeding . . . to another country" (Statement of Changes of Immigration Rules (HC 169), para. 9). The "means" of a passenger for the purposes of this paragraph are not just the possession of a ticket or the financial facilities to obtain one, but also the transport available to take him to his destination (*R.* v. *Secretary of State for the Home Department, ex p. Caunhye, The Times*, April 21, 1988).

(Health and Social Services and Social Security Adjudications Act 1983 (c. 41), s.17). For the purposes of s.17(3) of the 1983 Act, "means" meant the financial resources of a person, namely assets, sources of income, liabilities and expenses and realisable assets, so that an indemnity by a health authority against any liability for the cost of health care services provided to a disabled person meant that the person had the means to pay for them (*Avon County Council* v. *Hooper* [1997] 1 All E.R. 532).

(Construction (Working Places) Regulations 1966 (S.I. 1966 No. 94), reg. 36). "Other suitable means" meant some kind of preventative protective device, and a code of practice or system of work based on instructions did not discharge an employer's obligation under the regulation (*R.* v. *Rhone-Poulenc Rorer Ltd* [1996] I.C.R. 1054).

MEASURES. "Measures which the company . . . envisages it will take in connection with the transfer" (Dockyard Services Act 1986 (c. 52), s.1(6)(*d*)). Manpower projections were not "measures" within the meaning of this section, although steps taken to achieve planned reductions in manpower levels, otherwise than by natural wastage, would be. "Measures," however, are not confined to those which are inevitable or non-negotiable, since that would ignore the element of uncertainty produced by the word "envisages" (*Institution of Professional Civil Servants* v. *Secretary of State for Defence* [1987] 3 C.M.L.R. 35).

(European Convention on Extradition Order 1990 (S.I. 1990 No. 1507), Sched. 1, art. 14(2)). "Any measures necessary" to remove an extradited person from the requesting state was sufficiently wide to include re-extradition to a third state as well as deportation (*R.* v. *Secretary of State for the Home Department, ex p. Johnson* [1999] 2 W.L.R. 932).

MECHANICALLY. "Mechanically propelled vehicle" (Road Traffic Act 1972 (c. 20), s.190(1)). A motor vehicle remains a mechanically propelled vehicle unless and until the evidence shows that there is no longer any reasonable prospect of its ever being made mechanically mobile again (*Reader* v. *Bunyard* [1987] RTR 406).

MEDICAL. "Medical reasons" (Road Traffic Act 1972 (c. 20), s.8(3)(*a*) as substituted by Transport Act 1981 (c. 56), Sched. 8; now Road Traffic Act 1988 (c. 52), s.7(3)(*a*)). In considering whether a medical reason put forward by a motorist for not providing a specimen of breath was a proper one within the terms of this section, a constable did not have to determine whether it was a medically recognised condition, only whether it could be, and whether he had reasonable cause to believe that for medical reasons a specimen could not be provided or should not be required (*Dempsey* v. *Catton* [1986] RTR 194). A reason which did not go to a driver's medical ability to provide a specimen of breath was capable of amounting to a "medical reason" within the meaning of this section (*Davies* v. *DPP* [1989] RTR 391). Fear of the needle is not a "medical reason" for the purposes of this section (*Andrews* v. *DPP, The Times,* May 2, 1991). Intoxication by alcohol is capable of amounting to a "medical reason" within the meaning of this section (*Young* v. *DPP* [1992] RTR 328).

"Medical treatment" in the context of the Mental Health Act 1983 (c. 20) means psychiatric treatment and treatment for mental disorder and would not cover a pregnancy termination (*T.* v. *T.* [1988] 1 All E.R. 613).

"Medical treatment" in a hospital for the purposes of the Mental Health Act 1983 (c. 20), s.72(1)(*b*) included nursing, care and medical supervision and was not confined to the administration of specific drugs and therapies (*R.* v. *Canons Park Mental Health Tribunal, ex p. A.* [1994] 3 W.L.R. 630).

(Mental Health Act 1983 (c. 20), s.63). "Medical treatment" referred to treatment calculated to alleviate or prevent a deterioration of a mental disorder from which a patient was suffering, including such acts which prevented the patient from harming herself or which alleviated the symptoms of the disorder, so that feeding through a nasogastric tube in order to prevent a deterioration of the patient's condition constituted medical treatment for the purposes of s.63 (*B.* v. *Croydon Health Authority* [1995] 2 W.L.R. 294).

"Medical treatment." Stat. Def., Mental Health Act 1983 (c. 20), s.145(1); Social Security Contributions and Benefits Act 1992 (c. 4), s.122; Social Security Administration Act 1992 (c. 5), s.191.

(Mental Health (Scotland) Act 1984, s.125(1)). "Medical treatment" was wide enough in s.125(1) to include treatment which alleviated or prevented a deterioration of the symptoms of mental disorder rather than merely treating the disorder itself (*Reid* v. *Secretary of State for Scotland* [1999] 1 All E.R. 481).

"Medical claim" (Food Labelling Regulations 1984 (No. 1305)). To advertise that a product helped "reduce excess cholesterol levels cutting down the risk of heart disease" constituted a "medical claim" for the purposes of these Regulations (*Cheshire County Council* v. *Mornflake Oats* (1993) 12 Tr.L.R. 111).

MEDICINAL PRODUCT. A product which was to be administered with a view to restoring, correcting or modifying physiological functions could be a "medicinal product" within the definition contained in EEC Directive 65/65, Art. 1(2) even though it was not intended to cure or prevent illness and fell also within the definition of "cosmetic product" in Directive 76/678, Art. 1(1) (*The Upjohn Company* v. *Farzoo Inc., The Times*, June 3, 1991).

MEDICINE. Ordinary food in liquid form was not "medicine," which was identified by its chemical composition, within the meaning of the Mental Health Act 1983 (c. 20), s.58 (*B.* v. *Croydon Health Authority* [1995] 2 W.L.R. 294).

MEMBER. Stat. Def., Companies Act 1985 (c. 6), s.22; Insolvency Act 1986 (c. 45), s.250; Courts and Legal Services Act 1990 (c. 41), s.119; Trade Union and Labour Relations (Consolidation) Act 1992 (c. 52), s.70.

"In his character as a member" (Insolvency Act 1986 (c. 45), s.74(2)(f)). Damages in a claim by a member of a company for a misrepresentation inducing him to purchase shares in the market were not due to him "in his character as a member" (*Soden* v. *British and Commonwealth Holdings plc* [1997] 2 W.L.R. 206).

(Rent Act 1977 (c. 42), Sched. 1, para. 3(1)). The survivor of a homosexual relationship was not a member of the original tenant's family for the purposes of Sched. 1, para. 3(1) (*Fitzpatrick* v. *Sterling Housing Association Ltd* [1997] 4 All E.R. 991).

"Member of a mission," see MISSION.

MEMBERS OF A MISSION. (State Immunity Act 1978 (c. 33), s.16). Members of staff employed in the administrative and technical service of a mission within the meaning of Art. 1 of the Vienna Convention on Diplomatic Relations (1961) were "members of a mission" for the purpose of s.16 of the 1978 Act (*Arab Republic of Egypt* v. *Gamal-Eldin* [1996] I.C.R. 130.

A member of embassy staff employed in the administrative and technical service of the embassy was a "member of the mission" regardless of nationality or whether they had actually or notionally been sent from abroad by the state or whether their appointment had been notified to the Foreign Office (*Ahmed* v. *Government of the Kingdom of Saudi Arabia* [1996] I.C.R. 25).

MEMORANDUM. Stat. Def., Companies Act 1985 (c. 6), s.744.

MENACE. (5) "Menaces" (Theft Act 1968 (c. 60), s.21(1)). Where threats might affect the mind of an ordinary person of normal stability, but did not affect the person actually addressed, they could nevertheless amount to menaces (see *R.* v. *Clear* [1968] 1 Q.B. 670). Where threats affected the mind of the victim, although they would not have affected the mind of a person of normal stability, they could amount to "menaces" if it could be shown that the accused was aware of the likely effect of his actions on the victim (*R.* v. *Garwood* [1987] 1 W.L.R. 319).

MENTAL CONDITION. "Fitness to practise . . . by reason of his . . . mental condition" (Medical Act 1983 (c. 54), s.37). Mental condition is not synonymous with mental disorder, so that where the fitness of a medical practitioner to practise is called into question by reason of his mental condition it is not necessary to prove that he was suffering mental disorder or mental illness (*Crompton* v. *General Medical Council* (*No.* 2) [1985] 1 W.L.R. 885).

MENTAL IMPAIRMENT. Stat. Def., Disability Discrimination Act 1995 (c. 50), Sched. 1, para. 1(1); Protection of Children Act 1999 (c. 14), s.12(1).

MENTAL DISORDER. (Social Security (Hospital In-Patients) Regulations 1975, reg. 2, as amended). Severe mental handicap amounted to "mental disorder" within the meaning of reg. 2 of the 1975 Regulations, as amended (*Botchett* v. *Chief Adjudication Officer, The Times*, May 8, 1996).

MERCHANTABLE. (2) "Merchantable quality" (Sale of Goods Act 1979 (c. 54), ss.14(2), 14(6)). Where the plaintiff, without specifying the use for which he required them, purchased from the defendant a number of plastic buckets for the purpose of transporting a compound to Kuwait, and the buckets collapsed on being left in their container on the quayside in Kuwait in a temperature of 70 degrees centigrade, it was held that there was no express or implied term that the buckets were to be fit for the journey to Kuwait, and that they could still be fit for the purposes for which they might be "commonly bought" and therefore of "merchantable quality" within the meaning of this section (*M/S Aswan Engineering Establishment Co.* v. *Lupdine* [1987] 1 W.L.R. 1). A new car, which on delivery had a minor defect which was likely to, and subsequently did, cause the engine to seize up while the car was being driven was not of "merchantable quality" (*Bernstein* v. *Pamsons Motors* (*Golders Green*) [1987] 2 All E.R. 220). Nor was a Range Rover which, when sold as new, had defective engine, gearbox, bodywork and oil seals which, although none of them rendered the vehicle undrivable or unroadworthy, necessitated the carrying out of repairs (*Rogers* v. *Parish* (*Scarborough*) [1987] Q.B. 933). In considering whether an article is of "merchantable quality" within the meaning of this section the court should first ask what the purchaser was entitled to think he was buying. Thus a car which, had the purchaser known that at some time in its history it had been an insurance write-off, would never have been bought, was held not to have been of merchantable quality notwithstanding that it performed reasonably well (*Shine* v. *General Guarantee Corporation* [1988] 1 All E.R. 911). In considering whether a second-hand car was of "merchantable quality" for the purposes of the 1979 Act the appropriate test was not to be limited to its state of roadworthiness but should also include the wider definition contained in s.14(6) that required all the circumstances to be taken into consideration (*Business Application Specialists* v. *Nationwide Credit Corporation* [1988] RTR 332).

MERITS. For the circumstances in which a procedural decision of the Dutch Court of Appeal, on whether the court had jurisdiction to entertain and adjudicate on a claim, was held, by the House of Lords, to be a decision "on the merits" for the purposes of the application of the doctrine of issue estoppel, see *The Sennar* [1985] 2 All E.R. 104.

(R.S.C., Ord. 59, r.10(2)). In the context of an application to set aside a statutory demand in bankruptcy proceedings, the merits in question were the potential defences specified in paras. (a) to (d) of r.6.5(4) of the Insolvency Rules 1986, so that there could only be a hearing on the merits where the application to set aside had failed and where it had succeeded, there could not have been a hearing on the merits (*AIB Finance Ltd* v. *Debtors* [1997] 4 All E.R. 677).

MESSAGE. (Wireless and Telegraphy Act 1949 (c. 54), s.19(6)). Although the emissions of radar speed guns sent signals or signs of significance to another person, they did not constitute a warning or information within the meaning of s.19(6) since messages could only be sent between two human beings (*R.* v. *Knightsbridge Crown Court, ex p. Foot, The Times*, February 18, 1998).

METHOD OF DISPOSAL. See DISPOSAL.

MILK. Stat. Def., Food Safety Act 1990 (c. 16), s.53.
"Milk production," see AREA.

MILE. Stat. Def., "means international nautical miles of 1,852 metres" (Environment Act 1995 (c. 25), s.6(8)).

MILITARY HOSPITAL. Stat. Def., Road Traffic (NHS Charges) Act 1999 (c. 3), s.15(2).

MINE. In context of munitions, Stat. Def., Landmines Act 1998 (c. 33), s.1.

MINERAL RESOURCE. Stat. Def., "any natural resource that is neither living nor renewable"—(Antarctic Act 1994 (c. 15), s.6(5)).

MINERALS. Stat. Def., Town and Country Planning Act 1990 (c. 8), s.336.

MINICAB. See PRIVATE HIRE VEHICLES.

MINISTER. Stat. Def., includes head of a Northern Ireland Department (Criminal Appeal Act 1995 (c. 35), s.22(3)(*b*)).

MINOR. "Minor relocation" (National Health Service (General Medical and Pharmaceutical Services) Amendment (No. 2) Regulations 1987 (No. 401), reg. 26(3)(*a*)). In deciding whether or not a move of premises was a "minor relocation" within the meaning of this regulation, consideration should primarily be given to the effect on the service to the public, rather than its impact on competitors. The geographical element depends on local knowledge of the location (*R.* v. *Cumbria Family Practitioner Committee, ex p. Boots the Chemists* [1989] C.O.D. 322).

"Minor interests" (Land Registration Act 1925 (c. 21), s.3(xv)). A purely contractual interest in the proceeds of a resale of property is not a "minor interest" within the meaning of this section (*Lynton International* v. *Noble* (1991) 63 P. & C.R. 452).

MINORITY SHAREHOLDER. A 50 per cent. shareholder could be a "minority shareholder" within the exceptions to the rule in *Foss* v. *Harbottle* (1843) 2 Hare 461 (*Barrett* v. *Duckett* [1993] B.C.C. 778).

MISCONDUCT. The word "misconduct" in s.8 of the Pharmacy Act 1954 (c. 61) does not necessarily connote moral censure. A single serious error could constitute "misconduct" for the purpose of disciplinary proceedings under this section (*R.* v. *Pharmaceutical Society of Great Britain, ex p. Sokoh, The Times*, December 4, 1986).

"Serious professional misconduct" (Dentists Act 1984 (c. 24), s.27(1)) is not restricted to dishonesty or moral turpitude but includes all professional misconduct, whether by omission or commission (*Doughty* v. *General Dental Council* [1987] 3 W.L.R. 769).

(Medical Act 1983 (c. 54), s.36(1)). "Serious professional misconduct could include seriously negligent treatment measured by objective professional standards (*Doughty* v. *General Dental Council* [1988] A.C. 164 applied) (*McCandless* v. *General Medical Council* [1996] 1 W.L.R. 167).

MISLEADING. "Misleading as to the price" (Consumer Protection Act 1987 (c. 43), s.20(1)). An advertisement promising to better any competitor's price by £20 became "misleading" within the meaning of this section as soon as the person placing the advertisement refused to honour it, and even though he did so on one occasion only (*Warwickshire County Council, ex p. Johnson* (1992) 11 Tr.L.R. 76).

Stat. Def., Consumer Protection Act 1987 (c. 43), s.21.

MISREPRESENT. "Any person has misrepresented . . . any material fact" (Social Security Act 1986 (c. 50), s.53(1). Failure to declare receipt of income support when claiming unemployment benefit constituted a misrepresentation within the meaning of this section (*Jones* v. *Chief Adjudication Officer; Sharples* v. *Same* [1993] 1 All E.R. 225).

MISREPRESENTATION. (Misrepresentation Act 1967 (c. 7), s.2(1)). To advertise a used motorcar with serious mechanical defects as "absolutely immaculate" was a misrepresentation. The defence that "absolutely immaculate" related only to the appearance of the car failed (*Ward* v. *Stevens* [1993] 5 C.L. 183).

MISSION. "Member of a mission" (Immigration Act 1971 (c. 77), s.8(3)). An employee of a foreign embassy whose appointment had not been notified to the Foreign Office was not a "member of a mission" for the purposes of this section (*R.* v. *Immigration Appeals Tribunal, ex p. Ali* [1989] C.O.D. 203).

MOBILE HOME. Stat. Def., Housing Grants, Construction and Regeneration Act 1996 (c. 53), s.78(5).

MODIFICATIONS. Stat. Def., "includes amendments, additions and omissions" (Finance Act 1996 (c. 8), s.202(10)); Armed Forces Act 1996 (c. 46), s.10(3); Housing Act 1996 (c. 52), s.63(1); Education Act 1996 (c. 56), s.579(1); Finance Act 1998 (c. 36), s.32(12).

MODIFY. Stat. Def., "includes amend or repeal" (Scotland Act 1998 (c. 46), s.126(1)).

MOLEST. (5) The term "molesting," whether or not used in the context of proceedings brought under the Domestic Violence and Matrimonal Proceedings Act 1976 (c. 50), applies in its ordinary connotation to any conduct which intentionally causes such a degree of harassment as calls for the intervention of the court (*Johnson* v. *Walton* [1990] 1 F.L.R. 350).

MONEY. Stat. Def., "includes cheques, banknotes, postal orders, money orders and foreign currency" (Criminal Justice (Scotland) Act 1995 (c. 20), s.72(6)).

MONEY'S WORTH. (Trade Marks Act 1938 (c. 22), s.68 as added by the Trade Marks (Amendment) Act 1984 (c. 19), Sched. 1, para. 25(2)(*c*)). "Money's worth" means "equivalent to money" in the sense of something essentially material, and not emotional or spiritual reward (*Gideon's International Service Mark* [1991] R.P.C. 141).

MONOPOLY. See ATTRIBUTABLE.

MONUMENT. Stat. Def., "includes a tombstone or other memorial and any fixtures or furnishings" (Town and Country Planning (Scotland) Act 1997 (c. 8), s.197(5)); Care of Places of Worship Measure 1999 (No. 2), s.6(1).

MORE THAN ONE DISQUALIFICATION. (Road Traffic Offenders Act 1988 (c. 53) (as substituted by the Road Traffic Act 1991 (c. 40), s.29)). Two disqualifications imposed at the same time by the same court to run concurrently was one disqualification and not "more than one disqualification" within the meaning of s.29 (*Learmont* v. *DPP* [1994] R.T.R. 286).

MORTGAGE. Stat. Def., Building Societies Act 1986 (c. 53), s.119; Landlord and Tenant Act 1987 (c. 31), s.60; Town and Country Planning Act 1990 (c. 8), s.336.
   "Mortgage debt," Stat. Def., Building Societies Act 1986 (c. 53), s.119(1) as amended by Building Societies Act 1997 (c. 32), Sched. 7, para. 53(1).

MORTGAGE ACTION. (R.S.C., Ord. 88, r.1(1)(a)). An action to recover the debt on a running account, which had been secured by a mortgage, was a simple contract debt and not a "mortgage action" which should have been commenced in the Chancery Division (*National Westminster Bank plc* v. *Kitch* [1996] 1 W.L.R. 1316).

MOTHER. Stat. Def., Human Fertilisation and Embryology Act 1990 (c. 37), s.27.

MOTOR. (14) "Motor accessory." For a long list of items which have been held not to be motor accessories for the purposes of the Fifth Schedule to the Shops Act 1950 (c. 28), see *Hadley* v. *Texas Homecare* (1987) 86 L.G.R. 577).

"Motor car," "motor cycle," "motor vehicle." Stat. Def., Road Traffic Act 1988 (c. 52), s.185; Capital Allowances Act 1990 (c. 1), s.36.

MOTORBICYCLE, MOTORCYCLE, MOTORTRICYCLE. Stat. Def., Vehicle Excise and Registration Act 1994 (c. 22), Sched. 1, para. 2(3).

MOTOR TRACTOR. (Road Traffic Regulation Act 1984 (c. 27), s.136(6)). A recovery vehicle with an arm which towed and bore a substantial part of the weight of a broken down vehicle was held not to be a "motor tractor" within the meaning of this section (*DPP* v. *Holtham*, [1990] Crim.L.R. 600. See also LOAD.

MOTOR VEHICLE. An articulated lorry trailer did not become a "motor vehicle" for the purposes of the Road Vehicles (Construction and Use) Regulations 1986 (No. 1078), reg. 100 by virtue of being attached to a tractor. It remained a trailer (*N.F.C. Forwarding* v. *DPP* [1989] RTR 239). See INTENDED.

MOVING PICTURES. "Exhibition of moving pictures" (Cinematograph Act 1909 (c. 30), s.1(3)) as amended by the Cinematograph Act 1982 (c. 33), s.10) does not include the operation of a video amusement game (*British Amusement Catering Trades Association* v. *Westminster City Council* [1988] 2 W.L.R. 485).

MUNITIONS. Stat. Def., Northern Ireland (Emergency Provisions) Act 1996 (c. 22), s.20(9).

MUSIC. "Music and dancing" in s.76(2)(*a*) (*b*) of the Licensing Act 1964 (c. 26) is to be understood as meaning any music and dancing, licensed or not, and is not restricted in its application to public music and dancing (*Edwards* v. *DPP* (1991) 155 J.P.N. 506).
    Stat. Def., "includes sounds wholly or predominantly characterised by the emission of a succession of repetitive beats" (Criminal Justice and Public Order Act 1994 (c. 33), s.63(1)); Licensing (Scotland) Act 1976 (c. 66), s.18A(9) inserted by Licensing (Amendment) (Scotland) Act 1996 (c. 36), s.1(1).

MUSICAL. "Musical work." Stat. Def., Copyright, Designs and Patents Act 1988 (c. 48), s.3.

MUST. "Must be made" (Finance Act 1971 (c. 68), s.23(2)). As used in this section "must" is mandatory and not merely directory (*Ward-Stemp* v. *Griffin* [1988] S.T.C. 47).
    The requirement in R.S.C., Ord. 18, r.8(1), that in any pleading subsequent to a statement of claim a party "must" specifically plead any matter showing illegality, is mandatory (*Shell Chemicals UK* v. *Vinamul (formerly Vinyl Products)* (1991) 135 S.J. 412).
    "Application . . . must be made within six weeks" (Housing Act 1974 (c. 44), Sched. 8, para. 2(3)). "Must" is mandatory, so that a tenant who was out of time, and was refused an extension of time by the county court, could not initiate the procedure over again by serving a second notice (*Mayhew* v. *Free Grammar School of John Lyon* [1991] E.G.C.S. 61).

N

NATIONAL ASSEMBLY FOR WALES or CYNULLIAD CENEDLAETHOL CYMRU. Stat. Def., Government of Wales Act 1998 (c. 38), s.1(1).

NATIONAL HEALTH SERVICE. See NHS BODY; and NHS TREATMENT.

NATIONAL ORIGINS. The term "national origins" in s.1(3) of the Race Relations Act 1976 (c. 74), refers to race rather than citizenship or residence (*Tejani* v. *Superintendent Registrar for the District of Peterborough* [1986] IRLR 502).

NATIONAL SECURITY. "In the interests of national security, territorial integrity or public safety" (Convention for the Protection of Human Rights and Fundamental Freedoms 1953 (Cmd. 8969), Art. 10). The protection of the efficiency and reputation of M.I.6 was not sufficient reason in the national interest to justify, under this article, the continuation of injunctions preventing newspapers from purveying information on a matter of legitimate public concern, after the publication of that matter elsewhere (*The Observer and The Guardian* v. *United Kingdom* (1992) 14 E.H.R.R. 153).

NAVIGATION. "Vessel in navigation", See VESSEL.

NEAR. "In or near the area" (Coroners (Amendment) Act 1926 (c. 59), s.18). A death likely to have occurred eight to nine miles offshore had not occurred "near the area" within which the coroner had jurisdiction (*R.* v. *Coroner for East Sussex, ex p. Healy* [1988] 1 W.L.R. 1194).
See also AT OR NEAR.

NEAREST. "Nearest available route," see AVAILABLE.

NECESSARY. (18) "Necessary . . . for disposing fairly of the cause or matter" (R.S.C., Ord. 24, r.13(1)). Disclosure of documents containing answers to questions put by the police during an investigation into the death of a person was held to be "necessary" for "disposing fairly" of an action by the mother of the deceased against the Commissioner of Police of the Metropolis (*Peach* v. *Commissioner of Police of the Metropolis* [1986] Q.B. 1064). The test for making an order for the production and inspection of documents under this rule is not whether the documents are relevant but whether the order is necessary for disposing fairly of the cause or matter (*Dolling-Baker* v. *Merrett* [1990] 1 W.L.R. 1205).
"Necessary for avoiding a substantial risk of prejudice to the administration of justice" (Contempt of Court Act 1981 (c.49), s.4(2)). In forming a view as to whether it was "necessary" to make a postponement order under this section the court must have regard to the competing public considerations of ensuring a fair trial and of open justice (*Ex p. The Telegraph plc, The Times*, March 16, 1993).
Where in civil proceedings the evidence was uncontroversial, the risk of sensational reporting of any evidence was slight and where the likelihood that there would be little or no reporting of the trial, there was no

substantial risk that pending criminal proceedings would be prejudiced by reporting of the civil actions to justify an order under s.4(2) (*MGN Pension Trustees* v. *Bank of America National Trust and Savings Association* (*Serious Fraud Office intervening*) [1995] 2 All E.R. 355).

"Necessary in the interests of justice . . . or for the prevention of . . . crime" (Contempt of Court Act 1981 (c. 49), s.10). The words "in the interests of justice" were given the meaning "in the technical sense of the administration of justice in the course of legal proceedings in a court of law; expediency, however great, is not enough; section 10 requires actual necessity to be established" (*per* Lord Diplock in *Secretary of State for Defence* v. *Guardian Newspapers* [1985] A.C. 339, 340): this case was followed in *Maxwell* v. *Pressdram* [1987] 1 W.L.R. 298). "Necessary" as used in this section means "really needed" and, according to the facts in any particular case, lies somewhere between "indispensable" on the one hand and "useful" or "expedient" on the other (*Re an Inquiry under the Company Securities* (*Insider Dealing*) *Act 1985* [1988] 2 W.L.R. 33). "Interests of justice" is used in s.10 in the sense that persons should be enabled to exercise important legal rights or to protect themselves from serious legal wrongs, and is not confined to legal proceedings in a court of law. So that where a company sought disclosure of a journalist's notes so as to identify a person who gave him, in breach of confidence, information in which there was no public interest in publication but publication of which would severely damage its business, then disclosure was held to be "necessary in the interests of justice" (*X Ltd.* v. *Morgan-Grampian* (*Publishers*) [1990] 2 W.L.R. 1000). An order for disclosure of the source of information in the interests of justice was not "necessary" for the purposes of this section where the applicant had failed to make personal inquiries in order to discover the source of a leak of confidential information, and where there was insufficient evidence to show that the source would have been revealed if inquiries had been made (*Broadmoor Hospital* v. *Hyde, The Times*, March 18, 1994). See also REASONABLE EXCUSE; PREVENTION.

An order for disclosure of documents which would enable an employer to discover the identity of a disloyal employee may be "necessary in the interests of jsutice" (*Camelot Group plc* v. *Centaur Communications Ltd* [1998] 2 W.L.R. 379).

The words "where necessary" in condition 11(5) of the National Conditions of Sale mean "necessary under the lease" (*Bickel* v. *Courtenay Investments* [1984] 1 W.L.R. 795).

"Necessary for the proper performance of the employee's duties that he should reside in the accommodation" (Finance Act 1977 (c. 36), s.33(4)(*a*)). For the purposes of this section the necessity must be based on the relationship between the proper performance of duties and the dwelling-house, and not on the personal exigencies of the taxpayer and his difficulty in finding other suitable accommodation (*Vertigan* v. *Brady* [1988] S.T.C. 91).

"Necessarily in the performance of duties of employment." Journalists reading newspapers purchased from an allowance paid by their employers was not an activity performed "necessarily in the performance of their duties" but was an activity merely preliminary to the performance of such work and not deductible under the Income and Corporation Taxes Act 1970 (c. 10), s.189(1) (*Fitzpatrick* v. *I.R.C.*, 1994 S.L.T. 836).

National Health Service (Pharmaceutical Services) Regulations 1992 reg. 4). The words "necessary" and "desirable" did not have to be construed disjunctively (*R.* v. *Yorkshire RHA, ex p. Baker, The Times*, May 6, 1996).

"To do all such other things as may be necessary for winding up the company's affairs and distributing its assets" (Insolvency Act 1986 (c. 45), Sched. 4, para. 13). The power contained in Sched. 4, para. 13 was not wide enough to cover an agreement reached with a company to assign the fruits of an action for wrongful trading in return for the company agreeing to fund the litigation (*Re Oasis Merchandising* [1997] 2 W.L.R. 764).

NEED. (Company Directors Disqualification Act 1986 (c. 46)). "Need" had to be interpreted as a practical need, related to the interests of the company; for example, where the involvement of the director was critical to investor or consumer confidence (*Re Tech Textiles Ltd* [1998] 1 BCLC 259).

NEEDS. In considering the suitability of alternative accommodation offered under s.34(3)(*a*)(*b*) of the Housing Act 1980 (c. 51) it is right to regard the need for a garden and facilities for pursuing a hobby as a tenant's "needs" within the meaning of paras. 1 and 2 of Pt. II of Sched. 4 to the 1980 Act (*Enfield London Borough Council* v. *French* (1984) 83 L.G.R. 750).

"The meet other needs" (Social Security Act 1986 (c. 50)(, s.32(2)(*b*)) does not mean "all other needs," so that such needs have to be in accordance with directions given or guidance issued by the Secretary of State, as provided for in the subsection (*R.* v. *Secretary of State for Social Service, ex p. Stitt* [1992] C.O.D. 335).

(Insolvency Act 1986 (c. 45), s.310). Private school fees and other educational expenses could amount to the "reasonable needs of the bankrupt and his family" (*Re, Rayatt, The Times*, May 4, 1998).

NEGLECT. "Neglect on the part of any director" (Trade Descriptions Act 1968 (c. 29), s.20(1)). Where the managing director of a garage company is entitled to delegate work to senior staff and to expect it to be completed in accordance with his instructions, he is not guilty of "neglect" within the meaning of this section if he does not check that the work is correctly carried out (*Lewin* v. *Bland* [1985] RTR 171). When the first of two co-directors asked the other to make inquiries as to the legality of a product they were proposing to market, and then, relying absolutely on the assurances of the other, put it on the market, he was guilty of "neglect" under the section when it turned out that the product was illegal (*Hirschler* v. *Birch* [1987] RTR 13).

"Neglect" meant continuous or non-transient neglect so that death from cerebral anoxia because of an obstructed airway could not give rise to a verdict of death as a result of neglect (*R.* v. *H.M. Coroner for North Humberside and Scunthorpe, ex p. Jamieson* [1995] Q.B. 1 applied) (*R.* v. *Surrey Coroner, ex p. Wright* [1997] 1 W.L.R. 16).

"Wilfully . . . ill-treats, neglects . . . " see ILL-TREAT.

NEGOTIATIONS. (Consumer Credit Act 1974 (c. 39), s.56(1)(*b*)). A wide construction should be given to the words "negotiations" in s.56(1)(*b*), since it provided that all antecedent negotiations and communications should be taken into account, from the time when the debtor, hirer and negotiator first entered into communication (*Forthright Finance Ltd* v. *Ingate* [1997] 4 All E.R. 99).

NEIGHBOUR. (Housing Act 1985 (c. 68), Sched. 2), "Neighbours" within the meaning of the 1985 Act were not confined to adjoining occupiers but covered those people sufficiently close to the behaviour creating a nuisance or annoyance to be adversely affected by it (*Northampton Borough Council* v. *Lovatt, The Independent*, November 14, 1997).

NEIGHBOURHOOD. (National Health Service (Pharmaceutical Services) Regulations 1992 (S.I. 1992 No. 662), reg. 4). A shopping and leisure centre was a "neighbourhood" within the meaning of reg. 4 even though no persons lived there and an assessment of the adequacy of provision of pharmaceutical services required consideration of the various needs of the shoppers who visited the centre and whether the needs of the shoppers could be met by existing pharmacies (*R.* v. *Family Health Services Appeal Authority, ex p. Boots The Chemist plc, The Times*, June 28, 1996).

NET ASSETS. Stat. Def., Companies Act 1985 (c. 6), ss.152, 154, 264.

NET PROCEEDS. Stat. Def., "the amount accruing on the disposal less any expenditure reasonably incurred for the purposes of making it" (Education Act 1996 (c. 56), s.70(4)).

NEW. A so-called "new" vehicle could not properly be so described for the purposes of a retail sale where there was clear evidence that the extent of damage suffered prior to sale was such that the vehicle could not be restored to the condition that a purchaser might reasonably expect for a "new" vehicle (*Raynham Farm Co.* v. *Symbol Motor Corporation, The Times*, January 27, 1987). It was open to a jury to find that the application by a dealer of the word "new" to a car should indicate that it had not had any previous owner, and that he had infringed s.1 of the Trade Descriptions Act 1968 (c. 29) when selling as "new" a car which had been temporarily registered in his own name; notwithstanding that the car had been sold in mint condition and with low delivery mileage only (*R.* v. *Anderson* (1988) 152 J.P. 373).
   "New facts or evidence" (Coroners Act 1988 (c. 13), s.13(1)(*b*)). Evidence will qualify as "new" within the meaning of this section if it was not available at the time of the original inquest, would have been admissible had it been available and was credible and relevant to an issue of significance (*Re Fletcher, The Times*, March 27, 1992).
   "New claim means . . . any claim involving either (a) the addition or substitution of a new cause of action; or (b) the addition or substitution of a new party . . ."
   (Limitation Act 1980 (c. 58), s.35(2)). Section 35(2) did not include the substitution of a party who had succeeded to a claim or liability which already represented in existing proceedings and which did not involve a new cause of action (*Yorkshire Regional Health Authority* v. *Fairclough Building Ltd and anr* [1996] 1 All E.R. 519).
   "New claim . . . made after the expiry of any time limit under this Act" (Limitation Act 1980 (c. 58), s.35(3)). The relevant date for expiry under

s.35(3) was the date when the amendment was made rather than the date when leave to amend was granted (*Welsh Development Agency* v. *Redpath Dorman Long* [1994] 4 All E.R. 10).

(Criminal Justice Act 1988 (c. 33), s.133). A conviction that was wrongful because of the subsequent discovery of a judicial error did not amount to "new or newly discovered fact" within the meaning of s.133 (*R.* v. *Secretary of State for the Home Department, ex p. Bateman and Howse* (1995) 7 Admin.L.R. 175).

NEWSPAPER. Stat. Def., Local Government (Access to Information) Act 1972 (c. 70), s.100K as inserted by Local Government Act 1985 (c. 43), s.1.

NHS BODY. Stat. Def., National Health Service Act 1977 (c. 49), s.22(1A) inserted by Health Act 1999 (c. 8), s.27(1).

NHS TREATMENT. Stat. Def., Road Traffic (NHS Charges) Act 1999 (c. 3), s.1(6).

NOISE. Stat. Def., Environmental Protection Act 1990 (c. 43), s.79.

NOMADIC. "Persons of a nomadic habit of life" (Caravan Sites Act 1968 (c. 52), s.16). A person who establishes a residential base, and merely departs from it seasonally from time to time can nevertheless be said to be following a "nomadic" way of life as a gipsy, notwithstanding that he regularly returns for part of the year to the same place where he might be said to have a fixed abode or permanent residence (*Greenwich London Borough Council* v. *Powell* [1989] 2 W.L.R. 7). See also GIPSIES. Members of an erstwhile nomadic family did not cease to be "persons of a nomadic habit of life notwithstanding that they had not travelled since 1974 when their last horse died (*R.* v. *Shropshire County Council, ex p. Bungay* [1990] C.O.D. 392). The words "nomadic habit of life" import more than just the habit of wandering or travelling; they import moving from place to place with a purpose in mind as a necessary and characteristic part of their lives (*R.* v. *South Hams District Council, ex p. Gibb, The Times,* November 15, 1993). The notion of economic independence, or at least a desire for economic independence, is inherent in the idea of nomadic life, as is the notion that the nomad's living is to be made in an activity in which he has to go from place to place (*R.* v. *Dorset County Council, ex p. Rolls, The Times,* February 1, 1994).

NOMINAL PLAINTIFF. A plaintiff had to be deliberately duplicitous and acting for the benefit of another to be regarded as a "nominal plaintiff" (*C.A. Envis* v. *Thakkar, The Times*, May 2, 1995).

NON-COMBUSTIBLE MATERIAL. Stat. Def., Merchant Shipping (Fire Protection: Large Ships) Regulations 1998 (No. 1012), reg. 1(2).

NON-POLITICAL CRIME. Indiscriminate atrocities, which were disproportionate to, or have insufficiently direct causal connection with any genuine political objective were not "political crimes" (*T.* v. *Secretary of State for the Home Department* [1995] 2 All E.R. 1042).

NORMAL. (34) "Normal retiring age" (Employment Protection (Consolidation) Act 1978 (c. 44), s.64(1)(*b*) as amended by s.3(1) of the Sex Discrimination Act 1986 (c. 59)). Where the contractual retiring age of 60 was extended by a temporary administrative policy to the age of 65, the "normal retiring age," within the meaning of this section, reverted to 60 when the policy ended (*Hughes* v. *Department of Health and Social Security* [1985] A.C. 776). A civil servant aged 63 at the date of his dismissal was held to be entitled to bring a complaint of unfair dismissal on the ground that a purported reduction in the normal retiring age from 65 to a band "between 62 and 63" was insufficiently definite to constitute a "normal retiring age," so that the statutory alternative of 65 applied. (*Swaine* v. *Health and Safety Executive* [1986] IRLR 205). To establish what is, in any particular circumstances, the "normal retiring age" within the meaning of this section the tribunal should consider the statistical as well as the contractual situation; so that, in a case where a company normally retained employees beyond the 60 years provided for by their contracts of employment, it was held that the "normal retiring age" was the statutory 65 (*Mauldon* v. *British Telecommunications* [1987] I.C.R. 450). In determining "normal retiring age" for the purposes of this section it is necessary to establish what, at the effective date of termination of the employee's employment, and on the basis of the facts then known, was the age at which employees of all age groups in the employee's position could reasonably regard as the normal age of retirement applicable to the group (*Brooks* v. *British Telecommunications* [1991] I.C.R. 286). Where employers had a genuine and clearly stated policy as to normal retiring age this was not undermined by the granting of a few limited and temporary exceptions (*Barclays Bank* v. *O'Brien* [1993] I.C.R. 347). Where certain employees had a variety of expectations as to their retirement ages before they received a letter from their employer stating that it was proposed to reduce the retirement ages of all with a retirement age over 60 from 64 to 60 in progressive stages, it was permissible to have regard to the letter in determining whether there was a group of employees with a "normal retiring age" for the purposes of this section (*Barber* v. *Thames Television* [1992] I.C.R. 661). Where there was a contractual retirement age applicable to all or nearly all of a group of employees holding the same or similar positions, there was a rebuttable presumption that the contractual retirement age was the "normal retirement age" (*Barclays Bank* v. *O'Brien* [1995] 1 All E.R. 438). There can be no concept of a normal retiring age when an employee's position is unique (*Patel* v. *Nagesan* [1995] I.C.R. 988).

"Normal gross income" (Family Income Supplements Act 1970 (c. 55), s.4(1); Family Income Supplements (General) Regulations 1980 (No. 1437), reg. 2). A family's "normal" gross income for the purposes of calculating supplementary benefit means the usual income of the family and does not include an unusual or abnormal income, as for instance when the earner is on strike (*Lowe* v. *Rigby* [1985] 1 W.L.R. 1108).

"Normally based" (Council Directive (72/1166/EEC), Arts. 1(4), 2(2), 7(2). When a vehicle bore a properly issued registration plate it had to be regarded as "normally based" in the territory of the state of registration, even if at the material time authorisation to use the vehicle had been withdrawn (*Gambetta Auto S.A.* v. *Bureau Central Français* [1985] RTR 129).

(2) "Normally used" (Value Added Tax (Cars) Order 1980 (No. 442), art. 2). In deciding whether a motor vehicle was one "of a kind normally used" within the meaning of this article the approach should not be by reference to the variety of the particular model, but by determining whether it was part of a normally accepted class (*Withers of Winsford* v. *Commissioners of Customs and Excise* [1988] S.T.C. 431).

"The full extent normal in his case" (Social Security (Unemployment, Sickness and Invalidity Benefit) Regulations 1983 (No. 1598), reg. 7(1)(*e*)). A person who worked a regular two-and-a-half days a week under a community programme scheme was employed to "the full extent normal in his case," and was, therefore, not entitled to unemployment benefit in respect of the rest of the week (*Chief Adjudication Officer* v. *Brunt* [1988] 2 W.L.R. 511). Whether a claimant's pattern of work was "normal in his case" for the purposes of this regulation depended on what was normal for the particular claimant rather than what was normal for the particular employment he held (*Riley* v. *Chief Adjudication Officer* [1988] 1 All E.R. 457).

"Normal residence" (Council Directive 83/182/EEC, Art. 7(1)) corresponds to the permanent centre of interest of the person concerned, and that place is to be determined by reference to all the criteria available and all relevant factual circumstances. So that a person who spent nights and weekends with his girlfriend in a different member state had not moved his "normal residence" to that state (*Rigsadvokaten* v. *Ryborg, The Times*, May 2, 1991).

NORTHERN IRELAND ASSEMBLY. Stat. Def., Northern Ireland Act 1998 (c. 47), s.4(5).

NORTHERN IRELAND LEGISLATION. Stat. Def., Northern Ireland Act 1998 (c. 47), s.98(1).

NORTHERN IRELAND ZONE. In fishing context, Stat. Def., Northern Ireland Act 1998 (c. 47), s.98(1).

NOT LESS THAN. (Landlord and Tenant Act 1954, (c. 56), s.29(3)). Where the landlord had served a notice to quit on March 23, an application for a new tenancy made on May 23 was made exactly two months after the service of the notice, and was therefore made "not less than two months" after the service and complied with the requirements of this section (*Riley (E.J.) Investments* v. *Eurostile Holdings* [1985] 1 W.L.R. 1139).

See also WITHIN.

NOT SUCH AS TO AFFECT THE PRODUCTION OF THE DOCUMENT OR THE ACCURACY OF ITS CONTENTS. (Police and Criminal Evidence Act 1984 (c. 60), s.69(1)(b)). The malfunctioning of a computer (for example: in its recording of the time of a test) in a way which was not relevant to the issue did not affect the admissibility of a statement generated by it. A malfunction was relevant if it affected the way in which the computer processed, stored or retrieved the information used to generate the statement tendered in evidence (*DPP* v. *McKeown* [1997] 1 All E.R. 737).

NOTICE. "Notice in writing" (Immigration Act 1971 (c. 77), s.4(1)). An immigration officer's stamp in a passport cannot be regarded as an effective "notice in writing" for the purposes of this section unless it could reasonably be expected to be understood by persons of the class to which the particular immigrant belonged (*R.* v. *Secretary of State for the Home Office, ex p. Betancourt, The Times,* October 5, 1987; *R.* v. *Secretary of State for the Home Department, ex p. Tolba* [1988] Imm.A.R. 78). A partially illegible stamp on an immigrant's passport, which did not make clear to the immigrant the length of time he was allowed to remain in the United Kingdom, was not a valid notice in writing for the purposes of this section (*R.* v. *Secretary of State for the Home Department, ex p. Minton* [1990] C.O.D. 101). "Notice . . . refusing leave" (Immigration Act 1971 (c. 77), Sched. 2, para. 6(1)). The belief of an immigration officer as to the nature of a letter purporting to be a notice of refusal of leave to enter is irrelevant to the question whether it is a proper "notice" within the meaning of this paragraph (*Ramaiah (Rubeena)* v. *Secretary of State for the Home Department* [1992] Imm.A.R. 263).

A facsimile transmission on a tenant of notice to exercise a rent review clause by a landlord and simultaneous delivery of the notice to the tenant's agents was sufficient "notice in writing" (*E.A.E. (R.T.)* v. *E.A.E. Property* (O.H.), 1994 S.L.T. 627).

"Without notice of any intention" (Matrimonial Causes Act 1973 (c. 18), s.37). A constructive notice could be sufficient for the purposes of this section (*Kemmis* v. *Kemmis* [1988] 1 W.L.R. 1307).

"Notice of appeal" (Employment Appeal Tribunal Rules 1980 (No. 2035), r.3(1)). A letter from solicitors giving notice of an intention to appeal from an industrial tribunal's decision could not be accepted as a "notice of appeal" for the purpose of this rule (*Martin* v. *British Railways Board* [1989] I.C.R. 24).

"The insurer had notice of the proceedings" (Road Traffic Act 1972 (c. 20), s.149(2)(*a*)). A letter from solicitors advising insurers that, unless the claim was satisfied, they proposed to recommend to their client that he institute proceedings, did not constitute a "notice" for the purposes of this section (*Harrington* v. *Link Motor Policies at Lloyd's* [1989] RTR 345).

A telephone conversation between the insured's solicitors and the insurers in which the solicitor intimated that a court action had been brought in order to avoid time bar and where the date of bringing the proceedings was inaccurate by one day could amount to a "notice of the bringing of proceedings" under the Road Traffic Act 1988 (c. 53), s.152(1) (*Orme* v. *Ferguson* (1995) S.C.L.R. 752).

(Child Abduction and Custody Act 1985 (c. 60), Sched. 1, Art. 16). Where a court became aware either expressly or by necessary implication that there had been a wrongful removal or retention of a child within the meaning of Art. 3 of the Hague Convention, that constituted "notice" of that removal or retention within the meaning of Art. 16 (*R.* v. *R. (Residence Order: Child Abduction)* [1995] 3 W.L.R. 425).

(R.S.C., Ord. 65, r.4(3)). An order for substituted service should not be made where there was no likelihood of bringing the notice to the attention of the defendant himself (*Abbey National plc* v. *Frost (Solicitors' Indemnity Fund Intervening)* [1998] 2 All E.R. 321).

NOXIOUS. "Noxious . . . thing" (Firearms Act 1968 (c. 27), s.5(1)(*b*)). A discharge of electricity can be a "noxious" thing within the meaning of this section (*Flack* v. *Baldry* [1988] 1 W.L.R. 393).

O

OBJECT. (Transfer of Undertakings (Protection of Employment) Regulations 1981 (S.I. 1981 No. 1794), reg. 5). The word "object in reg. 5(4)A should be construed as meaning a refusal to accept a transfer, which had to be conveyed to the transferor or transferee before the date of the transfer. The objection could be conveyed by word or deed or both, and each case depended on its facts to determine whether there was a sufficient state of mind on the part of the employee to consent to the transfer (*Hay* v. *George Hanson (Building Contractors) Ltd* [1996] IRLR 427).

OBJECTIVE. (Road Traffic Act 1988 (c. 52), s.11(3)). The "objective" of carrying out the roadside breath test was to obtain a reliable positive or negative reading, not to obtain a reading which was reliable in some circumstances but not in others (*DPP* v. *Heywood* [1998] RTR 1).

OBLIGATION. "Any obligation assumed" (Civil Liability (Contribution) Act 1978 (c. 47), s.7(2). These words cannot apply to a duty of care arising out of a particular relationship and imposed by law (*Lampitt* v. *Poole Borough Council, Taylor (Third Parties)* [1990] 3 W.L.R. 179).

(Interpretation Act 1978 (c. 30), s.16(1)(*c*)). Failure to comply with a requirement in a notice served under statutory powers amounting to a criminal offence created an "obligation or liability" under s.16(1)(*c*) which applied to both civil and criminal proceedings (*Aitken* v. *South Hams District Council* [1994] 3 All E.R. 400).

Inheritance (Provision for Family and Dependents) Act 1975 (c. 63), s.3(1)(*d*) referred to obligations and responsibilities which the deceased had immediately before his death and could not include a past failure to discharge an obligation which was now defunct (*Re Jennings (Deceased)* [1994] 3 All E.R. 27).

(Civil Jurisdiction and Judgments Act 1982 (c. 27), Sched. 3C, art. 5(1)). "Obligation in question." A pre-contractual obligation not to misrepresent a risk under a reinsurance contract was not "an obligation" within the meaning of art. 5(1) (*Trade Indemnity* v. *Forsakringsaktiebolaget Njord (in liq.)* [1995] 1 All E.R. 796).

(Lugano Convention on Jurisdiction and the Enforcement of Judgments in Civil and Commercial Matters 1988, Art. 5). Art. 5 drew no distinction between obligations arising in the context of a contract and obligations arising under or after the contract, so that the duty to make a fair presentation of the reinsurance risk amounted to an "obligation" (*Agnew* v. *Lansforsakringsbolagens AB* [1996] 4 All E.R. 978).

(Lugano Convention on Jurisdiction and Enforcement of Judgments in Civil and Commercial Matters 1988, Art. 5(1)). An "obligation in question" under Art. 5 referred to the matter relating to the contract or the particular dispute under the contract (*Trade Indemnity plc* v. *Forsakringsaktiebolaget*

Njord [1995] 1 All E.R. 796 considered) (*Agnew* v. *Lansforsakringsbolagens AB* [1997] 4 All E.R. 937).

"Place of performance of the obligation," see PLACE.

OBSCENE. (Obscene Publications Act 1959 (c. 66), ss.2(1), 2(4)). Exhibiting a model head, to each of the ears of which there was attached an earring made out of a freeze dried human foetus, although constituing the common law offence of outraging public decency, was held to be unlikely to deprave or corrupt and was not therefore "obscene" within the meaning of this section (*R.* v. *Gibson* [1990] 3 W.L.R. 595).

(3) "Obscene articles" (Obscene Publications Act 1959 (c. 66), s.3). Articles of sexually explicit nature are not necessarily obscene (*Darbo* v. *DPP, The Times,* July 11, 1991).

OBSTRUCT. (6) "Wilfully obstructs" (Highways Act 1980 (c. 66), s.137). An offence under this section is committed where as a matter of fact and degree a particular use of the highway is so unreasonable as to amount to an obstruction. Thus the accused who, while working as a tout for a Soho club, approached small groups of pedestrians, engaging them in conversation, and thus forcing other pedestrians into the highway, was held to have obstructed "the free passage along a highway" within the meaning of this section (*Cooper* v. *Metropolitan Police Commissioner* (1986) 82 Cr.App.R. 238). In concluding that a supermarket had not obstructed the highway by placing three parallel rows of shopping trolleys along the pavement outside its premises justices were held to have erred in over-emphasising the service to shoppers the trolleys provided, and the fact that no one had complained (*Devon County Council* v. *Gateway Foodmarkets* [1990] C.O.D. 324). Gates, tied by twine to hedges and held closed by a loop of twine, barring the entire breadth of a bridleway, but which could be opened easily, nevertheless constituted an obstruction contrary to this section (*Durham County Council* v. *Scott* [1990] Crim.L.R. 784).

(Highways Act 1980 (c. 66), s.149(1)). "Obstruction" is caused where a pavement is made difficult to pass by reason of an obstruction (*Cornwall County Council* v. *Blewett* [1994] C.O.D. 46).

(19) (Police Act 1964 (c. 48), s.51(3)). A man who told his brother repeatably, and in colourful language, to say nothing to police officers seeking to question him in the street did not thereby obstruct the police in the execution of their duty (*Green* v. *DPP* [1991] Crim.L.R. 782). But refusal of entry to premises, accompanied by verbal abuse and giving a false name was held to be obstructing the police (*Ledger* v. *DPP* [1991] Crim.L.R. 439). An intervener who sought to assist the prevention of an arrest which, in the circumstances, was not a lawful arrest within s.25 of the Police and Criminal Evidence Act 1984 (c. 60) could not be charged with wilful obstruction of a police officer in the execution of his duty contrary to s.51(3) of the 1964 Act (*Edwards* v. *DPP, The Times*, March 29, 1993).

(30) (Removal and Disposal of Vehicles Regulations 1986, reg. 3). An offence of obstruction under s.137 was established where any part of the highway had been wilfully and without lawful excuse obstructed so as to deny access by persons to that part and so constitute an unreasonable use of the highway; that the words "position", "condition" and "circumstances" in reg. 3 of the Removal and Disposal of Vehicles Regulations 1986

qualified obstruction and had no reference to user of the highway. In the absence of any qualification as to reasonableness, "obstruction" in reg. 3 did not have the same meaning as obstruction in s.137, but meant obstruction to the use of the road by persons who were using or might be expected to use it (*Carey* v. *Chief Constable of Avon and Somerset* [1995] RTR 405).

OBSTRUCTION. (Factories Act 1961 (c. 34), s.28). Pieces of wood which had been placed deliberately on the floor in order to block access to a specific area and which were clearly visible, posed a clear risk to persons using the floor and so constituted an "obstruction" within the meaning of s.28(1) of the 1961 Act (*Erskine* v. *Falcon Catering Equipment Ltd* 1997 G.W.D. 4–166).

OBTAIN. "Information which he knowingly obtained" (Company Securities (Insider Dealing) Act 1985 (c. 8), s.1(3)(*a*)). For the purposes of this section the word "obtained" has a wider meaning than acquired by purpose or effort. It would cover the situation where a person came by the information without any positive action on his part (*R.* v. *Fisher* (1988) 4 B.C.C. 360; *Attorney-General's Reference* (*No. 1 of 1988*) [1989] 2 W.L.R. 729).

"Obtained" connoted a process rather than one single act so that the mere fact that a divorce was finalised in one country could not dissociate the process of "obtaining" it from the proceedings in which it was obtained (*R.* v. *Secretary of State for the Home Department, ex p. Ghulam Fatima* [1996] A.C. 527 followed).

An overseas divorce would only be recognised in England if it was "obtained" for the purposes of the Family Law Act 1986 (c. 55), s.46 in the country in which proceedings had been instituted (*Berkovits* v. *Gringberg* (Att.-Gen. intervening) [1995] 2 All E.R. 681); [1995] 1 F.L.R. 477).

OCCASIONAL. "Occasional residence abroad" (Income and Corporation Taxes Act 1970 (c. 10), s.49). A taxpayer with business interests in the United States, after being ordinarily resident in the United Kingdom for a number of years, spent the whole of the 1978–79 tax year abroad. This absence was held to be more than mere "occasional residence abroad" (*Reed* v. *Clark* [1985] 3 W.L.R. 142).

OCCUPATION. (10) "Actual occupation" (Land Registration Act 1925 (c. 21), s.70(1)(*g*)). A person can be in "actual occupation" of a house even though her physical presence was neither exclusive nor continuous and uninterrupted. A wife who was in the matrimonial home at least some part of nearly every day was held to be in "actual occupation," notwithstanding that the house was in her husband's name (*Kingsnorth Finance Co.* v. *Tizard* [1986] 1 W.L.R. 783). The appropriate time to consider whether there was a person in "actual occupation" of land so as to give rise to an overriding interest was when the conveyance was completed and not when it was registered. And a semi-derelict house, in process of restoration, is capable of being under "actual occupation" for the purposes of this section (*Lloyds Bank* v. *Rossett* [1988] 3 W.L.R. 1301). In order to establish an overriding interest by "actual occupation" the occupation had to be at such a time and of such a nature as to put a lender on enquiry as to the amount that he should lend. "Actual occupation" means established or settled occupation and must exist at the date of the completion giving rise to the right (*Abbey National Building Society* v. *Cann* [1990] 2 W.L.R. 833); *Lloyds Bank* v. *Rosset* [1990] 2 W.L.R. 867). An option to purchase amounted to "actual occupation" and could be an overriding interest enforceable against a registered proprietor of the land (*Ferrishurst Ltd* v. *Wallcite Ltd* [1999] 2 W.L.R. 667).

(16) "Occupation" (Landlord and Tenant Act 1954 (c. 56), s.37(2)) means actual occupation, even if that differs from what might be authorised under the lease (*Department of the Environment* v. *Royal Insurance* (1987) 54 P. & C.R. 26).

Management and control functions by a market operator of a market hall who was not physically present in the premises amounted to "occupation" under the Landlord and Tenant Act 1954 (c. 56), s.23(1) (*Graysim Holdings* v. *P. & O. Holdings* [1994] 1 W.L.R. 992).

See RATEABLE OCCUPATION.

OCCUPATIONAL PENSION. (Social Security (No. 2) Act 1980 (c. 39), s.5(3)). A claim by a retired civil servant that the pension he received was not "occupational" because he had funded the whole amount of the pension by taking a reduced salary, failed on the ground that, on the balance of probability, the employer had discharged some at least of the cost (Social Security Decision No. R(U) 1/89).

OCCUPATIONAL PENSION SCHEME. (Pensions Act 1993 (c. 48), s.1). A scheme for payment of industrial injury allowances, which included a provision whereby benefits were payable otherwise than on termination of service, could amount to an "occupational pension scheme" given the wide scope of s.1 of the Pensions Act 1993 (*City and County of Swansea* v. *Johnson* [1999] 2 W.L.R. 683).

Stat. Def., Financial Services Act 1986 (c. 60), s.207.

OCCUPATIONAL QUALIFICATION. "Genuine occupational qualifica-tion" (Sex Discrimination Act 1975 (c. 65), s.7). Being a woman was held not to be a genuine occupational qualification for working in a women's clothing shop, so that failure to consider a man for the job was discrimina-tion (*Etam* v. *Rowan* [1989] IRLR 150). A centre for children of ethnic minority origin was entitled to rely on the defence of "genuine occupational qualification" where the duties of an advertised post required an employee of the same racial group who could carry them all out (*Tottenham Green Under Fives Centre* v. *Marshall (No. 2)* [1991] I.C.R. 320).

OCCUPIER. (16) (General Rate Act 1967 (c. 9), s.16). The fact that a person enjoys sole actual occupation of premises does not necessarily mean that he also has exclusive occupation for the purposes of deciding whether he is an "occupier" within the meaning of s.16. Thus the tenants in sole occupation of a warehouse were not occupiers in exclusive occupation because the owners shared control over access and retained the right to allow other persons to store goods there (*Channel Shipping (Newport)* v. *Newport Borough Council* [1988] 16 E.G. 87). An agreement permitting occupation of residential premises in common with a stated number of others who might be granted a like right is capable of preventing a grant of exclusive occupation (*A.G. Securities* v. *Vaughan*; *Antoniades* v. *Villiers* [1988] 3 W.L.R. 1205).

(4) "Occupier of every factory" (Explosives Act 1875 (c. 17), s.23). Receivers in their capacity as managers of a factory can be "occupiers" for the purposes of this section (*Lord Advocate* v. *Aero Technologies* (*In Receivership*, 1991 S.L.T. 134).

"Occupier" (Wildlife and Countryside Act 1981 (c. 69), s.28) refers only to a person who has some interest in the land, such as a tenant, and not someone with a transitory interest who is doing some work on the land for the owner (*Southern Water Authority* v. *Nature Conservancy Council* [1992] 1 W.L.R. 775).

"Occupier of the land" (London Local Authorities Act 1990, s.21(2)(*j*)). A trader who set up trestle tables in the forecourt of a store, with the permission of the manager of the store, was not the "occupier" of the forecourt for the purposes of this section (*O'Gorman* v. *Brent London Borough Council, The Times*, May 20, 1993).

"Occupier of the premises" (Landlord and Tenant Act 1954 (c. 56), s.23(1)). A market operator letting stalls in an enclosed hall adjacent to a shopping precinct was an occupier of the premises for the purposes of s.23(1), and entitled as a protected tenant to the grant of a new tenancy (*Graysim Holdings* v. *P. & O. Property Holdings, The Times*, March 2, 1994, C.A.).

(Fire Precautions Act 1971 (c. 40), s.7(1)). A person who was temporarily away on holiday remained an "occupier" for the purposes of the 1971 Act, so that he was liable for any use of the premises for which a fire certificate was required when none was in force during his absence, although he might not be an occupier if his absence was measured in months rather than weeks (*Bamber* v. *Mackinnon*, 1996 S.L.T. 1180).

(Misuse of Drugs Act 1971 (c. 38), s.8). A cohabitee of nine years standing who lived in a property of which his girlfriend was the tenant could be the "occupier" of the property for the purposes of s.8 of the 1971 Act since he had the power to exclude persons who wished to smoke cannabis in the property (*Read* (*Keith Paul*) v. *DPP* [1997] 10 C.L. 120).

Stat. Def., Housing Act 1985 (c. 68), s.558; Local Government Finance Act 1988 (c. 41), s.65; Food Safety Act 1990 (c. 16), s.53.

OCCUPY; OCCUPIED. (6) "Occupied by the tenant . . . for the purposes of a business carried on by him" (Landlord and Tenant Act 1954 (c. 56), s.23(1)). A property containing self-contained flats, occupied by persons employed at National Health Service hospitals, and managed by the local Health Authority, was held to have been occupied by the authority. As the authority was acting on powers delegated by the Secretary of State the property was occupied for the purposes of a government department within the meaning of this section. (*Linden* v. *Secretary of State for Social Services* [1986] 1 W.L.R. 164). A small park was "occupied" for the purposes of this section by the local authority to whom it was let (*Singh* v. *Wandsworth London Borough Council* [1992] 4 Admin.L.R. 1). A market operator who let out stalls inside a covered enclosed hall adjacent to a shopping precinct "occupied" the premises for the purposes of this section (*Graysim Holdings* v. *P. & O. Property Holdings, The Times*, March 2, 1994).

(7) "Occupy . . . for the purposes . . . of a business" (Landlord and Tenant Act 1954 (c. 56), s.30(1)(*g*)). A landlord could not oppose the grant of a new business tenancy on the ground that she wished to relet part of the building as residential flats, since she could not then be said to be occupying them (*Jones* v. *Jenkins* (1985) 277 E.G. 644).

(11) "Occupies the dwelling-house as his residence" (Rent Act 1977 (c. 42), s.2(1)(*a*)). A tenant who lived and worked in Malaysia and occupied a flat in England for between 9 and 26 days a year did not occupy it as his "residence" for the purposes of this section (*D.J. Crocker Securities (Portsmouth)* v. *Johal* [1989] 42 E.G. 103). The fact that a room occupied by the landlord did not contain a cooker did not prevent the room being a "dwelling-house," and the fact that the landlord did not sleep there did not prevent his occupying it "as his residence" (*Palmer* v. *McNamara* (1990) 23 H.L.R. 168).

Homeless persons who were temporarily accommodated in bed and breakfast premises by the local authority were "occupying" those premises for the purposes of ss.15 and 19 of the Housing Act 1961 (c. 65), notwithstanding that the premises called themselves an hotel (*R.* v. *Hackney London Borough Council, ex p. Thrasyvoulou* (1986) 84 L.G.R. 823).

(12) "Occupied the dwelling-house as his residence" (Rent Act 1977 (c. 42), Sched. 15, Case 11). For the purposes of Case 11 it is not necessary for the landlord to show that he had occupied the premises as his home. Occupation as a residence, which might have been temporary or intermittent, would be enough (*Mistry* v. *Isidore* [1990] 31 E.G. 43).

"Occupied together with agricultural land" (Rating Act 1971 (c. 39), s.2(2)(*b*)). For a building to qualify as an agricultural building for rating purposes by being "occupied together with agricultural land" it had to be occupied together with that land so as to form in a real sense a single agricultural unit. The distance of separation would be a relevant factor (*Hambleton District Council* v. *Buxted Poultry* [1993] 2 W.L.R. 34).

"Occupied as a private dwelling" (Housing Act 1985 (c. 68), Sched. 24, Part 1, 2(1)(*a*)). To be "occupied", for the purposes of this schedule, it is not necessary that the owner should be personally resident in the house at the relevant time, provided that he had begun the process of occupation by installing his furniture and personal possessions (*Singh (Kabal)* v. *Sandwell Metropolitan Borough Council* (1992) 64 P.&C.R. 323).

"To occupy the mobile home as his only or main residence" (Mobile Homes Act 1983 (c. 34), s.1(1)(*b*)). In order to determine whether a mobile home is occupied as an only or main residence, the court must consider the situation at the date on which the matter comes before them for hearing, and not at the date on which the originating application for re-possession of the pitch was made (*Omar Parks* v. *Elkington*; *Ron Grundy (Melbourne)* v. *Bonhevo* [1992] 1 W.L.R. 1270).

"Jointly occupies" (Housing Benefit (General) Regs. 1987 (No. 1971), reg. 3(2)(*d*)). These words refer to occupation under legal rights enjoyed jointly with one or more persons and do not include persons who merely reside together (*R.* v. *Chesterfield Borough Council, ex p. Fulwood, The Times,* June 15, 1993).

"Occupy the premises" (London Local Authorities Act 1990 (c. vii), ss.21(2)(*j*), 38(1)(*a*)). A street trader selling temporarily from trestle tables set up on the forecourt of a shop, with the permission of the manager of the shop, did not "occupy the premises" for the purposes of these sections (*O'Gorman* v. *Brent London Borough Council, The Times,* May 20, 1993).

OCCUR. "In the courts for the place where the harmful event occurred" (Civil Jurisdiction and Judgments Act 1982 (c. 27), Sched. 1, art. 5(3)). Negligence which originated abroad but which had a harmful effect in this country could be said to have "occurred" in this country for the purposes of this article (*Minster Investments* v. *Hyundai Precision Industry Co.* [1988] 2 Lloyd's Rep. 621).

OF. "Of and incidental to," see INCIDENTAL.

OFFENCE. (Magistrates' Courts Act 1980 (c. 43), s.125(4)). The breach of a community service order was held to be an "offence" within the meaning of this section (*Jones* v. *Kelsey* [1987] Crim.L.R. 392). But a warrant issued for the arrest of the accused for defaulting on a fine was held not to be issued in "connection with an offence" for the purposes of this section (*DPP* v. *Peacock* [1989] Crim.L.R. 372).

"He shall be guilty of an offence" (Town and Country Planning Act 1971 (c. 78), s.89(5)). Using land in contravention of an enforcement notice, contrary to this section, is an offence of absolute liability. It is not necessary to establish that the user of the land knew of the existence of the enforcement notice in respect of which he has been charged (*R.* v. *Collett, The Times,* October 29, 1993).

"Relevant offence," see RELEVANT.
"Conduct Offence" See CONDUCT.

OFFENDER. "Deprive the offender of his rights . . . in the property" (Powers of Criminal Courts Act 1973 (c. 62), s.43(3)). A person can still be an "offender" for the purposes of this section notwithstanding that he was not the user of the relevant property (*R.* v. *Colville-Scott* [1990] 1 W.L.R. 958).

OFFENSIVE WEAPON. (2) A police truncheon is an "offensive weapon" for the purposes of s.1(1) of the Prevention of Crime Act 1953 (c. 14) (*Houghton* v. *Chief Constable of Greater Manchester* (1987) 84 Cr.App.R. 319). But neither a machete in a scabbard nor a powerful catapult came within the definition of "offensive weapon" contained in s.1(4) (*Southwell* v. *Chadwick* (1987) 85 Cr.App.R. 235). A sword-stick is an offensive weapon even though primarily carried to correct a difficulty in walking (*R.* v. *Butler* [1988] Crim.L.R. 695). A domestic carving knife is not an "offensive weapon" for the purposes of s.1(4) where there was no evidence that the person carrying it intended to hurt others with it but there was evidence that he intended to harm himself. Section 1(4) of the 1953 Act should be so construed as to require an intention to cause injury to some person other than oneself (*R.* v. *Fleming* [1989] Crim.L.R. 71). A rice flail can be an "offensive weapon" within the meaning of this section (*Copus* v. *DPP* [1989] Crim.L.R. 577).

OFFER. "To . . . offer to supply a controlled drug to another" (Misuse of Drugs Act 1971 (c. 38), s.4(1)(*b*)). The offence of offering to supply a controlled drug is complete under this section when the offer is made. It was no defence to show that the accused had not intended to supply the drug (*R.* v. *Goddard* [1992] Crim.L.R. 588).

(Insolvency Act 1986 (c. 45), s.271(3)). A debtor could make an "offer" of less than half the debt to his one creditor "to secure or compound for a debt" in respect of which a bankruptcy petition had been presented under s.271(3) (*Re A Debtor* (*No. 32 of 1993*) [1995] 1 All E.R. 628).

OFFICE. (21) "Office or employment" (Income and Corporation Taxes Act 1970 (c. 10), s.181). Payments made to a barrister for part-time lecturing were held to be emoluments from an "office or employment" and therefore assessable to income tax under Schedule E (*Sidey* v. *Phillips* [1987] S.T.C. 87). A self-employed senior barristers' clerk was held not to be the holder of an "office" within the meaning of this section (*McMenamin* v. *Diggles* [1991] S.T.C. 419). See also EMOLUMENTS.

The words "office or employment" should be considered in their ordinary sense rather than confined to strictly defined contracts of service, so that a self-employed accountant fell within the subsection (*R.* v. *Callender* [1992] 3 All E.R. 51). A freelance vision mixer involved in the production of television programmes was held not to be the holder of an "office" within the meaning of the section (*Hall* v. *Lorimer, The Times,* November 18, 1993).

"Office or employment" (Theft Act 1968 (c. 60), s.16(2)(*c*)). The tenancy of a public house granted to a tenant who made several false statements in his tenancy application was held not to be an "office or employment" for the purposes of this section (*R.* v. *McNiff* [1986] Crim.L.R. 57).

"Office activities," Stat. Def., Health and Safety (Enforcing Authority) Regulations 1998 (No. 494), reg. 2(1).

"Office-holder," Stat. Def., "includes employee or other post-holder" (Scotland Act 1998 (c. 46), s.15(3)); and see EMPLOYMENT.

In the execution of his office, see EXECUTION.

OFFICER. "Officer of a company" (Companies Act 1985 (c. 6), s.727). An administrator is an "officer of a company" within the meaning of this section and can therefore be the subject of an order absolving him from possible liability (*Re Home Treat* [1991] BCC 165).

A London Underground ticket collector is "an officer" of the Company for the purposes, under s.5(2) of the Regulation of Railways Act 1889 (c. 57), of detaining a person who had failed to produce a ticket and refused to supply her name and address (*Moberly* v. *Alsop* [1992] C.O.D. 190).

"Assaults an officer of the court" (County Courts Act 1984 (c. 28), s.14(1)), see ASSAULT.

In relation to body corporate, Stat. Def., Social Security Administration Act 1992 (c. 5), s.121C(9) inserted by Social Security Act 1998 (c. 41), s.64.

In relation to public authority, Stat. Def., Civil Evidence Act 1995 (c. 38), s.9(4).

In relation to body corporate, Stat. Def., Competition Act 1998 (c. 41), s.59(1).

OFFSHORE INSTALLATION. Stat. Def., Merchant Shipping (Salvage and Pollution) Act 1994 (c. 28), s.8(5).

OIL. Stat. Def., Income and Corporation Taxes Act 1988 (c. 1), s.502.

Stat. Def., Merchant Shipping Act 1995 (c. 21), s.173(10)).

"Oil or gas," Stat. Def., "means (a) any mineral oil or any relative hydrocarbon which, in its natural state, is not a solid; or (b) methane or any other natural gas" (Coal Industry Act 1994 (c. 21), s.9(6)).

"Crude oil," Stat. Def., Merchant Shipping (Fire Protection: Large Ships) Regulations 1998 (No. 1012), reg. 1(2).

OMISSION. For the purposes of s.153(1) of the Employment Protection (Consolidation) Act 1978 (c. 44) "omission" has to be given its ordinary and natural meaning, so that the non-payment of money or the denial of a benefit can be an "omission," notwithstanding that there was no obligation on the part of the employer to make the payment or grant the benefit (*National Coal Board* v. *Ridgway* [1987] 3 All E.R. 582).

ON ACCOUNT OF. "On account of another" (Theft Act 1968 (c. 60), s.5(3)). Although a publican had contracted to sell on his employer's premises only beer supplied by the employer, payment received by the publican for the sale of beer clandestinely obtained elsewhere was not received "on account of" the employer (*Att.-Gen.'s Reference (No. 1 of 1985)* [1986] A.C. 909).

ON ANY OCCASION. "On any occasion" under the Contempt of Court Act 1981 (c. 49), s.14(1) meant the date upon which sentence was passed regardless of the number of applications which were before the court on that date (*Villiers* v. *Villiers* [1994] 2 All E.R. 149).

ON BEHALF. (7) *Gaspet* v. *Ellis* [Main Work, p. 1762], appeal dismissed ([1987] 1 W.L.R. 769).

ONE EVENT. An underwriter's negligence in failing on a number of occasions to investigate an underlying problem of asbestosis each time he underwrote a policy could not fall within the ordinary meaning of "one event" so as to qualify for an indemnity (*Caudle* v. *Sharp*, Lloyd's List, August 3, 1995).

ON DEMAND. Money payable "on demand" was payable immediately upon demand being made, allowing only such time as was necessary to implement the mechanics of payment (*Bank of Baroda* v. *Panesar* [1986] 3 All E.R. 751.

ON DUTY. "Period . . . on duty," see PERIOD.

ON THE LIFE OF ANY PERSON. To qualify as a policy of insurance "on the life of a person," a sum of money or other benefit had to be payable on an event uncertain as to its timing or as to its happening at all and dependent on the contingencies of human life so that a sum payable on the surrender of the policy was not a contract of insurance on the life of a person (*Fuji Finance Inc.* v. *Aetna Insurance Co.* [1994] 3 W.L.R. 1280).

OPEN. "Open to the public." A solicitor who practised from his home, corresponding with clients from that address, which had no nameplate, and meeting them where necessary elsewhere, did not have an office "open to the public" within the meaning of rule 2(*b*) of the Solicitors Practice Rules 1975 (*Re a Solicitor* (1987) 131 S.J. 1086).

"Open to the public" (Council Regulation No. 3820/85/EEC (OJ 1985 No. L370 pl), Art. 1(1)). The roads at Heathrow Airport owned by the British Airport Authorities are "open to the public" for the purposes of this article, and tachograph regulations applied to goods vehicles using those roads (*DPP* v. *Cargo Handling* [1992] RTR 318).

OPEN MARKET. For the purposes of s.34 of the Landlord and Tenant Act 1954 (c. 56) "open market" includes a situation to create a market, a willing lessor and a willing lessee, a reasonable period in which to negotiate the letting, the negotiations to be at arm's length, the property to be freely exposed to the market, and no account to be taken of any higher rent that might be paid by a potential lessee with a special interest (*Baptist* v. *Masters of the Bench and Trustees of the Honourable Society of Gray's Inn* [1993] 42 EG 287).

OPEN SPACE. A building which was used for country recreation and which enhanced the beauty of an open space was capable of forming "part of an open space" for the purposes of the Town and Country Planning Act 1959 (c. 53), s.26(2) as amended by the Local Government Planning and Land Act 1980 (c. 65), Sched. 23 (*R.* v. *Plymouth City Council, ex p. Freeman* (1987) 19 H.L.R. 328).

"Open space" (Local Government Act 1972 (c. 70), s.123(2A) as amended by the Local Government Planning and Land Act 1980 (c. 65), Sched. 23, Pt. V). Doncaster Common, or Town Moor, is an "open space" within the meaning of this section (*R.* v. *Doncaster Metropolitan Borough Council, ex p. Braim* (1987) 85 L.G.R. 233).

A pattern of private gardens is capable of being an "open space" for the purposes of the Secretary of State's Circular No. 8 of 1987 which designated "open spaces," *inter alia*, as capable of contributing to the special character of a conservation area, and therefore requiring "special attention" under s.277 of the Town and Country Planning Act 1971 (c. 78) (*Ward* v. *Secretary of State for the Environment* [1990] 1 P.L.R. 85).

Stat. Def., Channel Tunnel Rail Link Act 1996 (c. 61), s.5(6).

OPENING. (2) A three-sided loading bay at one end of a factory was not an "opening in the floor" within the meaning of s.28(4) of the Factories Act 1961 (c. 34) (*Allen* v. *Avon Rubber Co.* [1986] I.C.R. 695).

OPERATE. "Operate private hire vehicles" (Local Government (Miscellaneous Provisions) Act 1976 (c. 57), s.55(1)). A mini-cab operator whose offices were based outside a controlled district, within which an operator's licence was required under this section, did not "operate" within the controlled area merely by advertising his firm in a directory which circulated in the controlled area (*Windsor and Maidenhead Royal Borough Council* v. *Khan* [1994] R.T.R. 87).

The term "operate" in the Local Government (Miscellaneous Provisions) Act 1976 (c. 57), s.46(1)(*e*) should be given the narrow interpretation provided in s.80(1) (*Adur District Council* v. *Fry* (CO25/95), April 7, 1995).

A ship was being "operated" not only when at sea but also when in port, afloat, whether under repair or loading or unloading cargo (*Littlejohn* v. *Wood & Davidson* (O.H.), *The Scotsman*, December 6, 1995).

OPERATION. The word "operation" in s.29 of the Wildlife and Country-side Act 1981 (c. 69) is wide enough to include agricultural activities (*Sweet* v. *Secretary of State for the Environment* [1989] 2 P.L.R. 14).

"Other operations in, on, over or under land" (Town and Country Planning Act 1971 (c. 78), s.22(1)), see DEVELOPMENT.

"Supplied to a ship for her operation," see GOODS.

In military context, Stat. Def., "includes exercises and other activities" (Landmines Act 1998 (c. 33), s.5(7)).

OPPRESSION. (Police and Criminal Evidence Act 1984 (c. 60), s.76(2)(*a*)). Merely holding someone in police custody cannot amount to "oppression" for the purposes of this section (*R.* v. *Fulling* [1987] 2 W.L.R. 923). A series of police procedural irregularities, preceding the accused's confession, were held to have amounted to "oppression" (*R.* v. *Davison* [1988] Crim.L.R. 442).

OPTION. Stat. Def., includes right of first refusal (Landlord and Tenant (Covenants) Act 1995 (c. 30), s.1(7)).

OR. "Knowingly contravenes or . . . fails to comply" (Housing Act 1985 (c. 68), s.369(5)). "Or" is here used disjunctively so that the subsection creates two separate offences (*Wandsworth London Borough Council* v. *Sparling* (1988) 20 H.L.R. 169).

(Material Causes Act 1973 (c. 42), s.31). "Or until further order" in s.31 envisaged the making of a further order before original order ceased to have effect (*G* v. *G* [1997] 2 W.L.R. 614).

ORAL EVIDENCE. Stat. Def., Civil Evidence Act 1995 (c. 38), s.13.

ORALLY. "Orally or in a document" (Civil Evidence Act 1968 (c. 64), s.2). Statements recorded without the speaker's knowledge were made "orally" not "in a document" and were inadmissible unless proved as required by direct oral evidence. Statements recorded with knowledge and consent were made "in a document" and "orally" (*Ventouris* v. *Mountain* (*No. 2*); *The Italian Express* [1992] 3 All E.R. 414).

ORDER. "Order appointing a receiver or sequestrator of land" (Land Charges Act 1925 (c. 22), s.6(1)(*b*)). Such orders were not limited to receiverships which could bind a purchaser but applied to any receivership of land. Thus, an order appointing a receiver to manage a block of flats would be registrable under this Act (*Clayhope Properties* v. *Evans* [1986] 2 All E.R. 795).

An order of the court in ancillary relief proceedings following divorce was not an "order" made under s.24 of the Matrimonial Causes Act 1973

(c. 18) (*R.* v. *Rushmoor Borough Council, ex p. Barrett* [1986] 2 All E.R. 795).

(Matrimonial Causes Act 1973 (c. 18), s.23(1), as amended by the Matrimonial and Family Proceedings Act 1984 (c. 42), s.5(2)). The words "or until further order" meant "further order in the meantime" and could not revive an order for periodical payments after the term for repayment had expired. Further the provision in s.23(1) of the 1973 Act that "the court could make any one or more of the following orders" including not only the orders in paragraphs (a) to (f) but any one or more of the orders within a paragraph (*G.* v. *G. (Periodical Payments)* [1997] 2 W.L.R. 614).

Undertakings expressed to last "until trial of further order" came to an end or were discharged upon determination of the action, or as soon as it was automatically struck out under C.C.R., Ord. 17, r.11(9) (*Patel* v. *Patel* [1996] 7 C.L. 80).

The relevant part of a sentence fixed by the trial judge under the Criminal Justice Act 1991 (c. 53), s.34 amounts to an "order" (*R.* v. *Dalton* [1995] 2 W.L.R. 377).

ORDINARILY RESIDENT. (12) "Ordinarily resident" (British Nationality Act 1981 (c. 61), s.7(2)(*c*)). A person who overstayed a limited leave to remain in the United Kingdom was here unlawfully, even if he had acted inadvertently and was not criminally liable. He was, therefore, for the purposes of this section, not "resident" during the relevant period (*Chelliah* v. *Immigration Appeal Tribunal* (1986) 83 L.S.Gaz.) A United Kingdom citizen, who left to begin new employment in Hong Kong, ceased to be "ordinarily resident" in the United Kingdom on the date of departure, notwithstanding that he received payment from his United Kingdom job up to a date beyond the day of departure (*R.* v. *Immigration Appeal Tribunal, ex p. Ng* [1986] Imm.A.R. 23).

(12) For the purposes of the Immigration Act 1971 (c. 77), s.2 and the Immigration Rules made under that Act it is possible for a person to be "ordinarily resident" in two places at once. The requirement for ordinary residence is a settled purpose, specific or general, such as, in this case, the intention to establish a home for the family and to live in it permanently (*Britto* v. *Secretary of State for the Home Department* [1984] Imm.A.R. 93).

(17). Where a person was so mentally handicapped that she was totally dependent on a parent or guardian she was, for the purposes of the National Assistance Act 1948 (c. 29), ss.21(1), 24 and the National Health Service Act 1977 (c. 49) "ordinarily resident" with the parent or guardian (*R.* v. *Waltham Forest London Borough Council, ex p. Vale, The Times,* February 25, 1985; *R.* v. *Redbridge London Borough Council, ex p. East Sussex County Council* [1993] C.O.D. 256).

A person who tries repeatedly to obtain leave to enter the U.K. but is prevented by reason of the Secretary of State's decisions against him could not be said to be "ordinarily resident" in the U.K. within the meaning of the Immigration Act 1971 (c. 77), ss.3(5)(*b*), 71(1) (*R.* v. *Secretary of State for the Home Department, ex p. Butta (Mohammed)* [1994] Imm.A.R. 197).

A corporation was "ordinarily resident" outside the jurisdiction for the purposes of R.S.C., Ord. 23, r.1(1)(*a*) if the central management and control of the company abides and is exercised overseas (*Re Little Olympian Each Ways* [1995] 1 W.L.R. 560).

"Ordinarily Resident" (Education (Mandatory Awards) Regulations 1983 (No. 1135), reg. 5(4)). The applicant for a study grant, who had lived for 13 years in Hong Kong where her father was employed, was not "ordinarily resident" in Lancashire, notwithstanding that the family came from there, intended to return there, and had a house there (*R.* v. *Lancashire County Council, ex p. Huddleston* [1986] 2 All E.R. 941).

Where a child subject to a care order was not resident in any local authority, s.31(8)(*b*) of the Children Act 1989 (c. 41) should be interpreted as if it read "where the child does not ordinarily reside" in a local authority area, otherwise any child who was resident but not ordinarily resident within a local authority area would fall between s.31(8)(*a*) and (*b*) (*Gateshead MBC* v. *B.*, *The Times*, March 19, 1996).

ORDINARILY WORKS. "Ordinarily works outside Great Britain" (Employment Protection (Consolidation) Act 1978 (c.44), s.141(2)). A merchant seaman employed under a crew agreement entered into in England for employment on a ship registered in Great Britain, but used solely for Caribbean cruising, worked "ordinarily" outside Great Britain for the purposes of this section (*Wood* v. *Cunard Line* [1990] IRLR 281). An employee did not "ordinarily" work outside Great Britain just because his contract of employment required him to work wherever in the world his employer specified (*Somali Bank* v. *Rahman* [1989] I.C.R. 314). A man who, at the time of his dismissal, had been required to work in the U.K. was held to have worked "ordinarily" in Great Britain, notwithstanding that for a substantial part of the previous two years he had been required to work in Germany (*Weston* v. *Vega Space Systems Engineering* [1989] IRLR 429).

ORDINARY. Where the terms of a Mareva injunction restrained the defendant from dealing with any of his assets, save for a fixed sum for ordinary living expenses, "ordinary living expenses" meant the ordinary expenses necessary to sustain the standard of living to which he was reasonably accustomed. They did not cover exceptional expenses such as legal fees (*T.D.K. Tape Distributor (U.K.)* v. *Videochoice* [1985] 3 All E.R. 345).

Any application other than an originating application was an "ordinary application" under the Insolvency Rules 1986 (No. 1925), r.7.2 (*Port* v. *Auger* [1994] 3 All E.R. 200).

"Ordinary share capital." Stat. Def., Income and Corporation Taxes Act 1988 (c. 1), s.832.

ORDINARY COURSE OF BUSINESS. Plaintiffs who were suing architects for professional negligence could not obtain an injunction under the *Mareva* jurisdiction to restrain the architects from settling claims under their professional indemnity insurance policy without the plaintiff's consent, since the bona fide settlement of such claims would be a transaction in the "ordinary course of business" (*Normid Housing Association* v. *Ralphs and Mansell* [1989] 1 Lloyd's Rep. 265 & 274).

Expenditure incurred defending an unfair prejudice petition was held not to have been incurred in the "ordinary course of business" for the purposes of the Insolvency Act 1986 (c. 45) (*Re Crossmore Electrical and Civil Engineering* (1989) 5 BCC 37).

Whether a transaction had taken place "in the ordinary course of business" was a matter to be determined objectively by reference to business practices in the commercial world, the ordinary operational activities of a business as a going concern, the past practices of a company and its dealings with creditors. A payment made to secure the consent or a lessor to the assignment of the lessee's interest in circumstances where the lessee was disposing of his interest in the business was not made "in the ordinary course of business" *Countrywide Banking Corporation Ltd* v. *Dean* [1998] 2 W.L.R. 441).

ORGAN. "Organs of the state" (EEC Equal Treatment Directive 76/207, Art. 5(1)) could include a body, whatever its legal form, which had been made responsible for providing a public service under the control of the State and had for that purpose special powers beyond those applicable in relations between individuals (*Foster* v. *British Gas* [1991] 2 W.L.R. 1075; *Doughty* v. *Rolls-Royce* [1992] IRLR 126).

ORGANISE. "Organised daytime study" (Immigration Rules 1983, H.C. 169, paras. 21, 22, 107). "To be organised there must be the organiser making the rules and the organised who adheres to the rules. The organiser must set the task and, it seems to be in context, require it to be done at a specific time, at a specific place and under supervision". *Per* Henry J. (*R.* v. *Immigration Appeal Tribunal, ex p. Idiaro* [1991] Imm.A.R. 546).

ORIGINAL. "An original set-off or counterclaim" (Limitation Act 1980 (c. 58), s.35(3)). A claim by one defendant against another defendant for contribution was not "an original set-off or counterclaim" within the meaning of this section (*Kennet* v. *Brown* [1988] 1 W.L.R. 582).

(Copyright Act 1956 (c. 74), s.2). "Original" does not require original or inventive thought but only that the work should not be copied and should originate from the author (*Bookmakers' Afternoon Greyhound Services* v. *Wilf. Gilbert* (*Staffordshire*) [1994] F.S.R. 723).

The words "original buildings of 1909–1915 only" referred not only to the period of their construction but also to the period of planning, conception, design and, to an extent, the realisation of the designer's work (*City of Edinburgh Council* v. *Secretary of State for Scotland* [1998] 1 All E.R. 174).

ORIGINAL PURPOSES. (Charities Act 1960 (c. 58), s.13). Where the charitable purpose of a gift of land for use as playing fields for the benefit and enjoyment of the inhabitants of an area could be carried on on other land, it was held that the retention of the existing site was not part of the "original purposes" of the charity, so that the court had power to authorise the sale or exchange of any part of the land (*Oldham Borough Council* v. *Att.-Gen.* (1992) 136 S.J.(LB) 252).

ORIGINATING CAUSE. A "cause" could amount to a continuing state of affairs while the time, place and occurrence of an "event" was particular to it (*Axa Reinsurance (U.K.) plc* v. *Field* [1996] 1 W.L.R. 1026).

OTHER. "Other evidence" (Affiliation Proceedings Act 1957 (c. 55), s.4(1) as amended by Affiliation Proceedings (Amendment) Act 1972 (c. 49), s.1(1)). A report of the result of blood tests can be "other evidence" capable of corroborating the evidence of the mother of an illegitimate baby in proceedings under this Act (*Turner* v. *Blunden* [1986] Fam. 120). As also can the failure of the alleged father to comply with a direction that he submit to a blood test (*McVeigh* v. *Beattie* [1988] 2 W.L.R. 992).

"Other offences" (Magistrates' Courts Act 1980 (c. 43), s.128(8)(*a*)). These words are not to be construed as referring only to offences unrelated to those already charged. So that where the accused were already charged with conspiracy to rob, which could encompass a number of individual robberies then those individual robberies could be considered "other offences" within the meaning of the section (*R.* v. *Bailey*; *R.* v. *Smith, The Times*, March 22, 1993).

"Other needs" (Social Security Act 1986 (c. 50), s.32) does not mean "all other needs" (*R.* v. *Secretary of State for Social Services, ex p. Stitt; R.* v. *Same, ex p. Healey; R.* v. *Social Fund Inspector, ex p. Ellison* [1992] C.O.D. 335).

"Other instrument" (Education (Mandatory Awards) Regulations 1990 (No. 1628), Sched. 3, para. 5(5)). These words were held to be sufficiently wide to include an order of the county court made without the parties' consent (*R.* v. *Sheffield City Council, ex p. Parker, The Times*, June 29, 1993).

"Other legal proceedings" (Companies Act 1985 (c. 6), s.726). This phrase refers to any matter in which the jurisdiction of the court is invoked by an originating process, other than a writ. It applies to a person who has invoked the jurisdiction by whatever originating process, including a petition. The word "plaintiff" in s.726 covers such a person. Accordingly an application for security for costs can be made against a person who brings a petition under s.459 of the 1985 Act (*Re Unisoft Group No. 1; Saunderson Holdings* v. *Unisoft Group* [1993] BCLC 1292).

A limited company which presented a petition under s.459 was a plaintiff in an action of "other legal proceedings" within the meaning of s.726(1) and could be ordered to give security for costs (*Re Unisoft Group E* [1994] B.C.C. 11).

"Other legal process" within the meaning of the Insolvency Act 1986 (c. 45), s.11(3)(*d*) did not include the taking of a non-judicial step, such as the service of a notice under the contract of a lease (*Scottish Exhibition Centre* v. *Mirestrop (In Administration) (No. 2)*, 1996 S.L.T. 8).

(Insolvency Act 1986 (c. 45), s.11(3)). The words "proceedings" and "legal process" in s.11(3) embraced all legal proceedings from the initiation of proceedings to the enforcement of judgment but did not include non-judicial steps such as the levying of distress, so that peaceable re-entry by a landlord which had not required the assistance of the court did not require leave under s.252(2) (*A Debtor, Re: No. 13A/10/95 and A Debtor, Re; No. 14A/10/95*) [1996] 1 All E.R. 691).

Pre-trial proceedings are "other proceedings" within the meaning of Legal Aid in Criminal and Care Proceedings (General) Regulations 1989 (No. 344), reg. 10 (*R.* v. *Liverpool City Magistrates' Court, ex p. Pender (No. 2)* [1994] 2 All E.R. 897). Complaints and applications to an industrial tribunal were "other proceedings" in the Insolvency Act 1986 (c. 45), s.11(3)(*d*) and an application made without the prior consent of the administrator was not a nullity (*Carr* v. *British International Helicopters (in administration)* [1994] I.C.R. 18).

"If . . . the court is satisfied, on other grounds," (Insolvency Rules 1986 (No. 1925)r.6.5(4)(*d*)). A debtor's offer to give security over shares held by him but not presently realisable, did not constitute "other grounds" within the meaning of this rule (*Re a Debtor (No. 415/SD/1993)* [1994] 1 W.L.R. 917).

(Local Government Finance Act 1988 (c. 41)). A demountable aerial ropeway used by pedestrians to cross a harbour during the summer months was a road crossing over a watercourse within the meaning of Sched. 5, para. 1A of the 1988 Act, and was accordingly not a rateable hereditament, but amounted to an "other construction" under Sched. 5, para. 18A. The fact that it was dismountable was irrelevant to the issue (*Griffin* v. *Sansom (Valuation Officer)* [1996] R.A. 454).

"Other records" (Bankers' Books Evidence Act 1879 (c. 11), s.9), see BANKER (5).

"Other financial resources," see FINANCIAL RESOURCES.

"Other legal process," see LEGAL PROCESS.

"Other payment," see PAYMENT.

OTHER PERSON. "To kill that other or a third person" (Offences against the Person Act 1861 (c. 100), s.16 as substituted by the Criminal Law Act 1977 (c. 45), Sched. 12). A foetus *in utero* was held not to be an "other or a third person" within the meaning of this section (*R.* v. *Tait* [1989] 3 W.L.R. 891).

"Other person lawfully acting in the execution of this Act," see LAW-FULLY. "Act or default of some other person," see ACT.

OTHER SIMILAR OFFICER. (R.S.C. 1981 Ord. 65, r.3(1)). An employee of a foreign body corporate carrying on business in England, who was in England and was in charge of its business there, albeit as a junior employee, fell within the description of "other similar officer" on whom personal service on the body corporate could properly be effected pursuant to Ord. 65, r.3(1) (*Kuwait Airways Corp.* v. *Iraqi Airways Co. and ors* [1995] 3 All E.R. 694).

OTHER PROCEEDINGS. See PROCEEDINGS.

OTHERWISE. "Otherwise than for profit" (Value Added Tax Act 1983 (c. 55), Sched. 6, Group 6, Item 2). A company which carried on, as its only activity, an educational establishment was held to provide education "otherwise than for profit," notwithstanding that it budgeted for and achieved a surplus of income over expenditure, the surplus being applied for educational charitable purposes only (*Customs and Excise Commissioners* v. *Bell Concord Educational Trust* [1989] 2 W.L.R. 679).

"Whether fraudulently or otherwise" (Social Security Act 1986 (c. 50), s.53(1) means "whether fraudulently or not." A claim that "otherwise" should be construed *ejusdem generis* with fraudulently failed (*Page* v. *Chief Adjudication Officer, The Times,* July 4, 1991).

"Otherwise than in consequence of the accident" (Social Security Administration Act 1992 (c. 5), s.98(1)(*b*)).

Post-accident benefits recouped by the Secretary of State out of agreed compensation for an accident were paid as a direct result of that accident

(*Hassall and anr* v. *Secretary of State for Social Security* [1995] 3 All E.R. 911).

OUTER SPACE. Stat. Def., Outer Space Act 1986 (c. 38), s.13.

OUTHOUSE. (Leasehold Reform, Housing and Urban Development Act 1993 (c. 28), s.62). A storeroom which was within the curtilage of the building, although not within the curtilage of the flat itself, was an "appurtenance" although it was not an "outhouse" since it was within the same building and not outside it or in the grounds of the block (*Cadogan* v. *McGirk* [1996] 4 All E.R. 643).

OUTRAGING PUBLIC DECENCY. The offence of outraging public decency consists of the deliberate and actual commission of an act which is, *per se,* lewd or obscene; evidence of motive or intent cannot supply the element of lewdness or obscenity to an act which itself lacked it (*R.* v. *Rowley* [1991] 1 W.L.R. 1020).

OUTSIDE. "Duties ... performed ... outside the United Kingdom" (Finance Act 1977 (c. 36), Sched. 7, para. 2(1)(*a*)). Periods spent within the U.K. on days off cannot be attributed to duties performed "outside" the U.K. (*Leonard* v. *Blanchard, The Times*, February 16, 1993).

"Supplied outside the United Kingdom" (Value Added Tax Act 1983 (c. 55), s.6(3)). Where U.K. customers visited overseas premises to inspect a machine in working order, and the machine was then dismantled, transported to the U.K. and reassembled it was held to have been "supplied outside the United Kingdom" within the meaning of this section (*George Kuikka* v. *Customs and Excise Commissioners* (1990) 3 VATTR 185).

"The person who made the statement is outside the United Kingdom" (Criminal Justice Act 1988 (c. 33), s.23(2)(*b*)(i)). A consular official who was unwilling to give evidence in a criminal trial was not, by virtue of her diplomatic status which might make her immune to the process, deemed to be "outside the United Kingdom" for the purposes of this section (*R.* v. *Jiminez-Paez* (1994) 98 Cr.App.R. 239).

OUTSTANDING DEBT. A tax liability which was not immediately payable and was to be discharged from year to year in the ordinary manner was not an "outstanding debt" (*McCormick* v. *McCormick* (O.H.), 1994 S.C.L.R. 958).

OVERCROWDING. Stat. Def., Housing Act 1985 (c. 68), s.324.

OVERRIDING INTEREST. The interest of tenants in common who were in actual occupation of registered land was an "overriding interest" within the meaning of s.70(1)(*g*) of the Land Registration Act 1925 (c. 21) (*City of London Building Society* v. *Flegg* [1986] 2 W.L.R. 616). The interest of a wife in occupation of the matrimonial home, who had paid money to a company under the control of herself and her ex husband, and which had purchased that home, was an "overriding interest" within the meaning of the section (*Winkworth* v. *Edward Baron Development Co.* (1986) 130 S.J. 72). An agreement made pursuant to s.38 of the Housing Act 1980 (c. 51) created a public right which was an "overriding interest" within the meaning of s.70 of the 1925 Act. So that where an owner of land entered into an agreement with a highway authority, pursuant to the section, whereby land was to be dedicated as a public highway maintainable at the public expense at some future date, and before that date was reached the land was transferred to a subsequent purchaser, and the agreement had not been registered in the charges register, the subsequent purchaser was bound by the agreement (*Overseas Investment Services* v. *Simcobuild Construction, The Times,* November 2, 1993).

(Family Law Act 1986 (c. 55), s.46). A Jewish "get" divorce, written in England but delivered to the other spouse in Israel was a transnational divorce and could not be recognised as an "overseas divorce" within the meaning of s.46 of the 1986 Act (*Berkovits* v. *Grinberg (Attorney-General intervening)* [1995] 1 FLR 477).

OVERSEAS. "Overseas institution," Stat. Def., Banking Act 1987 (c. 22), s.74.

"Overseas securities," Stat. Def., Finance (No. 2) Act 1997 (c. 58), s.26(5).

OWE. "Any sum owed" (Consumer Credit Act 1974 (c. 39), s.129(2)(*a*)) means any sum already in arrears, and not those payable but not yet due (*Ashbroom Facilities* v. *Bodley* [1992] CCLR 31). "Any sum owed" could include the whole sum due when considering an application under the Consumer Act 1974 (c. 39), s.129 (*Murie McDougall* v. *Sinclair*, 1994 S.L.T. (Sh.Ct.) 74).

OWNER. (Housing Benefits Regulations 1982 (No. 1124), r.2(1)). A person who was one of three trustees for sale in respect of the property in which she resided, and who held a beneficial interest in the property as one of the tenants in common, was not the "owner" for the purposes of this regulation (*R.* v. *Sedgemoor District Council Housing Benefit Review Board, ex p. Weaden* (1986) 84 L.G.R. 850).

(48)–(50) "Owner" in section 21(4)(*b*) of the Supreme Court Act 1981 (c. 54) means "registered owner" and is to be contrasted with "beneficial owner" in paragraphs (i) and (ii) of that section (*The EVPO Agnic* [1988] 1 W.L.R. 1090).

"Owner" was capable of meaning the person liable under a bill of lading (*The Stolt Loyalty* [1995] 1 Lloyd's Rep. 598).

(Road Traffic Act 1991 (c. 40), s.82(3)). A disposition of a vehicle sufficient to rebut the presumption of ownership had to be such so as to require notification of a change of ownership under the Road Vehicles (Registration and Licensing) Regulations 1971 so that merely leaving a vehicle at a garage for repair did not amount to its disposition (*R.* v. *Parking Adjudicator, ex p. Wandsworth LBC* [1998] RTR 51).

(Local Government and Housing Act 1989 (c. 42), s.104(2)). An equitable interest in property was sufficient to give an "owner's interest" within the meaning of s.104(2) (*R.* v. *Tower Hamlets LBC, ex p. von Goetz* [1999] 2 W.L.R. 582).

Stat. Def., Housing Act 1985 (c. 68), s.237; Copyright Designs and Patents Act 1988 (c. 48), s.173; Road Traffic Act 1988 (c. 52), s.192; Road

Traffic Offenders Act 1988 (c. 53), s.68; Local Government and Housing Act 1989 (c. 42), s.138; Town and Country Planning Act 1990 (c. 8), s.336; Water Industry Act 1991 (c. 56), s.219; Water Resources Act 1991 (c. 57), s.221; Local Government Finance Act 1992 (c. 14), s.6.

"Owner of a vehicle," Stat. Def., Road Traffic Act 1991 (c. 40), s.82(2).

In relation to land, Stat. Def., Goods Vehicles (Licensing of Operators) Act 1995 (c. 23), s.58(1); Environment Protection Act 1990 (c. 43), s.78A(9) inserted by Environment Act 1995 (c. 25), s.57.

"Owner's interest," Stat. Def., Housing Grants, Construction and Regeneration Act 1996 (c. 53), s.140(1).

OWNER OCCUPIER. Stat. Def., Housing Act 1985 (c. 68), s.237.

P

PACKAGE. (Hague Rules, Art. IV, r.5). For the purposes of Art. IV, r.5 of the Hague Rules, where parcels of cargo were loaded in containers, it was the parcels and not the containers which constituted the relevant "packages" (*The River Gurara* [1997] 4 All E.R. 498). "Packages" under the Hague Rules Art. IV, r.5 referred to the number of items in each container rather than the number of containers themselves since the purpose of the Hague Rules was to prevent shipowners from restricting liability for losses by the terms of their contracts (*The River Gurara* [1998] Q.B. 610).

Stat. Def., Weights and Measures Act 1985 (c. 72), s.68.

PACKINGS. In the Annex to EEC Council Reg. 950/68 as amended by Reg. 333/83 "packings" included beer barrels, beer bottles and plastic crates for beer barrels, and this was held to apply even where those containers were to be returned to the seller of the beer in a non-EEC country (*Firma Albert Schmid* v. *Hauptzollamt Stuttgart-West (No. 357/87)* [1990] 1 C.M.L.R. 605).

PAID. (Child Support Act 1991 (c. 48), s.6(1)). "Paid" in s.6(1) meant "actually paid" rather than "lawfully paid" so that even if state benefits were being unlawfully claimed by a parent with care, the Secretary of State was still entitled to recover maintenance from the absent parent (*Secretary of State for Social Security* v. *Harmon, The Times,* June 10, 1998).

PARENT. The unmarried cohabitee of a mother was not a "parent" for the purposes of the financial provisions for children contained in Sched. 1 to the Children Act 1989 (c. 41) (*J.* v. *J.* (*A Minor; Property Transfer*) [1993] 2 F.L.R. 56). A person who had had his or her parental rights removed remained a parent for the purposes of the Children Act 1975 (c. 72) until an adoption order was pronounced (*D.* v. *Grampian Regional Council,* 1994 S.L.T. 1038). A court order under the Adoption Act 1976 (c. 36) freeing a child for adoption removed any parental responsibility that a natural father might have had so that he was not a "parent" for the purposes of the Children Act 1989 (c. 41) (*Re C (Minors) (Adoption): Residence Order*), *The Times,* November 19, 1992).

(Adoption Act 1976 (c. 36), s.16). A putative father is not a "parent" for the purposes of this Act (*Re L (a Minor) (Adoption)* [1991] 1 F.L.R. 171).

The natural mother of an adopted child with whom she had had no contact for three and a half years was not a "parent" within the meaning of s.10 of the 1989 Act (*Re S (a Minor), The Times,* March 8, 1993). Once an adoption order has been made a natural parent is no longer a "parent" for the purposes of s.10 of the 1989 Act and accordingly would require leave to apply for a contact order under s.8 (*Re C. (A Minor) (Adopted Child: Contact)* [1993] 3 W.L.R. 85).

(Adoption Act 1976 (c. 36), s.72 as amended by Children Act 1989 (c. 41), Sched. 10). "Parent" under s.72(1) of the 1976 Act meant a parent with parental responsibility for the child under the Children Act 1989 unless the context otherwise required (*Re C. (A Minor) (Adoption: Parties)* [1995] 2 FLR 483).

"Parent" meant biological parent rather than someone exercising a parental role (*R. v. Governors of La Sainte Union Convent School, ex p. T.* [1996] ELR 98).

Before the enactment of the Human Fertilisation and Embryology Act 1990 (c. 37) a male parent meant a biological parent (*M (Child Support Act: Parentage), Re* [1997] 2 F.L.R. 90).

Education Act 1993 (c. 35), s.169). A parent was one who had full time care on a settled basis for a child so that a foster parent could be included in the definition even though the local authority exercised parental responsibility for the child (*Fairpo v. Humberside C.C.* [1997] 1 All E.R. 183).

PARENTAL RESPONSIBILITY. An order remanding a young person to local authority accommodation under the Children and Young Persons Act 1969 (c. 54), s.23 did not confer parental responsibility on a local authority (*North Yorkshire County Council v. Selby Youth Court Justices* [1995] 1 W.L.R. 1).

PARENT COMPANY. Stat. Def., Companies Act 1989 (c. 40), s.21.

PARLIAMENT. "Parliament" in s.4(1) of the Rates Act 1984 (c. 33) means the House of Commons (*R. v. Secretary of State for the Environment, ex p. Greenwich London Borough Council, The Times,* December 19, 1985).

PART. "Parts, pertinents and others" in a lease covered all heritable property but could not apply to moveables such as floor coverings (*Lowe v. Quayle Munro Ltd,* 1997 S.C.L.R. 701).

"Part of a business," see BUSINESS.

PART WITH. "Part with possession" (Firearms Act 1968 (c. 27), s.57(4)). A person who left two shotguns for safekeeping at the home of another while they went on holiday together had "parted" with possession within the meaning of this section (*Hall v. Cotton* [1986] 3 W.L.R. 681).

See ANY PART.

"Part of an open space," see OPEN SPACE.

PARTICIPATE. "Participate in any treatment" (Abortion Act 1967 (c. 87), s.4(1)). A medical receptionist, required to type letters referring patients for abortion, could not, in so doing, be held to be participating in the treatment for termination of pregnancy authorised by this Act (*R.* v. *Salford Health Authority, ex p. Janaway* [1988] 3 W.L.R. 1350).

PARTICIPATOR. Stat. Def., Income and Corporation Taxes Act 1988 (c. 1), s.417.

PARTICULAR CIRCUMSTANCES. (Animals Act 1971 (c. 22), s.2(2)(*b*)). The tendency of a dog to defend its territory fiercely can amount to "particular circumstances" under this section, even when the animal is known to be generally docile (*Curtis* v. *Betts* [1990] 1 W.L.R. 459).

PARTICULAR SOCIAL GROUP. The members of a group had to share an attribute which existed independently of the feared persecution, which united them and set them apart from the rest of society and which was recognised by society generally in order to qualify as a "particular social group" within the meaning of the Convention and Protocol relating to the Status of Refugees (1951), Art. 14, and women who had been accused of adultery and had been abandoned by their husbands so that they faced persecution in the form of emotional and physical abuse and social ostracism could not form a "particular social group" for the purposes of the Convention (*R.* v. *Immigration Appeal Tribunal, ex p. Shah* [1998] 1 W.L.R. 74).

Persons who shared a common employment did not constitute a social group within the meaning of Art. 1A(2) since the defining characteristic of a social group had to be one which was fundamental to the individual identities or conscience of its members (*Ex p. Shah* [1998] 1 W.L.R. 74 distinguished) (*Ouanes* v. *Secretary of State for the Home Department* [1998] 1 W.L.R. 218).

PARTNER. Stat Def., Housing Grants, Construction and Regeneration Act 1996 (c. 53), s.101.

PARTY. "Party to the action" (R.S.C., Ord. 16, r.8(1)). Where, in an action for damages for negligent damage to cargo, the proceedings against the charterers, the second defendants, had been stayed it was held that, notwithstanding that the proceedings against them had been stayed, they remained a "party to the action" for the purposes of this rule (*Lister (R.A.) & Co.* v. *Thomson (E.G.) (Shipping) (No. 2)* [1987] 1 W.L.R. 1614).

"Party to the proceedings" (R.S.C., Ord. 15, r.12(3)). Represented parties in a representative action were not "party to the proceedings" within the meaning of this rule (*Ventouris* v. *Mountain* (1990) 140 New L.J. 666).

(R.S.C., Ord. 27, r.3). R.S.C., Ord. 27, r.3 required an admission to be made by a party to an action, but did not require that party to be a party to the action at the time the admission was made (*Ellis* v. *Allen* [1914] 1 Ch. 904 followed) (*Standerwick* v. *Royal Ordinance plc* [1996] 8 C.L. 83).

A child, who was a beneficiary of litigation rather than a litigant was not a "party to proceedings" within the meaning of the Tribunals and Inquiries

Act (c. 53), s.11(1) (*S. (A Minor)* v. *Special Educational Needs Tribunal* [1996] 1 W.L.R. 382; [1996] 1 All E.R. 171).

"Proceedings involving . . . the same parties" (Convention on Jurisdiction and the Enforcement of Judgments in Civil and Commercial Matters 1968, Art. 21). "Parties" is not restricted to those domiciled in the contracting states (*Overseas Union Insurance* v. *New Hampshire Insurance*, *The Times*, September 27, 1988).

Where there was sufficient identity between an insurer and his insured that any judgment against one would be regarded as *res judicata* against the other, the insurer and the insured would be considered as the same party for the purposes of Art. 21 of the Convention (*Drouot Assurances SA* v. *Consolidated Metallurgical Industries (CMI Industrial Sites)* [1998] All E.R. (E.C.) 483).

Where some of the parties to an action in a contracting state are the same as those in a subsisting action in another contracting state, the second court must stay its proceedings in respect of those parties, although the proceedings can continue between the other remaining parties (*The Tatry* [1999] 2 W.L.R. 181).

(Supreme Court Act 1981 (c. 54), s.51(6) and (7), as amended by Courts and Legal Services Act 1990 (c. 41), s.4(1)). The term "party" was not an open-ended category and was limited to a person who had been served with notice of, or had intervened in, proceedings by virtue of rules of court or other statutory provision so that a person who elects to oppose an ex parte application for leave to move for judicial review was not a "party" within the meaning of s.51(6) and (7) and 151 of the 1981 Act, and could not apply for a wasted costs order against an unsuccessful applicant's legal representatives (*R.* v. *Camden London Borough Council, ex p. Martin* [1997] 1 W.L.R. 359).

"Party" (Supreme Court Act 1981 (c. 54), s.151). The fact that someone is served with a notice of a party's intention to seek ancillary relief does not automatically make that person a "party" to the proceedings (*T.* v. *T. (Financial Provision)* (1990) 1 F.L.R. 1).

(Tribunals and Enquiries Act 1992 (c. 53), s.11). A "party to proceedings" for the purposes of s.11 of the 1992 Act was a person who was properly before the tribunal according to the terms of any legislation prescribing who might be parties before that tribunal.

(Civil Jurisdiction and Judgments Act 1982 (c. 27), Art. 21). A mere licensee who happened to be working for a plaintiff could not be regarded as the same party as the plaintiff since it was a wholly different legal person and enterprise (*Mecklermedia Corp.* v. *D.C. Congress GmbH* [1998] 1 All E.R. 148).

See ANY PARTY.

PASS. "Shall not pass a custodial sentence" (Criminal Justice Act 1991 (c. 53), s.1(2)). Activating a suspended sentence was not passing a sentence for the purposes of this section (*R.* v. *Crawford* (1994) 98 Cr.App.R. 297).

PASSENGER. (Town Police Causes Act 1847 (c. 89, s.28). Police officers who had been stationed in a public lavatory following complaints, and there witnessed a man masturbating, were not "passengers" within the meaning of this section (*Cheeseman* v. *DPP* [1991] 2 W.L.R. 1105).

(Carriage by Air Acts (Application of Provisions) Order 1967 (S.I. 1967 No. 480), Sched. 1). A policeman killed in a helicopter crash, which had been chartered by the police force for the purposes of surveillance work, was a passenger so that the helicopter operators were liable under the Warsaw Convention 1929 (*Herd* v. *Clyde Helicopters* 1996 S.L.T. 976).

Stat. Def., Convention relating to the Carriage of Passengers and their Luggage by Sea, Article 1(4), reproduced in Sched. 6 to Merchant Shipping Act 1995 (c. 21).

PASSENGER IN TRANSIT. (Immigration Act 1971 (c. 77), s.14). A foreign citizen who was a member of a tour party in Europe was not a "passenger in transit" (*Low (Fui-Chun)* v. *Secretary of State for the Home Department* [1995] Imm.A.R. 435).

PASSPORT. "United Kingdom passport" (Immigration Act 1971 (c. 77), s.3(9) as substituted by Immigration Act 1988 (c. 14), s.3(1)). A British Visitors Passport is not a passport to which this section applies (*R.* v. *Secretary of State for the Home Department, ex p. Minta, The Times,* April 14, 1992).

PATIENT. (3) "At a hospital as a patient" (Road Traffic Act 1972 (c. 20), s.9 as substituted by schedule 8 to the Transport Act 1981 (c. 56)). A motorist who, after an accident, was taken to hospital where he was X-rayed and then discharged, was not still a "patient" at the hospital when requested to provide a breath test in the hospital car park, notwithstanding that he had not yet left the hospital precincts (*Askew* v. *DPP* [1988] RTR 303).

"Any such patient" (Mental Health Act 1983 (c. 20), s.73(2)). A patient who was the subject of a restriction order under s.41 but was found by a mental health review tribunal not to be suffering from a mental illness nevertheless remained a "patient" for the purposes of this section until such time as he was absolutely discharged (*R.* v. *Merseyside Mental Health Review Tribunal, ex p. K* [1990] 1 All E.R. 694).

PAY. (7) An entitlement to benefits under an occupational pension scheme was "pay" for the purposes of Art. 119 EEC Treaty (*Bilka-Kaufhaus GmbH* v. *Weber von Hartz* (No. 170/84) [1987] I.C.R. 110). But a state pension was not (*Roberts* v. *Birds Eye Walls* [1991] I.C.R. 43). In this context "pay" should be given a wide meaning and would include a redundancy payment made under a contractual redundancy scheme (*Hammersmith and Queen Charlotte's Special Health Authority* v. *Cato* [1988] 1 W.L.R. 132; *Barber* v. *Guardian Royal Exchange Assurance Group* [1990] 2 All E.R. 660; *McKechnie* v. *U.B.M. Building Supplies (Southern)* [1991] IRLR 283). But neither a statutory redundancy payment, nor a statutory payment made by the Secretary of State out of the redundancy fund under s.106 of the Employment Protection (Consolidation) Act 1978 (c. 44), were "pay" for the purposes of Art. 119 (*Secretary of State for Employment* v. *Levy* [1989] IRLR 469). Pension payments made under a contracted-out private scheme are "pay" whereas payments made under a statutory social security scheme are not (*Griffin* v. *London Pension Fund Authority* [1993] IRLR 248).

"Pay" (EEC Treaty, Art. 119) does not include unemployment benefit (*Social Security Decision No. R(U) 10/88*).

Compensation for unfair dismissal was "pay" under the EEC Treaty, Art. 119 (*Mediguard Services* v. *Thame* [1994] I.R.L.R. 504 and *R.* v. *Secretary of State for Employment, ex p. Seymour-Smith* [1997] All E.R. 97).

Sums payable by an employer to an employee for failing to give notice to which the employer was entitled were "pay" even though the payments were made after the termination of the employment relationship and made by a person other than the employer for the purposes of Art. 119 of the EEC Treaty (*Clark* v. *Secretary of State for Employment* [1995] I.C.R. 673).

(Employment Protection (Consolidation) Act 1978 (c. 44), ss.54, 64, Sched. 13, paras. 4, 5; E.C. Treaty, Art. 119). Compensation for unfair dismissal constituted "pay" under Art. 119 of the E.C. Treaty (*Warren* v. *Wylie and Wylie* [1994] IRLR 316 and *Methilhill Bowling Club* v. *Hunter* [1995] IRLR 232).

(11) A protective award was "pay" for the purposes of Dir. 80/987 under the Trade Union and Labour Relations (Consolidation) Act 1992 (c. 52), ss.189(3) and 190(5).

PAYABLE. "No remuneration was payable" (Employment Protection (Consolidation) Act 1978 (c. 44), Sched. 14, para. 6(3)). Where an employee agreed to work for whatever the company could afford to pay him it was held that no remuneration was "payable," within the meaning of this paragraph, during those weeks when, as a result of this arrangement, he received nothing at all (*Secretary of State for Employment* v. *Crane* [1988] IRLR 238).

"Payable" (Social Security (Unemployment, Sickness and Invalidity Benefit) Regulations 1983 (No. 1598), reg. 7(1)(k)(iii)) means "due and owing" rather than "has been or will be paid." Thus compensation for unfair dismissal was "payable" for the purposes of this regulation notwithstanding that the claimant was highly unlikely to receive the sums due from her former insolvent employer (*Morton* v. *Chief Adjudication Officer* [1988] IRLR 444).

A sum was "payable" within the meaning of the Powers of Criminal Courts Act 1973 (c. 62), s.35(3)(*b*)(ii) when it was due for payment and also when it would fall due to be paid in the future (*DPP* v. *Scott* (*Thomas*) [1995] RTR 40).

"Payable" in s.35(3)(*b*)(ii) of the Powers of Criminal Courts Act 1973 (c. 62) can refer to compensation which might become payable at a future date, so that the power of magistrates to award compensation is limited to £175 since the other loss is payable by the motor Insurers Bureau (*DPP* v. *Scott* (*Thomas*) [1995] RTR 40).

PAYMENT. "Payment or reward for . . . the adoption" (Adoption Act 1958 (c. 5), s.50(1)). The payment of a sum of money by a childless couple to the natural mother in a surrogacy arrangement is not a "payment or reward" within the meaning of the section, provided there is no element of profit or financial gain (*Re An Adoption Application* (*Surrogacy*) [1987] 2 All E.R. 826).

"The time the . . . payment is received" (Value Added Tax Act 1983 (c. 55), s.5(1)). The transfer of funds into a company's deposit account, on terms that sums could be transferred to that company's current account, constituted a "payment" within the meaning of this section (*Dormers Builders (London)* v. *Customs and Excise Commissioners* [1988] S.T.C. 735). A sum paid for services to be performed at a later date, and then immediately lent back to the payer, was still a "payment" for the purposes of this section (*Customs and Excise Commissioners* v. *Faith Construction* [1989] 3 W.L.R. 678). A payment may be "received" for the purposes of this section notwithstanding that the money is not yet under the control of the payee (*Nevisbrook* v. *Customs and Excise Commissioners* [1989] S.T.C. 192).

"Payment" (Income and Corporation Taxes Act 1988 (c. 1), s.338). The debiting of interest through computer entries does not necessarily constitute "payment" (*Minsham Properties* v. *Price*; *Lysville* v. *Same* [1990] S.T.C. 718).

"Payment or other reward" (Drug Trafficking Offences Act 1986 (c. 32), s.1(3)). The potential market value of a drug found in the possession of a first time drug trafficker before any sale could be made by him could not be regarded as a "payment or other reward" within the meaning of this section (*R.* v. *Butler, The Times*, December 29, 1992).

"Payments other than a periodical payment" (Income Support (General) Regulations 1987 (No. 1967)). A payment of £10,500 by a former husband to his ex-wife 13 months after he stopped making weekly payments of £40 following his redundancy was a payment "other than a periodical payment" within the meaning of these regulations (*Bolstridge* v. *Chief Adjudication Officer, The Times*, May 5, 1993). (Employment Protection (Consolidation) Act 1978 (c. 44), s.73(9)). An *ex gratia* payment made by an employer expressed to incorporate an employee's "statutory redundancy entitlement" did not have to be deducted from the basic award made by an industrial tribunal after a finding that the employee had been unfairly dismissed (*Boorman* v. *Allmakes Ltd* [1995] I.C.R. 842).

"Payment in respect of expenses" (Wages Act 1986 (c. 48), s.7). A payment in respect of a mileage allowance did not cease to be "in respect of expenses" just because it was generous and the words "in respect of" meant "referring to" or "relating to" and did not require precise numerical equivalence (*Southwark London Borough Council* v. *O'Brien* [1996] IRLR 420).

(Housing Act 1985 (c. 68), s.398(6)(b)). "Other payments" were monies, other than rent, received by a landlord in the ordinary course of a lease, and included monies received from utilities' meters (*Jacques* v. *Liverpool City Council* [1996] 7 C.L. 398).

(Employment Rights Act 1996 (c. 18), s.214(2)). A "redundancy payment" in s.214(2) referred to a statutory rather than a voluntary redundancy payment (*Senior Heat Treatment Ltd* v. *Bell* [1997] IRLR 614).

PEACE. See BREACH OF THE PEACE.

PECUNIARY ADVANTAGE. A person who had retained shares in defiance of a court order and who had drawn dividends from the shares, which had increased in value, had obtained a "pecuniary advantage" within the meaning of s.71(1)(b) of the Criminal Justice Act 1988 (Designated Territories) 1991 (*United States Government* v. *Montgomery* [1999] 1 All E.R. 84).

PECUNIARY INTEREST. "Pecuniary interest . . . in any . . . other matter" (Education (School Government) Regulations 1987 (No. 1359), Sched. 2, para. 2(1)). A proposal to close two schools and replace them with city technology colleges was an "other matter" in which the schools' teacher governors had a "pecuniary interest" which barred them from participating in discussions about the proposal or voting on it (*Bostock* v. *Kay* (1989) 133 S.J. 749). Where governors of a county school proposed applying to alter its status to that of a grant maintained school, there was no evidence that such a change would alter the financial position of the teacher governors. Accordingly those governors who were members of the school's staff had no "pecuniary interest" in the proposal for the purposes of this paragraph (*R.* v. *Governors of Small Heath School, ex p. Birmingham City Council* [1990] C.O.D. 23).

PEDLAR. (3) A person who regularly supplements his own income selling goods for a charity by going from house to house is a "pedlar" within the meaning of s.3(1) of the Pedlars Act 1871 (c. 96) (*Murphy* v. *Duke* [1985] 2 W.L.R. 773). A pedlar is an itinerant seller who trades as he travels as distinct from one who merely travels to trade. Thus a trader who sold wrapping paper from a portable stand in a stationary position in a street market was not a "pedlar" (*Watson* v. *Malloy, Watson* v. *Oldrey* [1988] 1 W.L.R. 1026).

There was nothing in s.3(1) nor in the ordinary meaning of "pedlar" to exclude a person using a device to assist with the transportation of his goods (*Shepway District Council* v. *Vincent* [1994] C.O.D. 451).

PENALISE. "Penalising him for doing so" (Employment Protection (Consolidation) Act 1978 (c. 44), s.23(1)(*a*)). Granting, pay rises only to employees who accepted an offer of personal contracts in lieu of collective bargaining by their trade union "penalised", within the meaning of this section, those employees who did not accept the offer (*Associated British Ports* v. *Palmer, The Times*, May 5, 1993).

PENALTY. (Rehabilitation of Offenders Act 1974 (c. 53), s.5(8)). An endorsement of a driving licence was not a "penalty" for the purposes of s.5(8) (*Power* v. *Provincial Insurance plc* [1998] RTR 61).

PENDING. (R.S.C., Ord. 4, r. 9(1)). An action is "pending" if the writ has been issued, irrespective of whether it has been served on the defendant (*Arab Monetary Fund* v. *Hashim (No. 4)* [1992] 1 W.L.R. 1176).

"Pending development of the land" (Housing Act 1985 (c. 68), Sched. 1, para. 3). Where permission had been refused for proposed development of land, that development could no longer be said to be "pending" (*Lillieshall Road Housing Co-operative* v. *Brennan* (1991) 24 H.L.R. 195).

"Proceedings which are pending" (Children Act 1989 (c.41), Sched. 14, para. 1(1)). A judge's order to authorise a short-term placement and to adjourn a long-term placement qualified the proceedings as "pending" proceedings which were therefore preserved by this paragraph (*Re H. (Wardship: Pending Proceedings)* (1992) 156 L.G.Rev. 548). Pending proceedings mean genuine, active applications in wardship, whether the hearing of an originating summons or an ancillary application (*C. (A Minor) (Children Act 1989: Transitional Provisions)* [1992] 1 FLR 628).

PENDING LAND ACTION. (Land Charges Act 1972 (c. 61), s.17(1)). An action for damages for breach of a landlord's repairing covenant in a lease, even though coupled with a claim for a mandatory order to complete the repairs, was not a "pending land action" within the meaning of this section because it was not a claim "relating to . . . any interest in . . . land" (*Regan and Blackburn* v. *Rogers* [1985] 1 W.L.R. 870). An action by a servient landowner, asserting that an easement over his land has ceased to exist, is a "pending land action" within the meaning of this section, and so can be protected by a caution registered against the dominant owner's registered land pursuant to s.59(1) of the Land Registration Act 1925 (c.21) (*Willies-Williams* v. *National Trust* (1993) 65 P. & C.R. 359).

PENSION. (Income and Corporation Taxes Act 1970 (c. 10), s.181(3)). Regular monthly disability benefits, paid by the trustees of the employer's pension fund to a former employee who had been declared redundant while absent from work through illness, constituted "pension" payments for the purposes of this section. The fact that the payments were made on account of the taxpayer's disability rather than on account of his past services was immaterial (*Johnson* v. *Farquhar* [1992] S.T.C. 11).

Stat. Def., includes lump sum, allowance or gratuity and return of contributions with or without interest or other addition—(Coal Industry Act 1994 (c. 21), Sched. 5, para. 1(1)).

PERFORMANCE. "Performance of the said duties," see WHOLLY AND EXCLUSIVELY.

Stat. Def., Copyright, Designs and Patents Act 1988 (c. 48), s.180.

PERIL OF THE SEA. This expression describes a proximate cause which might, as a matter of definition, arise with or without negligence (*J. Lauritzen A/S* v. *Wijsmuller BV* [1989] 1 Lloyd's Rep. 148).

PERIOD. "Period . . . on duty" within the meaning of s.103(1) of the Transport Act 1968 (c. 73) is a question of fact in each case, and a driver was held not to be "on duty" during two half-hour periods of rest and refreshment (*Carter* v. *Walton* [1978] RTR 378).

"Act extending over a period" (Race Relations Act 1976 (c. 74), s.68(7)(*b*)). A condition of employment by which an employee's pension entitlement was less favourable than that of other employees was a disadvantage which continued throughout the period of the employment and was therefore an "act extending over a period" within the meaning of this section (*Barclays Bank* v. *Kapur* [1991] 2 W.L.R. 401). But where a black staff nurse complained that she had been discriminated against when her employees regraded her at a lower grade, with consequent lesset pay than her white comparator, but had not asserted that they had acted in pursuance of a discriminatory policy, the act of which she complained was, for the purposes of s.68(7), once-for-all and did not extend "over a period" (*Sougrin* v. *Haringey Health Authority* [1992] IRLR 416).

"Period of account" (Finance Act 1981 (c. 35), Sched. 9). A claim for stock relief for a 104-week period which encompassed periods covered by earlier claims, and had been adopted solely for the purposes of making an out-of-time election for transitional relief under Sched. 10, was not a "period of account" within Sched. 9 (*Bass Holdings* v. *Money, The Times*, March 12, 1993).

Where the executive had power to detain persons pending their removal from the country, it was to be implied that the power could ony be exercised during such period as was reasonably necessary to effect removal and that if it became apparent that removal could not be effected within a reasonable time, further detention was not authorised (*Tan Te Lam* v. *Tai Chau Detention Centre* [1996] 2 W.L.R. 863).

See TRIAL PERIOD.

"Daily working period." See WORKING.

PERIODIC. "Periodic licence to occupy premises" (Housing Act 1988 (c. 50), s.32(1)(1A)). A licence under the terms of which an employee was granted exclusive possession of a bungalow belonging to his employer, so that he could better perform the duties of his employment, was a service licence, notwithstanding that the employee was in fact never in a position to perform those duties. It was not a "periodic licence" for the purposes of s.5 of the Protection from Eviction Act 1977 (c. 43) (*Norris (trading as J. Davies & Son)* v. *Checksfield* (1991) 135 S.J. 542).

PERIODICAL. "Periodical payment", see PAYMENT.

PERMANENT. "Permanently displaced" (Land Compensation Act 1973 (c. 26), s.29(3A) as amended by the Housing Act 1974 (c. 44), Sched. 13). A person could be said to have been "permanently displaced" from his dwelling within the meaning of this section where the improvements carried out to the dwelling were so radical as to cause it to lose its original identity (*R.* v. *Islington London Borough Council, ex p. Casale, The Times*, December 14, 1985).

"The intention of permanently depriving the other of it" (Theft Act 1968 (c. 60), s.6(1)). A person who removed a pair of doors from the property of a landlord and fitted them to another property was held to have had "the intention of permanently depriving" the landlord of the doors, notwithstanding that both properties were owned by the same landlord (*DPP* v. *Lavender (Melvyn), The Times,* June 2, 1993).

(Value Added Tax Act 1994 (c. 23), Sched. 8) ("Permanently adapted"). An adaptation to a motor vehicle did not have to be either irreversible or such as to preclude other use in order to qualify as being "permanently adapted" and zero-rated for VAT purpose (*Customs and Excise Commissioners* v. *Help the Aged* [1998] RTR 120).

PERMISSIBLE MAXIMUM WEIGHT. "Permissible maximum weight" referred to an aggregate of the maximum weight of the vehicle and any trailer in use, in relation to the requirement that a vehicle should be fitted with a tachograph (*Small* v. *DPP* [1995] R.T.R. 95).

PERMIT. (31) "Permitted the contravention" (Transport Act 1968 (c. 73), s.96(11)). An employer who paid a fee to a self-employed traffic manager was nevertheless held to have "permitted" a driver to exceed the hours of continuous driving permitted by this section, as the knowledge of the traffic manager could be imputed to the employer (*Worthy* v. *Gordon Plant (Services)* [1989] RTR 7).

A transport manager, who issued repeated written warnings to drivers time and again that they were in breach of Council Regulation 3820/85, Arts. 6(1) and 7(1) without ensuring that the warnings were carried on to the next stage of disciplinary action "permitted" the contravention contrary to the Transport Act 1968 (c. 73), s.96(11A) (*Light* v. *DPP* [1994] R.T.R. 396).

"Permit any other person to use a motor vehicle" (Road Traffic Act 1988 (c.52), s.143(1)(*b*)). Where the owner lent his car on condition that the person he lent it to found someone to drive it who was properly insured it was held that the imposition of that condition was insufficient to avoid the owner's strict liability under this section of permitting an uninsured person to drive the vehicle, even though he was at the time unaware that the person found to drive the car was uninsured (*DPP* v. *Fisher* [1991] Crim.L.R. 787).

PERSECUTION. (United Nations Convention 1951). "Persecution" should be given its ordinary English meaning (*Kagema* v. *Secretary of State for the Home Department* [1997] Imm. A.R. 137).

Persecution should be defined within the context of recognised human rights standards and included discrimination, however caused. Discrimination perpetrated or condoned by the state amounted to persecution. (*Horvath (Milan)* v. *Secretary of State for the home Department* [1999] Imm. AR 121).

PERSISTENT. "Persistently in default" (Companies Act 1948 (c. 38), s.188(1)(*b*); as amended by Companies Act 1981 (c. 62), s.93; now Companies Act 1985 (c. 6), s.297(1)). Repeated failure by a liquidator to comply with the "relevant requirements" as to the filing of returns and accounts was sufficient to amount to his being "persistently in default," notwithstanding that at no stage was an enforcement order made or a conviction obtained. Culpability is irrelevant. "Persistently" connotes some degree of continuance or repetition either in the same default or in a series of defaults. In this case 27 defaults in two years was held to amount to persistent default (*Re Arctic Engineering* [1986] 1 W.L.R. 686).

"Persistence" meant a degree of repetition by more than one invitation to a person or invitations to different persons (*R.* v. *Tuck* [1994] Crim.L.R. 375).

PERSON. (50) A group of people controlling more than one company can be a "person" within the meaning of s.153(4) of the Employment Protection (Consolidation) Act 1978 (c. 44) (*Harford* v. *Swiftrim* (1987) 84 L.S.Gaz. 820).

"The person having control of the house" for the purposes of s.9(1A) of the Housing Act 1957 (c. 56) (as inserted by Housing Act 1969 (c. 33), s.72 now Housing Act 1985 (c. 68), s.190) is not the person entitled to the freehold reversion but is he who is entitled to receive the hypothetical rack rent. To determine who that might be the court had to consider the actual estates in the property, and where, as here, ground rent was less than the rack rent, it would be the occupying tenant who would receive the rack rent, and it was therefore he who would be the "person having control" for the purposes of this section (*Pollway Nominees* v. *Croydon London Borough*

Council [1986] 2 All E.R. 849). A long leaseholder would qualify as the person having "control" for the purposes of this section (*R.* v. *Lambeth London Borough Council, ex p. Clayhope Properties* [1987] 3 All E.R. 545). But a statutory tenant of a flat in a house in disrepair was held not to be the "person having control of the house" for the purposes of this section (*White* v. *Barnet London Borough Council* [1989] 3 W.L.R. 131).

"Person within the jurisdiction" (R.S.C., Ord. 49, r.1(1)). A woman who agreed to accept service of garnishee proceedings on her solicitors was a "person within the jurisdiction" for the purposes of this rule, notwithstanding that she had left the jurisdiction by the time the order nisi was made (*S.C.F. Finance Co.* v. *Masri (No. 3) (Masri, Garnishee)* [1987] 1 All E.R. 194).

The word "person" in reg. 11(*c*) and (*d*) of the Supplementary Benefit (Conditions of Entitlement) Regulations refers only to a natural person and not a corporate or unincorporate body such as the local authority (*Decision No. R (S.B.) 2/87*).

"A person, an institution or any other body" (Child Abduction and Custody Act 1985 (c. 60), Sched. 1, art. 3) would, in proceedings under this Act, include the court itself (*Re J. (a Minor)* (1989) 133 S.J. 876).

(Child Abduction Act 1984 (c. 37), s.2(1)). Children who were deflected by some action from that which they were doing with parental consent were removed from the lawful "control" of their parents without necessarily involving a geographical removal (*R.* v. *Leather* (1994) 98 Cr.App.R. 179).

"Person" (Development Land Tax Act 1976 (c. 24), s.28(1)(3)). As no contrary intention is indicated an unincorporated association is a "person" for the purposes of this section, following the definition in Schedule 1 to the Interpretation Act 1978 (c. 30) (*Worthing Rugby Football Club Trustees* v. *I.R.C.* [1987] 1 W.L.R. 1057).

"Person likely to be caused harassment, alarm or distress" (Public Order Act 1986 (c. 64), s.5(1)). A police constable could be such a "person" for the purposes of this section (*DPP* v. *Orum* [1988] 3 All E.R. 449). It is possible for a person to be caused "harassment, alarm or distress" within the meaning of this section in circumstances where he is concerned for the safety of some person other than himself (*Lodge* v. *DPP* [1989] C.O.D. 179).

"Such person as may be so specified" (Matrimonial Causes Act 1973 (c. 18), s.23(1)(*f*)). The Accountant General was a "person" as well as an office for the purposes of this section and could order funds paid into court to be administered by the court funds' office (*F.* v. *F. (Financial Provision)* [1990] 2 F.L.R. 374).

"No person shall drive" (Greater London Council (Restrictions of Goods Vehicles) Traffic Order 1985). A limited company cannot be a "person" within the meaning of this Order (*Richmond upon Thames London Borough Council* v. *Pinn and Wheeler* (1989) 133 S.J. 389).

"Any person" (Transport Act 1982 (c. 49), s.36(1)) can include an unincorporated association (*R.* v. *Clerk to the Croydon Justices, ex p. Chief Constable of Kent* [1989] Crim.L.R. 910).

"Where a person dies in consequence of personal injuries sustained by him" (Damages (Scotland) Act 1976 (c. 13), s.1(1)). A foetus is not a "person" for the purposes of this section (*Hamilton* v. *Fife Health Board, The Times,* January 28, 1992).

"Person lawfully acting in the execution of this Act" (Immigration Act 1971 (c. 77), s.26(1)(c)) would include an entry clearance officer (*R.* v. *Secretary of State for the Home Department, ex p. Saffummensah (Kwadwo)* [1991] Imm.A.R. 43).

"Person making the payment" (Income and Corporation Taxes Act 1988 (c. 1), s.203(1)). A third party paying emoluments to a person with whom there was no employer-employee relationship was a "person making the payment" for the purposes of this section and was therefore required to make deductions of tax at source under Schedule E (*Booth* v. *Mirror Group Newspapers* [1992] STC 615).

"The person carrying out the work" (Building Regulations 1985 (No. 1965), reg. 14(3)) could be the owner of the premises if he had authorised and commissioned the work. The regulation does not necessarily apply solely to the person who physically carried out the work (*Blaenau Gwent Borough Council* v. *Sabz Ali Khan, The Times,* May 4, 1993).

"Persons . . . charged with the duty of investigating offences" (Police and Criminal Evidence Act 1984 (c. 60), s.67(9)). A store detective could be such a person (*R.* v. *Bayliss* (1994) 98 Cr.App.R. 235).

A supervisory manager for the Bank of England was not a "person charged with the duty of investigating offences" within the meaning of the Police and Criminal Evidence Act 1984 (c. 60), s.67(9) (*R.* v. *Smith (Wallace)* [1994] 1 W.L.R. 1398).

(Housing Act 1985 (c. 68), s.75). The ordinary and natural meaning of "person" is "living person", excluding an unborn child.—(*R.* v. *Newham London Borough Council, ex p. Dada* [1995] 3 W.L.R. 540.

"Any person" within the meaning of the Licensing Act 1964 (c. 26), s.20A included bodies corporate and incorporate (*R.* v. *Maidstone Crown Court, ex p. Harris* [1994] C.O.D. 514).

The phrase "a person representing a party" in r.44(1)(e) of the Immigration Appeals (Procedure) Rules 1984 (S.I. 1984 No. 2041), r.44(1)(e) applied to the person held out by the party to the appeal as being his representative (*R.* v. *Immigration Appeal Tribunal, ex p. Flores (Ruiz Pablo)* [1995] Imm.A.R. 85).

A body responsible for laying sound boards at the time of refurbishment could be the "person responsible" for a nuisance under the Environment Protection Act 1990 (c. 43), s.80 even though subsequently it had no right of entry into the premises from which the nuisance emanated or into where the noise was having an effect (*Network Housing Association Ltd* v. *Westminster City Council* 93 L.G.R. 280).

A deceased person was not a "person" within the meaning of the Criminal Appeal Act 1968 (c. 19), ss.1 and 9 (*R.* v. *Kearley (No. 2)* [1994] 3 All E.R. 246).

(Housing Act 1985 (c. 68), s.75). An unborn child was a "person who might reasonably be expected to reside with a pregnant homeless woman for the purposes of s.75 (*R.* v. *Newham London Borough Council, ex p. Dada* [1995] All E.R. 522).

(Housing Act 1985 (c. 69), Sched. 24). A "person" in Sched. 24, Part II meant the claimant and joint claimants would both have to occupy the property during the qualifying period (*Hussain* v. *Blackburn Borough Council* [1997] 37 RVR 36).

(Children and Young Persons Act 1933 (c. 12), s.39). A child, who was the victim of an alleged criminal act, which gave rise to criminal proceedings, was a person "in respect of whom criminal proceedings were taken" (*Re R. (A Minor) (Wardship: Restrictions on Publication*) [1994] 3 W.L.R. 36).

"Person from abroad" (Income Support (General) Regulations 1997, reg. 21(3)(*h*). A letter from the Home Office requesting a foreign national to make arrangements to leave the country, but which did not affect their immigration status until all appeals had been exhausted and a deportation order made did not make its addressee a "person from abroad" for the purposes of eligibility for income support under reg. 21(3)(*h*) (*R.* v. *Secretary of State for Social Security, ex p. Remilien* [1997] 1 W.L.R. 1640).

A letter which required a foreign national to leave the country but which stated that no steps to deport would be taken and so that foreign national did not come within Sched. 7(h) of the 1987 regulations, which stated that "a national of a member state . . . is required by the Secretary of State to leave the United Kingdom" and was not entitled to income support (*Remelien* v. *Secretary of State* (see above) distinguished) (*R.* v. *Oxford Social Security Appeal Tribunal, ex p. Wolke* [1996] 8 C.L. 643).

(Industrial Tribunals Act 1996 (c. 17), s.11). The fact that someone may be embarrassed by allegations did not, without more, make him a "person affected by" an allegation of sexual misconduct so that he would be entitled to an order restricting the reporting of proceedings in an industrial tribunal (*R.* v. *London (North) Industrial Tribunal, ex p. Associated Newspapers Ltd, The Times*, May 13, 1998).

An industrial tribunal had the power to make a restricting order binding on a body corporate under the Industrial Tribunals Act 1996 (c. 17), s.11 (*M* v. *Vincent* [1998] I.C.R. 73).

Stat. Def., "means a natural person"—(Carers (Recognition and Services) Act 1995 (c. 12), s.2(3)).

"Person to whom . . . a sum is due" (Insurance Companies Act 1982 (c. 50), s.96(1)(*b*)), see POLICYHOLDER.

"Person absolutely entitled," see ABSOLUTELY ENTITLED.

"Person aggrieved," see AGGRIEVED.

See AGGRIEVED; ANOTHER PERSON; ANY PERSON; OTHER PERSON.

PERSON INTERESTED. "Person interested in the charity" (Charities Act 1960 (c. 58), s.28(1)). A person who could not in any circumstances be a beneficiary of a charity, or take any interest under the trusts applicable to the property of the charity, could not be a "person interested" in that charity within the meaning of this section (*Bradshaw* v. *University College of Wales, Aberystwyth* [1988] 1 W.L.R. 190). To qualify as a "person interested" a person generally needed to have an interest in the charity concerned materially greater than or different from that possessed by ordinary members of the public (*Richmond upon Thames London Borough Council* v. *Rogers* [1988] 3 W.L.R. 513).

"Any person interested" (Law of Property Act 1925 (c. 20), s.30); A person entitled to a charging order on the share of a co-owner in the proceeds of sale of land has a proprietary interest in that share and is, therefore, a "person interested" within the meaning of this section (*Midland Bank* v. *Pike* [1988] 2 All E.R. 434).

"Person interested in the property" (Insolvency Act 1986 (c. 45), s.316). An original tenant who has assigned a lease is not a "person interested" in it for the purposes of this section (*MEPC* v. *Scottish Amicable Life Assurance Society*; *Eckley* (*Third Party*) [1993] 5 C.L. 219).

The Secretary of State was "a person interested in" the restoration of a company to the register under the Companies Act 1985 (c. 6), s.651 in the necessary performance of his statutory duties in the regulation of companies (*Re Townreach* (*No. 002081 of 1994*); *Re Principle Business Machines*, [1994] 3 W.L.R. 983).

PERSONAL CARE. (Registered Homes Act 1984 (c. 23), ss.1, 20). The fact that residents of a residential care home did not receive assistance with bodily functions did not prevent them from being persons who required or were provided with "personal care" within the meaning of this Act (*Harrison* v. *Cornwall County Council* (1991) 90 L.G.R. 81).

PERSONAL CIRCUMSTANCES. The availability to housing associations of grants from local funds against depreciation of equipment is a "personal circumstance" to be disregarded by rent assessment committees when assessing a fair rent under s.70(1) of the Rent Act 1977 (c. 42) (*Royal British Legion Housing Association* v. *East Midlands Rent Assessment Panel* [1989] 23 E.G. 84).

PERSONAL INJURY. Witnesses of a disturbance in a street involving damage to property had not suffered a "personal injury" within the meaning of s.35(1) of the Powers of Criminal Courts Act 1973 (c. 62) (*R.* v. *Vaughan* (1990) Cr.App.R.(S.) 46).

(Social Security Contributions and Benefits Act 1992 (c. 4), s.94(1)). Post-traumatic distress disorder suffered by a fireman, who had attended a number of fatal accidents during his career, was a "personal injury caused by accident" even though it was foreseeable that these events might cause trauma (*Chief Adjudication Officer* v. *Faulds* 1998 S.C.L.R. 719).

Stat. Def., "any disease or impairment of a person's physical or mental condition and includes the prolongation of any disease or such impairment" (National Health Service Act 1977 (c. 49), s.43C(3) inserted by Health Act 1999 (c. 8), s.9(1)).

See INJURY.

PERSONAL NATURE. "evidence of a personal nature," Stat. Def., Industrial Tribunals Act 1996 (c. 17), s.12(7).

PERSONAL REPRESENTATIVE. "Personal representative" did not signify the existence of a relationship of or akin to agency (*Advocate* (*Lord*) v. *Chung*, 1995 S.L.T. 65).

PERSONAL SERVICES. "Provides persons of that racial group with personal services" (Race Relations Act 1976 (c. 74), s.5(2)(*d*)). This section, as an exception to s.4, should not be construed too widely (*Tottenham Green Under Fives' Centre* v. *Marshall* (1989) IRLR 147). "Personal services" envisages circumstances where there is direct contact and where language and cultural understanding are of material importance (*Lambeth London Borough Council* v. *Commission for Racial Equality* [1989] I.C.R. 641).

PERSONALLY. (5) The decision of the Employment Appeal Tribunal in *Mirror Group Newspapers* v. *Gunning* [1985] 1 W.L.R. 394 [see the Main Work] was reversed by the Court of Appeal on the grounds that, although it was doubtless anticipated that under the agreement to distribute newspapers the work would be personally carried out, there was no obligation in the agreement to that effect (*Mirror Group Newspapers* v. *Gunning* [1986] 1 W.L.R. 546).

PEST. Stat. Def., Food and Environment Protection Act 1985 (c. 48), s.16(15).

PETROLEUM. Stat. Def., Petroleum Act 1998 (c. 58), s.1; Offshore Petroleum Production and Pipe-lines (Assessment of Environmental Effects) Regulations 1998 (No. 968), reg. 2(1).

PETROLEUM FIELD. Stat. Def., National Minimum Wage Act 1998 (c. 39), s.42(5).

PETTY SESSIONS. "Petty Sessions area." Stat. Def., Justices of the Peace Act 1979 (c. 55), s.4 as amended by Local Government Act 1985 (c. 51), s.12(2).

PHOTOGRAPH. A computer disk which contained data which could be converted into a screen image and into a print exactly reproducing an original photograph from which it was derived, came within the definition of "photograph" for the purposes of the Protection of Children Act 1978 (c. 37), ss.1 and 7, even though this technology had not been anticipated when the Act was passed (*R.* v. *Fellows* [1997] 1 Cr.App.R. 244).
Stat. Def., Copyright, Designs and Patents Act 1988 (c. 48), s.4.
"Pseudo-photograph," Stat. Def., Protection of Children Act 1978 (c. 37), s.7 as amended by Criminal Justice and Public Order Act 1994 (c. 33), s.84(3).

PIECE RATE. Stat. Def., Wages Act 1986 (c. 48), s.26.

PILOTAGE SERVICES. (Value Added Tax Act 1994 (c. 23), Sched. 3, Group 15, item 5, note 9). "Pilotage services" referred specifically to shipping and could not be applied to the provision of pilots for a helicopter service (*Medical Aviation Services Ltd* v. *Customs and Excise Commissioners* [1998] B.V.C. 2103).

PLACE. (15) "Place of business . . . in Great Britain" (Companies Act 1948 (c. 38), s.412; now Companies Act 1985 (c. 6), s.695). A company established a place of business in Great Britain if it carried on any part of its business there, however small. Thus the branch of a foreign bank can be a place of business for the purposes of this section (*South India Shipping Corp.* v. *Export-Import Bank of Korea* [1985] 2 All E.R. 219). The showing and storage of works of art at certain premises could be sufficient to establish those premises as a "place of business" of the owners, notwithstanding that there were also on the premises works of art belonging to others (*Cleveland Museum of Art* v. *Capricorn International* (1989) 5 BCC 860).

(15)(c) A field in which a car boot sale was held every Sunday was a "place" for the purposes of section 58 of the Shops Act 1950 (c. 28) as the sale was an occurrence which had a sufficient degree of permanence and regularity. But the boot of the car of one of the unknown sellers was not (*Palmer* v. *Bugler* (1989) 87 L.G.R. 382).

(21) "The place where the employee was so employed" (Employment Protection (Consolidation) Act 1978 (c. 44), s.81(2)(*a*)). This is not restricted to the place where an employee actually worked. It would also include any place where he might be contractually required to work (*Rank Xerox* v. *Churchill* [1988] IRLR 280).

"Last-known place of abode." Due service under s.196(3) of the Law of Property Act 1925 (c. 20) or s.23(1) of the Landlord and Tenant Act 1927 (c. 36) would be effected if the notice was left at the place, nearest to that in which the person was last known to have lived, to which a member of the public or a postman could go (*Trustees of Henry Smith's Charity* v. *Kyriakou* (1989) 29 RVR 106).

"Place of performance of the obligation" (Convention on Jurisdiction and the Enforcement of Judgments in Civil and Commercial Matters 1968, Art. 5(1)) refers to the place of performance of the obligation which formed the actual basis of the proceedings. "Obligation" refers to the contractual obligation forming the basis of the legal proceedings (*Medway Packaging* v. *Meurer Maschinen GmbH* [1990] 2 Lloyd's Rep. 112).

(Civil Jurisdiction and Judgment Act 1982 (c. 27), art. 5(1)). The expression "place of performance or the obligation in question" meant the intended place of performance of the supposed obligation (*Kleinwort Benson Ltd* v. *Glasgow City Council* [1996] 2 All E.R. 257).

In an action for negligent misstatement, the place where the statement had been made, whether oral or in writing, rather than where it had been received was the "place where the harmful event occurred", since it was the statement itself which defined the event which set the tort in motion (*Domicrest Ltd* v. *Swiss Bank Corporation* [1999] 2 W.L.R. 364).

"Place of work" (Local Government Act 1972 (c. 70), s.79(1)). A retired person whose only work consisted of his duties as a local councillor was entitled to claim that the council offices were his "place of work" (*Parker* v. *Yeo*, 90 L.G.R. 645).

"Place of business." Stat. Def., Companies Act 1985 (c. 6), s.744.

"Place of business" (Firearms Act 1968 (c. 27), s.33(3)). For the purposes of this Act the "place of business" of a firearms dealer included the place where he stored firearms and ammunition (*R.* v. *Bull, The Times,* August 18, 1993).

The cab of a fork-lift truck was a "place" within the meaning of the Factories Act 1961 (c. 34), s.29(1) and "plant" and "place" were not to be regarded as mutually exclusive (*Gunion* v. *Roche Products, The Scotsman,* October 19, 1994).

(Civil Jurisdiction and Judgments Act 1982 (c. 27), art. 5(3)). "Place where the harmful event occurred." Since the Brussels Convention 1968, Art. 5 did not define "harmful event", it was a matter which should be determined by the national court applying its substantive law (*Shevill* v. *Presse Alliance S.A.* [1996] 3 All E.R. 929).

The definition could not encompass any place where the adverse consequences of an event that had already caused damage elsewhere could be felt and so did not include the place where a victim claimed to have suffered financial loss consequential on initial damage arising and suffered by him in another contracting state (*Marinari* v. *Lloyds Bank plc* [1996] 2 W.L.R. 159).

(Construction (Working Places) Regulations 1966 (S.I. 1966 No. 64), reg. 6). "Place" had to be given its ordinary meaning and although not confined to a permanent structure it would be incompatible with the ordinary use of language to describe the dumper truck where the plaintiff had sustained his accident as his "place of work" (*Sweeney* v. *MacKenzie Construction Ltd* (1997) Rep. L.R. 35).

See also ESTABLISH.

PLAINTIFF. "Plaintiff" in the Supreme Court of Judicature (Consolidation) Act 1925 (c. 49), s.225 means the plaintiff in the proceedings as a whole and a defendant who makes an interlocutory application does not become the plaintiff against whom an application can be made for security for costs (*CT Bowring & Co. (Insurance) Ltd* v. *Corsi Partners Ltd* [1994] 2 Lloyd's Rep. 567).

(Companies Act 1985 (c. 6), s.726). See OTHER.

PLANNING UNIT. The question of whether a shop was an appropriate "planning unit" was a question of fact and degree for the Secretary of State to determine in accordance with the rule in *Burdle* v. *Secretary of State for the Environment* [1972] 1 W.L.R. 1207 (*Church Commissioners for England* v. *Secretary of State for the Environment* (1996) 71 P. & C.R. 73).

PLANT. (8) "Plant" (Finance Act 1971 (c. 68), ss.41(1), 44(1); now Capital Allowances Act 1990 (c. 1), ss.22(1), 24(1)). Glass shop fronts and items of internal decoration, installed in fast-food restaurants for the purpose of promoting trade, were not "plant" within the meaning of this section (*Wimpey International* v. *Warland*; *Associated Restaurants* v. *Same* [1989] S.T.C. 273). Expenditure on constructing permanent quarantine kennels for cats and dogs was held not to have been incurred on the provision of "plant" within the meaning of this section (*Carr* v. *Sayer* [1992] S.T.C. 396). Expenditure by wholesaler distributors on installing mezzanine platforms in their single-storey warehouses so as to increase storage space was incurred on "plant" within the meaning of this section, but ancillary lighting required as a consequence of the installation did not qualify (*Hunt* v. *Henry Quick*; *King* v. *Bridisco* [1992] STC 633).

PLANT VARIETY. Stat. Def., Plant Varieties Act 1997 (c. 66), s.1(3).

PLANTARIA. A plantaria or greenhouse used for nurturing and protecting growing plants but which also allowed customers to walk among benches where plants were growing was not "plant" for capital allowance purposes because it formed part of the premises in which the business was carried on (*Gray (Inspector of Taxes)* v. *Seymours Garden Centre (Horticulture)* [1995] STC 706).

(Town and Country Planning Act 1990 (c. 8), s.336).

PLANT (HORTICULTURAL). A carillon clock was not "plant and machinery" under s.336 (*Kennedy* v. *Secretary of State for Wales* [1996] EGCS 17). Stat. Def., Food and Environment Protection Act 1985 (c. 48), s.24.

PLEADING. (R.S.C., Ord. 18, r.19). An ordinary application, as defined by r.7(2) of the Insolvency Rules 1986 (No. 1925), was not a "pleading" within the meaning of r.19 (*Re Port (a Bankrupt) (No. 516 of 1987)*).

PLY FOR HIRE. A driver of a marked mini-cab, whose vehicle was not a licensed hackney carriage, plied for hire within the meaning of the Town Police Clauses Act 1847 (c. 89) if he was approached by a member of the public and then entered into negotiations for the hire of the vehicle (*Nottingham City Council* v. *Woodings* [1994] R.T.R. 72).

POLICE. "Deceased was in police custody" (Coroners Act 1988 (c. 13), s.8(3)(*b*)). A prisoner who was serving his sentence at a police station because of prison overcrowding remained in "police custody" for the purposes of this section when, after becoming seriously ill, he was taken to hospital where he died (*R.* v. *Coroner for Inner North London, ex p. Linnaine* [1989] 1 W.L.R. 395).

POLICE FORCE. Stat. Def., Criminal Appeal Act 1995 (c. 35), s.22(2)(*a*).

POLICYHOLDER. (Policyholders Protection Act 1975 (c. 75), s.8(2)). A person who was not the legal holder of a policy of insurance but who had a contingent claim under the policy on the insurance company's liquidation was not a "person to whom . . . a sum is due" within the meaning of s.96(1)(*b*) of the Insurance Companies Act 1982 (c. 50) and was not therefore a "policyholder" entitled under s.8(2) of the 1975 Act to compensation from the Policyholders Protection Board (*Scher* v. *Policyholders Protection Board (No. 2); Ackman* v. *Same (No. 2)* [1994] 2 All E.R. 37). A person was only a "policyholder" within the meaning of the Insurance Companies Act 1982 (c. 50), s.96 if all the preconditions of liability to the insurance company have been satisfied (*Scher* v. *Policyholders Protections Board* [1994] 2 All E.R. 37).

POLITICAL. The promotion of the observance of human rights by campaigning to change the laws or policies of a government was a "political object" within the meaning of s.92(2) (*R.* v. *Radio Authority, ex p. Bull* [1997] 3 W.L.R. 1094).

United Nations Convention Relating to the Status of Refugees (1951). A crime committed with the object of overthrowing or changing the government of a state or inducing it to change its policy is to be regarded as a "political crime" provided the commission of the crime is not too remote from its objective (*R.* v. *Governor of Pentonville Prison, ex p. Cheng* [1973] A.C. 931 applied) (*T.* v. *Secretary of State for the Home Department* [1995] Imm.A.R. 142).

(European Convention on Mutual Assistance in Criminal Matters 1959). Making payments by way of bribes or illicit donations to politicians or political parties with a view to bringing about a change in government policy were not "political offences" within the meaning of Art. 2 of the

European Convention on Mutual Assistance in Criminal Matters 1959 (*R. v. Secretary of State for the Home Department, ex p. Finninvest S.p.A.* [1997] 1 W.L.R. 743).

POLLUTION OF THE ENVIRONMENT. Stat. Def., Environmental Protection Act 1990 (c. 43), s.1.
"Marine pollution." See MARINE POLLUTION.

POSSESSION. (48) (Firearms Act 1968 (c. 27), s.2(1)). Where a person left his shotgun at another's house for cleaning and safekeeping while both of them were on holiday, the recipient was in possession of the shotgun within the meaning of this section (*Hall* v. *Cotton* [1986] 3 W.L.R. 681). Where, to oblige a friend, a man looked after a bag which, without him knowing it, contained a sawn-off shotgun, he was guilty of possession a firearm without a certificate contrary to this section. The offence is one of strict liability (*R.* v. *Waller* [1991] Crim.L.R. 381).

(Theft Act 1968 (c. 60), s.5(1)). "Possession" in s.5(1) of the 1968 Act meant in the custody of or actual control, so that a medical institution, from whom body parts had been stolen, had possession of those body parts at the time they were taken (*R.* v. *Kelly* [1999] 2 W.L.R. 384).

(49) "Controlled drug in his possession" (Misuse of Drugs Act 1971 (c. 38), s.5(2)). A man who put a small quantity of cannabis into his wallet, knowing what it was, remained in "possession" of it within the meaning of this section even though he had long forgotten it was there (*R.* v. *Martindale* [1986] 1 W.L.R. 1042). A woman who did no more than live with a man at a time when he possessed and dealt in drugs was not herself guilty of possession, notwithstanding that she must have known what he was doing (*R.* v. *Bland* [1988] Crim.L.R. 41). Where an accused was apprehended while delivering a box containing cannabis resin to a co-defendant, he was held to be guilty of having a "controlled drug in his possession," notwithstanding his claim that he thought the box contained pornographic videos (*R.* v. *McNamara* (1988) 87 Cr.App.R. 246). In construing the word "possession" the question to be asked was whether on the facts the defendant had been proved to have, or ought to have imputed to him, the intention to possess what was in fact a controlled drug (*R.* v. *Lewis* (1988) 87 Cr.App.R. 270).

"Lawful possession of the land" (Land Compensation Act 1973 (c. 26), s.37(2)(*a*)). "Possession" here means actual physical occupation with the intention to exclude intruders (*Wrexham Maelor Borough Council* v. *Mac-Dougall, The Times*, April 7, 1993).

"Goods in the company's possession under any hire-purchase agreement" (Insolvency Act 1986 (c. 45), s.11(3)(*c*)). Where a company was in possession of goods which came into its possession under the terms of a leasing agreement they remained "goods in the company's possession under any hire-purchase agreement" within the meaning of this section notwithstanding that the leasing agreement terminated on or before presentation of a petition by the company for an administration order (*Re David Meek Access; Re David Meek Plant* [1993] BCC 175).

(Law of Property Act 1925 (c. 20), s.54(2)). A lease to commence at a future date was not a lease "taking effect in possession" within the meaning of section 54(2) (*Long* v. *Tower Hamlets London Borough Council* [1996] 3 W.L.R. 317).

(Local Government Finance Act 1988 (c. 41), s.65(1)). Receivers who had been appointed agents under debentures were not by reason of their appointment "entitled to possession" of premises and were thus not owners liable for the unoccupied property rates (*Brown* v. *City of London Corporation* [1996] 1 W.L.R. 1070).

"Part with possession," see PART.

POSSESSIONS. (European Convention on Human Rights 1950, Protocol 1, Art. 1). Unchallenged rights over disputed land, which provided revenue might qualify as possessions within the meaning of Protocol 1, Art 1. (*Matos E. Silva LDA* v. *Portugal* (1997) 24 E.H.R.R. 573).

POST. "In the ordinary course of post" (Companies Act 1948 (c. 38), Sched. 1, Table A, art. 131). These words are not confined to post within the United Kingdom (*Parkstone* v. *Gulf Guarantee Bank* [1990] BCC 534).

POST-NUPTIAL SETTLEMENT. (Matrimonial Causes Act 1973 (c. 18), s.24(1)(*c*)). A sole member pension scheme entered into by a husband with the intention of providing financial support for himself and his wife during retirement with benefits available to the wife in the event of his death was a post-nuptial settlement capable of variation under the 1973 Act (*Brooks* v. *Brooks* [1994] 3 All E.R. 257).

POTATO. Stat. Def., "any tuber or true seed of *Solanum tuberosum L.* or other tuber-forming species or hybrid of the genus *Solanum L.*" (Potatoes Originating in Egypt Regulations 1998 (No. 201), reg. 2).

POTENTIAL BENEFIT. See BENEFIT.

POVERTY. The expression "poverty" in s.53 of the General Rate Act 1967 (c. 9) does not apply to a body corporate (*Hummingbird Entertainments* v. *Birmingham City Council* [1991] R.A. 165).

POWER. The documents of an insolvent company were not "in the power of" the Secretary of State of Trade and Industry within the meaning of R.S.C., Ord. 24, r.7 so as to entitle a former director of the company, against whom the Secretary of State was seeking a disqualification order to require the Secretary of State to make a further affidavit stating whether specified documents or classes of documents had at any time been in his power (*Re Lombard Shipping and Forwarding* [1992] BCC 700).

"Power to sell any of the company's property by public auction or private contract." An agreement that backers to litigation should receive half the proceeds recovered in the action in return for financing the litigation was a "sale" for the purposes of the Insolvency Act 1986 (c. 45), Sched. 4, para. 6 and was champertous (*Grovewood Holdings* v. *James Capel & Co.* [1994] 4 All E.R. 417).

POWER OF ENTRY TO DEAL WITH OR PREVENT A BREACH OF THE PEACE. (Police and Criminal Evidence Act 1984 (c. 60), s.17(6)). The power to enter property to deal with or prevent a breach of the peace was not restricted to places where public meetings were held but could apply to private property (*McLeod* v. *Commissioner of Police of the Metropolis* [1994] 4 All E.R. 553).

POWER TO ENJOY. (Income and Corporation Taxes Act 1970 (c. 10) s.478(2)). A taxpayer consultant chartered surveyor who had arranged for his fees to be paid to a Jersey company, which employed him, with specific arrangements as to salary, was held still to have the "power to enjoy" the income of the company within the meaning of this section (*I.R.C.* v. *Brackett* [1986] S.T.C. 521).

PRACTICABLE. "So far as practicable" (Social Security Act 1975 (c. 14), s.99(1)). In determining practicability for the purposes of this section regard may be had not only to matters internal to the claim for social security benefit, but also to extrinsic factors (*R.* v. *Secretary of State for Social Services, ex p. Child Poverty Action Group*, *The Times*, February 15, 1988).

"As soon as reasonably practicable" (Public Order Act 1986 (c. 64), s.39(2)). Where, by virtue of their powers under this section, the police directed squatters to leave premises occupied by them, the requirement to do so "as soon as reasonably practicable" related only to the practicability of moving out (*Krumpa* v. *DPP* [1989] Crim.L.R. 295).

"Not practicable to communicate" (Police and Criminal Evidence Act 1984 (c. 60), Sched. 1, para. 14(*a*)). "Practicable" is to be construed as wider than just "feasible" or "physically possible" (*R.* v. *Leeds Crown Court, ex p. Switalski* [1991] Crim.L.R. 559).

"As soon as practicable," see As SOON AS.

PRACTICE AND PROCEDURE. (Supreme Court Act 1981 (c. 54), s.84(1) and (2)). For the purposes of s.84(1) and (2), costs were a matter of practice and procedure so that the provisions of R.S.C., Ord. 62, r.18(3) were not ultra vires but were reasonable provisions defining and regulating the rights of a litigant in person to recover costs (*Mainwaring* v. *Goldtech Investments Ltd* [1997] 1 All E.R. 467).

PRE-PACKED. Stat. Def., Weights and Measures Act 1985 (c. 72), s.94.

PRECIOUS METAL. Stat. Def., "means gold or silver" (Treasure Act 1996 (c. 24), s.3(1)).

PREFERENCE. "Given a preference" (Insolvency Act 1986 (c. 45), s.239). Where an employee is entitled on the liquidation of a company to some level of compensation for redundancy or breach of contract, a payment far in excess of that sum could amount to a "preference" voidable under this section (*Re Clasper Group Services* (1988) 4 BCC 673). A debenture granted to a bank by a company three months before the company went into creditors' voluntary liquidation was held not to be a "preference" which could be set aside under this section (*Re M. C. Bacon* [1990] BCC 78).

"Preference dividend." Stat. Def., Income and Corporation Taxes Act 1988 (c. 1), s.832.

See also FRAUDULENT PREFERENCE.

PREGNANCY. See CONNECTED WITH.

PREJUDICE. A purchaser who was sold meat described as minced beef or minced steak which contained a percentage of other meats, had it sold to him to his "prejudice" within the meaning of s.2 of the Food and Drugs Act 1955 (c. 16) (*Shearer* v. *Rowe* (1985) 84 L.G.R. 296).

"Prejudice" (Limitation Act 1980 (c. 58), s.33(1)). On an application under this section the court is entitled, in considering all the circumstances, to take into account the existence, or lack of, prejudice to both parties (*Donovan* v. *Gwentoys* [1990] 1 W.L.R. 472).

(Environmental Protection Act 1990 (c. 43), s.79). "Prejudicial to health", defined as meaning "injurious or likely to cause injury to health" in s.79(7) of the 1990 Act did not mean bodily injury, so that a steep internal staircase which might cause accidental injury was not capable of giving rise to a statutory nuisance, since s.79 was aimed at dealing with premises which had an adverse effect on people's health because of their unwholesome and filthy condition (*R.* v. *Bristol City Council, ex p. Everett* [1999] 2 All E.R. 193).

See also SUBSTANTIALLY; UNFAIR.

PREMISES. (14) "Premises" for the purposes of ss.92 and 93 of the Public Health Act 1936 (c. 49) means the premises which are affected by the nuisance prejudicial to health, not the premises causing the nuisance, in cases where they are not the same (*Pollway Nominees* v. *Havering London Borough Council* (1989) 21 H.L.R. 462).

(19) "Part of premises ... let as a whole" (Rent Act 1977 (c. 42), s.137(3)). Where Part II of the Landlord and Tenant Act 1954 (c. 56) applied to the tenancy of premises, part of which were residential and the rest business premises, the residential part was not "premises" within the meaning of this section (*Pittalis* v. *Grant* [1989] 1 All E.R. 622).

"Consumption on the premises" (Value Added Tax Act 1983 (c. 55), Sched. 5, Group 1, Note (3)). Where food was supplied from a snack bar in a small room in a large building, and was consumed elsewhere in the building, it was not consumed on the premises, as "premises" in this schedule must be taken to refer to the room from which the snack bar was operated and not the whole building (*R.* v. *Customs and Excise Commissioners, ex p. Sims (T/A Supersonic Snacks)* [1988] S.T.C. 210). See also CATERING.

(Landlord and Tenant Act 1987 (c. 31)). Whether a relevant disposal of premises had taken place within the meaning of the 1987 Act was to be determined on a building by building basis and did not include a disposal of an adjoining building which had been purchased by a landlord at the same time and held under a separate registered title as the premises in question (*Kay Green* v. *Twinsectra Ltd* [1996] 4 All E.R. 546).

"Premises" (Landlord and Tenant Act 1987 (c. 31), s.46). In this section "premises" would include agricultural tenancies which included a dwelling, so that a sporting estate of 940 acres could be "premises" for the purposes of this section (*Dallhold Estates (U.K.)* v. *Lindsey Trading Properties, The Times,* December 15, 1993.

(35) (London Government Act 1963 (c. 33), Sched. 12). "Premises" in Sched. 12 included "any place" and so covered Leicester Square (*R. v. Bow Street Magistrates' Court, ex p. Mcdonald, The Times,* March 27, 1996).

(Protection from Eviction Act 1997 (c. 43), s.5). Premises let as an agricultural holding were not "premises let as a dwelling for the purposes of the 1977 Act (*National Trust for Places of Historic Interest or Natural Beauty* v. *Knipe* [1997] 4 All E.R. 627).

Premises which were let for business purposes under Part II of the Landlord and Tenant Act 1954 and sublet for residential use qualified for protection under the Rent Act 1977, s.137(3) (*Wellcome Trust Ltd* v. *Hammad* [1998] 1 All E.R. 657).

Stat. Def., Drug Trafficking Offences Act 1986 (c. 32), s.29; Consumer Protection Act 1987 (c. 43), s.45; Food Safety Act 1990 (c. 16), s.1.

Stat. Def., "includes any place and, in particular, includes—(a) any vehicle, vessel, aircraft or hovercraft; (b) any offshore installation; and (c) any tent or movable structure" (Criminal Justice and Public Order Act 1994 (c. 33), s.139(12); see also Jobseekers Act 1995 (c. 18), s.33(11)); "includes any land, vehicle, vessel or mobile plant" (Environment Act 1995 (c. 25), s.108(16)); "includes land, buildings, moveable structures, vehicles, vessels, aircraft and hovercraft" (Arbitration Act 1996 (c. 23), s.82(1)); Education Act 1996 (c. 56), s.311(1); Knives Act 1997 (c. 21), s.5(6); "includes land (including buildings), moveable structures, vehicles and aircraft" (Landmines Act 1998 (c. 33), s.27(1)).

PREMIUM. Payments made by a lessee to reimburse development costs incurred by the lessor, in consideration for future rent reduction, constituted a "premium" or "any like sum" within the meaning of paragraphs 2 and 10 of Schedule 3 to the Capital Gains Tax Act 1979 (c. 14) (*Clarke* v. *United Real (Moorgate)* [1988] S.T.C. 273).

"The payment of any premium" (Rent Act 1977 (c. 42), s.119). A sum paid by a prospective tenant to a sitting tenant in consideration of the latter's surrender of his protected tenancy was an unlawful "premium" for the purposes of this section (*Saleh* v. *Robinson* [1988] 36 E.G. 180).

PREPARATION. "Preparation or other product containing a substance" (Misuse of Drugs Act 1971 (c. 38), Sched. 2, Pt. I, para. 5). It is for the jury, applying the ordinary and natural meaning of the word, to decide what constitutes a "preparation." The mere picking of a certain type of scheduled mushroom did not constitute a "preparation" (*R. v. Walker* [1987] Crim.L.R. 565). Although "magic" mushrooms picked, packaged and frozen did not, in that state, amount to a "preparation" they did come within the meaning of the word "product" or within the phrase "or other product" (*Hodder* v. *DPP; Matthews* v. *DPP* [1990] Crim.L.R. 261).

"Preparation . . . of . . . preserved food" (Food Act 1984 (c. 30), s.16). The slicing of cooked meats does not amount to "preparation" for the purposes of this section (*Leeds City Council* v. *Dewhurst* [1990] Crim.L.R. 725).

(Food Safety Act 1990 (c. 16), s.53(1)). The chilling of meat was not "preparation" for sale of meat to the consumer since the word "preparation" had to be construed according to the context in which it was used (*MacNeill* v. *Sutherland* 1998 S.C.C.R. 474).

PREPARATORY. "More than merely preparatory," see ATTEMPT.

PRESENT. (11) "Complaint . . . presented to the tribunal" (Employment Protection (Consolidation) Act 1978 (c. 44), s.67(2)). An originating application pushed under the door (which had no letter box) of an industrial tribunal regional office on the day after a bank holiday, which was the final day for presenting an unfair dismissal complaint, had been "presented" in time for the purposes of this section (*Ford* v. *Stakis Hotels and Inns* [1987] I.C.R. 943).

"Present at the same time" (Wills Act 1837 (c. 26), s.9(c) (as substituted by the Administration Act 1982 (c. 53), s.17). Where a witness had attested a will in the presence of the testator, but in the absence of the second witness, who later witnessed the will in the presence of the first witness and the testator, the protestations of the first witness in front of the second witness amounted to an acknowledgment of her earlier signature so that the testator had acknowledged his signature in the presence of two witnesses present at the same time, who had both duly attested and the will was validly executed (*Couser* v. *Couser* [1996] 1 W.L.R. 1301).

PRESENT IN G.B. To qualify for an attendance allowance under the Social Security Act 1975 (c. 14), s.35(2B), (2C) and Social Security (Attendance Allowance) (No. 2) Regulations 1975 (No. 590), reg. 2(1) a person had to have an independent existence and could not be an unborn child and had to be "present in G.B." for 26 weeks of the 12 months preceding the commencement of an attendance allowance (*Social Security Decision No. R(A) 1/94*).

PRESERVATION. "Proper preservation of the building" (Town and Country Planning Act 1971 (c. 78), s.115). "Preservation" of a listed building, for the purposes of this section, means preserving it in the state it was in when first listed and not when the repairs notice was served (*Robbins* v. *Secretary of State for the Environment* [1989] 1 All E.R. 878).

PRESERVE. "Preserving the assets" (Companies (Winding Up) Rules 1949, r.195(1)) denotes some positive action, not mere inaction by the liquidator (*Re Linda Marie (In Liquidation)* (1988) 4 BCC 463).

"Desirability of preserving" (Town and Country Planning Act 1971 (c. 78), s.277(5)). The word "preserving" has to be interpreted in the wide sense of not causing harm rather than the narrow sense of making some positive contribution. Building developments which left the character or appearance of land in a conservation area unharmed did "preserve" that character or appearance within the purposes of this section (*South Lakeland District Council* v. *Secretary of State for the Environment* [1992] 2 W.L.R. 204).

"Establishing, preserving or defending his title," see ESTABLISH.

PREVENT. "For the purpose of preventing or detecting serious crime" (Interception of Communications Act 1985 (c. 56), s.2(2)). Whereas the

Secretary of State may issue a warrant requiring the interception of communications "for the purpose of preventing or detecting serious crime" that phrase was held not to extend to the *prosecution* of such crime (*R.* v. *Preston, The Times,* November 8, 1993).

PREVENTION. "Necessary . . . for the prevention of . . . crime" (Contempt of Court Act 1981 (c. 49), s.10). The phrase "prevention of crime" is to be construed in its wider or more natural sense rather than the restricted sense of prevention of a particular crime (*Re an Inquiry under the Company Securities (Insider Dealing) Act 1985* [1988] 2 W.L.R. 33). See also NECESSARY; REASONABLE EXCUSE.

PREVIOUSLY. The word "previously" in rule 195 of the Companies (Winding-up) Rules 1949 (No. 330 (L4)) means previously to the making of the winding-up order and not previously to the presentation of the petition (*Re A. V. Sorge & Co.* [1986] PCC 380).

PRIMA FACIE. The use of the phrase "prima facie" in s.50(3) of the Sale of Goods Act 1979 (c. 54) entitles the court to depart from a literal construction of the subsequent language in order to determine what would, in all the circumstances, be a fair price on the day in question (*Shearson Lehman Hutton* v. *Maclaine Watson & Co.* [1989] 2 Lloyd's Rep. 570).

PRIMARY LEGISLATION. Stat. Def., Human Rights Act 1998 (c. 42), s.21(1).

PRINCIPAL. Where the jurisdiction clause in a bill of lading provided for disputes to be settled in the country where the carrier had its "principal place of business", it was held that "principal" does not mean "main" but "chief" or "most important" and the principal place of business does not necessarily mean the place where most of the business is carried out; so that the principal place of business of shipowners (incorporated in Liberia but domiciled in Germany) of a ship managed from Hong Kong was Germany (*The Rewia* [1991] 2 Lloyd's Rep. 325).
"Principal place of business" (R.S.C., Ord. 81, r.3(1)), see SERVE.
Principal home, see HOME.

PRINCIPLES. The "principles" of the Treaty of Waitangi Act 1975 (No. 114 of 1975) were the underlying mutual obligations and responsibilities, reflecting the intent of the Treaty as a whole, and included the obligation by the Crown to protect and preserve the Maori language (*New Zealand Maori Council* v. *Att.-Gen. of New Zealand* [1994] 2 W.L.R. 254).

PRIOR WRITTEN AGREEMENT. (State Immunity Act 1978 (c. 33), s.2(2)). ("A State may submit . . . by a prior written agreement . . .") A solicitor's letter expressing an opinion for the benefit of the official to whom it was addressed and which was not an agreement in writing between an employee and the government nor an agreement purporting to submit to the jurisdiction of the English courts did not amount to a "prior" written agreement" within the meaning of s.2(2) of the 1978 Act (*Ahmed* v. *Government of the Kingdom of Saudi Arabia* [1996] I.C.R. 25).

PRIORITY NEED. See DEPENDENT.

PRISON. (2) A magistrates' court is not a "prison or other institution" for the purposes of s.39 of the Prison Act 1952 (c. 52) (*R.* v. *Moss and Harte* (1986) 82 Cr.App.R. 116).

Stat. Def., Sexual Offences (Protected Material) Act 1997 (c. 39), s.2(1); Water Industry Act 1991 (c. 56), Sched. 4A, para. 13(2), inserted by Water Industry Act 1999 (c. 9), s.1(2).

"Life Prisoner." See LIFE PRISONER.

PRIVACY. "Unwarranted infringement of privacy" (Broadcasting Act 1990 (c. 42), s.143(1)(*b*)). A broadcast can still be an infringement of privacy within the meaning of this section notwithstanding that the matter broadcast had previously been reported and was in the public domain (*R.* v. *Broadcasting Complaints Commission, ex p. Granada Television, The Times,* May 31, 1993).

PRIVATE COMPANY. Stat. Def., Companies Act 1985 (c. 6), s.1.

PRIVATE DWELLING-HOUSE. A house being used to accommodate former mental in-patients being returned to the community was not being used as "a private dwelling house" contrary to the terms of a restrictive covenant (*C. & G. Homes* v. *Secretary of State for Health* [1991] 2 W.L.R. 715).

PRIVATE HIRE VEHICLE. (Local Government (Miscellaneous Provisions) Act 1976 (c. 57), s.80(1)). A vehicle was operated as a "private hire vehicle" within the meaning of this section, notwithstanding that there was no payment of money, when the operator, being understaffed, asked his wife to drive pre-booked customers in her car. It was sufficient that he had obtained a commercial benefit by protecting the goodwill of the business (*St. Albans District Council* v. *Taylor* [1991] Crim.L.R. 852).

Stat. Def., Private Hire Vehicles (London) Act 1998 (c. 34), s.1(1)(a). See also HACKNEY CARRIAGE.

PRIVATE INVESTOR. Def. Financial Services Act 1986 (Restriction of Right of Action) Regs. 1991 (No. 489).

PRIVATE LEGISLATION. Stat. Def., includes provisional order, Confirmation Bill relating to provisional order, and local or personal Bill—(Local Government etc. (Scotland) Act 1994 (c. 39), s.121(4)).

PRIVATE POLICYHOLDER. (Policy Holders Protection Act 1975 (c. 75), s.6(7)(*b*)). A partnership does not qualify as a private policyholder if a member of the partnership is a corporate partner (*Scher* v. *Policyholders Protection Board (No. 2); Ackman* v. *Same (No. 2)* [1993] 3 W.L.R. 1030).

PRIVATE STUDY. (Copyright Act (Singapore), ss.35 and 39). "Study" meant the devotion of time and attention to acquiring information or knowledge. "Private" meant being kept or removed from public knowledge, even if the purpose were commercial in nature (*Aztech Systems Pte Ltd* v. *Creative Technology Ltd* [1996] F.S.R. 54).

PRIVATE VEHICLE. (Finance Act 1976 (c. 40), s.72(5)(*a*)(ii)). A motor vehicle that was specially equipped and fitted with a flashing blue light, and that a county fire officer was provided with and required to use, was "a vehicle of a type not commonly used as a private vehicle and unsuitable to be so used" for the purposes of this section, and was not, therefore, a "car" (*Gurney* v. *Richards* [1989] 1 W.L.R. 1180).

PRIVATELY. "Privately" (Patents Act 1977 (c. 37), s.60(5)) is not synonymous with secretly, so that experiments done in the High Court or Patent Office could be done "privately" for the purposes of this section (*Smith Kline Laboratories* v. *Evans* [1989] F.S.R. 513).

PRIVILEGED COMMUNICATION. The test whether a communication between a solicitor and his client was privileged was whether the communication or document was made confidentially for the purposes of legal advice. Those purposes had to be construed broadly, so that, where there was a continuum of communication and meetings during which information was passed for the purposes of keeping both parties informed, so that advice could be given and sought, privilege would attach to such communications (*Balabel* v. *Air India* [1988] 2 W.L.R. 1036). Copies of documents sent to a legal adviser to obtain legal advice could be privileged even if the originals were not (*R.* v. *Board of Inland Revenue, ex p. Goldberg* [1988] S.T.C. 524). But this Divisional Court decision was doubted by the Court of Appeal, which decided that privilege could not be claimed in respect of a copy of an affidavit, taken for the purposes of legal advice, when the original affidavit was not privileged (*Dubai Bank* v. *Galadari* [1989] 3 W.L.R. 1044). Documents held by a solicitor which the client intended to use for a criminal purpose were not "items subject to legal privilege" within the meaning of s.10(2) of the Police and Criminal Evidence Act 1984 (c. 60) and ss.27(4)(ii) and 29(2) of the Drug Trafficking Offences Act 1986 (c. 32), notwithstanding that the client was the innocent tool of a third party (*R.* v. *Central Criminal Court, ex p. Francis and Francis* [1988] 3 W.L.R. 989). There was no waiver of privilege where documents prepared for the purposes of civil proceedings were made available for the purposes of criminal proceedings (*British Coal Corporation* v. *Rye* (*No. 2*) [1988] 1 W.L.R. 1113). A note made by the plaintiff's solicitor of a telephone conversation between him and the defendant's solicitor, which merely recorded the substance of the conversation and contained nothing in the nature of a communication to the plaintiff, was not a privileged document even if the subject matter of the conversation was "without prejudice" (*Parry* v. *News Group Newspapers* (1990) 140 New L.J. 1719). In deciding whether to order disclosure of documents for which legal professional privilege was claimed, the court had to weigh the public policy on which the privilege was founded, namely, the necessity for a party to be able to make a clean breast to his legal adviser, against the gravity of the charge of fraud or dishonesty made (*Derby* v. *Weldon* (*No. 7*) [1990] 1 W.L.R. 1156). Where a party deployed material in an interlocutory application, privilege could be treated as waived altogether, with the result that the party could not then assert privilege for the same material at the subsequent trial (*Derby & Co* v. *Weldon* (*No.10*) [1991] 2 All E.R. 908). Legal professional privilege could not be claimed for original documents which were not previously in the possession, custody or power of a party to litigation, actual or contemplated, and which had not come into existence for the purposes of that litigation but which had been obtained by the solicitors of that party for that purpose (*Ventouris* v. *Mountain*, [1991] 1 W.L.R. 607). Letters asserting a claim under an insurance policy and letters written in response by the insurers were not protected by "without prejudice" privilege as at that point there was no dispute (*Standrin* v. *Yenton Minster Homes, The Times*, July 22, 1991). Where a party to litigation would not have been liable to disclose a relevant original document, for example, because he never had it, a copy of that document, secured by that party for the purposes of the litigation, could not be protected from disclosure on the grounds of professional privilege (*Lubrizol Corporation* v. *Esso Petroleum* [1992] *Gazette*, 22 July, 33). Information provided to a social security adjudication officer by a person applying for benefit was not covered by absolute privilege, and therefore allegations made by an employee against her former employer could be the subject of an action for libel (*Purdew* v. *Seress-Smith* (1992) 136 S.J. (LB) 244). A bank cannot claim legal professional privilege in respect of documents prepared by its auditors in the course of investigating problem loans (*Price Waterhouse* (*A firm*) v. *BCCI Holdings* (*Luxembourg*) *S.A.* [1992] BCLC 583). Where proceedings had initially been conducted by a party receiving advice from a firm of personnel consultants, that advice was not privileged from discovery since it was not covered by legal professional privilege (*New Victoria Hospital* v. *Ryan* [1993] I.C.R. 201). Medical reports, obtained confidentially by a plaintiff for the purposes of personal injury litigation, which were inadvertently disclosed on discovery to the defendants could be used by them at the trial. The plaintiff could not rely on his solicitor's mistake to claim that the reports were protected by privilege (*Pizzey* v. *Ford Motor Co.*, *The Times*, March 8, 1993). The mere service of witness statements under an order of the Court did not waive privilege in connected documents, (*Balkanbank* v. *Taher, The Times*, February 19, 1994). The paramountcy of a child's interests under the Children Act 1989 (c. 41) and the wardship jurisdiction override the legal professional privilege that attaches to a ligitant's medical report (*Oxfordshire County Council* v. *M, The Times*, November 2, 1993).

See also WITHOUT PREJUDICE.

PROCEED. "Lessor . . . proceeding . . . to enforce . . . a right of re-entry or forfeiture" (Law of Property Act 1925 (c. 20), s.146(2)). Relief against forfeiture could still be sought under this section where the landlord had physically re-entered the premises, without obtaining a court order, since the landlord was still "proceeding" to enforce his rights of forfeiture under this section until he obtained a judgment for possession (*Billson* v. *Residential Apartments* [1992] 2 W.L.R. 15).

PROCEEDING; PROCEEDINGS. (1) Interlocutory proceedings brought by a plaintiff against a third party were not a "proceeding in the High Court" within the meaning of R.S.C., Ord. 23, rule 1 and the court, therefore, had no jurisdiction to order the plaintiff to provide security for costs of the third party (*Taly N.D.C. International N.V.* v. *Terra Nova Insurance Co.* [1986] 1 All E.R. 69).

"A stay of the proceedings" (R.S.C., Ord. 53, r.3(10)). A decision made by the Secretary of State could be a "proceeding" which, under this rule, would be stayed on the granting of leave to apply for judicial review (*R.* v. *Secretary of State for Education and Science, ex p. Avon County Council* [1990] C.O.D. 349).

(Supreme Court Act 1981 (c. 54), s.9(7)). The trial of remaining counts in an indictment did not constitute "proceedings arising out of" that trial for the purposes of s.9(7) (*R.* v. *Lord Chancellor, ex p. Maxwell* [1996] 4 All E.R. 751).

"Costs of and incidental to all proceedings" (Supreme Court Act 1981 (c. 54), s.51(1)). Applications for leave to move for judicial review cannot constitute "proceedings" within the meaning of this section (*R.* v. *Test Valley Borough Council, ex p. Goodman* [1992] C.O.D. 101). But in *R.* v. *Darlington Borough Council, ex p. Association of Darlington Taxi Owners and Another (No. 2), The Times,* April 14, 1994 it was held that an application for leave to apply for judicial review "clearly constituted" "proceedings" for the purpose of this section.

"Proceedings" in s.63(1) of the Administration of Justice Act 1982 (c. 53) commence when the accused comes to the court to answer the charge, and not the time the charge is made (*R.* v. *Elliott* (1985) 81 Cr.App.R. 115).

(40)–(46) "In connection with any proceedings" (Legal Aid (General) Regulations 1980 (No. 1894), reg. 65). "Proceedings" here refer only to that part of the proceedings for which the legal aid certificate has been granted, and cannot be deemed to cover the whole action (*Littaur* v. *Steggles Palmer* [1986] 1 W.L.R. 287).

(54) "Proceedings" (Recognition of Divorces and Legal Separations Act 1971 (c. 53), ss.2, 3(1), as amended by Domicile and Matrimonial Proceedings Act 1973 (c. 45), s.15(2)) means a single set of proceedings that has to be instituted in the same country as that in which the divorce is ultimately obtained. So that, where a Pakistani produced talaq in England against his wife resident in Pakistan, and then, as required by Pakistan law, sent a written notice to the chairman of his local council in Pakistan, these were not "proceedings" under this Act (*R.* v. *Secretary of State for the Home Department, ex p. Ghulam Fatima* [1986] A.C. 527). See also *Maples* v. *Maples* [1987] 3 W.L.R. 487 where it was held that a Jewish divorce (*get*) was an extra-judicial proceeding which did not, under English law, dissolve the marriage.

(54) "Proceedings" under the Recognition of Divorces and Legal Separations Act 1971, as amended, meant a single set of proceedings which had to be instituted in the same country in which the divorce was ultimately obtained and despite different wording in the Family Law 1986 (c. 55), it was clear from the legislative history that the 1986 Act had not intended to change the law in relation to transnational divorces (*R.* v. *Secretary of State for the Home Department, ex p. Ghulam Fatima* [1986] A.C. 527 followed) (*Berkovits* v. *Grinberg (Attorney-General intervening)* [1995] 1 FLR 477).

"In any proceedings" (Police and Criminal Evidence Act 1984 (c. 60), ss.78(1), 80(5)) means any proceedings that take place after the section came into effect, and would therefore permit a former wife to give evidence of what had occurred during the marriage and before the Act came into force (*R.* v. *Cruttenden* [1991] 2 W.L.R. 921). The words "in any proceedings" in these sections cover committal proceedings (*R.* v. *Oxford City Justices, ex p. Berry* [1988] Q.B. 507; *R.* v. *King's Lynn Justices, ex p. Holland, The Times,* April 6, 1992).

"Proceedings in the courts" (Protection from Eviction Act 1977 (c. 43), s.3) is directed to the premises in respect of which possession is sought. It does not require that separate actions should be taken against every occupant (*Thompson* v. *Elmbridge Borough Council* [1987] 1 W.L.R. 1425).

"To institute and carry on such proceedings" (Shops Act 1950 (c. 28), s.71(1)). "Proceedings", for the purposes of this section are not restricted to criminal proceedings and can embrace civil proceedings for an injunction (*Kirklees Borough Council* v. *Wickes Building Supplies* [1992] 3 W.L.R. 170).

"No other proceedings" (Insolvency Act 1986 (c. 45), s.11(3)(*d*)). The detention by a creditor of the debtor's aircraft was not an "other proceeding" for the purposes of this section (*Re Paramount Airways*) [1990] BCC 130).

"Proceedings which are pending" (Children Act 1989 (c. 41) Sched. 14, para. 1(1)). All genuine active applications made in wardship proceedings which had been issued before October 14, 1991 were "proceedings" which were "pending" within the meaning of this paragraph (*Re C (a Minor)* [1992] F.C.R. 169).

"Proceedings of Parliament" (Bill of Rights 1688, art. 9). The process of appointing a chairman and membership of Parliamentary Committees formed part of the "proceedings of Parliament," and evidence about them fell within the privileges of Parliament and could not be adduced without the authority of Parliament (*Rost* v. *Edwards* [1990] 2 W.L.R. 1280); note also "Parliamentary proceedings," Stat. Def., Olympic Symbol etc. (Protection) Act 1995 (c. 32), s.4(16).

"Proceedings for the recovery or administration of any property" (Theft Act 1968 c. 60), s.31(1)(*a*) would not embrace bankruptcy proceedings (*R.* v. *Kansal* [1992] *Gazette,* 15 July, 35

"Proceedings in the nature of an appeal" (Race Relations Act 1976 (c. 74), s.54(2)). The right of review of a decision of the General Medical Council to refuse to grant full registration of a doctor qualified in Pakistan was a "proceeding in the nature of an appeal" within the meaning of this section (*Khan* v. *General Medical Council, The Times,* March 29, 1993).

The term "proceedings . . . against the defendant" within the meaning of the Drug Trafficking Offences Act 1986 (Designated Countries and Territories) Order 1990, Sched. 3 included proceedings *in rem* in which the standing of a person with financial interest in the proceedings was plainly recognised (*SL Re;* [1995] 4 All E.R. 159).

(Council Directive 72/166 relating to insurance against civil liability in respect of the use of motor vehicles, Art. 3). "Bringing of proceedings". The "bringing of proceedings" was when the court prepared, issued and sealed the summons for service (*Silverton* v. *Goodall and Motor Insurers Bureau* [1997] 5 C.L. 81).

"Proceedings in public" (Defamation Act 1952 (c. 66), s.7(3). The final report of a special inquiry amounted to "proceedings in public" where the status and procedure of the inquiry was such that its final report, being its judgment, even if not made public, formed part of the proceeding in public (*Tsikata* v. *Newspaper Publishing plc* [1997] 1 All E.R. 655).

"Conclusion of proceedings", Stat. Def., Criminal Justice and Public Order Act 1994 (c. 33), s.67(9)).

"Decision in proceedings on an appeal," see DECISION.

"Judicial proceedings," Stat. Def., Olympic Symbol etc. (Protection) Act 1995 (c. 32), s.4(16).

"Other legal proceedings," see OTHER.

Action or proceeding, see ACTION.

PROCEEDS. "Proceeds of drug trafficking" (Drug Trafficking Offences Act 1986 (c. 32), s.2(1)). "Proceeds," for the purposes of this section, are not limited to profits (*R.* v. *Smith* (*Ian*) [1989] 1 W.L.R. 765).

"Proceeds" (Theft Act 1968 (c. 60), s.5(4)). Cash handed over by a third party for a cheque represents the "proceeds" of the cheque; so that where a person received two cheques by mistake instead of one, and cashed them both, the cash received represented the "proceeds" of "property" got "by another's mistake" within the meaning of this section (*R.* v. *Davis* (1989) 88 Cr.App.R. 347).

(Drug Trafficking Act 1994 (c. 37)). "Proceeds" did not mean profit but sale price (*R.* v. *Banks* (*David Malcolm*) [1997] 2 Cr.App.R.(S.) 117).

PROCESS. "Process" (Factories Act 1961 (c. 34), s.175(1)) denotes a continuous activity and would not cover a single operation such as, as in this case, the demolition and removal of a kiln (*R.* v. *A.I. Industrial Products* [1987] I.C.R. 418). This case was overruled by the House of Lords when it held that the demolition of a factory was a "process" within the meaning of the Asbestos Regulations 1969 (No. 690), reg. 76(1) (*Nurse* v. *Morganite Crucible* [1989] 2 W.L.R. 82). Dry sweeping asbestos was the undertaking of a "process" within the meaning of these regulations (*Edgson* v. *Vickers and Another* [1994] I.C.R. 510).

See also ARTICLE.

PRODUCE. "The produce of the deposits" (Trustee Savings Bank Act 1981 (c. 65), s.1(3)). The "produce" within the meaning of this section is restricted to the amount of the deposits and interest contractually due under the contracts of deposit and does not require the bank to pay over any increase in the assets of the bank attributable to the employment of the deposits in their business (*Ross* v. *Lord Advocate* [1986] 3 All E.R. 79).

"Shall produce the warrant to him" (Police and Criminal Evidence Act 1984 (c. 60), s.16(5)(*b*)). For the purposes of this section a warrant card was "produced" when the occupier was given an opportunity to inspect it (*R.* v. *Longman* [1988] 1 W.L.R. 619).

"Produces goods" (Value Added Tax Act 1983 (c. 55), Sched. 2, para. 2). The application of a permanent pleating process to fabrics made so significant a change in the character of the fabrics that it could be regarded as a production of goods for the purposes of this paragraph (*Customs and Excise Commissioners* v. *Ali Baba Tex, The Times,* June 4, 1992)

PRODUCT. "Any preparation or other product," see PREPARATION.

PRODUCTION. "The production of such a drug" (Misuse of Drugs Act 1971 (c. 38), s.4(2)(*b*)). Conversion of one form of Class A drug into another form of the same genus might be "production" within the meaning of this section (*R.* v. *Russell* (1992) 94 Cr.App.R. 351).

PROFESSIONAL ASSOCIATION. (Value Added Tax Act 1983 (c. 55), Sched. 6, Group 6, Item 1(*b*)). An association of directors of polytechnics in England and Wales is not "a professional association, membership of which is wholly or mainly restricted to individuals who have or are seeking a qualification appropriate to the practice of the profession concerned" (*Committee of Directors of Polytechnics* v. *Customs and Excise Commissioners* [1992] S.T.I. 909).

PROFESSIONAL MISCONDUCT. See MISCONDUCT.

PROFIT. "Otherwise than for profit" (Value Added Tax Act 1983 (c. 55), Sched. 6, group 6, item 2). Profit means a surplus of income over expenditure, and it does not cease to be "profit" within the meaning of this schedule even if achieved by an educational establishment which ploughed the whole of it back into the business (*Customs and Excise Commissioners* v. *Bell Concord Educational Trust* [1988] S.T.C. 143).
Stat. Def., Income and Corporation Taxes Act 1988 (c. 1), s.6.

PROHIBITED. "Prohibited weapon," see DESIGNED.

PROMISSORY NOTE. (1) A document containing an undertaking to repay a loan "by" a certain date or "on or before" a certain date is not a "promissory note" within the meaning of s.83 of the Bills of Exchange Act 1882 (c. 61). Undertakings in such terms as these have been held not to satisfy the definition in the section which requires that the signatory should undertake to pay on demand or at a "fixed or determinable future time" (*Williamson* v. *Rider* [1963] 1 Q.B. 89, followed by *Claydon* v. *Bradley* [1987] 1 All E.R. 522).

PROPER. (County Court Rules 1981, Ord. 1, r.3). "Proper officer" could only mean the district judge or chief clerk ofthe county court or other officer acting on his behalf (*Kent* v. *Grant* [1997] 7 C.L. 79).
"Proper instrument of transfer," see INSTRUMENT.

PROPERLY. (1) must be shown to have foreseen that the particular kind of harm might be d(R.S.C., Ord. 11, r.1(*j*)). An action against a defendant out of the brought" within the meaning of this rule (*Amanuel* v. *Alexandros Shipping Co., The Alexandros P* [1986] Q.B. 464).
"Properly payable" (Wages Act 1986 (c. 48), s.8(3)). Where there is a dispute as to what wages are "properly payable" within the meaning of this section the Employment Appeal Tribunal has jurisdiction to determine the matter by applying common law and relevant statutory provisions (*Greg May (CF & C)* v. *Dring* [1990] 1 R.L.R. 19; *Kournavous* v. *J. R. Masterson & Sons* [1990] I.C.R. 387). Where there was an agreement to pay a sum in lieu of notice and the only dispute was as to which of two sums was appropriate, the claim was for a liquidated sum "properly payable" as wages within the meaning of s.8(3) rather than for unliquidated damages for breach of contract (*Janstorp International (UK)* v. *Allen*, [1990] I.C.R. 779).

"Properly interested person" (Coroners Rules 1984 (No. 552), r.20(2)(h)). At an inquest the brother of the deceased is not necessarily a "properly interested person" within the meaning of this rule (*R.* v. *Portsmouth Coroner, ex p. Keane* [1990] C.O.D. 7).

"Not properly executed" (Consumer Credit Act 1974 (c. 39), s.61). A consumer hire agreement which failed to bring to the attention of the hirer the duties imposed on him by the agreement and his liability to pay accelerated payments in the event of breach was held to have been "not properly executed" within the meaning of this section (*Rank Xerox* v. *Hepple* [1993] 11 C.L. 73.

A landlord will have acted "properly" in the discharge of his obligation to insure premises against specified risks in some insurance office of repute if the insurance rate is representative of the market rate, or the contract was negotiated at arm's length and in the market-place (*Havenridge* v. *Boston Dyers* [1994] 49 E.G. 111).

(Environmental Protection Act 1990 (c. 43), s.82(12)). Expenses "properly incurred" included the costs of proving the existence of a statutory nuisance and complying with the statutory requirements before a complaint could be made as well as those expenses incurred in preparation for and at the hearing, as long as the amount did not exceed what was warranted by the particular proceedings (*R.* v. *Dudley Magistrates' Court ex p. Hollis* [1999] 1 W.L.R. 642).

PROPERTY. (37) "Money or other property" (Theft Act 1968 (c. 60), s.34(2)(a)). The liquid in a hypodermic syringe can be "property" within the meaning of this section (*R.* v. *Evans (R.)*, *The Times*, December 1, 1987). The equitable interest which a bank retained in drafts it had issued upon another's mistake was "property" within the meaning of the Theft Act 1968 (c. 60) (*R.* v. *Hamid Shadrokh-Cigari*, [1988] Crim.L.R. 465). A sum of money represented by a figure in an account was within the phrase "other intangible property" for the purposes of s.4(1) of the Theft Act 1968 (*R.* v. *Crick, The Times,* August 18, 1993).

(Theft Act 1968 (c. 60), s.4). Parts of corpses were capable of being property if they had acquired different attributes by virtue of the application of a skill such as dissection or preservation, for exhibition or educational purposes (*R.* v. *Kelly* [1999] 2 W.L.R. 384).

Quotas, issued by the Hong Kong Department of Trade and Industry and held by a company which exported textiles, were saleable with the approval of the Department and were "property" within the meaning of the Hong Kong Theft Ordinance, ss.2(1), 5(1) (*Att.-Gen. of Hong Kong* v. *Chan Nai-Keung* [1987] 1 W.L.R. 1339).

"Such property as may be so specified" (Guardianship of Minors Act 1971 (c. 3), s.11B as inserted by s.12 of the Family Law Reform Act 1987 (c. 42). A father's joint tenancy with the mother can be "property" for the purposes of this section (*K.* v. *K.* [1992] 1 W.L.R. 530).

(Matrimonial Causes Act 1973 (c. 18), s.37(2)(b)). An interest in a subsisting periodic tenancy was "property" within the meaning of s.37(2)(b) but a tenancy which had expired could not be revived for the purposes of the section (*Newlon Housing Trust* v. *Alsulaimen* [1998] 4 All E.R. 1).

"Property" (Insolvency Act 1986 (c. 45), s.436). A non-assignable secure periodic tenancy under Part IV of the Housing Act 1985 (c. 68) gave the tenant a mere personal right to remain in possession of the premises and was not "property" which was capable of passing to (and hence being disclaimed by) a trustee in bankruptcy of the tenant under the 1986 Act (*London City Corporation* v. *Brown* [1990] 22 H.L.R. 32). The expectation of an award which may or may not materialise did not form part of a bankrupt's property for the purposes of the Insolvency Act 1986 (c. 45) (*A Bankrupt No. 145/95 In Re; The Times*, December 8, 1995).

"Property" for the purposes of the 1986 Act could only describe an existing item at the time of the bankruptcy order, so that an award of damages from the Criminal Injuries Compensation Board made after a person had been adjudicated bankrupt was not "property" which vested in the trustee in bankruptcy pursuant to ss.283(1) and 306(1) of the 1986 Act (*Re Campbell, (a Bankrupt)* [1996] 3 W.L.R. 626).

"Property which is not property of the company" (Insolvency Act 1986 (c. 45), s.234) applies only to tangible property and does not cover choses in action (*Welsh Development Agency* v. *Export Finance Company* [1992] BCC 270).

(Finance Act 1986 (c. 41), s.102). "Property" in s.102 referred to a particular interest in property, which could exist alongside other interests in the same physical object (*Ingram (Executors of the Estate of Lady Ingram)* v. *IRC* [1998] B.T.C. 8047).

"Onerous property" (Insolvency Act 1986 (c. 45), s.315). A licence to assign a lease under which the assignee covenants with the landlord to observe the covenants in the lease for the remainder of the term is "property" for the purposes of this section (*MEPC* v. *Scottish Amicable Life Assurance Society; Eckley (Third Party)* [1993] 5 C.L. 219).

(Insolvency Act 1986 (c. 45), s.178). A waste management licence could not continue in force if disclaimed so that a conflict arose between the powers of a liquidator under s.178 of the 1986 Act and the general purpose of the Act to promote the interests of good administration of business and commerce, especially when combined with the wide and more far-reaching concerns of the Environment Agency who granted the licence. Accordingly the waste management licence could not be disclaimed as "onerous property" under s.178 (*Environment Agency* v. *Stout* [1999] 1 All E.R. 746).

(Insolvency Act 1986 (c. 45), s.436). A waste management licence could be transferred and generally marketed with the effect that it amounted to "property" within the meaning of s.436 of the 1986 Act (*Environment Agency* v. *Stout* [1999] 1 All E.R. 746).

(Insolvency Act 1986 (c. 45), Sched. 4, para. 6). The fruits of a claim for wrongful trading were not the property of the company at the commencement of the liquidation but were acquired by the liquidator through the exercise of his statutory rights (*Re Oasis Merchandising Ltd* [1997] 2 W.L.R. 764).

"Any property which . . . has been used for the purpose of committing . . . any offence" (Powers of Criminal Courts Act 1973 (c. 62), s.43(1)(*a*)). This is to be construed as meaning offence taken into consideration was not a "relevant period" for the purposeW.L.R. 1340). See also USE.

"Property" (R.S.C., Ord. 29, r.2). A be ordered by the court under Ord. 50, r.3 (*Tudor Accumulator Company* v. *China Mutual Steam Navigation Company* [1930] W.N. 200; *Ash* v. *Buxted Poultry, The Times*, November 29, 1989).

"Property recovered or preserved" (Solictors Act 1974 (c. 47), s.73). The word "property" should be construed widely, and can include a liquidated sum due under an unsatisfied judgment, and an order for costs (even where those costs have not yet been taxed). Such property may be the subject of a solictor's charging order under the Act (*Fairfold Properties* v. *Exmouth Docks (No. 2)* [1993] 2 W.L.R. 241).

An unsevered interest under a joint tenancy did not form part of the "property" of a debtor or his personal representative at the date of the insolvency administration order under the Insolvency Act 1986, s.283 (*Re Palmer (Deceased) (A Debtor)* [1994] 3 All E.R. 835).

"Property recovered or preserved in proceedings" (Legal Aid Act 1988 (c. 34), s.16). The effect of an order postponing sale in proceedings brought under the Law of Property Act 1925, s.30 was to enlarge the beneficial interest by transforming the transient right to remain in possession for as long as the parties agreed to postpone sale into a right to enjoy possession for a substantial period and to have the occupation protected by an enforced postponement of sale so that the beneficial interest of one party would attract the statutory charge under s.16 as "property preserved" in proceedings (*Parkes* v. *Legal Aid Board* [1996] 4 All E.R. 271).

In the case of an insured property development company which carried out its business mainly by the employment of independent contractors who designed and constructed the buildings, the words "property used by the insured at the premises" in a consequential loss policy could not properly be restricted to property owned by the developer or physically in its possession, and so included the architects' drawings which formed an integral part of the development which had been destroyed by fire (*Glengate-KG Properties Ltd* v. *Norwich Union Fire Insurance Society Ltd* [1996] 2 All E.R. 487).

"Company's property" (Insolvency Act 1986 (c. 45), Sched. 4, para. 6). Rights acquired by a liquidator in the course of his statutory powers were not the company's property within the meaning of Sched. 4, para. 6 (*Oasis Merchandising Services Ltd, Re* [1997] 2 W.L.R. 764).

(Criminal Justice Act 1988 (c. 33), s.71(6)). "Realisable property" was the amount that might be realised at the time the order was made, so that a court was entitled to consider the value of property and the amount required to discharge any incumbrance over the property (*R.* v. *Harvey* [1999] 1 All E.R. 710).

"Realisable property", Stat. Def., Criminal Justice (Scotland) Act 1995 (c. 20), s.72.

Stat. Def., Insolvency Act 1986 (c. 45), s.436; Criminal Justice Act 1988 (c. 33), s.102.

Stat. Def., "includes a thing in action, and any interest in real or personal property"—(Law of Property (Miscellaneous Provisions) Act 1994 (c. 36), s.1(4)).

Stat. Def., "includes rights and interests of any description" (Scotland Act 1998 (c. 46), s.126(1)).

"Deal with any property." See DEAL WITH.

"Inspection . . . of property." See INSPECTION.

See also DAMAGES; DOCUMENT.

PROPOSAL. "A proposal to acquire" within the meaning of s.8 of the Caravan Sites Act 1968 (c. 52) could exist without there being a formal resolution or an unequivocal intention to acquire land by a county council for a caravan site (*R*. v. *Secretary of State for the Environment, ex p. North Hertfordshire District Council* [1989] 21 H.L.R. 588).

PROPOSES. (Landlord and Tenant Act 1987 (c. 31), s.5). The expression "proposes" in s.5 denoted a state of mind between mere consideration of a possible course of action and a fixed and irrevocable determination to pursue that course of action, so that the conclusion of a contract with a third party to sell premises amounted to a "proposal" (*Mainwaring* v. *Trustees of Henry Smith's Charity* [1996] 2 All E.R. 220).

PROPRIETARY. "Proprietary right or interest" (Theft Act 1968 (c. 60), s.5(1)). An employee, in breach of a contract made with his employer to sell on the employer's premises only goods supplied by the employer, made a personal profit by selling goods obtained elsewhere. It was held that these circumstances did not have the effect of giving the employer a "proprietary right or interest" in that profit within the meaning of this section (*Att.-Gen.'s Reference (No. 1 of 1985)* [1986] A.C. 909).

PROSECUTION. "The prosecution" (Prosecution of Offences Act 1985 (c. 23), s.22(3)(*b*)), for the purposes of this section, includes both the investigating police and the Crown Prosecution Service (*R*. v. *Birmingham Crown Court, ex p. Ricketts* [1990] Crim.L.R. 745).
"Prosecution for an offence" within the meaning of s.5(4) of the Dangerous Dogs Act 1991 (c. 65) can include a prosecution which had been commenced but discontinued (*R*. v. *Walton Street Justices, ex p. Crothers, The Times,* June 30, 1992).

PROSPECTIVE PURCHASER. A prospective purchaser for the purposes of the Price Marking Order 1991 (No. 1382) was someone who contemplated making a purchase (*Drewery* v. *Ware-Lane* [1960] 3 All E.R. 529 applied) (*Allen* v. *Redbridge London B.C.* [1994] 1 All E.R. 728).

PROSPECTUS. Stat. Def., Companies Act 1985 (c. 6), s.744.

PROSTITUTE. The term "common prostitute" in s.1(1) of the Street Offences Act 1959 (c. 57) applies exclusively to female prostitutes—(*DPP* v. *Bull* [1994] 3 W.L.R. 1196).

PROSTITUTION. "Live wholly or in part on the earnings of prostitution" (Sexual Offences Act 1956 (c. 69), s.30(1)). A woman who offered sexual services and took the money but failed to provide the services was nevertheless engaged in "prostitution" within the meaning of this section (*R*. v. *McFarlane* [1994] Q.B. 419). See also EARNINGS.

PROTECTED SITE. A "protected site" for the purposes of s.1(2) of the Mobile Homes Act 1983 (c. 34) means one where planning permission has been granted for one or more mobile homes to be set up upon it (*Balthasar* v. *Mullane* (1986) 84 L.G.R. 55). Sites provided for gipsies by local authorities under ss.6, 16 of the Caravan Sites Act 1968 (c. 52) are outside the definition of "protected site" in s.5(1) of the 1983 Act (*Greenwich*

London Borough Council v. *Powell* [1989] 2 W.L.R. 7). A site long used for caravans but in respect of which the relevant planning permission had lapsed was not a "protected site" (*Adams* v. *Brown* [1989] L.S.Gaz., December, 39). A site owned and occupied by a county council as a caravan site providing accommodation for gypsies pursuant to a duty under s.6 of the Caravan Sites Act 1968 is not a "protected site" within the meaning of s.1(2) (*Stoke on Trent City Council* v. *Frost & Frost* (1991) 24 H.L.R. 290).

PROTECTED TENANCY. (Rent Act 1977 (c. 42), s.1.) A lease of premises, which included living accommodation, to which Part II of the Landlord and Tenant Act 1954 (c. 56) applied, could not be turned into a "protected tenancy" under the 1977 Act by unilateral action on the part of the lessee (*Wagle* v. *Trustees of Henry Smith's Charity Kensington Estate* [1989] 2 W.L.R. 669).

PROTECTION. "Protection of property," see LAWFUL EXCUSE.

PROVE. The word "proves" in s.1(5) of the Leasehold Property (Repairs) Act 1938 (c. 34) does not connote proof by the landlord on the balance of probabilities, but merely the establishing of a prima facie or arguable case, without the need for evaluation of any rebutting evidence put forward by the tenant (*Associated British Ports* v. *Bailey* (*C.H.*) [1989] 49 E.G. 53).

PROVIDE. "Provided by the employer with work" (Employment Protection (Consolidation) Act 1978 (c. 44), s.87). Where work was made available to an employee on a piecework basis the employee was held to have been "provided" with work within the meaning of this section, notwithstanding that he had failed to agree a rate of pay for the work with the employer (*Spinpress* v. *Turner* [1986] I.C.R. 433).

"Services . . . provided in the course of any trade or business" (Trade Descriptions Act 1968 (c. 29), s.14(1)(ii)). A false statement about services already provided was within this section of it was connected or associated with the supply of the services in question (*R.* v. *Bevelectric* (1992) 142 New L.J. 1342).

(Income and Corporation Taxes Act 1988 (c. 2), s.154). A benefit was not "provided" until it became available to be enjoyed by the taxpayer, so that arrangements between an employer and a builder to build a loft conversion in which the taxpayer could work from home were not relevant in determining whether a benefit had been provided (*Templeton (Inspector of Taxes)* v. *Jacob* [1996] 1 W.L.R. 1433).

PROVISION. "The provision . . . for any building . . . of . . . heating" (Industrial Training (Construction Board) Order 1980 (No. 1274), Sched. 1, para. 1(*a*)(viii)) would include all routine maintenance (*Systems Servicing (Prop. Martway)* v. *Construction Industry Training Board* [1988] I.C.R. 764).

It was immaterial any particular contract of private hire, whether made by telephone or in any other way, when determining whether a defendant had made "provision for the invitation or acceptance of bookings for a private hire vehicle" for the purposes of the Local Government (Miscellaneous Provisions) Act 1974 (c. 57), ss.46(1)(*d*) and 80(1) (*Windsor and Maidenhead Royal Borough Council* v. *Khan* [1994] R.T.R. 87).

(Defective Premises Act 1972 (c. 35), s.1). The phrase "the provision of a dwelling" in s.1 of the Defective Premises Act 1972 connoted the creation of a new dwelling and did not include works of rectification to an existing building (*Jacobs* v. *Moreton* 72 BLR 92).

(Allotments Act 1925 (c. 61), s.8) "Adequate provision" under s.8 meant a site upon which allotment gardening could reasonably be undertaken by persons displaced by a decision to dispose of allotment land and did not require the provision of a site which was at least as advantageous to the plot holders as that which they were required to leave (*R.* v. *Secretary of State for the Environment, ex p. Gosforth Allotments and Gardens Association* (CO/294/94) May 23, 1995, Laws J.).

(Local Government (Miscellaneous Provisions Act 1976 (c. 57), s.19). The providing of time share accommodation did not constitute provision of recreational facilities and the words "assistance of any kind" in section 19(1) had to be construed in that context in which the power to provide buildings was part of the power to provide facilities, and the intended beneficiaries were those intended to use or enjoy the recreational facilities and did not extend to assisting those providing the facilities (*Credit Suisse* v. *Allerdale Borough Council* [1996] 3 W.L.R. 894).

The term "provision" in a Himalaya clause in a bill of lading took its character from the terms "exceptions, limitations, . . . conditions and liberties" with which it was grouped, all of which shared the same characteristics that they were not as such rights which entailed correlative obligations on the cargo-owners (*The Mahkutai* [1996] 3 All E.R. 502).

(Housing Benefit (General) Regulations 1987 (No. 1971), Sched. 1). The "provision of adequate accommodation" extended to general counselling and support services which helped a tenant to maintain the property's fabric but did not include services which were designed to keep the tenant in the property, such as ensuring that rent was paid on time and providing for the physical or personal needs of the tenant (*R.* v. *Sutton London Borough Council, ex p. Harrison, The Times,* August 22, 1997).

(Value Added Tax (Input Order) 1992 (S.I. 1992 No. 3222) art. 5). "Provision for" was to be construed as "to" rather than "for the benefit of" so that Customs were entitled to disallow expenses for guests at a staff dinner dance as business entertainment (*KPMG* v. *Customs and Excise Commissioners* [1997] V. & D.R. 192).

PROVOCATION. (1) The crying and restlessness of a 17-day-old baby could constitute provocation sufficient to enable a defendant to raise it as a defence in a murder case (*R.* v. *Doughty* [1986] Crim.L.R. 625).

Self-induced provocation is still provocation within the meaning of the Homicide Act 1957 (c. 11), s.3 (*R.* v. *Johnson (Christopher)* [1989] 1 W.L.R. 740). The defence of provocation in a murder trial is only available when there has been a sudden and temporary loss of self-control, which need not be immediate (*R.* v. *Ahluwalia* [1992] 4 All E.R. 889). A self-induced glue sniffing addition was not a characteristic which could raise the defence of provocation in a murder trial as it was inconsistent with the concept of the reasonable man (*R.* v. *Morhall* [1993] 4 All E.R. 888). Provocation requires a sudden and temporary loss of control, resulting in the accused being unable to restrain himself from doing what he did. A direction to the effect that provocation requires a complete loss of control to the extent that an accused does not know what he is doing was a misdirection (*R.* v. *Richens* [1993] 4 All E.R. 877).

PSYCHOLOGICAL HARM. These words in article 13(*b*) of Schedule 1 to the Child Abduction and Custody Act 1985 (c. 60) mean substantial and not trivial psychological harm (*A.* v. *A.*, *Re A* (*a Minor*), *The Times*, June 13, 1987).

PUBLIC AUTHORITY. "As public authorities" (Council Directive 77/388 [Sixth VAT Directive], Art. 4(5)). Activities carried out "as public authorities," within the meaning of Art. 4(5), were those carried out by bodies governed by public law in the context of the legal order peculiar to them, and excluded activities which they carried out under the same legal conditions as traders in the private sector (*Ufficio Distrettuale delle Imposte Dirette di Fiorenzuola d'Arda* v. *Comune di Carpaneto Piacentino, The Times*, November 15, 1989).

Stat. Def., Civil Evidence Act 1995 (c. 38), s.9(4); Human Rights Act 1998 (c. 42), s.6.

In Northern Ireland, Stat. Def., Northern Ireland Act 1998 (c. 47), s.75(3).

PUBLIC BODY. Stat. Def., Criminal Appeal Act 1995 (c. 35), s.22(1).

PUBLIC CAPACITY. (General Medical Council Preliminary Proceedings Committee and Professional Conduct Committee (Procedure) Rules 1980 (No. 858), r.6(2), Appendix, r.2). An officer of a family practitioner committee is a person acting in a "public capacity" for the purposes of these rules (*Prasad* v. *General Medical Council* [1987] 1 W.L.R. 1697).

PUBLIC COMPANY. Stat. Def., Companies Act 1985 (c. 6), s.1.

PUBLIC CONCERN. "Not of public concern and . . . not for public benefit" (Defamation Act 1952 (c. 66), s.7). Whether a publication lost the protection of qualified privilege under s.7(3) because it was "not of public concern . . . and not for public benefit" was a question of fact to be decided in each case (*Tsikata* v. *Newspaper Publishing plc* [1997] 1 All E.R. 655).

PUBLIC CORPORATION. Stat. Def., Finance (No. 2) Act 1997 (c. 58), s.5(1).

PUBLIC DOCUMENT. See DOCUMENT.

PUBLIC ENTERTAINMENT. An "acid house" party open to members of two clubs who had bought tickets in advance was a "public entertainment" within the meaning of the Local Government (Miscellaneous Provisions) Act 1982 (c. 30), s.1 (*Lunn* v. *Colston-Hayter* [1991] Crim. L.R. 467).

PUBLIC GOOD. "Conducive to the public good" (Immigration Act 1971) (c. 77), s.3(5)(*b*)). It could not be claimed that the exclusion of a returning resident, who had originally obtained leave to enter the United Kingdom by deception, but had since done nothing to warrant deportation, was "conducive to the public good" (*R. v. Immigration Appeal Tribunal, ex p. Patel* [1988] 2 W.L.R. 1165). The deportation of a person after five drug-related convictions was upheld on the basis of it being "conducive to the public good", notwithstanding that the Parole Board on releasing him had made no recommendation that he should be deported (*R. v. Secretary of State for the Home Department, ex p. Anderson* [1991] C.O.D. 38).

PUBLIC HOLIDAY. Stat. Def., Arbitration Act 1996 (c. 23), s.78(5).

PUBLIC HOUSE. A public house which provided a dance floor, disc jockey and other "theme" activities ancillary to the main purpose of selling intoxicating liquor, did not thereby cease to be a "public house" within the terms of a condition in a change of use planning permission (*Shepway District Council and South Coast Leisure* (1988) 3 P.A.D. 178).

PUBLIC OFFICE. Stat. Def., National Parks and Access to the Country-side Act 1949 (c. 97), s.11A(4) inserted by Environment Act 1995 (c. 25), s.62(1).

PUBLIC PLACE. "Public place" (Road Traffic Act 1972 (c. 20), ss. 5, 6; now Road Traffic Act 1988 (c. 52), ss.4, 5). An off the road parking bay with no physical barrier between it and the road was a "public place" for the purposes of this section (*Capell* v. *DPP* (1991) 155 J.P.N. 139). A caravan park where entry could only be obtained by those who had registered and were using or visiting the site was nevertheless held to be a public place (*DPP* v. *Vivier* [1991] RTR 205). As was a multi-storey car park without a barrier (*Bowman* v. *DPP* [1991] RTR 263). The lane leading from the berth of a cross-Channel ferry through the immigration and docking terminal with access excluded to all but passengers was nevertheless a "public place" for the purposes of these sections, and accordingly a driver breathalyzed on that lane was properly convicted (*DPP* v. *Coulman* [1993] RTR 230). (Road Traffic Act 1988 (c. 52), ss.2 and 3). School grounds, which were used as a leisure park outside school hours were a public place, where members of the public might be expected to be found, *Roger* v. *Normand*, 1994 S.C.C.R. 861.

"Public place" (Criminal Justice Act 1967 (c. 80), s.91). The landing of a block of flats that was secure and locked, accessible only with a key or by means of an entry phone security system, was not a "public place" for the purposes of this section (*Williams (Richard)* v. *DPP* (1992) 95 Cr.App.R. 415).

"Public place" (Dangerous Dogs Act 1991 (c. 65), s.10(2)). A garden path is not a "public place" within the meaning of this section (*Fellowes* v. *DPP* [1993] Crim.L.R. 523). A dangerous dog, as defined by s.1 of this Act, in a private car which was on a public highway was in a "public place" within the meaning of s.10(2) (*Bates* v. *DPP* (1993) 157 J.P. 1004).

Land owned by a local authority could be inferred to be for use by the public so that a dog which attacked in such a place could be said to have been dangerously out of control in a public place (*Cummings* v. *DPP, The Times,* March 26, 1999).

A private club's car park was not a "public place," if of such a size that it would not be generally regarded as a public place (*Havell* v. *DPP* [1993] Crim.L.R. 621).

(Environmental Protection Act 1990 (c. 43), s.87). A telephone kiosk was not a "public place" within the meaning of the 1990 Act, s.87(4) (*Felix* v. *DPP*, *The Times*, May 5, 1998).

Stat. Def., Public Order Act 1986 (c. 64), s.16; Criminal Justice Act 1988 (c. 33), s.139; Prevention of Terrorism (Temporary Provisions) Act 1989 (c. 4), s.3; "includes any highway and any other premises or place to which at the material time the public have or are permitted to have access (whether on payment or otherwise)" (Criminal Justice and Public Order Act 1994 (c. 33), s.167(6)); Northern Ireland (Emergency Provisions) Act 1996 (c. 22), s.58.

PUBLIC PROCESSION. Stat. Def., Public Processions (Northern Ireland) Act 1998 (c. 2), s.17(1).

PUBLIC RECORDS. "Welsh public records," Stat. Def., Government of Wales Act 1998 (c. 38), s.118.

PUBLIC REGISTER. (Civil Jurisdiction and Judgments Act 1982 (c. 27), Sched. 1, art. 16). A company's share register is a register to which the public have access and is therefore a "public register" within the meaning of this article (*Re Fagin's Bookshop* [1992] BCLC 118).

PUBLIC REVENUE. "Public revenue dividend" (Income and Corporation Taxes Acts 1970 (c. 10), ss.93, 107 and 1988 (c. 1), ss.17, 45). Interest on damages payable by the Crown as tortfeasor was not a "public revenue dividend" for the purposes of taxation under Sched. C (*Esso Petroleum Co.* v. *Ministry of Defence* [1989] 3 W.L.R. 1129).

PUBLIC ROAD. Stat. Def., Vehicle Excise and Registration Act 1994 (c. 22), s.62(1).

PUBLIC-SECTOR BODY. Stat. Def., "means the Treasury or any Minister of the Crown, the [Coal] Authority, a local authority, any company which is wholly owned by the Crown or any body which is not a company but is established by or under any enactment for the purpose of carrying out functions conferred on it by any enactment or subordinate legislation"— (Coal Industry Act 1994 (c. 21), Sched. 4., para. 1(2)).

PUBLIC SERVICE. Employment as a foreign language assistant in a university was not employment in the "public service" within the meaning of Article 48(4) of the EEC Treaty (*Alluè* v. *Università degli Studi di Venezia*, [1989] E.C.R 1591).

PUBLIC SERVICE VEHICLE. (Public Passenger Vehicles Act 1981 (c. 14), s.1(1)). A person who used his privately owned motor vehicle to carry girls to school, receiving payment of petrol money, and who was undertaking a systematic carrying of passengers for reward which went beyond the bounds of social kindness, was held to have been "carrying passengers for hire or reward" for the purposes of this section and, therefore, of operating a "public service vehicle" (*DPP* v. *Sikondar* [1993] RTR 90). Courtesy coaches provided by a hotel for use by its customers were "public service vehicles" carrying passengers for hire or reward within the meaning of this section (*Rout* v. *Swallow Hotels* [1993] RTR 80).

PUBLIC TRUSTEE. (Public Trustee Act 1906 (c. 55), s.5(1)). When appointed the sole trustee of a trust, the Public Trustee may exercise the discretions and discretionary powers conferred on the trustees by the trust instrument even though the instrument expressly provides that those powers should not be exercisable at a time when there are less than two trustees (*Duxbury's Settlement Trusts, Re;* [1995] 3 All E.R. 145).

PUBLICATION. (13). "Publication" (Obscene Publications Act 1959 (c. 66), s.2(6)). The act of developing, printing and selling photographic films depicting obscene acts was capable of amounting to an act of publication within the meaning of this section (*R.* v. *Taylor (Alan), The Times,* February 4, 1994).
    Stat. Def., Copyright, Designs and Patents Act 1988 (c. 48), s.175; Knives Act 1997 (c. 21), s.10.

PUBLICLY OWNED. Stat. Def. (in relation to shares), Finance (No. 2) Act 1997 (c. 58), s.5(1).

PUBLISH. Stat. Def., "In relation to journalistic, literary or artistic material, means make available to the public or any section of the public" (Data Protection Act 1998 (c. 29), s.32(6)).

PUBLISHER. Stat. Def., Defamation Act 1996 (c. 31), s.1(2).

PUNISHMENT. "Punishment or measure prescribed by its own law" (Convention on the Transfer of Sentenced Persons 1983 (Cmnd. 9617), Art. 10, para. 2) does not mean the maximum punishment prescribed by law but what would normally be given for the same offence (*R.* v. *Secretary of State for the Home Department, ex p. Read* [1988] 2 W.L.R. 236).

PUPIL. Stat. Def., Further and Higher Education Act 1992 (c. 13), s.14.

PURCHASE. "Money applied in purchasing the estate" (Finance Act 1972 (c. 41), Sched. 9, para. 1). Where a term loan is raised to pay off an overdraft it cannot be said that the money is applied in "purchasing" property, notwithstanding that the overdraft had been negotiated by a property developer to finance the purchase and development of properties (*Lawson* v. *Brooks* [1992] S.T.C. 76).
    "And the landlord did not become landlord by purchasing the dwelling-house" (Rent Act 1977 (c. 42), Sched. 15, case 9). Where parents transferred their interest in a flat to their son in consideration of mutual love and affection but subject to a covenant by the son to keep up mortgage instalments on the flat, the transaction was not one of purchase for the purposes of case 9 (*Mansukhani* v. *Sharkey* [1992] 24 H.L.R. 600). The payment of money by a person when acquiring a house does not necessarily show that it is being acquired by "purchase", but, where a plaintiff bought the property from his employer's estate, even though he did so with money left to him by his employer, it was nonetheless a purchase and the plaintiff became a landlord by purchase (*Amaddio* v. *Dalton* [1991] 23 H.L.R. 332).

PURCHASE PRICE. Where there was an agreement for the payment of commission to an estate agent of a percentage of the "purchase price" it was held that the purchase price included not only the cash sum but also the value of the house taken in part exchange (*Connell Estate Agents* v. *Begej* [1993] EG 125).

PURPOSE. "The purposes for which it was acquired" (Land Compensation Act 1973 (c. 26), s.29(1)(*c*)). Where land was compulsorily acquired for the purposes of council housing development and was then, after the abandonment of the scheme, in process of being cleared so that it could be sold for private development, it was at that time still held for "the purposes for which it was acquired" within the meaning of this section (*Greater London Council* v. *Holmes* [1986] 1 All E.R. 739).

"Larger purpose" (Companies Act 1985 (c. 6), s.153(1)(*a*), 2(*a*)). A narrow definition should be applied to these words so as to prevent the mischief at which the provisions of this part of the Act were aimed, namely allowing an individual to gain control of a public company by using the company's own funds (*Brady* v. *Brady* [1988] 2 W.L.R. 1308).

"Purpose of any business" (Value Added Tax Act 1983 (c. 55), s.14(3(*b*)). Where, in order to achieve the necessary standard of fitness for his career as an actor, the appellant joined a health club, it was held that his subscription was incurred for a "business" purpose within the meaning of this section (*Anholt (Anthony)* v. *Customs and Excise Commissioners* [1989] V.A.T.T.R. 297). Legal expenses incurred by a taxable person arising out of court proceedings wholly unrelated to his business use were not incurred "for the purpose of any business" within the meaning of this section (*Customs and Excise Commissioners* v. *Rosner, The Times,* January 4, 1993).

"Purposes of a government department." See OCCUPY: OCCUPIED.

"For the purpose of restricting or regulating the development or use of the land," see RESTRICT.

(Employment Protection (Consolidation) Act (c. 44), s.23(1)(*b*)). "For the purposes of" within the meaning of s.23(1)(*b*) connoted an object which the employer desired or sought to achieve so that an insistence on managerial experience before promotion to a manager's post an employee who was full-time trade union official was not action taken "for the purpose of" preventing him from continuing on his trade union activities (*Department of Transport* v. *Gallecher* [1994] I.C.R. 967).

A new building which was physically connected with the existing church could be described as being built "for the purpose of enlarging the church" so that it did not contravene the Disused Burial Grounds Act 1884 (c.72), s.3 (*St. Michaels and All Angels, Tettenhall Regis, In Re;* [1996] 2 W.L.R. 385).

PURSUANCE. "In pursuance of a contract" (Finance Act 1981 (c. 35), s.111(7)). Expenditure by the taxpayer company in reimbursing its agents in respect of costs incurred as a result of contracts made by them as agents of the taxpayer was made "in pursuance of" the original contract between the taxpayer and its agents, and not in pursuance of the contracts made by the agents (*I.R.C.* v. *Mobil North Sea* [1987] 1 W.L.R. 1065).

"In pursuance of any instrument made under any enactment" (Race Relations Act 1976 (c. 74), s.41(1)(*a*)). These words are to be construed in the narrow sense in that they refer only to acts done in the necessary performance of an express obligation contained in the instrument. They do not extend to acts done in the exercise of a power or discretion granted by the instrument (*Hampson* v. *Department of Education and Science* [1990] 3 W.L.R. 42). The General Medical Council, in exercising its power to test the knowledge of English of an applicant for registration, pursuant to the Medical Act 1983 (c. 54), was held not to have been acting "in pursuance of . . . any enactment" within the meaning of s.41(1)(*a*) (*General Medical Council* v. *Goba* [1988] IRLR 425).

"In pursuance of a contract" (Leasehold Reform Act 1967 (c. 88), s.3(1), as amended by Housing Act 1980 (c. 51), Sched. 21, para. 3(*a*)). Where a contract did no more than permit the mesne landlord to underlet it could not be said that an underletting was made "in pursuance" of that contract so as to remove it from the ambit of the Act (*Proma* v. *Curtis* [1989] 2 E.G. 74).

PURSUE. "Whom he is pursuing" (Police and Criminal Evidence Act 1984 (c. 60), s.17(1)(*d*)). For a constable to have the right to enter and search premises for the purpose of recapturing someone he is pursuing the pursuit must be continuous and almost contemporaneous with the entry into the premises. "Pursuing" for the purposes of this section connotes a chase (*D'Souza* v. *DPP* [1992] 1 W.L.R. 1073).

Q

QUALIFY. "Qualified in full for any capital allowance" (Finance Act 1968 (c. 44), Sched. 12, para. 1(2), now Capital Gains Tax Act 1979 (c. 14), s.127(1)(*b*)). Machinery which was sold having never been used, and in respect of which capital allowances had been withdrawn retrospectively, had not "qualified" for any capital allowance within the meaning of this regulation (*Burman* v. *Westminster Press* [1987] S.T.C. 669).

(4) A Canadian can be a "qualified person" for the purposes of s.3(2) of the Copyright Act 1956 (c. 74) (*Milltronics* v. *Hycontrol* [1990] F.S.R. 273).

(Pension Schemes Act 1993 (c. 48), s.1). "Qualifying service" meant no more than service which qualifies for relevant benefits (*City and County of Swansea* v. *Johnson* [1999] 2 W.L.R. 683).

QUALIFYING WORKER. (Rent (Agriculture) Act 1976 (c. 80)). An agricultural mechanic was employed in agriculture (*McPhail* v. *Greensmith* [1993] E.G.L.R. 228).

QUALITY. "Nature or quality of medicinal products" (Medicines Act 1968) c. 67, s.93(7)(*b*)). "Quality" applies not only to a commercial quality or grade, but could also mean the medicine's character, characteristics or an attribute (*R.* v. *Roussel Laboratories*; *R.* v. *Good* (1989) 88 Cr.App.R. 140).

R

RACIAL. "Racial group" (Race Relations Act 1976 (c. 74), s.3(1)). English-speaking Welsh and Welsh-speaking Welsh do not have separate ethnic origins and are not therefore of different "racial groups" within the meaning of this section. So that refusing to employ a person because she could not speak Welsh was not racial discrimination (*Gwynedd County Council* v. *Jones* [1986] I.C.R. 833). Gipsies are a "racial group" within the meaning of this section as being identifiable by reference to their ethnic origins (*Commission for Racial Equality* v. *Dutton* [1989] 2 W.L.R. 17). Rastafarians are not a racial group in that their origins are religious and not ethnic (*Dawkins* v. *Crown Supplier (PSA)* [1993] IRLR 284).   See also ETHNIC.

(Race Relations Act 1976 (s.74), ss.1 and 3). The historic separation of the nations of Scotland and England means that the Scots and the English are "racial groups" defined by reference to national origins. Secondly since neither the Scots nor the English possessed common characteristics of a racial nature they could not comprise a racial group within the meaning of s.3 on the basis of ethnic origins alone (*Northern Joint Police Board* v. *Power* [1997] IRLR 610).

"Racial group" (Race Relations Act 1976 (c. 74), s.5(2)). In this section "racial group" is to be narrowly construed as one ethnic group and was not satisfied by a group described as "Afro-Caribbean and Asian" (*Lambeth London Borough Council* v. *Commission for Racial Equality* [1989] I.C.R. 641).

"Racial hatred." Stat. Def., Public Order Act 1986 (c. 64), s.17.

"Racial group," Stat. Def., Crime and Disorder Act 1998 (c. 37), s.28(4).

RACK RENT. "Rack rent" meant the full annual valuation of a property (*Ashworth Frazer Ltd* v. *Gloucester City Council* [1997] EGCS 7).

RADIO. See LOCAL RADIO STATION.

RAILWAY PASSENGER SERVICE. A service which was unlikely to benefit the travelling public and which was introduced simply to avoid the statutory closure procedure coming into operation was not a "railway passenger service" within the meaning of the Railways Act 1993 (c. 43) (*Highland Regional Council* v. *British Railways Board, The Times*, November 6, 1995).

RAILWAY. Stat. Def., Transport and Works Act 1992 (c. 42), s.67.

RAISE IN ISSUE. (Asylum and Immigration Appeals Act 1993 (c. 23), Sched. 2, para. 5(3)(*a*)). The expression "does not raise any issues" refers to a situation where it was unnecessary for the Secretary of State to decide whether a claimant was a refugee since he could be returned to to a third country in which he did not fear persecution (*R.* v. *Secretary of State for the Home Department, ex p. Mehari* [1994] 2 All E.R. 494).

RAPE. (Also male rape and buggery), Stat. Def., Sexual Offences Act 1956 (c. 69), ss. 1 and 12 as substituted and amended by Criminal Justice and Public Order Act 1994 (c. 3), ss. 142 and 143.

RATE. Stat. Def., Local Government Act 1986 (c. 10), s.1.

RATEABLE OCCUPATION. (1) A husband who had separated from his wife and left the matrimonial home was not in "rateable occupation" for the purposes of the Rate Acts notwithstanding that the home remained in his name (*Doncaster Metropolitan Borough Council* v. *Lockwood* (1987) 17 Fam. Law 241). A person who occupied premises as a squatter, either alone or jointly with other squatters, could be in "rateable occupation" of the premises for the purposes of the General Rate Act 1967 (c. 9) (*Westminster City Council* v. *Tomlin* (1988) 28 RVR 196). The owners of a warehouse were held to be in "rateable occupation" of a bay in the warehouse which, although empty, was open for business (*Calmain Properties* v. *Rotherham Metropolitan Borough Council* [1988] E.G. 127). A property company was held not to be in "rateable occupation" of a sports ground which it had bought, with its original equipment, with a view to selling at a profit (*Sheafbank Property Trust* v. *Sheffield Metropolitan District Council* [1988] R.A. 33).

REACHABLE. The words "reachable on arrival" in a voyage charter should be construed in the ordinary sense, and they do not apply solely to cases where a berth was not reachable on arrival by reason of congestion (*K/S Arnt J. Moerland* v. *Kuwait Petroleum Corporation*; *The Fjordaas* [1988] 1 Lloyd's Rep. 336), or non-availability of tugs and bad weather (*Palm Shipping* v. *Kuwait Petroleum*; *The Sea Queen* [1988] 1 Lloyd's Rep. 500).

REALISABLE PROPERTY. (Drug Trafficking Offences Act 1986 (c. 32), s.4(3)). A contingent interest under a will is realisable property under s.4(3) (*R.* v. *Walbrook and Glasgow* [1994] 15 Cr.App.R.(S.) 783).

READINESS. To be valid a notice of "readiness to discharge" issued by a ship must indicate readiness to discharge the whole cargo and not merely a part of it (*Unifert International SARL* v. *Panous Shipping Co.* (*The Virginia M*), [1989] 1 Lloyd's Rep. 603).

REASON. A statement by an immigration officer that he is not satisfied that the potential visitor is genuinely seeking entry for only the limited period specified is a sufficient statement of "reasons" for his decision to refuse entry for the purposes of reg. 4(1)(*a*) of the Immigration Appeals (Notices) Regulations 1984 (No. 2040) (*R.* v. *Secretary of State for the Home Department, ex p. Swati* [1986] 1 All E.R. 717). A declared decision to deport an alien on the ground of national security was a "sufficient statement" of the "reasons" for deportation (*R.* v. *Secretary of State for the Home Department, ex p. Cheblak* [1991] 2 All E.R. 319).

REASONABLE. "Accommodation . . . reasonable for him to continue to occupy" (Housing Act 1985 (c. 68), s.58(2A), as inserted by s.14 of the Housing and Planning Act 1986 (c. 63)). The risk of violence in a particular neighbourhood could affect the reasonableness of occupation of the accommodation available to a woman (*R.* v. *Broxbourne Borough Council, ex p. Willmoth* (1989) 21 H.L.R. 415). When considering whether it is reasonable for an applicant to continue to occupy accommodation, the authority should not confine their enquiries to the state of the accommodation itself but should have regard to its location (*R.* v. *Wycombe District Council, ex p. Queenie Homes and Dean Homes* (1990) 22 H.L.R. 150). In determining whether it was "reasonable" for a applicant to continue to occupy her accommodation, the housing authority must have regard not only to the physical condition but also the suitabiltity of the premises for all those (including in this case a new-born baby) affected by their decision (*R.* v. *Medina Borough Council, ex p. Dee* (1992) 24 H.L.R. 562). Prior to reaching a decision on whether it was "reasonable" for an applicant to continue to occupy accommodation an authority should make a determination about the truth of relevant allegations (*R.* v. *Northampton Borough Council, ex p. Clarkson* (1992) 24 H.L.R. 529), and undertake sufficient enquires as to why a homeless applicant had left her accommodation (*R.* v. *Tynedale District Council, ex p. McCabe* (1992) 24 H.L.R. 384).

(Administration of Justice Act 1970 (c. 31), s.36; Administration of Justice Act 1973 (c. 15), s.8). The outstanding term of a mortgage should, in the absence of exceptional circumstances, be the starting point in determining how long it would be reasonable to keep a mortgagee out of possession so as to give the mortgagor time to pay any sums due under the mortgage (*Cheltenham and Gloucester Building Society* v. *Norgan* [1996] 1 W.L.R. 343; [1996] 1 All E.R. 449) The question of what amounted to a "reasonable period" was a matter for the court to determine on the facts of each case (*National and Provincial Building Society* v. *Lloyd* [1996] 1 All E.R. 630).

"Measures . . . reasonable for a person . . . to take" (Health and Safety at Work etc. Act 1974 (c. 37), s.4(2)). When a person made non-domestic premises available as a place of work for persons not his employees, the reasonableness of the measures which he was required to take to ensure the safety of those premises, as required by this section, was to be determined in the light of his knowledge of the expected use for which the premises had been made available and the extent of his control and knowledge of the actual use thereafter (*Austin Rover Group* v. *Inspector of Factories* [1988] Crim.L.R. 752).

"His conduct was reasonable" (Public Order Act 1986 (c. 64), s.5(3)(*c*)). The reasonableness of conduct as a defence under this section is to be viewed objectively (*DPP* v. *Clarke* [1991] 135 S.J. 135). It might be "reasonable" for the accused to use threatening behaviour in circumstances where he had been told by the police, in excess of their powers, that his property was being seized (*Kwasi Poku* v. *DPP, The Times,* January 19, 1993).

"As the Tribunal may determine to be reasonable in the circumstances" (Copyright, Designs and Patents Act 1988 (c. 48), s.119(3)). In determining what was "reasonable" under this section the Tribunal has a wide discretion. The rate which would have been paid by a willing buyer to a willing seller for the right to use the copyright work in public performances is a useful approach, but not a fixed or exclusive criterion of what would be "reasonable" (*Working Men's Club and Institute Union* v. *The Performing Rights Society* [1992] R.P.C. 227).

"Reasonable to expect of him as a solicitor" (Solicitors Act 1974 (c. 47), Sched. 1A as inserted by Sched. 15 to the Courts and Legal Services Act 1990 (c. 41)). Prejudice to a client does not need to be shown before the professional services provided by a solicitor are found to have been not "of the quality which it is reasonable to expect."

See also ACCOMMODATION; AVAILABLE; HOMELESS.

REASONABLE AMOUNT. (Rules of the Supreme Court 1981, Ord. 62, r.12). The words "reasonable amount" in Ord. 62, r.12 should be taken to represent the hypothetical solicitor having regard to the costs incurred by other solicitors in the locality for similar work based on the taxing officer's own knowledge and experience, but bearing in mind that his past taxations could be out of date (*L.* v. *L. (Legal Aid Taxation)* [1996] 1 FLR 873).

REASONABLE CARE. (Patents Act 1977 (c. 37), s.28(3)(*a*)). The proprietor of a patent, who gave clear and unambiguous instructions to an agent to renew the patent within the prescribed time, was held to have taken "reasonable care" to see that the renewal fee was paid as required under this section, even though the agent failed to carry out the instruction (*Re Textron* [1989] R.P.C. 441).

REASONABLE CAUSE. (13) "Reasonable cause to believe that for medical reasons a specimen of breath cannot be provided" (Road Traffic Act 1972 (c. 20), s.8(3)(*a*), as substituted by Sched. 8 to the Transport Act 1981 (c. 56)). For a constable to have "reasonable cause to believe" under this section it is not necessary that he should determine whether the medical reason is a medically recognised condition, only whether it could be (*Dempsey* v. *Catton* [1986] RTR 194). What was a "reasonable cause to believe" was a question of fact to be objectively decided by the magistrate, and, if it was objectively determined as a matter of fact that there was a reasonable cause, it was immaterial whether the police constable actually believed it or not (*Davis* v. *DPP* [1988] RTR 156; *White* v. *Proudlock* (Note) [1988] RTR 163).

"Without reasonable cause" (Bail Act 1971 (c. 63), s.6(1)). A defendant who handed his charge sheet to his solicitor without making any note of the date on which he was to surrender to custody, and mistakenly formed the opinion that he was to surrender on a later date, was held not to have "reasonable cause" for not surrendering on the due date (*Laidlaw* v. *Atkinson, The Times,* August 2, 1986).

REASONABLE EXCUSE. (8) (Prevention of Crime Act 1953 (c. 14), s.1(1)). A police truncheon is an offensive weapon, but wearing one as part of a police uniform for a fancy dress party was held to be a "reasonable excuse" for having it in a public place for the purposes of this section (*Houghton* v. *Chief Constable of Greater Manchester* (1987) 84 Cr.App.R. 319). Forgetfulness of possession is not a "reasonable excuse" for the purposes of this section (*R.* v. *McCalla* (1988) 87 Cr.App.R. 372). The defence of "reasonable excuse" is not open to individuals who arm themselves to repel violence which they themselves provoke by creating a situation in which violence is likely to occur (*Malnik* v. *DPP* [1989] Crim.L.R. 451).

(11) "Without reasonable excuse, fails to provide a specimen" (Road Traffic Act 1972 (c. 20), s.8(7), as amended by Transport Act 1981 (c. 56), Sched. 8; now Road Traffic Act 1988 (c. 52), s.7(6)). Repugnance on the

part of the accused was capable of providing a "reasonable excuse" for not providing a blood sample for analysis under the requirements of this section if it amounts to a phobia recognised by medical science (*West Yorkshire Metropolitan Police* v. *Johnson* [1986] Crim.L.R. 66). Physical inability to provide a breath specimen in spite of strenuous efforts to do so could amount to a "reasonable excuse" for failure (*Cotgrove* v. *Cooney* [1987] RTR 124). But the fact that a breath test machine is difficult to use is not a reasonable excuse for failing to provide a specimen of breath (*Dawes* v. *Taylor* [1986] RTR 81). The question whether a defendant has a "reasonable excuse" for not providing a specimen does not arise until he attempts to provide one (*Teape* v. *Godfrey* [1986] RTR 213). Section 58 of the Police and Criminal Evidence Act 1984 (c. 60) (giving a person in custody the right to see a solicitor) did not provide a "reasonable excuse" for refusing to provide a specimen until after the arrival of the solicitor (*DPP* v. *Billington* [1988] 1 W.L.R. 535; *Francis* v. *Chief Constable of Avon and Somerset* [1988] RTR 250; *Grennan* v. *Wescott* [1988] RTR 253). Fear of AIDS is not a "reasonable excuse" (*DPP* v. *Fountain* [1988] RTR 385). The fact of having just given a blood sample for hospital purposes was not a "reasonable excuse" for not giving another when required to do so by a constable (*Kemp* v. *Chief Constable of Kent* [1987] RTR 66). An unlawful arrest did not provide a "reasonable excuse" for refusing to provide a specimen (*Hartland* v. *Alden* [1987] RTR 253). The statement by the accused that he was incapable of doing so was not in itself a "reasonable excuse" for failing to provide a sample of breath; some additional evidence, such as that of a doctor, was necessary to show that he was unable to do so (*Grady* v. *Pollard* [1988] RTR 316). The fact that the accused had offered a urine specimen could not constitute a "reasonable excuse" for refusing to supply a blood specimen (*Grix* v. *Chief Constable of Kent* [1987] RTR 193). The absence of a warning of the consequences of a failure to supply a specimen, or the failure to understand that warning, could be a "reasonable excuse" within the meaning of this section (*Chief Constable of Avon and Somerset Constabulary* v. *Singh* [1988] RTR 107). The fact that a request to provide a specimen of blood had previously been made did not constitute a "reasonable excuse" for refusing to comply with a request for a breath specimen (*DPP* v. *Boden* [1988] RTR 188). Where the accused had not been told that in some circumstances a urine sample might be acceptable he was held to have had a "reasonable excuse" for failing to provide a blood sample (*DPP* v. *Gordon*; *DPP* v. *Griggs* [1990] RTR 71). Insistence by a motorist that he should first be permitted to read the code of practice dealing with the detention, treatment and questioning of persons by police officers was not a "reasonable excuse" for refusing to supply a breath specimen when requested to do so before he had finished reading it (*DPP* v. *Cornhill* [1990] RTR 254). Stress following a motor accident is not a "reasonable excuse" (*DPP* v. *Eddowes* [1990] Crim.L.R. 428). An unlawful arrest does not provide a defendant with a "reasonable excuse" for failing to provide a specimen (*R.* v. *Thomas* [1990] Crim. L.R. 269). Following a solicitor's advice is not a "reasonable excuse" for failing to provide a specimen (*Dickinson* v. *DPP* [1989] Crim.L.R. 741). A defendant was held to have had a "reasonable excuse" for failing to provide specimens of breath until after he had seen a solicitor in a case where he had been provided with forms stating that he had a right to see a solicitor "at any time" (*Hudson* v. *DPP*, *The Times*, May 28, 1991). It was not a "reasonable excuse" for failing to provide a breath specimen for analysis that the defendant's self-induced intoxication had rendered him unable to understand the procedure (*DPP* v. *Beech* [1992] Crim. L.R. 64. Stress caused by self-precipitated agitation was not sufficient "reasonable excuse" for failure to comply with this section (*DPP* v. *Ambrose* (*Jean-Marie*) [1992] RTR 285). A mistaken belief that he was entitled to read the codes of practice before providing a breath specimen was not a "reasonable excuse" for the accused's refusal to supply one (*DPP* v. *Whalley* [1991] RTR 161). The defendant had a "reasonable excuse" for failing to provide a specimen under s.7(6) of the 1988 Act where justices found, without medical evidence, that shock and inebriation rendered him physically incapable of doing so (*DPP* v. *Pearman* [1992] RTR 407). A genuine phobia of catching AIDS amounted to a "reasonable excuse" (*De Freitas* v. *DPP* [1993] RTR 98; *DPP* v. *Kinnersley* [1993] RTR 105. The fact that the motorist had tried as hard as he could to provide the requested specimen was not of itself a "reasonable excuse" for failure (*Smith* (*Nicholas*) v. *DPP* [1992] RTR 413). It was not a "reasonable excuse" for failing to provide a specimen of breath for a motorist to insist on seeing a solicitor before doing so (*Salter* v. *DPP* [1992] RTR 386). The fact that the motorist was driving on private land when requested to provide a breath specimen was not a reasonable excuse for failing to comply (*Hawes* v. *DPP* [1993] RTR 116). The fact that the accused had been treated for nervous asthma was not a "reasonable excuse" (*DPP* v. *Curtis* [1993] RTR 72). Being of a nervous disposition and waiting for a solicitor's advice was not a reasonable excuse for failing to provide a specimen (*DPP* v. *Kirk* [1993] C.O.D. 99). Hyperventilation can be a "reasonable excuse" for the purposes of this section (*DPP* v. *Szarzynski* [1993] RTR 364). Failure by a defendant to provide a breath specimen because of the pain occasioned by a road traffic accident although he had earlier provided a sample of breath was not a "reasonable excuse" (*DPP* v. *Radford* [1995] R.T.R. 86).

"Did without reasonable excuse refuse to . . . answer such question" (Financial Services Act 1986 (c. 60), s.178(2)). A financial journalist who refused to disclose the sources of his information concerning insider-dealing in the City could not claim that the protection granted by s.10 of the Contempt of Court Act 1981 (c. 49) provided a "reasonable excuse" for so doing where such disclosure was necessary for the prevention of crime. (*Re an Inquiry under the Company Securities* (*Insider Dealings*) *Act 1985* [1988] 2 W.L.R. 33). See also NECESSARY; PREVENTION.

"Reasonable excuse" (Finance Act 1985 (c. 54), ss.15, 33). Ignorance of the requirement to do so is not a "reasonable excuse" for failure to notify the Commissioners of Customs and Excise of a liability to be registered for value added tax (*Neal* v. *Commissioners of Customs and Excise* [1988] S.T.C. 131). Where a person honestly and reasonably believes that his activities do not amount to the carrying on of a business he has a "reasonable excuse" for failure to notify liability for VAT registation (*Prior* (*M.J.*) *and Prior* (*K.E.*) v. *Customs and Excise Commissioners* [1992] S.T.I. 912).

"Reasonable excuse" (Finance Act 1985 (c. 54), ss.14(6), 19(6)(*b*), 33(2)). An insufficiency of funds by itself was not a "reasonable excuse" for the non-payment of value added tax, except in the rarest of cases; but insuffiency by reason of unforeseeable misfortune might be a reasonable excuse. (*Commissioners of Customs and Excise* v. *Harris*; *Same* v. *Salevon* [1989] S.T.C. 907. The non-receipt of a surcharge liability notice was not a "reasonable excuse" for the purposes of this section (*Customs and Excise Commissioners* v. *Medway Draughting and Technical Services*; *Same* v. *Adplates Offset* [1989] S.T.C. 346). The fact that funds were available when a cheque might be expected to be presented did not provide a "reasonable excuse" for its dishonour on a later presentation (*Customs and Excise Commissioners* v. *Palco Industry Co.* [1990] S.T.C. 594). Financial difficulties brought about by late payment or non-payment on the part of debtors could amount to a "reasonable excuse" within the meaning of this section (*Customs and Excise Commissioners* v. *Steptoe* [1992] S.T.C. 757). Where taxpayers adopted a system of payment by credit-transfer under which the Commissioners allowed them an extra seven days they were entitled to believe that their obligations had been satisfied and had, therefore, a "reasonable excuse" for late payment (*Barney & Freeman* v. *Customs and Excise Commissioners* [1990] VATTR 19). To provide "a reasonable excuse" for a misdeclaration of VAT the default must be the result of unforeseen events, not failure in management oversight of the accounting system (*Merseyside Police Authority* v. *Customs and Excise Commissioners* (1991) 2 VATTR 152). The inaccuracy of a subordinate employee relied upon to prepare a return did not provide a "reasonable excuse" for a misdeclaration within the meaning of s.14(6) (*Victoria Alloys (U.K.)* v. *Customs and Excise Commissioners* (1992) 2 VATTR 163). An honest error based on an incorrect assumption which was corrected within the time limit for furnishing the return could constitute a "reasonable excuse" (*T. & D. Kennedy* v. *Customs and Excise Commissioners* (1991) 2 VATTR 157). Where a taxpayer formed a mistaken view of the date of a transaction of an unfamiliar type on the advice of his accountant he had a "reasonable excuse" for a misdeclaration (*Enterprise Safety Coaches* v. *Customs and Excise Commissioners* (1991) 1 VATTR 74). The fact that an error is made by an employee working without supervision does not necessarily preclude a company from relying on a defence of "reasonable excuse" for a misdeclaration (*Fritz Bender Metals (U.K.)* v. *Customs and Excise Commissioners* (1991) 1 VATTR 80).

"Any person who without reasonable excuse fails to comply" (Banking Act 1987 (c. 22), s.39(11)). A notice issued by the Bank of England under s.39(3)(*a*) of this Act requiring the production of documents overrode a High Court injunction against the disclosure of the documents; so that the existence of the injunction could not provide a "reasonable excuse" for failure to comply with the notice (*A* v. *B Bank (Bank of England intervening)* [1992] 1 All E.R. 778).

"Any person who without reasonable excuse fails to comply" (Banking Act 1987 (c. 22), s.42(4)). Fear of self-incrimination is not a "reasonable excuse" for failure to comply with a requirement imposed by this section (*Bank of England* v. *Riley, The Times*, November 1, 1990).

"Without reasonable excuse" (Control of Pollution Act 1974 (c. 40), s.58(4)). A birthday celebration was not a "reasonable excuse" for nuisance by noise (*Wellingborough District Council* v. *Gordon* [1991] J.P.L. 874).

"Reasonable excuse for not doing anything required to be done" (Taxes Management Act 1970 (c. 9), s.118(2)). Where a taxpayer knew that no assessment had been raised although substantial gains had been realised, it was open to a commissioner to infer neglect for which there was no "reasonable excuse" within the meaning of this section (*Kingsley* v. *Billingham* [1992] S.T.C 132).

"Any person who without reasonable excuse . . ." (Criminal Justice Act 1987 (c. 38), s.2(13)). The fact that a person has been charged with a criminal offence is not a "reasonable excuse" for failing to comply with a requirement imposed on him under this section (*Re Bishopsgate Investment Management, The Times*, April 26, 1993).

(Firearms Act 1968 (c. 27), s.19). A belief that a firearms' certificate was valid and constituted lawful authority was not capable of amounting to a "reasonable excuse" under s.19, since a belief in lawful authority based on facts which is true could not amount to lawful authority, was not capable of being a defence of reasonable excuse to a charge under s.19 (*R.* v. *Jones* [1995] 3 All E.R. 139).

REASONABLE FINANCIAL PROVISION. (Inheritance (Provision for Family and Dependants) Act 1975 (c. 63), s.1(1)). In considering whether "reasonable financial provision" had been made in a will the court was not entitled to take into account legally unenforceable assurances given by other beneficiaries under the will (*Rajabally* v. *Rajabally* (1987) 17 Fam. Law 314). The test for considering whether the disposition of a deceased's estate fails to make "reasonable financial provision" for a surviving spouse, having regard to all of the matters listed in s.3, is objective (*Moody* v. *Stevenson* [1992] 2 W.L.R. 640).

(Inheritance (Provision for Family and Dependants) Act 1975 (c. 63), s.1(1). Past failure to discharge obligations which were now defunct could not give rise to a claim for "reasonable financial provision." The need to reduce or discharge a mortgage did not amount to "reasonable financial provision" required for maintenance (*Re Jennings (Deceased)* [1994] Ch. 286).

The financial needs of an applicant were just one of the factors to be taken into account when determining a claim under the 1975 Act (*Re Krubert (dec'd)* [1996] 3 W.L.R. 959).

REASONABLE GROUNDS. (Occupiers' Liability Act 1984 (c. 3), s.1). Whether an occupier of land had "reasonable grounds to believe" that a trespasser might come into the vicinity of a danger on the land was to be determined by considering the actual state of affairs on the ground when the injury occurred (*White* v. *St. Albans City and District Council, The Times*, March 12, 1990).

"Reasonable grounds to believe" meant that it was necessary to demonstrate that the occupiers had actual knowledge of a relevant fact or knew facts which provided grounds for a relevant belief established by evidence (*Swain* v. *Puri* [1996] 10 C.L. 499).

(Prevention of Terrorism (Temporary Provisions) Act 1984 (c. 8), s.12). Instructions from a superior officer to effect arrest did not give the arresting officer "reasonable grounds" for suspecting a person to be involved in acts of terrorism. When deciding whether an arresting officer had "reasonable grounds" the court was not required to look beyond what was in the officer's mind, and his suspicion did not need to be based on his own observations but could be based on what he had been told, and it was not necessary for him to prove that the facts founding his suspicions were true (*O'Hara* v. *Chief Constable of the Royal Ulster Constabulary* [1997] 1 All E.R. 129).

REASONABLE MAN. (Homicide Act 1957 (c. 11), s.3). A defendant's history or the circumstances in which he was placed at the relevant time might be taken into acocunt when deciding whether an accused was provoked enough to make a reasonable man do as he did, so that the accused's addiction to glue-sniffing, which was said to be the subject of the provocation, should have been taken into account when considering whether the provocation was enough to cause a man possessed of an ordinary man's power of self-control to act as the defendant did however discreditable the characteristic (*R.* v. *Morhall* [1995] 3 All E.R. 659).

REASONABLE PERIOD. (Child Care Act 1980 (c. 5), s.12B(5), as added by Sched. 1 to the Health and Social Services Adjudications Act 1983 (c. 41)). Although a local authority has power under this subsection to postpone for a "reasonable period" the making of a decision concerning parental access to a child under its care, it must nevertheless reach a decision with some urgency so as not to deny the parents their rights (*R.* v. *Bolton Metropolitan Borough Council, ex p. B* (1986) 84 L.G.R. 78).

REASONABLE PRECAUTIONS. "All reasonable precautions and . . . all due diligence" (Consumer Protection Act 1961 (c. 40), s.2; Trade Descriptions Act 1968 (c. 29), s.24; Consumer Safety (Amendment) Act 1986 (c. 29), s.12). Defendants had to do some positive act in order to satisfy the criteria required by these sections. It is not enough, if charged with selling goods that fail to satisfy statutory requirements, to show that the orders placed with the wholesalers were on condition that the goods conformed with those requirements (*Riley* v. *Webb* [1987] Crim.L.R. 477). A system whereby the sampling of imported goods was at the rate of one packet in 10,000 dozen, and the results were only reported to the importer if they were adverse, did not satisfy the standard of care required by these Acts (*Rotherham Metropolitan B.C.* v. *Raysum (U.K.), The Times*, April 27, 1988).

"All reasonable precautions and . . . all due diligence" (Food Safety Act 1990 (c. 16), s.21(1)). A meat trader who placed reliance on a meat inspector's certificate was held to have complied with the requirements of this section (*Carrick District Council* v. *Taunton Vale Meat Traders, The Times,* February 15, 1994).

"All reasonable precautions to ensure the safety of passengers" (Public Service Vehicles (Conduct of Drivers, Conductors and Passengers) Regulations 1936 (No. 619), reg. 4(c)). A driver who, knowing that his bus could not be started without a jerk, nevertheless drove off before all passengers were seated, had not taken "all reasonable precautions" within the meaning of this regulation (*Steff* v. *Beck* [1987] RTR 61).

REASONABLE STEPS. An owner of a vehicle which was deliberately left unattended temporarily in a car park with the keys in the ignition was in breach of a condition in the policy that "all reasonable steps should be taken to protect the vehicle against loss or damage" when the car was stolen and damaged, even though the owner underestimated or did not contemplate the risk of theft or though his absence would only be short (*Devco Holder and Burrows & Paine* v. *Legal & General Assurance Society* [1993] 2 Lloyd's Rep. 567). An assured who had considered the security position of leaving jewellery worth £24,000 in the glove compartment of his car while leaving the car unattended for a short time but keeping it in his view was not reckless and had taken "all reasonable steps to safeguard his property" (*Sofi* v. *Prudential Assurance Co.* [1993] 2 Lloyd's Rep. 559).

REASONABLE TIME. "After the lapse of a reasonable time" (Sale of Goods Act 1979 (c. 54), s.35(1)) means a reasonable time to inspect the goods and try them out generally. The nature of a defect discovered *ex post facto* was irrelevant in assessing what was a "reasonable time" within the meaning of this section. So that the purchaser of a new car, which had a minor defect which subsequently caused the engine to seize up and render it not of merchantable quality, was not entitled to rescission of the contract and repayment of the purchase price as he had by then retained the car for a reasonable time within the meaning of this section (*Bernstein* v. *Pamson Motors* (*Golders Green*) [1987] 2 All E.R. 220).

"Within such reasonable time" (Companies Act 1985 (c. 6), s.212(4)). One and a half working days was not "reasonable" for the purposes of this section (*Re Lonrho* [1990] Ch. 695).

Where the parties to a contract for the sale of land were obliged to complete within a "reasonable time" what was "reasonable" was determined by the facts of the case, and not always the period set out in *Johnson* v. *Humphrey* ([1946] 1 All E.R. 1990) measured by "the legal business which has to be performed in connection with the investigation of title and the preparation of documents" (*Dean* v. *Upton, The Times*, May 10, 1990).

"Within a reasonable time" (Landlord and Tenant Act 1988 (c. 26), s.1(3)). A landlord who failed for nearly three months to respond to the tenant's request for leave to assign, and had then delayed further, had failed to communicate his decision "within a reasonable time," as required by this section (*Midland Bank* v. *Chart Enterprises* [1990] 44 E.G. 68).

"Reasonable time" (Uniform Customs and Practice for Documentary Credits (1983 Revision), art. 16) was held to include time necessary in the circumstances for consultation with experts or with the applicant for credit (*Bankers Trust Co.* v. *State Bank of India* [1991] 2 Lloyd's Rep. 443).

REASONABLENESS. "Requirement of reasonableness" (Unfair Contract Terms Act 1977 (c. 50), s.2(2)). An exclusion clause in a plant hire agreement providing for the hirer to be liable for the negligence of the owners' employee operating the plant, was held not to satisfy the "reasonableness" required by this section (*Phillips Products* v. *Hyland* (Note) [1987] 1 W.L.R. 659). A disclaimer of liability for negligence by a valuer instructed by a mortgagee, in circumstances where it was known that the valuation would probably be relied upon by the prospective purchaser, did not satisfy the "requirement of reasonableness" imposed by this section (*Smith* v. *Bush* (*Eric S.*); *Harris* v. *Wyre District Council* [1989] 17 E.G. 68).

REASONABLY. (11) "Acted reasonably in treating it as a sufficient reason for dismissing the employee" (Employment Protection (Consolidation) Act 1978 (c. 44), s.57(3)). Employers who denied an employee his contractual right to appeal against his dismissal had not "acted reasonably" within the meaning of this section (*West Midlands Co-operative Society* v. *Tipton* [1986] 1 All E.R. 513). The test of reasonableness in determining the fairness of a dismissal under this section is purely objective and it is not necessary for an employer to have considered consultation for a dismissal to be fair (*Duffy* v. *Yeomans & Partners* [1993] I.C.R. 862).

"Could reasonably be expected to have known" (Social Security Act 1975 (c. 14), s.152(4)). A director cannot rely on his lack of business acumen or his lack of interest in the company's affairs for his lack of knowledge of the company's failure to make payments due under this section, because any reasonable director would have known (*Department of Health and Social Security* v. *Evans* [1985] 2 All E.R. 471).

"Person who might reasonably be expected to reside with him" (Housing (Homeless Persons) Act 1977 (c. 48), s.16). Where an applicant for accommodation under this Act had known a man for 10 years and had had a son by him, it was reasonable to expect that he would reside with her (*R.* v. *Wimbourne District Council, ex p. Curtis* (1985) 18 H.L.R. 79).

"Reasonably be expected to live with the respondent" (Matrimonial Causes Act 1973 (c. 18), s.1(2)(*b*)). The test of reasonableness is nothing more than whether an intelligent person, knowing the parties and the circumstances, would consider it reasonable for the petitioner to live with the respondent (*Buffery* v. *Buffery* [1988] 2 F.L.R. 365). A sensitive wife could not "reasonably" be expected to continue to live with a dogmatic and chauvinistic husband (*Birch* v. *Birch* [1992] 1 FLR 564).

REASONABLY NECESSARY. (Local Government (Miscellaneous Provisions) Act 1976 (c. 57), s.47). The imposition of a condition of the issue of new licences for taxis that they must be adapted to take wheelchairs was held to be "reasonably necessary" within the meaning of this section (*R.* v. *Manchester City Council, ex p. McHugh* (1989) 153 J.P.N. 593).

REASONABLY OBTAINABLE. By virtue of s.37(3)(*e*) of the New Towns Act 1981 (c. 64) as substituted by s.1(4) of the New Towns and Urban Development Corporations Act 1985 (c. 5), the Commission for New Towns had to dispose of surplus land for the "best reasonably obtainable" consideration. The use of the word "reasonably" was held not to imply that the Commission could, on moral or ethical grounds of supposed fairness to the persons from whom it had been compulsorily acquired, take a price for the land that was below the best obtainable (*Tomkins* v. *Commission for the New Towns* (1988) 28 RVR 219).

REASONABLY PRACTICABLE. (11) "Reasonably practicable" (Employment Protection (Consolidation) Act 1978 (c. 44), s.67(2)). The advice of a third party that the claimant should delay putting in a claim for unfair dismissal until the internal appeal processes had been exhausted was not a ground for contending that it was not "reasonably practicable" to present a claim in time (*Croydon Health Authority* v. *Jaufurally* [1986] I.C.R. 4). But where a claimant only discovered too late that her dismissal had not, as she had thought, been for reasons of redundancy, it was held that it had not been "reasonably practicable" for her to present the complaint in time (*Machine Tool Industry Research Association* v. *Simpson* [1988] IRLR 212).

In considering whether, in the circumstances, it had or had not been "reasonably practicable" to present a case of unfair dismissal before the expiry of the statutory time limit the expression "reasonably practicable" should be looked at in a common sense way, and an industrial tribunal was entitled to fix a reasonable period after the expiry of the statutory time limit (*James W. Cook and Co. (Wivenhoe)* v. *S. Tipper* [1990] IRLR 386). There is no general principle that a claimant could not rely on erroneous advice from a third party to establish that it was not "reasonably practicable" to present a case of unfair dismissal within the time limits prescribed by this section (*Jean Sorelle* v. *Rybak* [1991] I.C.R. 127). A decision to await the outcome of criminal proceedings was not a ground for contending that it was not "reasonably practicable" to present a claim for unfair dismissal in time (*Trevelyans (Birmingham)* v. *Norton* [1991] I.C.R. 488). Where an application was posted to the tribunal on Friday, May 19, but did not arrive until Tuesday, May 23, *i.e.* one day out of time, it was held that the tribunal had not erred in finding on the evidence that it was not reasonably practicable for the applicant to have presented his application within time. The tribunal were entitled to find as a matter of fact that the applicant could reasonably have expected his application to be delivered within time in the ordinary course of the post (*St. Basil's Centre* v. *McCrossan* [1991] IRLR 455). It was held that a tribunal was entitled to find that it was not reasonably practicable for a complainant to present his complaint on time in circumstances where he had been misled by both a solicitor and an employee of the tribunal (*London International College* v. *Sen* [1993] IRLR 333). But confusion between an employee and his union as to which of them was to initiate the employee's claim for unfair dismissal was not a matter which rendered it impracticable to have presented the application in time (*Dowty Aerospace Gloucester* v. *Ballinger, The Times*, March 5, 1993). Where an employee, who had made a complaint of unfair dismissal more than three months after the termination of his employment after learning of the matters on which he based the complaint, subsequently learnt of other matters and amended his complaint, the industrial tribunal accepted that it had not been reasonably practicable for the employee to present his claim on time (*Marley (UK)* v. *Anderson* [1994] I.C.R. 295). Where a claim for unfair dismissal was sent by post but never arrived, and had to be re-submitted out of time, it was held that it would have been reasonable to check before time ran out whether the original claim had been received by the tribunal (*Capital Foods Retail* v. *Corrigan* [1993] IRLR 430).

"Not reasonably practicable for the complaint to be presented before the end of . . . three months" (Employment Protection (Consolidation) Act 1978 (c. 44), s.67(2)). The reasonable practicability of presenting a complaint depended upon awareness of the specific grounds of complaint, not awareness of a right to complain (*Marley (U.K.) Ltd* v. *Anderson* [1996] I.C.R. 728).

"Not reasonably practicable to secure his attendance" (Police and Criminal Evidence Act 1984 (c. 60), s.68(2)(*a*)(ii)). The question whether it was reasonably practicable to secure the attendance of a witness was to be considered not only as at the time when the trial commenced but against the whole background to the case (*R.* v. *Bray* (1989) 88 Cr.App.R. 354). It was not possible to claim that it was "not reasonably practicable" to secure the attendance of two witnesses from Bogota in circumstances where it was held that the prosecution should have done more to discover the reason for the refusal to attend and to make it clear that the Crown would pay the witnesses' fares and expenses (*R.* v. *De Arango* (*Gonzales*); *Same* v. *Orozco* (*Restrepo*); *Same* v. *Loaiza* (*Medina*) (1993) 96 Cr.App.R. 399). The reasonable practicability of securing the attendance of a witness, on an application by the prosecution to allow his statement to be read, was to be judged as at the date of the application (*R.* v. *French*; *Same* v. *Gowhar*, *The Times*, March 25, 1993).

It was "reasonably practicable" for a complainant to bring an action for unfair dismissal within three months of the effective date of termination of her employment even though the law at that time afforded no protection against unfair dismissal for those working less than 21 hours per week (*Biggs* v. *Somerset County Council*, *The Times*, January 29, 1996).

The phrase requiring a party to comply with the terms of an order of the court as far as was "reasonably practicable" was sufficiently general to embrace financial considerations as well as those which were physically feasible (*Jordan* v. *Norfolk County Council* [1994] 4 All E.R. 218). See also AS SOON AS PRACTICABLE; PRACTICABLE.

REASONABLE PROSPECT. Where it was to be determined whether a landlord had a reasonable prospect of obtaining planning permission, the correct test was whether there was a real chance rather than whether it was more likely than not that permission would be granted (*Cadogan* v. *McCarthy and Stone (Developments) Ltd*, *The Independent*, June 17, 1996).

REASONABLY SUSPECTED. (Public Order Act 1936 (c. 6), s.7(3)). In circumstances where a constable has to make a spur-of-the-moment decision in an emergency it is reasonable for him to suspect that a mere disturbance might develop into a breach of the peace (*G.* v. *Chief Superintendent of Police*, *Stroud* [1987] Crim.L.R. 269).

REBATE. See DISCOUNT.

RECALL. "Is recalled to duty" (Police Regulations 1987 (No. 851), reg. 28). A change in rostered starting time resulting in a change which straddled two "days" under reg. 26(5) was held not to be a "recall" within the meaning of reg. 28 (*R.* v. *South Yorkshire Police, ex p. Middup*, *The Times*, May 1, 1989).

(Mental Health Act 1983 Part II (c. 20), s.42). The word "recall" should not be regarded in purely physical terms as meaning the bringing back of a person to where he once was, but should be viewed as reinstating the restrictive regime of control under s.41 of the 1983 Act (*Dlodlo* v. *Mental Health Review Tribunal for the South Thames Region* [1966] 8 C.L. 474).

RECEIVE. "Persons receiving or entitled to the income" (Income and Corporation Taxes Act 1970 (c. 10), s.114(1)). Where no beneficiary had an absolute vested interest in the income of a trust the trustees were the persons "receiving or entitled to the income" for the purposes of this section (*Dawson* v. *I.R.C.* [1989] 2 W.L.R. 858).

"The return . . . is received by the Commissioners" (Finance Act 1985 (c. 54), s.20(1)(*b*)). A claim that a return was "received" when posted, on the basis that the Post Office was acting as agents for the Commissioners, failed (*Customs and Excise Commissioners* v. *W. Timms & Son* (*Builders*) [1992] STC 374).

"The time the . . . payment is received," see PAYMENT.

See ENTITLED.

RECEIVING APPARATUS. See TELEVISION.

RECKLESS. (5) "Drives . . . recklessly" (Road Traffic Act 1972 (c. 20), s.2 as substituted by Criminal Law Act 1977 (c. 45), s.50(1), now Road Traffic Act 1988 (c. 52), s.2). Reckless driving is not confined to the actual way a vehicle is driven, and a person who drove a lorry with an insecure load, which he knew might fall off and injure someone, and deliberately ran the risk, was guilty of reckless driving (*R.* v. *Crossman* [1986] RTR 49). A person driving with excess alcohol does not automatically drive recklessly (*Hand* v. *DPP* [1991] RTR 225).When directing a jury on reckless driving the judge should use Lord Diplock's definition of recklessness in *R.* v. *Lawrence* [1982] A.C. 510 [see Main Work, p. 2185] (*R.* v. *Lamb* (*Charles*) (1990) 91 Cr.App.R. 181; *R.* v. *Reid* [1991] Crim.L.R. 269; *R.* v. *Fisher* (*Paul*) [1993] RTR 140). Recklessness in the context of reckless driving includes an objective test that is "heedlessness of the presence of a risk as well as disregard of a recognised risk" (*R.* v. *Reid* [1992] 1 W.L.R. 793). The fact that the accused had been drinking before driving was not relevant to the first part of the test of recklessness as laid down by Lord Diplock in *Lawrence* (*supra*), namely whether the accused "was in fact driving the vehicle in such a manner as to create an obvious and serious risk of causing physical injury". Simply to drink in excess and then drive was not sufficient and a direction which suggested to the jury that it might be was defective (*R.* v. *Welburn* [1992] Crim.L.R. 203).

(6) "Causes death . . . by driving . . . recklessly" (Road Traffic Act 1972 (c. 20), s.1 as substituted by Criminal Law Act 1977 (c. 45), s.50(1), now Road Traffic Act 1988 (c. 52, s.1). On the trial of an offence of causing death by reckless driving the jury, in their deliberations, may consider to what extent, to the knowledge of the defendant, the consumption of alcohol affected the manner of his driving (*R.* v. *Clarke* (1990) 91 Cr.App.R. 69). On a charge of causing death by reckless driving the prosecution must show that the manner of driving created an obvious and serious risk. It was not enough to show only that the motorist had drunk to excess and then driven (*R.* v. *Bennett* [1992] RTR 397). Where, on a charge of causing death by reckless driving, the defendant was, at the time, in a state described as driving without awareness induced by motorway driving over a long period, that did not amount to automatism sicne there was no destruction, nor total absence of, voluntary control on the part of the defendant in his driving (*Att.-Gen.'s Reference (No. 2 of 1992)* [1993] 3 W.L.R. 982). On a charge of causing death by reckless driving proof was required that the motorist was driving in such a manner as to create an obvious and serious risk of causing physical injury or substantially damaging property and driving with excess alcohol was not of itself sufficient (*R.* v. *Peters* (*Anthony Raymond*) [1993] RTR 133).

(17) There are two types of recklessness in English law. There is the subjective test which is to be applied to cases under ss.18 or 20 of the Offences against the Person Act 1861 (c. 100), and for which the definition of Mr. Justice Byrne in *R.* v. *Cunningham* [1957] 2 Q.B. 396 is the authority, by which the accused himself must be shown to have foreseen that the particular kind of harm might be done, and has nevertheless been reckless enough to have gone ahead and taken the risk. Then there is the objective test which is to be applied to cases under s.1 of the Criminal Damage Act 1971 (c. 48), and for which the definition of Lord Diplock in *R.* v. *Caldwell* [1982] A.C. 341 is the authority, where the accused himself has not given any thought to the possibility of there being any risk, but has done an act which an ordinary prudent person could foresee might endanger property (*R.* v. *Morrison* (1989) 89 Cr.App.R. 17). On a charge of attempted arson in the aggravated form contemplated by s.1(2) of 1971 Act, in addition to establishing a specific intent to cause damage by fire, it was held to be sufficient to prove that the defendant was reckless as to whether life would thereby be endangered (*Att.-Gen.'s Reference (No. 3 of 1992), The Times,* November 18, 1993). A defendant who failed to give thought to the possibility that his actions might give rise to a risk of causing another person actual bodily harm was not guilty of an offence under s.47 of the 1861 Act. The test of recklessness under this section was that laid down in *R.* v. *Cunningham (supra)* that the accused had foreseen that the particular kind of harm might be done and yet had gone on to take the risk of it (*R.* v. *Spratt* [1990] 1 W.L.R. 1073; *Berrelly* v. *DPP* [1991] C.O.D. 184). On a charge under s.20 of the 1861 Act the accused must be shown to have intended to cause the particular kind of harm specified or to have been reckless as to whether he did so (*R.* v. *Parmenter* (1991) 92 Cr.App.R. 68). See also ASSAULT.

It is open to a trial judge to use the word "reckless" in its ordinary meaning as part of an exposition of gross negligence in cases of manslaughter by criminal negligence (*R.* v. *Adomako* [1994] 3 W.L.R. 288).

(18) "Reckless as to whether any property would be ... damaged"; "reckless as to whether the life of another would be thereby endangered" (Criminal Damage Act 1971 (c. 48), s.1(2)(*a*)(*b*)). In considering whether a certain act is "reckless" within the meaning of this section the question to be asked is whether an ordinary prudent bystander would have perceived an obvious risk that property of value or life would thereby be endangered (*R.* v. *Sangha* [1988] 1 W.L.R. 519).

The word "recklessness" in article 3(2) of the Sea Fishing (Enforcement of Community Control Measures) Order 1985 (No. 487) should be given its ordinary English meaning, as it was in the context of the tort of fraud (*Ministry of Agriculture Fisheries and Food* v. *Mainprize* [1989] Crim.L.R. 213).

"Recklessly to make a statement which is false" (Trade Descriptions Act 1968 (c. 29), s.14(1)(*b*)). A statement concerning past services could fall within the ambit of this section if it was made in connection with the transaction in question, as, for example, a device to persuade the customer to enter into the transaction (*R.* v. *Bevelectric* (1992) 142 New L.J. 1342).

(Data Protection Act 1984 (c. 35), s.5). "Recklessness" required consideration of the defendant's foresight of the consequences set out in the Data Protection Act 1984, s.5 (*Data Protection Registrar* v. *Amnesty International (British Section), The Times,* November 23, 1994).

RECOGNITION AND ENFORCEMENT

RECOGNITION AND ENFORCEMENT. These words in Art. 10(1) of the European Convention on Recognition and Enforcement of Decisions concerning Custody of Children and on the Restoration of Custody of Children are to be construed disjunctively (*Re H (a Child) (Foreign Order)*, *The Times*, November 19, 1993).

RECONSTRUCTION. The erection of a new building as part of the phased redevelopment of a site was not capable of constituting the "reconstruction . . . of any existing building" within the meaning of Schedule 5, group 8 to the Value Added Tax Act 1983 (c. 55), as amended by s.10 and Sched. 6, para. 5 to the Finance Act 1984 (c. 43) (*Wimpey Group Services* v. *Commissioners of Customs and Excise* [1988] S.T.C. 625).

(9) "Substantial work of reconstruction" (Landlord and Tenant Act 1954 (c. 56), s.30(1)(*f*)). Non-structural internal works to update an old building did not amount to substantial "reconstruction" within the meaning of this section (*Barth* v. *Pritchard* [1990] 20 E.G. 65). For works to qualify as "reconstruction" within the meaning of this section it must be shown that they are works of rebuilding (including preparatory or ancillary works) involving a substantial interference with the structure of the building, but not necessarily confined to the outside or load bearing walls (*Romulus Trading Co.* v. *Henry Smith's Charity Trustees* [1990] E.G. 41).

(4) "Reconstruction" (Finance Act 1927 (c. 10), s.55). A partition of assets does not constitute a "reconstruction" for the purposes of this section (*Swithland Investments* v. *I.R.C.* [1990] S.T.C. 448).

RECORD. "Recorded or stored" (Forgery and Counterfeiting Act 1981 (c. 45), s.8(1)(*d*)). Passwords or control numbers used to gain unauthorised access to a computer system had not been "recorded or stored" within the meaning of this section (*R.* v. *Gold*; *R.* v. *Schifreen* [1988] 2 W.L.R. 984). See also DEVICE.

"Record compiled by a person acting under a duty" (Police and Criminal Evidence Act 1984 (c. 60), s.68). Neither the depositions of two witnesses in Ireland (who were too scared to attend), nor the statement of a witness made to a police officer in the United States, could be a "record" for the purposes of this section (*R.* v. *O'Loughlin* [1988] 3 All E.R. 431). Attendance notes of interviews with and statements of witnesses in Swaziland made by a defendant's solicitor, and coming into existence only because he was preparing the defendant's case for trial, did not fall within the restricted meaning of "record" in s.68, and were, therefore, not admissible in evidence in the proceedings (*R.* v. *Cunningham* [1989] Crim.L.R. 435). Confession statements made by persons other than the accused can form part of a "record" within the meaning of this section (*R.* v. *Iqbal* [1990] 1 W.L.R. 756). Application forms for accounts at a bank, completed by a person who might have been a defendant but for the fact that she could not be found, were capable of forming part of a record compiled by bank officials and were therefore part of a "record" within the meaning of this section (*R.* v. *Bow Street Stipendiary Magistrate, ex p. DPP* (1990) 91 Cr.App.R. 283).

(Copyright, Designs and Patents Act 1988 (c. 48), s.182). "Recording" in s.182 covered a recording and a record of the recording (*Bassey* v. *Icon Entertainment plc)* [1995] E.M.L.R. 596).

RECORDING. Stat. Def., Copyright, Designs and Patents Act 1988 (c. 48), s.180.

RECORDS. Stat. Def., Consumer Protection Act 1987 (c. 43), s.45; "in relation to a council, means any documents which—(a) belong to the council or of which they have custody; and (b) have been retained for reference and research purposes or because of their likely historical interest"—(Local Government (Wales) Act 1994 (c. 19), s.60(7)); "includes registers, maps, plans and accounts, as well as computer records and other records kept otherwise than in documentary form"—(Coal Industry Act 1994 (c. 21), s.57(8)); Civil Evidence Act 1995 (c. 38), s.9(4).

See ACCOUNTING RECORDS.

RECOVERY VEHICLE. (Vehicles (Excise) Act 1971 (c. 10), s.16(8)). Appropriately constructed vehicles are not prevented from being "recovery vehicles" within the meaning of this section just because they are being used to transport disabled vehicles (*Harvey (T.L.)* v. *Hall* [1986] RTR 334). See also BREAKDOWN VEHICLE; SPECIALISED.

Stat. Def., Finance Act 1987 (c. 16), Sched. 1, Pt. II, para. 2.

REDEVELOPMENT. Demolition of houses and site clearance undertaken by a local authority, so that it could be sold for private development, was "redevelopment" within the meaning of s.29 of the Land Compensation Act 1973 (c. 26) (*Greater London Council* v. *Holmes* [1986] Q.B. 989). So also was the demolition of a block of flats by the local authority landlord when it became dangerous (*Bulger* v. *Knowsley Borough Council* [1989] 10 C.L. 372).

REDUNDANCY. Stat. Def., Trade Union and Labour Relations (Consolidation) Act 1992 (c. 52), s.195.

"By reason of redundancy", see DISMISS.

RE-ESTABLISHING ONESELF IN THE COMMUNITY. (Social Security Act 1986 (c. 50); Social Fund Directions, direction 4). An applicant who had been previously resident in Ethiopia was refused a discretionary grant from the social fund on the grounds that she could not be said to be "re-establishing herself in the community" (*R.* v. *Social Fund Inspector, ex p. Ali*) (1994) 6 Admin.L.R. 205).

REFERENCE. "Reference is made to any document" (R.S.C., Ord. 24, r.10(1)). This means a direct allusion. It would not cover a reference by inference (*Dubai Bank* v. *Galadari (No. 2)* [1990] 1 W.L.R. 731).

(Law of Property Act 1925 (c. 20), s.141). "Reference to the subject matter." Covenants to carry on the business of a petrol station, to keep the station open all day for the sale of the landlord's products and to purchase from the landlord on his standard terms affected the mode of user of land and ran with it by virtue of s.141 (*Caerns Motor Services* v. *Texaco* [1995] 1 All E.R. 247).

REFUGEE. The term "refugee" does not have the same meaning throughout the Geneva Convention 1951 (*R.* v. *Secretary of State for the Home Department, ex p. Jahangeer (Shala)* [1994] Imm.A.R. 564).

For the purposes of the Geneva Convention, Art. 31, "refugee" included a bona fide asylum-seeker whose application had yet to be decided (*Khaboka* v. *Secretary of State for the Home Department* [1993] Imm.A.R. 585).

Stat. Def., Education (Student Loans) Regulations 1998 (No. 211), reg. 3(1); Education (Mandatory Awards) Regulations 1998 (No. 1166), reg. 2.

(Convention and Protocol relating to the Status of Refugees, Art. 1A(2)). An applicant had to have a current well-founded fear of persecution in order to be recognised as a refugee and it was not sufficient that he had such fear when he left his country of origin. In the context of a civil war, an applicant had to show a fear of persecution which was over an above the risks of clan warfare (*Adan* v. *Secretary of State for the Home Department* [1998] 2 All E.R. 453).

REFUSE. (5) "House refuse" (Public Health Act 1936 (c. 49), s.72). Refuse generated by the occupants of a university hall of residence was held not to be "house refuse" within the meaning of this section (*Mattison* v. *Beverley Borough Council* (1987) 151 J.P. 499). Rubbish, which included mildewed carpeting, an old tin bath and various pieces of wood, metal and plastic, and which had accumulated on the balcony of council premises, was not "house refuse" within the meaning of this section (*Dear* v. *Newham London Borough Council* [1988] 20 H.L.R. 348).

REFUSED. "The grant of a licence may be refused" (Transport Act 1985 (c. 67), s.16). A decision by a local authority to defer, for a few weeks, its decision whether or not to grant hackney carriage licences, pending a survey to determine whether there was an unmet demand for hackney carriages in the area, was not a refusal for the purposes of this section (*R.* v. *Middlesborough Borough Council, ex p. I.J.H. Cameron (Holdings)* [1992] C.O.D. 247).

REGISTER. "The register" in rule 77(1)(*a*) of the Land Registration Rules 1925 (No. 1093 (L28)) does not mean the global register of all registered land but refers only to the register of the individual title in question (*Dunning (A.J.) & Sons (Shopfitters)* v. *Skyes & Son (Poole)* [1987] 2 W.L.R. 167).

REGISTERED. Rights of common were registered within the meaning of the Commons Registration Act 1965 (c. 64) whether the registration was provisional or final (*Dynevor (Lord)* v. *Richardson* [1994] 3 W.L.R. 1091).

In relation to political party, Stat. Def., Registration of Political Parties Act 1998 (c. 48).

REGULARLY. "Regularly works" (Social Security (Unemployment, Sickness and Invalidity Benefit) Regulations 1983 (No. 1598), reg. 7(2)(*b*)). "Regularly" imports the concept of uniform re-occurrence or repetition as distinct from that which occurs casually or intermittently (*Decision No. R.(V)* 2/88).

REGULATE. "For the purpose of restricting or regulating the development or use of the land," see RESTRICT.

REGULATION. "Regulations . . . shall not be made unless a draft . . . has been laid before Parliament" (Supplementary Benefits Act 1976 (c. 71), s.33(3)(*c*) as substituted by Social Security Act 1980 (c. 30), Sched. 2, para. 28). An explanatory booklet issued to explain their operation was not a part of the regulations themselves (*R.* v. *Department of Health and Social Security, ex p. London Borough of Camden, The Times,* March 5, 1986).

REINSTATE. "Reinstate the former residential occupier" (Housing Act 1988 (c. 50), s.27(7)(*b*)). The offer of a key to a wrecked room did not amount to reinstatement within the meaning of this section (*Tagro* v. *Cafane* [1991] 2 All E.R. 235).

RELATE. "Which relates to the carrying out of such operations" (Town and Country Planning Act 1971 (c. 78), s.87(4)(*b*)). Where planning permission was granted for the construction of a replacement bungalow conditional on the existing bungalow being destroyed, it was held that the condition related to the carrying out of building operations—the replacement bungalow—and thus satisfied the conditions of this section (*Harvey* v. *Secretary of State for Wales and Cardiff City Council* (1990) 88 L.G.R. 253). The time limit for enforcement imposed by this section applies only to the structure of the building, that is, that had something to do with the physical and visible characteristics. A breach of a condition relating to occupation was not protected (*Newbury District Council* v. *Secretary of State for the Environment, The Times,* July 19, 1993).

"Relate to the offence" (Misuse of Drugs Act 1971 (c. 38), s.27). Only money or property shown to be connected with the crime for which a person has been convicted can be said to "relate to the offence," and therefore forfeitable under this section; it would not include working capital held for the purpose of buying further drugs (*R.* v. *Llewellyn* (1985) 7 Cr.App.R.(S.) 225; *R.* v. *Simms* (1988) 9 Cr.App.R.(S.) 418).

RELATED ACTIONS. The term "related actions" within the meaning of the Convention on Jurisdiction and the Enforcement of Judgments in Civil and Commercial Matters 1968, Art. 21 was to be given a wide meaning and included actions commenced in different jurisdictions by different parties, which arose out the same cause of action (*The Maciej Rataj* [1995] E.C. All E.R. 229).

RELATING. "Relating only to costs" (Supreme Court Act 1981 (c. 54), s.18(1)(*f*)). An appeal against a decision of the High Court or a county court that a solicitor is or is not to be personally liable for costs under R.S.C., Ord. 62, r.8 is not an appeal "relating only to costs," but is one relating to the conduct of the solicitor (*Thompson* v. *Fraser* [1986] 1 W.L.R. 17).

(12) "Matters relating to trial on indictment" (Supreme Court Act 1981 (c. 54), s.29(3)). Orders made by a crown court judge that an indictment should lie on the file not to be proceeded with without the leave of that court or the Court of Appeal were "matters relating to trial on indictment" within the meaning of this section (*R.* v. *Central Criminal Court, ex p. Raymond* [1986] 1 W.L.R. 710). See also DISPOSE OF. A crown court, when issuing a witness summons under s.2(1) of the Criminal Procedure (Atten-

dance of Witnesses) Act 1965 (c. 69), was exercising its jurisdiction in a matter "relating to trial on indictment" within the meaning of s.29(3) of the 1981 Act (*Ex p. Rees, The Times,* May 7, 1986). The forfeiture order relating to two cars which the applicant had lent to his son, and which had been used on journeys to supply prohibited drugs, was not a matter "relating to trial on indictment" within the meaning of this section because it was not an order which affected the conduct of the son's trial (*R. v. Crown Court at Maidstone, ex p. Gill* [1987] All E.R. 129). A legal aid contribution order made by a magistrates' court, or a crown court, under s.7(1) of the Legal Aid Act 1982 (c. 44) was not a matter "relating to trial on indictment" for the purposes of this section (*Sampson v. Crown Court at Croydon* [1987] 1 All E.R. 609). An application to stay a criminal trial on the ground of abuse of process was not a matter "relating to trial on indictment" since such an application determined whether there should ever be a trial and did not affect the conduct of the trial (*R. v. Central Criminal Court, ex p. Randle* [1991] C.O.D. 227). The decision of a crown court whether or not to exercise its power under s.39 of the Children and Young Persons Act 1933 (c. 12) to allow publication of particulars identifying a young person was not a matter "relating to trial on indictment" (*R. v. Leicester Crown Court, ex p. S.* [1991] C.O.D. 231). Whether a trial should be stayed because of delay in bringing the accused to trial was not a matter "relating to a trial on indictment" within the meaning of s.29(3) (*R. v. Norwich Crown Court, ex p. Belsham, The Daily Telegraph,* March 22, 1991). A costs order made against the prosecution in the Crown Court after verdicts of not guilty had been recorded in the defendants' favour under s.17 of the Criminal Justice Act 1967 (c. 80) was not a matter relating to trial on indictment (*R. v. Wood Green Crown Court, ex p. Director of Public Prosecutions* [1993] 1 W.L.R. 723). A decision by a trial judge determining whether or not the Crown Court had jurisdiction to try an indictment was held to be a matter "relating to trial on indictment" within the meaning of this section (*R. v. Manchester Crown Court, ex p. DPP* [1993] 1 W.L.R. 1524). A decision made under s.6 of the Criminal Justice Act 1987 (c. 38) to dismiss charges before the trial begins is not part of a trial and is not therefore a matter relating to a trial on indictment (*R. v. Central Criminal Court, ex p. Director of Serious Fraud Office* [1993] 1 W.L.R. 949). The refusal by a Crown Court judge to fix a date for the trial of a charge of the possession of drugs was a "matter relating to a trial on indictment" (*R. v. Liverpool Crown Court, ex p. Mende* [1991] C.O.D. 483). The decision of a Crown Court judge to reinstate a prior legal aid order was a matter "relating to" a trial on indictment (*R. v. Isleworth Crown Court, ex p. Willington* [1993] 1 W.L.R. 713). An order of the Crown Court that the whole or part of an indictment should be stayed as an abuse of process was a decision "relating to trial on indictment" under this section (*R. v. Manchester Crown Court and Ashton, ex p. DPP* [1993] 2 W.L.R. 846).

A decision after argument as to the date of a trial on indictment was a matter "relating to trial on indictment," and was not susceptible of judicial review (*R. v. Southwark Crown Court, ex p. Ward, The Times,* August 19, 1994).

The arraignment of a defendant and the conduct of a plea and directions hearing were matters relating to a trial on indictment since the purpose of the arraignment was to determine the plea that he wished to enter in relation to the trial, so that provided the arraignment were properly conducted, the High Court had no jurisdiction to intervene by way of judicial review (*DPP* v. *Crown Court at Manchester and Ashton* [1993] 2 W.L.R. 846 followed) (*R.* v. *Crown Court at Maidstone, ex p. Hollstein* [1995] 3 All E.R. 503 and *R.* v. *Crown Court at Maidstone, ex p. Clark* [1995] 3 All E.R. 513 not followed) (*R.* v. *Crown Court at Leeds, ex p. Hussain* [1995] 3 All E.R. 527).

"Relating to" (Landlord and Tenant Act 1954 (c. 56), s.10(1)). Where a covenant in a tenancy agreement required someone to contribute to the cost of insuring property or of repairing it or of lighting cleaning and maintaining it or even employing a caretaker to look afer it the covenant could fairly be described as a term of the tenancy "relating to" that property within the meaning of this section (*Blatherwick (Services)* v. *King* [1991] Ch. 218).

"In respect of, or relating to, any land" (County Courts Act 1984 (c. 28), s.22(1)). A tree preservation order is an order relating to land for the purposes of this section (*Newport Borough Council* v. *Khan (Sabz Ali)* [1990] 1 W.L.R. 1185).

"Information relating to the proceedings" (Administration of Justice Act 1960 (c. 65), s.12). Publication of the fact that a named person had applied to a mental health review tribunal did not disclose "any information relating to the proceedings" contrary to this section (*Pickering* v. *Liverpool Daily and Echo Newspapers* [1991] 2 A.C. 370).

"In matters relating to a contract" (Civil Jurisdiction and Judgments Act 1982 (c. 27), Sched. 4, art. 5(1)). The special jurisdiction conferred by this article in respect of "matters relating to a contract" requires either an actual contractual relationship or a consensual relationship closely akin to a contract (*Barclays Bank* v. *Glasgow City Council* [1992] 3 W.L.R. 827).

The expression "matters relating to a contract" in Sched. 1, art. 5 of the Civil Jurisdiction and Judgments Act 1982 (c. 27) was not to be interpreted by reference to the classification of causes of action in domestic law, and "contract" included a contract void *ab initio* (*Kleinwort Benson Ltd* v. *Glasgow City Council* [1996] 2 W.L.R. 655).

A claim for restitution of monies paid under a purported agreement which was later accepted as void *ab initio* was not a matter "relating to a contract" within the meaning of Art. 5(1), nor being based on unjust enrichment was it a matter relating to tort or delict within the meaning of Art. 5(3) (*Kleinwort Benson Ltd* v. *Glasgow City Council* [1997] 3 W.L.R. 923).

A claim which could be brought under contract and also, in English law, independently of the contract on the same facts was a "matter relating to a contract" within the meaning of Art. 5(1) (*Source Ltd* v. *T.U.V. Rheinholding A.G.* [1997] 3 W.L.R. 365).

RELATING TO THE ADOPTION OF A CHILD. An application for leave to issue a notice to remove a child from foster-parents was an application "relating to the adoption of a child" under the Adoption Act 1976 (c. 36), s.6 (*Re C. (A Minor) (Adoption Notice: Local Authority)* [1994] 1 W.L.R. 1220).

RELATION. See In Relation to.

RELATIVE. A great uncle is not a "relative" for the purposes of s.72(1) of the Adoption Act 1976 (c. 36) (*Re C. (Minors)* (1989) 133 S.J. 20).

Stat. Def., Income and Corporation Taxes Act 1988 (c. 1), s.417; Children Act 1989 (c. 41), s.105; Family Law Act 1996 (c. 27), s.63(1); Housing Act 1996 (c. 52), s.178(3); (including great-great-grandparents, etc.), Council Tax (Exempt Dwellings) Order 1992 (No. 558), Art. 2(5) substituted by Council Tax (Exempt Dwellings and Discount Disregards) (Amendment) Order 1998 (No. 291), Art. 2.

Stat. Def., "the person's parent or grandparent, child or grandchild, sibling, aunt or uncle or niece or nephew or someone with whom he lives as a couple" (Breeding of Dogs Act 1973 (c. 60), s.4A(6), inserted by Breeding and Sale of Dogs (Welfare) Act 1999 (c. 11), s.7).

See CLOSE RELATIVE.

RELEASE. "Releases or writes off the whole or part of the debt" (Income and Corporation Taxes Act 1970 (c. 10), s. 287(1) and 1988 (c. 1), s.421(1)). Where the sale of the participators' shares in a closed company to a fellow participator included a novation of outstanding debts there was a "release" of those debts for the purposes of these sections (*Collins* v. *Addies; Greenfield* v. *Bains* [1991] STC 445).

RELEVANT. "In conjunction with any other relevant matters" (Sexual Offences (Amendment) Act 1976 (c. 82), s.1(2)). "Relevant matters" in this section are restricted to mean relevant matters properly before the jury, and would not permit any evidence to be adduced about any previous sexual experience of the complainant in a rape case, as this is expressly excluded by s.2(1) (*R.* v. *Barton* [1987] Crim.L.R. 399).

"Relevant factor"; "relevant circumstances" (Statement of Changes in Immigration Rules (H.C. Paper (1982–83) No. 66), paras. 156, 158 Immigration Rules 1983 (H.C. 169), r.58). The adverse effect of a person's deportation on third party interests, which could ultimately extend to the interests of the public as a whole, was a "relevant factor" or "relevant circumstance" within the meaning of these rules (*Singh* v. *Immigration Appeal Tribunal* [1986] 2 All E.R. 721). Failure to understand the significance of the stamps in a passport was held not to be a "relevant circumstance" within the meaning of r.58 (*R.* v. *Secretary of State for the Home Department, ex p. Islam* [1990] C.O.D. 177).

A workshop designed to evaluate a person's "true worth, potential value, skills and aspirations" rather than to find work was not a "relevant course" within the meaning of the Income Support (General) Regulations 1987 (No. 1967), reg. 22(1) (*Fowkes* v. *Adjudication Officer* (unreported).

"Relevant employees" (Employment Protection (Consolidation) Act 1978 (c. 44), s.62(4)(*b*)(i) as amended by Employment Act 1982 (c. 46), s.9, Sched. 3, para. 18). The test of who were "relevant employees" within the meaning of this section was a retrospective one, and, where there had been a lock-out, the tribunal had to consider who were the employees directly interested at the date of the lock-out (*Campey (H.) & Sons* v. *Bellwood* [1987] I.C.R. 311).

(11) "Relevant offence" (Fugitive Offenders Act 1967 (c. 68), s.3(1)). A "relevant offence" for the purposes of this Act is one where, if the elements of the foreign offence were proved, an offence would have occurred against

English law if the events had occurred in the U.K. The court was not entitled to receive evidence to determine whether the fugitive's conduct would found criminal charges in England (*Government of Canada* v. *Avonson* [1989] 3 W.L.R. 436).

The "relevant part" of a discretionary life sentence within the meaning of the Criminal Justice Act 1991 (c. 53), s.34(3) was the period before the Parole Board considered the case and not the period before the prisoner was to be released (*R. v. Fox, The Times*, November 24, 1994). The "relevant part" of a discretionary life sentence amounts to an order (*R.* v. *Dalton* [1995] 2 All E.R. 349).

"Relevant period" (Criminal Justice Act 1967 (c. 80), s.67, as amended by Police and Criminal Evidence Act 1984 (c. 60), s.49). Time spent in custody in connection with an offence taken into consideration was not a "relevant period" for the purposes of this section. (*R.* v. *Towers* (1988) 86 Cr.App.R. 355). The period spent in custody awaiting trial in respect of one robbery was not a "relevant period" for the purposes of the sentence to be imposed for another different robbery (*R.* v. *Secretary of State for the Home Office, ex p. Read* (1987) 9 Cr.App.R.(S.) 206).

Only one period of remand in custody which constituted a "relevant period" within s.67(1) and (1A) of the 1967 Act so that a prisoner was entitled to a deduction of the period of remand in respect of his sentence in respect of the first sentence imposed only (*R.* v. *Secretary of State for the Home Department, ex p. Naughton* [1977] 1 W.L.R. 121 and *R.* v. *Governor of Brockhill Prison, ex p. Evans* [1997] 2 W.L.R. 236).

For the purposes of s.67(1) and 67(1)(A) only one period of remand in custody could be credited against consecutive terms of imprisonment where there had been concurrent remands in custody (*R.* v. *Secretary of State for the Home Department, ex p. Naughten* [1997] 1 W.L.R. 118).

"Relevant time" (Insolvency Act 1986 (c. 45), ss.239, 240). The "relevant time" at which a company gives a preference, for the purposes of s.239, is the time when the decision to grant it was made, not the time when it was actually created (*Re M. C. Bacon* [1991] Ch. 127).

"Relevant circumstances" (Statement of Changes in Immigration Rules 1983 (H.C. 169), rules 52, 58). Emotional needs could be a "relevant" factor in deciding whether a parent was dependent upon a child for the purposes of rule 52 (*R.* v. *Immigration Appeal Tribunal, ex p. Khatum*, [1989] Imm.A.R. 482). Assurances received by a student from a Home Office official, when she applied for an extension of time, that there would be no difficulty in her re-entering the U.K. after a trip abroad were "relevant circumstances" within the meaning of rule 58 (*R.* v. *Secretary of State for the Home Department, ex p. Oloniluyi* [1989] Imm.A.R. 135). The expression "all relevant circumstances" in para. 60 of H.C. 251 cannot give an immigration officer a wider discretion than that which is contained in the rest of the Immigration Rules (*Secretary of State for the Home Department* v. *Patel (Veena)* [1992] ImmAR 486).

"Relevant to any issue" (Police and Criminal Evidence Act 1984 (c. 60), s.74(1)). Evidence of identification can be "relevant" for the purposes of this section (*R.* v. *Grey* (1989) 88 Cr.App.R. 375).

"Relevant association with a visiting force" (Local Government Finance Act 1988 (c. 41), Sched. 1, para. 2). A British citizen residing in the U.K., who was named to a visiting serviceman and dependent upon him, was held not to be exempt from the personal community charge as she did not have a "relevant association with a visiting force". For the purposes of this paragraph and within the meaning of s.12 of the Visiting Forces Act 1952 (c. 67) (*Cherwell District Council* v. *Oxfordshire Valuation and Community Charge Tribunal, The Times,* November 18, 1991).

"Relevant notice" (Agricultural Holdings Act 1986 (c. 5), Sched. 3, Case G). The return by a tenant's execution of a rent demand together with a cheque was held not to have amounted to a "relevant notice" within Case G (*Lees* v. *Tatchell* [1990] 23 E.G. 62). A notice in the "deaths" column of the local newspaper was not a "relevant notice"; nor was a letter from a firm of solicitors informing the landlord's manager that the tenant had died (*BSC Pension Fund Trustees* v. *Downing* [1990] 19 E.G. 87).

"Any relevant requirement has not been complied with" (Acquisition of Land Act 1981 (c. 67), s.23(2)(*b*)). Where a compulsory purchase order has been made there is a "relative requirement" within the meaning of this section that the decision maker should consider and important objection by the person aggrieved (*Bolton Metropolitan Borough Council* v. *Secretary of State for the Environment and Greater Manchester Waste Disposal Authority* (1990) 61 P. & C.R. 343). The words "any relevant requirement" in this section should not be construed as applying to procedural matters only (*Greenwich London Borough Council* v. *Secretary of State for the Environment*; *Yates* v. *Secretary of State for the Environment, The Times,* March 2, 1993).

"The relevant date" (Wages Act 1986 (c. 48), Sched. 6, para. 9) is the date of expiry of the statutory redundancy notice which the employers are required to give under s.49(1) of the Employment Protection (Consolidation) Act 1978 (c. 44) (*Staffordshire County Council* v. *Secretary of State for Employment* [1981] I.C.R. 664).

"Other relevant information" (Legal Aid in Criminal and Care Proceedings (Costs) Regs. 1989 (No. 343), reg. 9(1)). When determining counsel's fees in the Crown Court the sum of the fees paid to the opposing party is "other relevant information" within reg. 9(1) (*Lord Chancellor* v. *Wright* [1993] 4 All E.R. 74).

"Unaware of any relevant fact," see HOMELESS.

(Immigration Act 1971 (c. 77), s.14). Entry clearance could be the "relevant document" for the purposes of s.14(2A) so long as it related to the reason that the application (*R.* v. *Secretary of State for the Home Department, ex p. Ahmed (Ashfaque)* [1995] ImmAR 590).

"Relevant locality," see LOCALITY.

(Income and Corporation Taxes Act 1988 (c. 1), ss.619(1) and 623(2)). ("Relevant earnings . . . means . . . any income . . . chargeable to tax . . . immediately derived by him from the carrying on or exercise by him of his trade . . .). Income received by a tax-payer from syndicates at Lloyds where he was an external Name and where the trade of underwriting was undertaken by the syndicate's agent was not derived by the taxpayer from the carrying on or exercise by him of his trade as an individual and so did not qualify him for relief from income tax (*Koenigsberger* v. *Mellor* (1995) T.C. Leaflet No. 3438).

"Relevant disposal," see DISPOSAL.

"Relevant local government service," see LOCAL GOVERNMENT SERVICE.

RELIABLE DEVICE. (Road Traffic Act 1972 (c. 20), s.8(3)(*b*), as substituted by Sched. 8 to the Transport Act 1981 (c. 56)). These words are to be construed subjectively as meaning a device which the operator reasonably believes to be reliable (*Thompson* v. *Thynne* [1986] RTR 293). Spelling mistakes in the elements of a Lion Intoximeter do not make it an unreliable device (*Burditt* v. *Rogers (Note)* [1986] RTR 391). But an error in the date on the printout of a Lion Intoximeter was held to be sufficient basis for the constable to decide that the device was unreliable (*Slender* v. *Boothby (Note)* [1986] RTR 385).

RELIEF. "Relief" included the exemption of the income of a charity applied for charitable purposes or the exemption of the income of an approved pension scheme from its investments as a relief from tax, which would otherwise have been payable (*Commissioners of Inland Revenue* v. *Universities Superannuation Scheme Ltd* (1996) T.C. Leaflet No. 3499).

In judicial context, Stat. Def., "includes any remedy or order (other than in criminal proceedings)" (Human Rights Act 1998 (c. 42), s.12(5)).

REMOVAL. "The removal or the retention of a child" (Child Abduction and Custody Act 1985 (c. 60), Sched. 1, art. 3). For the purposes of this article the words "removal" and "retention' refer to mutually exclusive single events occurring on a specific occasion (*Re H. (Minors) (Abduction: Custody Rights)* [1991] 3 W.L.R. 68).

"So as to remove him from the lawful control of any person having lawful control" (Child Abduction Act 1984 (c. 37), s.2 (1)(*a*)). These words do not contemplate the geographical removal of the child, but the removal of the control of the child from the parent, or other person having lawful control, to the accused (*R.* v. *Leather, The Times*, January 21, 1993).

REMUNERATION. (Estate Agents Act 1979 (c. 38), s.18(2)). A discount of 18 per cent. obtained by an estate agent on his client's newspaper advertising was in effect a "remuneration" which the agent was required by this section to disclose to his client (*Solicitors' Estate Agency (Glasgow)* v. *MacIver*, 1990 S.C.L.R. 595).

(Wages Act 1986 (c. 48), s.16). Sums payable by the employer only counted as remuneration for the purposes of the 1986 Act, so that amounts paid by employers to employees in respect of cheque and credit card tips constituted remuneration (*Nerva* v. *R. L. & G. Ltd* [1997] I.C.R. 11).

Stat. Def., "includes remuneration in kind" (Data Protection Act 1998 (c. 29), Sched. 8, para. 6(5)).

RENT. Unless there is an express agreement to the contrary the payment of household bills does not constitute the payment of "rent" for the purposes of the Rent Acts (*Bostock* v. *Bryant* [1990] 39 E.G. 64).

(Housing Benefit (General) Regulations 1987 (No. 1971), regs. 10(1), 11(2)(*c*)). "Rent" should be construed widely to include any service charges of other payments expressly mentioned in reg. 10(1) (*R.* v. *East Yorkshire Borough of Beverley Housing Benefits Review Board, ex p. Hare, The Times*, February 28, 1995).

"Rent" under the Supreme Court Act 1981 (c. 54), s.38 and the County Courts Act 1984 (c. 28), s.138 was a periodical sum paid in return for the occupation of land, issuing out of the land where a distress would be levied for non-payment (*Escalus Properties Ltd* v. *Robinson* [1995] 3 W.L.R. 525).

"All the rent in arrear" in s.138(2) and (3) of the County Courts Act 1984 referred to rent in arrears at the date of issue of proceedings and rent claimed as means profits on the date of a court order (*Maryland Estates Ltd* v. *Bar-Joseph* [1998] 3 All E.R. 193).

Stat. Def., Landlord and Tenant Act 1985 (c. 70), s.31.

Term relating to rent, see TERMS.

REORGANISATION. "Reorganisation of a company's share capital" (Finance Act 1965 (c. 25), Sched. 7, para. 4). The increase in a company's share capital followed by the allotment of the new shares to its parent company for cash constituted a "reorganisation" of the company's share capital within the meaning of this paragraph (*Dunstan* v. *Young, Austen and Young* [1989] S.T.C. 8).

REPAIR. "Keep in repair" (Housing Act 1961 (c. 65), s.32(1); now Landlord and Tenant Act 1985 (c. 70), s.11). The landlord's statutory duty to keep the premises in "repair" does not extend to improving the standard of accommodation built some time ago in accordance with the standards which prevailed at the time (*Quick* v. *Taff-Ely Borough Council* [1985] 3 All E.R. 321). Works carried out by the landlord of a house which involved the replacement of the entire front and rear elevations, and of the roof, and the fitting of new windows and doors were not works of "repair" falling within this section (*McDougall* v. *Easington District Council* (1989) 21 H.L.R. 310). The replacement of plaster saturated by condensation could be covered by the landlord's duty to "repair" under this section (*Staves* v. *Leeds City Council* [1990] 11 C.L. 339). The statutory duty to "keep in repair" an ancient listed Grade 1 building was satisfied in circumstances where the landlords had over the years carried out running repairs to the roof, even though they knew it needed replacing (*Trustees of the Dame Margaret Hungerford Charity* v. *Beazeley, The Times*, May 17, 1993).

A repairing covenant in standard form contained in a lease of commercial premises did not impose liability on the tenant to remedy defects in the original construction of the building (*Post Office* v. *Aquarius Properties* (1987) 281 E.G. 798). Substantial works to the roof of a building were to be regarded as "repair or replacement" within the terms of a repairing covenant, rather than an improvement (*New England Properties* v. *Portsmouth New Shops* [1993] 23 EG 130).

(Highways Act 1980 (c. 66), s.56). The presence of vegetation on a bridleway did not render it "out of repair" (*Westley* v. *Hertfordshire County Council, The Times*, March 5, 1998).

"Repair" (Industrial Tribunal Training (Construction Board) Order 1980 (No. 1274), Sched. 1, para. 1(*a*), (*c*), as amended by Industrial Training (Construction Board) Order 1964 (Amendment) Order 1982 (No. 922)), see ALTERATION.

REPORT. (Education Act 1944 (c. 31), Sched. 1, Part II, para. 7). A bare recommendation from the education committee of a local authority relating to a school closure was not sufficient to constitute a "report" for the purposes of this paragraph (*R.* v. *Kirklees Metropolitan Borough Council, ex p. Molloy* (1988) 86 L.G.R. 115). But a report by the sub-committee of an education committee, which was considered but not adopted by the education committee, was held to be sufficient to constitute a "report" by the education committee (*R.* v. *Secretary of State for Education and Science, ex p. Threapleton, The Times*, June 2, 1988). So also was a report by a director of education which the education committee adopted and submitted to the council (*Nichol* v. *Gateshead Metropolitan Borough Council* (1989) 87 L.G.R. 435).

(Defamation Act 1952 (c. 66), Sched. 1, para. 5). A "report" of proceedings did not have to be a contemporary report or item of recent news, and later events did not have any impact on its fairness or accuracy, which was to be measured by reference to that to which it purported to relate (*Tsikata* v. *Newspaper Publishing plc* [1997] 1 All E.R. 655).

REPRESENT. "Represented to the court" (Police and Criminal Evidence Act 1984 (c. 60), s.76(2)). A suggestion during cross-examination that an alleged confession was improperly obtained is not a representation within the meaning of this section (*R.* v. *Liverpool Juvenile Court, ex p. R.* [1988] Q.B. 1).

"Represented for the purposes of sentence" (Powers of Criminal Courts Act 1973 (c. 62), s.21). An offender is not "represented" within the meaning of this section if, having been represented by counsel when he was arraigned and pleaded guilty, he is not so represented when sentence is passed (*R.* v. *Hollywood (Paul)* (1990) 12 Cr.App.R.(S.) 325).

REPRESENTATION. "Representation which he knows to be false" (Immigration Act 1971 (c. 77), s.26(1)(*c*)). Presentation to the immigration officer of a passport and a fraudulently obtained entry clearance was a "representation" within the meaning of this section, notwithstanding that nothing was said (*R.* v. *Secretary of State for the Home Department, ex p. Patel* [1986] Imm.A.R. 515, distinguishing *R.* v. *Secretary of State for the Home Department, ex p. Addo, The Times*, April 18, 1985).

REPRODUCTION. (3) "Reproduction" (Copyright Act 1956 (c. 74), s.48(1)). The direct copying of a three-dimensional object is the indirect copying of the manufacturer's drawings and was held to be "reproduction" (*L.B. (Plastics)* v. *Swish Products* [1979] F.S.R. 145) (knock-down drawers for the furniture industry), (*British Leyland Motor Corporation* v. *Armstrong Patents Co.* [1986] 2 W.L.R. 400) (car's exhaust pipe).

(Income Support (General) Regulations 1987, reg.3, Sched. 2). "Resides with" meant living in the same house and there was no requirement that either the claimant or the other person should have the legal interest in the property (*Bate* v. *Chief Adjudication Officer, The Times*, May 17, 1996).

REQUIRE. "A constable in uniform may require" (Highways Act 1980) (c. 66), s.140(2)). A request under this section must be made by personal confrontation. A telephoned request is not sufficient (*R.* v. *Worthing Justices, ex p. Waste Management* [1989] RTR 131).

"Any document . . . required for any accounting purpose" (Theft Act 1968 (c. 60), s.17(1)(*a*)). Where, for accounting purposes, a telephone operator had a duty to complete a standard printed form recording each call, that document became a document "required for any accounting purpose" and could be "falsified" within the meaning of this section if no document was completed (*R.* v. *Shama* [1990] 1 W.L.R. 661).

"Land is required" (Town and Country Planning Act 1971 (c. 78), s.112(1)). "Required" here means "needed" for the accomplishment of one of the activities or purposes set out in the section (*R.* v. *Secretary of State for the Environment, ex p. Sharkey* [1991] N.P.C. 112).

(Town and Country Planning Act 1990 (c. 8), s.226). "Required" in the context of s.226 means more than "convenient" and less than "indispensable" (*R.* v. *Leeds City Council, ex p. Leeds Industrial Co-operative Society Ltd* (1997) 73 P. & C.R. 70).

REQUIREMENT. (5) "Requirement or condition" (Race Relations Act 1976 (c. 74), s.1(1)(*b*)). These words connote a mandatory requirement which, in the employment context, constitutes an absolute bar to employment if the applicant is unable to comply with it (*Perera* v. *Civil Service Commission (No. 2)* [1983] I.C.R. 428; *Meer* v. *Tower Hamlets London Borough Council* [1988] IRLR 399).

"Requirement or condition" (Sex Discrimination Act 1975 (c. 65), s.1(1)(*b*)). The need for a candidate for a job to be within a particular age range could be a "requirement" within the meaning of this section (*University of Manchester* v. *Jones* [1992] I.C.R. 52).

Management or supervisory experience, which was a material requirement in a job, could be a "requirement or condition" within the meaning of s1(1)(*b*) of the 1975 Act (*Falkirk Council* v. *Whyte* [1997] IRLR 166).

"Requirement of reasonableness," see REASONABLENESS.

RESIDE. (43) "Residing with" (Rent Act 1968 (c. 23), Sched. 1, para. 7; Rent Act 1977 (c. 42), Sched. 1, para. 3). To qualify as a statutory tenant by succession under this schedule a person had to show that he or she had made a home at the premises and had become a part of the household of the deceased relative. So that a woman who moved in with her mother in order to nurse her through a terminal illness, but still retained the tenancy of her own house, where her son continued to live, was held to have been "residing with" her mother within the meaning of this paragraph (*Swanbrae* v. *Elliott* (1987) 19 H.L.R. 87; *Hildebrand* v. *Moon* [1989] 37 E.G. 123). Where a person resided with a statutory tenant with the joint intention that that person should become a permanent member of the household, the fact that the tenant was temporarily absent for four months did not mean that the person was not "residing with" the tenant during that period (*Hedgedale* v. *Hards* (1991) 23 H.L.R. 158).

"Resided with the tenant throughout" (Housing Act 1980 (c. 51), s.30(2)(*b*); Housing Act 1985 (c. 68), s.87) requires a connection with the property and not merely a close relationship with the tenant (*South Northamptonshire District Council* v. *Power* [1987] 1 W.L.R. 1433). For section 87 to apply the secure tenant and his successor need not have resided throughout the 12-month period in the actual premises of which the tenant was the secure tenant at the date of his death (*Waltham Forest London Borough Council* v. *Thomas* [1992] 3 W.L.R. 131).

"Person with whom dependent children reside" (Housing Act 1985 (c. 68), s.59(1)(*b*)). It is not necessary for the dependent child to "reside" wholly and exclusively with the homeless person in order to fall within this section (*R.* v. *Lambeth Borough Council, ex p. Vagliviello* (1990) 22 H.L.R. 393).

(Children Act (c. 41), s.31(8)(b)). It was necessary to construe s. 31(8)(b) as though the word "ordinarily" was expressly included between the words "not" and "reside" (*Gateshead Metropolitan Borough Council* v. *L* [1996] 3 All E.R. 264).

(Income Support (General) Regulations 1987 (S.I. 1987 No. 1967), reg. 3(1)). "Resides with" in reg. 3(1) should be given its ordinary meaning, that the claimant and the other person lived in the same residence or household and the claimant did not have to have a legal interest in the house (*Bate v. Chief Adjudication Officer* [1996] 1 W.L.R. 814).

"With whom dependent children reside," see DEPENDENT.

RESIDENCE. (34)–(36) A tent or a vehicle can be a "residence" for the purposes of s.5 of the Representation of the People Act 1983 (c. 2) regardless of its standard or legality (*Hipperson* v. *Electoral Registration Officer for the District of Newbury* [1985] 3 W.L.R. 61).

The residence of a subsidiary company in a foreign country was not residence by the parent company for the purpose of giving a foreign court jurisdiction over the parent company (*Adams* v. *Cape Industry* [1990] Ch. 433).

To determine the ordinary residence of a company the courts consider where central management and control actually lies. So a non-trading company incorporated in Jersey with a Jersey-registered office, Jersey-resident shareholders and a Jersey board and Secretary which had operated its powers within what it conceived to be Jersey law was "ordinarily resident" outside the jurisdiction for the purposes of R.S.C., Ord. 23, r.1(1)(*a*)—(*Re Little Olympian Each Ways* [1995] 1 W.L.R. 560).

"Normal residence," see NORMAL.

"Occupies as his residence," see OCCUPY (11).

See alo MAIN RESIDENCE.

RESIDENT. (36) "Resident there on the qualifying date" (Representation of the People Act 1983 (c. 2), s.1(1)(*a*)). Seven women who camped on highway land and common land were, in the absence of injunctions requiring them to vacate, which would have made the residence unlawful, held to be resident within the meaning of this section, and therefore "entitled to vote" (*Hipperson* v. *Electoral Registration Officer for the District of Newbury* [1985] 3 W.L.R. 61).

Stat. Def., Local Government Finance Act 1992 (c. 14), s.6; Taxation of Chargeable Gains Act 1992 (c. 12), s.9.

RESIDENTIAL ACCOMMODATION. "Let by him as residential accommodation" (Finance Act 1980 (c. 48), s.80(1)). Accommodation provided for short-term holiday lets was "residential" within the meaning of this section (*Owen* v. *Elliott* [1990] 3 W.L.R. 133).

"Provides . . . residential accommodation" (Registered Homes Act 1984 (c. 23), s.1(1)). For the purposes of this Act "residential accommodation" was provided also to persons in residential care homes who intended staying only on a temporary basis (*Swindells* v. *Cheshire County Council* (1993) 91 L.G.R. 582). Elderly people who came with their carers only during the day to a home registered under this Act were not "resident" there (*Cotgreave* v. *Cheshire County Council* (1992) 156 J.P.N. 762).

(National Assistance Act 1948 (c. 29), ss.21 and 26; National Health Service Act 1977 (c. 49), Sched. 8, para. 2(1); Income Support (General) Regulations 1987 (S.I. 1987 No. 1967), Sched. 4, para. 6(1)). Where a residential home was transferred from local authority control to a voluntary organisation and arrangements made for the local authority to make payments to the organisation at rates determined under the agreement, "residential accommodation" was not provided if the arrangements did not include a provision which satisfied s.26(2) (*Chief Adjudication Officer* v. *Quinn* [1996] 4 All E.R. 72 and *Steane* v. *Chief Adjudication Officer* [1996] 4 All E.R. 83).

"Residential accommodation" was a place where a person lived and did not mean accommodation with an institutional quality or where board or other services were provided (*R.* v. *Newham London Borough Council, ex p. Medical Foundation for the Care and Victims of Torture* (1998) 1 CCLR 227).

Stat. Def., Home Energy Conservation Act 1995 (c. 10), s.1(1).

RESIDENTIAL CARE HOME. Stat. Def., Water Industry Act 1991 (c. 56), Sched. 4A, para. 8(2), inserted by Water Industry Act 1999 (c. 9), s.1(2).

RESIDENTIAL TRIP. Stat. Def., Education Act 1996 (c. 56), s.462(2).

RESIDUARY ESTATE. "Residuary estate" (Administration of Estates Act 1925 (c. 23), s.46). A surviving spouse's rights to a statutory legacy under this section are not affected by her rights in the deceased's estate in another country. A claim that "residuary estate" included foreign property failed (*Re Collens* (*Dec'd*); *Royal Bank of Canada* (*London*) v. *Krogh* [1986] 1 All E.R. 611).

RESORT. (Licensed Premises (Exclusion of Certain Persons) Act 1980 (c. 32), s.1(1)). An accused person need not be convicted of a specifically violent offence but rather one in which violence was involved (such as resisting arrest) for an exclusion order in respect of licensed premises to be imposed (*Barr* (*Stewart Martin*) v. *H.M. Advocate*, 1997 S.L.T. 1004).

RESORTING TO PREMISES. (Betting and Gaming Duties Act 1981 (c. 63), s.26(3)). A person "resorted to premises" from the moment of entry and including the period of time spent on the premises (*R.* v. *Customs and Excise Commissioners, ex p. Ferrymatics, The Times,* February 23, 1995).

RESOURCES. "Other financial resources," see FINANCIAL.
"Actual resources," see ACTUAL.

RESTAURANT. "The carrying on of a restaurant" (Landlord and Tenant Act 1954 (c. 56), s.43 as substituted by s.2(6) of and para. 5 of Sched. 2 to the Finance Act 1959 (c. 58)). Where the tenant of a public house provided the facilities of a restaurant he was "carrying on" a restaurant within the meaning of this section, so that the tenancy was one to which Part II of the 1954 Act applied (*Taylor* v. *Courage* [1993] 44 EG 116).

REST PERIOD. (Transport Act 1968 (c. 73), s.95). A driver who worked overtime, although not driving, worked during a daily working period and not a "rest period" (*Prime* v. *Hosking*, C.O. 2703/94 D.C., December 12, 1994).

RESTRICT. "For the purpose of restricting or regulating the development or use of the land" (Town and Country Planning Act 1971 (c. 78), s.52). A local authority was entitled to enter into a covenant under this section to restrict or to regulate the development or use of land, either permanently or for such a period as was prescribed by the agreement, even though the purpose could not be achieved by the imposition of a planning condition under s.29 of the 1971 Act (*Re L (Minors: Parties), The Times,* November 11, 1993).

RESTRICTION. (Restrictive Practices Act 1976 (c. 34), Sched. 3, para. 2(*b*)). The words "term" and "restriction" referred to the same matter under Sched. 3 of the 1976 Act (*Associated Dairies* v. *Baines* [1995] I.C.R. 296).

RESTRICTIONS. Clauses in franchise agreements which resulted in a division of markets between franchisor and franchisee, or between franchisees, constituted "restrictions of competition" contrary to Art. 85(1) of the EEC Treaty (*Pronuptia de Paris GmbH, Frankfurt am Main* v. *Schillgallis* (No. 161/84) [1986] 1 C.M.L.R. 414). A prohibition by a Member State on the distribution of information relating to the availability of abortions in another Member State was not a restriction on the freedom to provide services within the meaning of Art. 59 of the EEC Treaty, where that information was not distributed on behalf of an economic operator established in the second state (*Society for the Protection of Unborn Children (Ireland)* v. *Grogan, The Times,* October 7, 1991).

RESULT. "As a result of his death" (Fatal Accidents Act 1976 (c. 30), s.4, as substituted by the Administration of Justice Act 1982 (c. 53), s.3). An allowance based on the husband's pension and paid by his former employers to his widow following his death was a benefit which accrued to the widow "as a result of his death" within the meaning of this section (*Pidduck* v. *Eastern Scottish Omnibuses* [1990] 1 W.L.R. 993).

"Obtains property as a result of" the commission of an offence (Criminal Justice Act 1988 (c. 33), s.71(4)). Where the authors of a book about an escaped spy had been charged with the offence of aiding him escape, payments made to them by the publisher were (should they be found guilty) held to be property obtained "as a result of" the commission of an offence within the meaning of this section (*Re R.* [1991] C.O.D. 369).

RETAIL. Persons who paid to gain entry to a field regularly used on Sunday for car boot sales, and there sell goods from their car boots, were not necessarily carrying on a "retail trade or business" within the meaning of the Shops Act 1950 (c. 28), ss.47, 58, 59 (*Palmer* v. *Bugler* [1989] Crim.L.R. 385). A planning permission granted for a warehouse club selling a wide variety of goods in bulk packages and in a manner genuinely designed to ensure that those eligible to use the facility were restricted to a class did not a amount to permission for "retail" use (*R.* v. *Thurrock Borough Council, ex p. Tesco Stores, The Times,* November 5, 1993).

(Value Added Tax Act 1983 (c. 55), Sched. 4, para. 3). Goods which were sent by a supplier to persons, who acted on their own account rather than as agents, some of which would be sold to customers and some of which would have been earmarked for distribution for their own use or to be given as presents, when the supplier were unaware as to which goods would be used for which purpose, were "goods to be sold by retail" and so a taxable supply (*Fine Art Developments plc* v. *Customs and Excise Commissioners* [1996] 1 All E.R. 888).

"Retail employment"; "retail transaction." Stat. Def., Wages Act 1986 (c. 48), s.2.

"Sale by retail." Stat. Def., Licensing (Retail Sales) Act 1988 (c. 25), s.1.

RETAIN. "May be retained so long as it is necessary" (Police and Criminal Evidence Act 1984 (c. 60), s.22(1)). The word "retained" meant that the customs officer was entitled to keep back the produced material as against the owner for as long as permitted, and did not preclude the Commissioners for Customs and Excise from sending the material to a law enforcement agency investigating drug trafficking (*R.* v. *Southwark Crown Court, ex p. Commissioners of Customs and Excise* [1989] L.S.Gaz., December 6, 49).

RETENTION. "The removal or the retention of a child." See REMOVAL.

RETIREMENT. For the purposes of a pension fund rule, termination of employment by dismissal could still constitute "retirement from the service by reason of incapacity" (*Harris* v. *Lord Shuttleworth (Trustees of the National & Provincial Building Society Pension Fund), The Independent,* November 26, 1993).

"Provision in relation to . . . retirement," see IN RELATION TO.

RETURN DAY. (County Courts Act 1984 (c. 28), s.138(2)). For the purposes of this section the "return day" is the date specified for the hearing in the possesssion summons (*Swordheath Properties* v. *Bolt* [1992] 38 EG 152).

RETURNED UNSATISFIED. A writ of *fieri facias* returned after failing to gain access to the premises where it was to be executed, execution was not "returned unsatisfied" within the Insolvency Act 1986 (c. 45), s.268(1)(*b*) to entitle creditors to present a bankruptcy petition (*Re A Debtor (No. 340 of 1992), The Times,* March 6, 1995).

RETURNING OFFICER. (Representation of the People Act 1983 (c. 2), s.128(2)). The "returning officer" referred to the person in charge of the election procedure whether or not a poll was taken (*Absalom* v. *Gillett* [1995] 1 W.L.R. 128).

REVENUE. See CAPITAL

REVERSION. Stat. Def., "means the interest expectant on the termination of a tenancy" (Landlord and Tenant (Covenants) Act 1995 (c. 30), s.28(1)).

REVIEWABLE. "Reviewable disposition" (Matrimonial Causes Act 1973 (c. 18), s.37(2)). Where an order had been made which, on the face of it, discharged an injunction which had restrained a husband from disposing of his properties, the disposition by him of the properties was nevertheless a "reviewable disposition" within the meaning of this section (*Sherry* v. *Sherry* [1991] 1 F.L.R 307).

REVOLVER. Stat. Def., Firearms (Amendment) Act 1988 (c. 45), s.25.

RIDING. A person is "riding" a motorcycle contrary to s.72 of the Highways Act 1835 (c. 50) even if he merely sits astride it and propels it with his feet. This section forbade the riding of a motorcycle on a footpath by the side of a road made or set apart for the accommodation of foot passengers, and was held not to apply to footpaths in general (*Selby* v. *DPP* [1994] R.T.R. 157).

RIFLE. Stat. Def., Firearms (Amendment) Act 1988 (c. 45), s.25.

RIGHT; RIGHTS. "Residuary . . . rights and liabilities" (Local Government Act 1985 (c. 51), s.62). The right to acquire land by compulsory purchase was a "right" within the meaning of this section (*Central Property Investment Co.* v. *Camden London Borough Council, The Times*, April 18, 1989).

"Rights *in rem*" An action for a declaration that a person held immovable property as trustee and for an order requiring that person to execute such documents as should be required to vest the legal ownership in another was not an action *in rem* for the purposes of the Civil Jurisdiction and Judgments Act 1982 (c. 27), Sched. 1, art. 16(1) (*Webb* v. *Webb* [1994] 3 All E.R. 911).

The claim of a trustee in bankruptcy that a half-share in property formed part of the bankrupt's estate was a right in rem of immoveable property since it was a claim in legal ownership (*Re Hayward (dec'd),* [1997] 1 All E.R. 32).

(European Convention on Human Rights 1950, Art. 6). A dispute over a "civil right" had to be genuine and serious, and may relate not only to the existence of the right but also to its scope and the manner of its exercise and the outcome of proceedings must be directly decisive for the right in question before there could be a violation of Art. 6 (*Hamer* v. *France* (1997) 23 E.H.R.R. 1).

"Rights in property arising out of a matrimonial relationship" (Convention on Jurisdiction and the Enforcement of Judgments in Civil and Commercial Matters, Art. 1). An order which is solely concerned with the division of property between spouses was a decision concerned with the rights of property arising out of a matrimonial relationship and not enforceable under the Brussels Convention (*Van den Boogaard* v. *Laumen* [1997] 3 W.L.R. 308).

RIGHT OF WAY. (15) Rights of Way Act 1932 (c. 45), s.1(1)(8)). Section 1(1) does not apply to rights of navigation on non-tidal waters (*Att.–Gen. (ex rel. Yorkshire Derwent Trust)* v. *Brotherton* [1991] 3 W.L.R. 1126). See also WAY.

(Law of Property Act 1925 (c. 20), s.193(1)). For the purposes of s.193(1), rights of access to commons for air and access were not confined to access on foot but extended to riding which was a normal way of taking air and access in 1925 (*R.* v. *Secretary of State for the Environment, ex p. Billson* [1998] 2 All E.R. 587).

RIGHTS OF COMMON. This phrase as used in s.14 of the Military Lands Act 1892 (c. 43) as amended by the Criminal Justice Act 1982 (c. 48) is restricted to legal rights. It is not wide enough to embrace any general practice of taking air and exercise over common land (*DPP* v. *Hutchinson* [1989] 3 W.L.R. 281).

RIGHTS OF CUSTODY. See CUSTODY.

RIOTOUSLY. "Persons riotously and tumultuously assembled together" (Riot (Damages) Act 1886 (c. 38), s.2(1)). The words "riotously and tumultuously" involve two concepts, both of which must be fulfilled to render the section applicable. For an assembly to be tumultuous it should be of considerable size and should be an excited and emotionally aroused assembly and generally, although not necessarily, should be accompanied by noise (*Edmonds (D.H.)* v. *East Sussex Police Authority, The Times*, July 15, 1988).

RISK. "Exposed to risks to their health or safety" (Health and Safety at Work etc. Act 1974 (c. 37), s.3(1)). In a case involving legionella pneumophila the prosecution did not have to prove that members of the public had actually inhaled the bacterium or that it had actually been there to be inhaled. It was sufficient if there had been a risk of it being there (*R.* v. *Board of Trustees of the Science Museum, The Times*, March 15, 1993).

ROAD. (6) "Road" in s.196 of the Road Traffic Act 1972 (c. 20); now Road Traffic Act 1988 (c. 52), s.191, is, by definition, any highway and can therefore include bridleways or footpaths in so far as they are highways (*Lang* v. *Hindhaugh* [1986] RTR 271). A pavement which is both publicly and privately owned can still be a "road" if the public use and pass over the whole of it (*Price* v. *DPP* [1990] RTR 413). The car park of a rest home was not a "road" within the meaning of s.192(1) (*Severn Trent Water* v. *Williams and the Motor Insurers' Bureau* [1995] 10 C.L. 638).

(13) The building of an hotel service yard amounted to "laying out or constructing a road" within the meaning of s.43(2)(*d*) of the Town and Country Planning Act 1971 (c. 78) (*Hillingdon London Borough Council* v. *Secretary of State for the Environment* [1990] J.P.L. 575).

(Road Traffic Act 1988 (c. 52), s.192). The definition of "road" in s.192 was intended to include roads which did not qualify as highways whilst excluding roads to which the public had no access, so that a car park which had a roadway for the passage of vehicles entering and leaving parking bays which had conventional traffic signs and markings and to which the public had access, and where the risk of cars causing injuries could hardly be said to be less than that on other types of road and amounted to a "road" (*Cutter* v. *Eagle Star Insurance Co. Ltd, The Times,* December 3, 1996).

Where a car park was used for "through" traffic and not merely by pedestrians and vehicles to obtain access to and from a parking space, it could be properly be regarded as a "road" (*Clarke* v. *Kato* [1997] 1 W.L.R. 208).

Whether a car park was a road was a matter of fact, but where a pub car park was used by customers of the pub, by walkers and by users of an adjacent garage, the car park was a road within the meaning of the Act (*O'Connor* v. *Royal Insurance* [1996] 12 C.L. 463).

A road linking the docks with a town, owned by the port authority who had restricted access to it by means of a byelaw was a "road" within the meaning of section 192 (*Renwick* v. *Scott* 1996 S.L.T. 1164).

Stat. Def., Road Traffic Act 1988 (c. 52), s.192; Road Traffic Offenders Act 1988 (c. 53), s.98); Horses (Protective Headgear) Act 1990 (c. 25), s.3; Goods Vehicles (Licensing of Operators) Act 1995 (c. 23), s.58(1); Private Hire Vehicles (London) Act 1998 (c. 34), s.36; Road Traffic (NHS Charges) Act 1999 (c. 3), s.17.

ROAD TRAFFIC. Stat. Def., Road Traffic Reduction (National Targets) Act 1998 (c. 24), s.1.

ROBBERY. (4) (Theft Act 1968 (c. 60), s.8). Stealing food from a victim of violence, but without knowledge of the violence, which had taken place in a different room, was held not to be "robbery" within the meaning of this section (*R.* v. *Harris, The Times,* March 4, 1988).

ROLE OF A CHURCH AS A LOCAL CENTRE OF WORSHIP AND MISSION. It is permissible to consider the interests of the regular members of the congregation who do not reside within the parish as well as the interests of local parishioners when constructing the words "the role of the church as a local centre of worship and mission" in the Care of Churches and Ecclesiastical Jurisdiction Measure 1991, s.1 (*Re St. Luke the Evangelist, Maidstone* [1995] 1 All E.R. 321).

ROOF. "Roofed accommodation" (Car Tax Act 1983 (c. 53), s.2(1)(*c*)(ii)). A roofed space behind the driver's seat of a pick-up truck which had side windows, but which was not reasonably capable of accommodating a person, was not "roofed accommodation" within the meaning of this section (*R.* v. *Commissioners of Customs and Excise, ex p. Nissan (U.K.), The Times,* November 23, 1987).

ROUND. A "round" (Motor Vehicles (Wearing of Seat Belts) Regulations 1982 (No. 1202), reg. 4) means a series of visits or calls. A newsagent was not on a "round" within the meaning of this regulation when driving his van every morning to the same pick-up point to collect bundles of newspapers (*Webb* v. *Crane* [1988] RTR 204).

ROYAL COMMISSION. Stat. Def., Olympic Symbol *etc.* (Protection) Act 1995 (c. 32), s.4(16).

S

SACRAMENT HOUSE. A "sacrament house" to reserve the sacrament is not an illegal ornament but an article consistent with and subsidiary to the ministrations of the church (*S. Thomas, Pennywell, Re;* [1995] 2 W.L.R. 154).

SADDLER. Stat. Def., Medicines (Exemption for Merchants in Veterinary Drugs) Order 1998 (No. 1044), Art. 2(1).

SAFE; SAFETY. "Safe means of access" (Factories Act 1961 (c. 34), s.29(1)). An employer who had an established system for ensuring safe access at his factory was not in breach of his duty under this section by failing to ensure in severe weather conditions that every area had been gritted by the start of the working day (*Gitsham* v. *C. H. Pearce & Sons, The Times*, February 11, 1991). The test of keeping a place of work safe for any person working there, under s.29(1), is a strict one, and there is no obligation in a claim for breach of statutory duty under the section for the claimant to establish that the question of reasonable foreseeability arises in consideration of whether the place of work is safe (*Larner* v. *British Steel, The Times*, February 19, 1993).

"Secure that the ship is operated in a safe manner" (Merchant Shipping Act 1988 (c. 12), s.31(1)). A shipowner is under a duty to take all reasonable steps to ensure that his ship is operated in a safe manner but, in the absence of evidence relating to decisions by the company's management, liability is not imposed on the owner for every error or omission of every employee, however junior (*Seaboard Offshore* v. *Secretary of State for Transport* [1993] 1 W.L.R. 1025).

"Safe system of work." The mere fact that a system of work was hazardous did not render it unsafe (*Nilsson* v. *Redditch Borough Council* [1994] 12 C.L. 467).

The word "safe" should not be equated with "not dangerous" simply because they were antonyms but should be construed with reference and an employer's obligation was to prevent any risk of injury arising from the state or condition of the work place and not just to prevent risks that were reasonably foreseeable (*Mains* v. *Uniroyal Englebert Tyres (I.H.), The Scotsman*, June 14, 1995), and applied in *R.* v. *Secretary of State for the Home Department, ex p. Kara (Hussein)* [1995] Imm.A.R. 584.

Stat. Def., Consumer Protection Act 1987 (c. 43), s.19(1).

SAFE BERTH. A berth hung with fenders which, because of their construction, damaged the hull of a ship was not a "safe berth" (*Prekookeanska Plovidba* v. *Felstar Shipping Corp.; The Carnival, The Independent*, January 23, 1992).

SAFE PORT. "Safe port" (Shelltime 3 Form of Charter, clause 3). A port which had only suffered one seaborne guerilla attack on shipping nevertheless be categorised as an unsafe port within the meaning of this clause" (*The Saga Cob, The Financial Times*, July 9, 1991).

SAFELY. "Can safely be administered" (Medicines Act 1968 (c. 67), s.28(3)(*g*)). There is no absolute standard of safety. Few drugs are entirely free from the risk of inducing side effects in some patients. The question has always to be whether the degree of risk is sufficiently low to be acceptable, and that cannot be considered without an appreciation of the benefits to be gained from taking a risk of that degree (*R.* v. *Medicines Commission, ex p. Organon Laboratories* [1990] C.O.D. 272).

SAID. "Anything said or done" (Police and Criminal Evidence Act 1984 (c. 60), s.76(2)(*b*)) is limited to something external to the person making the confession, and to something which is likely to have influenced him (*R.* v. *Goldenberg* (1989) 88 Cr.App.R. 285). See also UNRELIABLE.

SALE; SELL; SOLD. "Where goods are sold" (Sale of Goods Act 1979 (c. 54), s.21). Where there was an agreement to sell a car, the car did not by virtue only of that agreement become "sold" within the meaning of this section (*Shaw* v. *Commissioner of Police of the Metropolis* [1987] 1 W.L.R. 1332).

Where a husband and wife, as beneficial owners of the matrimonial home, purported to transfer the property to the wife absolutely this was not a "sale" within the meaning of s.205 of the Law of Property Act 1925 (c. 20) (*Monarch Aluminium* v. *Rickman* [1989] 10 C.L. 136).

"Sale . . . of an interest in land" (Law of Property (Miscellaneous Provisions) Act 1989 (c. 34), s.2). An option to buy land could be described as a contract for the sale of land conditional upon the exercise of the option (*Spiro* v. *Glencrown Properties* [1991] Ch. 537; *Armstrong and Holmes* v. *Holmes, The Times*, June 23, 1993).

"The shares are to be sold" (Companies Act 1948 (c. 38), s.174(3A)(*b*), see now Companies Act 1985 (c. 6), s.456). "Sold" here means sold for cash. The power of the court under this section does not extend to ordering the transfer of shares in one company in exchange for those in another (*Re Westminster Property Group* [1985] 1 W.L.R. 676).

"Sold" (Copyright Act 1956 (c. 74), s.21(1)(*b*)). The question whether a sale had been completed was not to be decided on a consideration of the minds of the parties to see if they shared the same intention but on the objective consideration of what passed between them (*Phillips* v. *Holmes* [1988] R.P.C. 613).

"On the completion of the sale." Where an agency agreement had stipulated a commission of 3 per cent on the purchase price "on the completion of the sale" a part-exchange was capable of being a "sale" provided that the cash element of the transaction was not merely nominal (*Connell Estate Agents* v. *Begej, The Times*, March 19, 1993).

Stat. Def., Food Safety Act 1990 (c. 16), s.2.

"Sale of a cause of action" (Insolvency Act 1986 (c. 45), Sched. 4, para. 6). An agreement to transfer half the proceeds recovered from an action in return for financing that action was a "sale of a cause of action" (*Grovewood Holdings* v. *James Capel & Co.* [1994] 4 All E.R. 417).

"Sale by retail." Stat. Def., Licensing (Retail Sales) Act 1988 (c. 25), s.1.

"Sale of goods by description," see DESCRIPTION.

SALMON. Stat. Def., Salmon Act 1986 (c. 62), s.40.

SALVAGE. "Salvage for services rendered to a ship" (Supreme Court of Judicature (Consolidation) Act 1925 (c. 49), s.22(1)(v)). The jurisdiction of the Admiralty Court under this section does not extend to the rendering of services to vessels in peril in non-tidal inland waters (*The Goring* [1987] 2 W.L.R. 1151).

SAME. (17) "Committed on the same occasion" (Transport Act 1981 (c. 56), s.19(1)). Where the accused kept two uninsured vehicles which he parked on the road outside his house, one being used to provide parts for the other, the two offences of using uninsured vehicles were held to have been "committed on the same occasion" within the meaning of this section (*Johnston* v. *Over* [1985] RTR 240).

"The locality . . . was in the same state" (General Rate Act 1967 (c. 9), s.20(1)(b)), "State" should be given a wide construction so as to include intangible as well as physical advantages and disadvantages. Thus, the locality in part of which an enterprise zone had been designated, was not "in the same state" as before the designation (*Clement* v. *Addis* [1988] 1 W.L.R. 301).

(Civil Liability (Contribution) Act 1978 (c. 47), s.1(1)). "The same damage" referred to the damage suffered by the person to whom the party seeking contribution was liable, so that the physical defects in a reservoir suffered by a water authority and the damage suffered by the building and civil engineering contractor who suffered the financial loss of having to construct a second reservoir for the water authority were not "the same damage" within the meaning of s.1(1) of the 1978 Act (*Birse Construction Ltd* v. *Haiste Ltd Watson (Third Parties)* [1996] 1 W.L.R. 675).

SAME POSITION. The provision of s.13(1) of the Housing Act 1980 (c. 51) (replaced by s.136(1) of the Housing Act 1985 (c. 68)) that where a new tenant inherits from a secure tenant the new tenant shall be "in the same position" as was the secure tenant, means that where the secure tenant had arranged a price for purchasing his council house, including a discount for length of residence, the new tenant inherits not only the right to buy but also the right to the discount (*McIntyre* v. *Merthyr Tydfil Borough Council* (1989) 21 H.L.R. 320).

SAMPLE. (9) "Sample" (Food and Drugs Act 1955 (c. 16), s.91). Defective food, *e.g.* a piece of cheese containing a piece of metal, handed in by a purchaser who had bought it for home consumption, was not a "sample" within the meaning of this section (*Arun District Council* v. *Argyle Stores* [1986] Crim.L.R. 685).

"Bodily sample," Stat. Def., Child Support Act 1995 (c. 34), s.21(4).

"Intimate sample" and "non-intimate sample," Stat. Def., Criminal Justice and Public Order Act 1994 (c. 33), s.58(2) and (3) (amending s.65 of Police and Criminal Evidence Act 1984 (c. 60)).

SANCTIONS. "Sanctions . . . shall be available" (Health and Medicines Act 1988 (c. 49), s.17(1)(c)). The use of the word "sanctions" shows that it is intended that there should be a pend element in addition to what is required to compensate the National Health Service for Loss suffered as a result of the medical practitioner's defamation (*R.* v. *Secretary of State for the Department of Health, ex p. Hickey, The Times,* June 25, 1992).

SANDWICH COURSE. Stat. Def., Education (Student Loans) Regulations 1998 (No. 211), reg. 3(1).

SATISFY; SATISFIED. "Where . . . the court is satisfied" (Children Act 1975 (c. 72), s.37(1)). To be satisfied that a child's welfare "would not be better safeguarded and promoted by the making of an adoption order . . . than it would be by the making of a custodianship order" the court would have to be satisfied that the child's welfare would be better served by custodianship. If the balance of advantage was exactly equal the court could not be so satisfied (*Re S. (a Minor)* [1987] 2 W.L.R. 977).

"If a magistrates' court is satisfied" (Magistrates' Courts Act 1980 (c. 43), s.129(1)). Justices could only be "satisfied" that a person who had been remanded was unable by reason of illness or accident to appear or be brought before the court at the expiration of the period for which he had been remanded if they had solid grounds on which they could reasonably found a reliable opinion (*R. v. Liverpool City Justices, ex p. Grogan* [1991] C.O.D. 148).

SCANDALOUS. "Scandalous, frivolous or vexatious" (Industrial Tribunals (Rules of Procedure) Regulations 1985 (No. 16), Sched. 1, r.12(2)(*e*)). These words refer to the contents of a claimant's application, not to his behaviour at the hearing (*O'Keefe* v. *Southampton City Council* [1988] I.C.R. 419).

SCHOOL. Stat. Defs., Further and Higher Education Act 1992 (c. 13), s.14; Finance Act 1994 (c. 9), s.84(3) (new inserted s.32(11) of Finance Act 1991 (c. 31)).

"School teacher," Stat. Def., Teachers' Pay and Conditions Act 1987 (c. 1) s.7.

SCOTS CRIMINAL LAW. Stat. Def., Scotland Act 1998 (c. 46), s.126(1).

SCOTS PRIVATE LAW. Stat. Def., Scotland Act 1998 (c. 46), s.126(1).

SCOTTISH ADMINISTRATION. Stat. Def., Scotland Act 1998 (c. 46), s.126(1).

SCOTTISH LEGISLATION. Stat. Def., Scotland Act 1998 (c. 46), s.70(9).

SCOTTISH SEAL. Stat. Def., Scotland Act 1998 (c. 46), s.2(6).

SCOTTISH ZONE. In relation to fishing, Stat. Def., Scotland Act 1998 (c. 46), s.126(1).

SCULPTURE. (Copyright, Designs and Patents Act 1988). "Sculpture" should be given its ordinary, natural meaning in the 1988 Act (*Metix (UK) Ltd* v. *G. H. Maughan (Plastics) Ltd* [1997] F.S.R. 718).

SEA. Stat. Def., Food and Environment Protection Act 1985 (c. 48), s.24; "includes any estuary or arm of the sea" (Merchant Shipping Act 1995 (c. 21), s.131(4)).

SEARCH.. "Intimate search," Stat. Def., "a search which consists of the physical examination of a person's body orifices other than the mouth" (Police and Criminal Evidence Act 1984 (c. 60), s.65 as inserted by Criminal Justice and Public Order Act 1994 (c. 33), s.59(1)).

SEASON. "During a particular season" (Caravan Sites and Control of Development Act 1960 (c. 62), Sched. 1, para. 7). These words are intended to apply to agricultural workers engaged in seasonal work and should not be construed as applying to workers involved in agricultural operations throughout the year (*Vale of White Horse District Council* v. *Mirmalek-Sani, The Times*, February 10, 1993).

SECRET. The term "trade secret" was not restricted to information relating to particular scientific or technical processes but could include information gained in the course of business about customers or business activities (*TSB Bank plc* v. *Connell*, 1997 S.L.T. 1255).

SECURE. "Load carried . . . shall . . . be so secured" (Road Vehicles (Construction and Use) Regulations 1986 (No. 1078), reg. 100). In considering whether a load had been adequately secured it was necessary to consider not only the actual securing of the load but also such matters as the positioning of the load, the weather and road conditions, including the clearance below any bridges on the route (*Walker–Trowbridge* v. *DPP, The Times*, March 3, 1992).

SECURITIES. Stat. Def., "in relation to a company, includes shares, debentures, bonds, and other securities of the company, whether or not constituting a charge on the assets of the company" (Coal Industry Act 1994 (c. 21), s.65(1)).

Stat. Def., Crown Agents Act 1995 (c. 24), s.14; Pensions Act 1995 (c. 26), s.40(2); Atomic Energy Authority Act 1995 (c. 37), s.13(1); Finance Act 1996 (c. 8), s.186(2); Income and Corporation Taxes Act 1988, s.181A(t) as inserted by Finance Act 1996 (c. 8), Sched. 29, para. 1.

Stat. Def., "shares, stock, debentures, debenture stock, loan stock, bonds, and other securities of any description" (Cash Ratio Deposits (Eligible Liabilities) Order 1998 (No. 1130), Art. 2(1)); Bank of England (Information Powers) Order 1998 (No. 1270), Art. 1(2).

See also OVERSEAS SECURITIES.

SECURITY. "Any security in respect of the debt" (Insolvency Rules 1986 (No. 1925), r.6.1(5)) was to be construed as having the same meaning as in ss.383 and 385(1) of the Insolvency Act 1986 (c. 45). Accordingly, the "security" that had to be referred to in the statutory demand served on a debtor by a bank was security "over any property of the person by whom the debt was owed" and therefore did not include the security of third persons (*Re a Debtor* (*No. 310 of 1988*) [1989] 1 W.L.R. 452).

(Insolvency Act 1986 (c. 45), s.383(2)). A landlord's right to peaceable re-entry for non-payment of rent was not a "security" for the purposes of s.383(2) (*Razzag* v. *Pala* [1997] 1 W.L.R. 1336).

Stat. Def., Taxation of Chargeable Gains Act 1992 (c. 12) ss.104, 132; "means any mortgage, charge or other security" (Housing Act 1996 (c. 52), s.39(2)); "shares, stock, debentures, debenture stock, loan stock, bonds, units of a collective investment scheme and other securities of any description" (Building Societies Act 1986 (c. 53), s.9A(9) inserted by Building Societies Act 1997 (c. 32), s.10).

SEISED. "Court other than the court first seised" (Civil Jurisdiction and Judgments Act 1982 (c. 27), Sched. 1, arts. 21, 22). An English Court is "seised" of proceedings for the purposes of this article on the day the issue of proceedings is served on a defendant (*Dresser UK* v. *Falcongate Freight Management* [1992] 2 W.L.R. 319). For the purposes of article 21 and English court became definitively seised of proceedings on the service of the writ (*Nestle Chemicals SA* v. *DK Line SA, The Times,* April 4, 1994).

SELECT. "Selected for dismissal," see DISMISS; DISMISSAL.

SELF. "Self-employed persons" (EEC Regulation No. 1408/71, Art. 1(a)(iv), as amended by Regulation No. 1390/81). A missionary priest who was supported as to his daily needs by contributions from his parishioners remained a "self-employed" person for the purposes of this article, notwithstanding that his parishioners were the beneficiaries of the service he provided (*Van Roosmalen* v. *Bestuur van de Bedrijfsvereniging voor de Gezondheid* (No. 300/84) [1988] 3 C.M.L.R. 471).

"Self-employed" (Conduct of Employment Agencies and Employment Businesses Regulations 1976 (No. 715). A person engaged by an employment agency as a contract worker for another company was "self-employed" for the purposes of these regulations (*Ironmonger* v. *More- field t/a Appointments* [1988] IRLR 461).

A freelance vision mixer who worked for 20 companies on short-term contracts lasting one or two days and who was registered for VAT was "self-employed" for the purposes of assessment to income tax (*Hall (Inspector of Taxes)* v. *Lorimer, The Times,* November 18, 1993).

SELF-CONTAINED UNIT. (Council Tax (Chargeable Dwellings) Order 1992, Art. 2). The concept of "self-contained" unit in Art. 2 did not require any analysis of its future saleability. The terms of planning consent could be relevant when determining whether a granny-flat annex was a "self-contained unit". However the level of community living was an irrelevant consideration (*Batty* v. *Burfoot and ors* [1995] 2 EGLR 142).

SELL. Stat. Def., "includes offer or expose for sale and includes have in possession for sale" (Bread and Flour Regulations 1998 (No. 141), reg. 2(1)).

SELLER. (Factors Act 1889 (c. 45), s.9). Although, for the purposes of this section, the "seller" of the goods does not have to be the owner, a person whose possession of goods was derived from the unlawful posession of a thief cannot pass a good title as a "seller" under this section (*National Employers Mutual General Insurance Association* v. *Jones* [1987] 3 All E.R. 385).

SEND. The "sending" of a writ by post for the purposes of service under R.S.C., Ord. 81, r.3(1)(c) does not refer merely to the initial dispatch of the writ but connotes the whole process of dispatch, transmission and delivery to the receiver (*Austin Rover Group* v. *Crouch Butler Associates* [1986] 1 W.L.R. 1102).

"Send" (Industrial Tribunal (Rules of Procedure) Regulations 1985 (No. 16), Sched. 1, r.5). A notice of hearing is "sent" under this rule when it is received or deemed to have been received. "Send" here does not refer to the date of posting (*Derrybaa* v. *Castro-Blanco* [1986] I.C.R. 546).

"Sent by post" (Immigration Appeals (Notices) Regulations 1972 (No. 1683), reg. 6) means dispatched by post and not "received" (*R.* v. *Secretary of State for the Home Department, ex p. Yeboah* [1987] 3 All E.R. 999).

SENTENCE. "May appeal . . . against any sentence" (Criminal Appeal Act 1968 (c. 19), s.9). A confiscation order made on the conviction of the accused of possessing prohibited drugs with intent to supply was an order made on sentence, and could therefore be treated as part of the "sentence" for the purposes of this section, and therefore the subject of an appeal (*R.* v. *Johnson* [1990] 3 W.L.R. 745).

"Deferred sentence" (Criminal Appeal Act 1968 (c. 19), s.50(1); Criminal Justice Act 1988 (c. 33), ss.35(6), 36). A deferred sentence was a sentence for the purposes of appeal (*Att.-Gen.'s Reference (No. 22 of 1992)* [1994] 1 All E.R. 105) and was a "sentence" within the meaning of s.50, as amended and therefore capable of challenge (*R.* v. *L (deferred sentence)* [1999] 1 W.L.R. 479).

(Criminal Justice Act 1967 (c. 80), ss.67 and 102). The expression "sentence of imprisonment in s.67(1) was like the expression "term of imprisonment" in s.104(2) and to be construed as referring to the aggregate of any consecutive sentences imposed at the same trial, so that any period spent on remand should be deducted from the total sentence and not from each consecutive sentence (*R.* v. *Secretary of State for the Home Department, ex p. Naughton* [1997] 1 All E.R. 426).

(Criminal Justice Act 1967 (c. 80), s.67 and Criminal Justice Act 1991 (c. 53), s.33). The relevant sentence for determining whether an individual is a long-term or short-term prisoner under s.33(1) of the 1991 Act is the sentence imposed by the court and not the sentence as reduced by time spent on remand (*R.* v. *Secretary of State for the Home Department, ex p. Probyn* [1998] 1 All E.R. 357).

(Rehabilitation of Offenders Act 1974 (c. 53), s.5(8)). An endorsement of a driving licence was not a "sentence" within the meaning of s.5(8) (*Power* v. *Provincial Insurance plc* [1998] RTR 61).

SENTENCED. See CONVICTED.

SEPARATE CHARGE. (Supplementary Benefit (Requirements) Regulations 1983 (No. 1399), reg. 9(4A), introduced by the amendment in para. 2 of the Supplementary Benefit (Requirements and Resources) Amendment and Uprating Regulations 1987 (No. 659)). Where, under the terms of reg. 9(4A), in addition to the weekly amount for board and lodging in a nursing or residential care home, a "separate charge" is made for additional services, "separate charge" is restricted to one made by those providing the board and lodging. It could not be one made by a third party (*Pearce* v. *Chief Adjudication Officer, The Times*, May 10, 1990).

SEPARATE DWELLING. (3) "Let as a separate dwelling" (Rent Act 1977 (c. 42), s.1). Where 39 days before the expiry of the headlease of a block of flats, the tenant sub-let the basement to the appellant for a term of three years at a rent of £2,400 p.a., it was held that the basement had not been let to the appellant as a "separate dwelling" within the meaning of this section (*Grosvenor Estate Belgravia* v. *Cochran* [1991] 44 E.G. 169).

"Let as a separate dwelling" (Housing Act 1985 (c. 68), s.79). Accommodation comprising a bedroom, small bathroom and shared kitchen in a hostel managed by a registered housing association which provided various services, including bed linen, towels, hot water and central heating, was not let as a "separate dwelling" within the meaning of this section (*Central YMCA Housing Association* v. *Saunders* (1990) 23 H.L.R. 212). A furnished bedroom with its own bathroom and W.C., but with no cooking facilities, in a hostel run by the local authority was not "let as a separate dwelling" (*Central YMCA Housing Association* v. *Goodman* (1991) 24 H.L.R. 98).

SERIES. "Series of similar actions" (Employment Protection (Consolidation) Act 1978 (c. 44), s.24(2)). Weekly payments showing a variation in pay between union and non-union employees were held not to be a "series of similar actions," but a continuation of the first one which established the differential (*Adlam* v. *Salisbury and Wells Theological College* [1985] I.C.R. 786).

"Series of two or more offences" (Magistrates' Courts Act 1980 (c. 43), s.22(1)). Where, of the three preferred charges which subsisted at the time of the appellant's election for trial, two were dropped before committal, the third was held not to form part of a "series" within the meaning of this section (*R.* v. *Braden* [1988] Crim.L.R. 54).

(3) "Series of offences of the same or a similar character" (Indictment Rules 1971 (No. 1253), r.9). Where the alleged offences (in this case indecent assault on a boy) were linked by a sufficiently close nexus it was held that two offences only, and spaced nine years apart, could form a "series" for the purposes of this rule (*R.* v. *Baird* (1993) 97 Cr.App.R. 308).

"Series of like or similar events" (Value Added Tax Act 1983 (c. 55), Sched. 6). Seven performances in a week of a play put on as a fund-raising event was held to be a "series" for the purposes of this Schedule and so did not qualify for VAT exemption (*Northern Ireland Council for Voluntary Action* v. *Customs and Excise Commissioners* (1991) 1 VATTR 32).

SERIOUS. "The offence . . . was so serious that a non-custodial sentence . . . . cannot be justified" (Criminal Justice Act 1982 (c. 48), s.1(4A)(*c*), as amended by s.123(3) of the Criminal Justice Act 1988 (c. 33)). This phrase comes to this: "The kind of offence which when committed by a young person would make all right thinking members of the public, knowing all the facts, feel that justice had not been done by the passing of any sentence other than a custodial one" (*per* Lord Justice Lawson in *R.* v. *Bradbourn* (1985) 7 Cr.App.R.(S.) 180). To justify a custodial sentence under this section there must be an individual offence which was so serious that a non-custodial sentence for it could not be justified; so that where the accused pleaded guilty to one offence of handling stolen goods and three of theft, and asked for 136 similar offences to be taken into consideration, it was held that as there was no one single offence so serious that a non-custodial sentence could not be justified, the accused should be conditionally discharged (*R.* v. *Choudhury (Javed Aktar)* (1992) 13 Cr.App.R.(S.) 290). The conclusion that a young offender intended using a stolen credit card to obtain credit was enough to justify holding that the offence was "so serious" as to justify a custodial sentence under this section (*R.* v. *Bumrungpruick* [1992] Crim.L.R. 674). Attempted rape by a boy aged 14 was held to be not "so serious" (*R.* v. *Hallett (Paul David)* (1990) 12 Cr.App.R.(S.) 552. But stealing mail from mail bags carried on trains was "so serious" within the meaning of the section (*R.* v. *Joseph (Anthony)* (1990) 12 Cr.App.R.(S.) 531). The offence committed by a 17-year-old of previous good character, who acted as look-out while his accomplices burgled a house, was held not to be "so serious" within the meaning of this section (*R.* v. *Mole* (1991) 12 Cr.App.R.(S.) 371). The offence committed by a 20-year-old of previous good character, who pleaded guilty to wounding his ex-cohabitee's new boyfriend by punching him and pushing him down a flight of stairs was held not to be "so serious" within the meaning of this section (*R.* v. *Grant (Lee)* (1990) 12 Cr.App.R.(S.) 441). Burglary or attempted burglary have been held to be offences "so serious" that non-custodial sentences could not be justified (*R.* v. *Bray (Shaun Peter)* (1991) 12 Cr.App.R.(S.) 705; *R.* v. *Stokoe (Dennis Amos)* (1991) Cr.App.R.(S.) 726; *R.* v. *Webster (Marlon)* (1991) 12 Cr.App.R.(S.) 760. Placing an imitation bomb in a department store (*R.* v. *Wilburn* [1992] Crim.L.R. 129); robbing a man of £40 in a public lavatory (*R.* v. *Whittle* [1992] Crim.L.R. 220) and robbery with intimidation (*R.* v. *Robinson (Darren Lee)* (1992) 13 Cr.App.R.(S.) 104; *R.* v. *Golding (Calvin Dale)* [1992] 13 Cr.App.R.(S.) 142) were all held to be "so serious" within the meaning of this section. As also were indecent assault (*R.* v. *Powell* [1992] Crim.L.R. 132) and unlawful wounding (*R.* v. *Bray (Martin)* [1992] 13 Cr.App.R.(S.) 5). In deciding whether an offence is so serious that a non-custodial sentence is not justified it is necessary for the sentencer to consider each offence separately (*R.* v. *Thompson* (1989) 11 Cr.App.R.(S.) 246; *R.* v. *Hawker (Gary Alan)* (1992) 123 Cr.App.R.(S.) 694). So that where an accused made 15 guilty pleas and asked for 45 other offences to be considered it was held that none of them was "so serious" as to justify a custodial sentence (*R.* v. *Hawker* [1992] Crim.L.R. 521). The following offences have been considered "so serious" within the meaning of s.1(4A): impersonating police officers (*R.* v. *Lewes Crown Court, ex p. Charles* (1992) 13 Cr.App.R.(S.) 231); possession of cannabis with intention to supply (*R.* v. *Black (Jason George)* (1992) 13 Cr.App.R.(S.) 262; robbery of schoolboys of small sums by juveniles (*R.* v. *Pretty (Martin Allan)* (1992) 13 Cr.App.R.(S.) 280); theft of substantial sums by employee (*R.* v. *Fuzzey (Claire Ann)* (1992) 13 Cr.App.R.(S.) 169). Burglary of £400 worth of parts from a motor dealer's storeroom was not "serious" enough to warrant a custodial sentence (*R.* v. *Akehurst (Edwin Alexander)* (1992) 13 Cr.App.R.(S.) 568). Conspircy to aid a prisoner to escape was "serious" enough to warrant a custodial sentence (*R.* v. *O'Neill (Justin Paul)* (1992) 13 Cr.App.R.(S.) 730).

"So serious that only such a sentence [custodial] can be justified" (Criminal Justice Act 1991 (c. 53), s.1(2)(*a*)). Robbery by a 22-year-old in a small shop at knife-point was held to be "serious" enough to justify a custodial sentence (*R.* v. *Cunningham, The Times,* December 3, 1992). A burglary at the home of a person whose recent death had been announced in the newspapers was held to be "so serious" that only a custodial sentence could be justified (*R.* v. *Lewis (John)*, *The Times*, March 29, 1993). As also were a series of indecent assaults (*R.* v. *Powell (Shane)* (1992) 13 Cr.App.R.(S.) 202). Theft of money from a telephone kiosk could be "so serious" within the meaning of this section (*R.* v. *Decino*, *The Times*, May 10, 1993).

"Serious harm" under the Children and Young Persons Act 1969 (c. 54), s.23 as substituted by the Criminal Justice Act 1991 (c. 53), s.60, required an assessment of the nature of offences committed, the manner in which they had been committed, as well as the risk of repetition (*R.* v. *Croydon Youth Court, ex p. G. (A Minor)*, *The Times*, May 3, 1995).

(Criminal Justice Act 1991 (c. 53), s.2(2)(*b*). An assault on a member of the public which fractured his nose when he tried to intervene to prevent another assault was not sufficiently serious to render it necessary to protect the public from serious harm within the meaning of s.2(2)(*b*) (*R.* v. *Gardiner (Dean Norman William)* [1994] Cr.App.R.(S.) 747). A conviction for grievous bodily harm was "serious physical harm" within the meaning of the Criminal Justice Act 1991 (c. 53), s.31(3) (*R.* v. *Ely* [1994] Crim.L.R. 539).

For a crime to be political for the purposes of Art. 1F(b) it had to be sufficiently closely and directly linked to the political purpose, regard being had to the means used to achieve the political end, to whether the crime was aimed at a government or military target or a civilian one and whether it was likely to involve the indiscriminate killing or injuring of members of the public with no connection with the government of the state, so that the bombing of an airport where 10 civilians had been killed could not amount to a "serious non-political crime" (*T.* v. *Immigration Officer* [1996] 2 W.L.R. 766).

"Serious enough to warrant such a sentence" [Community sentence] (Criminal Justice Act 1991 (c. 53), s.6(1)). Reckless driving was serious enough to warrant such a sentence (*R.* v. *Cox (David Geoffrey)*, *The Times*, December 3, 1992).

"Serious deterioration" (Supreme Court Act 1981 (c. 54), s.32A), see CHANCE.

"Serious professional misconduct," see MISCONDUCT.

See also HISTORY.

SERVANT. (Licensing Act 1964 (c. 26), s.169). The fact that a servant of a company exercised control over another company servant did not render the latter the servant of the former (*Russell* v. *DPP* (1997) 161 J.P.N. 184).

SERVE; SERVICE (Notice). (11) "Served on him" (Road Traffic Act 1972 (c. 20), s.10(5), as amended by the Transport Act 1981 (c. 56), Sched. 8). Service accepted by defendant's counsel is a valid service for the purposes of this section (*Penman* v. *Parker* [1986] 1 W.L.R. 882).

"Writ . . . served . . . by . . . post . . . to . . . principal place of business" (Rules of the Supreme Court, Ord. 81, r. 3(1)). A writ was held to have been "served" within the meaning of this rule when it was delivered to the principal place of business although not addressed to it (*Austin Rover Group* v. *Crouch Butler Savage Associates* [1986] 1 W.L.R. 1102).

"Sufficiently served" (Companies Act 1985 (c. 6), s.695(1)). A writ served on one of the persons whose names and addresses had (as required by Part XXIII of the Act) been delivered by an overseas company to the Registrar of Companies as authorised to accept service was held to have been "sufficiently served," notwithstanding that the company had ceased to have a place of business in Great Britain (*Punjab National Bank* v. *Rome and Bathurst* [1989] F.L.R. 380).

The service of a writ, defence or counterclaim by facsimile transmission of documents (fax) was good service if it could be proved that a legible copy of the document, which otherwise met the rules, came into the hands of the party to be served (*Ralux NV/SA* v. *Spencer Mason, The Times*, May 18, 1989). Service by fax of documents that are not originating process is good service if the transmission results in a legible document (*Hastie and Jenkerson* v. *McMahon* [1990] 1 W.L.R. 1575).

Service of a court order on a plaintiff at his last known address was not properly effected by delivery of it to his London address when the solicitors serving the words "within the jurisdiction" refer to the defendant and not to the writ for service. So that, where it was established that within seven days of the placing of a writ through the defendant's letter box he came to know of its existence on returning from abroad, the service was valid, notwithstanding that at the time the writ was placed in his letter box he had been outside the jurisdiction (*Barclays Bank of Swaziland* v. *Hahn* [1989] 1 W.L.R. 506). A writ must be served personally on each defendant by the plaintiff or his agent (R.S.C., Ord. 10, r.1). But there is nothing in the Rules of the Supreme Court prohibiting agreement by the parties on a mode of service outside the provisions of Order 10 (*Kenneth Allison* v. *A.E. Limehouse & Co.* [1991] 3 W.L.R. 671. A writ contained in a sealed envelope inserted through the letter box of the English home of the defendant, at a time when she was in India was, in the absence of a statement by the plaintiff that in his opinion the writ would have come to the knowledge of the defendant within seven days of the date of insertion in the letter box, not served to the satisfaction of the court (*India Videogram Association* v. *Patel* [1991] 1 All E.R. 214).

"Service of any document" (R.S.C., Ord. 65, r.5(1)). The use of facsimile transmission of a document (other than one required to be served personally or one originating process) constituted good "service" provided that it could be proved that the document, in a complete and legible state, had in fact been received by the person on whom service was to be effected (*Hastie and Jenkerson* v. *McMahon* [1990] 1 W.L.R. 1575).

"Service of a summons" (County Court Rules 1981 (No. 1687), Ord. 7, r.10(1)). Service had to be made to an address at which the defendant had some continuing presence. That could not include a place where he was never present even though it had a direct and immediate connection with him (*Willowgreen* v. *Smithers, The Times*, December 14, 1993).

But a summons posted to a defendant's last known address in England and posted on by a friend to the defendant who had moved to Spain was held to have been properly served under this rule (*Rolph* v. *Zolan* [1993] 1 W.L.R. 1305).

(Law of Property Act 1925 (c. 20), s.196(3)). A notice was sufficiently served for the purposes of s.196(3) if it was left at the last known place of abode or address even though it never came to the attention of the intended recipient (*Kinch* v. *Bullard* [1998] 4 All E.R. 650).

Where a tenant occupied a bed-sitting room in a building in multiple occupation, delivery of a notice to the common front entrance by the postman amounted to "service" for the purposes of s.196(3) of the Law of Property Act 1925 (c. 20) (*Henry Smith's Charity Trustees* v. *Kyriakou* [1989] 50 E.G. 42).

"Shall serve a notice" (Control of Pollution Act 1974 (c. 40), s.58(1)). Service of an abatement notice by inserting it through the letter box of the relevant premises is good service for the purposes of this section (*Lambeth London Borough Council* v. *Mullings* (1990) RVR 259).

"Served . . . at his usual or last known place of residence, or his place of business" (Taxes Management Act 1970 (c. 9), s.115(2)). A notice sent to a place of business no longer occupied was not duly "served" within the meaning of this section (*Re A Debtor (No. 1240/SD/91, ex p. The Debtor* v. *I.R.C.* [1992] S.T.C. 771).

(State Immunity Act 1978 (c. 33), s.12(1)). Service on a diplomatic mission was not service on the state of that mission for the purposes of s.12(1) of the 1978 Act and service was not effected until the document had been transmitted to the government department responsible for foreign affairs of the relevant state and had been received by that department (*Kuwait Airways Corp.* v. *Iraqi Airways Co. and ors* [1995] 3 All E.R. 694).

"Already serving . . . a term of imprisonment" (Magistrates' Courts Act 1980 (c. 43), s.82(3) (as amended by the Criminal Justice Act 1982 (c. 48), s.77 Sched. 14, para. 52). A custodial sentence took effect as soon as it was pronounced so that justices were entitled to commit a fine defaulter to prison in the exercise of their powers under s.82(3) of the 1980 Act as he was "already serving a term of imprisonment (*R.* v. *Grimsby and Cleethorpes Justices, ex p. Walters* [1997] 1 W.L.R. 89).

(Race Relations Act 1976 (c. 74), s.20). Those parts of a police officer's duties involving assistance to, or protection of members of the public entailed the provision of services to the public and fell within the scope of s.20.

See also GIVE.

SERVICE CHARGE. A fixed sum, which was subjet to an indexed escalation clause, payable as a contribution towards the cost of repairs and maintenance without any reference to actual costs incurred or about to be incurred was not a service charge within the meaning of the Housing Act 1985 (c. 68), Sched. 6, para. 16A (*Coventry City Council* v. *Cole* [1994] 1 All E.R. 997).

SERVICE MARK. See SERVICE.

SERVICES. (EEC Treaty, Arts. 59, 60). Courses provided in a technical institute of secondary education in the context of a national education system could not be regarded as "services" within the meaning of Art. 59 (*Belgian State* v. *Humbel* (No. 263/86), [1988] ECR 5365). Medical termination of pregnancy, performed in accordance with the law of the state where it is carried out is a "service" within the meaning of articles 59 and 60 of the EEC Treaty (*Society for the Protection of Unborn Children (Ireland)* v. *Grogan, The Times,* October 7, 1991). Lottery activities were "services" within the meaning of Art. 60 of the EEC Treaty. However, a prohibition on the importation of materials relating to a lottery organised in another Member State could not be regarded as a measure involving an unjustified interference with the freedom to provide services (*Commissioners of Customs and Excise v. Gerhart Schindler* [1994] Q.B. 610).

Lottery activities, including the importation of advertisements and tickets with a view to the participation by residents of one state in a lottery operated in another Member State were "services" under the EEC Treaty, Art. 60 (*Customs and Excise Commissioners v. Schindler* [1994] Q.B. 610).

See also SUPPLY.

"Used in relation to services" (Trade Marks (Amendment) Act 1984 (c. 19), s.1(7) as substituted by s.2(1)(*b*) of the Patents, Designs and Marks Act 1986 (c. 39)): for a service to fall within the definition of "service mark" in this section it had to be charged for separately and as such (*Re Boots Co.* [1989] 3 All E.R. 948).

A seaman's entitlement to severance payment on termination of his employment is not remuneration for services to a ship and cannot constitute a maritime lien against the ship (*The Tacoma City* [1991] 1 Lloyd's Rep. 330).

SETTLED. (9) (Settled Land Act 1925 (c. 18)). Where the facts showed that it was the intention of the parties that the defendant cohabitee of the plaintiff would have the right to occupy a house for life, it was held that it was "settled land," that she was the tenant for life and that she was entitled to a vesting deed (*Ungurian v. Lesnoff* (1989) 133 S.J. 946).

"Settled in the United Kingdom" (Immigration Act 1971 (c. 77), s.2(1)(*c*)). An applicant who had obtained entry to the U.K. through a deception, and who had knowledge of the deception, was not entitled to be treated as "settled" in the U.K. within the meaning of this section (*R. v. Secretary of State for the Home Department, ex p. Miah* [1990] 2 All E.R. 523).

(European Convention on Human Rights, Art. 8). "Settled was to be given the same meaning as in the immigration legislation of the U.K. so that a person who was in the U.K. pending the outcome of an asylum application was not "settled" for the purposes of the Home Office's Policy Document entitled "Marriage and Children" (*R. v. Secretary of State for the Home Department, ex p. Sekhon (Paramjit)* [1995] Imm.A.R. 338).

"Settled accommodation" (Housing Act 1985 (c. 68), Pt. III). Accommodation provided in a hostel for the homeless as a first stage in the discharge of the duty under the Housing Act 1985, s.65(2) towards permanent accommodation was not "settled accommodation" (*R. v. Rushcliffe Borough Council, ex p. Summerson and Buckley* (1993) 25 H.L.R. 577).

"Settled accommodation" did not have to be suitable permanent accommodation but a material consideration had to be the assumption by a local authority of a duty under the Housing Act 1985, s.65(2) (*R. v. Brent London Borough Council, ex p. Awua HL* (1994) 26 H.L.R. 539). An assured shorthold tenancy granted by a private landlord which might reasonably be expected to be renewed at the end of its fixed term could qualify as "settled accommodation" (*R. v. Wandsworth London Borough Council, ex p. Crooks, The Times,* April 12, 1995).

"Settled intention" as an element of habitual residence related to a decision to live in a particular place rather than settlement in the sense of permanent or long-term residence, since habitual residence could be for a limited period (*Moran* v. *Moran*, 1997 S.L.T. 541).

SETTLEMENT. "Settlement" (Income and Corporation Taxes Act 1970 (c. 10), ss.437(1), 444(2)). Where a husband covenanted under a deed of separation with his wife to pay maintenance to their children, the deed of separation, containing as it inevitably must an element of bounty, was held to be a "settlement" within the meaning of these sections (*Harvey* v. *Sivyer* [1985] 3 W.L.R. 261). A complicated arrangement whereby dividend income was paid to infant children in respect of their shareholdings in a company formed for that purpose, and managed by their fathers, was an "arrangement" within the meaning of s.444(2) and, containing as it did an element of bounty, was held to be a "settlement" under s.437(1). The income therefore came to be treated for tax purposes as that of the fathers (*Butler* v. *Wildia* [1988] L.S.Gaz., December 14, 43).

"What is to be taken for the purposes of capital transfer tax to be a settlement" (Finance Act 1975 (c. 7), Sched. 5, para. 1). The five successive steps taken to implement an elaborate scheme, devised to avoid liability to capital transfer tax, evolving round the settled property provisions of Sched. 5, were effective and achieved their purpose. As the steps were not pre-ordained and thus could not constitute a single composite transaction they were not struck down by the anti-avoidance principles laid down in *Ramsay* v. *I.R.C.* [1982] A.C. 300 (*Fitzwilliam* v. *I.R.C.* [1993] 3 All E.R. 184).

An exclusive right to occupy property for life did not necessarily constitute a life interest in property under the 1925 Act but depended on the context in which the right to occupy had been granted, so that an undertaking by which an exclusive occupation of property for life had been granted in order to formalise existing family arrangements rather than effect a restructuring of an estate did not create a "settlement" (*Dent* v. *Dent* 1 All E.R. 659).

SETTLEMENT (Residential). "Admitted for settlement" (The Statement of Immigration Rules for Control on Entry 1973 (H.C. 81), r.38(c)) connotes a present intention to settle in the U.K. So that the wife of a person already settled in the U.K., who brought their child with her from Pakistan, with the intention of staying a short while before returning alone to Pakistan, had not been "admitted for settlement" within the meaning of this rule (*R.* v. *Immigration Appeal Tribunal, ex p. Rashida Bibi* [1988] Imm.A.R. 298). See also FOR.

SEVERAL. "Several" meant more than two (*Clowes Development (U.K.) Ltd* v. *Secretary of State for the Environment* [1996] EGCS 163).

SEVERE. (1) "Severe financial hardship" (Legal Aid Act 1974 (c. 4), s.13(3)). In considering whether a successful unassisted defendant would suffer "severe financial hardship" within the meaning of this section if required to meet his total costs, the capital and income of his spouse can be taken into account (*Adams* v. *Riley* [1988] 2 W.L.R. 127). There is no reason why a local authority or any other large body should not be able to make a claim under this section on the grounds that costs in legal proceedings would cause "severe financial hardship;" but these are strong words and indicate some impairment of the ability to function normally (*R. v. Greenwich London Borough Council, ex p. Lovelace (No. 2)* [1992] 1 Q.B. 155).

"Severe impairment of intelligence" (Sexual Offences Act 1956 (c. 69), s.45, as substituted by s.127(*b*) of the Mental Health Act 1959 (c. 72) as amended by s.65(1) and Sched. 3, para. 29 of the Mental Health (Amendment) Act 1982 (c. 51)) is to be measured against the standards of normal persons, and the opinions of medical experts, if admissible at all, have no bearing (*R. v. Hall (J.H.)* (1988) 86 Cr.App.R. 159).

"Severe discomfort" (Mobility Allowance Regulations 1975 (No. 1573), reg. 3) is not synonymous with "severe pain or distress" (*Cassinelli v. Secretary of State for Social Services, The Times,* December 6, 1991).

SEWER. (8) (Public Health Act 1936 (c. 49), s.343). A sewer is nonetheless a "sewer" within the meaning of this section whether or not it is in use as a sewer. The word is descriptive of the pipes' function and not of their actual use at any time (*J. Pullan & Sons v. Leeds City Council* (1991) 7 Const.L.J. 222).

Stat. Def., Water Industry Act 1991 (c. 56), s.219.

SEX. "Discriminates . . . on the ground of . . . sex," see DISCRIMINATE.

(Council Directive 75/117). "Sex" in the Equal Pay Directive did not extend to sexual orientation and the word should be given the same meaning as in the Equal Treatment Directive (*R. v. Secretary of State for Defence, ex p. Perkins (No. 2), The Times,* July 16, 1998).

SEXUAL DEVIANCY. (Mental Health Act 1983 (c. 20), s.1(3)). Sexual deviancy, for the purposes of this section, means the practice, not merely the inclination (*R. v. Mental Health Review Tribunal, ex p. Chatworthy* [1985] 3 All E.R. 699).

SEXUAL MISCONDUCT. Stat. Def., Industrial Tribunals Act 1996 (c. 17), s.11(6).

SEXUAL OFFENCE. Attempted rape came within the definition of "sexual offence" for the purposes of the Criminal Justice Act 1991 (c. 53), s.31(1) (*R. v. Robinson, The Times,* December 3, 1992).

Stat. Def., Criminal Justice Act 1991 (c. 53), s.31(1) as amended by Criminal Justice and Public Order Act 1994 (c. 33), Sched. 9, para. 45; Industrial Tribunals Act 1996 (c. 17), s.11(6); Sexual Offences (Protected Material) Act 1997 (c. 39), s.2(1).

Stat. Def., in relation to Scottish law, Criminal Procedure (Scotland) Act 1995 (c. 46), s.210A(10) inserted by Crime and Disorder Act 1998 (c. 37), s.86(1).

SHALL. "The Secretary of State shall consult with organisations . . . concerned" (Social Security and Housing Benefits Act 1982 (c. 24), s.36(1)). "Shall" in this section is mandatory (*R. v. Secretary of State for Social Services, ex p. Association of Metropolitan Authorities* [1986] 1 All E.R. 164).

"The rules shall be so framed" (Immigration Act 1971 (c. 77), s.1(5)). "Shall" is here mandatory (*R.* v. *Immigration Appeal Tribunal, ex p. Ruhul* [1987] 1 W.L.R. 1538; *R.* v. *Secretary of State for the Home Department, ex p. Zalihe Huseyin, The Times,* October 31, 1987). See also FREE.

"Shall not begin later than" (Supreme Court Act 1981 (c. 54), s.77(2)(*b*)). "Shall" is here directory and not mandatory (*R.* v. *Governor of Spring Hill Prison, ex p. Sohi* [1988] 1 All E.R. 424).

"The company shall" (Insolvency Act 1986 (c. 45), ss.98, 99). "Shall" is here permissive and not mandatory (*Re Salcombe Hotel Development Co.* (1989) 5 BCC 807).

"The tribunal shall make an additional award" (Employment Protection (Consolidation) Act 1978 (c. 44), s.71(2)(*b*)). The word "shall" in this section is directory not mandatory (*Conoco (U.K.)* v. *Neal* [1989] IRLR 51).

"Shall give not less than 10 days' notice" (Company Directors Disqualification Act 1986 (c. 46), s.16(1)). "Shall" here is directory and not mandatory, so that failure to give the 10 days' notice did not render the application for a disqualification order either void or voidable (*Secretary of State for Trade and Industry* v. *Langridge* [1991] 2 W.L.R. 1343).

"Shall . . . supply . . . such information" (Adoption Act 1976 (c. 36), s.51(1)). In interpreting Acts of Parliament which impose statutory duties in apparently absolute terms the courts should look to what was intended by Parliament and, as Parliament was presumed not to have intended that those terms should enable someone to benefit from his own serious crime, it was held that there was no absolute duty to provide the information requested under this section (*R.* v. *Registrar-General, ex p. Smith* [1991] 2 Q.B. 393).

"Shall tell . . . shall proceed" (Magistrates' Courts Act 1980 (c. 43), s.21). "Shall" is mandatory and so, once a trial on indictment is ordered under this section, there is no power to vary the decision save as set down by s.25 (*R.* v. *Liverpool Justices, ex p. Crown Prosecution Service* (1990) 90 Cr.App.R. 261).

"The High Court . . . shall . . . order that they be struck out" (County Courts Act 1984 (c. 28), s.40(1) as amended by s.2(1) of the Courts and Legal Services Act 1990 (c. 41)). This section does not impose a mandatory requirement on the High Court to strike out proceedings which were wrongly stated in the High Court. There remains the option to transfer the proceedings to a County Court (*Restick* v. *Crickmore, The Times,* December 3, 1993).

(Housing Benefit (General) Regulations 1987, reg. 11(2)). Notwithstanding the use of the word "shall" in reg. 11(2) of the 1987 Regulations, there remained a discretion as to the reduction of the eligible rent to an amount considered appropriate, which was to be determined in accordance with the facts of each case, including the cost of suitable alternative accommodation, the health of the applicant and any other difficulties in having to find alternative accommodation (*R.* v. *City of Westminster Housing Benefit Review Board, ex p. Mehanne* [1999] 2 All E.R. 317).

SHAM. Where a landlord let a flat to a company, bought for that purpose by the prospective occupier, instead of to that person and it was established that it was the intention of both parties, with all knowledge of what that involved, that the flat should be let to the company and not the occupier, it was held that a subsequent claim by the occupier that the transaction was a "sham" failed, and that the landlord had achieved his purpose, which was to avoid constituting the occupier a statutory tenant (*Hilton* v. *Plustitle* [1988] 3 All E.R. 1051). Similarly, a series of lettings of a flat to companies with which the occupier was associated were held not to be "shams" and therefore avoided conferring security of tenure on the occupier (*Estavest Investments* v. *Commercial Express Travel* [1988] 49 E.G. 73).

A device for avoiding security of tenure, whereby a tenancy of an agricultural holding was granted to a nominee tenant who then granted a sub-tenancy to the person who wished to farm the land, although not strictly a "sham" in the sense envisaged by Diplock L.J. in *Snook* v. *London and West Riding Investments* [1967] 2 Q.B. 786 [see Main Work, p. 2411] was an artificial scheme intended to achieve what the Agricultural Holdings Act 1948 (c. 63) forbad, and therefore failed (*Gisborne* v. *Burton* [1988] 38 E.G. 129).

SHARE. Stat. Def., Companies Act 1985 (c. 6), s.744; Income and Corporation Taxes Act 1988 (c. 48), s.229; Companies Act 1989 (c. 40), s.22; "includes stock" (Atomic Energy Authority Act 1995 (c. 37), s.13(1)).

"British ship," "United Kingdom ship," Stat. Def., Merchant Shipping Act 1995 (c. 21), s.1.

SHARED ACCOMMODATION. A landlord and tenant who shared a kitchen resided together so as to disentitle the tenant from receiving housing benefit under the Housing Benefit (General) Regulations 1987 (No. 1971), reg. 3 (*Thamesdown Borough Council* v. *Goonery (James)*, February 13, 1995, C.A.).

SHELLFISH. Stat. Def., Food and Environment Protection Act 1985 (c. 48), s.24; Food Safety (Fishery Products and Live Shellfish) (Hygiene) Regulations 1998 (No. 994), reg. 2(1).

SHIP. Stat. Def., Aviation and Maritime Security Act 1990 (c. 31), s.17.

"Sailing ship," Stat. Def., Merchant Shipping (Fire Protection: Small Ships) Regulations 1998 (No. 1011), reg. 1(2).

SHIP DUES. (Harbours, Docks and Piers Clauses Act 1846, s.44). Mooring charges were not "ships dues", which had traditionally been applied to charges for the use of a harbour or the infrastructure or essential installations of a harbour and not for the use of additional or optional services, such as moorings (*R.* v. *Carrick DC, ex p. Prankerd* [1999] 2 W.L.R. 489).

SHIPPING SERVICES. Stat. Def., Shipping and Trading Interests (Protection) Act 1995 (c. 22), s.5(8).

SHOP. A travel agency was not a "shop" within the meaning of s.74 of the Shops Act 1950 (c. 28) (*Erewash Borough Council* v. *Ilkeston Consumer Co-operative Society* 87 L.G.R. 96).

Stat. Def., "any premises where there is carried on a trade or business consisting wholly or mainly of the sale of goods"—(Sunday Trading Act 1994 (c. 20), Sched. 1, para. 1).

SHORTHOLD TENANCY. (Housing Act 1988 (c. 50), s.34). A tenancy could only be treated as a protected shorthold tenancy in possession proceedings and s.34 should not be read as excluding from transitional protection a tenancy "which if proceedings for possession under the mandatory shorthold ground had been brought would have been treated as a protected shorthold tenancy" (*Thalmann* v. *Evans* [1996] 8 C.L. 420).

SHORT LEASE. Stat. Def., Companies Act 1985 (c. 6), Sched. 4, para. 83, Sched. 9, para. 34.

SHOULD BE REFUSED. The expression "should be refused" for the purposes of the Immigration Rules (H.C. 251) para. 111 stated a rule fixed subject to the Secretary of State's discretion outside the rules (*Pearson* v. *Immigration Appeal Tribunal* [1978] Imm.A.R. 212 applied) (*R.* v. *Secretary of State for the Home Department, ex p. Okello* [1995] Imm.A.R. 269).

SHOW. "Tending to show" (Criminal Evidence Act 1898 (c. 36), s.1(*f*)). "To show" in this section is to be construed as "revealed" (*R.* v. *Anderson* [1988] 2 W.L.R. 1017).

SHOWN. The word "shown" in a conveyance was not a word of limitation (*Wright Davies* v. *Marler* [1995] 10 C.L. 122).

SICKNESS. "Incapable of work in consequence of sickness" (Employment Protection (Consolidation) Act 1978 (c. 44), Sched. 13, para. 9(1)(*a*)). Where an employee retired early for medical reasons and was then, after a period of ten days, re-employed in a less stressful position, the ten day gap was held not to be a period where he was incapable of work due to sickness within the meaning of this paragraph, which requires a causal link between the absence from work and the incapacity due to sickness (*Pearson* v. *Kent County Council* [1993] IRLR 165).

SIGN. "Sign the bill" (Administration of Justice (Miscellaneous Provisions) Act 1933 (c. 36), s.2(1)). Merely to initial a bill of indictment is not to "sign" it within the meaning of this section (*R.* v. *Morais* [1988] 3 All E.R. 161).

(Statute of Frauds 1677; Law of Property Act 1925 (c. 20), s.40); Law of Property (Miscellaneous Provisions) Act 1989 (c. 34), s.2) The provisions of the Statute of Frauds 1677 and the Law of Property Act 1925 (c. 20), s.40 should no longer govern the meaning of the word "signed" in the 1989 Act as they did not interpret "signed" in the way understood today. Where a document was required to be signed, the signatory had to write his own name in his own hand (*Firstpost Homes* v. *Johnson* [1995] 1 W.L.R. 1567).

(Insolvency Rules 1986 (S.I. 1986 No. 1925), r.8.2(3)). A proxy form was signed for the purposes of rule 8(2)(3) if it bore upon it some distinctive or personal marking which had been placed there by or with authority of, the creditor so that a faxed form which had been signed by the transmitting creditor satisfied the provisions of the rules (*Re a Debtor (No. 2021 of 1995), ex p. Inland Revenue Commissioners* v. *The Debtor* [1996] 2 All E.R. 345).

SIGNIFICANT. "Business which consists to a significant degree of selling
. . . sex articles" (Local Government (Miscellaneous Provisions) Act 1982
(c. 30), Sched. 3, para. 4). In considering what degree of business is
"significant" within the meaning of this paragraph the relevant factor is the
proportion of sales of sex articles relative to the total turnover of the shop.
To be "significant" this proportion should be more than what would just be
needed to prevent it from being brushed aside as *de minimis*, and annual
turnover of sex articles representing 1 to 1.5 per cent. of total sales was held
not to be significant (*Lambeth London Borough Council* v. *Grewal* (1985) 82
Cr.App.R. 301).

(Children Act 1989 (c. 41), s.31). An abandoned baby was suffering
"significant harm" immediately before it was rescued so as to justify an
application for, and the granting of a care order (*Re M (Care Order:
Parental Responsibility*) [1996] 2 FLR 84).

(Limitation Act 1980 (c. 58), s.14(1)). For the purposes of s.14(1)
"significant" was defined as an injury sufficiently serious to cause severe
pain and sufficiently disabling to go to an Accident and Emergency
Department for investigation (*Shah* v. *Dexion Group Ltd* [1998] 1 C.L. 53).

SIMILAR. (E.C. Council Directive 65/65, Art. 4.8(a)(iii)). A medicinal
product was "essentially similar" to another if it had the same qualitative
and quantitative composition in respect of its active principles, the same
pharmaceutical form and was bioequivalent, unless it could be shown to be
significantly different in terms of safety or efficacy (*R.* v. *Licensing
Authority, ex p. Generics (UK) Ltd, The Times,* January 4, 1999).

"Series of similar actions," see SERIES.

SINGLE PAYMENT. (Supplementary Benefits Act 1976 (c. 71), s.3(1) as
amended by Sched. 2 to the Social Security Act 1980 (c. 30)). These words
are limited to exceptional expenditure on a single occasion or on several
occasions over a limited period (*Vaughan* v. *Social Security Adjudication
Officer* [1987] 151 J.P.N. 15). See also EXCEPTIONAL.

SINGLE TERM. (Criminal Justice Act 1991 (c. 53), s.51(2)). Where a
prisoner commits a new offence during his release on licence with the result
that the original offence is activiated but a new sentence of imprisonment
imposed, the order for return to prison whether served before or concurrently with the new term amounts to a "single term" within the meaning of
s.51 (*R.* v. *Secretary of State for the Home Department, ex p. Probyn* [1998] 1
All E.R. 357).

SITE. "The site . . . to which the balloon is attached" (Town and Country
Planning (Control of Advertisements) Regulations 1984 (No. 421),
reg. 2(4)). For the purposes of these regulations the "site" can be any
object on the premises heavy enough to prevent the balloon blowing away,
such as, in this case, a motor vehicle (*Wadham Stringer (Fareham)* v.
Fareham Borough Council (1987) 53 P. & C.R. 336).

(Town and Country Planning (Control of Advertisements) Regulations
1989 (S.I. 670) reg. 8, Sched. 3). "Site" in the 1989 Regulations referred to
the whole premises on which the advertisements were displayed rather than
just the specific area of the premises covered by the advertisement (*Barking*

& *Dagenham London Borough Council* v. *Mills and Allen Ltd Co.* [1997] 1 C.L. 535).

SLAUGHTERHOUSE. Stat. Def., Food Safety Act 1990 (c. 16), s.53.

SMALL. A capital distribution representing 15.58 per cent. of the value of shares in respect of which it was made was not "small, as compared with the value of the shares in respect of which it is distributed" within the meaning of s.72(2) of the Capital Gains Tax Act 1979 (c. 14) (*O'Rourke* v. *Binks* [1991] S.T.C. 455).

SMOKE. Stat. Def., Environmental Protection Act 1990 (c. 43), s.79.

SNOWBALL SCHEME. A "snowball scheme" by which money paid by members was redistributed to scheme members with founder members receiving the most, amounted to a lottery for the purposes of the Lotteries and Amusements Act 1976 (c. 32) but was not regarded as a "game" by any of the participants and so did not amount to "gaming" within the meaning of the Gaming Acts 1845 or 1968 (*One Life Ltd (in liquidation)* v. *Roy, The Times,* July 12, 1996).

SOCIAL. "Social reasons" (Council Directive (67/228/EEC), Art. 17). The European Court held that there were good "social reasons" within the meaning of this article for applying a zero rate of VAT to the construction of buildings for housing (*E.C. Commission* v. *U.K.* (No. 416/85) [1988] 3 W.L.R. 1261).

"Social services function" (Local Authority Social Services Act 1970 (c. 42), s.7D). It was not clear whether the duty to consult over the proposed closure of a residential home for the elderly was a "social services function" within the meaning of s.7D of the 1970 Act and so it was particularly appropriate for decision by the courts rather than the Secretary of State (*R.* v. *Devon County Council, ex p. Baker* [1995] 1 All E.R. 73).

SOIL. (Protection of Badgers Act 1992 (c. 51), s.8). The purpose of s.8 of the 1992 Act was to enable huntsmen to stop up entrances to badgers' setts to prevent use by foxes during a hunt, but not in such a way as to prevent badgers from gaining access or egress to their setts. The materials specified in s.8(5) were, by definition, all light, easily removable and not permanently obstructive so that "loose soil" had to be of the same nature, which would be a question of fact in each case. Clay-based soil would have to be broken up sufficiently in order to fall within the defence afforded by s.8(5) (*Lovett* v. *Bussey, The Times,* April 24, 1998).

SOLD. (Inheritance Tax Act 1984 (c. 51), Part VI). The meaning of "sold" for the purposes of inheritance tax relief depended on its context and could mean either "agreed to be sold" as under a specifically enforceable contract for the sale of land or "conveyed or transferred on completion of sale" (*Jones* v. *Inland Revenue Commissioners* [1997] STC 358).

SOLE. "Sole or main residence," see MAIN RESIDENCE.

"Sole responsibility" (Immigration Rules (H.C. 160), r.50(e) and (f)). The absence of day-to-day care was not determinative of "sole responsibility" (*Bain* v. *Hugh L.S. McConnell* 1991 S.L.T. 691 applied) (*Alagon* v. *Secretary of State for the Home Department* (O.H.), 1995 S.L.T. 381).

SOLELY. "Solely on the evidence of one witness" (Road Traffic Regulation Act 1984 (c. 27), s.89(2)). A person convicted of speeding on the evidence of a police officer based on his opinion of speed calculated from physical and material data such as skid marks, burn marks and vehicle damage, was held not to have been convicted "solely on the evidence of one witness" within the meaning of this section (*Crossland* v. *DPP* [1988] RTR 417).

SOLICIT. "Persistently solicits a woman" (Sexual Offences Act 1985 (c. 44), s.2(1)). The act of persistently driving a motor vehicle late at night round an area frequented by prostitutes did not of itself constitute an act of soliciting. Not only is evidence of persistence indispensable for a conviction under this section, it is also necessary for the prosecution to prove that the man said to have been soliciting a prostitute had given some indication, by act or word, to the prostitute, that he required her services (*Darroch* v. *Director of Public Prosecutions* (1990) 91 Cr.App.R. 378).

SOLICITOR. "Acting as a solicitor" (Solicitors Act 1974 (c. 47), s.25(1)). An unqualified person who represented a party in an arbitration was held not to have "acted as a solicitor" within the meaning of this section (*Piper Double Glazing* v. *D.C. Contracts (1992) Co.* [1994] 1 All E.R. 177).

SOUND EQUIPMENT. Stat Def., "means equipment designed or adapted for amplifying music and any equipment suitable for use in connection with such equipment"—(Criminal Justice and Public Order Act 1994 (c. 33), s.64(6)).

SOUVENIR. Not every item bought by a tourist becomes for that reason, a "souvenir" within the meaning of ss.47 and 59 of the Shops Act 1950 (c. 28), as amended by s.31 of the Criminal Justice Act 1972 (c. 71). Sweaters and vases were held not to be "souvenirs" within the meaning of these sections (*York City Council* v. *Little Gallery, The Times*, December 2, 1985).

SOVEREIGN. Jersey is not a "sovereign state" for the purposes of the Carriage of Goods by Road Act 1965 (c. 37) (*Chloride Industrial Batteries* v. *F. & W. Freight* [1989] 1 W.L.R. 823).

"Done by it in the exercise of sovereign authority" (State Immunity Act 1978 (c. 33), s.14(2)(*a*)). The forcible confiscation and retention of ten civilian aircraft from Kuwait by Iraqi Airways Co. (a corporation owned by the Republic of Iraq), at the direction of the government, was an activity done in the exercise of "sovereign authority" within the meaning of this section (*Kuwait Airways Corp.* v. *Iraqi Airways Co., The Times*, October 27, 1993).

SPECIAL CIRCUMSTANCES. "Because of special circumstances" (Housing Act 1985 (c. 68), s.61(1)(*d*)). The desirability for children with reading difficulties to continue to attend the same school could be a "special circumstance" for concluding that there was a "local connection" with a particular authority within the meaning of this section (*R. v. Harrow London Borough Council, ex p. Carter, The Times*, November 3, 1992).

A large damages claim, high costs and a narrow margin between the amount of the final judgment and payments into court could amount to "special circumstances" which could justify an award of costs in favour of a defendant even where a plaintiff had beaten the payment in (*Charm Marine Inc. v. Elbourne Mitchell* [1997] 10 C.L. 61).

SPECIAL CONSIDERATION. In giving "special consideration" under paragraph 51 of the Statement of Changes in Immigration Rules 1983 (H.C. 169) to the needs of a fully dependent and unmarried daughter over 18 and under 21, who applied for entry to the U.K., the immigration appeal tribunal should adopt an approach of broad humanity, so as not to disregard her needs for a home and financial support simply on the narrow ground that her sponsor in the U.K. was already providing both abroad (*R. v. Immigration Appeal Tribunal, ex p. Kara* [1989] Imm.A.R. 20).

SPECIAL DIET. (Supplementary Benefit (Requirements) Regulations 1983 (No. 1399), reg. 11, Sched. 4, para. 14), see CONDITION.

SPECIAL EDUCATIONAL NEEDS. In relation to children and adults, Stat. Def., Education Act 1994 (c. 30), s.19(3).

SPECIAL EDUCATIONAL PROVISION. A "special educational provision" within the meaning of s.1(3) of the Education Act 1981 (c. 60) is one which was called for by a learning difficulty, such as, as in this case, dyslexia, and is not limited to educational provision available only in independent schools. Provision available within a local education authority's schools could be a "special educational provision" within the meaning of this section (*R. v. Hampshire County Council, ex p. J.*, *The Times*, December 5, 1985). Speech therapy would be a "special educational provision" within the meaning of this Act (*R. v. Lancashire County Council, ex p. C.M. (A Minor)* (1989) 19 Fam. Law 395).

SPECIAL OCCASION. (Licensing Act 1964 (c. 26), s.74(4)). The frequency of any occasion is relevant to the question whether it is "special" for the purposes of this section, and plainly the greater the frequency of any occasion the less "special" it is likely to be (*Paulson v. Oxford City Magistrates' Court* [1989] C.O.D. 464).

SPECIAL POLICE SERVICES. (Police Act 1964 (c. 48), s.15(1)). The provision of police officers to attend inside the football ground when matches were being played there was the provision of "special police services" within the meaning of this section (*Harris v. Sheffield United Football Club* [1987] 3 W.L.R. 305).

SPECIAL REASON. (2) "Special reasons" (Road Traffic Act 1972 (c. 20), s.93(1); Road Traffic Offenders Act 1988 (c. 53), s. 34(1)). Where a driver is liable to disqualification for a second offence, circumstances special to the first offence cannot be "special reasons" for the second (*Bolliston v. Gibbons*

[1985] RTR 176). When a defendant in a laced drink case seeks to avoid disqualification by adducing special reasons, the court must consider whether he should have realised, as in this case, that he was unfit to drive (*Pridige* v. *Gant* [1985] RTR 196). A medical or other emergency which compels a motorist to drive is capable of amounting to "special reasons" for not disqualifying, but the test is objective as to whether such an emergency in fact existed (*Thompson* v. *Diamond* [1985] RTR 316). Where a defendant was convicted of driving with excess alcohol on the evidence of one specimen, and was also convicted of failing to provide a second specimen, the circumstances did not constitute "special reasons" for failing to disqualify or indorse on the second offence (*Denneny* v. *Harding* [1986] RTR 350). Conflict between the blood/alcohol level figures provided by blood and breath specimens could amount to a "special reason" for not disqualifying (*Smith* v. *Geraghty* [1986] RTR 222). The fact that a motorist drives only a very short distance is capable of being a "special reason" for not disqualifying him from driving under this section. Thus, where a drinking passenger drove a car back on to the road and parked it, after the original driver had crashed it into a field, there was a "special reason" (*Chatters* v. *Burke* [1986] 1 W.L.R. 1321). And, where the drinking husband backed the car out of a parking space preparatory to the wife driving them home, there was also a special reason for not disqualifying (*Redmond* v. *Parry* [1986] RTR 146). Ignorance of the overnight effect of alcohol consumed 12 hours before driving did not constitute a "special reason" for not disqualifying (*DPP* v. *O'Meara* [1989] RTR 24). Justices were held to have erred in finding "special reasons" for not disqualifying a driver who had an accident on his way home after attending an emergency situation as the emergency could have been met by means other than driving (*DPP* v. *Waller* [1989] RTR 112). A motorist who pleads, as a "special reason" under this section, that his drink has been laced has to satisfy the justices, first, that the drink has been laced and, secondly, that the excess alcohol was attributable to that which had been added without his knowledge (*James* v. *Morgan* [1988] RTR 85). Fear by a motorist for the safety of his wife if he did not drive to escape the threatening behaviour of her former husband could be a "special reason" for not disqualifying him (*Williams* v. *Tierney* [1988] RTR 118). Where the first of two breath tests produced a negative result that was not a "special reason" for not disqualifying when a second test proved positive (*DPP* v. *White* [1988] RTR 267). Dealing with an emergency can be a "special reason" for the purposes of s.93 but only for the period of the emergency. It no longer protected a driver on his way home after he had dealt with the emergency (*DPP* v. *Feeney* (1989) 89 Cr.App.R. 173, D.C.). Ignorance of the accused as to what she was doing, through the influence of a laced drink given her by a friend, could be a special reason for non-disqualification (*DPP* v. *Barker* [1990] RTR 1). The fact that a drunken driver had only driven 40 yards in order to be able to park his car safely, and that there was no danger to any member of the public, was held to be a "special reason" for non-disqualification (*DPP* v. *Corcoran* [1991] RTR 329). The fact that the defendant had not had a "reasonable excuse" for not providing a specimen under s.8(7), as substituted, did not necessarily mean that there would also not be special reasons for not disqualifying under s.93 (*Daniels* v. *DPP, The Times*, November 25, 1991). If a motorist relies on the fact that his drink was laced as a special reason under this section then he has to show that his drink was in fact laced, that he did not known that it was laced and that he would not otherwise have exceeded the prescribed limit (*DPP* v. *Connor*; *Same* v. *Allat*; *Same* v. *Connor*; *Same* v. *Chapman*; *R.* v. *Chichester Crown Court, ex p. Moss*; *Moss* v. *Allen* [1992] RTR 66). A genuine fear of contracting AIDS as a result of blowing into a police breath test device was capable of amounting to a special reason for not disqualifying a driver who had refused to provide a specimen of breath (*DPP* v. *Kinnersley, The Times*, December 29, 1992). Fear for her own personal safety and the possibility of further damage to her car did not amount to a special reason for non-disqualification in circumstances where the motorist had deliberately taken a decision to drink when she knew she would be driving (*DPP* v. *Doyle* [1993] RTR 369).

The circumstances which led justices to decide not to disqualify a motorist, even after accepting his plea of guilty to a charge of failing to provide a specimen of breath, could provide a "special reason," within the meaning of s.101(2) of the Road Traffic Act 1972 (c. 20) (now Road Traffic Offenders Act 1988 (c. 53), s.44), for not ordering the obligatory number of penalty points to be indorsed on his licence (*McCormick* v. *Hitchins* (1986) 83 Cr.App.R. 11). The fact that consecutive offences of permitting uninsured use of a vehicle might have been avoided had the defendant been aware of the first constituted a "special reason" for not indorsing his licence for the subsequent offences (*Barnett* v. *Fieldhouse* [1987] RTR 266). Ignorance of the terms of an insurance policy cannot be a "special reason" for the purposes of this section (*East* v. *Bladen* [1987] RTR 291). But justices were held to be entitled to find that there were "special reasons" not to indorse the licences of motorists who performed U-turns across the central reservation of a motorway in circumstances where their lane was blocked and there had been no on-coming traffic in the opposite carriageway for a considerable time (*DPP* v. *Fruer* [1989] RTR 29). A solicitor speeding on the motorway in answer to an urgent call by his clerk did not have "special reasons" to avoid indorsement of his licence (*Robinson* v. *DPP* [1989] RTR 42). Participation by a police officer on duty in a police training exercise which required him to try to keep another police car under a surveillance was not a "special reason" for non-endorsement of licence under s.101(2) (*Agnew* v. *DPP* [1991] RTR 144). Where the accused rode his child's mechanically propelled motorcycle along a road and struck a car, and pleaded guilty to a charge fo careless driving, the fact that he regarded the cycle as a toy was not a "special reason" for not endorsing his licence (*DPP* v. *Powell* [1993] RTR 236).

Driving friends who had been injured in a disturbance to hospital, having been informed that there were no ambulances available and that a taxi would not convey them amounted to "special reasons" for non-disqualification (*DPP* v. *Upchurch* [1994] RTR 366). Driving home to relieve a 14-year-old babysitter who had received a number of telephone calls in which the caller had threatened to use a knife, having failed to find alternative means of transport home, amounted to "special reasons" for non-disqualification (*DPP* v. *Knight* [1994] RTR 374).

Circumstances which did not amount to a reasonable excuse for failing to provide a specimen of breath for analysis could afford a "special reason" under s.34 but the court had to be in a position to accept the factual basis although finding that the factual basis did not amount to a reasonable excuse (*DPP* v. *Daley (No. 2)* [1994] RTR 107). An emergency situation requiring the defendant to escape further assault by driving could provide "special reasons" but once a number of options, including not driving, became open to him any further journey could not amount to "special reasons" (*DPP* v. *Goddard* [1998] RTR 463).

(9) "Some other special reason" (Arbitration Act 1979 (c. 42), s.1(7)(*b*)). A change in the law, as opposed to a discovery of new facts, subsequent to the hearing of an action, could constitute a "special reason" for a decision of the High Court to be considered by the Court of Appeal under this section (*Arnold* v. *National Westminster Bank* [1988] 3 All E.R. 977).

"Some special reason why such a notice was not given" (Arbitration Act 1979 (c. 42), s.1(6)(*b*)). At a rent review, a failure by the tenant's surveyor to recognise a challenge by the landlord to the basis on which the revised rent had been assessed at an earlier rent review was not a "special reason" for the tenant's failure to give notice to the arbitrator that a reasoned award was required (*Leeds Permanent Building Society* v. *Latchmere Properties* [1989] 20 E.G. 128).

(Housing Act 1985 (c. 68), s.59). "Other special reason" should not be construed using the ejusdem generis rule. The word "special" pointed to the fact that the circumstances of the applicant had to be particularly serious and different from other homeless persons and the financial impecuniosity of an asylum seeker, while not a special reason on its own, should be considered together with the absence of family or friends in the U.K. and an inability to speak English (*R.* v. *Kensington and Chelsea R.L.B.C. ex p. Kihara, The Independent,* July 3, 1996).

SPECIALISED. "Specialised vehicles" (Community Road Transport Rules (Exemptions) Regulations 1978 (No. 1158), reg. 4(3)) are vehicles whose construction, fitments and other permanent equipment guaranteed that they were used primarily for one of the operations specified in that regulation, such as door-to-door selling. The mere fact of being used for a specified operation did not of itself make the vehicle "specialised" within the meaning of this regulation (*Gaunt* v. *Nelson* [1978] RTR 1).

"Specialised breakdown vehicle" (EEC Regulation 543/69, Art. 4(9)). The exemption from the tachograph regulations in respect of specialised breakdown vehicles was conditional only on the nature of the vehicle concerned regardless of the use to which it was put. In this case the transport of old unroadworthy cars (*Hamilton* v. *Whitelock* [1988] RTR 23).

See also BREAKDOWN VEHICLE; RECOVERY VEHICLE.

SPECIALITY. (Limitation Act 1980 (c. 58), s.8(1)). An action for damages for breach of a contract under seal (a "speciality") was governed by s.8(1) of the 1980 Act and so subject to a 12 year limitation period (*Aiken* v. *Stewart Wrightson Members Agency Ltd* [1995] 1 W.L.R. 1281; [1995] 2 Lloyd's Rep. 618).

SPECIES. "Species of dog in s.2(2)(*b*) of the Animals Act 1971 (c. 22) means "breed," not dogs generally.

The presence of the word "includes" in s.11 of the Animals Act 1971 (c. 22) (the interpretation section) allowed "sub-species" to be substituted for "species" (*Hunt* v. *Wallis,* [1994] P.I.Q.R. P128).

SPECIFIC ISSUE ORDER. (Children Act 1989 (c. 41), s.8). An application for a specific issue order could not be made to determine rights of occupation in a property (*Pearson* v. *Franklin* [1994] 2 All E.R. 137).

SPECIFICITY PRINCIPLE. A grant from the European Social Fund which was utilised by a public body for purposes which had nothing to do with projects earmarked for the grant but which had already been funded by the body's own domestic arrangements did not breach the "specificity principle" contained in the E.C. regulations governing the administration of the European Social Fund (*Birmingham City Council* v. *Birmingham College of Food and Sutton Coldfield College; Cheshire County Council* v. *Halton College* [1996] ELR 1).

See also ADDITIONALITY PRINCIPLE.

SPECIFIED. A period is sufficiently specified for the purposes of s.1(1) of the Perpetuities and Accumulations Act 1964 (c. 55) if it is made unambiguously clear what that period is to be; so that where a will specified a period not expressed as a number of years, but which could become a number of years by calculation it was held that the period had been sufficiently "specified" for the purposes of this section (*Re Green's Will Trusts* [1985] 3 All E.R. 455).

Where a landowner granted a licence for an indefinite period in contemplation that the land would be used for grazing, that was held to have created a seasonal grazing licence "during some specified period of the year" within the meaning of s.2(1) of the Agricultural Holdings Act 1948 (c. 63) (*Watts* v. *Yeend* [1987] 1 W.L.R. 323).

(Taxes Management Act 1970 (c. 9), s.20). The words "specified or described" in s.20(8D) should be given their ordinary and natural meaning and not a more restricted interpretation (*R.* v. *Inland Revenue Commissioners, ex p. Ulster Bank Ltd* [1997] STC 832).

SPECIFIED OPERATION. (Town and Country Planning Act 1971 (c. 78), s.43). The question whether work carried out on a site for which planning permission had been granted for a limited time constituted a "specified operation" within the meaning of s.43(2) was one of purpose and not degree (*Thayer* v. *Secretary of State for the Environment* [1991] 3 P.L.R. 104). See also *R.* v. *Elmbridge Borough Council, ex p. Oakimber* [1991] 3 P.L.R. 35).

SPECIFIED PERSON. (Employment Act 1990 (c. 38), s.7(3)(*b*)). The requirement under this section that a call for industrial action be made by a "specified person" (in this case the union's general secretary) was met where the general secretary gave a regional union official authorisation to strike should the negotiations with the employers, set for the following day, break down (*Tanks and Drums* v. *Transport and General Workers Union* [1991] IRLR 372).

SPECIFIED PROCEEDINGS. (Children Act 1989 (c. 41), ss.37, 41; Family Proceedings Rules 1991 (S.I. 1991 No. 1247), rr.4.10–4.11, 9.2A, 9.5). Proceedings ceased to be "specified proceedings" once a local authority had decided not to apply for a public law order after completion of an investigation under s.37(1) (*CE (Section 37 direction), Re;* [1995] 1 FLR 26).

SPORT. Stat. Def., Fire Safety and Safety of Places of Sport Act 1987 (c. 27), ss.42, 43.

SPOUSE. "Spouse" in EEC Regulations 1612/68, Art. 10(1)(*a*) was held to refer only to a relationship based upon marriage, and could not be extended to cover other types of partner however stable the relationship (*The Netherlands* v. *Ann Florence Reed* (No. 59/85) [1987] C.M.L.R. 448).

STAGE. "At any stage of the proceedings" (R.S.C., Ord. 15, r.6(2)). A stay of proceedings, even where ordered by consent upon all the parties agreeing terms of settlement, was not the equivalent of a dismissal or discontinuance of the proceedings, so that they remained at a "stage of the proceedings" for the purposes of this rule (*Rofa Sport Management AG* v. *DHL International (U.K.)* [1989] 2 All E.R. 743).

STAMP. Stat. Def., Weights and Measures Act 1985 (c. 72), s.94.

STATE. "Same state," see SAME.

STATE AUTHORITY. (E.C. Collectives Redundancy Directive 75/129). A privatised water company, having regard to it powers and duties and the control to which it was subject, was an authority of the state (*Foster* v. *British Gas* followed; *Doughty* v. *Rolls Royce* considered) (*Griffin* v. *South West Water Services* [1995] IRLR 15).

STATED OFFENCE. A warrant to search premises and seize goods was valid even though it did not state the particular offence for which the warrant was sought but was still in the terms authorised by the magistrate granting it, who had been told orally of the suspected offence (*R.* v. *Chief Constable of Warwickshire, ex p. Fitzpatrick* [1999] 1 W.L.R. 573).

STATEMENT. "Statement of the reasons" (Immigration Appeals (Notices) Regulations 1984 (No. 2040), reg. 4(1)(*a*)). A statement by an immigration officer that she was not satisfied that the applicant was genuinely seeking entry only for the one week asked for was a sufficient "statement of the reasons" for the purposes of this regulation (*R.* v. *Secretary of State for the Home Department, ex p. Swati* [1986] 1 All E.R. 717).

"Any statement made by or taken from a child" (Magistrates' Courts Act 1980 (c. 43), s.103, as substituted by Criminal Justice Act 1988 (c. 33), s.33). A transcript made from a video-tape of a police interview with a child was held to be a "statement" within the meaning of this section (*R.* v. *H.* (1991) 155 J.P. 561).

"Statement contained in a document produced by a computer" (Police and Criminal Evidence Act 1984 (c. 60), s.69(1)). Records of telephone calls made by the accused, recorded automatically and shown on computer print-outs were held not to be "statements" for the purposes of this section and could therefore be admitted in evidence (*R.* v. *Spiby* (1990) 91 Cr.App.R. 186).

"Statement made by a person in a document" (Criminal Justice Act 1988 (c. 33), s.23(1)). Where a person had been injured and died before the trial but after having made a statement to a police officer, recorded by him at the time, that statement was a "statement" in a "document" within the meaning of this section (*R.* v. *MacGillivray* (1993) 97 Cr.App.R. 232, C.A.).

"A statement prepared . . . for the purpose . . . of a criminal investigation" (Criminal Justice Act 1988 (c. 33), s.24(4)). A supermarket receipt recording a certain purchase as evidence of the facts recorded in it was not a "statement" so prepared within the meaning of this section (*R.* v. *Murphy, Wiseman and Maron* [1992] Crim.L.R. 883).

Stat. Def., Civil Evidence Act 1995 (c. 38), s.13; "words, pictures, visual images, gestures or any other method of signifying meaning" (Defamation Act 1996 (c. 31), s.17(1)).

STATUTORY BODY. Stat. Def., Armed Forces Act 1996 (c. 46), s.21(5).

STATUTORY DEMAND. See DEMAND.

STATUTORY FUNCTIONS. Stat. Def., "functions conferred by virtue of any enactment" (Northern Ireland Act 1998 (c. 47), s.44(10)).

STATUTORY PROVISION. Stat. Def., Industrial Tribunals Act 1996 (c. 17), s.42(1); Defamation Act 1996 (c. 31), s.17(1).

Stat. Def., including Measures, National Institutions Measure 1998 (No. 1), s.12(1).

STATUTORY UNDERTAKERS. Stat. Def., Regional Development Agencies Act 1998 (c. 45), s.19(10).

STATUTORY UNDERTAKING. Stat. Def., Local Government etc. (Scotland) Act 1994 (c. 39), s.59(9).

STEP. (1) "Steps in the proceedings" (Arbitration Act 1950 (c. 27), s.4). The filing of an affidavit and attendance before the master to defend a summons issued by the plaintiffs for leave to enter summary judgment under R.S.C., Ord. 14 were "steps in the proceedings" within the meaning of this section (*Turner and Goudy* v. *McConnell* [1985] 2 All E.R. 34). A defendant who ticked the boxes in the form acknowledging service of a writ, to indicate that he wished to apply for a High Court action commenced in a district registry to be transferred to London or to another district registry, was held not to have taken a "step in the proceedings" (*Skopos Design Group* v. *Homelife Nursing, The Times*, March 24, 1988). Seeking to stay or dismiss a third party action under the inherent jurisdiction of the court and under R.S.C., Ord. 18, r.19(1) did not amount to taking a "step" in the third party proceedings (*RGE (Group Services)* v. *Cleveland Offshore* (1986) 11 Con.L.R. 77).

(Arbitration Act 1950 (c. 27), s.5) A consent order (in this case consent to an interpleader payment) did not amount to "a step in the proceedings" which could prevent a stay of those proceedings in favour of arbitration (*Hickie* v. *Alternative Software Ltd* [1996] 6 C.L. 40).

"Steps . . . to enforce any security" (Insolvency Act 1986 (c. 45), s.11(3)(c)). In the case of an ordinary possessory lien, the assertion by the lien holder of a right to retain constituted the taking of a "step" to enforce his security within the meaning of this section (*Bristol Airport* v. *Powdrill* [1990] 2 W.L.R. 1362). The detention by a creditor of a debtor's aircraft was a step to enforce a security within the meaning of this section (*Re Paramount Airways*) [1990] BCC 130).

(2) "Step to commence arbitration proceedings" (Arbitration Act 1950 (c. 27), s.27). Where a rent review clause provided for arbitration and stipulated certain time limits to be of the essence, a late notice was invalid and not therefore "a step to commence arbitration proceedings" within the meaning of this section (*Richurst* v. *Pimenta* [1993] 1 W.L.R. 159).

STOCK. Stat. Def., "includes any marketable security" (Finance Act 1986 (c. 41), s.80B(2) inserted by Finance Act 1997 (c. 16), s.97(1)).

STORAGE. "Storage" implied a degree of permanence and could not include property placed temporarily (*Plews* v. *Plaisted*, 1997 S.L.T. 1371).

STORM. While the word "storm," used in the insured perils clause of an insurance policy, might involve an element of violence in the sense of rapid movement of air or water, it was not to be restricted to that meaning, nor to the particular technical significance of the Beaufort Scale. It could also properly be used to cover an extreme or unusually intense precipitation (*Glasgow Training Group* (*Motor Trade*) v. *Lombard Continental, The Times*, November 21, 1988).

JCT Standard Form of Building Contract (1980) Private Edition with Quantities, cl.22C.) Heavy rainfall could amount to "storm" although this was a question of fact and degree (*Nimmo (William) & Co.* v. *Russell Construction* (O.H.) 1995 S.L.T. 1282).

STREET. "Street" (Town Police Clauses Act 1847 (c. 89), s.38, as amended by Sched. 3 to the Criminal Justice Act 1967 (c. 80) and ss.39 and 46 of, and Sched. 3 to, the Criminal Justice Act 1982 (c. 48)). Land was not a "street" for the purposes of this section unless the public, including taxi drivers, had a legal right of access to it. Accordingly the taxi rank at Birmingham Airport on land owned by the airport authority and subject to its by-laws was not a "street" (*Young* v. *Scampion* [1989] RTR 95).

Stat. Def., Sexual Offences Act 1985 (c. 44), s.4; Housing Act 1985 (c. 68), s.622; Gas Act 1986 (c. 44), Sched. 4, para. 6; New Roads and Street Works Act 1991 (c. 22), s.48; Transport and Works Act 1992 (c. 42), s.67.

STREET TRADING. (Pedlars Act 1871 (c. 96) s.3). It was not necessary to set up a pitch in order to be convicted of street trading (*Prentice* v. *Normand*, 1994 S.C.C.R. 55).

(London Local Authorities Act 1990, ss.21, 38). Exposing goods for sale outside a shop which were to be paid for inside the shop amounted to street trading in London, although such an activity was specifically excluded elsewhere under the Local Government (Miscellaneous Provisions) Act 1982 (*Wandsworth LBC* v. *Rosenthal, The Times*, March 28, 1996).

STRIKE. Overtime bans and bans on rest day working were "strikes" within the meaning of s.246 of the 1992 Act, since a refusal to work for periods of time during which employees were normally employed constituted a "strike" (*Connex South Eastern Ltd* v. *National Union of Maritime and Transport Workers* [1999] IRLR 249).

Stat. Def., Employment Act 1988 (c. 19), s.1; Trade Union and Labour Relations (Consolidation) Act 1992 (c. 52), s.246; Employment Rights Act 1996 (c. 18), s.235(4).

STRUCTURE. (5) A caravan used for the storage and mixing of cattle food was not a "structure" for the purposes of the Town and Country Planning Acts (*Wealden District Council* v. *Secretary of State for the Environment* (1988) 56 P.&C.R. 286).

"The structure . . . of the dwelling-house" (Landlord and Tenant Act 1985 (c. 70), s.11(1)(*a*)). The plaster on the walls can be part of the "structure" for the purposes of this section (*Staves and Staves* v. *Leeds City Council* (1990) 23 H.L.R. 95). The "structure" in this sentence consists of those elements which give it its essential appearance, stability and shape; it is not limited to those parts of the dwelling-house which are load-bearing, but any particular part must be a material or significant element in the overall construction (*Irvine* v. *Moran* (1991) 24 H.L.R. 1).

"Structure fixed to a building" (Town and Country Planning Act 1971 (c. 78), s.54(9)). "Structure" in this section is limited to such structures as are ancillary to the building itself, and is not intended to cover some other complete building in its own right, such as, as in this case, one connected by a bridge and a tunnel (*Debenhams* v. *Westminster City Council* [1986] 3 W.L.R. 1063).

"Structure . . . forming part of the land and comprised within the curtilage of a building" (Town and Country Planning Act 1971 (c. 78), s.54(9)). A ha-ha was held to be such a structure (*Watson-Smyth* v. *Secretary of State for the Environment and Cherwell District Council* (1991) 64 P.&C.R. 156).

"No fresh structures," see CARAVAN.

STRUCTURED SETTLEMENT. Stat. Def., Damages Act 1996 (c. 48), s.5.

STUDENT. (Income Support (General) Regulations 1987, reg. 61). For the purposes of reg. 61 of the 1987 Regulations, a "student" had to attend a full-time course from the time of enrolment through such terms as were periods of terms or vacation within it (*Chief Education Officer* v. *Webber* [1997] 4 All E.R. 274).

STUDENTS' UNION. Stat. Def., Education Act 1994 (c. 30), s.20(1).

STUDY. "Study . . . evaluation . . . jobs" (Equal Pay Act 1970 (c. 41), s.1(5)). To be effective the "study" had to analyse the various factors necessary for the effective performance of the job, and then compare the result with other similar jobs performed by other workers (*Bromley* v. *Quick* (*H. & J.*) [1988] IRLR 249).

SUBJECT. In constitutional context, Stat. Def., "a person not acting on behalf of the Crown" (Scotland Act 1998 (c. 46), s.99(5)).

SUBJECT TO. "Subject to the tenancy," see TENANCY.

(Race Relations Act 1976 (c. 74), s.4(2)(c)). An employer "subjected" an employee to racial harassment if he caused or permitted the harassment to occur in circumstances in which he could control, whether the harassment was caused by a third party. The test was whether the event in question was sufficiently under the control of the employer that he could have prevented the harassment or reduced its extent (*Burton* v. *De Vere Hotels Ltd* [1997] I.C.R. 1).

SUBJECT TO DETAILS/LOGICAL AMENDMENTS. The term "subject to details" was a well-known term on the context of a bill of lading and "logical amendment" should be treated as illustrative and/or supplemental rather than restrictive in intention (*CPC Consolidated Pool Carriers GmbH* v. *CTM CIA Transmediterranea SA* [1994] 1 Lloyd's Rep. 68).

SUBMIT TO. "Submit to the jurisdiction" (Convention on Jurisdiction and the Enforcement of Judgments in Civil and Commercial Matters 1968, Art. 18). Neither the acknowledgment of service of a writ nor an application to stay an action could amount to a submission to the jurisdiction for the purposes of this Convention (*The Sydney Express* [1988] 2 Lloyd's Rep. 257).

SUBORDINATE LEGISLATION. Stat. Def., Human Rights Act 1998 (c. 42), s.21(1).

SUBSIDIARY. "Or any of its subsidiaries" (Companies Act 1985 (c. 6), s.151). "Subsidiaries" here means English subsidiaries and did not prevent a foreign subsidiary from giving financial assistance for the acquisition of shares in its English parent company (*Arab Bank* v. *Mercantile Holdings* [1994] Ch. 71).

"Subsidiary company." Stat. Def., Companies Act 1985 (c. 6), s.736; Companies Act 1989 (c. 40), s.144.

SUBSTANCE. Stat. Def., Consumer Protection Act 1987 (c. 43), s.45; Water Act 1989 (c. 15), s.189.

SUBSTANTIAL. "Substantial risk that the course of justice . . . will be seriously . . . prejudiced" (Contempt of Court Act 1981 (c. 49), s.2(2)). These words refer not to the acts or omissions relied on as giving rise to liability but to the casualty caused by the acts or omissions. So that where, in a libel action against a newspaper the defence of justification was relied on, it was held that repetition of the allegations by another newspaper 11 months before the earliest date set for the trial did not pose a "substantial risk" of prejudice (*Att.-Gen.* v. *News Group Newspapers* [1986] 3 W.L.R. 365). In considering whether the strict liability rule applied under section 2(2) in respect of a publication, the court had to ask in each case whether in the circumstances the publication created at the time of its publication a substantial risk that the course of justice could be seriously impeded or prejudiced. The risk had to be a practical risk (*Att.–Gen.* v. *Guardian Newspapers* [1992] 3 All E.R. 38).

A court could not be satisfied that there was a "substantial risk that the course of justice . . . will be seriously . . . prejudiced" where despite very noteworthy information, a broadcast in a news bulletin had been very brief, ephemeral in nature and where there had been a relatively small circulation of the information in newspapers in an area well away from the place of trial nine months' later (*Att.-Gen.* v. *Independent Television News* [1995] 1 All E.R. 370).

Where there had been saturation coverage of a news item in the months before an incident which led to court proceedings, further intense news coverage concerning that incident did not necessarily create a greater risk of prejudice than that which already existed; each publication had to be considered separately as at the date of publication and the impact on a potential juror at the time of trial assessed (*Att.-Gen.* v. *Mirror Group Newspapers Ltd* [1997] 1 All E.R. 456). The fact that a judge had stayed criminal proceedings suggested that the publication of a newspaper article, which had not named the defendants, but had suggested that a notorious murder had been carried out by a gang involved in drug dealing, had created a substantial risk that the original trial was seriously prejudiced (*Att.-Gen.* v. *Birmingham Post and Mail Ltd* [1998] 4 All E.R. 49).

"A substantial part of the United Kingdom" (Fair Trading Act 1973 (c. 41), s.64(3)) means a part of such size, character or importance as to merit consideration. It need not necessarily be a large part (*R.* v. *Monopolies and Mergers Commission, ex p. South Yorkshire Transport* [1993] 1 W.L.R. 23).

"Substantial links" (Secretary of State's Statement of Policy, July 25, 1990). The fact that an asylum-seeker has friends in the United Kingdom does not in itself amount to "substantial links" with the United Kingdom for the purposes of this statement (*R.* v. *Secretary of State for the Home Department, ex p. Dursun (Huseyin)* [1991] Imm.A.R. 297

"Substantial part of the whole rent" (Rent Act 1977 (c. 42), s.7(2)). The amount of rent attributed to the provision of a full laundry service can be a "substantial" part of the whole for the purposes of this section (*Nelson Developments* v. *Taboada* (1992) 24 H.L.R. 462).

"Some other substantial reason of a kind such as to justify . . . dismissal" (Employment Protection (Consolidation) Act 1978 (c. 44), s.57(1)(*b*)). An expression of an intention to resign by an employee could qualify as a reason for dismissal under this section (*Ely* v. *YKK Fasteners (UK)* [1994] I.C.R. 164).

A "substantial" amount of contributory negligence meant a considerable amount (*Calder* v. *Simpson*, 1994 S.L.T. 32).

(Public Order Act 1986, (c. 64), s.4).

A "substantial cause" should be more than merely "*de minimis.*" The conduct of a person, charging at a police officer, who put out his leg to stop him, thereby suffering an ankle injury, was the substantial cause of the officer's injury (*R.* v. *Hennigan* (1971) 55 Cr.App.R. 262 approved and *R.* v. *Roberts (Kennedy)* (1972) 56 Cr.App.R. 95 followed by (*R.* v. *Notman* [1994] Crim.L.R. 518).

(Civil Jurisdiction and Judgments Act 1982 (c. 27), s.41(3)(*b*)). Enforced presence by reason of a condition of bail that he should remain in the United Kingdom did not indicate that a defendant had a "substantial connection" with the UK for the purposes of s.41(3)(*b*) of the 1982 Act (*Petrograde Inc.* v. *Smith* [1998] 2 All E.R. 346).

"Substantial work of reconstruction." See RECONSTRUCTION.

SUBSTANTIALLY. A building could be "substantially completed" within the meaning of para. 9 of Sched. 1 to the General Rate Act 1967 (c. 9) notwithstanding that the architect had not yet issued a certificate of practical completion (*London Merchant Securities* v. *Islington London Borough Council* [1986] R.A. 81). But see the report of the appeal to the House of Lords ([1987] 3 W.L.R. 173).

"Substantially prejudiced" (Town and Country Planning Act 1971 (c. 78), s.84(4)(*b*)). For parties to establish that they had been "substantially prejudiced" by a local authority's failure to serve them directly with enforcement notices they must prove that the position they are in would have been materially different had they been properly served (*Mayes* v. *Secretary of State for Wales* [1989] J.P.L. 848).

SUCCESSOR. (Housing Act 1985 (c. 68), s.88). Where a council entered a new tenancy agreement with a wife after her husband had terminated his part of their joint tenancy, she was not a "successor" to the joint tenancy under this section, and her son was, therefore, entitled on her death to suceed her as the successor and therefore became a secure tenant under s.87 (*Bassetlaw District Council* v. *Renshaw* (1991) 23 H.L.R. 603).

SUCH. "Such directions," see DIRECTIONS.

AS SUCH. (Law of Property Act 1925 (c. 20), s.199(1)(ii)(*b*)). Facts which came to the attention of solicitors who were acting for a husband and wife remained with them and could not be treated as coming to them again when they were instructed by lenders so that s.199(1)(ii)(*b*) precluded the solicitors' knowledge of relevant facts or matters being imputed to the lender (*Halifax Mortgage Services* v. *Stepsky* [1996] 2 W.L.R. 230).

SUE. The charterers of a ship that is the subject of an action *in rem* were being "sued" for the purposes of the 1968 Convention on Jurisdiction and the Enforcement of Judgments in Civil and Commercial Matters and Sched. 1 to the Civil Jurisdiction and Judgments Act 1982 (c. 27) (*The Deichland* (1989) 133 S.J. 596).

See IF SUED.

SUFFER. "Anything suffered," "that thing is suffered" (Crown Proceedings Act 1947 (c. 44), s.10(2)). Where, during tests on nuclear weapons being carried out by the Atomic Energy Authority, serving soldiers suffered radiation injuries through the negligence of the scientists employed by the Authority in failing to give the soldiers proper advice as to their safety, the thing "suffered" was the actual exposure to radiation not the continuing acts or omissions of the scientists (*Pearce* v. *Secretary of State for Defence* [1988] 2 W.L.R. 144; overruling *Bell* v. *Secretary of State for Defence* [1986] Q.B. 322).

See also IS SUFFERING.

SUFFICIENT CAUSE. There is "sufficient cause" under s.12 of the Extradition Act 1870 (c. 52) for not conveying a person committed in custody out of the U.K. within two months if the delay in surrender of the person is due to the British Government's seeking assurances that the death penalty will not be imposed (*Re Soering* [1990] C.O.D. 162).

A French law which prohibited discovery which had never been used in England to justify the restriction of discovery and which had not prevented French companies in English commercial disputes from giving discovery so that there was no risk that an offence would be committed or that prosecution would ensue was not "sufficient cause" to revoke a discovery order under R.S.C., Ord. 24, r.17 (*Partenreederei M/S "Heidberg" (A Body Corporate)* v. *Grosvenor Grain and Feed Co.; Heidberg, The* [1993] 2 Lloyd's Rep. 324).

SUFFICIENT INTEREST. (R.S.C., Ord. 53, r.3(7)). A respected environmental presssure group, with 2,500 supporters in the area affected by the application, who might otherwise have an effective means of bringing their concerns to the court and who sought an order of certiorari had "sufficient interest" in an application for judicial review under R.S.C., Ord. 53, r.3(7) where the court should look at the nature of the applicant, the extent of his interest in the subject-matter of the application, the court had to look at the nature of the applicant, the extent of his interests in the issues raised, the remedy sought to be achieved and the nature of the relief sought (*R.* v. *Pollution Inspectorate, ex p. Greenpeace (No. 2)* [1994] 4 All E.R. 329).

(Supreme Court Act 1981 (c. 54), s.31(3). Leave to make an application for judicial review would be refused if a person had no interest whatsoever in the subject-matter of the application and was no more than a meddlesome busybody (*R.* v. *Monopolies and Mergers Commission, ex p. Argyll Group* [1986] 1 W.L.R. 763 applied) (*R.* v. *Pollution Inspectorate, ex p. Greenpeace* [1994] 4 All E.R. 329).

The importance of the vindication of the rule of law, the significance of the issues raised, the likely absence of any other possible challenger, the nature of the breach of duty against which relief was sought and the prominent role of the applicant in giving advice guidance and assistance to aid were all factors to be considered when determining whether an applicant had sufficient interest (*R.* v. *Inland Revenue Commissioners, ex p. National Federation of Self-Employed and Small Businesses* [1982] A.C. 617; *R.* v. *Secretary of State for Social Services, ex p. Child Poverty Action Group* [1990] 2 Q.B. 544 and *R.* v. *Secretary of State for Foreign and Commonwealth Affairs, ex p. Rees-Mogg* [1994] Q.B. 552 applied) (*R.* v. *Secretary of State for Foreign and Commonwealth Affairs, ex p. World Development Movement* [1995] 1 W.L.R. 386).

SUFFICIENT LIGHTING. "Effective provision" of "sufficient and suitable lighting" (Factories Act 1961 (c. 34), s.5(1)). These words impose an absolute duty on employers, which will be breached even by the mere failure of a light bulb just before the occurrence of an accident (*Davies* v. *Massey Ferguson Perkins* [1986] I.C.R. 580).

SUFFICIENT SECURITY. (Companies Act 1985 (c. 6), s.726(1)). "Sufficient security" for costs in this section does not mean complete security but security of a sufficiency, in all the circumstances of the case, to be just (*Innovare Displays* v. *Corporate Booking Services* [1991] BCC 174).

SUFFICIENT UNDERSTANDING. A child who could give instructions to a solicitor and make decisions as the need arose had "sufficient understandign" within the meaning of the Family Proceedings Rules 1991 (No. 1247), r.9.2A to continue proceedings without a guardian *ad litem* or next friend (*Re H. (A Minor) (Guardian ad litem: Requirement)* [1994] 4 All E.R. 762).

SUIT. (Hague Rules, Art. III, r.6). A "suit" encompassed an action in tort or contract (*Anglo Irish Beef Processors International* v. *Federated Stevedores Geelong* [1997] 1 Lloyd's Rep. 207).

SUITABLE. (9(*g*)) "Suitable alternative . . . accommodation" (Land Compensation Act 1973 (c. 26), s.39(1)). Temporary accommodation, without a promise of permanent accommodation to follow, and which could not accommodate all the members of the family was still held to be "suitable" within the meaning of this section (*R.* v. *East Hertfordshire District Council, ex p. Smith* (1991) 23 H.L.R. 26).

"Suitable accommodation" (Housing Act 1985 (c. 68), s.69, as amended by s.14(3) of the Housing and Planning Act 1986 (c. 63)). In determining whether an offer of accommodation was an offer of "suitable accommodation" the authority should have regard not only to the accommodation itself, but also to the individual circumstances of the homeless person and her family (*R.* v. *Brent London Borough Council, ex p. Omar* (1991) 23 H.L.R. 446). In assessing the suitability of accommodation a local authority could separate medical needs from social needs by those qualified in each area, provided that the ultimate decision was the result of a composite assessment of all relevant factors (*R.* v. *Lewisham London Borough Council, ex p. Dolan* (1992) 25 H.L.R. 68). An offer of accommodation was not "suitable" where the authority had failed to take into account material available to them about the extent of racial harrassment in the vicinity of the premises (*R.* v. *Tower Hamlets London Borough, ex p. Subhan* (*Abdul*) (1992) 24 H.L.R. 541). A local authority failed to make an offer of suitable accommodation in a case where the applicant was required to accept or refuse the offer before a potentially relevant factor, medical evidence relating to the applicant's children, had been assessed by the authority (*R.* v. *Wycombe District Council, ex p. Hazeltine, The Times*, March 8, 1993). The provision of "suitable" accommodation for the purposes of this section could entail more than one short-term stay, so that the intended final accommodation could be reached in stages (*R.* v. *Brent London Borough Council, ex p. Macwan, The Times*, April 6, 1994).

"Suitable alternative accommodation" (Rent Act 1977 (c. 42), Sched. 15, Pt. IV). Where the tenant of a flat in a quiet road in Hampstead was offered alternative accommodation on a busy commercial road in Kilburn it was held that the alternative accommodation was not "suitable" within the meaning of this schedule (*Dawncar Investments* v. *Plews* (1993) 25 H.L.R. 639).

Where an applicant for accommodation was married with children, the obligation was to provide accommodation for the entire family and was not discharged where the accommodation was split between two dwellings (*R.* v. *Ealing LBC, ex p. Surdonja* [1999] 1 All E.R. 566).

(16) "Suitable arrangements" (Education Act 1944 (c. 31), s.39). "Suitable" refers to the suitability of the transport arrangements, not the suitability of the school (*R.* v. *East Sussex County Council, ex p. D.* [1991] C.O.D. 374).

"Suitable available vacancy," see AVAILABLE.

(Children and Young Persons Act 1933, s.53, as amended). A flexible approach to the sentencing of young persons under s.53 was required so that the word "suitable" was not confined to the length of sentence imposed but enabled the Secretary of State to place a young person in a place where the period of detention was no longer than the original sentence but which was more suited to the needs of the individual (*R.* v. *B (a minor) (sentence: jurisdiction)* [1999] 1 W.L.R. 61).

SUM. (Limitation Act 1980 (c. 58), s.9(1)). Compensation for compulsory purchase even if not quantified was a "sum recoverable by virtue of . . . enactment" and so subject to a six year limitation period under s.9(1) (*Hillingdon LBC* v. *A.R.C. Ltd* [1998] 1 W.L.R. 174).

SUM DUE. (Insolvency Act 1986 (c. 45), s.411; Insolvency Rules 1986 (S.I. 1986 No. 1925), reg. 13.12). "Sum due" included a claim for unliquidated damages in tort (*Soden* v. *British and Commonwealth Holdings plc* [1997] 2 W.L.R. 206).

SUMMARILY. "Begun to try the information summarily" (Magistrates' Courts Act 1980 (c. 43), s.25(2)). This phrase should be given a narrow interpretation. It refers to the process of determining the guilt or innocence of the accused. So that a stipendiary magistrate who committed a defendant for crown court trial at a preliminary hearing, reversing a previous decision of lay justices that the defendant be tried summarily, was acting in excess of his powers (*R.* v. *Birmingham Magistrates' Court, ex p. Webb* [1992] C.O.D. 315).

SUM OWED. (Consumer Credit Act 1974 (c. 39), ss.129, 136). The "sum owed" related to every sum owed under the loan agreement (*Southern and District Finance* v. *Barnes, The Times,* April 19, 1995).

SUPERIOR COURT. The Crown Court was a "superior court" for the purposes of the Supreme Court Act 1981 (c. 54), ss.1(1) and 45 (*R.* v. *Crown Court, ex p. Essex Chief Constable* [1994] 1 All E.R. 325).

SUPERVISION. "Continual supervision throughout the night" (Social Security Act 1975 (c. 14), s.35(1)(*b*)(ii)). A person constantly present and ready to intervene to assist a sufferer from epilepsy in the event of an attack might for that reason alone be exercising "continual supervision" within the meaning of this section. It is not necessary that the supervisor shall be constantly awake (*Moran* v. *Secretary of State for Social Services, The Times,* March 14, 1987).

Where it was a term of an insurance holiday that an unqualified person carrying out a structural survey was to be "supervised", the degree of supervision required was that which was regarded as good practice in the profession. It was not essential for the supervising surveyor to attend the site being inspected (*Summers* v. *Congreve Horner & Co.* [1992] 40 EG 144).

(Value Added Tax Act 1994 (c. 23), Sched. 9, Group 9, note (2)). A qualified ophthalmologist who supervised eye examinations when on the premises and was available for consultation on the telephone when not on the premises, provided optician's services under direct supervision and so was exempt under the 1994 Act (*Land (t/a Crown Optical Centre)* v. *Customs and Excise Commissioners* [1998] B.V.C. 2277).

"Supervision, direction or control," see CONTROL.

SUPPLY. (8)–(9) The word "supply" in ss.4(1)(*b*) and 4(3)(*a*) of the Misuse of Drugs Act 1971 (c. 38) implies an act designed to benefit the recipient of the drug and not the supplier. There was, therefore, no "supply" of a drug where one person gave it to another for safekeeping (*R.* v. *Dempsey* (1985) 82 Cr.App.R. 291). But a person in unlawful possession of a controlled drug which has been deposited with him for safekeeping has the "intent to supply it to another" within the meaning of s.5(3) if his intention is to return the drug to the person who deposited it with him (*R.* v. *Maginnis* [1987] 2 W.L.R. 765). Where an addict purchased a small quantity of heroin for immediate consumption by himself and a friend, it was held that there had been an act of supply, although on a very small scale (*R.* v. *Spinks* [1987] Crim.L.R. 786). To support a conviction of the offence of conspiring to offer to supply a controlled drug it is necessary to prove that the conspirators intended that the drug be supplied (*R.* v. *Gill, The Times*, January 13, 1993).

(12) "Supply of goods or services" (Value Added Tax Act 1983 (c. 55), ss.1, 2 E.C. Council Sixth Directive 77/388). A company carrying on a charge card or credit card operation made a "supply" to the retailer of a financial service for a consideration for the purposes of value added tax. Although the agreement between the card operators and the retailer provided only for the purchase of debts at a discount it was held that there was a provision of facilities to the retailer in exchange for the discount which amounted to a "supply" within the meaning of this section (*Customs and Excise Commissioners* v. *Diners Club* [1989] 2 All E.R. 385). The provision of in-flight catering to passengers on domestic flights was an integral part of the transport, and not a separate "supply" for the purposes of this section (*Customs and Excise Commissioners* v. *British Airways* [1990] STC 643. A merchant bank was, for VAT purposes, "supplying" the financial services it rendered to an Isle of Man company in issuing, placing and underwriting the issue of its shares (*Singer & Friedlander* v. *Customs and Excise Commissioners* [1989] 1 C.M.L.R. 814). Where vouchers are sold to a retailer with an agreement that they will be redeemed at a discount, the discount is a consideration for the supply of services which are taxable under these sections (*High Street Vouchers* v. *Customs and Excise Commissioners* [1990] STC 575). Trophies presented at the annual Professional Footballers' awards dinner were supplied for a consideration included in the price of the dinner and therefore were not a VAT taxable supply (*Customs and Excise Commissioners* v. *Professional Footballers' Association (Enterprises), The Times*, February 2, 1993). Equipment delivered and installed, but without final payment having been made, was "supplied" for value added tax purposes under s.5(1) (*Tas-Stage* v. *Customs and Excise Commissioners* [1988] STC 436). The operation of a hostel providing nightly accomodation for homeless persons was exempt by virtue of Art. 13A(1)(*g*) of the Sixth Directive being the "supply of services linked to welfare and social security work by a body governed by public law" (*Lord Mayor of London and Citizens of the City of Westminster* v. *Customs and*

Excise Commissioners [1989] VATTR 71). On a road building contract the contractor supplied all raw materials but engaged a sub-contractor to provide the labour. The fees paid to the sub-contractor were calculated by charging for work done including materials but deducting the cost of materials borne by the contractor. It was held that this arrangement did not constitute a "supply" of materials by the sub-contractor to the contractor (*Hopkins J. (Contractors)* v. *Customs and Excise Commissioners* [1989] VATTR 107). Unlawful trading by a bankrupt can be a "supply" for the purposes of value added tax (*J. E. Scally* v. *Customs and Excise Commissioners* [1989] VATTR 245. Accomodation provided by a company to a representative solely for the purposes of the business was not a taxable "supply" by the business (*Stormseal (UPVC) Windows Co.* v. *Customs and Excise Commissioners* [1989] VATTR 303). Where credit notes were issued in relation to services which had not been or would not be supplied there was no taxable "supply" (*Securicor Granley Systems* v. *Customs and Excise Commissioners* [1990] VATTR 9). A driving school whose instructors were self-employed and who paid to the school a proportion of the fees charged was, nevertheless, held to be supplying a service within the meaning of this section, on the grounds that the instructors were not in business on their own and were providing the driving tuition on behalf of the driving school (*Cronin (t/a Cronin Driving School)* v. *Customs and Excise Commissioners* [1991] STC 333). Classes given by individual members of a string quartet may contribute part of a "supply" by the quartet collectively, but where they are provided by a university for its students the quartet acts as its agent and the supplies are exempt under Sched. 6, Group 6. (*Alberni String Quartet* v. *Customs and Excise Commissioners* (1990) 3 VATTR 166). When a hotel agreed to guarantee the availability of a room for a customer, and the customer had not occupied or cancelled the room before the end of the reservation period a taxable "supply" had been made for the purposes of s.2 of the 1983 Act. The supply took place when the company made the room available and any charge made for it was subject to VAT (*Customs and Excise Commissioners* v. *Bass* [1993] STC 42). The provision of free meals by a motorway service station to the drivers of coaches who brought their coaches to the service station was a "supply" within the meaning of the Act (*Granada Group* v. *Customs and Excise Commissioners* (1991) 2 VATTR 104). The provision of a wide range of diplomatic services was not a single composite "supply" of services (*Bophuthatswana National Commercial Corp.* v. *Customs and Excise Commissioners* [1992] STC 741). The settlement of another's liability under a hire-purchase agreement in return for the transfer of the assets concerned gives rise to a taxable "supply" either by way of reimbursement or in consideration of the payment (*Phillip Drakard Trading* v. *Customs and Excise Commissioners* [1992] STC 568). An agreement to purchase goods subject to conditions, including onward sale, and leaving the vendor with the right and obligation to keep them in the interim, did no constitute a "supply" of the goods (*Creditgrade* v. *Customs and Excise Commissioners* (1991) 1 VATTR 87). Where supplies are made by self-employed individuals it is permissible to infer that they made the supplies directly to customers and not as agents for the person with whom they have a contract for services (*Customs and Excise Commissioners* v. *MacHenrys (Hairdressers)* [1993] STC 170). Estate agents' fees payable under a home sale incentive scheme were deductible by a building contractor as a supply of services paid for by him (*Customs and Excise Commissioners* v. *Redrow Group plc* [1999] 1 W.L.R. 408).

(11) "Supply to him" (Road Traffic Act 1972 (c. 20), s.10(6)). Part of a blood sample is "supplied" within the meaning of this section even if it is incorrectly labelled, so long as there is nothing to deter or prevent the defendant from having it analysed (*Butler* v. *DPP* [1990] RTR 377).

Stat. Def., Consumer Protection Act 1987 (c. 43), s.46.

"Goods . . . supplied to a ship for her operation," see GOODS.

SURGICAL. "Any surgical operation" (Mental Health Act 1983 (c. 20), s.57(1)(*a*)). Treatment by administering the drug gosevelin by injection using a conventional hypodermic syringe could not be described as a "surgical operation" (*R.* v. *Mental Health Commission, ex p. W.*, *The Times*, May 27, 1988).

SURNAME. Stat. Def., Companies Act 1985 (c. 6), ss.289, 305, Sched. 1, para. 4; Business Names Act 1985 (c. 7), s.8.

SURRENDER. "Surrender to custody" (Bail Act 1976 (c. 63), s.6(1)). Once a defendant had reported to the apropriate official at the appropriate time he had surrendered to bail and was then in "custody" within the meaning of this section; notwithstanding that he had then left the building before his case was called (*DPP* v. *Richards* [1988] 3 W.L.R. 153). A surrender into custody only occurs when the defendant himself surrenders or puts himself at the direction of the court or of an officer of the court (*R.* v. *Central Criminal Court, ex p. Guney*, *The Times*, February 1, 1994).

SURVEYOR. Stat. Def., Cathedrals Measure 1999 (No. 1), s.35(1).

SUSPECT. "Suspects that an arrestable offence had been committed" (Criminal Law Act 1967 (c. 58), s.2(4)). Suspicion for the purposes of this section is a state of conjecture or surmise where proof is lacking, and is not to be confused with the actual provision of evidence (*Holtham* v. *Commissioner of Police for the Metropolis*, *The Times*, November 28, 1987).

"The Director may investigate any suspected offence" (Criminal Justice Act 1987 (c. 38), s.1(3)). A suspected offence does not cease to be "suspected" once charges are preferred, so that a suspected offender who has been charged can still be "investigated" under this section (*R.* v. *Director of the Serious Fraud Office, ex p. Saunders* (1988) 138 New L.J. 243).

SUSTAIN. "Sustains a loss," see LOSS.

T

TABLE. A cylindrical piece of marble 3ft 5ins high, 8 feet in diameter and 10 tons in weight can be a "table" for the purposes of Canon F2 of the Revised Canons Ecclesiastical (*Re St. Stephen Walbrook* [1987] 2 All E.R. 578).

TAKE. "Taken from him" (Magistrates' Courts Act 1980 (c. 43), s.48). These words apply only to property found on a person, and not to property taken from his home (*R.* v. *Southampton Magistrates' Court, ex p. Newman* [1988] 3 All E.R. 669).

"Bird . . . had not been . . . taken" (Wildlife and Countryside Act 1981 (c. 69), s.1(3)(*a*)). "Taken" means captured and contemplates a live bird (*Robinson* v. *Everett* [1988] Crim.L.R. 699).

"Take any conveyance" (Theft Act 1968 (c. 60), s.12(1)) A person taking a conveyance without authority was guilty under this section notwithstanding that the vehicle had at that time been abandoned by someone else who had unlawfully taken it (*DPP* v. *Spriggs, The Times*, January 28, 1993).

TAKING PART. "Taking part in a strike" (Employment Protection (Consolidation) Act 1978 (c. 44), s.62(1)(*b*)). An employee who was absent ill when her fellow workers went on strike could not be said to have taken part in the strike unless that was a clear factual finding that had she not been ill she would have supported the industrial action (*Rogers* v. *Chloride Systems* [1992] I.C.R. 198).

TAX. A director's account which was substantially overdrawn to enable the taxpayer company to make loans to participators in a close company was "tax" for the purposes of the Taxes Management Act 1970 (c. 9), s.109 (*Joint (Inspector of Taxes)* v. *Bracken Developments* (1994) T.C. Leaflet No. 3389).

TAX ADVANTAGE. Where loans had been made by a company to its shareholders the shareholders had "obtained a tax advantage" within the meaning of the Income and Corporation Taxes Act 1970 (c. 10), s.460 (see now Income and Corporation Taxes Act 1988 (c. 1), s.703) in that they had received consideration in the non-taxable form of loans when they might have received it in the taxable form of capital dividends (*Bird* v. *Inland Revenue Commissioners* [1988] 2 W.L.R. 1237). No "tax advantage", within the meaning of this section, was obtained by a scheme to benefit a charity with a family company's dividend payments (*Sheppard* v. *I.R.C.; I.R.C.* v. *Sheppard* [1993] STC 240).

Stat. Def., Income and Corporation Taxes Act 1988 (c. 1), s.709.

TAX AVOIDANCE. (Income and Corporation Taxes Act 1988 (c. 1), s.741). For the purposes of s.741, tax avoidance was a course of action designed to conflict with or defeat the clear intention of Parliament and not the acceptance of an offer of freedom from tax which Parliament had deliberately made (*IRC* v. *Willoughby* [1997] 4 All E.R. 65).

TAX CREDIT. (Double Taxation Relief (Taxes on Income) (United States of America) Order 1980 (No. 568), art. 10(2)(*a*)). The term "tax credit" in this article has to be read as a "tax credit" under section 86 of the Finance Act 1972 (c. 41) (*Union Texas International Corporation* v. *Critchley* [1988] S.T.C. 691).

TAX EVASION. (Value Added Tax Act 1983 (c. 55), s.39(1)). For the purposes of s.39(1) it was unnecessary to prove an intention to make permanent default (*R.* v. *Dealy* [1995] 1 W.L.R. 658).

TAXABLE PERSON. (Sixth Directive No. 77/388/EEC of the Council of May 17, 1977, Art. 17), see EXPLOITATION.

TAXI. Stat. Def., Disability Discrimination Act 1995 (c. 50), s.32(5).

TAXIMETER. Stat. Def., Private Hire Vehicles (London) Act 1998 (c. 34), s.11(3).

TEACHER. "Teacher in further education." Stat. Def., Teachers' Pay and Conditions Act 1987 (c. 1), s.7. See also SCHOOL.

TELEVISION. An ordinary television set in a long-distance motor coach remained a "television receiving apparatus" within the meaning of reg. 143(2) of the Motor Vehicles (Construction and Use) Regulations 1978 (No. 1017) notwithstanding that it was only used for showing video recorded films (*Target Travel (Coaches)* v. *Roberts* [1986] RTR 120).

TEMPORARILY. "Temporarily employed outside . . . the British Islands" (Education (Mandatory Awards) Regulations 1983 (No. 1135), reg. 5(4)). A man who worked for 13 years in Hong Kong was not "temporarily" employed there for the purposes of these regulations, notwithstanding that he had a house in the United Kingdom and intended to return to it in due course (*R.* v. *Lancashire County Council, ex p. Huddleston* [1986] 2 All E.R. 941).

"Temporarily absent" (Social Security Benefit (Persons Abroad) Regulations 1975 (No. 563), reg. 2(1)). The fact that the absence of a person in receipt of benefit from the U.K. becomes indefinite does not necessarily mean that he is not "temporarily absent" for the purpose of this regulation (*R.* v. *Social Security Commissioner, ex p. Akbar* [1992] C.O.D. 245). It would be wrong to construe the word "temporarily" as synonymous with "not permanent" (*Chief Adjudication Officer* v. *Ahmed, The Times,* April 6, 1994).

TEMPORARY. (5) "Temporary cessation of work" (Employment Protection (Consolidation) Act 1978 (c. 44), Sched. 13, para. 9(1)(*b*)). Where the contract of a university lecturer expired on July 31 and was, through lack of funds, not renewed until October, it was held that, as "work" in this paragraph should be construed as being limited to "paid work," continuity of employment was not broken in August/September and there had only been a "temporary cessation of work" within the meaning of this paragraph (*University of Aston in Birmingham* v. *Malik* [1984] I.C.R. 492). In considering whether the gaps in the employment of applicants for redundancy payments constituted mere "temporary cessations of work," within the meaning of this paragraph, it was wrong simply to carry out the mathematical exercise of comparing lay-off periods with periods of employment. The correct approach was to look at the entire history of each applicant's employment and the circumstances surrounding it. Thus an employee who was intermittently absent from work, in an irregular pattern over a period of years prior to dismissal, could be considered only temporarily absent for the purposes of this paragraph, and therefore "continuously employed" for the purposes of s.81(1) (*Flack* v. *Kodak* [1987] 1 W.L.R. 31). Employment which is not pursuant to contracts in the same series is irrelevant in assessing whether an interval constitutes a "temporary cessation" (*Surrey County Council* v. *Lewis* [1987] 3 W.L.R. 927). A fuel delivery driver regularly employed for seven months a year over 15 years was held not to have been continuously employed, since the breaks in his employment were more than a "temporary cessation of work" (*Sillars* v. *Charrington Fuels* [1989] I.C.R. 475). "Temporary cessations" had to be relatively short to fall within para. 9(1)(*b*), and the 29 weeks that fishermen employed for the salmon netting season were laid off each year was not a temporary cessation (*Berwick Salmon Fisheries Co.* v. *Rutherford* [1991] IRLR 203).

See also CONTINUOUSLY.

TENANCY. "Subject to the tenancy" (Leasehold Reform Act 1967 (c. 88), s.9(1A)(*a*) as amended by the Housing Acts 1974 (c. 44) and 1980 (c. 51)). In this section "tenancy" means existing tenancy. So that where a tenant applying to purchase the freehold of a house under this section had previously obtained an extended lease, the price to be paid was to be calculated subject to the extended lease (*Mosley* v. *Hickman* (1986) 278 E.G. 728).

(6) (Rent Act 1977 (c. 42), s.1). A number of agreements each purporting to grant a mere individual licence did not collectively create a joint "tenancy" for the purposes of this Act (*Stribling* v. *Wickham* [1989] 27 E.G. 81). Where the monetary obligations of two parties to a renting agreement were not joint obligations there was no complete unity of interest and therefore no joint tenancy (*Mikeover* v. *Brady* (1989) 139 New L.J. 1194). A "licence" to occupy premises purportedly without exclusive possession was held to create a tenancy, since in reality the parties had contemplated that exclusive possession would be enjoyed (*Nicolaou* v. *Pitt* [1989] 21 E.G. 71). An arrangement whereby a builder who had carried out works of refurbishment on a property was permitted to take over the property, and use it as he liked until the owner paid for the works, created a "tenancy" in favour of the builder despite the element of uncertainty (*Canadian Imperial Bank of Commerce* v. *Bello* [1991] N.P.C. 123).

The granting of accommodation to an occupier for a limited period by a housing authority in discharging its duties under s.65(3) of the Housing Act 1985 (c. 68) did not create a statutory tenancy (*Ogwr Borough Council* v. *Dykes* [1989] 1 W.L.R. 295). But in a case where the housing association was under no such statutory duty, and a homeless person was referred by the council to the housing association, which housed her in temporary accommodation under an agreement promising sole occupancy, a tenancy was created, notwithstanding that the association retained a key for the purposes of offering support and inspecting the state of repair (*Family Housing Association* v. *Jones* [1990] 1 All E.R. 385). The effect of agreeing to purchase a property at one third of its true value and guaranteeing the vendors the right to remain in it for the rest of their lives was to create a tenancy (*Skipton Building Society* v. *Clayton, The Times*, March 25, 1993).

"Tenancy" (Housing Act 1985 (c. 68), s.79(1)). A homeless person who was provided with temporary accommodation by a housing association was a tenant and not a licensee (*Family Housing Association* v. *Jones* [1989] 22 H.L.R. 45). A licence to occupy a self-contained bedsitting room in a single men's hostel run by the council was not a tenancy within s.79(1), but was a licence to occupy within s.79(3) (*Westminster City Council* v. *Clarke, The Times,* February 13, 1992).

"Tenancy" (Landlord and Tenant Act 1954 (c. 56)). An agreement which reserved to the landlady the right to enter the premises for occasional inspections, and under which the tenant paid a sum to have the landlady clean the premises, created a tenancy rather than a licence (*Vandersteen* v. *Agius* (1992) 65 P. & C.R. 266).

Stat. Def., Housing Act 1985 (c. 68), s.621; Landlord and Tenant Act 1985 (c. 70), s.36; Landlord and Tenant Act 1987 (c. 31), s.59; Landlord and Tenant Act 1988 (c. 26), s.5; includes licence (Housing Act 1996 (c. 52), s.158(1)).

TENANT. Where a potential purchaser was granted possession of the premises in question for a term at a rent, he was a tenant and not merely a licensee, notwithstanding that neither he nor the owner intended that a tenancy should be created (*Bretherton* v. *Paton* (1986) 278 E.G. 615). An occupier, allowed to occupy a council house for a fixed period in the performance of a statutory duty imposed on the council, and allowed to remain in occupation after the fixed period, was a licensee and not a tenant (*Ogwr Borough Council* v. *Dykes* [1989] 1 W.L.R. 295). Occupants of flats intended to be short-life housing were short-term licensees and not tenants (*Camden London Borough Council* v. *Shortlife Community Housing* [1992] N.P.C. 52).

"The tenant" (Agricultural Holdings (Notices to Quit) Act 1977 (c. 12), s.2(1)(*b*)). In the case of a joint tenancy "the tenant" for the purposes of this section means the joint tenancy and not the joint tenants or any one of them (*Featherstone* v. *Staples* (1986) 278 E.G. 867).

(7) (Agricultural Holdings Act 1948 (c. 63), s.24(1)). Where a tenancy and sub-tenancy of agricultural land were created simultaneously, and it was contemplated by all parties that the sub-tenant would farm the land, the sub-tenant became the "tenant" entitled to security of tenure under this section (*Gisbourne* v. *Burton* [1988] 3 W.L.R. 921).

Stat. Def., Housing Act 1985 (c. 68), s.621; Landlord and Tenant Act 1987 (c. 31), s.59; Landlord and Tenant Act 1988 (c. 26), s.5; Landlord and Tenant (Covenants) Act 1995 (c. 30), s.28(1).

TERM. A rent review clause in an underlease provided that the revised rent, "having regard to the terms of this underlease (other than those relating to rent)," was to be what could be expected in the open market. It was held that in this context the rent review clause was not a term "relating to rent" (*MFI Properties* v. *BICC Group Pension Trust* [1986] 1 All E.R. 974).

A rent review clause was operable during the contractual term of the lease and could not be relied upon once the term had been determined (*Willison* v. *Cheverell Estates Ltd* [1995] NPC 101).

"Term of the contract" (Equal Pay Act 1970 (c. 41), s.1(2)). "Term" means a distinct provision or part of the contract comparable, from the point of view of benefits conferred, with a similar part or provision of another contract (*Hayward* v. *Cammell Laird Shipbuilders* [1988] 2 All E.R. 257).

"Such terms . . . as the court thinks fit" (Adoption Act 1976 (c. 36), s.12(6)). On making an adoption order it was open to the court to grant, as a "term" of the order, an injunction restraining the natural father from communicating with the child or adoptive parents (*Re Adoption Application No. 77/88, The Times*, June 4, 1990).

"Term of years" (Agricultural Holdings Act 1986 (c. 5), s.1(5)). A tenancy of agricultural land for a term of more than 12 and less than 24 months is a letting for a "term of years" within the meaning of this section (*E.W.P.* v. *Moore* [1992] 2 W.L.R. 184).

(Local Government and Housing Act 1989 (c. 42), s.109). The reference to a "term of years absolute" in the 1989 Act applied to equitable and legal interests (*R.* v. *Tower Hamlets London Borough Council, ex p. von Goetz* [1998] 3 C.L. 377).

(Employment Rights Act 1996 (c. 18), s.197(1)). The reference to a fixed term included a contract which had been varied by an extension of the term under the same contract (*BBC* v. *Kelly-Phillips* [1998] 2 All E.R. 845).

(Restrictive Trade Practices Act 1976 (c. 34), s.9(3)). For the purpose of s.9(3) every agreement for the supply of goods, however made, the part which dealt exclusively with the supply of goods should be disregarded and in order to decide whether the Act applied, the remainder only should be taken into account (*M.D. Foods plc (formerly Associated Dairies Ltd)* v. *Baines* [1997] 2 W.L.R. 364).

TERM OF IMPRISONMENT. See SENTENCE.

TERMINATION. Stat. Def. "in relation to a tenancy, means the cesser of the tenancy by reason of effluxion of time or from any other cause"— (Agricultural Tenancies Act 1995 (c. 8), s.38(1)).

TERMINATED. Teachers' Superannuation (Consolidation) Regulations 1988, reg. E4(7)). The words "was terminated" had a transitive meaning and referred to an act which brought employment to an end, and did not refer to the expiration of a fixed term contract (*Teachers Pensions Agency* v. *Hill* [1998] 4 All E.R. 865).

TERRORISM. (Offences against the Person Act 1864 (c. 268), s.2(1)(f), as substituted by the Offences against the Person (Amendment) Act 1992 (No. 14 of 1992), s.2).

A murder committed with the sole intention of killing the victim and where there was a consequential frightening of occasional bystanders was not a murder committed "in the course of furtherance of an act of terrorism" (*Lamey* v. *R.* [1996] 1 W.L.R. 902).

Stat. Def., Northern Ireland (Emergency Provisions) Act 1996 (c. 22), s.58.

TESTAMENTARY DISPOSITION. The nomination by a member of a company pension scheme of a beneficiary to receive the death benefit payable under the scheme on the member's death before retirement was not a testamentary disposition by the member, and so the nomination was valid despite non-compliance with the statutory requirements for such dispositions (*Baird* v. *Baird* [1990] 2 W.L.R. 1412).

TESTIMONY. (Criminal Justice Act 1988 (c. 33), s.33(2A), as amended by the Criminal Justice Act 1991 (c. 53) and the Criminal Justice and Public Order Act 1994 (c. 33). A child who could both understand questions and answer them in a manner which was coherent and comprehensible was capable of giving "intelligible testimony" (*DPP* v. *M* [1998] 2 W.L.R. 604).

THEFT. Where goods are given to another in exchange for a stolen cheque, the loss of those goods is a loss "caused by theft" within the meaning of a clause in an insurance policy (*Dobson* v. *General Accident Fire and Life Assurance Corp.* [1989] 3 W.L.R. 1066).

THERE AND THEN. "There and then" in the Water Act 1989 (c. 15), s.148(1) meant at or proximate to the site where a sample was taken and on the occasion of the taking of the sample (*Att.-Gen's Reference (No. 2 of 1994)* [1994] 1 W.L.R. 1579).

THEREBY. "Thereby endangered" (Criminal Damage Act 1971 (c. 48), s.1(2)(*b*)). The word "thereby" relates to the damage to property and not to the act which caused the damage. So that the intention or recklessness charged under this section must be directed to the possible dangers caused by the destroyed or damaged property, and not to the dangers inherent in the method of causing the destruction or damage (*R.* v. *Streer* [1987] 3 W.L.R. 205). But, distinguishing this case, it has since been held that the word "thereby" relates to the damage or destruction intended by the accused and not to the actual damage or destruction caused (*R.* v. *Dudley* [1989] Crim.L.R. 57).

THEREFROM. "In respect of any office or employment on emoluments therefrom" (Income and Corporation Taxes Act 1970 (c. 10), s.181(1)). A fee paid to a professional footballer by his club as an inducement to him to consent to his transfer to another club was an emolument flowing "from" his employment by the second club, and was therefore chargeable to Schedule E income tax under this section (*Shilton* v. *Wilmshurst* [1991] 2 W.L.R. 530).

THING. "That thing is suffered," see SUFFER.

THIRD COUNTRY. (Asylum and Immigration Appeals Act 1993 (c. 23), Sched. 2, para. 5(6); H.C. 251, para. 180K). The phrase "third country" in H.C. 251, para. 180K was not a term of art as long as an asylum seeker can be removed to a safe country, which may be the applicant's country of nationality (*R.* v. *Special Adjudicator, ex p. Abudine (Mohammed Siad Ahmed)* [1995] Imm.A.R. 60).

THIRD PERSON. See ANOTHER PERSON; OTHER PERSON.

THREATEN. "Threatening abusive or insulting words or behaviour" (Public Order Act 1986 (c. 64), s.4(1)(*a*)). The offence under this section requires that the accused must intend or be aware that his words or behaviour are threatening, abusive or insulting and must be directed at another person (*Winn* v. *DPP* (1992) 142 New L.J. 527).

TICKET. Stat Def.,—"a document or documents evidencing an agreement (wherever made) for the carriage of any person"—(Finance Act 1994 (c. 9), s.43(1)).

TIDAL WATER. (Merchant Shipping Act 1894 (c. 60), ss.546, 742). Gravesend Reach of the River Thames is a "tidal water" within the meaning of these sections and not, therefore, a "harbour" (*The Powstaniec Wielhopolski* [1988] 3 W.L.R. 723).

TIME. See AT THE TIME.

TIME OFF. "Take time off . . . to undergo training" (Employment Protection (Consolidation) Act 1978 (c. 44), s.27). In this section "time of" means those hours when the employee would normally have been at work and which it is reasonable that he should be allowed to take off to attend a training course (*Hairsine* v. *Kingston upon Hull City Council* [1992] I.C.R. 212).

TIME WORKER. Stat. Def., Wages Act 1986 (c. 48), s.26.

TITLE. The phrase "good marketable title" was not to be construed as a title free from all encumbrances, so that a solicitor who failed to inform the bank who had promised a loan to the purchaser that there was a right of way over the land was not in breach of contract but refers only to the quality of evidence which a purchaser can regard as enough to satisfy the vendor's obligation to deduce good title to the property (*Barclays Bank plc* v. *Weeks Legg & Dean* [1998] 3 All E.R. 213).

TOGETHER WITH. "Together receiving treatment services" (Human Fertilisation and Embryology Act 1990 (c. 37), s.4 and Sched. 3, para. 5(1)). Once a donor had died, the use of his sperm in the course of providing treatment services to a woman could not be regarded as provided for the "woman and man together" within the meaning of s.4(1)(b) (*R.* v. *Human and Fertilisation and Embryology Authority, ex p. Blood* [1997] 2 W.L.R. 806).
    "Occupied together with," see OCCUPY: OCCUPIED.

TO OR FOR THE VICTIM. (Social Security Administration Act 1992 (c. 5), s.82(1)). Benefit paid to the victim was not limited to that part of the benefit for the claimant's support but included those parts which were calculated for the support of his wife and children (*Hassall and anr* v. *Secretary of State for Social Security* [1995] 3 All E.R. 909).

TOTAL. "Total number of hours which are not concurrent" (Powers of Criminal Courts Act 1973 (c. 62), s.14(3)) means the total number of hours ordered, not the total number of hours left to serve (*R.* v. *Anderson* [1990] Crim.L.R. 130).

TOUCH. (3) A covenant by a surety to accept a lease replacing a lease disclaimed on behalf of an insolvent tenant "touched and concerned the land" demised, so that the benefit of the covenant ran with the reversion and did not have to be expressly assigned (*Coronation Street Industrial Properties* v. *Ingall Industries* [1989] 1 W.L.R. 304).

TOWARDS. "Towards a child" (Indecency with Children Act 1960 (c. 33), s.1(1)). "Towards" here means more than just "in the presence of." The act of gross indecency must be directed at the child who must be aware of what is going on (*R.* v. *Francis* (1989) 88 Cr.App.R. 127).

"Uses towards another person" (Public Order Act 1986 (c. 64), s.4(1)(*a*)). These words connote present physical presence. The person "towards" whom threatening, abusive or insulting words are used must, for the purposes of this section, perceive with his own senses the threat, abuse or insult; so that a threat made by a person in a house against another person outside the house, who had not even heard it, had not been made "towards" that person (*Atkin* v. *DPP* [1989] Crim.L.R. 581).

TOXIC. "Toxic chemical", Stat. Def., Chemical Weapons Act 1996 (c. 6), s.1(5).

TRADE. (7) "Gains arising . . . from any trade" (Income and Corporation Taxes Acts 1970 (c. 10), s.108; 1988 (c. 1), s.18). A company whose main purpose was to assume responsibility for foreign loans for ship-building was not "trading" for the purpose of these sections, so that losses made on currency exchange were not trading losses available to the group in computing corporation tax (*Overseas Containers (Finance) Ltd.* v. *Stoker* [1989] 1 W.L.R. 606). A company that acquired two loans secured on real property, and then carried on activities relating to the securities, was thereby carrying on a "trade" for corporation tax purposes (*Torbell Investments* v. *Williams, Whiteway Laidlaw & Co.* v. *Same* [1986] S.T.C. 397. The profit from a one-off transaction of purchase, development and resale of a property by a self-employed general dealer and contractor was not profit from a "trade" and not therefore assessable under Schedule D (*Kirkham* v. *Williams* [1991] 1 W.L.R. 863). A sum recovered, by way of damages, to compensate a trader for having paid a rent which was, owing to the negligence of a firm of estate agents, more than could reasonably be expected, was held to be a trading receipt for corporation tax purposes (*Donald Fisher* v. *Spencer* [1989] S.T.C. 256). Earnings from prostitution are the earnings of a "trade" (*Inland Revenue Commissioners* v. *Aken* [1990] S.T.C. 497). A one-off purchase, and sale three months later, of land for a profit need not be an adventure in the nature of "trade" for the purposes of Sched. D (*Manson* v. *Morton* [1986] 1 W.L.R. 1343). But where a bank subscribed for shares of a customer company in difficulties it was held that, although the bank always intended to sell the shares as soon as conditions permitted, the bank's profits when the shares were later sold amounted to a gain arising from "trade" (*Waylee Investment* v. *I.R.C.* [1991] S.T.C. 780). Fees received by a skilled freelance vision mixer involved in the production of television programmes were "gains arising from any trade" for the purposes of this section (*Hall* v. *Lorimer, The Times,* November 18, 1993). Where a taxpayer bought 10 acres of land and an old mill for the purpose of providing himself with office and storage space, and subsequently built a house on the land, it was held that the land was not "trading stock" and its acquisition was not an "adventure in the nature of trade;" so that when selling it at a profit the taxpayer was not liable to schedule D income tax (*Kirkham* v. *Williams* [1991] 1 W.L.R. 863). A farm worker organising a group, which included himself, to provide potato merchants with pickers and graders was not in business on his own account and so was not assessable under Schedule D. Nor was he an "employer" for PAYE purposes within the meaning of reg. 29 of the Income Tax (Employment) Regulations 1973 (No. 334) (*Andrews* v. *King* [1991] S.T.C. 481).

"By way of trade" (Copyright Act 1956 (c. 74), s.21(4A) as amended by s.1 of the Copyright Act 1956 (Amendment) Act 1982 (c. 35)) means for the purposes of trading, so that a person who purchased infringing copies of cinematograph films from a trader for his own use could not be liable under this section (*Reid* v. *Kennet* (1986) 150 J.P. 109).

"Carrying on a trade" (Finance Act 1971 (c. 68), s.41(1)). Where a taxpayer company entered into a series of transactions under which two limited partnerships were set up to finance the continued production of two films, it was held that the expenditure incurred in acquiring master film negatives was incurred in "carrying on a trade" within the meaning of this section (*Ensign Tankers (Leasing)* v. *Stokes* [1992] 1 A.C. 655).

Where a company which carried on the trade of leasing equipment bought and leased two films, the distribution agreements were held to be entered into in the ordinary course of a trade notwithstanding that they were made with companies which were part of the same group and under the same ultimate control (*Barclays Mercantile Industrial Finance* v. *Melluish* [1990] S.T.C. 314).

"In the course of a trade or business" (Trade Descriptions Act 1968 (c. 29), s.1(1)). The supply by an agent of a motorcar belonging to another which was not supplied in the ordinary course of the agent's business and for which the agent received no payment, was nevertheless supplied "in the course of a trade or business" within the meaning of this section (*Kirwin* v. *Anderson* (1992) 11 Tr.L.R. 33).

"Earnings from any trade, professional, vocation" (Income and Corporation Taxes Act 1988 (c. 1), s.619(1)). Income received by the taxpayer from the syndicates at Lloyd's, to which he belonged as an external name, was not income derived "from any trade" within the meaning of this section (*Koenigsberger* v. *Mellor, The Times*, May 25, 1993).

Stat. Defs., Income and Corporation Taxes Act 1988 (c. 1), ss.6, 229; "includes any business or profession"—(Trade Mark Act 1994 (c. 26), s.103)).

"Trade effluent," Stat. Def., Water Resources Act 1991 (c. 57), s.221.

TRADE DESCRIPTION. See FALSE TRADE DESCRIPTION.

TRADE DISPUTE. "In . . . furtherance of a trade dispute" (Trade Union and Labour Relations (Consolidation) Act 1992 (c. 52), s.219). Action taken by teachers who refused to carry out certain duties in relation to national curriculum assessment which they considered unreasonable was a "trade dispute" within the meaning of this section (*Wandsworth London Borough Council* v. *National Association of School Masters and Union of Women Teachers* [1994] I.C.R. 81).

A dispute concerning the terms and conditions of employment of employees with a third party who had never been employed by that party was not a "trade dispute" within the meaning of s.244 of the 1992 Act (*University College London Hospitals NHS Trust* v. *Unison* [1999] I.C.R. 204).

Stat. Def., Social Security Contributions and Benefits Act 1992 (c. 4), s.27; Trade Union and Labour Relations (Consolidation) Act 1992 (c. 52), s.218; Jobseekers Act 1995 (c. 18), s.35(1).

TRADE-MARK. (7)–(8) "Mark" (Trade Marks Act 1938 (c. 22), s.68) is something which is apt only to distinguish goods. The goods themselves are not "marks" for the purposes of this section; so that a bottle, however distinctive its shape, is a container, not a "mark" (*Re Coca-Cola Co.* [1986] 1 W.L.R. 695).

TRADE MARK. Stat. Def., "any sign capable of being represented graphically which is capable of distinguishing goods or services of one undertaking from those of other undertakings"—(Trade Marks Act 1994 (c. 26), s.1(1)).

TRADE OR BUSINESS. "Carry on any trade or business in a Park" (Royal and Other Parks and Gardens Regulations 1977 (No. 217)). A person can be carrying on a "trade" within the meaning of this regulation even though no actual goods are present or change hands. Thus a photographer photographing or offering to photograph passing pedestrians for a price can be carrying on a trade (*Burgess* v. *McCracken* (1986) 150 J.P. 529).

"In the course of a trade or business" (Trade Descriptions Act 1968 (c. 29), s.1). The first sale by a proprietor of a taxi firm of one of his two cars could not be said to amount to a normal practice and was therefore not "in the course of a trade or business" for the purposes of this section (*Devlin* v. *Hall* [1990] RTR 320).

"Trade or business" (Trade Descriptions Act 1968 (c. 29), s.14(1)). The Law Society do not carry on a "trade or business" within the meaning of this section and cannot therefore be accused of making a false advertisement (*R.* v. *Bow Street Magistrates' Court, ex p. Joseph* (1986) 130 S.J. 593). A car, which the seller had used as a taxi, sold to a buyer who gave the seller another car in part exchange, had not been sold in the course of "trade or business" within the meaning of this section (*Devlin* v. *Hall* [1990] RTR 320).

TRADE UNION. Stat. Def., Trade Union and Labour Relations Act 1992 (c. 52), s.1.

TRADE UNION ACTIVITY. (Employment Protection (Consolidation) Act 1978 (c. 44), s.28(1)). A TUC lobby of Parliament in connection with proposed legislation affecting the teaching profession was held not to be a "trade union activity" for the purposes of this section (*Luce* v. *Bexley London Borough Council* (1990) 88 L.G.R. 909). Attending a meeting of a district co-ordinating committee set up by a single union was held to be "taking part in any trade union activity" within the meaning of this section (*London Ambulance Service* v. *Charlton* [1992] IRLR 510).

TRADING COMPANY. Stat. Def., Finance Act 1985 (c. 54), Sched. 20, para. 1(2); Income and Corporation Taxes Act 1988 (c. 1), ss.229, 576, 756. See WHOLLY OR MAINLY.

TRADING GROUP. Stat. Def., Finance Act 1985 (c. 54), Sched. 20, para. 1(2); Income and Corporation Taxes Act 1988 (c. 1), ss.229, 576; Taxation of Chargeable Gains Act 1992 (c. 12), Sched. 6, para. 1(2).

TRADING INCOME. See INCOME.
    (Pension Scheme Act 1993 (c. 48), s.146(1)). "Trustees or managers in s.146(1) should be given their ordinary and natural meaning (*Century Life* v. *Pensions Ombudsman* [1995] 11 C.L. 585).

TRADING LOSS. See LOSS.

TRADING STOCK. (3) The decision in *General Motors Acceptance Corporation* v. *I.R.C.* [1985] S.T.C. 408 [see Main Work, p. 2672] was upheld by the Court of Appeal [1987] S.T.C. 122. Supplies of spare parts, motor tyres and diesel fuel held by a company in the road transport business constituted "trading stock" for the purposes of paras. 29, 30 of Sched. 5 to the Finance Act 1976 (c. 40) (*Ashworth* v. *Mainland Car Deliveries* [1987] S.T.C. 481).
    Loans acquired by a company for the purpose of safeguarding its credibility as a bank were held to be "trading stock" for the purposes of the Income and Corporation Taxes Act 1970 (c. 10) (*Torbell Investments* v. *Williams, Whiteway Laidlaw* v. *Same* [1986] S.T.C. 397).

TRAFFIC. Stat. Def., New Roads and Street Works Act 1991 (c. 22), s.105.

TRAFFIC CASUALTY. Stat. Def., Road Traffic (NHS Charges) Act 1999 (c. 3), s.1(1).

TRAILER. An articulated mobile crane is in effect one vehicle and cannot be said to be a front part towing a "trailer" within the meaning of the Motor Vehicles (Authorisation of Special Types) General Order 1979 (No. 1198), art. 25(2) (*DPP* v. *Evans and Hewden Stuart Heavy Cranes*, *The Times*, November 13, 1987). But an articulated lorry trailer remained a "trailer" for the purposes of s.40(5)(*b*) of the Road Traffic Act 1972 (c. 20) even when attached to a tractor unit (*N.F.C. Forwarding* v. *DPP* [1989] RTR 239).

TRAINING. Stat. Def., in relation to teachers, includes "any training or education with the object of fitting persons to be teachers, or better teachers,"—so includes continuing professional education (Education Act 1994 (c. 30), s.19(4); "includes education" (Nurses, Midwives and Health Visitors Act 1997 (c. 24), s.22(1)).

TRAMWAY. Stat. Def., Transport and Works Act 1992 (c. 42), s.67.

TRANSACTION. "Transaction" (Finance Act 1973 (c. 51), Sched. 19, para. 10(1)). Where one company acquired over 75 per cent. of the shares of another company by aggregating a number of share allotments, each allotment was a separate "transaction" within the meaning of this paragraph (*Rothschild (J.) Holdings* v. *I.R.C.* [1988] S.T.C. 645).

"Transaction" or "arrangement" (Dairy Produce Quotas Regulations 1984 (No. 1047), para. 17(3)). A verbal arrangement which is not legally enforceable is capable of amounting to a "transaction" or "arrangement" within the meaning of this paragraph (*R.* v. *Dairy Produce Quota Tribunal for England and Wales, ex p. Lifely* [1988] 27 E.G. 79).

The term can attract a wider or narrower construction depending on the context: thus Morritt J. in *Hambro* v. *Duke of Marlborough* [1994] 3 W.L.R. 341 at 349,—"the principle to which Lord Wilberforce referred applies where the wide construction, if adopted, would bring within the scope of the Act transactions which Parliament could not have intended to be included. But in this case the wide words are not uncontrolled because of the other requirements of the section. I see no reason for the adoption of a restricted interpretation when the transaction may only be carried out if the court considers it for the benefit of the land or the beneficiaries to do so. If that condition is satisfied then there is every reason for giving the words the widest meaning they can reasonably bear". A unilateral act of imposing on land a trust for sale which freed the land and the life tenant was a "transaction" for the purposes of the Settled Land Act 1925 (c. 18), s.64(2) (*Hambro* v. *Duke of Marlborough* [1994] 3 All E.R. 332).

(Companies Act 1985 (c. 6), s.322(3)(b)). "Transaction" within the meaning of s.322(3)(b) referred merely to the acquisition of property and not the means by which such property had been acquired, so that the cost of repaying compound interest to a bank, which had lent money to purchase the property in question, was not recoverable in damages for breach of s.320(1)(b) (*Duckwari plc (No. 3), The Times,* January 7, 1999).

Stat. Def., Insolvency Act 1986 (c. 45), s.436.

Stat. Def., "includes any agreement, arrangement or understanding, whether or not legally enforceable, and a series of transactions" (Finance Act 1998 (c. 36), Sched. 20, para. 22(1).

TRANSFER. (Firearms Act 1968 (c. 27), s.57(4)). The leaving of a shotgun at another's house for cleaning and safekeeping while both parties were on holiday constituted a "transfer" within the meaning of this section (*Hall* v. *Cotton* [1986] 3 W.L.R. 681).

"A transfer from one person to another of an undertaking" (Transfer of Undertakings (Protection of Employment) Regulations 1981 (No. 1794), reg. 3(1)). In order to decide whether there was a "transfer" of an "undertaking" for the purposes of this regulation an industrial tribunal would have to carry out an appraisal of all the relevant factors, with no single factor being definitive, to decide whether there was an identifiable economic unit and a transfer of that unit (*Dines* v. *Initial Healthcare Services* [1993] I.C.R. 978). Similarly, in considering whether work contracted out by a local council involved the transfer of an undertaking within these Regulations, an industrial tribunal should take into account all surrounding circumstances to see whether there was a recognisable economic activity carried on by the transferor and continued by the new employer (*Wren* v. *Eastbourne Borough Council* [1993] I.C.R. 955). In considering whether work contracted out by a local council involved the transfer of an undertaking in the nature of a commercial venture for the purposes of these Regulations, an industrial tribunal should take into account all surrounding circumstances to see if there was a recognised economic activity carried on by the transferor and continued by the new employer (*Wren* v. *Eastbourne Borough Council, The Times,* August 18, 1993). Where one company took over the provision of services from another company as a result of competitive tendering, the business or undertaking of the first company did not come to an end so that there was a "transfer of undertaking" for the purposes of the Regulations (*Dines* v. *Initial Healthcare Services* [1995] I.C.R. 11). In considering whether there had been a "transfer of undertaking" the court had to identify the economic activity engaged in before the alleged transfer, and compare the activities, assets and staff before and after the transfer to ascertain whether the economic entity first identified still existed. A business which consisted of labour only and where the transferor was the immediate beneficiary even though day-to-day control was exercised by another to whom the services were being provided, was capable of being transferred within the meaning of the 1981 Regulations (*Scilly Isles Council* v. *Brintel* [1995] I.C.R. 249). There had been a "transfer of undertaking" where a third party took over responsibility for the provision of school cleaning from the council, employing 60 per cent of the existing workforce, replaced the equipment and materials and introduced new shift patterns, allocations of work, procedures and quality control systems although the council retained a degree of control over the manner in which the cleaning serviecs were provided (*Kelman* v. *Care Contract Services* [1995] I.C.R. 260).

(Council Directive 77/187, Arts. 1 and 4). The transfer of the assets of a company in liquidation to another amounted to a "transfer" within the meaning of Directive 77/187 since the transfer was intended to ensure that the undertaking continued and the continuity of the business was assured (*Jules Dethier Equipment SA* v. *Dassy* [1998] All E.R. 346).

"Immediately before the transfer" (Transfer of Undertakings (Protection of Employment) Regulations 1981 (No. 1794) r.5). "Transfer," in the case of a sale, was held to refer to the whole period of a transaction from contract to final completion (*Kestongate* v. *Miller* [1986] I.C.R. 672). But it has now been established that the date of the "transfer" for the purposes of these Regulations is the completion date (*Secretary of State for Employment* v. *Spence* [1986] I.C.R. 651, followed by *Brook Lane Finance Co.* v. *Bradley* [1988] I.C.R. 423). See also IMMEDIATELY.

"If a . . . business . . . is transferred from one person to another" (Employment Protection (Consolidation) Act 1978 (c. 44), Sched. 13, para. 17(2)). Where it was agreed in principle that various aspects of the business of a technically insolvent undertaking would be transferred to another company, and the deal was subsequently called off, it was held that there had, nevertheless, been a transfer of the business within the meaning of this paragraph, and that therefore the continuity of employment of an employee, transferred in anticipation of the deal, had been preserved (*Dabell* v. *Vale Industrial Services* (*Nottingham*) [1988] IRLR 439). See also CONTINUOUSLY.

"Transfer of the whole property in goods" (Value Added Tax Act 1983 (c. 55) Sched. 2, para. 1(1)). To effect a transfer of the property in goods for the purposes of value added tax it is not necessary for the transferee to hold the goods for a measurable period of time (*Philips Exports* v. *Customs and Excise Commissioners* [1990] S.T.C. 508).

The completion of a transfer was a process which could occur over a period of time rather than at a particular moment (*Clark and Tokely Ltd* v. *Oakes* [1999] I.C.R. 276).

"Transfer of value," see VALUE.

"Proper instrument of transfer," see INSTRUMENT.

TRANSMISSION. (RSC, Ord. 62, r.5(2B)(b)). "Transmission" meant the process from the moment the document was dispatched by the sender until the time when the entire document had been received by the recipient's fax equipment, with no reasonableness implied (*Lady Anson (t/a Party Planners)* v. *Trump* [1998] 3 All E.R. 331).

TRANSMITTER. Stat. Def., Northern Ireland (Emergency Provisions) Act 1996 (c. 22), s.20(9).

TRANSPORT. (E.C. Council Directive 77/388 (Sixth Directive) Art. 9(2)(*d*)) An ocean-going yacht is a form of "transport" for the purposes of this Directive notwithstanding its primary use for sporting purposes (*Hamann* v. *Finanzamt Hamburg-Eimsbuttel* (Case 51/88) [1991] S.T.C. 193).

TREASURE. Stat. Def., Treasure Act 1996 (c. 24), ss. 1 & 3.

TREAT. "Treated . . . as a child of the family," see CHILD.

TREATMENT. "Such other forms of treatment" (Mental Health Act 1983 (c. 20), s.57(1)(*b*)). Treatment by administering the drug gosevelin by injection using a conventional hypodermic syringe would not, within the ambit of this section, be covered by the phrase "such other forms of treatment." (*R.* v. *Mental Health Commission, ex p. W, The Times*, May 27, 1988).

TREATY. The "Treaty on European Union" referred to in the European Communities (Amendment) Act 1993 (c. 32), s.1 meant the whole of the Union Treaty including the protocols (*R.* v. *Secretary of State for Foreign and Commonwealth Affairs, ex p. Rees-Mogg* [1994] 1 All E.R. 457).

TRESPASSER. Stat. Def., Public Order Act 1986 (c. 64), s.39.

TRIAL. "Trial or hearing" (Magistrates' Courts Act 1980 (c. 43, s.121(1)). When a person is arrested and brought before a magistrate for breach of bail under s.7 of the Bail Act 1976 (c. 63), this is not a "trial or hearing " within the meaning of s.121(1) (*R.* v. *Liverpool City Justices, ex p. DPP* [1992] 3 W.L.R. 20.

(Magistrates' Courts Act 1980 (c. 43), s.6). The words "for trial" in s.6(3)(*b*) were to be interpreted as meaning "for the purposes of trial" and any bail granted by the magistrates ended if the defendant surrendered himself into custody at arraignment or at any other hearing before the Crown Court (*R.* v. *Maidstone Crown Court, ex p. Jodka, The Times*, June 13, 1997).

(Crown Court Rules 1982, r.24A). "All or part of a trial" meant all or part of the trial process, which would include a pre-application (*Ex p. Guardian Newspapers Ltd* [1999] 1 All E.R. 65).

"Relating to trial on indictment," see RELATING.

TRIAL PERIOD. (Employment Protection (Consolidation) Act 1978 (c. 44), s.84(3)(4)). The "trial period" in relation to the new contract of employment is strictly limited to the four weeks prescribed by this section, and cannot be extended by virtue of the fact that due to holiday closures no work was available for much of that time (*Benton* v. *Sanderson Kayser* [1989] I.C.R. 136).

TRISHAW. (Local Government (Miscellaneous Provisions) Act 1976 (c. 57), s.47). Trishaws were licensable under the Local Government (Miscellaneous Provisions) Act 1976, since they were wheeled vehicles "standing or plying for passengers to be carried for hire at separate fares" and could not be regarded as omnibuses, which were exempt from licences (*R.* v. *Cambridge City Council, ex p. Lane, The Times,* October 13, 1998).

TROPICAL STORM. Stat. Def., "means a hurricane, typhoon, cyclone, or other storm of a similar nature" (Merchant Shipping Act 1995 (c. 21), s.91(7)).

TRUST. "Breach of trust" A musician and his manager, who agreed that the latter would manage his business affairs and receive 20 per cent of the musician's income, were in a fiduciary relationship and so not subject to the limitation period imposed by the Limitation Act 1980 (c. 58), s.21(1)(b) (*Nelson* v. *Rye* [1997] 2 All E.R. 186).

Stat. Def., Recognition of Trusts Act 1987 (c. 14), Sched., art. 2; Building Societies Act 1986 (c. 53), s.6B(8) inserted by Building Societies Act 1997 (c. 32), s.6.

TRUST CORPORATION. Stat. Def., Enduring Powers of Attorney Act 1985 (c. 29), s.13.

TRUSTEE. (R.S.C., Ord. 62, r.6(2)). A maintenance trustee who managed flats and administered a maintenance fund made up of tenants' contributions was not acting as "trustee" for the tenants but as agent of the landlord when he tried to enforce the tenants' repairing covenants (*Holding and Management* v. *Property Holding and Investment Trust* [1988] 1 W.L.R. 644).

TUMULTUOUSLY. See RIOTOUSLY.

TURNOVER. Stat. Def., Companies Act 1985 (c. 6), Sched. 4, para. 95; Companies Act 1989 (c. 40), s.22.

TYPE. "Any dog of the type known as the pit bull terrier" (Dangerous Dogs Act 1991 (c. 65), s.1(1)(a)). "Type" is not synonymous with "breed". It has a wider meaning (*R.* v. *Knightsbridge Crown Court, ex p. Dunne* [1994] 1 W.L.R. 296).

U

UNABLE. The words "unable to walk or virtually unable to do so" (Social Security Act 1975 (c. 14), s.37A, as inserted by Social Security Pensions Act 1975 (c. 60), s.22(1)) did not cover a person who, being blind and suffering from other disabilities, was only able to walk outside with the help of an adult guide (*Lees* v. *Secretary of State for Social Services* [1985] 2 W.L.R. 805). The meaning of "virtually unable to walk" is a question of law. The base point is a total inability to walk, which can be extended to take in people who can technically walk but only to an insignificant extent. An inability or virtual inability to walk cannot be established merely on the bases of for instance, an inability to walk to the shops or to a bus stop (Social Security Decision No. R (M) 1/91).

"The company is unable to pay its debts" (Insolvency Act 1986 (c. 45), s.123(1)(*e*)). Failure to pay a debt which there were no substantial grounds for disputing was sufficient evidence of inability to pay for the purposes of this section (*Taylor's Industrial Flooring* v. *M. & H. Plant Hire (Manchester)* [1990] B.C.C. 44).

The test for inability to pay one's debts within the meaning of s.272(1) of the 1986 Act was whether or not one was able to pay those debts at the time they were due, rather than whether one's assets exceeded liabilities (*Re Coney (a bankrupt)* [1998] B.P.I.R. 333).

UNAMBIGUOUS, EASILY IDENTIFIABLE AND CLEARLY LEGIBLE. The requirements of the Price Marking Order 1991 (No. 1382), arts. 3 and 8 were satisfied if the price was clearly and unmistakably indicated on or alongside goods with or without assistance from the retailer (*Drewery* v. *Ware-Lane* [1960] 1 W.L.R. 1204 applied) (*Allen* v. *Redbridge London Borough Council* [1994] 1 W.L.R. 139).

UNAUTHORISED. "Unauthorised access" (Computer Misuse Act 1990 (c. 18). s.17). No offence under s.17(5) of the 1990 Act was committed where police officers, who were entitled to secure access to the Police National Computer extracted information from it for their own personal use (*DPP* v. *Bignell* [1998] 1 Cr.App.R. 1).

UNCONSCIONABLE BARGAIN. Old age with accompanying diminution of judgment can satisfy the requirements for setting aside a sale at an undervalue as an unconscionable bargain; requirements which were laid down in *Fry* v. *Lane* (1888) 40 Ch.D. 312 (*Watkin* v. *Watson-Smith*, *The Times*, July 3, 1986).

UNDER. Offences set out in an enactment were offences "under" that enactment, and the offence of conspiracy was excluded from being "under" the Act by implication (*R.* v. *Secretary of State for the Home Department, ex p. Gilmore* [1998] 1 All E.R. 264).

UNDERTAKING. A public official was an "undertaking" within the meaning of the Treaty of Rome 1957, Art. 86 and subject to competition rules where he was engaged in an economic activity (*Miller & Bryce Ltd* v. *Keeper of the Registers of Scotland*, 1997 S.L.T. 1000).

"Conduct his undertaking," see CONDUCT.
Stat. Def., Companies Act 1989 (c. 40), s.22.
See TRANSFER.

UNDUE DELAY. Failure to act "promptly" in applying for judicial review
is still "undue delay" within the meaning of s.31(6) of the Supreme Court
Act 1981 (c. 54), notwithstanding that there was "good reason" for
extending the time under R.S.C., Ord. 53, r.4(1) (*R. v. Stratford-on-Avon
District Council, ex p. Jackson* [1985] 1 W.L.R. 1319). Whenever there was a
failure to act promptly, or within three months as prescribed by Ord. 53,
rule 4(1), there was "undue delay" within the meaning of s.31(6) of the
1981 Act (*R. v. Dairy Produce Quota Tribunal, ex p. Caswell* [1990] 2 W.L.R.
1320). But where, on an *inter partes* hearing, there was a finding that an
application had been made promptly for the purposes of Ord. 53, r.4 it did
not rule out the possibility of a court finding at the substantive hearing that
there had been "undue delay" in making the application and exercising its
discretion under s.31(6)(*b*) to refuse to grant any relief (*R. v. Swale Borough
Council, ex p. Royal Society for the Protection of Birds* [1990] C.O.D. 263).
    An applicant who failed to apply promptly for judicial review was guilty
of "undue delay" even if he had good reason for the delay (*R. v. Secretary of
State for Health, ex p. Furneaux* [1994] 2 All E.R. 652).

UNDUE HARDSHIP. (2) (Arbitration Act 1950 (c. 27), s.27). "Hardship"
is caused when a justiciable claim which may succeed is barred by a time-
limit. "Undue hardship" is caused when that hardship is not warranted by
the circumstances (*Tote Bookmakers* v. *Development and Property Holding
Co.* [1985] Ch. 261).
    "Undue hardship" (Foreign Limitation Periods Act 1984 (c. 16), s.2(2)).
The word "undue" adds something more than just hardship. It means an
excessive hardship or a hardship greater than the circumstances warrant
(*Jones* v. *Trollope Colls Cementation Overseas, The Times*, January 26, 1990).
Where a contract is governed by foreign law which does not permit an
extension of time to sue, but the parties agree an extension that would have
been in accordance with the Hague-Visby rules, it could cause "undue
hardship" under this section if the extension were unenforceable (*Kominos,
S., The* [1990] 1 Lloyd's Rep. 541).

UNENFORCEABLE. "Unenforceable" (Bretton Woods Fund Agreement
Order 1946 (No. 36), Art. VIII, s.2(*b*)) means that the relevant exchange
contract cannot be enforced by the courts although the contract itself is not
rendered illegal thereby (*United City Merchants (Investments)* v. *Royal Bank
of Canada* [1983] 1 A.C. 168).

UNFAIR. (5) "Unfairly prejudicial to the interests of some part of the
members" (Companies Act 1985 (c. 6), s.459). In deciding whether or not
the conduct of a company's affairs is unfairly prejudicial consideration is
not limited to the members' strict legal rights. The use of the word
"unfairly" enables the court to have regard to wider equitable considerations (*Re a Company (No. 00477 of 1986)*, [1986] P.C.C. 372. The court
dismissed a motion to strike out a petition in which the petitioning
shareholders of a company claimed that the directors had acted in a

manner "unfairly prejudicial" to their interests by favouring a lower bid for the company's shares from a company promoted by the directors in preference to a higher bid from a competitor (*Re a Company (No. 008699 of 1985)* [1986] P.C.C. 296). A company's decision to delay holding an extraordinary general meeting requisitioned by two members until a date some seven months after the date of requisition, although not in breach of section 368 of this Act, was held to be "unfairly prejudicial" to the members concerned (*McGuinness* v. *Petitioners, The Times,* January 15, 1988). Conduct which was not discriminatory and affected all the members of a company equally could not be unfairly prejudicial to "some part" of the members; thus the failure of the directors to pay reasonable dividends could not constitute grounds for a petition under this section (*Re a Company (No. 00370 of 1987)* [1988] 1 W.L.R. 1068). But this case was not followed in *Re Sam Weller* [1989] 3 W.L.R. 923, where it was held that conduct that affected the rights of all members equally might be unfairly prejudicial to the interests of some of them, since "interests" is a wider term than "rights" and members might have different interests even though their rights were identical. In circumstances where the only income for some shareholders was dividends on their shareholdings in the company in question a policy of low dividend payment might for them be "unfairly prejudicial" (*Re a Company (No. 823 of 1987)* (1988) 133 S.J. 1297). A unilateral and secret exercise of the power of allotment of shares with the intention of reducing a shareholder's holding while increasing that of the party exercising the power was held to be blatantly "unfairly prejudicial" (*Re D.R. Chemicals* (1989) 5 BCC 39). An allotment of shares to a majority shareholder without notice to the minority shareholder could be "unfairly prejudicial" within the meaning of this section (*Re a Company (No. 005134 of 1986)*; *Ex p. Harries* [1989] BCLC 383). A valuation of a minority shareholding undertaken on the basis of a valuation of the whole block of shares, together with a premium if they would give control if sold, or a discount if they remained a minority, was held not to be "unfairly prejudicial" within the meaning of s.459 (*Re Castleburn* [1989] P.C.C. 386). The creation of shares at an extraordinary general meeting called without proper notice was "unfairly prejudicial" to the interests of those buying the shares. Failure to hold annual general meetings or prepare accounts was "unfairly prejudicial" to the interests of all the members of the company, not just some of them (*Re Company A (No. 00789 of 1987)*, *ex p. Shooter*; *Re Company A (No. 3017 of 1987)*, *ex p. Broadhurst* [1990] BCLC 384). The withholding of money owed to a subsidiary company by a parent company that exercised financial control over it was held not to be "unfairly prejudicial" to the interests of the minority shareholders in the subsidiary since the parent company withheld the payments in order to secure its own survival (*Nicholas* v. *Soundcraft Electronics* [1993] BCLC 360). Mismanagement of a company could, in certain circumstances, amount to unfairly prejudicial conduct, but the courts would only reach such a view on rare occasions (*Re Elgindata* [1991] BCLC 959).

"Not to be unfairly dismissed" (Employment Protection (Consolidation) Act 1978 (c. 44), s.57). Where a person was dismissed for the valid reason of redundancy the fact that he had not been consulted beforehand did not automatically render his dismissal unfair (*Polkey* v. *A. E. Dayton Services* [1987] 1 All E.R. 984). A six month delay between the conduct giving rise to dismissal and the actual dismissal does not necessarily make the dismissal "unfair" (*Dillett* v. *National Coal Board* [1988] I.R.C. 218). An employer's dismissal procedure is prima facie unfair if an employee is not allowed to know the contents of statements upon which the employer relies to justify dismissal (*Louies* v. *Coventry Hood and Seating Co.* [1990] I.C.R. 54). Where an employee was to be dismissed from particular employment for which he had become unsuitable it might be unfair for the purposes of this section for an employer to do so without first considering the possibility of alternative employment (*P* v. *Nottinghamshire County Council* [1992] IRLR 362). It was not unfair to dismiss an employee who had admitted making nuisance telephone calls to other members of the staff (*East Berkshire Health Authority* v. *Matadeen* [1992] IRLR 336). It was not unfair to dismiss the managing director of a company following the discovery by his fellow directors that he had been making plans to set up in competition (*Marshall* v. *Industrial Systems & Control* [1992] IRLR 294). It was not unfair to dismiss four nurses who had refused to accept a variation in their terms of employment, in circumstances where the new terms offered, considering all the surrounding circumstances, were reasonable (*St. John of God (Care Services)* v. *Brooks* [1992] IRLR 546). It was not unfair to dismiss an employee who had committed a deliberate fraud in circumstances where he had received a final warning for a similar fraud (*United Distillers* v. *Conlin* [1992] IRLR 503). It was unfair to dismiss an employee where the initial disciplinary hearing was defective because it had been convened with undue haste, notwithstanding that the defects had been cured at the appeal stage (*Byrne* v. *BOC* [1992] IRLR 505). It was not unfair to dismiss an employee who had indicated he would resign shortly to emigrate and then, after the employer had recruited and trained his successor, attempted to revoke his decision (*Ely* v. *YKK Fasteners (UK)* [1994] I.C.R. 164). An employee made redundant with immediate effect and without consultation was "unfairly dismissed" within the meaning of s.57 notwithstanding the employers' claim that there were exceptional circumstances which obviated the need to consult (*Heron* v. *Citylink Nottingham* [1993] IRLR 372). See also REASONABLY.

"Unfairly prejudicial to the interests of its creditors or members" (Insolvency Act 1986 (c. 45), s.27(1)(*a*)). A negligent sale of a company's assets at less than their true value by an administrator was held to be insufficient to establish a claim for unfair prejudice under this section (*Re Charnley Davies* [1990] BCC 605).

"Unfairly prejudices the interests of a creditor" (Insolvency Act 1986 (c. 45), s.262(1)(*a*)). A voluntary arrangement whereby a bankrupt's leasehold interest in a shop was to be sold was not unfairly prejudicial to the interests of the landlord, himself a creditor for rent arrears (*Re Mohammed Naeem (A Bankrupt) (No. 18 of 1988)* [1990] 1 W.L.R. 48).

UNFIT. "Unfit to be concerned in the management of a company" (Companies Act 1985 (c. 6), s.300; now Company Directors Disqualification Act 1986 (c. 46), ss.6(1)(*b*), 8(2)). Ordinary commercial misjudgement does not of itself constitute unfitness for the purposes of this section (*Re McNulty's Interchange* [1988] BCLC 376). The non-payment by a company of sums due to the Crown in respect of pay-as-you-earn, national insurance contributions and value-added tax could not of itself be treated as evidence that the directors are "unfit" to be directors (*Re Sevenoaks Stationers (Retail)* [1991] Ch. 164). Two company directors who transferred stock from a company that was insolvent to a new company, paying 10 per cent. of its value, were held to be "unfit" within the meaning of this section (*Keypack Homecare (No. 2)* [1990] BCC 117). A non-accountant director who relied upon an accountant co-director to produce audited accounts and file annual returns did not himself become "unfit" within the meaning of this section by virtue of the fact that no audited accounts were produced and no annual returns made by his co-director (*Re Cladrose* [1990] BCC 11). A director, chairman and the largest shareholder in a company, who treated the company as his own, ignored the shareholders, failed to keep accounting records, deliberately failed to prepare accounts in time and pursued a course of investment *ultra vires* of the company, was (not surprisingly) held to be "unfit to be concerned in the management of a company" (*Re Samuel Sherman* [1991] 1 W.L.R. 1070). A director who, in order to retain control of a company, deliberately played fast and loose with his powers as a director, was "unfit" within the meaning of s.6 notwithstanding that he was acting in what he saw as the company's best interests (*Re Looe Fish* [1993] BCC 348). To create, immediately, a company similar to a previous one which had gone into insolvency, and, when the second company had gone the same way, to create a third company which also became insolvent, was held to be evidence of unfitness for the purposes of s.6 (*Re Linvale* [1993] BCLC 654). Directors who caused the company to incur expenditure for a purpose not connected with its trading purposes and failed to exercise proper stewardship over the company's affairs were "unfit" within the meaning of this section (*Re A. & C. Group Services* [1993] BCLC 1297). As also was a director of two companies who failed to remit Crown moneys, failed to keep proper accounts and failed to keep clients' moneys separate from his own (*Re Burnham Marketing Services; Secretary of State for Trade and Industry* v. *Harper* [1993] BCC 518). "Unfitness meant general unfitness, and past conduct could be relevant to a finding of present unfitness in the management of a company (*Re Polly Peck International* [1993] B.C.C. 890).

The words "unfit to attend as a witness" in s.23(2)(*a*) of the Criminal Justice Act 1988 (c. 33) apply not only to a person's physical ability to attend at court but also to his mental capacity (*R.* v. *Setz-Dempsey; R.* v. *Richardson, The Times,* July 20, 1993.

"Unfit for human habitation." Stat. Def., Housing Act 1985 (c. 68), s.604.

UNION. "Students' union". See STUDENTS' UNION.

UNITARY AUTHORITY. Stat. Def., Water Resources Act 1991 (c. 57), s.91B(8) inserted by Environment Act 1995 (c. 25), s.58; Environment Act 1995 (c. 25), s.91(1).

UNITED KINGDOM. A policy was a "U.K. policy" under the Policyholders Protection Act 1975 (c. 75), s.4, if had any of the obligatioins under the contract evidenced by the policy been performed at the relevant time, such performance would have formed part of an insurance business which the insurer was authorised to carry on in the U.K., regardless of whether the obligations would have been performed in the U.K. (*Ackman* v. *Policyholders' Protection Board* [1993] 2 Lloyd's Rep. 533).

"United Kingdom Waters," Stat. Defs., Merchant Shipping (Salvage and Pollution) Act 1994 (c. 28), s.8(5); Police Act 1964 (c. 48), s.19(5A) added by Criminal Justice and Public Order Act 1994 (c. 33), s.160(1); Police Act 1996 (c. 16), s.31(5).

UNIVERSITY. Stat. Def., Further and Higher Education Act 1992 (c. 13), s.90(3); Education (Mandatory Awards) Regulations 1998 (No. 1166), reg. 2.

UNLAWFUL. "Entertainments which are not unlawful" (Local Government (Miscellaneous Provisions) Act 1982 (c. 30), Sched. 3, para. 3A(*c*), as amended). "Unlawful" in this schedule means "criminal." It cannot be extended to cover, for example, everything done against sound morality. (*McMonagle* v. *Westminster City Council* [1990] 2 W.L.R. 823). But on appeal the House of Lords held ([1990] 1 W.L.R. 823) that the words "which are not unlawful" were to be treated as surplusage in view of the evident intention of Parliament in enacting the relevant legislation; and accordingly the prosecution did not have to prove that the entertainment provided was not unlawful.

"Unlawful sexual intercourse with a woman who at the time of the intercourse does not consent to it" (Sexual Offences (Amendment) Act 1976 (c. 82), s.1(1)(*a*)). The House of Lords held that it was clearly unlawful to have sexual intercourse with any woman without her consent, whether within marriage or not, and that the use of the word "unlawful" in the subsection added nothing. There were no rational grounds for putting any gloss on the word and it should be treated as mere surplusage (*R.* v. *R.* [1991] 4 All E.R. 481).

"Unlawful wounding" (Offences against the Person Act 1861 (c. 100), s.20). To establish the offence of unlawful wounding under this section the prosecution must prove either that the defendant intended or that he actually foresaw that his act would cause physical harm to some person (*R.* v. *Savage; DPP* v. *Parmenter* [1991] 3 W.L.R. 914).

"Unlawfully at large" (Police and Criminal Evidence Act 1984 (c. 60), s.17(1)(*d*)). A person who, being detained in hospital for assessment under s.6(2) of the Mental Health Act 1983 (c. 20), went absent without leave was "unlawfully at large" within the meaning of s.17(1)(*d*) (*d'Souza* v. *DPP* [1992] 1 W.L.R. 1073).

UNLESS. "Unless the contrary is shown" (R.S.C., Ord. 10, r.1(3)(*a*)). These words shall be given their full meaning and not restricted to mean only "unless the contrary is shown by the defendant" (*Abu Dhabi Helicopters* v. *International Aeradio* [1986] 1 All E.R. 395; *Hodgson* v. *Hart District Council* [1986] 1 All E.R. 400).

UNMARRIED COUPLE. Stat. Def., Social Security Act 1986 (c. 50), s.20; "a man and woman who are not married to each other but are living together as husband and wife otherwise than in prescribed circumstances" (Jobseekers Act 1995 (c. 18), s.35(1)); "a man and woman who are not married to each other but are living together as husband and wife" (Social Fund Winter Fuel Payment Regulations 1998 (No. 19), reg. 1(2)).

UNNATURAL. "Has died . . . an unnatural death" (Coroners Act 1988 (c. 13), s.8(1)(*a*)). Where a natural death was accompanied by concurrent events, such as failure to provide medical care or emergency services, which themselves might be a cause of death, then the coroner should consider whether the death was thereby rendered "unnatural" within the meaning of this section. A death from asthma in a chronic asthmatic was held to be from natural causes and accordingly the coroner had no power to conduct an inquest (*R.* v. *Poplar Coroner, ex p. Thomas* [1993] 2 W.L.R. 547).

UNNECESSARY. "It appears . . . that a highway . . . is unnecessary" (Highways Act 1980 (c. 66), s.116). In deciding whether a public right of way was unnecessary for the purposes of a stopping-up order under this section the court must have regard to the use made of the way for recreational purposes as well as for getting to a specific destination (*Ramblers Association* v. *Kent County Council* (1990) 60 P. & C.R. 464).

UNOCCUPIED. "Unoccupied land" (Caravan Sites Act 1968 (c. 52), s.10(1)(*b*)). Land on which a gipsy stationed a caravan with the landowner's permission was not "unoccupied" for the purposes of this section (*R.* v. *Beaconsfield Justices, ex p. Stubbings* (1987) 85 L.G.R. 821).

UNREASONABLE. (Supreme Court Act 1981 (c. 54), s.51(7)). The issue of a writ without a letter before action to set aside an award of libel damages on the grounds that it had been obtained by fraud, where the pleading had been signed by both leading and junior counsel, could be unreasonable conduct to justify a wasted costs' order against the solicitor even though they acted free of charge (*Count Tolstoy-Miloslavsky* v. *Lord Aldington* [1997] 2 All E.R. 556).

UNREASONABLY. (1)–(9) The Court of Appeal reviewed at length the authorities on whether a landlord's refusal to permit the assignment of a lease was or was not unreasonable in those cases where the lessee had covenanted not to assign without licence, such licence "not to be unreasonably withheld." A number of propositions of law were deduced. In this case the withholding of consent was held to be unreasonable because of the disproportionate harm to the tenant compared to the minimum disadvantage suffered by the diminution in the value of the landlord's reversion (*International Drilling Fluids* v. *Louisville Investments* (*Uxbridge*) [1986] Ch. 513). In refusing consent to the underletting of two floors of a house let to a tenant on a long lease, on the grounds that, if the tenant moved out before the end of the lease, the underleases would acquire protection under the Rent Acts, the landlord had acted "unreasonably" (*Deverall* v. *Wyndham* [1989] 1 E.G. 70). The landlord's consent to an assignment had been reasonably withheld in a case where the tenant had not complied with a repairing covenant, where the house was in a ruinous condition, and where the proposed assignee would not agree to a timetable to carry out the works or provide the landlord with financial security for doing so (*Orlando Investments* v. *Grosvenor Estate Belgravia* [1989] 43 E.G. 175). A landlord who had failed for nearly three months to respond to the tenant's request for licence to assign, and had then delayed further, was held to have unreasonably withheld his consent (*Midland Bank* v. *Chart Enterprises* [1990] 44 E.G. 68).

(15) "Is withholding his agreement unreasonably" (Adoption Act 1976 (c. 36), s.16(2)(*b*)). Where the natural parents of a child, with whom they had had no contact, and after whom they were incapable of looking, refused to consent to the foster parents' application for adoption on the grounds that a custodianship order would suffice to secure the child's welfare and should satisfy the foster parents, it was held that the consent had been "unreasonably withheld" (*Re M (a Minor)* [1987] 1 W.L.R. 162). In similar circumstances it has been held that the parents had "unreasonably withheld" consent to adoption by the foster parents (*Re L. (a Minor)* (1990) 20 Fam. Law 98). A sense of grievance that a local authority had not attempted to rehabilitate a child with his mother was a factor to be considered in deciding whether the mother had "unreasonably" withheld her consent to the adoption of the child (*Re B (a Minor) (Adoption: Parental Agreement)* [1990] 2 F.L.R. 383). Again, in a case where the mother, who had done all she could to preserve contact with her two children taken into care, had a feeling of injustice because the local authority had changed its plans for the children and her access application had been adjourned, it was held that she had not withheld her consent to adoption "unreasonably" (*Re E. (Minors) (Adoption: Parental Agreement)* [1990] 2 F.L.R. 397). A parent's refusal of consent to adoption did not become "unreasonable" by virtue of delay which could not be attributed to him (*Re C. (Minors) (Adoption)* [1992] 1 FLR 115).

"Consent was unreasonably withheld" (Landlord and Tenant Act 1954 (c. 56), s.53). In determining whether, for the purposes of this section, a landlord's consent to a change of use was "unreasonably refused" the court should first seek to ascertain the reason on which the landlord had acted, and then consider whether, objectively, refusal for that reason was reasonable (*Tollbench* v. *Plymouth City Council* [1988] 23 E.G. 132).

On an appeal by a freeholder to an arbitrator against the refusal, by the managers of a scheme approved by the court under s.19 of the Leasehold Reform Act 1967 (c. 88), of consent to a proposed development, such consent being subject to a proviso that it "shall not be unreasonably withheld," it was for the freeholder to show that the refusal was one at which no body of managers, acting reasonably, could have arrived (*Estates Governors of Alleyn's College* v. *Williams, The Times,* January 21, 1994).

"Membership . . . unreasonably refused" (Employment Act 1980 (c. 42), s.4(2)(*a*)). In a case where there was an agreement that an employer would employ only members of a particular branch of a trade union, it was held that the refusal of the trade union to permit an employee, who was an established member of the union, to transfer from one branch of the union to the authorised branch was unreasonable (*Transport and General Workers Union* v. *Tucker, The Times*, March 2, 1988).

"Costs . . . incurred unreasonably or improperly" (R.S.C., Ord. 62, r.11). What was reasonable or unreasonable depended on the circumstances of each case. But it would seem that the principles requiring gross misconduct laid down in the older authorities were not applicable to an application under this modern rule (*Sinclair-Jones* v. *Kay* [1988] 2 All E.R. 611).

"Acting unreasonably" (Insolvency Act 1986 (c. 45), s.125(2)). A petitioner was held not to have acted "unreasonably" in seeking to have the company wound up in order to realise his shareholding, instead of exercising his rights relating to the purchase of his shares by other members of the company pursuant to a provision in the company's articles; nor had it been unreasonable of him to refuse an offer by the other members to buy his shares according to a provision in the articles (*Re Abbey Leisure* [1990] BCC 60). The reasonableness of a decision to withhold consent to an assignment must be judged, for the purposes of the Landlord Tenant Act 1988 (c. 26), s.1(3)(*a*) by reference to circumstances existing and known to the landlord when he made the decision (*CIN Properties* v. *Gill* [1993] 38 EG 152). It was held that landlords were acting reasonably in withholding consent to the assignment of a lease where they would suffer severe financial loss should the assignment take place (*Olympia & York Canary Wharf* v. *Oil Property Investment* [1993] NPC 108).

UNREGISTERED COMPANY. (Insolvency Act 1986 (c. 45), s.220). A football and social club which, in addition to providing various social amenities for its members, also promoted professional association football and provided benefits for non-members, was not an "unregistered company" within the meaning of this section (*Western Counties Construction* v. *Witney Town Football and Social Club, The Times,* November 19, 1993. See ASSOCIATION.

Stat. Def., Insolvency Act 1986 (c. 45), s.223.

UNRELIABLE. "Render unreliable any confession" (Police and Criminal Evidence Act 1984 (c. 60), s.76(2)(*b*)). "Unreliable" means "cannot be relied on as being the truth," and whether or not a drug addict undergoing withdrawal was fit to be interviewed in the sense that his answers could be relied upon was a matter for those present at the time (*R.* v. *Crampton* (1991) 92 Cr.App.R. 369). See also SAID.

UNSAFE. (4) "Conviction . . . unsafe or unsatisfactory" (Criminal Appeal Act 1968 (c. 19), s.2(1)). The words "unsafe" and "unsatisfactory," for the purposes of this section, are disjunctive and do not have different meanings from each other (*R.* v. *McIlkenny* (1991) 141 New L.J. 456).

UNSATISFACTORY. See UNSAFE.

UNSUITABLE. A trailer which was ordinarily suitable for the load it was carrying did not become "unsuitable" within the meaning of the Road Vehicle (Construction and Use) Regs. 1986 (No. 1078), r.100(3) merely because it had been badly loaded (*Young* v. *DPP* (1991) 155 J.P.N. 506).

(Education Act 1944 (c. 31), s.55(1)). The fact that a pupil had been selected for one school did not render another school closer to the pupil's home and which catered for her abilities "unsuitable" so as to render the local authority obliged to pay for free transport (*R.* v. *Kent County Council, ex p. C* [1998] ELR 108).

UNTIL. (2) Extension of cover on a marine insurance policy "until" a specified date is inclusive of that date (*The Kiel* [1991] 2 Lloyd's Rep. 546).

UNWANTED. (Sex Discrimination Act 1975 (c. 65), ss.6(2)(*b*); E.C. Recommendation and Code of Practice on Measures to Combat Sexual Harrassment). The word "unwanted" is essentially the same as "unwelcome" or "uninvited" (*Insitu Cleaning* v. *Heads* [1995] IRLR 4).

URGENCY. "By reason of the urgency of the matter" (Housing and Planning Act 1986 (c. 63), s.61(8)(*a*)). The "urgency" exemption from the duty to consult contained in this section does not apply to any urgency arising as a result of the minister's own failure to reach a decision until the last moment (*R.* v. *Secretary of State for Social Security, ex p. Association of Metropolitan Authorities, The Times,* July 23, 1992).

USE. (29) "Use . . . a motor vehicle on a road" (Road Traffic Act 1972 (c. 20), s.143; now Road Traffic Act 1988 (c. 52), s.143). A motor vehicle whose brakes were locked and whose wheels were unable to turn was held not to be in "use" within the meaning of this section as there was no element of controlling, managing or operating it as a vehicle (*Thomas* v. *Hooper* [1986] RTR 1). Although a thumb-print on the rear view mirror of a vehicle might be enough to show that the accused had been in it, it was not enough to establish "use" within the meaning of this section (*Chief Constable of Avon and Somerset Constabulary* v. *Jest* [1986] RTR 372). It is, for the purposes of this section, possible for more than one person to "use" a vehicle, and the user of a vehicle could, in some circumstances, include one whose vehicle was being used for his purposes or on his behalf under his instruction or control (*Hallett Silberman* v. *Cheshire County Council* [1993] RTR 32).

Where an offence involving use of a vehicle provided the alternative offence of causing or permitting another to use a vehicle, a person was only a user if he was the owner rather than the driver (*Jones (James)* v. *DPP* [1999] RTR 1).

(29) "Person . . . who uses on a road a . . . trailer" (Road Traffic Act 1972 (c. 20), s.40(5)). The owner of a defective trailer who provided it for another person to tow could be said to be "using" it for the purposes of this section, notwithstanding that neither he nor any servant of his was the driver (*NFC Forwarding* v. *DPP* [1989] RTR 239).

(33) "Use for trade" (Weights and Measures Act 1963 (c. 31), s.11(2)). The use of unstamped prescribed measuring equipment by the licensee and barman of a public house was held to be "use" by the employers for the purposes of this section (*Evans* v. *Clifton Inns* (1987) 85 L.G.R. 119).

"A person using the vehicle" (Motor Insurers Bureau (MIB) Agreement 1972, clause 6(1)(*c*)). A passenger in a car which was being driven by a driver whom he knew to be uninsured and who was involved in a joint enterprise with the driver was "using the vehicle" within the meaning of this clause (*Stinton* v. *Stinton, The Times,* August 5, 1992).

A passenger who assumed an element of control, management or operation of a vehicle could be a user of the vehicle within the meaning of cl.6(1)(c)(ii) of the Motor Insurers Agreement 1972 and user had the same meaning as in the Road Traffic Act 1988. The procurement of an uninsured vehicle by a passenger or an element of joint enterprise could give rise to the requisite amount of control to come within the scope of the clause (*O'Mahoney* v. *Jolliffe, The Times,* February 24, 1999).

"Used for the carriage . . . of the thing . . . liable to forfeiture" (Customs and Excise Management Act 1979 (c. 2), s.141(1)(*a*)). An aircraft which, unknown to the airline operators, carried in its cargo a container in which there was cannabis resin was being "used for the carriage" of the cannabis resin within the meaning of this section notwithstanding circumstances where the airline operators could not be said to be reckless in failing to discover its presence (*Commissioners of Customs and Excise* v. *Air Canada* [1991] 2 W.L.R. 344).

(59) "Uses any apparatus for wireless telegraphy" (Wireless Telegraphy Act 1949 (c. 54), s.1(1)). "Uses" in this section has its natural and ordinary meaning and cannot be extended to mean "has the use of" (*Rudd* v. *Secretary of State for Trade and Industry*, [1987] 1 W.L.R. 786; overruling *D* (*A Minor*) v. *Yates* [1984] Crim.L.R. 430). See also APPARATUS.

Retrieving computer-held data and observing its contents on a screen or by means of a printout could not without any further act thereafter constitute "use" contrary to s.5(2)(*b*) (*R.* v. *Brown (Gregory)* [1996] 1 All E.R. 545).

"Used for the purpose of committing . . . any offence" (Powers of Criminal Courts Act 1973 (c. 62), s.43(1)(*a*)). Money in the possession of a person convicted of supplying drugs had not been "used" by him but by those who had bought the drugs from him, and was therefore safe from forfeiture under this section (*R.* v. *Slater* [1986] 1 W.L.R. 1340).

"Use" (Patents Act 1949 (c. 87), s.32). Demonstrations of an invention for the purpose of obtaining finance or to seek licences did not amount to "use" within the meaning of this section (*Vax Appliances* v. *Hoover* [1991] F.S.R. 307).

Where the owner of a wine bar placed leaflets advertising the bar on the windscreens of cars parked in a council car park he was held to have "used" the vehicles for a purpose in connection with a trade or business contrary to an order made under s.35(1) of the Road Traffic Regulation Act 1984 (c. 27) (*Hickman* v. *Chichester District Council* 90 LGR 70).

"Use any such data held by him" (Data Protection Act 1984 (c. 35), s.5(2)(*b*)).

(60) (Road Traffic Act 1988 ss.47(1), 143(1), 185(1)). Where a vehicle which fell within the definition of vehicle in s.185(1) was on a road, the owner had "use" of it on a road whether or not at the material time it had wheels (*Pumbien* v. *Vines* [1996] RTR 37).

A chromolin used for the purposes of checking the quality of film used in the printing process could be something "used for the purposes of making a counterfeit note" under the Forgery and Counterfeiting Act 1981 (c. 45), s.17(1) (*R.* v. *Maltman, The Times,* July 14, 1994).

"Fraudulently alters or uses . . . any licence" (Vehicles (Excise) Act 1971 (c. 10), s.26(1)(*c*)). Exhibiting an altered vehicle excise licence on a car parked on private land was held not to amount to fraudulent use of the licence within the meaning of this section (*R.* v. *Johnson (Tony)* [1995] R.T.R. 15).

"Uses . . . causes or permits [land] to be used" (Town and Country Planning Act 1990 (c. 8), ss.179(6) and 285(2)).

(E.C. Council Directive 77/388 on a common system for VAT, Art. 6). The words "use of goods" in Art.6(2)(a) were subject to strict interpretation which precluded taxation of private goods forming part of a business for which the taxpayer was entitled to claim a VAT reduction (*Finanzamt Munchen III* v. *Mohsche (C193/91)* [1997] STC 195).

"Use as a village hall or similarly". The supplies in respect of refurbishment to a sports and fitness centre which operated in part as a business venture attracted a zero-rating for the purposes of VAT since its objective was to improve conditions of life for members of the local community (*Jubilee Hall Recreation Centre Ltd* v. *Customs and Excise Commissioners* [1997] STC 414).

(Coal Mining Subsidence Act 1991 (c. 41), s.30). Mere ownership of property did not amount to "use" for the purposes of a business within the meaning of s.30 (*Collins (Pontefract) Ltd* v. *British Coal Corporation* (1998) 76 P. & C.R. 219).

(Harbours Act 1964 (c. 40), s.57(1)). A ship is used in navigation if it is actually or potentially capable of being used for navigation, regardless whether it is a commercial or private vessel, so that a harbour authority was entitled to levy distraint for non-payment of harbour dues even though the vessel was privately owned and used solely as a holiday home (*R.* v. *Carrick DC, ex p. Prankerd* [1999] 2 W.L.R. 489).

See also PROPERTY.

"Uses threatening, abusive or insulting words," see WORDS.

"Uses towards another person," see TOWARDS.

"Change in the use of any land," see CHANGE.

USER. (Road Traffic Act 1988 (c. 52), Part VI and Motor Insurers Bureau (Compensation of Victims of Uninsured Drivers) Agreement 1972, cl.6(1)(*c*)(ii)).

A pillion passenger on an uninsured motorcycle was not a user of the vehicle within the meaning of cl.6(1)(*c*)(ii) of The 1972 Agreement in the absence of a sufficient degree of control of management of the vehicle (*Hatton* v. *Hall*, *The Times*, May 15, 1996).

The operation of an incinerator for the commercial destruction of hazardous waste was not within the "reasonable user" under Scottish law since it was not necessary for the common and ordinary use and occupation of the land (*Graham* v. *Rechem International Ltd* [1996] Env. L.R. 158).

USUAL WAY OF BUSINESS. (Partnership Act 1890 (c. 39), s.5). An undertaking, given in the context of an underlying transaction of a solicitorial nature, to provide security for a loan could be within the "usual way" of a solicitor's business. So that, where such undertakings were given fraudulently by a solicitor, they bound the partners of the firm for which he worked (*United Bank of Kuwait* v. *Hammond*; *City Trust* v. *Levy* [1988] 1 W.L.R. 1051).

V

VALID. "Valid as an enduring power of attorney" (Enduring Powers of Attorney Act 1985 (c. 29), s.6(5)(*a*)). A power was "valid" within the meaning of this section if the donor understood its nature and effect, notwithstanding that at the time of its execution she was incapable, by reason of mental disorder, of managing her affairs (*Re K, re F,* [1988] 2 W.L.R. 781).

"Will shall be valid" (Wills Act 1837 (c. 26), s.9(*b*), as substituted by s.17 of the Administration of Justice Act 1982 (c. 53)). Where a testator made a signature intending to "give effect to" his will before he made any dispositive provisions, that was a "valid" execution of a will so as to satisfy s.9(*b*), provided that the signing and subsequent dispositions all formed part of one transaction (*Wood* v. *Smith* [1992] 3 All E.R. 556).

VALUABLE. (2) "Valuable consideration" (Law of Property Act 1925 (c. 20), ss.77(1)(*c*), 205(xxi)). Where the assignee of a lease took on the liability of paying the rent and performing other obligations, thus conveying a benefit to the lessee, this was "valuable consideration" for the purposes of the Act notwithstanding that the stated consideration was only £1 (*Johnsey Estates* v. *Lewis and Manley* (*Engineering*) (1987) 284 E.G. 1240).

"Valuable security" (Theft Act 1968 (c. 60), s.20). Guidance to courts for determining by three stages whether the wide terms of this section applied to a document was provided by the Court of Appeal. The stages were: (i) to identify what the document did; (ii) then to ask whether it fell within any part of the definition of "valuable security" in s.20(3); (iii) if it did then to ask, bearing in mind the wide terms of s.20(2), whether, in respect in which the document was a valuable security, it had been executed.

A clearing house automated payment service is a "valuable security" within the meaning of s.20 (*R.* v. *King* [1991] 3 W.L.R. 246).

VALUE. (3) "For value" (Bills of Exchange Act 1882 (c. 61), s.29(1)(*b*)). The holder of a cheque, who had received it as indorsee from the payee in payment of an antecedent debt smaller than the amount of the cheque, and in anticipation of future debts, took it "for value" within the meaning of this section (*MacKenzie* v. *Buono, The Times*, July 31, 1986). See also HOLDER IN DUE COURSE.

"Transfer of value" (Finance Act 1975 (c. 7), s.20(4)). Where trustees of a discretionary settlement agreed to allow valuable paintings to go into the custody of a connected person, but one excluded from the beneficial interest, and then appointed a life interest in them to a beneficiary, there had been a "transfer of value" within the meaning of this section (*I.R.C.* v. *Macpherson* [1988] 2 W.L.R. 1261). See also ASSOCIATE.

"The value of the land" (Land Compensation Act 1961 (c. 33), s.5(4)) includes both the open market value an compensation for disturbance (*Hughes* v. *Doncaster Borough Council* [1991] 2 W.L.R. 16).

"Value" in an insurance policy did not mean market value and the proper measure of indemnity depended on the facts and circumstances (*Keystone Properties* v. *Sun Alliance and London Insurance*, 1993 S.C. 494).

VARIETY. See PLANT VARIETY

VARY. "Where . . . dispositions . . . are varied" (Finance Act 1978 (c. 42), s.68). There can only be one variation of a disposition. A further redirection of part of the deceased's estate failed because it did not vary a disposition of "property comprised in his estate immediately before his death" as required by the section (*Russell* v. *I.R.C.* [1988] 1 W.L.R. 834).

VEHICLE. A recovery vehicle towing a broken-down vehicle, where the bulk of the weight of the latter is borne by the former, is deemed to be a "vehicle itself constructed to carry a load" for the purposes of s.117(2) of the Road Traffic Regulation Act 1984 (c. 27) (*DPP* v. *Holtham* [1991] RTR 5).

A vehicle used for delivering and collecting skips, including builders' skips, was not used for "a general service performed in the public interest (*Swain* v. *McCaul* [1997] RTR 102).

(Road Vehicles Lighting Regulations 1989 (S.I. 1989 No. 1796) reg. 3, Table 4(4), 16). A vehicle adapted for the purposes of conveying the sick was an emergency vehicle for the purposes of reg. 16 of the 1989 Regulations even when the vehicle was being used for purposes other than as an ambulance when a blue light was fitted but not illuminated (*DPP* v. *Hawkins* [1996] RTR 160).

Stat. Defs., "means a mechanically propelled vehicle" (Vehicle Excise and Registration Act 1994 (c. 22), s.62(1)); in context of trespass, includes "any vehicle, whether or not it is in a fit state for use on roads, and includes any chassis or body, with or without wheels, appearing to have formed part of such a vehicle, and any load carried by, and anything attached to, such a vehicle" as well as caravans (Criminal Justice and Public Order Act 1994 (c. 33), s.61(9)); includes hovercraft (Northern Ireland (Emergency Provisions) Act 1996 (c. 22), s.58); "includes any means of conveyance" (United Nations Personnel Act 1997 (c. 13), s.2(3)).

(Council Regulation 3820/85 on the harmonisation of certain social legislation relating to road transport). The words "vehicle used in connection with . . . refuse collection and disposal" in Art. 4(6) must be interpreted as covering vehicles used for the collection of waste of all kinds which was not subject to more specific rules, and for the transportation of such waste over short distances within the context of a general service in the public interest provided directly by public authorities or by private undertakings under their control (*Criminal Proceedings against Groupil* (C39/45) and *Mrozek* v. *Jager* (C335/94) ECJ).

"Goods vehicle."—See GOODS VEHICLE.

"Recovery vehicle," Stat. Def., Vehicle Excise and Registration Act 1994 (c. 22), Sched. 1, para. 5(2).

VENISON. Stat Def., Deer Act 1991 (c. 54), s.16.

VESSEL. (6) "Vessel in navigation" (Merchant Shipping Act 1984 (c. 5), s.742). "Navigation" is not synonymous with movement on water, but means planned or ordered movement from one place to another. A sailing dinghy used on a reservoir for pleasure is not "in navigation" within the meaning of this section (*Curtis* v. *Wild* [1991] 4 All E.R. 172). Nor is a jet ski (*Steadman* v. *Scholfield* [1992] 2 Lloyd's Rep. 163).

Stat. Def., Dangerous Vessels Act 1985 (c. 22), s.7; "includes hovercraft" (Antarctic Act 1994 (c. 15), s.31(1)); "includes any ship or boat, or any other description of vessel used in navigation" (Merchant Shipping Act 1995 (c. 21), s.255(1)); "includes any ship or boat, or any other description of vessel used in navigation" (Merchant Shipping Act 1995 (c. 21), s.255(1)); "includes any ship, boat, barge, lighter or raft and any other description of craft, whether used in navigation or not" (British Waterways Act 1995 (c. i), s.2(1)).

"Pleasure vessel," Stat. Def., Merchant Shipping (Fire Protection: Small Ships) Regulations 1998 (No. 1011), reg. 1(2).

VETERINARIAN. (E.C. Council Directive 91/497 on health problems affecting intra community trade in fresh meat). The reference to "official veterinarian" in the Directive could not mean a qualified meat inspector or someone with lesser qualifications than a veterinarian (*Ministry of Agriculture, Fisheries and Food* v. *Webbs Country Foods Ltd* [1998] Eu. L.R. 359).

VICTIM. (European Convention on Human Rights 1950, Art. 25). Shareholders who alleged detriment to their financial interests as a result of government measures were not "victims" within the meaning of Art. 25 (*Agrotexim* v. *Greece* [1996] 21 E.H.R.R. 250).

VIDEO CAMERA. Stat. Def., Wireless Telegraphy (Control of Interference from Videosenders) Order 1998 (No. 722), Art. 3.

VIDEO RECORDER AND VIDEO RECORDING. Stat. Def., Wireless Telegraphy (Control of Interference from Videosenders) Order 1998 (No. 722), Art. 3.

VIDEO WORK. A game on computer disk, which if successfully completed, displayed a clip of moving naked women as a reward, amounted to "video work" within the meaning of the Video Recordings Act 1984 (c. 39), s.1. The clip was not a video game and thus exempt under s.2(1)(*c*) (*Kent County Council* v. *Multi Media Marketing (Canterbury), The Times,* May 9, 1995.

VIOLENCE. "Immediate unlawful violence" (Public Order Act 1986 (c. 64), s.4(1)). Distribution of copies of a book containing abusive and insulting writing was not likely to cause any person to believe that "immediate unlawful violence" will be used against him (*R.* v. *Horseferry Road Magistrates' Court, ex p. Siadatan* [1990] 3 W.L.R. 1006).
  "Crime of violence," see CRIME.
  Stat. Def., Public Order Act 1986 (c. 64), s.8.
  "Violence on that person" (Offences against the Person Act 1864 (c. 268), s.2(1)(f)(2), as amended). "Violence on that person" necessarily involved physical contact with the victim and did not include threatening or chasing him (*Daley* v. *The Queen* [1998] 1 W.L.R. 494).
  (Estate Agents Act 1979 (c. 38), s.3(1)(*a*)(i)). For the purposes of s.3(1)(*a*)(i) an offence of violence could include the application of force to a building (*Antonelli* v. *Secretary of State for Trade and Industry* [1998] 1 All E.R. 997).

VIOLENT. Where the phrase "entry to . . . premises by forcible and violent means" was used in an insurance policy "violent" was used in its ordinary sense, and accordingly entry to the insured's premises by using stolen keys was not violent (*Nash t/a Dino Services* v. *Prudential Assurance Co.* [1989] 1 All E.R. 422). See also FORCIBLE.
  "Violent offence" (Criminal Justice Act 1991 (c. 53), s.3(1)). Attempted rape where the victim suffered actual physical injury came within the definition of "violent offence" in s.31(1) (*R.* v. *Robinson, The Times,* December 3, 1992).
  Possession of a knife without intention to use it was not a "violent offence" within the meaning of the Criminal Justice Act 1991 (c. 53), s.31(2) (*R.* v. *Bibby* [1994] Crim.L.R. 610).

Use of an imitation firearm during the commission of a robbery was not a "violent offence" within the meaning of s.31(1) (*R.* v. *Palin (Gareth Wayne)* (1995) Cr.App.R.(S.) 888).

The carrying of a firearm which was unloaded and intended merely to frighten rather than to harm did not amount to a be a "violent offence" (*R.* v. *Khan (Touriq)* (1995) Cr.App.R.(S.) 180).

VIRTUALLY. "Virtually unable" to walk, see UNABLE.

VISITOR. For the purposes of the Occupiers' Liability (Northern Ireland) Act 1957 (c. 25), s.2, a person who used a public right of way was not a visitor to the land over which the right of way passes (*McGeown* v. *Northern Ireland Housing Executive* [1994] 3 W.L.R. 187).

VOCATION. Those years of an educational course which, taken in isolation, could not be regarded as "vocational training" within the meaning of the EEC Treaty were, none the less, to be so regarded if the whole course, of which they formed a part, constituted a preparation for a qualification for a particular profession, trade or employment, or which provided the necessary skills for such profession, trade or employment (*Gravier* v. *City of Liège* [1985] ECR 593; *Belgian State* v. *Humbel*, 263/86 [1988] ECR 5365). University education in veterinary medicine is "vocational training" (*Blaizot* v. *University of Liège* (No. 24/86) [1989] 1 C.M.L.R. 57).

VOLUNTARY. "Any voluntary payment" (Housing Benefit (General) Regulations 1987 (No. 1971), Sched. 4, para. 13(1)). Payments made to a miner's widow in lieu of concessionary coal was not "voluntary payments" within the meaning of, and for the purposes of this paragraph (*R.* v. *Doncaster Metropolitan Borough Council, ex p. Boulton* (1992) 25 H.L.R. 195).

Cash payments in lieu of concessionary coal which had been made in the expectation of improved industrial relations and efficiency were not "voluntary payments" (*Social Security Decision No. R (IS) 4/94* (1995) 9 C.L. 446).

VOLUNTARY ORGANISATION. Stat. Def., applying Stat. Def. in National Assistance Act 1948 (c. 29) (Carers (Recognition and Services) Act 1995 (c. 12), s.1(6)); Housing Act 1996 (c. 52), ss.2(6) and 180(3); National Minimum Wage Act 1998 (c. 39), s.44(4).

VOTING SHARE CAPITAL. Stat. Def., Cash Ratio Deposits (Eligible Liabilities) Order 1998 (No. 1130), Art. 2(1).

VULNERABLE. "Vulnerable as a result of old age, mental illness . . . or physical disability" (Housing Act 1985 (c. 68), s.59(1)(c)). The opinion of a single medical officer is not an adequate basis on which to judge vulnerability under this section (*R.* v. *Lambeth London Borough Council, ex p. Carroll* (1988) 20 H.L.R. 142). Vulnerable means vulnerable in a housing context (*R.* v. *Bath City Council, ex p. Sangermano* (1984) 17 H.L.R. 94). The mere fact that an applicant is an epileptic does not qualify him as vulnerable (*R.* v. *Reigate and Banstead Borough Council, ex p. Di Domenico* (1988) 20 H.L.R. 153).

A person who had a history of alcohol and drug dependence was not vulnerable since she could not show that she was less able to obtain suitable accommodation than the ordinary person (*Ortiz* v. *Westminster City Council* (1993) 27 H.L.R. 364).

W

WAGERING CONTRACT. See GAMING CONTRACT.

WAGES. "A deduction from his wages" (Wages Act 1986 (c. 48), ss.1, 5, 7, 8). Failure to pay a bonus was not a wage deduction within the meaning of s.5 (*Barlow* v. *A. J. Whittle* (*trading as Micro Management*) [1990] I.C.R. 270). Where an employer sought to recover an amount in excess of the wages due to an employee this could still be "a deduction" from the employee's "wages" for the purposes of this section (*Alsop* v. *Star Vehicle Contracts* [1990] I.C.R. 378; *New Centurion Trust* v. *Welch* [1990] I.C.R. 383; *Home Office* v. *Ayres, The Times,* October 22, 1991; *Murray* v. *Strathclyde Regional Council* [1992] IRLR 396). A payment in lieu of notice has been held not to be "wages" for the purposes of s.7 of this Act (*Kournavous* v. *Masterton* [1990] I.C.R. 387) so that where an employer stopped an employee's cheque for payment in lieu of notice this was not "a deduction from his wages" within the meaning of s.5. However, unpaid commission and holiday pay due under the employee's contract were held to be deductions from wages (*Delaney* v. *Staples* [1992] 2 W.L.R. 451). Where an employee's termination payment included "salary in lieu of notice" described as "net" and was less than the gross pay due in this regard, it was held that pay in lieu of notice did not fall within the definition of "wages" in s.7 so that the difference between the amount paid and the gross figure was not a "deduction" within the meaning of s.5 (*Foster Wheeler* (*London*) v. *Jackson* [1990] I.C.R. 757). But where there was an agreement to pay a sum in lieu of notice and the only dispute was as to which of two sums was appropriate, the claim was for a liquidated sum properly payable as wages within the meaning of s.8(3) rather than for unliquidated damages for breach of contract. Such payment in lieu could amount to "wages" within the meaning of the Act (*Janstorp International* (*UK*) v. *Allen* [1990] I.C.R. 779). The unilateral withdrawal of a wage supplement paid to an employee in respect of the loss of his right to cash pay after the abolition of the Trade Acts by the 1986 Wages Act constituted a "deduction from any wages" within the meaning of s.1(1) of the 1986 Act (*McCree* v. *Tower Hamlets London Borough Council* [1992] I.C.R. 99). Payment of commission which was expressed to be discretionary and non-contractual was held to come within the definition of "wages" in s.7 (*Kent Management Services* v. *Butterfield* [1992] I.C.R. 272).

Unpaid commissions could amount to "wages" within the meaning of s.7 and refusal to pay such commissions could amount to an unlawful deduction within the meaning of s.1(1) (*Blackstone Franks Investment Management Ltd* v. *Robertson, The Times,* May 4, 1998).

A ship's officer's severance pay under National Maritime Board terms is not "wages" giving rise to a lien over the ship (*Tacoma City* [1991] 1 Lloyd's Rep. 330).

Stat. Def., Wages Act 1986 (c. 48), s.7; includes emoluments (Merchant Shipping Act 1995 (c. 21), s.313(1)).
See also EMPLOYMENT; IN THE COURSE; PROPERLY.

WAIT. (City of Gloucester (Eastgate Street) (Waiting Regulations) Order 1982, arts. 3 & 5(1)). Where regulations permitted a licensed hackney carriage to "wait" at a hackney carriage stand, it was held that "wait" meant "waiting for a fare," and did not authorise the parking there of a locked and unattended licensed hackney carriage (*Rodgers* v. *Taylor* [1987] RTR 86).

WALES. Stat. Def., including certain seas, Government of Wales Act 1998 (c. 38), s.155(1) and (2).

WALKING DISTANCE. The "walking distance" to any school within the meaning of s.39 of the Education Act 1944 (c. 31) is to be measured along the shortest route which a child, accompanied if necessary, could walk with reasonable safety to school (*Rogers* v. *Essex County Council* [1986] 3 W.L.R. 689).
Stat. Def., Education Act 1996 (c. 56), s.444(5).

WALKING POSSESSING AGREEMENT. Stat. Def., Value Added Tax Act 1994 (c. 23), s.68(2).

WALL. "Party fence wall" and "Party wall," Stat. Def., Party Wall etc. Act 1996 (c. 40), s.20.

WARRANT. "Warrant to arrest a person in connection with an offence" (Magistrates' Courts Act 1980 (c. 43), s.125(4) as amended by Police and Criminal Evidence Act 1984 (c. 60), s.33). A warrant issued under s.16(1) of the Powers of Criminal Courts Act 1973 (c. 62) to arrest a person for the breach of a community service order was a "warrant" within the meaning of s.125(4) (*Jones* v. *Kelsey* [1987] Crim.L.R. 392).

WARRANTY. The term "warranty as to locality" included warranties about the vessel's location both at commencement and during the period of cover and applied to the trading limits provision (*Australia & New Zealand Banking Group* v. *Compagnie D'Assurances Maritimes Aeriennes Et Terrestres; Northern L, The* Lloyd's List, June 1, 1995).

WASTE. (Town and Country Planning General Development Order 1977 (No. 289), art. 8). "Waste" can include waste substances for reprocessing which, once reprocessed, are reusable and cease to be waste (*R.* v. *Rotherham Metropolitan Borough Council, ex p. Rankin* (1990) 1 P.L.R. 93).
Material which was unwanted in the hands of the original owners was "waste" within the meaning of the Control of Pollution Act 1974 (c. 40), s.30(1)(*a*) (*Friel (H.L.) & Son* v. *Inverclyde District Council,* 1994 S.C.L.R. 561).
(16) "Controlled waste" (Control of Pollution Act 1974 (c. 40), ss.3, 30). Material removed as waste from one site and deposited for a useful

purpose at another remained "waste" for the purposes of this Act, notwithstanding that it had been sorted and graded before re-use (*Kent County Council* v. *Queenborough Rolling Mills* [1990] Crim.L.R. 813). Seaweed was held not to be "controlled waste" within the meaning of this section, so that a disposal licence under s.5 of the Act was not required (*Thanet District Council* v. *Kent County Council* [1993] C.O.D. 308).

The definition of "waste" in Council Directive 85/442, Art. 1 included substances and objects which were capable of economic reutilisation (*Inter-Environnement Wallonie ASBL* v. *Region Wallonie* [1998] All E.R. (EC) 135).

(E.C. Council Directive 75/442). Materials which were to be re-used without any intermediate recovery operation were not to be treated as waste for waste licence management purposes, but materials to be re-cycled or reclaimed, where there was an intermediate recovery operation, were to be treated as "waste" (*Mayer Parry Recycling Ltd* v. *Environment Agency, The Times,* December 3, 1998).

Stat. Def., Environmental Protection Act 1990 (c. 43), Sched. 2B inserted eby Environment Act 1995 (c. 25), Sched. 22, para. 95.

WASTE LAND. "Waste land of a manor" (Commons Registration Act 1965 (c. 64), s.22(1)). Manorial waste is land which is parcel of a manor and uncultivated (*Re Britford Common* [1977] 1 W.L.R. 39; *Re Box Hill Common* [1980] 1 Ch. 109) and for these purposes mowing a race course or a golf course is not cultivation (*R.* v. *Doncaster Metropolitan Borough Council, ex p. Braim, The Times,* October 11, 1986). The mere fact that land is let to a series of tenants does not of itself prevent the land from being waste land of the manor and therefore a common (*Re TWM Barlwim Common, Risca and Rogerstone* (Ref. No. 273/D/106–107)). The decision of the Court of Appeal in *Re Box Hill Common* ([1980] Ch. 109) [see Main Work, p. 2831] that the words "waste land of a manor" could not comprehend land which had ceased to be connected with a manor before the date of registration, and that accordingly the land could not be registered as common land, has now been disapproved by the House of Lords in holding that "waste land of a manor" means "waste land now or formerly of a manor" or "waste land of manorial origin." Such land does not cease to be registrable under the Act on account of ceasing to be in the same ownership as the lordship of the manor (*Hampshire County Council* v. *Milburn* [1990] 2 W.L.R. 1240).

After a proposal to construct works had been abandoned, land over which the public had a right of acccess and which remained open, uncultivated and unoccupied was "waste land of a manor" (*Mid-Glamorgan County Council* v. *Ogwr Borough Council* [1995] 1 W.L.R. 313).

WASTING ASSET. "Wasting asset" (Capital Gains Tax Act 1979 (c. 14), s.37(1)). For the purposes of computing capital gains tax liability on the sale of a residential property, a lease having less than 50 years to run was to be treated as a "wasting asset" even though the tenant had had an option to extend the term under the provisions of the Leasehold Reform Act 1967 (*Lewis* v. *Walters* [1992] S.T.C. 97).

Stat. Def., Taxation of Chargeable Gains Act 1992 (c. 12), s.44.

WATCH. "Watch or beset" (Conspiracy and Protection of Property Act 1875 (c. 86), s.7), see BESET.

WATERCOURSE. (Public Health Act 1936 (c. 49), s.259). Although an estuary could be a watercourse at common law, within the context of ss.259–266 of the 1936 Act an estuary was not a "watercourse" (*R. v. Falmouth and Truro Port HA, ex p. South West Water Ltd, The Times,* May 6, 1999).

Stat. Defs., Water Industry Act 1991 (c. 56), s.219; Water Resources Act 1991 (c. 57), s.221; Land Drainage Act 1991 (c. 59), s.72.

WATERS. See INLAND WATERS.

WATERSIDE MANUFACTURER. Where two separate companies, which were both wholly-owned subsidiaries of a third, respectively owned and operated a wharf and manufacturing premises, but the manufacturing company's premises did not abut the waterside, it was not legitimate to pierce the corporate veil and treat them as a single entity so as to qualify as a "waterside manufacturer," and thus be exempt from the requirement to employ registered dock workers to carry out what would otherwise be port transport work (*National Dock Labour Board* v. *Pinn & Wheeler, The Times,* April 5, 1989). See also DOCK.

WAY. "A way over any land" (Highways Act 1980 (c. 66), s.31(1)). A non-tidal river over which there has been a public right of navigation cannot be a "way over any land" for the purposes of this section (which provides for the presumption of dedication as a highway of any way which has been actually enjoyed by the public for 20 years or more), it being held that what was dedicated could not be anything but the land itself (*Att.-Gen. ex p. Yorkshire Derwent Trust* v. *Brotherton* [1991] 3 W.L.R. 1126).

(Road Traffic Act 1988 (c. 52), s.192). A road restricted to the public by means of a byelaw and a notice but not physically blocked to members of the public is a "way to which the public has access" within the meaning of s.192 (*Renwick* v. *Scott* 1996 S.L.T. 1164).

See also RIGHT OF WAY.

WEAPON. (Firearms Act 1968 (c. 27), s.5(1)(*b*)). An electric stunning device is a "weapon" within the meaning of this section (*Flack* v. *Baldry* [1988] 1 W.L.R. 393). A CS gas canister is a "weapon" within the meaning of this section. The argument that the gas was the weapon and the canister merely its container failed. It was the combination of canister and contents that comprised the "weapon" (*R.* v. *Bradish* (1990) 154 J.P. 21). A gun did not cease to be a "weapon" within the meaning of this section just because, due to some unknown fault, it was not working (*Brown* v. *DPP, The Times,* March 27, 1992).

See DISCHARGE; NOXIOUS.

"Chemical weapons", see CHEMICAL WEAPONS.

WEEK. "A week's pay" (Employment Protection (Consolidation) Act 1978 (c. 44), Sched. 14, paras. 5(1), (2)). An employee's average rate of remuneration should be calculated by reference to all hours worked, including overtime, and all remuneration received including overtime pay stripped of any bonus element (*British Coal Corp.* v. *Cheesebrough and Secretary of State for Employment* [1988] IRLR 351).

"Period of four weeks" (Employment Protection (Consolidation) Act 1978 (c. 44), s.84(4)). "Weeks" here means calendar weeks, not working weeks (*Benton* v. *Sanderson Kayser* [1989] IRLR 19).

"Within six weeks" (Acquisition of Land Act 1981 (c. 67), s.23). A six week period beginning on a Tuesday ends six Tuesdays later and an act done on the sixth Tuesday is done within six weeks. A period measured in weeks ends at midnight on the corresponding day of the week to that on which the period commenced. The word "within" means the final moment of a period in time. Where a time limit could not be extended it was important not to construe the limit narrowly (*Omoregei* v. *Secretary of State for the Environment* [1997] 4 C.L. 541).

Stat. Def., "means any period of 7 days"—(Social Security (Incapacity for Work) Act 1994 (c. 18), s.3(1) (new inserted s.30C(7) of Social Security Contributions and Benefits Act 1992 (c. 4)).

WEIGHING. "Weighing or measuring equipment." Stat. Def., Weights and Measures Act 1985 (c. 72), s.94.

WELFARE. "Welfare of a minor" (Supreme Court Act 1981 (c. 54), s.18(1)(*h*)(i). Parental access is not part of "welfare" for the purposes of this section (*Re H* (*Minors*) (1989) 19 Fam. Law 349).
  See EDUCATION.

WELL-FOUNDED. "Owing to a well-founded fear of being persecuted" (Art. 1A(2) of the United Nations Convention (1951) and Protocol (1967) Relating to the Status of Refugees (Cmd. 9171 and Cmd. 3096)). Although the existence of a state of fear is clearly a subjective matter the question whether the fear is "well-founded" has to be assessed by the Secretary of State on an objective basis in the light of facts and circumstances known to him or established to his satisfaction (*R.* v. *Secretary of State for the Home Department, ex p. Sivakumaran* [1988] 2 W.L.R. 92; *R.* v. *Secretary of State for the Home Department, ex p. H., The Times,* June 20, 1988).

"Well-founded fear of persecution" (Immigration Rules 1983, H.C. 251, para. 75). Where an asylum-seeker had a fear of persecution in his home village, but not in any other part of his country of origin to which he might return, the fear was not "well-founded" to the extent of justifying a grant of asylum (*Yurekli* v. *Secretary of State for the Home Department* [1991] Imm.A.R. 153; *R.* v. *Secretary of State for the Home Department, ex p. Gunes (Hidir)* [1991] Imm.A.R. 278). There could be no "well-founded" fear of persecution for members of a sect who had not actually suffered religious persecution nor preached nor shown any intention to preach their religion; the mere existence of a law prohibiting the sect from seeking converts was not enough to found a fear of persecution (*R.* v. *Secretary of State for the Home Department, ex p. Ahmad* [1990] Imm.A.R. 61). In determining whether a person had a "well-founded" fear of being persecuted if he were deported to a particular country, information from that country's High Commissioner was relevant and could be taken into account (*R.* v. *Secretary of State for the Home Department, ex p. Mendis* [1990] Imm.A.R. 6).

Experience of a situation in Germany, where there had been sporadic neo-Nazi attacks, could not amount to a well-founded fear of persecution for the purposes of these Rules (*R.* v. *Secretary of State for the Home Department, ex p. Singh (Mangal)* [1992] Imm.A.R. 376; *Singh (Balbir)* v. *Secretary of State for the Home Department* [1992] Imm.A.R. 426).

In exceptional circumstances, the making of an application for asylum could create the possibility of an applicant being subject to persecution if returned to his country of origin and the making of a fraudulent claim could not necessarily act as a total barrier to the reconsideration of an applicant's status as a refugee (*M.* v. *Secretary of State for the Home Department* [1996] 1 W.L.R. 507).

WHEREBY. For circumstances in which a series of transactions failed as a tax avoidance scheme because one of them was held to be a "transaction whereby any other person . . . has received an abnormal amount by way of dividend" contrary to s.461C of the Income and Corporation Taxes Act 1970 (c. 10), see *Bird* v. *I.R.C.* [1985] S.T.C. 584).

WHETHER. The phrase "whether in berth or not" (wibon) incorporated into the laytime provisions of a berth charterparty applied only where a berth was not available. It did not apply where a berth was available but the ship was unable to reach it because of fog (*Bulk Transport Shipping Co.* v. *Seacrystal Shipping, The Kyzikos* [1988] 3 W.L.R. 858).

WHISKY. Stat. Def., Scotch Whisky Act 1988 (c. 22), s.3.

WHO. "A person who in the U.K. . . . . does any act with intent to cause a fire or explosion" (Explosive Substances Act 1883 (c. 3), s.3(1), as amended by s.7 of the Criminal Jurisdiction Act 1975 (c. 59)). The word "who" refers to the act done by a person and not to the person carrying out the act, creating a geographical limitation on the act. Therefore, any person who is an alien and does not enter the U.K., but conspires to cause an explosion in the U.K., is guilty of an offence under this section (*R.* v. *Ellis (Desmond)* (1992) Cr.App.R. 52).

WHOLE. Where business premises were empty for a very short period, it was unlikely that a court would find that they had not been occupied "for the whole of a five year period" (*Bacciocchi* v. *Academic Agency Ltd* [1998] 2 All E.R. 241).

(County Court Rules 1981 Order 11, rule 2). In unliquidated claims, the "whole amount" must mean the amount which the plaintiff was prepared to accept in satisfaction of his claim (*Mattison* v. *Ellis* [1998] 11 C.L. 72).

WHOLLY AND EXCLUSIVELY. (1) "Wholly and exclusively laid out or expended for the purposes of the trade, profession or vocation" (Income and Corporation Taxes Acts 1970 (c. 10), s.130(*a*), 1988 (c. 1), s.74(*a*)). Contributions made by a partnership towards the removal costs of those partners required to relocate were not incurred "wholly and exclusively" "for the purposes" of the "profession" (*MacKinlay* v. *Arthur Young McClelland Moores and Co.* [1989] 3 W.L.R. 1245). Payments by a company to trustees of a settlement set up to secure the company's future and the well-being of its employees were held to have been incurred "wholly and exclusively" for the purposes of the company's trade (*Bott E.* v. *Price* [1987] S.T.C. 100). Remuneration paid by a company, on the advice of its accountant, to the sole shareholder and director which was found to be excessive remuneration for the work she did and to represent in part a diversification of her husband's earnings to her fiscal purposes, was not deductible in computing the company's tax liability, not being incurred "wholly and exclusively" for the purposes of the trade under s.30 (*Earlspring Properties* v. *Guest, The Times*, May 25, 1993).

(2) "Wholly, exclusively and necessarily in the performance of the said duties" (Income and Corporation Taxes Acts 1970 (c. 10), s.189(1), 1988 (c. 1), s.198(1)). Expenses incurred by a general medical practitioner in travelling from his home or his surgery to hospital, or from one hospital to another, or to attend medical seminars, were not incurred in the "performance" of his duties within the meaning of this section (*Parikh* v. *Sleeman* [1988] S.T.C. 580). Although reading other newspapers was an integral part of a journalist's work, expenditure on such publications was nevertheless held not to have been incurred "wholly, exclusively and necessarily" in the performance of his duties of employment for the purposes of this section (*Smith* v. *Abbott* [1994] 1 W.L.R. 306).

See also CAPITAL.

WHOLLY OR MAINLY. "Wholly or mainly for the purpose of carrying on a trade" (Income and Corporation Taxes Act 1988 (c. 1), Sched. 19, para. 7). Where members of a management team borrowed money to enable them to acquire shares in a company formed by them to acquire and carry on the business of an existing company, the new company so formed was held to exist "wholly or mainly for the purpose of carrying on a trade" and was therefore a "trading company" within the meaning of the definition in para. 7 (*Lord* v. *Tustain*; *Same* v. *Chapple, The Times*, May 24, 1993).

WHOSE. "Whose . . . affidavit" (R.S.C., Ord. 24, r.10). These words extended to an affidavit sworn by a deponent who was not a party but which was procured by and used on behalf of a party (*Dubai Bank* v. *Galadari* (*No.2*) [1990] 1 W.L.R. 731).

WIFE. "Wives" (Immigration Act 1971 (c. 77), s.1(5)) cannot be construed as "husbands" for the purposes of this section. Accordingly, the husband of a Commonwealth citizen who was settled in the United Kingdom when the Act came into force could not rely on the provisions of this section to defeat removal directions made against him by the Home Secretary (*Singh (Bahadur)* v. *Immigration Appeal Tribunal* [1988] Imm.A.R. 582).

"Wife living with him or . . . wholly maintained by him" (Income and Corporation Taxes Act 1970 (c. 10), s.8(1)(*a*)). For the purposes of this section a "wife" is someone who has entered into a lawful marriage with a particular man, and does not include a so-called common law wife, however close or permanent the cohabitation might be (*Rignell* v. *Andrews* [1990] S.T.C. 410).

WILD BIRD. See DEAD WILD BIRD.

WILD MAMMAL. See MAMMAL.

WILFUL. "Wilful default . . . by or on behalf of any person" (Taxes Management Act 1970 (c. 9), s.36). Professional accountants employed by a taxpayer could commit "wilful default" on his "behalf" notwithstanding that the taxpayer himself was unaware of any misleading information in his tax return (*Pleasants* v. *Atkinson* [1987] S.T.C. 728).

To sustain a finding of "wilful default or culpable neglect" within the meaning of the Community Charges (Administration and Enforcement) Regulations 1989 (No. 438) it is necessary at least for there to be evidence that the non-payer has been offered employment which he has then rejected or refused (*R.* v. *Poole Magistrates, ex p. Benham; Benham* v. *Poole Borough Council* [1991] RVR 217).

"Wilful exposure to needless peril". An exclusion clause in these terms in a personal accident insurance policy could only be relied on in cases where either it could be shown that an insured injury was quite likely to occur or that the insured person clearly appreciated the risk of the injury occurring. A merely negligent or reckless act by the insured person did not fall within the exception clause (*Morley* v. *United Friendly Insurance, The Times*, February 8, 1993).

"Wilfully disturbs any spawn" (Salmon and Freshwater Fisheries Act 1975 (c. 51), s.2(4)). A riparian owner who caused gravel to be removed from the river bank in an area where spawning fish were to be found, and then caused lorries to cross, was guilty of an offence under this section (*National Rivers Authority* v. *Jones* (*John L.*) [1992] C.O.D. 351).

(Highways Act 1980 (c. 66), s.137). "Wilfully" meant intentionally as opposed to accidentally (*Kent County Council* v. *Upchurch River Valley Golf Course Ltd* [1998] 3 C.L. 347).

WILFULLY. "Wilfully obstructs," see OBSTRUCT.

"Wilfully assaults, ill-treats, neglects, abandons or exposes," see ILL-TREAT.

"Wilfully interrupts," see INTERRUPT.

WITH HIM. "Has with him," see HAS. See also POSSESSION; REASONABLE EXCUSE (8).

WITHIN. A notice to quit requiring the tenants to vacate premises "within a period of three months" did not necessarily require them to vacate before the end of that period, and was not therefore inconsistent with a clause in the lease specifying "not less than three months previous notice in writing" (*Manorlike* v. *Le Vitas Travel Agency* [1986] 1 All E.R. 573).

WITHIN THE JURISDICTION. (1) The question whether a defendant out of the jurisdiction who voluntarily submits to the jurisdiction after the writ is served is a "person . . . within the jurisdiction" for the purposes of R.S.C., Ord. 11, r.1(2) was discussed in *Amanuel* v. *Alexandros Shipping Co., The Alexandros P* [1986] Q.B. 464).

(1) "Service on a defendant within the jurisdiction" (R.S.C., Ord. 10, r.1(2)). The words "within the jurisdiction" apply to the defendant and not

to the writ for service (*Barclays Bank of Swaziland* v. *Hahn* [1989] 1 W.L.R. 506).

See also PROPERLY.

WITHOUT ANY DEDUCTION. The words "without any deduction" in a lease, in the absence of guidance as to the intended meaning, were insufficient to exclude a tenant's equitable right of set-off in subsequent litigation (*Famous Army Stores* v. *Meehan* [1993] 1 E.G.L.R. 73 not followed) (*Connaught Restaurants* v. *Indoor Leisure* [1994] 1 W.L.R. 501).

WITHOUT FOUNDATION. (Asylum and Immigration Appeals Act 1993, Sched. 2, para. 5(3)(*a*)). A claim for asylum was "without foundation" if it was unnecessary for the Secretary of State to decide whether a claimant was a refugee who ought to be admitted by virtue of Convention obligations because he could be removed to a third country in which he did not fear persecution (*R.* v. *Secretary of State for the Home Department, ex p. Mehari* [1994] Q.B. 474).

WITHOUT PREJUDICE. (1) The privilege attached to "without prejudice" correspondence ceases if and when the protected negotiations achieve their object in reaching a settlement. So that, where a plaintiff brought an action against two defendants, the "without prejudice" correspondence which had passed between the plaintiff and one of the defendants, and had resulted in a settlement of their claims, thereafter ceased to be privileged and became available to the other defendants (*Rush and Tompkins* v. *Greater London Council* [1988] 3 W.L.R. 939).

"Without prejudice" had more than one meaning depending upon the context in which it was used. When used in the compromise process it usually appeared in the heading of a letter rather than in the body of the text. Where it appeared in the text of a letter it did not indicate the commencement of litigation but merely indicated an intention to seek compromise without giving up the right to seek redress through the courts (*Peterborough City Council* v. *Mancetter Developments* [1996] EGCS 50).

See also PRIVILEGED COMMUNICATION.

WITHOUT PRIOR NOTICE. "Without prior notice" in a contract of employment should be construed as meaning "without advance notice" (*Bainbridge* v. *Circuit Foil U.K. Ltd, The Times,* February 26, 1997).

WITHOUT SUPPORT. (Coal Mining Subsidence Act 1991 (c. 45), ss.1(1), 2(1)). "Withdrawal of support" could cover passive as well as active loss of suport so that subsidence caused by the shifting of infill in a site previously used for lawful coal-mining operations could result in the loss of suport to land to found liability under s.2(1) (*British Coal Corporation* v. *Netherlee Trust Trustees* 1995 S.L.T. 1038).

WITNESS. "Solely on the evidence of one witness" (Perjury Act 1911 (c. 6), s.13). Two witnesses who testified to having heard the defendant admit falsity did not become "one witness" for the purposes of this section by virtue of the fact that they heard him on the same occasion (*R.* v. *Peach* [1990] 1 W.L.R. 976).

Stat. Def., Prosecution of Offences Act 1985 (c. 23), s.21.

WOODLAND. Stat. Def., Deer (Scotland) Act 1996 (c. 58), s.45(1).

WORDS. "Words or behaviour" (Public Order Act 1986 (c. 64), s.5(1)(*a*)). Delivering a letter to another, who opened it in the absence of the sender, was not using "words" within the meaning of this section (*Chappell* v. *DPP* [1989] C.O.D. 259).

WORK. "Incapable of work in consequence of sickness" (Employment Protection (Consolidation) Act 1978 (c. 44), Sched. 13, para. 9(1)(*a*)). The words "incapable of work" refer to the type of work which had been carried out by the employee prior to any interruption in continuity; so that, although he had undertaken a different sort of work during the period of interruption, he could still be "incapable of work in consequence of sickness" for the purposes of this paragraph (*Donnelly* v. *Kelvin International Services* [1992] IRLR 496).

"Place of work" (Local Government Act 1972 (c. 70), s.79(1)(*c*)). The word "work" for the purposes of this section is to be given its ordinary meaning and could, therefore, include duties performed as a councillor (*Parker* v. *Yeo* [1992] 90 LGR 645).

(Race Relations Act 1976 (c. 74), s.7). Work done by the employees of concessionaires operating within a department store was work done for the store, in that it was work done for the benefit of the store and ultimately under the store's control (*Harrods Ltd* v. *Remick* [1996] I.C.R. 846).

(Treaty of Rome 1957, Art. 119). Attendance at the annual conference of a union was not "work" in the usual sense, in that the employer had no control over the employee's activities whilst at the conference (*Arbeiterwohlfahrt der Stadt Berlin E.V.* v. *Botel*) (C360/90) [1992] IRLR 423 distinguished) (*Manor Bakeries Ltd* v. *Nazir* [1996] IRLR 604).

(Race Relations Act 1976 (c. 74), s.7). The employees of franchisees, who provided individuals to work in a large department store, worked for the store as well as for their employers, so that the store could be liable under the 1976 Act for acts of unlawful discrimination as principal (*Harrods Ltd* v. *Remick* [1998] I.C.R. 156).

See also AT WORK; TEMPORARY (5).

WORKER. (5) Persons involved in activities carried out in the context of a rehabilitation or retraining scheme for persons who were otherwise not capable of finding employment could not be regarded as "workers" within the meaning of Art. 48 of the EEC Treaty (*Bettray* v. *Staatssecretaris van Justitie* (No. 344/89) [1989] ECR 1621); see also, as to meaning in EEC Treaty, Art. 48, *Raulin* v. *Minister van Onderwijs en Wetenschappen* [1994] 1 C.M.L.R. 227.

A wife who undertook the care of her paraplegic husband but had neither given up work nor abandoned any attempts to seek work when she began to care for him, was not a member of the "working population" within the Council Directive 79/7 in equal treatment for men and women in matters of social security, Art. 2 (*Zuchner* v. *Handelskrankenkasse (Ersatzkasse) Bremen* (C77/95), *The Times,* December 9, 1996).

(Employment Rights Act 1996 (c. 18), s.200). A police officer serving with the Metropolitan Police was an office-holder rather than a "worker" within the meaning of s.200 (*Commissioner of Police* v. *Lowrey-Nesbitt* [1999] I.C.R. 401).

Stat. Def., Wages Act 1986 (c. 48), ss.8, 26; Trade Union and Labour Relations (Consolidation) Act 1992 (c. 52), s.296.

WORKING CLASSES. Although the words "working classes" no longer appear in housing legislation a covenant that obliged a landlord to use premises for housing the "working classes" was held not to be valid (*Westminster City Council* v. *Duke of Westminster* (1992) 24 H.L.R. 572).

WORKING DAY. (Council Regulation 3821/85 on recording equipment in road transport, Art. 15; Transport Act 1968 (c. 73), s.97). Driving home from work in any vehicle fitted with a tachograph comprised part of the "daily working period" covered by Art. 15 (*DPP* v. *Guy* [1998] RTR 82).

See DAY.

WORKS. "Works" within cll. 27.4.1 and 27.4.4 of the JCT Standard Form, 1980 ed. did not include snagging and remedial works undertaken after practional completion (*Emson Eastern* (*in receivership*) v. *EME Development* 26 ConLR 57).

(National Trust Act 1971 (c. 6), s.23). "Works" in s.23(1) should be construed widely to include the power to erect fences in appropriate cases and was not to be confined to the erection of buildings (*National Trust for Places of Historic Interest or Natural Beauty* v. *Ashbrook*, *The Times*, July 3, 1997).

Stat. Def., "includes any building, structure, excavation or other work on land" (Town and Country Planning (Scotland) Act 1997 (c. 8), s.251(6)).

WOULD. "Reckless as to whether the life of another would be thereby endangered" (Criminal Damage Act 1971 (c. 48), s.1(2)(*b*)). In this section "would" is used as going to the expectations of the normal prudent bystander. The fact that there were special features which prevented the risk of danger to another was irrelevant (*R.* v. *Sangha* [1988] 1 W.L.R. 519).

WRECK. See DERELICT.

Stat. Def., Merchant Shipping Act 1995 (c. 21), s.255(1).

WRITE. "Written report" (Insolvent Companies (Disqualification of Unfit Directors) Proceedings Rules 1987 (No. 2023), r.3(2)). A report by an Official Receiver providing evidence that a director is unfit for office was still valid for the purposes of this rule notwithstanding that it was written by the Official Receiver's deputy (*Re Homes Assured Corp.* [1993] BCC 573).

WRITING. Stat. Def., Copyright, Designs and Patents Act 1988 (c. 48), s.178. See also NOTICE.

"Agreement in writing", Stat. Def., Arbitration Act 1996 (c. 23), s.5(1).

WRITTEN PUBLICATION. Stat. Def., Criminal Procedure and Investigations Act 1996 (c. 25), s.59(2).

Y

YEAR. "In . . . the year of assessment" (Income and Corporation Taxes Act 1988 (c. 1), s.381(1)). The words "in . . . the year of assessment" should be given their ordinary and natural meaning and referred to a fiscal year (*Gascoine* v. *Wharton (Inspector of Taxes)* (1996) T.C. Leaflet No. 3498).

YEARLY INTEREST. Accrued sums payable by a subsidiary company to its parent company on a commercial loan were held to be "yearly interest" within the meaning of s.251(2) of the Income and Corporation Taxes Act 1970 (c. 10) (*Minsham Properties* v. *Price* [1990] S.T.C. 718).